THE ILIAD

HOMER

Translated by Rodney Merrill

THE UNIVERSITY OF MICHIGAN PRESS
Ann Arbor

THE ILIAD

Copyright © by the University of Michigan 2007
All rights reserved
Published in the United States of America by
The University of Michigan Press
Manufactured in the United States of America
⊗ Printed on acid-free paper

2010   2009   2008   2007   4   3   2   1

A CIP catalog record for this book is available from the British Library.

Library of Congress Cataloging-in-Publication Data

Homer.
    [Iliad. English]
    The iliad / Homer ; translated by Rodney Merrill.
        p.   cm.
    Includes bibliographical references.
    ISBN-13: 978-0-472-11617-1 (cloth : acid-free paper)
    ISBN-10: 0-472-11617-7 (pbk. : acid-free paper)
        1. Epic poetry, Greek—Translations into English.   2. Achilles
    (Greek mythology)—Poetry.   3. Trojan War—Poetry.   I. Merrill,
    Rodney, 1940–   II. Title.

    PA4025.A2M46   2007
    883'.01—dc22   2007020852

Dedication and Acknowledgments

While I was working on my translation of the *Odyssey*, the *Iliad* loomed as a yet higher peak to be scaled. In the event, it has taken me much less time, for I was able not only to draw on the skills I developed and the formulaic phrasing I worked out for that earlier undertaking but also to spend almost all my time on the task. I owe much of the credit for this happy state of affairs to my mother, Ivanelle Merrill, who has helped support me financially, and to my partner, Bruce Burton, who has given me support of many kinds. I dedicate this translation to them.

I must also acknowledge the indispensable contributions of commentators, translators, and lexicographers listed in the bibliography. I have constantly had at my side the versions of Richmond Lattimore and A. T. Murray—the latter revised by William F. Wyatt—and have plundered them freely for felicitous phrasing. I want especially to thank, among my friends, two learned devotees of Homer, J. K. Anderson and Stephen Daitz, who have read through the entire translation and given me valuable suggestions for improving it and the introduction. Thanks also to Gregory Nagy for his counsel and support, and to him and the members of his Berkeley seminar, Spring 2002, for admitting me to their stimulating discussions of ancient hexameter poetry. Michael Tillotson and Thomas R. Walsh have advised me on many matters of translation and interpretation, as well as helping me with matters introductory and bibliographical. They and the other members of the Berkeley Greek Club—Prof. Anderson, Frederick Amory, Louise Chu, Gary Holland, John Nickel, Christopher Simon, and Andrew Stewart—have heard me read many passages of the work and responded sympathetically and critically. Linda Anderson and Anne Stewart have commented helpfully on the introduction. Those who have encouraged me by their favorable response to my earlier translation are too numerous to name, but I must mention Kathryn Hohlwein, who, through The Readers of Homer, an organization she founded and still heads, advances a cause dear to my heart—the oral performance of Homeric epic in translation. I cannot overstate the importance of all these supporters to my sense of the undertaking. The errors and infelicities that remain in the work despite the best efforts of my counselors are all mine.

Contents

THE *ILIAD* OF HOMER

CONTENTS

Singing the *Iliad*

[Note: Readers who—quite reasonably—prefer to go straight to the Iliad *itself, leaving the introduction for later, may enjoy this translation more if they read aloud as much of it as possible and subvocalize the rest. This epic originated as song, and my aim has been to bring its aural quality—its music—into English so far as I could. The discussion of the meter on pp. 4–5 may help, but it is not essential. Commentators mentioned in this introduction are listed in the bibliography.]*

> "This have the gods brought forth: they have spun the destruction of
>   peoples,
> so that it might be a song for the men who live in the future."
>
> (*Odyssey* 8.579–80)

With these words, Alkínoös, king of the Phaiákians, seeks to assuage the sorrow of an anonymous guest who has been listening to the bard Demódokos sing of the culminating events of the war at Troy. The guest is Odysseus, and we are not surprised that the song has evoked his tears: though it concluded with his personal triumph, we know that the war, its aftermath, and even the victory brought so much grief to all who took part in it that weeping in remembrance would be only natural. But we may find it harder to take this view of the gods' purpose in bringing about these tragic events. Is entertainment for future mortals to be the only redemptive possibility they offer? His hosts have indeed been entertaining Odysseus with athletic contests, dancing, and a comic song about the love between Ares and Aphrodítè; this Trojan song climaxes those offerings of hospitality.

   In the Homeric world, however, the significance of song goes far beyond entertainment in the narrow sense. Before writing was known, the song was the vehicle by which the memory of the people was kept alive. Through the song, performers discovered coherence in events or imposed it on them. Songs enabled listeners to become fully aware of meanings and implications that would otherwise have remained nebulous. Songs provided them with some of what we have in vast libraries—history, philosophy, theology, ethics, law, literature, rhetoric, sociology, even science. When literacy became the common currency of civilization, the Homeric epics, these greatest of all the songs, were the progenitors of the arts and disciplines we see arising among the pre-Socratic thinkers and in the classical age of Athens, whose children literally went to school to Homer. The very identity of the Hellenic people—despite their linguistic, political, social, and geographical differences—was in large part due to their common possession of these two epics: anywhere in the Greek world, over much more than a thousand years, a reference to Homer would be instantly recognizable, forming a common bond among people of varying backgrounds.

Such fundamental cultural unity that accommodates wide diversity is the heritage bequeathed to us by the Homeric epic. We still live in a world shaped by attitudes that found their earliest supreme expression among the Homeric singers—a world where competition, not communal cooperation, is the rule; where disagreements and debates, not submission to a priestly or royal hierarchy, are the stuff of social and political intercourse; where people must come to terms individually with the conditions of their lives, making decisions in lonely and often tragic incertitude. The story of the wrath of Achilles remains the greatest exemplar of that predicament. After the great lord Agamemnon insults him by taking away the girl he won as his prize of honor, Achilles decides to abandon his Achaian comrades and sit out the war until Agamemnon is driven to recognize his mistake in slighting "the best of the Achaians" (*Iliad* 1.412). Only later does Achilles discover that however right, even inevitable, his decision seemed, it has led to the greatest loss he could suffer—the death of his beloved friend Patróklos. Moreover, as a consequence of this unforeseen catastrophe, this great hero turns into an uncontrollable savage, redeemed from his impieties only by the command of Zeus and the courage of his adversary Hektor's father, Priam.

This bare summary of the central tragedy of the *Iliad* does no justice to the splendidly complex working out of the narrative, whose scope extends far beyond the story of Achilles to the larger war against Troy and, beyond that, to the lives of both mortals and gods. The overall thrust of the narrative is not hard to grasp: Achilles' absence from the battlefield causes reverses for the Achaians despite brilliant displays of prowess from their leaders. Learning that the Trojans have breached the recently constructed trench and wall around the encampment and set the Achaians' ships on fire, Patróklos persuades Achilles to let him wear the latter's armor and go to his comrades' aid. But after Patróklos has been disabled by the Trojan Euphorbos and the god Apollo, Hektor kills him and takes the armor. The grief-stricken Achilles determines to revenge his dear comrade, and in new armor made by the god Hephaistos, he returns to the battle, massacres

2

countless Trojans, takes alive twelve youths to slit their throats on the funeral pyre of Patróklos, kills Hektor, and attempts to mutilate Hektor's body by dragging it around the tomb of Patróklos. Venturing out of Troy, Hektor's father, King Priam, beseeches Achilles to return his son's body for burial; Achilles consents, and Hektor receives his funeral rites. So concludes the epic, though not the war, and we know from the song itself that Achilles' own death and then the destruction of Troy will come not long after the events narrated.

Yet despite the powerful thrust of this storyline, the complications are such that it can be difficult for most people, even those who know the *Iliad* quite well, to hold the details clearly in mind. After Achilles leaves the fight, the Achaians try various schemes—single combats, the trench and wall, an embassy to persuade the hero to rejoin his comrades, a nocturnal spying expedition—to repair the damage his loss has caused. But their efforts are futile, for Zeus, king of the gods, has already been persuaded by Achilles' mother, Thetis, to make the Achaians face defeat: only in this way will Achilles' honor be restored. The Achaian and Trojan armies face each other in one engagement after another on the plain or near the ships. Various leaders—Diomédes, Ajax, Agamemnon—have their moments of glory. Many a soldier is slaughtered, often with retrospective details of his happy life at home. Sometimes the gods intervene for one side or the other; sometimes they are kept from intervening by Zeus, who sometimes keeps watch, sometimes neglects to do so, and sometimes is distracted by the wiles of his sister and wife, Hera. Thus, even if we can sense where the narrative is going, often we can feel at a loss—no doubt like earlier listeners—as to how current happenings serve to advance it. We are plunged into a confusion analogous to that of the warfare represented in the epic.

In this respect, the *Iliad* differs notably from its great companion epic, the *Odyssey*, whose clear, though intricate, narrative thread allows us easily to "place" all that happens: first with Odysseus' wife, Penelope, and son, Telémachos, in Ithaka and the latter's travels to get news of his father; then with Odysseus himself on his travels, most of which he himself relates. In the second half, back in Ithaka, the two strands converge to show how Odysseus regains his wife and patrimony. Even this comparatively straightforward story gains enormously from the epic's nature as song, by virtue of which musical coherence and vigor reinforce the narrative movement. My essay "Translating Homeric Song," which introduces my translation of the *Odyssey*, discusses this music in some detail. A shorter account will serve the purpose for the *Iliad*.

The preliterate bards who composed these works inherited a long and sophisticated tradition of epic singing. We are not sure exactly how such songs were performed, but we assume that the singers in the *Odyssey*—Phemios in book 1, Demódokos in book 8—represent a living tradition of singers accompanying themselves on the lyre. In the *Iliad* (9.186–89), we see Achilles himself playing a lyre to please his spirit while singing of men's glorious actions. The rhythm of epic song has come down to us in the epic meter, but the tune is less certain. The bards may have sung the words to a simple melody, repeated with minor variations. Or the melody may have followed the pitch accents, which were notated by the marks that Alexandrian scholars placed on Greek texts from about 200 BCE. Or there may not have been "tunes," properly speaking; the pitch accents, heightened in performance, would have made even a recitation melodious. In any case, even after the epics had been written down, public performances by rhapsodes, who appear on Athenian vases holding a staff rather than a lyre, remained central to the experience. Plato's *Ion* (535b–e) gives us a vivid description of the emotions that the rhapsode of the title feels and expects his audience to feel when performing such moving scenes as that of Achilles rushing at Hektor in *Iliad* 22. Even at this late date, Ion's interlocutor, Socrates, uses the Greek word for "sing" or "chant" (*aeidein*) beside the words for "say" (*eipein, legein*). So we can be sure that the rhapsode's voice was well removed from ordinary speech and that he took full advantage of the strong rhythm in casting his spell over his listeners. We can get a lively sense of such performances from Stephen Daitz's splendid recordings, dramatic chantlike recitations of the original epics, complete with pitch accents.

The rhythm of the Homeric epics—so powerful that it dominated the Western world's poetry, Greek and Latin, for over two thousand years—comes to us in a strict, yet flexible, medium: the quantitative dactylic hexameter verse. The verse is quantitative, as the measure is based on syllable duration, not heavy or light stress as in English. Its major rhythmical unit, or foot, is the dactyl, composed of one long and two short syllables, used in various combinations with the spondee of two long syllables. Each verse includes six (*hex*) of these feet, the last of which can be either long-long or long-short. A transliteration of the *Iliad*'s first seven lines, the Proem, follows. Slashes (/) show foot division, diereses (¨) occur over vowels pronounced separately, and macrons (¯) indicate long syllables. Note that *ēō* in *Pēlēiadeō* is pronounced as one long syllable and that *ēu* in proper names (e.g., *Achílleūs*) is a diphthong, making one long syllable; *a* is pronounced as in *father*; *āi* as in *aisle*, *āu* as in German *aus*, *ē* as in French *fête*, and *ī* as in *machine*.

Mēnin a/eīde, the/ā, Pē/lēïä/deō Akhi/leös
oūlomen/ēn, hē / mūri' A/khāiōis / alge' e/thēke,
pōllās / d'īphthī/moūs psū/khās Aï/dī proï/āpsen
hērō/ōn, āu/toūs de he/lōria / teūkhe ku/nēssin
ōiō/nōisi te / pāsi, Di/ōs d' ete/lēïeto / boūlē,
ēx hoū / dē tā / prōta di/āstēt/ēn eri/sānte
Ātreï/dēs te a/nax ān/drōn kāi / diös A/khíllēūs.

4

By saying these lines aloud, even the Greekless reader may get a sense of the beauty of this rhythm, as well as of the various ways the two sorts of feet—dactyls and spondees—can be combined, and of the flexibility (within strict rules) of the phrasing.

I make no claim to reproduce the Greek meter in English, which has no agreed-on measure of syllabic quantity. The dactylic hexameter I employ is accentual; word stresses determine its metrical shape, and unlike Greek quantities, these stresses depend on how we say words to express meaning, not on syllables as sound units. But by following the Homeric line in its shape as well as its meter, observing its composition in half-lines and shorter units, the English line can attain a similar musicality. Moreover, quantity, though not strictly measured, plays a part in the way the English line is composed, sounded out, and heard, as do the intonations of English speech. My rendering of the Proem follows. Heavy syllables bear an acute accent (´). Note that in proper names (e.g., Péleús, Zeús, Átreús), *eu* is a diphthong, making one heavy syllable, as it is in Greek.

> Síng nów, / góddess, the / wráth of A/chílles the / scíon of / Péleús,
> rúinous / ráge whích / bróught the A/chaíans un/coúnted af/flíctions;
> mány the / pówerful / soúls ít / sént to the / dwélling of / Hádes,
> thóse of the / héroes, and / spoíl for the / dógs ít / máde of their / bódies,
> plúnder for / áll of the / bírds, and the / púrpose of / Zeús was
>   ac/cómplíshed—
> síng from the / tíme whén / fírst stoód / hóstíle, / stárting the / cónflíct,
> Átreús' / scíon, the / lórd of the / peóple, and / nóble A/chílles.

Again, reading aloud may suggest how this English meter conveys the hexameter rhythm. Like any song, this one goes forward line by line with few syntactical complications, so listeners can easily follow it. Even when the sense runs over from one line to the next, the syntax is not difficult for a listener to capture "on the wing." When grammatical inversions occur—for example, when the subject follows, rather than precedes, the verb, as in the last two lines quoted—the meter helps to keep the sentence clear, as does the formulaic nature of the diction.

Reading these two versions of the *Iliad*'s proem aloud may bring out this other essential feature of the oral style, the numerous formulae that determine the texture and character of the epic, as the work of Milman Parry, Albert B. Lord, and their successors in oral-formulaic studies has shown. These formulae are determined by—and in turn do much to define—the meter; some believe that the meter itself arose from formulae. In *The Best of the Achaians*, Gregory Nagy has shown that formulae are of great antiquity and that, far from being arbitrary, they express the deep themes of the epic. Nevertheless, many who have rendered

Homer into prose or free verse have found it so difficult to accommodate formulaic phrases that, despite their importance, they have ignored or minimized them. Indeed, as can be seen from examples in the *Iliad*'s proem, formulae come into their own only in a fully musical setting; otherwise, they can seem otiose, mere "padding." One of the most common formulae, the patronymic plus name, occurs in line 1: *Pēlēïädeō Akhilēös*, "Achilles the scion of Peleus." Another formula, epithet plus name, occurs in line 7: *dīos Akhīlleūs*, "noble Achilles." The first half of line 7 combines a frequent epithet of the leader Agamemnon with his patronymic: *Ātreïdēs te anāx āndrōn*, "Atreus' scion, the lord of the people." In English as in Greek, the meter makes the formulae musical, so that when repeated, they seem not otiose but pleasurable.

Beyond such phrases are numerous entire lines for repeated events. For example, speech introductions consist of two half-lines—one with a verb meaning "said," "answered," or both; the other with an epithet and name—as in *Iliad* 1.84: *Tōn d'apameībomenōs prosephē / podas ōkus Akhīlleūs*, "Answering him in return spoke forth / swift-footed Achilles." This line occurs twelve times in the *Iliad*; the first half-line occurs twenty-four times with other epithet-name formulae. This example also shows how such formulae are common to all epic; I used the same phrase to translate the same "answering" half-line in my translation of the *Odyssey*. There are many other oft-repeated formulae like this: not only speaking but other recurrent events (e.g., sunrise and the coming of night) and "typical scenes" (e.g., eating, making sacrifice, and donning armor) have their systems of formulae, some of them consisting of two or more lines variously combined.

The essential point here is that such repetitions, which may seem redundant when read silently, are a major source of the pleasure of a sung, chanted, or even recited epic: as in all sorts of music, repetition delights by allowing us to enjoy the sound again, the more so here as we need not pay close attention to the sense. Yet by a seeming paradox, far from dispersing our concentration, such enjoyment heightens it, enabling the listener's mind to dwell on what is new, to take it in completely. We feel such pleasure because of the charming and continuous rhythm that unites our experience of this story with the basic rhythms of our lives, those of the heartbeat, of breathing, of walking and running, of chewing food, of sexual intercourse. Almost every pleasurable physical experience we have is imbued with these two complementary characteristics: an insistent but flexible rhythm and repetition with variations. The same is true of the world we experience—the waves on the seashore, the rising and setting of the sun, the phases of the moon, the procession of the seasons and the years, the generations of animals and of people. Aristotle put it well in saying that "nature herself . . . teaches us to select the meter appropriate to such a story" (*Poetics* 1460a3). The rituals of many peoples have noticed and celebrated these natural rhythms and repeated occurrences, and the Homeric epic has more than a touch of the ritual to it. Moreover, the nearly physical pleasure of such rhythmed repetition provides a powerful stimulus to the memory of both composer and listener.

Far from being merely ornamental, then, the rhythmed and formulaic repetitions are central to both the making and the experience of Homeric epic. Scholars of the Parry-Lord school have shown convincingly that even when a line does not appear from extant material to be formulaic, its shape and syntax are conditioned by what we may call the formulaic habit of mind, voice, and ear. Indeed, we may be confident that this great meter was the essential precondition of the composition of these monumental epics, giving the singers a stock of phrases, lines, passages, themes, and stories, and stimulating their energies and their memories to the task of constructing them in the very process of performance. During much of the early oral tradition, no two performances would have been exactly the same, for the singers would have responded to the needs of particular occasions, as in books 1 and 8 of the *Odyssey* Phemios and Demódokos suit their songs to the desires of their listeners. As for our fixed versions of the two epics, we are not sure what part writing may have played in their composition. Some scholars believe that such large works must have required writers who could reflect on their construction in the way that literate poets do. I myself incline to Nagy's view, according to which the wide Panhellenic diffusion of these oral compositions-in-performance gave rise to the standard "texts" of the two great monumental epics largely as they have come down to us. (See Nagy's *Poetry as Performance: Homer and Beyond*, 109ff., for a summary of his five-stage "evolutionary model" of Homeric text-fixation, or the discussion in Merrill and Walsh 11–15.) But the fluid and multiform tradition of singing may have left traces in the form of textual variants, two of which are signaled in my translation. In book 11, line 543 is bracketed because its Greek original appears in no extant manuscript or ancient commentary. Early editors brought it into the standard text from quotations in Aristotle and Plutarch, in whose versions of the epic (whether written or held in memory) this line must have appeared; later it was rejected as inappropriate to the context, and translators usually ignore it. But aside from Aristotle's authority—he surely knew Homeric epic better than most people, ancient or modern—the line deftly conveys psychological insight. Even in the midst of his Zeus-sanctioned rampage, Hektor avoids Ajax son of Telamon because he senses that Zeus begrudges it when he fights somebody stronger. Earlier (7.200–312) in single combat with the same hero he was flattened by a boulder and all but beaten, and later (15.402–20), when he forgets his caution, Ajax wounds and disables him with another boulder. Less discussion is needed for the other bracketed lines, 16.614–15, which simply recount in different terms the action of the preceding three lines; the two passages surely derive from different versions, but both survive in our text.

Aside from such comparatively minor variants of word, phrase, or line, the sources of the epics we possess—mainly manuscripts, the earliest of which dates from about 1000 CE—are remarkably uniform. Perhaps our *Iliad* attained its present form in the eighth, seventh, or sixth century BCE, when a great and self-confident singer who knew the Panhellenic version—we may as well call him "Homer," if we remember that he embodies a centuries-long tradition of singers—sat with a transcriber and sang as complete a performance as he could. But even after that, many other versions would have remained extant in the living song tradition. So it is more likely that the final "crystallization," as Nagy calls it, resulted from the editorial work of Aristotle and the commentators in the great library of Alexandria, culminating in Aristarchus of Samothrace in the middle of the second century BCE, from which emerged the authoritative text that later copyists followed.

Though this controversy may never be resolved to every scholar's satisfaction, it seems clear that the construction of these long works is grounded in a fully oral tradition of composition-in-performance. In that case, through these enormously influential epics and the Greek culture they fostered, the invention of the dactylic hexameter must rank high as a crucial contribution to our civilization. It is no new thing to say that civilization may have originated partly in music, through which the physical rhythms of the human animal were enlisted in the development of the intellect. But it is worth emphasizing how this Greek aspect of Western civilization and, beyond that, of the transition from oral to literate culture retains the strength of its musical origins even to our modern ears, if we listen for it.

Even those who might not give full credence to these larger claims cannot deny the power of the meter or its importance for both the composition and the experience of the original epics. What has been questioned is whether an English version of the meter can convey its power. Granted, it must fall short of the Homeric ideal—English does not have the polysyllables that make the Greek line so sonorous. But enough of the music comes across in the English meter to make intelligible and pleasurable the formulaic phrases and verses, the musical texture based on those formulae, and the longer repeated passages. English has its own strong sounds, not the equivalent of those in Greek, but equally striking to the ear; I have tried to take advantage of these. Despite being a more monosyllabic language, English can be organized in phrases to make a long line cohere and even sing. Though I cannot invent an "art language" like that of the oral epic, compiled by generations of singers from several dialects to meet the needs of the heroic story and the strict meter, I have tried to make the diction of my translation fit the formulaic phrasing without strain. This aim rules out the more colloquial features of English, and a few words may seem archaic, notably *scion*, with which I often render patronymics. But though unusual, *scion* is at least as accurate as *son* for translating Greek patronymics, since like them its reference can extend beyond the previous generation. For example, *Āiakidēs, scion of Aíakos*, identifies Achilles by reference to his grandfather Aíakos.

One feature of the original Greek does come into English: the proper names of people and places. This would be true of any translation, but the metrical setting of this translation better conveys their Greek sonority. For the sake of the meter, I use accent marks on names whose accentuation might be unclear. Beyond their ubiquitous appearance in epithet-name formulae, proper names can give much pleasure, as in the catalogs of book 2, where the survey of people and places sounds at times like a musical roll call. Sometimes a hero's prowess is evoked by several lines of names of his victims, as in 8.273–77:

> Then who first of the Trojans was killed by Teukros the faultless?
> First Orsílochos perished and Órmenos and Opheléstes,
> Daítora, Chrómios too, and as well godlike Lykophóntes,
> then Polyaímon's son Amopáon, and then Melaníppos—
> all to the nourishing earth he brought in rapid succession.

The last formulaic line occurs twice more in the *Iliad* (12.194, 16.418), after similarly melodious lists. The most extended passage of this sort comes in 18.39–48, just after Achilles has learned of the death of Patróklos. Thetis, deep in the sea, responds to her son's anguish, and her sea-nymph sisters throng about her, lamenting:

> . . . there then Glaukè was sitting and Kýmodokê and Thaleía,
> Speío, Nesaíë, and ox-eyed Háliè also, and Thóë,
> Kýmothoë and as well Aktaíë and Límnoreía,
> Mélitè too and Iaíra, Amphíthoë too and Agaúë,
> Dýnamené and Pheroúsa, as well as Doto and Proto,
> Déxamené, Amphínomè also, and Kállianeíra,
> Doris and Pánopè too, and the glorious nymph Galateía,
> Némertés and as well Apseúdes and Kállianássa;
> there too Klýmenè was, Ianeíra as well, Ianássa,
> Maíra and Óreithuía, the fair-tressed nymph Amatheía . . .

The thirty-three names of the sisters were surely chosen for their chiming sonorities as much as for their significance (many have to do with the sea) or mythical status; in their metrical setting, they become almost pure music, incantatory, inviting listeners to share in the grief. Some translators find English translations for these names; for me, the Homeric music must come first. Translations of these and other such names are given in the list of proper names at the back of this book.

The value of thinking of the *Iliad* as song appears above all from considering the grand sweep of the work. Of course, there are many passages whose depth and drama come through in any rendering—to name only a few, the opening quarrel between Achilles and Agamemnon, the meeting of Hektor and Andrómachè in book 6, the embassy to Achilles in book 9, and Priam's meeting with Achilles in the last book. These, too, profit greatly from the musical setting. But many readers, even as they are enchanted by the splendor of the epic, can find the narrative hard to follow in detail and sometimes even repetitious and monotonous in recounting the numerous battles. As to the first difficulty, E. T. Owens' *The Story of the Iliad* elucidates the logic of the narrative, helping the reader understand how the story line brings out major themes and works up to climactic moments. Mark W. Edwards' *Homer, Poet of the Iliad* continues and develops this effort. Yet while we are reading a poem or listening to a song, we cannot rely on a commentator to make us grasp its narrative coherence. Nor can such scholars offer much help as regards the individual battles that form so much of the narrative.

Yet these battle scenes are essential to our grasp of the scope and intensity of the *Iliad*. What can help us most is to approach them, like other features of the epic, in musical terms, as variations on a theme almost in the sense familiar from our own classical music. A variation is an aesthetic unit that builds from sameness to difference each time it occurs, and our pleasure in it depends as much on recognizing the repetition of basic elements as on perceiving new ones. This structuring principle underlies a large proportion of all music—the drum music of Africa or Japan, jazz, modern popular music. In Western classical music, imitative polyphony, the stanzaic song, the theme with variations, the fugue, the sonata form, and much else embody this basic organizing idea: new material derives musical significance from its relationship with an initial melody, harmony, or rhythm, while repeated material takes on new meanings from the ways it has been "developed." The *Iliad* is organized and apprehended mainly as a narrative, but much of our experience of the song resembles that of such variation forms, and the pleasure we get is aural, hardly more available to a visual reading of the epic than it is to a perusal of a Bach fugue on the page.

Even more to the point, in a silent reading or an unmetrical translation, the very characteristic that makes the epic music what it is—repetition with variations— may well seem redundant. Before we even get to the battles, book 2 of the *Iliad* introduces us to two ways in which this organizing principle operates. The first way is through a passage repeated with changes or accretions. Near the beginning of the book, Zeus decides to start honoring Achilles (as Thetis has asked him to do in book 1) by sending a "baneful dream" (2.8) to Agamemnon, telling it to speak thus:

"Bid him to arm for the battle the long-haired men, the Achaians, acting in haste, for the wide-wayed city of Trojans he now might

capture, because the immortals who live in Olympian dwellings
no more argue about it; for Hera has bent to her purpose
all of them, making her plea, and affliction is fixed on the Trojans."

(2.11–15)

As ordered, the dream appears to Agamemnon in the guise of the wise old counselor Nestor. At 2.23–28, it begins with this exhortation:

"Are you asleep, son of war-skilled Atreus tamer of horses?
Not the whole night should slumber a man who is weighted with counsel,
who has troops entrusted to him, and so much to concern him.
Now give heed to me quickly—from Zeus I bring you a message—
though at a distance from you, he feels much care and compassion—
bidding you arm for the battle . . ."

At 2.28–34, the dream repeats the words of Zeus almost verbatim, then concludes, omitting the period that appeared after the word *Trojans* in line 15:

". . . affliction is fixed on the Trojans
from Lord Zeus: keep this in your mind—let oblivion not take
hold of you, once this honey-sweet slumber releases and leaves you."

(2.32–34)

Agamemnon is well and truly deceived into thinking the gods will grant the victory this day. As he tells the dream to a council of elders (2.56–75), he prefaces what the dream said with lines describing its appearance as Nestor and concludes with the order itself:

"'. . . affliction is fixed on the Trojans
from Lord Zeus: keep this in your mind now.' Thus having spoken,
it went flying away, and at once sweet slumber released me.
Come, let us somehow arm for the battle the sons of Achaians."

(2.69–72)

But Agamemnon then proceeds to his own deceptive tactics, saying he will first bid the army flee for home, while the other leaders must try to hold them back.

The whole episode is richly comic in its confusions and cross-purposes on both the divine and the human level, a fitting preamble to the chaos of motivation and action that constitutes warfare. Beyond being aurally pleasing in themselves, the repetitions reinforce the comedy by helping us keep track of the intricate deception that is being practiced. Moreover, when the central passage recurs, it takes on new meaning from its context: first showing Zeus' deceptive intent, it becomes for Agamemnon a dream of wish fulfillment, responding to the anxiety hinted at in the dream's rebuke concerning his responsibility. Finally, it serves to validate Agamemnon's deluded order to arm the troops, despite the possible skepticism that the real Nestor expresses (2.80–81) before he adds his wise authority to it by repeating it verbatim (2.83). Such repetitions do not work well if, in reading silently, we fall into the literate habit of letting our eyes glide over them as not adding anything new.

Another important repeated passage comes in the embassy, Book 9, during which the Achaian leaders Phoinix, Ajax, and Odysseus appeal to Achilles to rejoin the fighting. Here, Odysseus quotes Agamemnon's long speech offering many and costly presents if Achilles will return to battle (9.121–61, 262–99), but he leaves out four crucial lines that first stigmatize as Hades-like Achilles' unyielding stance and then assert the king's preeminence—two remarks sure to antagonize Achilles and thereby abort the whole mission.

> "Let him but yield—ungentle and ever unyielding is Hades;
> therefore of all of the gods is he the most hated by mortals—
> let him be subject to me, inasmuch as I am the more kingly,
> then also as I claim to be older than he in my birth-date."
>
> (19.158–61)

Wily diplomat that he is, Odysseus both begins and ends his report of Agamemnon's offer by saying that Achilles must merely "cease from your anger" (9.261, 299) in order to get these lavish gifts, and then appeals to Achilles' affection for his comrades. Homeric scholars and critics naturally make much of this omission, while general readers—even perceptive ones—can easily miss it because they all but skip what they perceive as "mere" repetition, especially since they have read almost exactly the same lines just minutes ago. On the other hand, listeners with Agamemnon's recent speech ringing in their ears are almost sure to notice and relish the omission—even more so if they are alert to significant variations.

Beyond this overt change in the message, performance or reading aloud presents the situation so dramatically that listeners perceive that, while Agamemnon and wise Nestor (9.164) consider the offer a generous reparation, it must sound to Achilles like an extravagant bribe with something unspoken behind it, especially coming from Odysseus, whom Agamemnon himself has characterized as "excelling in evil deceit" (4.339). And Achilles' suspicion would be accurate: to accept the gifts would be to yield, to accede to Agamemnon's assertion of superiority, literally unspoken by Odysseus. Achilles will begin his reply by saying that he hates as much as Hades' gates "the man who / keeps one thing concealed in his mind while saying another" (9.312–13). Finally, the very extravagance of the offer, brought forcibly to our ears by being repeated, may remind Achilles of the greedy accumulation of prizes for which he rebuked the king (1.163–68).

No wonder he rejects the offer. Again, dramatic context transforms the meaning of the repeated material, if we but listen for it.

Listeners attuned to repetition and variation would notice another significant omission in book 24, after Iris, obeying Zeus' orders, has told Priam to go to Achilles and ransom Hektor's body. We hear the message twice, first when Zeus gives it (24.144–58) and then when Iris repeats it to Priam, almost verbatim (24.175–87), and it is firmly fixed in our auditory memory. So we notice that when Priam reports it to his wife Hékabè, he severely truncates it, omitting all the assurances he has just heard concerning his safe-conduct, with Hermes himself as guide, and his kindly reception by Achilles (24.181–87, repeated from 24.152–58). I leave the reader to consider the effect this omission—and our vivid sense of it—has on what follows, when Hékabè excoriates Priam for his rash venture and characterizes Achilles as "an eater of raw flesh" (24.207). It at least allows Priam to present himself as a potentially self-sacrificing devotee to his son's memory (24.224–27), as he "forgets" that he has just been told, definitely and authoritatively, that Achilles will not kill but protect him (24.185). Our awareness of this "forgetfulness" should counter our propensity to sentimentalize the old man. But though the complexity of our response qualifies our sense of his noble devotion, it does not invalidate but rather enriches it by giving us insight into the pathos of an old man who still wants to be a hero. If in reading silently we ignore or regard of no importance the omission from the message, we miss a splendid Homeric moment.

The second kind of variation introduced in book 2 involves refrainlike repeated lines. The catalogs of Achaian and Trojan forces that occupy most of the last half of the book (lines 484–759, 816–77) proceed as series of variations, often using similar language for each leader or set of leaders. Scholars point out that these lists constitute a survey of the world these people inhabit, and we certainly get from them a strong sense of the scope of the war effort. How far the survey is based on historical fact and whether it originally formed part of the *Iliad* need not concern us here—J. K. Anderson's "The Geometric Catalogue of Ships" illuminates these issues. The capsule descriptions of places, people, and activities can be of much interest. But simply as lists to be read, the catalogs have made many a reader impatient to "get on with the story." If we are aurally immersed in the music of the lines, however, the names of the leaders and places have full sonorous value, and the recurring epithets for places as well as people please the ear. Thus, somewhat as the overture to an opera may introduce the melodies we will later be hearing sung in arias, the catalogs prepares us for the epic narrative by setting forth the names and, in many cases, the backgrounds of the men whose actions we will later be hearing about, so we may be better able to "place" them. This "overture" could not come first—it was essential to get the plot started—but it fits well here, as the two sides are being marshaled for their first engagement in the epic.

Two features of theme-and-variation structure are especially prominent in the twenty-nine "entries" of the catalog of Achaians. Most of them begin by specifying the people in the contingent, often by naming their places of origin (e.g., "Those who possessed Euboía . . . ," 2.536; "Those who inhabited Athens . . . ," 2.546) and giving the leader afterward; a few begin by naming the people and their leader or leaders (e.g., "Léïtos led the Boiótians there," 2.494; cf. 517). At or near the end, many have a line or two summing up the number of ships in each contingent, sometimes with the number of men in each ship. Two lines are especially notable (the first occurs thirteen times, the second four times, both with varying numbers):

Forty the black ships were which followed along with these leaders.

(2.524; cf. 534, 545, 556, etc.)

Thirty in all were the hollow ships that with them were advancing.

(2.516; cf. 602, 680, 733)

These lines are like the refrains in a song, though with minor variations. They please the ear somewhat as the cadences in a piece of music do, fulfilling expectation and giving the passages musical closure. But they do not occur so often as to become routine or monotonous; the bards could achieve closure in other ways also.

The catalog of Trojans and their allies is shorter, and since these forces come from the mainland, this catalog lists no ships and has none of the refrains of the first catalog. In these sixteen entries, most of them quite brief, appear dazzling variations in the phrasing for leading and dwelling, which my translation attempts to suggest. One might almost say that the stately fugue of the first catalog, with its many well-developed "episodes," gives way to the freer fantasia of the second. In any case, the musical dimension of all these passages helps us to take in the content. We will probably not remember the details, but we have taken delight in musically surveying these vast forces and their origins.

This same way of experiencing the song helps us to enjoy the *Iliad*'s countless battle encounters, though it is harder to characterize them simply, for they range from a few lines to major battles between heroes. I have already suggested how we derive aural pleasure from a list of a hero's victims in a metrical setting. Most battle scenes go well beyond naming those who are slaughtered—indeed, they constitute an important species of the "typical scenes" discussed by such Homeric critics as Bernard Fenik, who treats them in terms of narrative technique. Like the catalog "entries" in book 2, the battle scenes resemble variations on a theme, in terms of both action and language. Typically in these scenes, warriors meet, exchange words (or not), and throw spears at each other. Perhaps the first misses and the second hits, or one misses his target but hits another warrior, or one of them is wounded and either leaves battle or is taken from it. Or perhaps a hero kills many men in succession by sword or spear, fatally wounding different parts of the body. We come to be familiar with the way these scenes are composed and with the intermingling of repeated and varied diction.

For these "typical" variations in the action, many lines in the *Iliad* serve almost like refrains, orienting listeners by pointing to the recurrent features of a chaotic activity. Here are a few of them, with notes on how Homer uses sound to reinforce sense, and how I have tried to follow him in this respect:

"So did he say, then brandished and threw his long-shadowing spear-shaft." This line (3.355) occurs seven times, and the last phrase fourteen more, conveying in sound—as in the Greek *dolikhōskion ēngkhos*—the sense of a long spear moving across space.

"Straightway he to the ground from his chariot leapt in his armor." This line (3.29) occurs eight times, the last phrase four more; as in the Greek *teūkhisin / ālto khamāze*, the strong break between *chariot* and *leapt* emphasizes the sudden vigor of the action.

"Falling he crashed to the ground, and around him clattered his armor." The whole line (4.504) occurs seven times, the first half-line twelve more, the second three more. Here too sound reinforces sense. In the Greek, *doūpēsēn de pesōn, arabēse de teūkhe' ep'aūtōi*, the strong plosives *p, b, t,* and *kh,* as well as the repeated *-e* sounds, long and short, convey the meaning as in English do the consonants *d, t, l,* and *r;* the clusters *cr, gr,* and *cl;* and the echoing vowels, short *a* and the diphthong *ou.*

"He from the chariot fell, and around him clattered his armor." This line (5.294) occurs twice, the first half-line seven more times. These last two examples show how the "refrain" can be varied by combining different half-lines.

The topic of sound as conveying sense could well be pursued further, but the preceding examples must suffice here; Edwards (in *Sound, Sense, and Rhythm*) and W. B. Stanford both have excellent discussions. The continuous musical energy of the *Iliad* takes us into battle scenes more completely than any poem since, making us experience the bloodshed, the cruel mercilessness of the victors, the despairing humiliation of the losers, the bloodlust, the excitement of battle, the delight in strength, the craving for glory, and the consummation of manhood. I have striven to capture this in my translation. Try reading aloud 20.455–503 with full attention to the sounds and the sense. In this passage, Achilles has been disappointed in his attacks on Aineías and Hektor—both rescued by gods—and is wreaking havoc in the ranks of the Trojans. The prowess of Achilles, the pathos of his victims, and the dire energy of the fight resound in the rhythm, as in these lines:

It was Deukálion next he struck—at the place where the elbow's
sinews are joined, there he with the bronze spear-point penetrated
right through his arm; he awaited his onset, the arm a mere burden,

seeing in front of him death; on the neck with his sword-blade the hero
struck, and the head with the helmet he hurled far away as the marrow
gushed up out of the spine, and he lay stretched out on the ground there.

(20.478–83)

Notice how, in reading aloud, the runovers help make the action vivid without
injuring the line's integrity, how the alliteration on *h* in line 482 captures the fe-
rocious energy of the throw, how the long syllables of "lay stretched out on the
ground there" paint the picture.

The conclusion of the passage doubly exemplifies another distinctively Ho-
meric kind of variation, the extended simile, which illuminates the action by com-
paring it with another quite different one:

As when rages the ravenous flame of a fire in the deep-carved
glens of a dry hot mountain and sets the deep timber to burning,
lashing it onward the wind whirls blazes in every direction,
so with a spear like a god he was rushing in every direction,
charging the men he slaughtered; the black earth streamed with their
    life-blood.
As when a man yokes oxen, his big males broad in the forehead,
then on the strong-built floor they tread white barley to thresh it,
quickly it gets husked under the feet of the bellowing oxen,
so now beneath great-hearted Achilles the single-hoofed horses
trampled alike dead bodies and shields; bespattered with blood were
all of the axle below and the rims that surrounded the car-box,
fouled by drops of the gore thrown up from the hooves of the horses
and from the rims of the wheels; and the scion of Peleus kept on
straining for glory; with gore his invincible hands were bespattered.

(20.490–503)

A Homeric simile may be termed a "variation" inasmuch as it begins in some as-
pect of likeness to the narrative action but often either changes focus to another
aspect or affects us most strongly by the contrast it offers; this passage exemplifies
both kinds of development. The forest fire in the mountains first drives home
Achilles' maniacal rage, but then the phrase *in every direction* (translating the
Greek *pantēi*), when repeated from the image of the fire, emphasizes the scope
of his destruction, thus rounding out the depiction of his savage acts. The image
of oxen threshing grain takes us to a scene of peaceable production that throws
into relief the violent action, as the oxen point to Achilles and his chariot-horses,
the barley to dead bodies and shields, and the grain that results from the thresh-
ing to the gore that spatters the chariot. Similarity and contrast join to highlight
the cruel wastefulness of warfare. The song-form mediates our apprehension and

our pleasure: in both cases the simile takes three lines, its application two—though in the second case the focus on gore continues another four lines to the end of the book. Each movement in this symmetrical series is indicated by *hōs*, which I render alternating *as* and *so*. The verbal music reinforces our vision, as in the heavy spondees of l. 496, speaking of the oxen, "then on the strong-built floor they tread white barley to thresh it." Both imagery and music draw us deeply into the tragic contradictions of warfare: valor and suffering, just retribution and arbitrary cruelty, glorious action and bestial havoc.

It is important that we be so involved, for Homer's great art is to make us admire and want to emulate the heroes even as we recognize their delusions and the destruction they bring about by supporting a dubious cause in which most of the participants have no stake. The very idea of heroism is largely founded on this epic. Alexander the Great is said to have taken Achilles as his model, and he was not alone in his admiration. In *The Best of the Achaeans*, Gregory Nagy has shown that this Panhellenic hero was venerated both when the epic was reaching its final form and in later local "hero-cults." As with those cults, the impulse behind this epic arises from the death of the great hero. Though Achilles does not die in the narrative, knowledge of his early death overshadows the whole story from book 1 (352–56, 415–18), when Achilles and his mother Thetis both insist on it: he has chosen a short life with the glory of heroism over the longer life he would get by keeping away from war. Patróklos substitutes for Achilles not only by fighting the Trojans but also by dying, and in mourning for his comrade's death, Achilles prospectively mourns his own, as do his mother and the sea-nymphs in the passage discussed earlier in this introduction.

This ideal of heroism is set forth in the speech of Sarpédon to Glaukos, the leaders of the Trojans' Lykian allies, in 12.310–28: their prominence and wealth in their own country require that they never slacken in their leadership, and, as with Achilles, the certainty of death motivates them to act valorously so as to win glory. Time and again we see this ideal in speech and action, when the heroes—Diomédes, Ajax, Agamemnon, Hektor, Patróklos, Achilles himself—have an *aristeia*, a rampage of killing for the sake of the glory they will win. On such deeds depends their status among fighters and the recognition they receive in the form of prizes. The subject of the epic, the wrath of Achilles, rises from Agamemnon's seizure from Achilles of such a prize, the captive daughter of Bríseus, to replace the daughter of Chryses, the priest of Apollo; under the god's scourge, Agamemnon has to return his own prize-girl to her father. Though, in book 9 (341–43), Achilles protests his love for the girl he has lost, Agamemnon's act is initially and mainly seen as an outrage to Achilles' merits and his reputation as the best of the Achaians. When Achilles comes back into the fight, the restoration of this prize-girl is a major sign of his restored status.

If the strong music helps us to feel, even more than understand, the power of this heroic ideal and the action it inspires, it also makes us able to take in the negative aspects of warfare—the confusion, the suffering and savagery, the questionable motives. Homer alludes to the first of these aspects in the hero Diomédes' *aristeia* at 5.85–94 ("nor as to Tydeus' son would you know which side he belonged to, / whether he battled along with the Trojans, or with the Achaians," 85–86) and compares his assault with a winter torrent that destroys all in its path. But confusion appears even more in the narration of numerous battles, when listeners may not be sure whether a fighter is Achaian or Trojan. Who is striking whom can be ambiguous grammatically, when a Greek relative pronoun is used to refer to one of two fighters or to both in turn, as in the passage on the killing of Deukálion cited earlier—in my translation, readers may have found the pronouns *he*, *him*, and *his* too numerous for comfort. Another example occurs in 13.566: until we hear, in lines 567–75, that the Achaian hero Mérionés pursued and killed him, we do not know whether the man who "shrank back to the band of his comrades" in line 566 was the Achaian Antílochos or the Trojan Ádamas. Usually, translators clarify such situations by repeating proper names when the Greek does not. I have avoided doing this, because I think the epic deliberately plunges listeners into the confusion of battle, if only momentarily. In such passages, the music is crucial—the strong rhythm keeps us fully involved and, in a sense, oriented even when references are not immediately clear. We are swept along in a spellbinding torrent of measured words, with moments of clarity amid the confusion. We are experiencing the chaos of battle, not merely being told about it. Yet our pleasure in the song never ceases.

The musical energy of Homer sounds, too, in the varieties of suffering and death, grimly precise in detail. No poet has looked more directly at the horrors of warfare. Men get struck in the back between the shoulders; through the buttocks into the bladder; through the neck and up through the teeth, severing the tongue; into the skull, shattering the brain. Arms get cut off, the blood gushing out; heads are severed and sent rolling through the army. It would not be accurate to say that the music softens or "aesthetically transmutes" the unpleasantness—on the contrary, it makes the wounds excruciatingly visible. But it keeps us fascinated in two ways: first, by letting us hear the matter in measured rhythm; second, by imparting an almost ritual quality to the actions on account of the sonorous noun-epithet formulae and other formulaic repetitions, including the various "refrains" already mentioned. Reading aloud a passage—for example, 5.35–83—will make these points clearer, as well as revealing how the grisly deaths are often both intensified and relieved by short accounts of the dead men's happy and prosperous lives before they came to Troy. These stories can also contribute to our sense of battle confusion by diverting our attention from the action.

Behind all the accounts of battle loom deep doubts on both sides as to the value of the enterprise. Such doubts are conveyed in the speeches for which Homer is outstanding among epic poets. As Aristotle says (*Poetics* 1460a8–12), Homer presents the people themselves, rather than merely describing their actions in the manner of other epic poets. Indeed, the speeches themselves can be actions—Richard Martin has shown how many speeches of heroes, such as commands and rebukes, can be acts as surely as are battlefield deeds. During one such "speech-act" reviling Agamemnon (1.149–71), Achilles shows his own doubts and, by implication, those of most of the Achaians at Troy—they have no quarrel with the Trojans but have come for the sake of Agamemnon and Meneláos. The cause of Atreus' sons is not much better: Helen herself (3.171–76) speaks of her shameful behavior in going with Paris (also called Alexander), abandoning Sparta and her husband, Meneláos, and thereby bringing on the conflict. We are left to wonder whether such a woman is worth this terrible war. Both Achilles and the lowborn Thersítes (2.225–42) suggest that Agamemnon is motivated more by greed of gain than by a concern for his own or his brother's honor.

On the other side, the Trojans know that they are allowing many brave lives and prospectively the whole city to be destroyed for the sake of this beautiful but faithless woman and her handsome but unprincipled lover, who will not allow her to be returned despite the pleas of his compatriots. How such doubts about the worth of their cause affect the minds of those who must defend it appears in a rebuke that Hektor addresses to Paris after the latter has first challenged Meneláos and then shrunk back into the ranks of the Trojans, avoiding the combat; it can serve also to show us the musical construction of such utterances.

Looking at him then Hektor rebuked him in words of derision:
"Paris the bane, best-seeming, you woman-mad cheat and deceiver,
would that you never were born or that you unmarried had perished!
This is what I would desire, and it surely would be much better
than to be thus—a disgraceful coward despised by the others.
Surely at us laugh loudly the long-haired men, the Achaians,
saying we have this chief as our champion only because in
looks he is handsome, but not in his heart is there valor or prowess.
Was it like this you were at the time in the seafaring galleys
you sailed over the seaway, assembling the trustworthy comrades,
mingling with alien people and taking a beautiful woman
out of a faraway country, the sister-in-law of great spearmen,
such huge pain to your father and city and all of the people,
but to our enemies pleasure, to you yourself so disgraceful?
Would you indeed not face Meneláos belovèd of Ares?

Then you would learn what strong man's blossoming wife you are holding.
Nor would the lyre be of use to you then, or the gifts Aphrodítè
gave you, the hair and the beauty, were you with the dust to be mingled.
No, we Trojans are terrible cowards, or else you had long since
put on a tunic of stone on account of the evil you wrought us."

(3.38–57)

Overall, this speech almost displays the "ring composition" critics such as Edwards (in his *Commentary on Iliad* 17–20, 44–48) have detected in many Homeric passages, building through ideas to a central one and then returning to the first idea in reverse order. After the vividly scornful first line sets the tone, the speech falls into three sections of six lines, each section composed for maximum effect. The first section (lines 40–45) builds from the one-line wish to two lines setting the possibility of being unborn or dying unmarried against the scorn of his compatriots, then climaxes in three lines on the scorn of the Achaians. The middle six lines (46–51) review the outrage Paris committed against the Achaians, building to its consequences, thereby giving yet deeper reasons for both sides to despise him. The last section (lines 52–57) begins with two one-line exclamations on the present situation, thereby recalling the Achaians' scorn. The next two lines refer once more to the gifts on which Paris relies instead of valor. In the two final lines, Hektor returns to how Paris' actions reflect on Hektor and his countrymen: now the scorn is directed at their own cowardice in allowing the cowardly Paris to have his way. This is the climactic thought: how easy it would be to end this destructive and futile war, yet the Trojans cannot do it. It also climaxes Hektor's feeling: he must despise himself, almost more than Paris, for supporting the cause in whose name he must act heroically.

Only a great bard could achieve such a far-ranging and subtle union of thought, rhetoric, and emotion in a short speech composed to bring out the complexity of the situation and of Hektor's feelings even as it comes across as a spontaneous outburst. But we should be aware how the traditional song makes this possible by giving the singer his tools. As we have seen, the construction of the lines themselves, whether singly or in multiples, governs the progress of thought. Then the elements of thought are balanced within many lines, following the pattern of formulaic construction in half-lines. Thus such lines may readily express alternative possibilities (e.g., unborn vs. died unmarried at 3.40) and antitheses (e.g., handsome in looks vs. no valor at heart at 3.45; pleasure to enemies vs. disgraceful to yourself at 3.51). Sometimes this thinking in alternatives extends to two lines, as in 3.40–41, which sets desirable death against the disgrace of cowardice. In the middle six lines of Hektor's speech (3.46–51), the half-lines present a narrative in clearly comprehended steps, each preparing for the next, giving a brief but forceful summary of the outrage.

From this analysis, we can get a hint of how the musical construction of Homeric epic may have helped shape Western habits of thinking, in which are deeply engrained the ways just outlined for dealing with the complexity of experience—comparison, antithesis, summary. Underlying them all is the conviction, which for us amounts almost to an instinct, that effective discourse proceeds in steps, each related to the one that precedes it (whether by logic or by association), rather than coming primarily in oracular pronouncements or in fables (of course, the *Iliad* also presents examples of both the latter two forms of authoritative discourse). Perhaps such habits are intrinsic to thought and would have arisen anyway, but in its musical orderliness, the epic presents the original and efficacious models: the Greek thinkers who founded our intellectual tradition surely learned them at least in part from their immersion in the Homeric epics. The Herodotean history, the Platonic dialogue, and the Aristotelian treatise all profited from this systematic way of presenting material.

They learned another habit yet deeper, yet more determinative for Western thought and life: the willingness—indeed, eagerness—to consider many points of view before reaching judgment. Herodotus' inclusion of the testimony of others even when he rejects it, Socrates' engagement of other thinkers in the Platonic dialogues, and Aristotle's vast intellectual systems erected on the thought of his predecessors all arise from the thought-training these men must have gained in part from Homer. Arguments, more or less formalized, constitute a major way of approaching this breadth of thought. Within the *Iliad*, we see both negatively and positively how the inevitable disputes among men can and should be fruitful: for example, in book 1, Agamemnon's rejection of Nestor's wise counsel (1.254–84) brings disaster on the Achaians; but later on, a chastened Agamemnon is ready to listen to young Diomedes reproaching him for giving up (9.31–49) and then to Nestor rebuking his earlier arrogance and giving counsel (9.103–13).

More important than its portrayals of disputes are the ways the *Iliad* arouses debates about its deepest significance. Even today, for every reader or listener who thinks the *Iliad* exalts the heroic virtues of the past it celebrates, another believes the epic to be deeply antimilitarist, showing heroism as self-delusion and savagery. Though most people recall the vividly characterized individuals of the epic, Simone Weil argues cogently that the real "hero" is "Force," which, in all its manifold cruel operations, reduces human beings to things. Readers and listeners disagree, too, about the status and power of the gods within the epic. They sometimes seem to be fully in charge—as in the Odyssean lines that began this introduction and in the opening lines of the *Iliad* ("the purpose of Zeus was accomplished," 1.5). At other times, they are clearly subordinate to fate: Hera reminds Zeus (16.439–57) that he cannot override, though he might postpone for a while, the destined end even of his own son Sarpedon. Since the gods are themselves at odds in their ideas and actions, even if Zeus has the final say, we often feel that human suffering comes at the whim of one god or another. Though critics rightly point out that a god's aid in a fight elevates a hero's status, ordinary readers and listeners cannot help thinking that the hero's valor of itself would not have accomplished the deed. When Hektor kills Patróklos, the glory of his action is compromised by Apollo's part in disarming his victim. This is not just our judgment: Patróklos himself insists on it in 16.843–54. Similarly, when Achilles kills Hektor, he does so only with the aid of Athena, who first lures Hektor to confront him (22.214–46) and then returns his spear to him after a failed spear-throw (22.273–77). Yet this death is destined beyond any action of gods or men, as was elaborately demonstrated when Zeus lifted his golden scales and the doomsday of Hektor sank to Hades (22.208–13). Zeus held the scales, but he did not tip them: the men's fate is their own. It seems we must take account of three levels of determination— that of fate, that of the gods, and that of human decisions and actions. What part has heroic valor in this? Never has the difficulty of knowing the real springs of action been better represented. Just because we get no clear answer, we are stimulated to debate this problem—and many others.

Such a problematic stance toward human existence is perhaps the greatest gift to our culture from this traditional song, whose many generations of singers contributed to setting forth the full complexity of individual and social life. The music was essential to this outcome: like Greek tragedy, which derived so much from the *Iliad* in both subject matter and dramatic means, the song charms us even as it puts us at an "aesthetic distance" from the subject matter, inviting us to understand issues before making judgment. Moreover, the song can rouse sympathy for even the least sympathetic view or person—even for Helen, despite her own self-contempt and our awareness that she is the root of the conflict. In her despair, she proposes the same purpose for her sordid and tragic predicament as the one Alkínoös gives Odysseus for "the destruction of peoples" (*Odyssey* 8.579). While inviting Hektor to take a rest, Helen speaks of how he has endured troubles

> "caused by the bitch I am and by Lord Alexander's delusion,
> us upon whom Zeus set evil destiny, so that hereafter
> we be subject of song for the men who live in the future."
>
> (*Iliad* 6.356–58)

For her, such musical infamy must be shameful; for us, it can console and even occasion celebration, for we know that the song resulting from their destiny and the war that followed has been of immeasurable benefit to us who live in their future. If readers come as near to singing the *Iliad* as is possible from the imperfect English representation I offer in this book, they may profit even more from the rich and instructive pleasure it gives.

Bibliography

This list provides references to the works—including editions and translations—that I consulted in translating the *Iliad*, as well as to sources mentioned in the introduction. Also included are suggestions for further reading, selected from the vast body of writing on Homer and the *Iliad*. Those who want to read more deeply in Homeric studies can find extensive bibliographies in many of the scholarly works listed, such as those of Louden and Walsh.

TEXTS, COMMENTARIES, WORDBOOKS, AND TRANSLATIONS

Cunliffe, R. J. *A Lexicon of the Homeric Dialect.* New ed. Norman, OK, 1963.
Kirk, G. S., general ed. *The* Iliad: *A Commentary.* 6 vols. Individual vols. by G. S. Kirk, Mark W. Edwards, J. B. Hainsworth, Richard Janko, and Nicholas Richardson. Cambridge, 1985–93.
Lattimore, Richmond, trans. *The* Iliad *of Homer.* Chicago, 1951.
Leaf, Walter, and Bayfield, M. A., eds. *The* Iliad *of Homer.* 2 vols. London, 1962.
Murray, A. T., trans. *Homer: The* Iliad. 2 vols. Revised by William F. Wyatt. Cambridge, MA, and London, 1999.
Monro, David B., and Thomas W. Allen, eds. *Homeri Ilias.* 2 vols. Oxford, 1908.
Prendergast, G. L. *A Complete Concordance to the* Iliad *of Homer.* Revised by Benedetto Marzullo. Hildesheim, 1962.
West, Martin L. *Homeri Ilias.* 2 vols. Stuttgart, 1998–2000.
Willcock, Malcolm M. *A Companion to the* Iliad: *Based on the Translation by R. Lattimore.* Chicago, 1976.
Willcock, Malcolm M., ed. *Iliad.* 2 vols. Bristol, 1999.

ESSAY COLLECTIONS

Atchity, Kenneth. *Critical Essays on Homer.* Boston, 1987.
Bloom, Harold, ed. *Homer: Modern Critical Views.* New York, 1986.
Bremer, J. M., I. J. F. de John, and J. Kalff, eds. *Homer, Beyond Oral Poetry: Recent Trends in Homeric Interpretation.* Amsterdam, 1987.

Cairns, Douglas L., ed. *Oxford Readings in Homer's* Iliad. Oxford, 2001.

Carter, Jane B., and Sarah P. Morris, eds. *The Ages of Homer: A Tribute to Emily Townsend Vermeule.* Austin, 1995.

Fowler, Robert, ed. *The Cambridge Companion to Homer.* Cambridge, 2004.

Morris, Ian, and Barry Powell, eds. *A New Companion to Homer.* Leiden, 1997.

Steiner, George, and Robert Fagles, eds. *Homer: A Collection of Critical Essays.* Englewood Cliffs, NJ, 1962.

Wace, Alan J. B., and Frank Stubbings, eds. *A Companion to Homer.* London, 1962.

Wright, John. *Essays on the* Iliad: *Selected Modern Criticism.* Bloomington, 1978.

BOOKS, ESSAYS, AND SOUND RECORDINGS OF SPECIAL INTEREST

Anderson, J. K. "The Geometric Catalogue of Ships." In Carter and Morris, 181–91.

Aristotle. *Poetics.* Trans. Ingram Bywater. In *The Basic Works of Aristotle,* ed. Richard McKeon, 1455–87. New York, 1941.

Arnold, Matthew. *On Translating Homer.* London, 1861.

Bernardete, Seth. *Achilles and Hector: The Homeric Hero.* South Bend, IN, 2005.

Beye, Charles Rowan. *Ancient Epic Poetry: Homer, Apollonius, Virgil: With a Chapter on the Gilgamesh Poems.* Wanconda, IL, 2006.

Bowra, C. M. *Homer.* London, 1972.

Camps, W. A. *An Introduction to Homer.* Oxford, 1980.

Daitz, Stephen, reader. *The* Iliad *of Homer in Ancient Greek.* Madison, CT: Audio-Forum, 1992. To hear Daitz reading *Iliad* 1.1–52, go to http://www.rhapsodes.fll.vt .edu/iliad1.htm.

Dalby, Andrew. *Rediscovering Homer: Inside the Origins of the Epic.* New York, 2006.

Edwards, Mark W. *Homer, Poet of the* Iliad. Baltimore, 1987.

Edwards, Mark W. *Sound, Sense, and Rhythm: Listening to Greek and Latin Poetry.* Princeton, 2002.

Fenik, Bernard. *Typical Battle Scenes in the* Iliad: *Studies in the Narrative Techniques of Homeric Battle Description.* Wiesbaden, 1968.

Ford, Andrew Laughlin. *Homer: The Poetry of the Past.* Ithaca and London, 1992.

Griffin, Jasper. *Homer on Life and Death.* Oxford, 1980.

King, Katherine Callen. *Achilles: Paradigms of the War Hero from Homer to the Middle Ages.* Berkeley, 1987.

Kirk, G. S. *The Songs of Homer.* Cambridge, 1962.

Lloyd-Jones, Hugh. *The Justice of Zeus.* Berkeley, 1984.

Lord, Albert B. *The Singer of Tales.* New ed., edited by Stephen Mitchell and Gregory Nagy. Cambridge, MA, 2000.

Louden, Bruce. *The* Iliad: *Structure, Myth, and Meaning.* Baltimore, 2006.

Martin, Richard P. *The Language of Heroes: Speech and Performance in the* Iliad. Ithaca, 1989.

Merrill, Rodney, and Thomas R. Walsh. "The *Odyssey:* The Tradition, the Singer, the Performance." In *The* Odyssey *of Homer,* trans. Rodney Merrill, 1–53. Ann Arbor, 2002. See also Rodney Merrill, "Translating Homeric Song," in idem, 54–73; and the Web site *Translating the* Odyssey, http://home.earthlink.net/~merrill_odyssey.

Mueller, Martin. *The Iliad.* London, 1984.

Nagler, Michael N. *Spontaneity and Tradition: A Study in the Oral Art of Homer.* Berkeley, 1974.

Nagy, Gregory. *The Best of the Achaeans: Concepts of the Hero in Archaic Greek Poetry.* Revised edition. Baltimore, 1999.

Nagy, Gregory. *Poetry as Performance: Homer and Beyond.* Cambridge, 1996.

Owens, E. T. *The Story of the* Iliad, *as told in the* Iliad. London, 1946. Reprint, Ann Arbor, 1966.

Page, Denys. *History and the Homeric* Iliad. Berkeley, 1959.

Parry, Milman. *The Making of Homeric Verse: The Collected Papers of Milman Parry.* Ed. Adam Parry. Oxford, 1971.

Plato. *Ion.* Trans. Lane Cooper. In *The Collected Dialogues of Plato,* ed. Edith Hamilton and Huntington Cairns, 216–28. New York, 1961.

Schein, Seth L. *The Mortal Hero: An Introduction to Homer's* Iliad. Berkeley, 1984.

Stanford, William Bedell. *The Sound of Greek: Studies in the Greek Theory and Practice of Euphony.* Berkeley, 1967.

Taplin, Oliver. *Homeric Soundings: The Shaping of the* Iliad. Oxford, 1992.

Thomas, Carol G., and Craig Conant. *The Trojan War.* Westport, CT, 2005.

Vivante, Paolo. *The* Iliad: *Action as Poetry.* Boston, 1991.

Walsh, Thomas R. *Fighting Words and Feuding Words: Anger and the Homeric Poems.* Lanham, MD, 2005.

Weil, Simone. "The *Iliad,* or The Poem of Force." Trans. Mary McCarthy. In *War and the* Iliad, 1–38. New York, 2005.

West, M. L. *Ancient Greek Music.* Oxford, 1992.

Whitman, Cedric H. *Homer and the Heroic Tradition.* Cambridge, MA, 1958.

Wilson, Donna F. *Ransom, Revenge, and Heroic Identity in the* Iliad. Cambridge, 2002.

ACHAIANS AND TROJANS

[BLACK SEA]

BOSPHOROS

[HELLESPONT (PROPONTIS)]

CENTRAL GREECE

EUBOIA

PAPHLAGONIANS

Kytóros
Sésamos
Parthénios R.

Chalkis
Kerinthos
Histiaía
Antron
PHTHIA
Áps
Opóeis
LOKRIS
Kephísos R.
Orchómenos
Aulis
Kopai
BOIOTIA
Thebes
Plataia
▲Mt.
Parnássos
PHOKIS
Pytho
Sikyon
Korinth
Kleônai
Mykênê
Argos
Tiryns
Pellênê
Epidauros
Troizen
Athens
Eretría
SALAMIS
AIGINA
C. Sounion

CYPRUS
Paphos

Sangários River

HALIZONIANS

PHRYGIANS

ASKANIA

SOLYMOI

THRACIANS

Adresteia
Zeleia
MYSIANS
⊗
Troy

Mt. Átnos
SAMOTHRACE
IMBROS
TENEDOS

LEMNOS

SKYROS
LESBOS

CHIOS

[AEGEAN SEA]

Hermos River

MAIONIANS ▲Mt. Tmôlos
Kaýstrios R.
Maiándros River
Miletos ▲Mt. Mýkalê
KARIANS

LYKIANS

Xánthos R.

[MEDITERRANEAN SEA]

KIKONIANS

PAIONIANS
Axios River
Amydon
▲Mt.
Olympos
Oloôsson
Dodóna
Trikkê R.
Penéiós
[THESSALY]
Phéra
Orménios
PHTHIA
MAGNETES]
Mt. Pélion
Iolkós
Meliboía
KALYDNAI
KOS
NISYROS
SYME
Kameiros
Kámeiros
RHODOS
Lindos
Iálysos
KRAPATHOS
KASOS

IKARIA

SAMOS
DOULICHION
ITHAKA
ZAKYNTHOS
Acheloös River
AITOLIANS
Kálydon
EPEIANS
BOUPRASION
ELIS
Kyparisséeis
Hymínê
Pylos
ARKADIA
Álpheos
LAKEDAIMON
Sparta
Helos
Oitylos
KYTHERA
C. Maleia

LOKRIS
PHOKIS
EUBOIA
BOIOTIA
Orchómenos
Áthens
Karystos
Hermíonê

CRETE
Knosos
Gortys
Phaistos
Miletos

TROAD
Pityeia
Perkótê
Arisbê
Abydos
Sestos
Simóeis R.
Troy
Skamánder River
DARDANIANS
Mt. Ída ▲
Kymêssos
Thebê
Larissa
Chrysê

[THESPROTIA]

THE *ILIAD* OF HOMER

BOOK 1

Sing now, goddess, the wrath of Achilles the scion of Peleus,
ruinous rage which brought the Achaians uncounted afflictions;
many the powerful souls it sent to the dwelling of Hades,
those of the heroes, and spoil for the dogs it made of their bodies,
5 plunder for all of the birds, and the purpose of Zeus was accomplished—
sing from the time when first stood hostile, starting the conflict,
Atreus' scion, the lord of the people, and noble Achilles.
    Which of the gods brought strife to the two men, set them to fighting?
It was the offspring of Leto and Zeus; for enraged at the king, he
10 roused in the army a baneful disease, and the people were slaughtered,
all on account of his priest, whom Atreus' scion dishonored,
Chryses. For he had arrived at the swift ships of the Achaians,
seeking to free his daughter and bringing a measureless ransom,
bearing in hand bay-garlands of great far-shooting Apollo
15 wound on a gold-wrought staff, and he pled with them, all the Achaians,
but above all the two scions of Atreus, marshals of people:
    "Atreus' scions as well as the rest, you well-greaved Achaians,
now may the gods who dwell in Olympian palaces let you
ransack the city of Priam and safely arrive in your homeland;
20 but as for my dear child, set her free and accept this ransom,
showing respect for the scion of Zeus, far-shooting Apollo."
    Thereat all of the other Achaians were shouting approval,
saying to honor the priest and accept the magnificent ransom;
yet this pleased not the spirit of Atreus' son Agamemnon;
25 roughly he sent him away, and he laid a strong order upon him:
"Old man, never may I by the hollow ships come upon you,
either now lingering on or returning again in the future,
lest no help to protect you the god's staff prove, nor his garland.
Her I will not give freedom; before, old age will assail her
30 there in our house in Argos and far from the land of her fathers,

where she will weave at a loom and will share my bed and affection.
Go now, do not provoke me, that you might go the more safely."
　　So he spoke, and the old man feared, and obeyed what he said and
silently went by the shore of the deep sea rumbling and booming.
35　Loudly the old man, once he had gone to a distance, addressed his
prayer to the lordly Apollo, whom Leto of beautiful hair bore:
"Hear me, god of the silvery bow, who stride around Chrysè
and around Killa the sacred, and Ténedos mightily govern,
Smíntheus, if a delectable temple I ever have built you,
40　or if savory fat thigh-pieces I ever have burnt you
either of bulls or of goats, then bring this boon to fulfillment:
make those Dánaäns pay for my tears by shooting your arrows."
　　So he spoke as he prayed; he was heard by Phoibos Apollo.
Down from the peaks of Olympos he came, enraged in his spirit,
45　holding his bow on his shoulders as well as a close-covered quiver.
Arrows were clattering loud on his shoulders as he in his anger
started impetuous motion, and like night he was advancing.
Then well away from the ships he sat, and an arrow he let fly;
dreadfully out of the silvery bow then started the clangor.
50　It was the mules and the swift-paced dogs that first he assaulted,
but then straight at the men themselves a sharp arrow he shot and
struck: and the pyres close-crowded were always ablaze with the corpses.
　　Nine days then through the army were ranging the god's dread arrows,
but on the tenth to assembly the people were called by Achilles,
55　for in his mind it was put by the goddess white-armed Hera,
since she pitied the Dánaän men as she saw they were dying.
Then when they had collected and all were gathered together,
standing among them, thus spoke out swift-footed Achilles:
"Scions of Atreus, now I believe we are sure to be driven
60　wandering back to our homes, if indeed we can even escape death,
if at the same time battle and pestilence crush the Achaians.
But come now, let us ask some prophet or priest of a temple,
or some seer of dreams, since also from Zeus does a dream come,
who might tell us the reason that Phoibos Apollo is angry,
65　if for a vow unachieved or a hecatomb lacking he blames us—
so, once he has received the smoke-savor of lambs and unblemished
goats, he may then be willing to keep us safe from destruction."
　　Thus having spoken he sat back down, and among them stood up
Kalchas the scion of Thestor, the best at interpreting bird-flights,
70　who knew what was at hand, what would be and formerly had been,

who had conducted to Ilion city the ships of the Achaians
through the prophetic endowment that Phoibos Apollo had granted;
he with benevolent wisdom addressed them, giving them counsel:
"You are demanding of me, Zeus-cherished Achilles, to speak out
75   now of the wrath of Apollo, the lord who shoots from a distance.
This indeed I will say—you heed me and swear me an oath that
you will be eager in words and in deeds of your hands to protect me,
since I think I am going to anger the man who is greatest
lord among all of the Argives, obeyed by all the Achaians.
80   Stronger a king is, when he is angry at someone beneath him,
since even if for the day itself he swallows his anger,
yet thereafter his rancor he holds, till he can fulfill it,
deep in his breast: take thought, say whether indeed you will guard me."
    Answering him in return spoke forth swift-footed Achilles:
85   "Now take courage, declare the divine will just as you know it.
No, by the lord Zeus-cherished Apollo, to whom you, Kalchas,
uttering prayers, for the Dánaän host make known the divine will,
no one as long as I live on the earth and am seeing the daylight,
here by the hollow galleys, will lay heavy hands on your body—
90   none of the Dánaän host, even if you mean Agamemnon,
who now boasts that he is far best among all the Achaians."
    Then did the faultless prophet again take courage and speak out:
"Not for a vow unachieved or a hecatomb lacking he blames us,
but on account of the priest, whom once Agamemnon dishonored—
95   neither his daughter he freed, nor the ransom for her he accepted;
therefore pains has the Far-shooter given, and still will he give them.
Nor will he thrust from the Dánaän army the shameful destruction
till we return to her own dear father the glancing-eyed maiden
quite without ransom or price, and a sacred hecatomb lead to
100   Chrysè; and then we might propitiate him and persuade him."
    So having spoken, he sat back down, and among them the hero
Atreus' son stood up, wide-governing Lord Agamemnon,
grievously pained, with a heart grown utterly black in its anger,
filled to the brim; and his eyes shone forth like radiant blazes.
105   Kalchas the first he addressed, with a glare which boded him evil:
"Prophet of banes, you do not say anything good for me ever;
always instead it pleases your spirit to prophesy evil;
never of anything good do you speak one word, nor achieve it.
So even now to the Dánaäns here you reveal the divine will,
110   why in fact the Far-shooter is visiting anguish upon them—

31

it is because I refused to accept for the daughter of Chryses
ransom splendid and huge, since I much rather would have that
maiden at home, for before even Klýtaimnéstra, my wedded
wife, I want to have her, since she is not any less worthy
115 either in form or in stature, not either in wit or achievements.
Even so, if it is better to give her back, I am willing—
I want rather my people to live than to come to destruction.
But straightway get ready a prize for me, so that I may not
be of the Argives alone without prize, since that is not seemly.
120 All of you witness to this, that the prize I had is gone elsewhere."
       Answering him then spoke swift-footed and noble Achilles:
"Atreus' glorious son, most greedy for gain of all people,
how are the great-souled Achaians to give you a prize for your honor?
Nowhere do we see communal stores laid up in abundance,
125 but those things we have plundered from cities have all been divided,
nor is it seemly to take them away from the troops and collect them.
But to the god you surrender the girl now; then we Achaians
three- or fourfold will requite you for her, should Zeus ever somehow
give us the well-walled city of Troy to be conquered and ransacked."
130   Answering him in return then spoke forth strong Agamemnon:
"Do not thus, although you are valorous, godlike Achilles,
try to beguile me, for neither will you outwit nor persuade me.
Or do you wish, so that you have a prize for yourself, that I sit here
just as I am, without one—this girl you exhort me to give back?
135 But if indeed some prize these great-souled Achaians will give me,
suiting it well to my wishes, so it will be just compensation,
good; if they do not give one, then I will myself go and take one,
either your own prize, or else Ajax's, or that of Odysseus,
seize and remove her; and he will be angry, whomever I visit.
140 Nevertheless, these things we can bring to discussion hereafter;
come now, down to the luminous sea let us drag a black galley,
gather the rowers in suitable numbers, a hecatomb also
put on the ship, and the fair-cheeked daughter of Chryses herself then
go on board; some man of the council should act as the leader—
145 let it indeed be Ajax, Idómeneus, noble Odysseus,
or you, Peleus' son, the most marvelous man among all men,
so you can gain us the grace of the Far-worker, offering victims."
       Looking from lowering brows spoke forth swift-footed Achilles:
"Oh you appareled in shamelessness, most greedy and guileful,
150 how, to obey your speeches, would any Achaian be eager

32

either to go on the road or with men to do strenuous combat?
For it was not on account of the Trojan spearmen that I came
here to do battle with them, since I did not have any reason,
for they never had driven away my cattle or horses,
155   nor had they ever in Phthia the fertile, nurturing people,
ravaged the fruit of the earth, since great is the distance between us,
shadowy mountains as well as the sea's loud-echoing waters.
But it was you, most shameful, we followed, so you would be happy,
seeking to win Meneláos his honor, and yours too, dog-face,
160   back from the Trojans; and this you neither regard nor remember;
no, and indeed you threaten to seize for yourself my prize for
which I labored so hard, and the sons of Achaians bestowed it.
Never do I have a prize that is equal to yours, when Achaians
conquer and sack some richly endowed citadel of the Trojans;
165   but as to most of the violent combat, mine are the hands which
carry it through, and whenever it comes to dividing the plunder,
yours is the prize far greater, and I with a small but a dear one
go back down to my galleys when I am exhausted with fighting.
Now am I leaving for Phthia, because it will be much better
170   going away in the well-curved ships—nor at all am I minded
here to remain dishonored and heap for you treasure and riches."
    Answering him then spoke Agamemnon, lord of the people:
"Run away then, if your heart is demanding it; never for my sake
I will entreat you to stay here—with me indeed there are others
175   who will show honor to me, Zeus Counselor even above all.
You are most hateful to me of the rulers belovèd of great Zeus;
always conflict is dear to your spirit, and battles and warfare.
If much stronger you are, it was surely a god who endowed you.
Then go away now, back to your home with your ships and your comrades,
180   govern the Mýrmidons there; not at all I heed or regard you,
nor do I trouble myself with your rancor; but thus do I warn you:
As from me Phoibos Apollo is taking the daughter of Chryses,
I will convey her back with a ship of my own and my comrades
thither, but I will then lead off the fair-cheeked daughter of Bríseus,
185   going myself to your cabin—your own prize—so that you know well
how much greater than you I am, and another will shrink from
speaking to me as an equal and vying with me in my presence."
    So he spoke, and in Peleus' son pain grew; in his shaggy
breast was the spirit divided and two ways pondered the matter,
190   whether to draw from the sheath on his thigh his keen-whetted sword-blade,

make the assembly disperse, then cut down Atreus' scion,
or to desist from his anger and put a strong curb on his spirit.
As he was pondering over these things in his mind and his spirit,
drawing his great sword out of its scabbard, Athena descended
195   down from the sky; she was sent by the goddess white-armed Hera,
who in her heart for them both felt equally loving and caring.
There behind Peleus' scion she stood, by his light hair drew him,
showing herself to him only, and none of the others could see her.
Then was Achilles amazed, and he turned in his place, and at once he
200   recognized Pallas Athena: her eyes were fearfully shining.
Raising his voice he spoke, and in these winged words he addressed her:
"Wherefore, offspring of Zeus of the aegis, have you now come here?
Is it to witness the outrage of Atreus' son Agamemnon?
But to you now I say, and I think this will be accomplished:
205   by such arrogant deeds he will soon be robbed of his life-breath."
     Speaking to him made answer the goddess bright-eyed Athena:
"I have come down to restrain your temper, if you will obey me,
here from the sky; I was sent by the goddess white-armed Hera,
who in her heart for you both feels equally loving and caring.
210   But come, leave off the strife, with your hand not drawing your sword out;
but in your words cast blame upon him as to how it will happen.
For I say to you plainly, and this will indeed be accomplished:
Someday you will possess three times such glorious presents
all on account of this outrage; but now hold back and obey me."
215   Answering her in return spoke forth swift-footed Achilles:
"Goddess, indeed this word of you both I must go along with—
though in my spirit I feel such rage—since so is it better;
who to the gods is submissive, to him they carefully listen."
     Thus, and the weight of his hand he laid on the silver-wrought sword-hilt,
220   back in the scabbard he thrust the great sword, and the word of Athena
he did not disobey, but the goddess was gone to Olympos,
joining the rest of the gods in the palace of Zeus of the aegis.
     Once more using contemptuous words then Peleus' scion
spoke out to Atreus' son—not yet did he leave off his anger:
225   "Wine-sodden man with the eyes of a dog and the heart of a roe deer,
never do you take arms with your people to enter the battle,
nor do you go with the noblest Achaians on ambushing parties;
you in your heart do not dare—that seems to you death and destruction.
No, far better for you in the widespread host of Achaians,
230   taking away his gift from a man who speaks out against you.

King who feed on the people, for those you govern are worthless—
otherwise, Atreus' son, this outrage now were your last one.
But I say to you this and a great oath swear you upon it:
by this scepter I hold, which never again will bear branches
235　nor any leaves, from the time it left its stump in the mountains,·
nor will it burgeon again, for the bronze blade utterly stripped it
both of its leaves and its bark—now at last do the sons of Achaians
bear it in hand to administer justice and keep in protection
customs established from Zeus—so the oath I swear you is mighty:
240　someday longing for Achilles will come to the sons of Achaians,
all of them; then you will not be able, in spite of your anguish,
ever to come to their aid, as before man-slaughtering Hektor
many are falling and dying; the heart in your breast you will rend in
furious wrath that you did not honor the best of the Achaians."
245　　So spoke Peleus' son; to the ground he dashed the great scepter
brilliantly studded with nails all golden, and he himself sat down.·
Atreus' son on the other side kept on raging; between them
stood up fair-spoken Nestor, the clear-voiced speaker of Pylos,
so were the words which flowed from his tongue much sweeter than honey.
250　He already had seen die two generations of mortal
men, those who with himself had been earlier reared and begotten
there in Pylos the sacred; he now ruled over the third one.
He with benevolent wisdom addressed them, giving them counsel:
"Oh what a shame—great sorrow has come on the land of Achaia!
255　Priam would surely be happy, and so would the children of Priam;
greatly as well would the rest of the Trojans rejoice in their spirits
should they learn all this of the two of you, how you are wrangling—
who in the council are best of the Dánaäns, best in the fighting.
But pay heed to me now—you are both much younger than I am.
260　For already have I in the past consorted with men who
were even better than you, and they did not once disregard me.
Never indeed have I seen such men, nor again will I see them,
as Peiríthoös was, as Druas the shepherd of people,
as Exádios, Kaíneus, and as godlike Polyphémos,
265　no, or as Theseus Aigeus' son, a man like the immortals.
Strongest of all men born on the earth those heroes were brought up;
strongest they were themselves, and as well they battled the strongest—
savages, mountain-bred Centaurs—and dreadfully routed and killed them.
Yes, those men were the ones I accompanied, going from Pylos
270　far, from a land a great distance away, since they themselves called me.

35

Then moreover I fought on my own, and against them would no one
now among mortals alive on the earth ever enter a battle.
Yes, and as well they heeded my counsels, obeyed what I told them.
Now you also obey me, because to obey is much better.

275 Do not you, great man though you are, rob him of his maiden,
leave her instead as the prize that the sons of Achaians first gave him;
nor do you, Peleus' scion, desire to contend with the king in
face-to-face wrangling, because not equal to others a sceptered
king is endowed with his honors, the one whom Zeus granted glory.

280 If in fact you are stronger, a goddess the mother who bore you,
yet this man is the greater, because more people he governs.
Atreus' scion, abandon your temper; indeed it is I who
plead with you, give up your wrath at Achilles, for he is the greatest
bulwark against the afflictions of battle for all the Achaians."

285   Answering him in return then spoke forth strong Agamemnon:
"Yes, of all this, old sir, you speak as is fitting and proper.
But now here is a man who wants to be over all others—
over us all he wants to hold power, of all to be ruler,
give us all orders; and yet I think one man will not heed him.

290 Even indeed if the gods who live always have made him a spearman,
therefore have they put forward for him these insults to utter?"
        Then in response thus spoke, interrupting him, noble Achilles:
"Certainly I would be called mere coward and counted for nothing
if in my every act I submit to whatever you tell me.

295 Lay these dictates of yours on others, but never to me give
orders, for I do not think that I will any longer obey you.
Something else I will tell you, and you keep this in your mind now:
I will indeed not fight with my hands on account of the maiden,
neither with you nor another, because you take her who gave her;

300 but of the other possessions of mine by the swift black galley,
nothing of them shall you seize and bear off while I am unwilling.
Come now, give it a trial, that these men also may know it:
then black blood will at once spurt out of you over my spear-shaft."
        So did the two men, when they had battled in quarrelsome speeches,

305 stand and disperse the assembly beside the Achaians' galleys.
Peleus' scion returned to his cabins and balanced galleys
taking Patróklos, Menoítios' son, and the rest of his comrades.
Atreus' son then dragged a swift ship down into the sea-brine,
chose out twenty good oarsmen for her, and a hecatomb put on

310 board for the god, and he led in the fair-cheeked daughter of Chryses;

then went on as commander Odysseus of many devices.
 They thus having embarked sailed out on the watery pathway;
Atreus' son then ordered the host to wash off the pollution.
So they washed it away, the defilements threw in the sea-brine,
315 then for Apollo they offered up hecatombs full and effective,
bulls and mature goats, there on the shore of the desolate sea-brine;
eddying round in the smoke their savor ascended to heaven.
 So were they busy around the whole army; and yet Agamemnon
did not forget the reprisal with which he had threatened Achilles,
320 but Talthýbios thus he addressed, and as well Eurybátes—
these two men were his heralds and ready and nimble retainers:
"Go straightway to the cabin of Peleus' scion Achilles;
taking the hand of the fair-cheeked daughter of Bríseus, bring her;
but if he will not give her, then I in person must take her,
325 going with plenty of men—and to him more dreadful will that be."
 So as he spoke he sent them and laid upon them a strong order.
They unwillingly went by the shore of the desolate sea-brine,
walking until they came to the Mýrmidons' cabins and galleys.
Him they came upon there by his cabin and near his black galley,
330 sitting; but not at all, seeing the two, was Achilles rejoicing.
Both men, stricken with terror and feeling respect for the king, just
stood there—neither a word they spoke nor a question they asked him.
But in his mind he knew of their business; thus he addressed them:
"Welcome, heralds, the messengers both of Lord Zeus and of mortals,
335 come near—not in the least do I blame you, but Agamemnon,
who sent both of you here on account of the daughter of Bríseus.
But come now, Zeus-cherished Patróklos, and lead out the maiden,
give her to them to take back. Yet witnesses let these two be,
both in the sight of the fortunate gods and of men who are mortal,
340 then of the king so harsh and relentless, if ever hereafter
need should arise for my aid in keeping a shameful destruction
off of the others, for he in his ruinous spirit is raving,
nor is he skillful in seeing at once the before and the after,
so the Achaians among their ships might battle in safety."
345 So he spoke, and Patróklos obeyed his belovèd companion—
out of the cabin the fair-cheeked daughter of Bríseus he led and
gave her to them to take back; they returned to the ships of the Achaians;
all unwilling the woman accompanied them. But Achilles,
weeping and drawing away from his comrades, sat on the seashore
350 there by the gray sea-brine, looking over the measureless seaway.

Much to his own dear mother he prayed, while stretching his hands out:
"Since you, mother, have given me birth, although to live briefly,
honor at least should Olympian Zeus who thunders above be
ready to grant me; but now not even a little he gives me,
355 seeing that Atreus' son, wide-governing Lord Agamemnon,
has dishonored me, since he has taken my prize and he keeps it."
      He spoke, shedding his tears; he was heard by the lady his mother
where she sat in the depths of the sea by her father, the Old Man.
Speedily out of the gray sea-brine like a mist she ascended,
360 there as he kept on shedding his tears she sat down beside him,
gave him a pat with her hand, and said these words, calling upon him:
"Why, my child, do you weep? What grief has come over your spirit?
Speak out, do not conceal it, in order that both of us know it."
      Heavily groaning, to her spoke forth swift-footed Achilles:
365 "You know—why should I tell you about all this when you know it?
We once went against Thébè, Eëtion's sacred city,
which we conquered and ransacked, and brought here all of the plunder.
This they distributed fairly among them, the sons of Achaians,
choosing the fair-cheeked daughter of Chryses for Atreus' scion.
370 Straightway Chryses, the priest of Apollo who shoots from a distance,
came to the swift-sailing galleys of those bronze-armored Achaians
seeking to free his daughter and bringing a measureless ransom,
bearing in hand bay-garlands of great far-shooting Apollo,
wound on a gold-wrought staff, and he pled with them, all the Achaians,
375 but above all the two scions of Atreus, marshals of people.
Thereat all of the other Achaians were shouting approval,
saying to honor the priest and accept the magnificent ransom;
yet this pleased not the spirit of Atreus' son Agamemnon;
roughly he sent him away, and he laid a strong order upon him.
380 Angrily then did the old man go back again; but Apollo,
heeding the priest as he prayed, since he exceedingly loved him,
shot at the Argives his arrow of evil, and now were the people
dying in rapid succession; the god's dread arrows were ranging
everywhere in the widespread host of Achaians; a prophet,
385 knowing it well, then told us about the Far-shooter's intention.
Quickly, the first, I urged that the god be propitiated;
straightway wrath seized Atreus' scion, and standing at once he
uttered a menacing word, and indeed that threat is accomplished.
For in a swift ship now have set forth quick-glancing Achaians
390 taking the maiden to Chrysè and bearing the lord their presents;

now too, heralds have gone from my cabin and taken away that
daughter of Bríseus given to me by the sons of Achaians.
But if in fact you can, to your own child grant your protection;
going aloft to Olympos, implore great Zeus, if you ever
395 either by word have gladdened the spirit of Zeus, or by action.
For in the halls of my father have I heard you very often
boasting, the times you said that you only among the immortals
kept from the dark-cloud scion of Kronos a shameful destruction;
that was the time when the other Olympians wanted to bind him,
400 Hera herself and Poseidon and also Pallas Athena.
But then, goddess, did you go and set him free from his bindings,
summoning quickly to lofty Olympos the hundred-handed
creature the gods Briáreus call, whereas all men name him
Aigaíon, for indeed he is greater in might than his father;
405 there by the scion of Kronos he sat, in his glory exulting;
then were the fortunate gods terrified, and they did not bind him.
Now sit down by him, grasping his knees, and remind him of these things,
should he perhaps be willing to come to the aid of the Trojans,
pen the Achaians together against the ships' sterns, by the sea-brine,
410 there to be killed, so that all may partake of the king's satisfaction,
also that Atreus' son, wide-governing Lord Agamemnon,
learn of his madness: he did not honor the best of the Achaians."
    Then in answer to him spoke Thetis, while letting her tears fall:
"Ah my child, why did I so cursèd in motherhood raise you?
415 How I wish you could sit by the ships unharmed and untearful,
since your destiny is to live briefly and not for a long time.
Now you are doomed to be swift in dying and wretched above all
men, so that I to a terrible fate bore you in the palace.
This word soon I will utter to Zeus the great thunderbolt-hurler—
420 going to snowy Olympos myself—if he might be persuaded.
Yet you now, as you sit by the swift-faring galleys, continue
angry against the Achaians and cease from the battle entirely;
for to the fine Ethiopian race at the Ocean did Zeus go
yesterday seeking a feast, and along with him all of the gods went;
425 but on the twelfth day he will be going again to Olympos,
then indeed I will go to the bronze-floored palace of great Zeus,
there by his knees I will hold him, and I think I will persuade him."
    Soon as she said these words, she took her departure and left him
there still angry at heart on account of the fair-girdled woman,
430 whom they were taking despite him, against his will. But Odysseus

meanwhile proceeded to Chrysè, the sacred hecatomb bringing.
Finally, when they arrived inside of the deepwater harbor,
furling the sails they lowered and stowed them within the black galley,
let down the mast with the forestays, positioning it on the mast-crutch
435 speedily; wielding their oars they rowed the ship in to the mooring.
They threw over the anchoring-stones, made fast the stern-cables,
then themselves disembarked on the tide-heaped sand of the seashore;
they unloaded the hecatomb then for far-shooting Apollo;
Chryses' daughter as well stepped out of the seafaring galley.
440 Leading her up to the altar, Odysseus of many devices
handed her into the arms of her father, and thus he addressed him:
"Chryses, to you Agamemnon the lord of the people dispatched me,
bringing to you your daughter and offering Phoibos a sacred
hecatomb here for the Dánaän host, so we may appease that
445 lord who has given the Argives to much lamentation and sorrow."
     So as he spoke, in his hands he placed her; rejoicing, he took his
dear child back. For the god they speedily stationed the sacred
hecatomb all in good order surrounding the well-built altar.
Then, having washed their hands, they took up the barley for sprinkling.
450 Chryses among them uttered a loud prayer, lifting his hands up:
"Hear me, god of the silvery bow, who stride around Chrysè
and around Killa the sacred and Ténedos mightily govern,
just as before one time you listened to what I was praying,
honoring me when strongly you struck at the host of the Achaians,
455 so once more for me now do you grant this boon that I pray for:
finally now ward off from the Dánaäns shameful destruction."
     So he spoke as he prayed; he was heard by Phoibos Apollo.
But then, when they had uttered a prayer and had sprinkled the barley,
drawing the heads back first, they slaughtered the victims and flayed them,
460 then they cut off the thighs and in thick fat covered them over,
making two layers, and morsels of flesh they fastened upon them.
These did the old man burn on the split wood, over them pouring
glistening wine, and the youths held five-pronged forks there beside him.
After the thighbones burned and the people partook of the entrails,
465 then they cut up the rest and on stakes they spitted the pieces;
carefully roasting the meat, they drew off all of the morsels.
Then when they had completed the work and had readied the dinner,
they dined, nor of the well-shared meal were their hearts at all wanting.
When they had quite satisfied their appetites, drinking and eating,
470 young men filled to the brim great wine bowls, ready for drinking,

then poured wine into all of the cups to begin the observance;
all day long with their singing the god they propitiated,
singing their beautiful paeans, the younger among the Achaians,
hymning the great Far-worker; he heard, in his mind took pleasure.

475 Soon as the sun went down and the shadows of night came upon them,
they lay down to their sleep on the shore by the ship's stern-cables.
Soon as the Dawn shone forth rose-fingered at earliest daybreak,
straightway they set sail for the widespread host of Achaians;
favoring them was a wind far-working Apollo had sent them.

480 Setting the mast upright, they hoisted and spread out the white sail;
wind poured into the sail's white belly, a wave purple-foaming
thundered loudly around the curved keel as the ship sailed onward;
so with the wave she was running, and so was achieving the journey.
Finally, when they came to the widespread host of Achaians,

485 straightway then they dragged the black ship up onto the dry land,
high up onto the sand, and they fixed tall props underneath her,
then they parted and scattered among their cabins and galleys.

There by the swift-sailing ships kept sitting, resentful and angry,
Peleus' scion descended of Zeus, swift-footed Achilles;

490 nor did he ever attend the assembly, in which men are honored,
nor did he ever go into the battle, but eating his heart out
stayed right there; but he always longed for the tumult and battle.

But then, soon as appeared thereafter the twelfth of the mornings,
finally back to Olympos proceeded the gods who live always,

495 all at one time, Zeus leading. Her son's entreaties had Thetis
never forgotten, but she rose out of the waves of the deep sea
early at dawn; to the great sky she went up, and Olympos.
Sitting apart from the rest the wide-thundering scion of Kronos
she found high on the loftiest summit of rocky Olympos.

500 Close to his side she sat down then, and his knees with her left hand
she embraced, and his chin from below she grasped with her right hand,
thus imploring she spoke to the lord Zeus, scion of Kronos:
"Zeus our father, if ever among the immortals I showed you
favor in word or in deed, then grant this boon that I pray for:

505 honor my son, who is doomed to be quickest in dying beyond all
others; but now in fact Agamemnon, lord of the people,
has dishonored him, since he has taken his prize, and he keeps it.
But now you give him honor, Olympian counselor, Lord Zeus—
just so long put might in the Trojans until the Achaians

510 grant my son a requital and render him wealthy in honor."

So she spoke; not a word to her said the cloud-gathering god Zeus,
but a long time sat silent; and Thetis, as then she had grasped his
knees, now held to them fast and again for a second time asked him:
"Either in full faith make me a promise and nod your agreement,
515 or else refuse, since nothing you fear now, so that I know well
how much I among all of the gods am the most dishonored."

Sorely displeased, thus spoke to her then the cloud-gathering god Zeus:
"Ruinous work this is, inciting me so to a fight with
Hera, when she with words of revilement troubles and taunts me.
520 Even the way things are, she always among the immortal
gods upbraids me and says I am aiding the Trojans in battle.
Nevertheless, go back again now, so that Hera will not learn
any of this; these things I will care for and so will achieve them.
Come, I will nod to you now with my head, so you may believe me,
525 for it is this that among the immortals is greatest in pledging
what I intend—my word is not revocable nor deceitful,
nor does it lack fulfillment when once with my head I have nodded."

Thus did Kronos' son speak, and he nodded his head with its dark brows,
and the ambrosial tresses were sweeping around from the deathless
530 head of the sovereign lord, so that mighty Olympos was shaken.

So having planned these matters the two separated, and she then
leapt down into the deep sea-brine from resplendent Olympos,
Zeus went back to his palace; and straightway all of the gods stood
up from their seats when faced with their father, and none of them dared to
535 stay in his place as he came, but they all stood, giving him greeting.
So on his throne he sat; but as soon as she saw him the goddess
Hera was not unaware that with him some scheme had been plotting
Thetis of silvery feet, the Old Man of the Sea's dear daughter.
Straightway in words of reproach she addressed Zeus, scion of Kronos:
540 "Which of the gods, you deceiver, with you some scheme has been plotting?
Always dear to your spirit it is, anytime I am absent,
thinking of secret affairs and deciding them, nor are you ever
willing to speak me a word forthrightly about your intentions."

Speaking to her then answered the father of gods and of mankind:
545 "Hera, do not keep hoping that you are to know about all my
counsels—for you they will be too hard, though you are my bedmate.
But if a thing be fitting to hear about, nobody then will
know it before you do, no one of the gods nor of mortals;
anything I quite apart from the gods might wish to consider,
550 neither should you inquire of the details nor ask me about it."

Speaking to him then answered the ox-eyed queen, Lady Hera:
"Most dread scion of Kronos, and what is this word you have spoken!
All too true that before I never inquired or asked questions,
but quite free of disturbance whatever you want you have plotted.
555 Now in my heart I dreadfully fear she has won you over,
Thetis of silvery feet, the Old Man of the Sea's dear daughter.
Early at dawn she sat beside you, by the knees she embraced you;
then I suspect you nodded a pledge unfailing that you will
honor Achilles, destroy many men by the ships of the Achaians."
560   Answering her in return spoke forth the cloud-gathering god Zeus:
"You strange woman, you always suspect—I never escape you;
nevertheless you cannot do anything, but you will be yet
farther away from my heart; and for you that is more to be dreaded.
If things are as you say, they surely will be to my pleasure.
565 But sit down and be silent, and heed this word I am saying,
lest no help to protect you will be all the gods on Olympos
should I approach you and lay invincible hands on your body."
    So he spoke; terrified was the ox-eyed queen, Lady Hera;
she sat down and was silent; her heart she bent to obey him.
570 Then in the palace of Zeus were the heavenly gods much troubled;
quickly among them Hephaistos renowned for his craft began speaking—
comfort he brought to his much-loved mother, the white-armed Hera:
"Surely disastrous, no longer endurable, will our affairs be,
if on account of those mortals the two of you thus are to wrangle,
575 dragging among us gods such brawls—no more in the noble
banquet will there be pleasure, for ever the worst is the winner.
I would advise my mother, although of herself she knows it,
comfort to bring to our dear father Zeus, so that not any longer
Father will quarrel with her and will thereby trouble our feasting.
580 For in fact if he wished, the Olympian thunderbolt-wielder
out of our places could thrust us, for he is much stronger than we are.
But now speak and address him in some soft word of appeasement;
straightway for us the Olympian lord will be kindly and gracious."
    So did he say, then sprang to his feet, and he put a two-handled
585 cup in the hands of his much-loved mother, and thus he addressed her:
"Be of good heart, dear mother, endure, although you are grieving,
lest with my own eyes I should behold you, as much as I love you,
smitten, and then in spite of my sorrowing I could not give you
succor, for terrible is the Olympian faced as a rival.
590 For already before, at a time I thought to defend you,

43

picking me up by the feet, from the marvelous threshold he threw me.
All day long I was dropping, until at the hour of the sunset
I fell down onto Lemnos, and small life yet was within me.
There did the Sintian people attend to me once I had fallen."

595 So he spoke, and the goddess white-armed Hera was smiling;
then with a smile, from the hand of her son she accepted the goblet.
Straightway for all of the rest of the gods from the left to the right he
started to pour sweet nectar that he dipped up from the wine bowl.
Then in the fortunate gods there arose unquenchable laughter,
600 as they observed how Hephaistos was bustling about in the palace.
 So it was that for that whole day till the hour of the sunset
they dined, nor of the well-shared meal were their hearts at all wanting,
nor of the sounds of the beautiful lyre that Apollo was holding,
nor of the Muses, who sang in lovely antiphonal voices.
605 Later, as soon as had set the god Helios' radiant sunlight,
then they departed to rest for the night, each one to his own house,
where for each one of the gods had Hephaistos the glorious twice-lame
cripple erected a palace with his ingenious cunning;
off to his bed went Zeus the Olympian thunderbolt-wielder,
610 where he had always lain when a sweet sleep came down upon him;
going up there he slept, with the gold-throned Hera beside him.

BOOK 2

So were the rest of the gods and the men who were chariot-marshals
sleeping the whole night through; sweet slumber did not hold the god Zeus,
but in his mind he was pondering over the way that he might now
honor Achilles and kill many men by the ships of the Achaians.
5 This is the plan which seemed to him then in his spirit the best one—
sending a baneful dream down to Atreus' son Agamemnon;
raising his voice he spoke, and in these winged words he addressed it:
"Go down, baneful dream, to the swift ships of the Achaians;
making your way to the cabin of Atreus' son Agamemnon,
10 tell him exactly and fully of all these things, as I charge you.
Bid him to arm for the battle the long-haired men, the Achaians,
acting in haste; for the wide-wayed city of Trojans he now might
capture, because the immortals who live in Olympian dwellings
no more argue about it; for Hera has bent to her purpose
15 all of them, making her plea, and affliction is fixed on the Trojans."
So he spoke, and the dream went down—to his word it had listened;
speedily then it arrived at the swift ships of the Achaians,
going to Atreus' son Agamemnon, and there in his cabin
found him asleep—ambrosial slumber was pouring around him.
20 Over his head it stood in the likeness of Neleus' scion
Nestor, whom Agamemnon respected the most of the old men;
likened to Nestor, the baneful dream spoke out and addressed him:
"Are you asleep, son of war-skilled Atreus tamer of horses?
Not the whole night should slumber a man who is weighted with counsel,
25 who has the troops entrusted to him and so much to concern him.
Now give heed to me quickly—from Zeus I bring you a message—
though at a distance from you, he feels much care and compassion—
bidding you arm for the battle the long-haired men, the Achaians,
acting in haste; for the wide-wayed city of Trojans you now might
30 capture, because the immortals who live in Olympian dwellings

no more argue about it; for Hera has bent to her purpose
all of them, making her plea, and affliction is fixed on the Trojans
from Lord Zeus; keep this in your mind—let oblivion not take
hold of you once this honey-sweet slumber releases and leaves you."

35   So having said, it parted from there, and it left Agamemnon
pondering things in his heart that in fact would not be accomplished,
since he believed he would capture the city of Priam on that day,
fool, nor at all did he know of the works that Zeus was devising,
since yet longer was he to inflict lamentations and sorrows
40   both on the Trojan and Dánaän hosts in the violent combats.
Out of his sleep he awoke, the divine voice drifting about him.
Rising, he sat upright, and at once put on a soft tunic,
beautiful, recently woven, and over it threw a great mantle;
under his glistening feet he fastened his beautiful sandals,
45   straightway around his shoulders he hung a sword studded with silver,
then took up the ancestral scepter, immortal forever;
carrying it, he went to the ships of the bronze-clad Achaians.
      Soon as the goddess Dawn went upward to lofty Olympos,
telling of daylight to Zeus and the rest of the gods who live always,
50   then the king ordered the clear-voiced heralds to make an announcement
summoning to the assembly the long-haired men, the Achaians;
they gave out the announcement; the men very quickly assembled.
      First he summoned a session of great-souled elders to council
close to the galley of Nestor, the king whom Pylos had brought forth.
55   These men calling together, he framed shrewd counsel among them:
"Hear me, friends; a divine dream came upon me in my slumber,
through the ambrosial night, and above anyone, noble Nestor
it most closely resembled in beauty and size and appearance.
It stood over my head, and it spoke this word and addressed me:
60   'Are you asleep, son of war-skilled Atreus tamer of horses?
Not the whole night should slumber a man who is weighted with counsel,
who has the troops entrusted to him and so much to concern him.
Now give heed to me quickly—from Zeus I bring you a message;
though at a distance from you, he feels much care and compassion,
65   bidding you arm for the battle the long-haired men, the Achaians,
acting in haste; for the wide-wayed city of Trojans you now might
capture, because the immortals who live in Olympian dwellings
no more argue about it; for Hera has bent to her purpose
all of them, making her plea, and affliction is fixed on the Trojans
70   from Lord Zeus; keep this in your mind now.' Thus having spoken,

it went flying away, and at once sweet slumber released me.
Come, let us somehow arm for the battle the sons of Achaians.
First I will give them a trial in words, as is fitting and proper:
yes, I will bid them flee with the galleys of numerous oarlocks;
75 you, one place or another, should hold them back with your speeches."

So having spoken he sat back down, and among them stood up
Nestor, the man who ruled as the king over sandy-soiled Pylos;
he with benevolent wisdom addressed them, giving them counsel:
"Oh dear friends and companions, the Argives' leaders and princes,
80 if it had been some other Achaian who told us of this dream,
we would declare it a falsehood, and certainly we would reject it.
Now the man boasting to be far best of the Achaians has seen it.
Come, let us somehow arm for the battle the sons of Achaians."

So having spoken, he led them to go forth out of the council;
85 then those kings bearing scepters, obeying the shepherd of people,
rose up onto their feet, and the troops came hastening after.
Just as a honeybee nation in swarms close-crowded emerges
out of a hollow rock, and afresh bees always are coming—
like thick clustering grapes they fly among flowers in springtime,
90 some of them flying in throngs one way, some flying another—
so were the numerous nations of men from the galleys and cabins
marching along in troops at the front of the deep wide seashore,
making their way to assembly; and Rumor was blazing among them,
urging them onward, the Zeus-sent messenger; so were they gathered.
95 Shaken indeed was the place of assembly; the earth underneath them
groaned as the people were seated in tumult, and all nine heralds
cried out loudly and tried to control them, so they would keep from
shouting and listen with care to the rulers belovèd of heaven.
After much trouble the people were seated and kept in their places,
100 putting a stop to the clamor. And then stood strong Agamemnon
holding the scepter in hand that Hephaistos had labored to fashion.
This had Hephaistos given to Lord Zeus, scion of Kronos,
then Zeus gave it in turn to the messenger, slayer of Argos;
Hermes the lord next gave it to Pelops, driver of horses;
105 Pelops in turn then gave it to Atreus, shepherd of people;
Atreus, perishing, left it again to sheep-wealthy Thyéstes,
then Thyéstes left it to Lord Agamemnon to carry
and to bear sway over numerous islands and over all Argos.
Leaning upon this now, these words he addressed to the Argives:
110 "Oh friends, Dánaän heroes and noble attendants of Ares,

47

Zeus son of Kronos has mightily bound me in grievous derangement,
cruel and harsh—he before made promise and nodded agreement,
after I ransacked strong-walled Ilion I would return home;
now instead he has plotted an evil deception and bids me
115 go back to Argos dishonored when I have lost many people.
Thus no doubt to all-powerful Zeus it will be very pleasing,
who already has ruined the citadels in many cities,
then yet more will he ruin, for his is the mightiest power.
For indeed it is shameful for men of the future to hear of,
120 thus in vain that so great and so valiant a host of Achaians
entered a war and engaged in battle without any outcome,
fighting against men fewer than they, never showing fulfillment.
For if indeed the Achaians and Trojans were willing to do it,
cutting a truce to be trusted, and both sides then being numbered,
125 then if the Trojans were counted according to those who have households,
while we Achaians in tens were divided and set in order,
each of our tens chose out as a wine-pourer one of the Trojans,
many among those tens of a pourer of wine would be lacking.
So much greater in number, I say, are the sons of Achaians
130 than are the Trojans who dwell in the city; but there are the allies,
men who are fine spear-wielders from numerous cities, who aid them.
They keep driving me back and will not let me, though I wish to,
capture and ransack Ilion's well-inhabited city.
Nine are the years of all-powerful Zeus which now have departed,
135 rotted away are the beams of the ships, and the cables are slackened;
while I suppose our bedmates as well as our innocent children
sit in our houses forever awaiting us; thus is our labor
now still quite unaccomplished, the matter for which we have come here.
But come, just as I say, let all of us heed and obey it:
140 let us take flight with our ships to the much-loved land of our fathers,
since there is hope no longer that wide-wayed Troy we will capture."
    So he spoke, and in them he roused up the heart in their bosoms,
all those many among them who had not heard him in council.
Then the assembly was stirred like the huge high waves of the deep sea
145 on the Ikárian seaway, when Notos and Euros the south-east
winds rush down from the clouds of the great father Zeus and arouse them.
As at its coming the west wind stirs the deep grain to commotion,
blustering, rushing on it, and the stalks with the ears are bent over,
so now all the assembly of people was stirred; with an outcry
150 they rushed down to the galleys; beneath their feet did the dust rise

48

billowing up in the air; and they bade each other at once to
lay their hands on the galleys and drag them down to the bright sea,
cleaning the keel-troughs out; and the noise reached up to the heavens,
as for their homes they parted, removing the props from the galleys.
155   Then beyond fate a return for the Argives might have befallen
had not Hera addressed these words to Athena and spoken:
"Well now, daughter of Zeus of the aegis, unwearying goddess,
thus indeed to their homes, to the much-loved land of their fathers,
now will the Argives take flight upon the broad back of the deep sea!
160 So would they leave as a trophy for Priam and all of the Trojans
Helen of Argos, the woman for whom so many Achaians
have been slaughtered in Troy, faraway from the land of their fathers.
But now go to the army of those bronze-armored Achaians;
speaking to each of the men, with your mild words stop the departure;
165 do not allow them to drag to the sea their tractable galleys."
    She spoke, nor disobeyed her the goddess bright-eyed Athena;
speedily she came down from the summit of lofty Olympos,
then she quickly arrived at the swift ships of the Achaians.
There she discovered Odysseus, the equal of Zeus in devices,
170 standing, and never had he laid hand on his dark-hued strong-benched
galley, for anguish had come upon him, in his heart and his spirit.
Standing beside him there, thus spoke to him bright-eyed Athena:
"Zeus-sprung son of Laërtes, Odysseus of many devices,
thus will you now to your homes, to the much-loved land of your fathers,
175 take flight, flinging yourselves in the galleys of numerous oarlocks?
So would you leave as a trophy for Priam and all of the Trojans
Helen of Argos, the woman for whom so many Achaians
have been slaughtered in Troy, faraway from the land of their fathers.
But now go to the host of Achaians—refrain no longer;
180 speaking to each of the men, with your mild words stop the departure;
do not allow them to drag to the sea their tractable galleys."
    So she said, and he heeded the words that the goddess had spoken;
he went running and throwing his mantle off—this did the herald
catch, Eurybátes the Ithakan man who attended upon him.
185 Going to meet face-to-face Agamemnon, Atreus' son, he
took from his hand the ancestral scepter, immortal forever,
held it and went by the galleys of those bronze-armored Achaians.
    There, whichever the king he encountered, or man of distinction,
standing beside him, he with his mild words stopped his departure:
190 "Good man, it is not seemly to make you afraid, like a coward,

but of yourself sit down, and the other men cause to be seated.
You do not yet know clearly the purpose of Atreus' scion;
now he is trying them; soon he will strike those sons of Achaians.
There in the council, did all of us not hear what he was saying?
195   May he in wrath not do any harm to the sons of Achaians!
Huge indeed is the temper of rulers belovèd of heaven,
straight from Zeus is their honor, and much Zeus Counselor loves them."

But whichever the man of the people he saw and found shouting,
him he would strike with the scepter, and with such words he would scold him:
200   "Good man, sit and be quiet, and hear what others are saying,
those who are better than you are, a coward unfit for a battle,
you who never are counted in combat nor in the council.
There is no way in which all the Achaians could be here as rulers—
it is not good that the many be lords; let one be the leader,
205   one king, he whom the scion of Kronos of crooked devices
gives both scepter and judgment, so he rules over the people."

Thus through the army he went as its leader, and to the assembly
place they rushed to return once more from the galleys and cabins,
clamoring, as when a wave from the deep sea rumbling and booming
210   thundering breaks on the great sea-beach, and the seaway is roaring.

So then all of the others were seated and kept to their places;
still Thersítes alone, unmeasured in speech, kept railing;
he in his mind knew numerous words, disorderly ones with
which he vainly, without due order, would wrangle with princes,
215   but whatever he thought would elicit a laugh from the Argives.
He was the ugliest man to have come beneath Ilion city,
dragging his feet—he was limping in one leg—both of his shoulders
rounded about his chest, all hunching together; above, his
head curved in to a point, and a sparse nap sprouted upon it.
220   Hateful he was to Achilles especially, and to Odysseus,
since those two he would often revile; but to great Agamemnon
he cried stridently, shouting abuse, and at him the Achaians
were exceedingly angry, resentful of him in their spirits.
Still he raucously shouted in words that reviled Agamemnon:
225   "Atreus' son, why now do you find fault? What are you lacking?
Filled are your cabins with bronzes; inside of your cabins are women
too, a great number, the choicest among them, whom the Achaians
gave you first of the leaders, whenever we captured a city.
Or do you still feel lacking in gold which one of the sons of
230   Trojans, the tamers of horses, from Ilion fetches as ransom,

one whom I or another Achaian have fettered and brought here,
or a young woman, that you might join her in bed and affection,
whom you keep for yourself and apart from us? It is not right for
you, their leader, to bring into harm these sons of Achaians.

235   Weaklings, disgraces, the daughters, no longer the sons, of Achaians,
let us indeed go home in our galleys, and let us allow this
man here in Troy to enjoy his prizes, that he may discover
whether or not we others are giving him any assistance,
who just lately Achilles, a man much better than he is,

240   has dishonored, because he has taken his prize, and he keeps it.
But in his heart no wrath has Achilles, but he is neglectful;
otherwise, Atreus' son, this outrage now were your last one."

    So Thersítes reviled Agamemnon, shepherd of people,
speaking abuse, but at once beside him stood noble Odysseus;

245   looking from lowering brows, with a harsh word thus he rebuked him:
"Reckless of speech Thersítes, although so clear-voiced a speaker,
hold back, and not by yourself keep wanting to wrangle with princes.
For as I think there is no man else any baser than you of
all who came beneath Ilion city with Atreus' scion.

250   Therefore do not have kings on your lips as you utter your speeches,
neither at them bring forward reproaches, or look for homecoming.
We do not yet know clearly the way these matters will happen,
whether we sons of Achaians will go home safely or badly.
Therefore Atreus' son Agamemnon, shepherd of people,

255   now you sit here reviling, because these Dánaän heroes
give him so much they have won: sheer mockery, all you are speaking.
But I say to you plainly, and this thing will be accomplished:
should I again come upon you playing the fool, as you now are,
may no longer the head of Odysseus sit on his shoulders,

260   nor any longer may I be known as Telémachos' father
then, if I do not seize you and strip off the clothes from your body,
mantle and tunic and all which cover it, hiding the privates,
then dispatch you whining and sniveling down to the swift ships,
striking you out of the place of assembly with strokes of abasement."

265   So he spoke; with the scepter he struck the man's back and his shoulders;
he bent double in pain, and a great tear fell from his eyelid.
Ruddy with blood was the welt that arose on his back, in the middle,
under the gold-wrought scepter, and he sat down again, frightened,
suffering anguish, and helplessly gazing and wiping his tears off.

270   Grieved as they were, at Thersítes the men were merrily laughing;

51

thus would one of them say as he looked at another beside him:
"Well now, thousands of excellent things has Odysseus accomplished,
taking the lead in superior counsels and marshaling battle;
this deed now is the best by far he has done for the Argives,
275　thus restraining from ranting the scurrilous hurler of speeches.
Certainly not, I believe, will his valorous spirit arouse him
ever again with words of revilement to wrangle with princes."

　　So was the multitude speaking; the sacker of cities Odysseus
stood up holding the scepter; beside him bright-eyed Athena,
280　making herself like a herald, commanded the host to be silent,
so that together the nearest and farthest away of the Argives
might be able to hear his words and take mind of his counsel.
He with benevolent wisdom addressed them, giving them counsel:
"Scion of Atreus, lord, the Achaians are wanting to make you
285　now a despicable thing in the sight of all men who are mortal,
nor will they bring to fulfillment the promise that they undertook when
hither they still were making their way from horse-nourishing Argos—
after they ransacked strong-walled Ilion they would return home.
For, as if they were but weak young children or husbandless women,
290　they to each other are wailing to go back now to their homeland.
Yes, and indeed there is labor to make a man leave in affliction,
since anyone who stays even one month far from his bedmate
chafes in his many-benched ship with impatience, a man whom the wintry
stormwinds thwart and confine, and the deep sea rising in billows.
295　But for ourselves, it is nine long years in the circle of seasons
we have been lingering here; so I do not blame the Achaians
by the curved galleys for chafing impatiently. Nevertheless most
shameful it is to remain so long and return empty-handed.
Take heart, friends, and remain for a time yet, so that we find out
300　whether the prophecy Kalchas has uttered is true or is not true.
For in my spirit I know this well, and indeed all of you are
witnesses, whom Death's agents have not gone taking you with them:
when but a day or two after the ships of the Achaians in Aulis
gathered to carry disaster to Priam and all of the Trojans,
305　we were at that time, close to the spring, on the sacred altar
making the deathless gods our hecatombs full and effective,
under a beautiful plane tree, from which ran shimmering water;
there then appeared a great omen, a snake with a back that was blood red,
dreadful and grim—the Olympian lord brought it to the daylight.
310　Darting from under the altar, it rose up onto the plane tree.

Therein then were the young of a sparrow, her delicate children—
under the leaves on the topmost branch they cowered in terror;
eight there were, and the ninth was the mother who bore those children.
All of the young it devoured most piteously as they twittered,
315　while their mother was fluttering round and lamenting her children.
Coiling to spring, by the wing it seized her shrieking about them.
Finally, when it had eaten the sparrow's children and her too,
then it was made a clear sign by the god who before had revealed it,
turned to a stone by the scion of Kronos of crooked devices.
320　Thereupon, standing about, we marveled at all that had happened.
So when the gods' sacrifices the dread portent interrupted,
Kalchas at once spoke out, prophesying, and thus he addressed us:
'Why are you hushed in silence, you long-haired men, you Achaians?
This great omen for us Zeus Counselor brought to our vision,
325　late come, late in fulfillment, the fame of it never to perish.
As this serpent has eaten the sparrow's children and her too,
eight there were, and the ninth was the mother who bore those children,
so the same number of years we will be there fighting our battles;
finally then in the tenth we will capture the city of wide ways.'
330　So he spoke to us then: all this is now being accomplished.
But come, all of you keep to your place, you well-greaved Achaians,
stay until we have captured and sacked the great city of Priam."

　　So he spoke, and the Argives shouted aloud, and the galleys
dreadfully echoed around to the clamorous sound of Achaians
335　crying approval and praise for the words of the godlike Odysseus.
Then spoke also among them the horseman Gerenian Nestor:
"Well now! It is indeed like children that you are assembled,
innocent youngsters to whom mean nothing the labors of warfare.
Where will the covenants fixed and the oaths we have sworn disappear to?
340　Into the fire let counsels be cast, and the plans of the fighters,
unmixed wine of libations, the right-hand grips we have trusted!
For it is only with words we wrangle, and never at all are
able to find any cure, though we have been here for a long time.
Atreus' son, as before, keep holding your purpose unshaken,
345　leading the Argives still in the midst of the violent combats.
Let them perish, the one or two men, whoever apart from
all the Achaians devise such schemes—they will not be accomplished—
now to go homeward to Argos, before, as to Zeus of the aegis,
they learn whether or not his promise is merely a falsehood.
350　For I say to you this: the all-powerful scion of Kronos

nodded his promise the day we left on the seafaring galleys,
all of the Argives, bearing destruction and death to the Trojans—
lightning he flashed on the right, so showing a favorable omen.
So let none of you be in a hurry to part for his homeland
355   ever, until he has lain in a bed with the wife of a Trojan,
thus exacting revenge for our struggles and groans over Helen.
Should any man be terribly anxious to part for his homeland,
let him at once lay hands on his well-benched dark-hued galley,
so that in front of the others he meets his death and his doomsday.
360   But Lord, take good counsel yourself, pay heed to another;
never to be discarded will be this word I address you.
Set in order the men by tribes and by clans, Agamemnon,
so that a clan gives help to its clansmen, a tribe to its tribesmen.
If in this way you work it, and if the Achaians obey you,
365   then will you learn which leaders are cowards, and which of the people—
also which are the noble, for they will each fight with their own band.
You will learn too if by heaven's intent you will not sack the city,
or if instead by men's cowardice and their folly in warfare."
     Answering him in return then spoke forth strong Agamemnon:
370   "Old sir, again in counsel you vanquish the sons of Achaians.
Oh Zeus, father of all, and Athena as well, and Apollo,
would that among the Achaians were ten such counselors near me!
Then very quickly the city of great Lord Priam would bow down
under our conquering hands, be taken and utterly ransacked!
375   But to me Kronos' son Zeus of the aegis has given afflictions,
he who has thrown me among such fruitless quarrels and conflicts.
For on account of a maiden have I and Achilles been fighting
violently in our speeches, and I was the first to be angry.
If to one counsel we ever agree, no longer will there be
380   then for the Trojans a respite from evil, not even a brief one.
Now go back to our dinner, that we may join in the warfare.
Carefully each man sharpen his spear, and his shield make ready;
carefully each put fodder before his swift-footed horses;
carefully each, looking over his chariot, meditate battle,
385   so that all day we contend in the warfare of odious Ares,
since no pause for a rest will there be, not even a brief one,
not until night comes on, separating the might of the fighters.
Then will a man's sweat dampen the baldric surrounding his chest to
hold the man-sheltering shield, and the hand on his spear will grow weary;
390   then will his steeds be wet, at the well-polished chariot straining.

Anyone I may discover apart from the battle, desiring
back there by the curved galleys to stay, no longer will he have
reason for hoping that he will escape from the dogs and the vultures."
    So he spoke, and the Argives shouted aloud, as the breakers
395 crash on a towering cliff when the south wind rises to drive them
onto the crag out-jutting, and never do waves from the stormwinds—
all of them—leave it alone, as they start up hither and thither.
They stood, rushed from assembly, and scattered away to the galleys,
kindled the fires at their cabins and then partook of their dinners.
400 Some to one, some to another immortal god offered a victim,
praying that they would escape their death and the struggle of Ares.
But a fat bull of five years Agamemnon, lord of the people,
offered as victim to Zeus, the all-powerful scion of Kronos,
after he summoned the elders and noblest of all the Achaians,
405 Nestor the first of them all, and the lord Idómeneus also,
then right after, the two Ajaxes and Tydeus' scion;
sixth among them was Odysseus, the equal of Zeus in devices.
But of himself came there the great crier of war Meneláos,
for in his heart he knew his own brother and how he was busied.
410 Circling the bull they stood, and the barley meal lifted above it;
raising a prayer, thus spoke out among them strong Agamemnon:
"Zeus most honored and mighty, the dark-cloud dweller of heaven,
now may the sun not set and the shadows of night come upon us,
ever, until I have thrown to the earth the great palace of Priam,
415 blackened with smoke, and have kindled its gates in fiery blazes,
and from about his breast I have riven the tunic of Hektor
with a bronze sword into shreds; let many companions around him
fall headlong in the dust, and the earth in their teeth be taken."
    So did he say; not yet would the scion of Kronos fulfill it,
420 but the oblations he took, and the ceaseless toil he augmented.
But then, when they had uttered a prayer and had sprinkled the barley,
drawing its head back first, they slaughtered the victim and flayed it,
then they cut off the thighs and in thick fat covered them over,
making two layers, and morsels of flesh they fastened upon them.
425 These they burned on pieces of split wood stripped of their leafage;
spitting the entrails, over the flame of Hephaistos they held them.
After the thighbones burned and the people partook of the entrails,
then they cut up the rest and on stakes they spitted the pieces;
carefully roasting the meat, they drew off all of the morsels.
430 Then when they had completed the work and had readied the dinner,

they dined, nor of the well-shared meal were their hearts at all wanting.
When they had quite satisfied their appetites, drinking and eating,
speaking among them opened the horseman Gerenian Nestor:
"Atreus' glorious son Agamemnon, lord of the people,
435 now let us talk no longer of these things, nor for a long time
put off doing the work that the god to our hands has entrusted.
But come now, let the heralds of these bronze-armored Achaians
summon the people and down by the ships call them to assembly;
meanwhile let us together among the broad host of Achaians
440 go, so that we more swiftly may rouse impetuous Ares."

He spoke, nor ignored him Agamemnon, lord of the people;
straightway he ordered the clear-voiced heralds to make an announcement
summoning into the battle the long-haired men, the Achaians.
They gave out the announcement; the men very quickly assembled.
445 Then did the kings, Zeus-nourished, around great Atreus' scion
make haste marshaling them, and among them bright-eyed Athena
holding aloft the magnificent aegis, immortal and ageless;
from it a hundred tassels entirely of gold were aflutter,
all well woven and each of a hundred oxen in value.
450 Brilliantly blazing with this she rushed through the host of Achaians,
stirring them up to go forward and rousing the vigor of each man's
heart inside him to battle implacably, fight without ceasing.
Quickly the battle became much sweeter to them than to go back
home in the hollow ships to the much-loved land of their fathers.

455 Just as a ruinous fire flames out in a measureless forest
high on the crest of a peak, and the brightness appears from afar off,
so as the army was marching the gleam of the marvelous brazen
arms shone out all around in the upper air, reaching to heaven.

Thus were they too: in the way that the winged birds' numerous nations,
460 either of geese or of cranes or of long-necked swans of the meadow,
there in the Asian country, around the Kaÿstrios' eddies,
hither and thither are flying, as they in their wings are exulting;
clamorous, ever advancing they settle, the meadow reechoes—
so those numerous nations of men from the galleys and cabins
465 poured forth into the plain of Skamánder; the ground underneath their
feet and the feet of their horses was terribly, loudly resounding.
There they took up a stand on the flowered Skamándrian meadow,
thousands of them, as the leaves and the flowers appear in their season.

Just as the numerous nations of flies keep buzzing and swarming,
470 flying around inside of the fold enclosing a sheep flock,

when in the springtime season the milk pours into the buckets,
just such numerous long-haired men, the Achaians, were standing
there on the plain and against those Trojans, desiring to smash them.
　　Thus were they too: as among wide flocks of their goats do the goatherds
475　easily separate them when they in the pastures have mingled,
so were the leaders dividing the men now, hither and thither,
as to the battle they went; and among them strong Agamemnon,
most in his eyes and his head like Zeus the great thunderbolt-hurler,
but in his loins like Ares, in chest most like to Poseidon.
480　Just as a bull in the herd stands out above all of the other
oxen, for he is distinguished whenever the cattle are gathered,
so it was that for that day Zeus made Atreus' scion,
most outstanding of many, distinguished among all the heroes.
　　Now speak out to me, Muses who live in Olympian dwellings,
485　since you goddesses always are present and know about all things—
we hear only the rumor and glory and know about nothing—
tell me who were the marshals and lords of the Dánaän forces.
All of the host I never could tell or enumerate fully,
not if I had ten tongues and as well ten mouths to recite them,
490　and an unbreakable voice, and the heart inside me were brazen,
ever, unless the Olympian Muses, the daughters of Zeus who
carries the aegis, recalled who came beneath Ilion city.
Now will I tell those leaders of galleys and all of the galleys.
　　Léïtos led the Boiótians there, and Penéleos also,
495　Árkesiláos as well, then Klonios and Prothoênor,
they who in Hyria had their abodes and in rock-strewn Aulis,
Schoinos also, and Skolos, and multiple-ridged Eteónos,
Théspeia also, and Graia, and spaciously broad Mykaléssa,
those who dwelt around Harma, Eilésion too, and Erýthrai,
500　those who inhabited Éleon, Péteon also, and Hylè,
those in Okálea dwelling and Médeon, solidly founded,
Kopai and Eútresis also and Thisbè of numerous dovecotes,
those who held Koroneía and meadow-endowed Haliártos,
those who abode in Plataía and those who inhabited Glísas,
505　those who held lower Thebes, that city of noble foundation,
then Onchéstos the sacred, the glorious grove of Poseidon,
those who inhabited Arnè of great vineyards, and Mideía,
sacred Nisa as well and Anthédon, away on the seashore.
Fifty in all were the galleys of theirs which came, and in each one
510　traveled a hundred and twenty of those young men of Boiótia.

They who Asplédon possessed and Orchómenos, Minyan city,
them Askálaphos led, and Iálmenos, scions of Ares
whom Astýochè bore in the palace of Ázeus' son Aktor—
she was a virtuous maiden who went with powerful Ares
515 into her upstairs chamber; in secret he lay there beside her.
Thirty in all were the hollow ships that with them were advancing.
Schédios then and Epístrophos led the contingent from Phokis—
they were the scions of great-souled Íphitos, Naúbolos' offspring—
those who possessed Kyparíssos and also Pytho the rocky,
520 sacred Krisa as well, and Panópeus also, and Daulis,
those who about Hyámpolis dwelt, and in Ánemoreía,
those who beside the Kephísos, the shimmering river, were dwelling,
those who Lilaía possessed close by the Kephísos' headwaters.
Forty the black ships were which followed along with these leaders.
525 Those who marshaled the ranks of the Phokians set them in order
near the Boiótian troops on the left flank, armed for the battle.
Leading the Lókrians came swift Ajax, son of Oïleus,
smaller, and no such man as the scion of Télamon Ajax
but far smaller, for he was a slight man armored in linen,
530 yet with the spear he surpassed all Héllenes and all the Achaians.
These inhabited Kynos and Kálliarós and Opóeis,
Bessa and also Skarphè, as well as delightful Augeíai,
Tarphè and Thrónion also, around the Boágrios' waters.
Forty the black ships were which followed along with this leader,
535 Lokrians, those who are living across from sacred Euboía.
Those who possessed Euboía, the furious-breathing Abántes,
Chalkis, Erétria too, Histiaía of many great vineyards,
seaside Kerínthos as well and the steep-built city of Dion,
those who abode in Karýstos and those who inhabited Styra,
540 all these men Elephénor, an offshoot of Ares, commanded,
Chálkodon's scion, the leader among the greathearted Abántes.
Following him were the rapid Abántes with hair back-flowing;
spearmen they were, most eager with outstretched weapons of ash wood
ever to shatter the breastplates surrounding the chests of the foemen.
545 Forty the black ships were which followed along with this leader.
Those who inhabited Athens, a city of noble foundation—
country of that great-hearted Eréchtheus whom had Athena,
daughter of Zeus, once reared, but the earth, grain-giving, had born him,
then she placed him in Athens, within her own sumptuous temple;
550 there with the bulls and the rams they bring, the Athenians' offspring

seek to propitiate him as the years come round to completion—
leader of their contingent was Péteos' scion Menéstheus.
Never had any man born on the earth been equal to him for
setting in order the shield-bearing men and the chariot-fighters;
555   Nestor alone was his rival, for he was of earlier birth date.
Fifty the black ships were which followed along with this leader.

    Ajax brought from the island of Sálamis twelve of the galleys,
led them and placed them where the Athenian forces were stationed.

    Those who inhabited Argos and Tiryns, secure in its huge walls,
560   then Hermíonè too, and Asínè, controlling a deep gulf,
Troizen as well, Eïónai, and vineyard-rich Epidaúros,
then those sons of Achaians who Mases possessed and Aigína,
leader of these men was the great crier of war Diomédes,
also Sthénelos, glorious Kápaneus' much-loved scion
565   then as a third with them came Euryalos, godlike in manhood—
he was the son of the lordly Mekísteus, Tálaös' scion;
but over all these led the great crier of war Diomédes;
eighty the black ships were which followed along with these leaders.

    Those who possessed Mykénè, a city of noble foundation,
570   prosperous Korinth also and splendidly founded Kleónai,
and in agreeable Áraithýrea dwelt, and Orneíai,
Síkyon too, where Adréstos had been the first king of the people,
those who held Hyperésia too, and steep-built Gonoéssa,
also Pellénè, and those who were all around Aígion dwelling,
575   those on the whole seacoast and about broad Hélikè also,
theirs were a hundred ships that were led by strong Agamemnon,
Atreus' scion; the most and the best by far of the host were
following him, and among them accoutered in glittering bronze he
carried himself with pride, stood out among all of the heroes,
580   since now he was the best, and he led by far the most people.

    Those who held Lakedaímon, the land of ravines in its valley,
Pharis and Sparta, and also Messa of numerous dovecotes,
those who dwelt in Bryseíai as well as delightful Augeíai,
those who Amýklai possessed and the seashore city of Helos,
585   those who Laäs possessed, those too around Oítylos dwelling,
these did his brother command, the great crier of war Meneláos,
sixty in all were his ships, and apart from the rest they were drawn up.
Trusting to his own valorous heart he was going among them,
rousing them up to the battle; for he above all in his heart was
590   eager to take his revenge for his struggles and groans over Helen.

Those who inhabited Pylos as well as delightful Arénè,
Thryon, the ford of the Álpheios also, and well-built Aipy,
those who in Kýparisséëis dwelt and in Ámphigeneía,
Ptéleon also, and Helos and Dorion—where when the Muses
595 met with Thamýris the Thracian as he from Oichália parted,
leaving Oichálian Eúrytos' house, they stopped him from singing,
for in his vaunts he had boasted that he would prevail if the very
Muses were singing, the daughters of Zeus who carries the aegis;
they in their anger had made him disabled, his marvelous songs had
600 utterly taken away, and had made him forget lyre-playing—
all these forces were led by the horseman Gerenian Nestor;
ninety in all were the hollow ships that with him were advancing.

    Those who Arkádia held, underneath the steep peak of Kyllénè,
close to the tomb of Aipýtos—the men all hand-to-hand fighters—
605 those who in Phéneos dwelt and Orchómenos, wealthy in sheep flocks,
Rhipè and Strátia too, and the blustery town of Eníspè,
those who Tegéa possessed and as well Mantineía the charming,
those who Stýmphalos held or were in Parrhásia dwelling,
leader of these was the child of Angkaíos, strong Agapénor;
610 sixty in all were their ships, and in each of the galleys did many
men of Arkádia come, well skilled in the fighting of battles.
For to these troops Agamemnon the lord of the people had given
well-benched galleys for voyaging over the wine-dark seaway,
Atreus' son, since nautical labors had never concerned them.

615   Those who within Bouprásion dwelt, and in Elis the noble,
all of it which Hyrmínè and Mýrsinos, off at the seashore,
and the Olénian rock and Alésion held in their confines,
four were the leaders of these contingents; with each of the men ten
swift ships followed along, and on them went many Epeíans.
620 Two of the tens Amphímachos captained and Thálpios also—
one, son of Ktéatos, one, son of Eúrytos, scions of Aktor;
ten by mighty Dióres were led, Amarýngkeus' scion;
as for the fourth ten, godlike Polýxeinos served as the leader—
he was the scion of lordly Agásthenes, son of Augeías.

625   Those men who from Doulíchion came and the sacred Echínai
islands that lie just over the water and opposite Elis,
these were the troops that Meges commanded, the equal of Ares,
Phýleus' son, who was sired by Phýleus, the Zeus-loved horseman,
who in his wrath at his father had settled Doulíchion island;
630 forty the black ships were which followed along with this leader.

Of the great-souled Kephallénian fighters Odysseus was leader,
those who in Ithaka dwelt and on Nériton, trembling with leafage,
those who inhabited rough Krokyleía and rocky Aigílips,
those who Zakýnthos possessed, those also who dwelt around Samos,
635 those who the mainland held, who dwelt on the opposite seacoast.
Leader of these was Odysseus, the equal of Zeus in devices;
twelve were the red-cheeked galleys that followed along with this leader.
    Of the Aitolians Thoas the son of Andraímon was leader,
those who inhabited Pleuron and Ólenos too, and Pylénè,
640 Chalkis as well, on the seacoast, and Kálydon rugged and rocky,
since no more were the sons of the great-souled Oíneus living,
nor was he living himself; light-haired Meleágros had perished.
Therefore to rule the Aitolians fell upon Thoas entirely;
forty the black ships were which followed along with this leader.
645   Then of the Cretans Idómeneus famed as a spearman was leader,
those who inhabited Knosos and Gortys, secure in its huge walls,
Lyktos as well as Milétos and silvery-shining Lykástos,
Phaistos, and Rhýtion too, all towns most pleasant to dwell in,
others as well who dwelt around Crete of the hundred cities;
650 so of these men Idómeneus famed as a spearman was leader,
Mérionés too, peer of Enyálios, killer of fighters;
eighty the black ships were which followed along with these leaders.
    Then Tlepólemos Herakles' son, stout-bodied and valiant,
led nine ships of the venturous Rhodians there out of Rhodos—
655 those who dwelt around Rhodos in triple division were ordered:
Lindos, Iálysos second, and silvery-shining Kameíros.
So of these men Tlepólemos famed as a spearman was leader,
he who to Herakles' might had been born by Ástyocheía;
he from Ephýra had brought her, away from the river Selléëis,
660 after he sacked many cities of Zeus-loved vigorous fighters.
When Tlepólemos reached manhood in the well-built palace,
he at once killed his own father's belovèd maternal uncle,
who already was aging, Likýmnios, scion of Ares.
Hastily he built ships, then, gathering numerous people,
665 parted in flight on the seaway, for at that time were the others
threatening him who of Herakles' might were the sons and the grandsons.
Then he arrived in Rhodos, a wanderer, suffering sorrows;
there they settled by tribes in triple division, belovèd
even of Zeus, who rules as the lord of the gods and of mankind.
670 Marvelous then was the wealth which Kronos' son showered upon them.

Níreus led there three of the balanced galleys from Symè,
Níreus, who was the son of Aglaía and lordly Charópos,
Níreus, handsomest man of the rest of the Dánaäns who came
underneath Ilion, after the faultless scion of Peleus,
675 but of small power he was, and the host which followed him little.
   Those who possessed Nisýros and Krápathos also, and Kásos,
also Eurýpylos' city of Kos and the isles of Kalýdnai,
all of these troops Pheidíppos and Ántiphos led to the warfare,
both of them sons of the great lord Théssalos, Herakles' scion;
680 thirty in all were the hollow ships that with them were advancing.
   Now then, those of the people who dwelt in Pelásgian Argos,
those who had their abodes in Álopè, Alos, and Trachis,
those who possessed broad Phthia and Hellas of beautiful women,
Mýrmidons these were called, and as well Héllenes and Achaians,
685 fifty in all were their ships, and of them was Achilles the leader.
Nevertheless, they took no thought of the dolorous warfare,
since there was no one now who could guide them in ranks for the battle.
For at his ships yet lay swift-footed and noble Achilles,
wrathful over the fair-tressed maiden, the daughter of Bríseus,
690 whom after many a toil he had taken away from Lyrnéssos,
when he had sacked Lyrnéssos and taken the ramparts of Thébè,
struck down Mynes as well, and Epístrophos, passionate spearmen
who were the sons of the lord Euénos, Selépios' scion;
it was for her that he lay there grieving, but soon he would rise up.
695   Those who Phýlakè held, with flowery Pýrasos also,
holy Deméter's allotment, and Iton the mother of sheep flocks,
seaside Antron, and also Ptéleon laid among meadows,
warlike Prótesiláos of all these towns was the leader,
while he was living; but then already the black earth held him.
700 So was his wife in Phýlakè left, both cheeks lacerated,
mourning her half-built home—a Dardánian fighter had killed him
just as he leapt from his galley, the first by far of the Achaians.
Yet not leaderless these troops were, though mourning their leader;
rather in ranks they were set by a scion of Ares, Podárkes,
705 offspring of Íphiklos wealthy in sheep flocks, Phýlakos' scion;
he was himself full brother to great-souled Prótesiláos,
later than he in birth; and the older was also his better,
Prótesiláos the warlike hero; but nevertheless no
leader did those men lack, though mourning a man so distinguished.
710 Forty the black ships were which followed along with this leader.

Those who inhabited Phérai and close to the lake Boibéïs,
Boibè and Gláphyraí, and Iólkos of noble foundation,
leading eleven of their ships came the dear son of Admétos,
Lord Eumélos, whom to Admétos the splendor of women
715 bore, Alkéstis, the noblest in beauty of Pélias' daughters.
     Those who dwelt in Methóna and in Thaumákia also,
those who possessed Meliboía and rugged and rocky Olízon,
these Philoktétes was leading, the man well skilled as an archer;
seven in all were their ships, and aboard each galley were fifty
720 oarsmen skillful as archers to fight in the strenuous combat.
But on an island he lay, still suffering mighty afflictions,
where in sacred Lemnos the sons of Achaians had left him
pained by a terrible wound from a murderous snake of the water.
There was he lying in anguish; but now quite soon were the Argive
725 forces beside their ships to remember the lord Philoktétes.
Yet not leaderless these troops were, though mourning their leader;
rather in ranks they were set by Medon, Oïleus' bastard
son whom Rhenè had born to the sacker of cities Oïleus.
     Those who Trikkè possessed and Ithómè the rugged and rocky,
730 and Oichália held, Oichálian Eúrytos' city,
both of the sons of the lord Asklépios served as their leaders,
excellent healers themselves, Podaleírios first, and Macháon.
Thirty in all were the hollow ships that with them were advancing.
     Those who Orménios held, those too by the spring Hypereía,
735 those who Astérion held and the white citadel of Titános,
these did Eurýpylos lead, the illustrious son of Euaímon;
forty the black ships were which followed along with this leader.
     Those who possessed Argíssa and those who dwelt in Gyrtónè,
Orthè, Elónè, and wide Oloösson, a city of white walls,
740 all these troops Polypoítes, steadfast in battle, was leading,
son of Peiríthoös, who had been sired by Zeus the immortal.
Glorious Híppodameía to great Peiríthoös bore him
that very day that he took his revenge on the hairy and savage
Centaurs, from Pelion drove them and brought them near the Aithíkes—
745 not by himself, for with him was a scion of Ares, Leónteus,
who was the son of high-hearted Korónos the scion of Kaineus.
Forty the black ships were which followed along with these leaders.
     Twenty-two galleys from Kyphos did Gouneus lead, and with him were
following bold Eniénes and battle-enduring Peraíboi,
750 those also who had made their homes around wintry Dodóna,

63

those who inhabited farms by the ravishing stream Titaréssos,
which casts into the river Peneíos its fair-flowing water,
yet it is not mixed into the silvery-swirling Peneíos,
but on the surface above it floats like oil of the olive,
755   since of the waters of Styx of the dread oath it is an outflow.
        Of the Magnétes the leader was Próthoös son of Tenthrédon,
those who around the Peneíos and Pélion, trembling with leafage,
had their dwellings; of them swift Próthoös was the commander;
forty the black ships were which followed along with this leader.
760   These men then were the marshals and lords of the Dánaän forces.
Which were the best by far among them—Muse, tell me the number—
both of the men and the steeds who were following Atreus' scions?
Easily best of the steeds were the mares of the scion of Pheres,
those that Eumélos drove, swift-footed as birds that are flying,
765   like in their manes and their ages, their backs as if plumb-line leveled;
these had Apollo of silvery bow brought up in Pereía,
both of them mares, both bearing the terror of Ares in battle.
Best of the men by far was the scion of Télamon Ajax,
while yet Achilles was angry; for he was far strongest among them,
770   as were the horses that carried the faultless scion of Peleus.
He however was now at his well-curved seafaring galleys
lying, and raging against Agamemnon, shepherd of people,
Atreus' son; and his men, on the tide-heaped sand of the seashore,
were entertaining themselves in hurling the disk and the goat-spear,
775   wielding their bows; and the horses were each by its chariot standing,
feeding on lotus as well as the celery grown in the marshes,
taking their ease, and the lords' own chariots, carefully covered,
lay in the cabins; the men, forlorn of their warlike commander,
wandering hither and thither all over the camp, were not fighting.
780   On went the others, as if strong fire were devouring the whole earth;
under them rumbled the earth, like Zeus the great thunderbolt-hurler
raging in storm, when he lashes the earth surrounding Typhóeus
where in the Árimoi's land, they say, is the bed of Typhóeus;
just so under their feet was the earth now mightily rumbling
785   as to the battle they went; and the plain they crossed very swiftly.
        Now to the Trojans a messenger came, swift wind-footed Iris,
bringing a terrible message from Zeus who carries the aegis;
they in assembly were gathered in front of the doorway of Priam,
all of them meeting together, the young men as well as the elders.
790   Standing beside them there, thus spoke to them swift-footed Iris;

she in her speaking resembled Políites a scion of Priam—
trusting the speed of his feet he sat as the guard of the Trojans
high on the burial mound of a hero of old, Aisyétes,
waiting for when the Achaians should set forth out of their galleys.

795 Likened to him then, thus spoke out to them swift-footed Iris:
"Old sir, always are dear to you words that are long and unmeasured,
as at a time in peace; but a war unabating has risen.
Certainly many the battles among men which I have entered,
yet I never have seen so splendid and mighty an army;

800 for it is most like leaves or again like sands of the seashore,
coming ahead through the plain to do battle in front of the city.
Hektor, especially you I order to do as I tell you:
for about this great city of Priam are numerous allies,
but among men so dispersed, some speak in one tongue, some in others;

805 let each man lay injunctions upon those troops that he captains,
leading them forth to the battle and setting his townsmen in order."

Thus; nor at all failed Hektor to know that a goddess had spoken;
quickly he closed the assembly, and they rushed back to their weapons.
All of the gates they opened, and out of them hastened the people

810 going on foot and with horses; and great was the tumult that rose up.

There in front of the city a distance apart is a steep hill
out on the plain, with a way around it one side and the other;
this is the place men call Batieía, the Hill of the Brier,
but the immortals the grave of Myrínè the far-leaping dancer.

815 There were the Trojans divided and marshaled, and so were their allies.

Leading the Trojans was great Hektor of glittering helmet,
scion of Priam; the most and the best by far of the troops were
following him, well armored and eager to enter the spear-fight.

Of the Dardánians there Aineías was leader—Anchíses'

820 excellent child that divine Aphrodítè had born to Anchíses
out on the spurs of Mount Ida, a goddess who lay with a mortal—
not by himself, for along with him came two sons of Anténor,
Ákamas and Archélochos, skilled in all manner of battle.

Those who dwelt in Zeleía beneath the low foothills of Ida,

825 rich men drinking the clear dark stream of the river Aisépos,
Trojans—the leader of these was the brilliant son of Lykáon,
Pándaros, he whose bow by Apollo himself had been given.

Those who Ádresteía possessed and the land of Apaísos,
who Pityeía possessed and the steep high peak of Tereía,

830 these were Adréstos commanding, and Ámphios, armored in linen,

both of them sons of Perkósian Merops, who above all men
knew of the means of divining and would not allow that his children
go into battle, destroyer of men; yet not in the least they
listened to him, for the spirits of black death guided them onward.

835   Those who were living around Perkótè, and Praktion also,
who held Sestos as well, and Abýdos and noble Arísbè,
Hýrtakos' son led them, Lord Ásios, marshal of people,
Ásios, Hýrtakos' son, whom there from Arísbè his horses
tawny and mighty had carried, away from the river Selléëis.

840   There Hippóthoös led the spear-loving Pelásgian tribesmen,
those who dwelt in the cloddy and fertile land of Laríssa;
them Hippóthoös led, and Pylaíos a scion of Ares,
both of them sons of Pelásgian Lethos, Teútamos' scion.
Ákamas came with the hero Peíroös, leading the Thracians,

845   those whom the powerful flow of the Hellespont held in its limits.
Then Euphémos among the Kikonian spearmen was leader—
he was the son of Troizénos, the Zeus-loved scion of Kéas.
There the Paiónians, curved-bow-fighters, Pyraíchmes had led from
faraway Ámydon town, from the Áxios, broad in its current,

850   Áxios, which spreads over the earth the most beautiful water.
Leading the Páphlagónians came Pylaímones, savage
hearted, from Énetoi country, in which wild mules are engendered,
those who Kytóros possess, those too around Sésamos dwelling,
those who about the Parthénios River in glorious houses

855   dwell, and in Krómnas and Aígialós, and in high Erythínoi.
Odios then and Epístrophos led Halizónians there from
Álybè far at a distance, the land where silver is brought forth.
Chromis the Mysians captained, and Énnomos, reader of bird-signs,
yet by his reading of birds he did not ward off a black doomsday—

860   but by the hand of the swift-footed scion of Aíakos he was
quelled in the river, in which also other Trojans were slaughtered.
Phorkys the Phrygians led, godlike Askánios too, from
distant Askánia, ready and eager to fight in the combat.
Of the Maiónians Mesthles and Ántiphos both were the leaders,

865   sons of Talaímenes, who had been born of the Lake of Gygaía;
they the Maiónians led who beneath Mount Tmolos were dwelling.
Nastes commanded the Karian forces of uncouth language,
those who Milétos possessed and the leaf-filled mountain of Phthires,
also the streams of Maiándros and Mýkalè's steep high headland;

870   these were the troops Amphímachos led as commander, and Nastes,

66

Nastes and strong Amphímachos, Nómion's glorious children.
Nastes came like a girl to the battle, in golden apparel,
fool, nor did that have power to guard him from wretched destruction,
but by the hand of the swift-footed scion of Aíakos he was
875 quelled in the river—his gold was all taken by war-skilled Achilles.
   Leading the Lykians came Sarpédon and Glaukos the faultless
out of the faraway Lykian land, from the eddying Xanthos.

BOOK 3

Finally, when each army was marshaled, along with its leaders,
then, with a clamor and din as of wild birds, on came the Trojans,
as at a time that the clamor of cranes goes up toward heaven
when they flee a tempestuous winter and measureless rainfall,
5   flying aloft amid clamorous cries to the streams of the Ocean,
thus to the dwarf-men, Pygmies, delivering death and destruction;
early at dawn they carry against them terrible conflict.
But the Achaians advanced in silence and furious-breathing,
each in his spirit determined to be a defense for the others.
10   As in the peaks of the mountains the south wind spreads a mist over,
not to the shepherd a friend, to the thief much better than nighttime—
somebody then sees only as far as the rock he hurls forward—
so in a dense cloud now from beneath their feet did the dust rise
as to the battle they went; and the plain they crossed very swiftly.
15   When in coming together the men were close to each other,
forth from the Trojans leapt to the front godlike Alexander,
wearing across his shoulders the skin of a leopard, a curved bow
too, and a sword; two spears he was brandishing, headed with sharp bronze
points, and he shouted a challenge to all of the best of the Argives
20   there to do battle with him man to man in terrible combat.
But then, when Meneláos belovèd of Ares perceived him
sallying forth in front of the army and moving with long strides,
just as a lion rejoices at coming upon a huge carcass,
either a full-horned stag that he happens to find, or a wild goat,
25   when he is famished, and eats it greedily even if there are
swift hounds rushing against him and youths in the prime of their vigor—
so Meneláos rejoiced as he saw godlike Alexander
with his own eyes; for he thought he would take his revenge on the culprit.
Straightway he to the ground from his chariot leapt in his armor.
30   But then, soon as the lord godlike Alexander observed him

showing himself in the forefront, the spirit within him was shaken;
he shrank back to the band of his comrades, avoiding destruction.
As when somebody seeing a snake starts up and jumps backward
in the ravines of a mountain and shivering seizes his body,
35 then he withdraws yet farther, his cheeks in the grip of green pallor,
so once more back into the host of the venturous Trojans
went in his terror at Atreus' son godlike Alexander.
    Looking at him then Hektor rebuked him in words of derision:
"Paris the bane, best-seeming, you woman-mad cheat and deceiver,
40 would that you never were born or that you unmarried had perished!
This is what I would desire, and it surely would be much better
than to be thus—a disgraceful coward despised by the others.
Surely at us laugh loudly the long-haired men, the Achaians,
saying we have this chief as our champion only because in
45 looks he is handsome, but not in his heart is there valor or prowess.
Was it like this you were at the time in the seafaring galleys
you sailed over the seaway, assembling the trustworthy comrades,
mingling with alien people and taking a beautiful woman
out of a faraway country, the sister-in-law of great spearmen,
50 such huge pain to your father and city and all of the people,
but to our enemies pleasure, to you yourself so disgraceful?
Would you indeed not face Meneláos belovèd of Ares?
Then you would learn what strong man's blossoming wife you are holding.
Nor would the lyre be of use to you then, or the gifts Aphrodítè
55 gave you, the hair and the beauty, were you with the dust to be mingled.
No, we Trojans are terrible cowards, or else you had long since
put on a tunic of stone on account of the evil you wrought us."
    Then in answer to him spoke forth godlike Alexander:
"Hektor, because you have justly rebuked me and not beyond justice—
60 always in you is a heart unwearying, much like an ax which
goes through timber, impelled by a man who uses his skill for
shaping the beam of a ship, and the ax augments the man's efforts;
so inside of your breast is the heart unflinching and fearless—
bring not against me the charming endowments of gold Aphrodítè;
65 not to be flung to the side are the gods' magnificent presents,
any that they might give, though one would not willingly choose them.
Now then, if you desire me to enter the fight and do battle,
order the rest of the Trojans and all the Achaians to sit down;
then set me and the lord Meneláos belovèd of Ares
70 there in the middle to fight over Helen and all her possessions.

Let whichever of us triumphs and is proven the stronger
duly receive and take home both all of the wealth and the woman;
as for the rest, first plighting your friendship and trustworthy pledges,
you keep dwelling in fertile Troy, and the others return to
75 Argos, nourishing horses, and Achaia of beautiful women."
       So did he say; much Hektor rejoiced at his word as he listened;
into the middle he went, and the ranks of the Trojans he held back,
holding his spear by the middle, and they all quickly were seated.
Shooting at him with their bows were the long-haired men, the Achaians;
80 aiming at him their arrows and stones, they were trying to hit him.
Then in a loud voice cried Agamemnon, lord of the people:
"Hold back, Argives, and do not shoot at him, sons of Achaians;
ready to speak us a word now is Hektor of glittering helmet."
       He spoke, and they held back from the battle and fell into silence
85 quickly, and Hektor between the two sides then spoke and addressed them:
"Listen to me now, Trojans and all you well-greaved Achaians,
hear what says Alexander, for whose sake strife has arisen.
As for the rest of the Trojans and all the Achaians, he bids them
on the much-nourishing earth put aside their beautiful weapons.
90 He himself and the lord Meneláos belovèd of Ares
here in the middle will fight over Helen and all her possessions.
Let whichever of them triumphs and is proven the stronger
duly receive and take home both all of the wealth and the woman.
As for the rest, we will plight our friendship and trustworthy pledges."
95   So did he say; then all of the people were hushed in silence.
Then spoke also among them the crier of war Meneláos:
"Listen to me now too, for upon my heart has the anguish
come above all, and I hope that at last now you will be parted,
Argives and Trojans, because you have suffered so many afflictions
100 all for this quarrel of mine and of Lord Alexander, who caused it.
So to whichever of us his death and his doom are apportioned,
let him indeed now die, and the others will separate swiftly.
Bring out two young sheep, a white ram and the other a black ewe
both for the earth and the sun; and to Zeus we will offer another.
105 Also lead out the might of Lord Priam, that he may himself now
pledge these oaths, for his sons are all arrogant, not to be trusted,
lest these oaths of Lord Zeus someone violate by a trespass.
Always in fact do the spirits in younger men flutter unsteady;
but with an elder among them, at once the before and the after
110 he can observe, so that things will become far better for both sides."

So he spoke, and the people rejoiced, both Achaians and Trojans,
hoping that they would at last leave off their dolorous warfare.
Holding the chariots back in ranks, their drivers dismounted,
stripped themselves of their armor, and laid it down on the ground there,
115 each piece close to the others, with small earth showing between them.
Straightway Hektor dispatched to the citadel two of his heralds
quickly to bring down offering lambs and to summon Lord Priam,
while Talthýbios too was dispatched by strong Agamemnon
down to the hollow galleys to go, and an offering lamb he
120 bade him to bring; nor did he disobey the renowned Agamemnon.
     Meanwhile to white-armed Helen descended the messenger Iris,
like to her sister-in-law, bedmate of the son of Anténor,
whom that son of Anténor, the strong Helikáön, had married—
she was Laódikè, noblest in form of the daughters of Priam.
125 Helen she found in her chamber, engaged in weaving a great cloak,
purple, to wear double-folded, inweaving the numerous fights of
Trojans, tamers of horses, against bronze-armored Achaians,
which for her sake those men had endured at the urging of Ares.
Standing beside her there, thus spoke to her swift-footed Iris:
130 "Come with me here, dear sister, to witness the marvelous deeds of
Trojans, tamers of horses, and those bronze-armored Achaians,
they who before in the plain were waging against one another
dolorous war and of ruinous battle were ever desirous;
now in silence do they all sit, as the battle is ended,
135 leaning against their shields, with the long spears planted beside them.
But Alexander and Lord Meneláos belovèd of Ares
on your account are about to engage in a battle with long spears.
Then of the one who triumphs will you be called the dear bedmate."
     So having spoken the goddess put into her heart sweet yearning
140 after her earlier husband, her city as well, and her parents.
Straightway, veiling herself in shimmering garments of linen,
out of the room she went as her tears flowed tender and swelling,
not by herself, for together with her went two of her handmaids,
Aithrè, the daughter of Pittheus, and ox-eyed Klýmenè also.
145 Speedily then they arrived at the Skaian Gates of the city.
     Priam and those at his side, Lord Pánthoös, noble Thymoítes,
Lampos and Klýtios and Hiketáon, offshoot of Ares,
then Anténor as well as Oukálegon, both of them thoughtful,
elders-in-chief of the folk, on the Skaian Gates were all seated;
150 they for old age had relinquished warfare, yet they were noble

71

speakers and counselors, like the cicadas that deep in a forest
sitting on trees throw forth the clear lilylike sound of their voices.
Such were the governing chiefs of the Trojans who sat on the tower.
Soon as they looked on Helen as she on the tower was coming,
155 speaking in winged words gentle and soft they addressed one another:
"There is indeed no blame on the Trojans and well-greaved Achaians,
over a woman like this so long a time suffering sorrows;
dreadfully like the immortal goddesses is she to look on.
Nevertheless, though she is like them, let her go in the galleys,
160 not be left as a bane for ourselves and our children hereafter."
       So did they say, but aloud spoke Priam and called out to Helen:
"Come here over to me, dear daughter, and sit down beside me,
so that you see your earlier husband, your friends and your kinsmen—
nor do I blame you at all, but the gods instead are blameworthy,
165 who stirred up for me dolorous warfare against the Achaians—
also that you may tell me the name of the man so enormous.
Who is that man stout-bodied and valiant among the Achaians?
Others indeed there are who are taller than he by a head-length,
yet I never have seen with my eyes a man equal in beauty,
170 neither in majesty equal; he seems like a man most kingly."
       Answering him in these words spoke Helen, the splendor of women:
"You in my heart, dear father-in-law, are revered and respected;
would that a terrible death had been pleasing to me at the time I
followed your son here, leaving my marriage-chamber and kinsmen,
175 also my grown-up child and the charming companions my own age.
But not so would it be—therefore I am wasted with weeping.
This I will say to you now as to what you question and ask me:
Atreus' scion is he, wide-governing Lord Agamemnon;
he is indeed both an excellent king and a powerful spearman;
180 once he was brother-in-law of my bitch-faced self, if it might be."
       So she spoke, and the old man marveled at him and addressed him:
"Atreus' fortunate son, born destiny-favored and god-blessed,
many are those subjected to you, those sons of Achaians.
Once in the past I traveled to Phrygia, wealthy in vineyards;
185 there I saw many Phrygian men of swift-glistening horses—
they were the people of Ótreus as well as of godlike Mygdon—
who on the banks of the river Sangários had their encampment;
for as an ally in battle was I then counted among them
that very day when the Amazons came, those peers of the heroes;
190 yet they were not so many as these quick-glancing Achaians."

Next, as he looked at Odysseus, the old man once again asked her:
"Come now, tell me of that man too, dear child—who can he be,
shorter indeed by a head than is Atreus' son Agamemnon,
yet he is broader appearing across his chest and his shoulders.
195 On the much-nourishing earth, in fact, though his armor is lying,
like a herd's bellwether he is reviewing the ranks of the soldiers.
Yes, even so, to a ram with a thick fleece I would compare him,
one who is ranging among the white-glimmering sheep of a great flock."
     Helen descended of Zeus then spoke to him, giving an answer:
200 "That is the son of Laërtes, Odysseus of many devices,
who was brought up in the country of Ithaka, though it is rocky,
skillful in every sort of contrivance and cunning in counsel."
     Thoughtful Anténor in turn spoke out to her, giving an answer:
"Lady, indeed this word you have spoken is surely a true one.
205 For some time ago here on an embassy noble Odysseus
came about you, and with him Meneláos belovèd of Ares.
Here in my halls I entertained them, and I treated them kindly,
so of them both I learned their size and their cunning in counsel.
But at the time they mingled among these Trojans assembled,
210 then if they stood, Meneláos by his broad shoulders was taller,
while if they both sat down, more lordly than he was Odysseus.
But any time they wove for us all their speeches and counsels,
then to be sure Meneláos would talk quite calmly and nimbly;
few were his words, but exceedingly clear—he was never loquacious,
215 nor did he stumble in speaking, although in his age he was younger.
But any time that Odysseus of many devices would rise up,
then he would stand and stare down, on the ground were his eyes fixed firmly,
nor would he brandish the staff he held either backward or forward,
but unmoving he gripped it, the way that an ignorant man would;
220 you would have thought him to be both churlish and utterly mindless.
But then, when the enormous voice from his chest he would send forth
and as the words came drifting across like snowflakes in winter,
then you would not think any man else could rival Odysseus;
nor did we then much wonder at seeing Odysseus' demeanor."
225   Third then, as he saw Ajax, the old man once again asked her:
"Who is that other Achaian, a man stout-bodied and valiant,
so outstanding among the Argives by his head and broad shoulders?"
     Answering him spoke long-robed Helen the splendor of women:
"That one there is enormous Ajax, the Achaians' protector;
230 next to him then Idómeneus stands like a god there among his

73

Cretans; around him too are assembled the chiefs of the Cretans.
Often would entertain him Meneláos belovèd of Ares,
there in our palace, whenever from Crete he would come on a visit.
Now I see all the others of those quick-glancing Achaians,
235 whom quite well I would know and of whose names I could inform you;
yet there are two that I cannot see, those marshals of people
Kastor the tamer of steeds, Polydeúkes the noblest of boxers,
who are my own blood brothers and born like me to one mother.
Either they have not come here and left Lakedaímon the lovely,
240 or else though they have followed along in the seafaring galleys,
into the combat of men they are now not minded to enter,
fearing the insults and many reproaches to which I am subject."
    So she spoke, but the life-giving earth already enclosed them
back there in Lakedaímon, the much-loved land of their fathers.
245   Now through the city the heralds were bringing the gods' secure pledges—
two young lambs and the wine, heart-gladdening fruit of the plowland,
in a container of goatskin; the herald Idaíos was bringing
thither a shimmering wine bowl as well as a gold-wrought goblet.
Standing beside the old man he spoke these words to arouse him:
250 "Rise, Laómedon's son, you are called by the noblest among our
Trojans, tamers of horses, and those bronze-armored Achaians
down to the plain to descend, so that trustworthy oaths you can pledge them,
since Alexander against Meneláos belovèd of Ares
now is about to do battle with long spears over the woman;
255 then both the wealth and the woman will follow whoever shall triumph;
as for the rest, first plighting our friendship and trustworthy pledges,
we would keep dwelling in fertile Troy, and the others return to
Argos, nourishing horses, and Achaia of beautiful women."
    So he spoke, and the old man shuddered and ordered his comrades
260 straightway to harness the horses; and they then quickly obeyed him.
Into the chariot Priam ascended, and drew the reins backward.
There beside him on the beautiful chariot mounted Anténor.
Out through the Skaian Gates to the plain they drove the swift horses.
But then, when they had come to the Trojans and to the Achaians,
265 on the much-nourishing earth from the chariot having dismounted,
they strode into the middle, between the Achaians and Trojans.
Straightway rose Agamemnon, the lord of the people, to greet them,
also Odysseus of many devices; the glorious heralds
gathered together the gods' oath-offerings, then in a wine bowl
270 mixed wine; over the kings' hands they poured water for washing.

Atreus' son then, seizing and drawing his knife with his hand from
where it was always hanging beside the great sheath of his sword-blade,
cut off the offering hairs from the heads of the lambs; and the heralds
straightway passed them around to the noblest Achaians and Trojans.

275 Atreus' son in a loud voice prayed for them, lifting his hands up:
"Father Zeus, ruling from Ida, the lord most honored and mighty,
Helios, who look down upon all things, listen to all things,
rivers as well, and the earth, and the gods down under the earth who
pay back men who have perished, whoever has sworn to a false oath,

280 witnesses all of you be and the faith of our oaths watch over:
If in fact Alexander it be who kills Meneláos,
let him in that case have both Helen and all her possessions;
we in the seafaring ships will at once go back to our homeland.
If light-haired Meneláos it be who kills Alexander,

285 then are the Trojans to give both Helen and all her possessions
back and to pay to the Argives a recompense that is fitting,
such as will stay in the minds of the men who live in the future.
If the requital Priam as well as the children of Priam
be not willing to pay me, although Alexander has fallen,

290 then indeed for the sake of the penalty I will do battle—
here will I stay, until I have arrived at the end of the warfare."
     Thus; with the pitiless bronze he cut right through the lambs' gullets.
There on the ground he laid the two lambs, now gasping their breath out,
being deprived of their lives; for their strength by the bronze had been taken.

295 When they had drawn off wine from the wine bowl into the goblets,
pouring it out, they raised their prayer to the gods who live always.
Thus someone would have spoken among the Achaians and Trojans:
"Zeus most honored and great, and the rest of the gods undying,
those whoever the first violate these oaths we have sworn here,

300 let their brains flow out on the ground, like the wine we are pouring,
both their own and their sons', and their wives be taken by others."
     Thus; but the scion of Kronos would not yet grant them fulfillment.
These words Priam the scion of Dárdanos spoke and addressed them:
"Listen to me now, Trojans and all you well-greaved Achaians;

305 I will again now to windswept Ilion take my departure
homeward, because no way can I bear to behold with my own eyes
that dear son of mine fight Meneláos belovèd of Ares;
Zeus, I suppose, is aware, and the rest of the deathless gods, to
which of the two men death's finality now is allotted."

310   So he spoke, and the lambs in the chariot placing, the godlike

man himself then mounted upon it and drew the reins backward;
there beside him on the beautiful chariot mounted Anténor.
Homeward the two men went, toward Ilion making the journey.
Hektor the scion of Priam as well as the noble Odysseus

315 started by measuring out a good space for the combat, and straightway
taking the two lots up, in a helmet of bronze they shook them,
so to decide which one would be first in throwing his bronze spear.
Then did the host all pray, to the gods they lifted their hands up;
thus someone would have spoken among the Achaians and Trojans:

320 "Father Zeus, ruling from Ida, the lord most honored and mighty,
now to whoever has caused these troubles between the two peoples,
grant that the man be killed, that he enter the palace of Hades,
while for the rest of us there be friendship and trustworthy pledges."
So they spoke; and the lots great Hektor of glittering helmet

325 shook while looking away; that of Paris was quickest to jump out.
Straightway then in their ranks were the troops all seated, where each man's
high-paced horses were standing and intricate armor was lying;
meanwhile over his shoulders his beautiful armor was put by
Lord Alexander, the husband of Helen of beautiful tresses.

330 First, strong greaves on the calves of his legs he carefully fastened,
fine ones skillfully fitted with silver-wrought ankle-protectors;
second in order, around his chest he put on the breastplate,
that of his brother Lykáon—to him also it was suited.
Over his shoulders he slung on the sword, all studded with silver,

335 fashioned of bronze, then also the great shield, massive and heavy.
Onto his powerful head he fitted the well-made helmet
crested with horsehair; the plume on top of it fearfully nodded.
Then he took up a powerful spear which fitted his handgrip.
So in the same way put on his arms warlike Meneláos.

340 Soon as the two, either side of the throng, were armed and accoutered,
they strode into the middle, between the Achaians and Trojans,
glaring their terrible stares; and astonishment seized the observers,
all of the Trojans, tamers of horses, and well-greaved Achaians.
Near each other they took their stand in the space that was measured,

345 shaking the shafts of their spears while raging against each other.
Then Alexander was first to let fly his long-shadowing spear-shaft,
square on the circular shield thus striking the scion of Atreus,
nor did the bronze break through, but the point of the spear bent backward
there in the strong round shield. Then next to attack with the bronze was

350 Atreus' son Meneláos, while praying to Zeus the great father:

76

"Lord Zeus, grant me to punish the man who first wrought me affliction,
this noble lord Alexander, and under my hand to subdue him,
so any man among those hereafter may shudder at doing
evil to one who receives him as guest and who gives him his friendship."

355   So did he say, then brandished and threw his long-shadowing spear-shaft,
square on the circular shield thus striking the scion of Priam.
Straight through the glittering shield penetrated the powerful spear-shaft,
thrusting its way on through the elaborate work of the breastplate;
grazing his flank very closely the spear-point then through the tunic

360   pierced, but he swerved to the side and avoided the blackest of doomsdays.
Atreus' son then, drawing his sword all studded with silver,
lifting his hand up, struck at the horn of the helmet; the sword-blade
shattered upon it and fell from his hand in three or four pieces.
Atreus' son groaned loudly as he looked up to broad heaven:

365   "Oh father Zeus, there is no other god more baneful than you are;
here I had thought I would punish the evil of Lord Alexander;
now instead has the sword in my hands been shattered, the spear has
wholly in vain flown out of my grasp, and I did not strike him."
       Thus, and he rushed him, and seizing his helmet crested with horsehair

370   turned him around, then dragged him away to the well-greaved Achaians,
so he was choked by the strap, most elegant, under his soft throat,
which stretched under his chin for securing the four-horned helmet.
He would have dragged him away now and won unspeakable glory,
had not keenly observed Aphrodítè the daughter of Zeus and

375   broken the strap of the hide of a bull by violence slaughtered.
Empty the four-horned helm in his stout hand went with the fighter,
this then after he whirled it around Meneláos the hero
threw to the well-greaved Achaians; the trustworthy comrades received it.
Quickly he rushed Alexander again, most eager to kill him

380   using his bronze-tipped spear; but away Aphrodítè removed him
easily—she was a goddess—and covered him over in thick mist,
then she set him again in his bedroom, fragrant with incense.
Straightway she went out to call Helen, and her she encountered
on the high tower, with women of Troy there crowded around her.

385   She with her hand laid hold of her fragrant apparel and twitched it,
spoke to her then in the guise of a woman of elderly years who
served as a dresser of wool; while yet Lakedaímon she lived in,
beautiful wool she had carded, and she had especially loved her—
so in the guise of that woman addressed her divine Aphrodítè:

390   "Come here now: Alexander is summoning you to go homeward.

Yonder is he in his room, in his bed ornamented with spirals,
radiant both in his beauty and garments, and you would not think that
he had returned from a fight with a man, no, rather was going
out to a dance, or had just now paused from the dancing and sat down."

395   So she spoke, and in her she incited the heart in her bosom;
soon as she knew the surpassingly beautiful neck of the goddess
and the desirable breasts and the eyes so brilliantly shining,
marveling then she spoke to her these words, calling upon her:
"Goddess obsessed, why still in this way are you anxious to trick me?

400   Will you to some place farther of well-inhabited cities
carry me hence, of Maiónia's lovely domain, or of Phrygia,
if there too is belovèd to you some man who is mortal?
Is it because Meneláos has now over great Alexander
triumphed, and he is desiring my hateful self to take homeward?

405   Therefore do you now stand with deceitful intention beside me.
You go sit there beside him, the gods' ways wholly renouncing;
never again on your feet turn back to the realm of Olympos;
rather forever be anxious for him, watch over him always,
up to the time he makes you his wife, or indeed a mere slave-girl.

410   Thither will I not go—it would be too shameful to do it,
sharing the bed of that man—hereafter the women of Troy would
jeer at me, all of them; measureless grief I have in my spirit."
    Wrathfully then in reply thus spoke to her bright Aphrodítè:
"Do not provoke me, wretch, lest I in my anger forsake you,

415   so that I hate you as much as I now exceedingly love you—
I would devise you a ruinous hatred between the two armies,
Trojans and Dánaäns, so by a terrible fate you would perish."
    Thus she spoke, so that Helen the offspring of Zeus was affrighted;
shrouding herself in a garment of shimmering white, she in silence

420   went unseen by the women of Troy, and the goddess was guiding.
    When they reached Alexander's surpassingly beautiful palace,
then did the women-attendants at once turn back to their labors,
while to the high-roofed chamber ascended the splendor of women.
Picking an armchair up, Aphrodítè the lover of laughter

425   took it for her, and the goddess placed it to face Alexander;
there then sat down Helen the daughter of Zeus of the aegis,
turning her eyes to the side, and in these words scolded her husband:
"You have returned from the fight—how I wish right there you had perished,
quelled by the hands of a mightier man, my earlier husband!

430   Verily, greater than Lord Meneláos belovèd of Ares

you once boasted to be in your might, with your hands and a sharp spear.
But now go and call forth Meneláos belovèd of Ares
once more to fight against you face to face. No, rather indeed I
urge you to leave off now and against light-haired Meneláos
435 not to contend any longer, or fight in a man-to-man combat
foolishly, lest by his spear you perhaps be speedily vanquished."
    Speaking in words like these then Paris addressed her an answer:
"Woman, do not scold me to my heart with your bitter reproaches,
since this time Meneláos has won with the aid of Athena;
440 some other time will I win, since there are gods also on our side.
But come now, let us get into bed to enjoy our affection,
since not ever before has desire so enveloped my senses,
not at the time when first we left Lakedaímon the lovely,
when, having snatched you away, I sailed in the seafaring ships to
445 Kránaë Island and mingled with you in bed and affection,
never, as now I love you and pleasing desire for you grips me."
    Thus, and he started away to his bed, and his bedmate followed.
So did the two lie down on the bedstead corded for bedding.
Atreus' son like a beast went ranging about through the army
450 hoping that he might somewhere descry godlike Alexander;
but then none of the Trojans or glorious allies could ever
show Alexander to Lord Meneláos belovèd of Ares.
Never would they out of love have concealed him, if any had seen him,
since by them all he was hated as much as the blackest destruction.
455 Then spoke also to them Agamemnon, lord of the people:
"Listen to me now, Trojans, Dardánians also, and allies:
clearly has triumphed here Meneláos belovèd of Ares;
then as for Helen of Argos, along with her all her possessions,
give them to us now, and pay us a recompense that is fitting,
460 such as will stand also among men who live in the future."
So spoke Atreus' son, and the other Achaians approved it.

BOOK 4

Now were the gods all seated beside Zeus, holding assembly
there on the gold-wrought floor, and among them Hebè the august
server of drink poured nectar; with goblets of gold the immortals
pledged each other and drank, as they looked on the town of the Trojans.
5   Straightway the scion of Kronos attempted to irritate Hera,
uttering words of derision, provoking her ire with a challenge:
"Two of the goddesses are the abettors of Lord Meneláos,
Argive Hera the queen and the guardian-goddess Athena.
But now sitting apart from the fray they are taking their pleasure
10   as they observe; meanwhile Aphrodítè the lover of laughter
always stands by the man she cherishes, wards off his doomsday.
So just now she has rescued the man who expected to perish.
Nevertheless triumphs Meneláos belovèd of Ares.
Let us ourselves take thought of the way these matters will happen,
15   whether again among them grim battle and terrible combat
we should arouse, or between the two sides cast peaceable friendship.
If to us all somehow this way should be welcome and pleasant,
still would the city of great Lord Priam be fit to inhabit,
while Meneláos would take back homeward Helen of Argos."
20   So he spoke, and against him muttered Athena and Hera;
they sat next to each other and planned great banes for the Trojans.
There in silence Athena remained, nor a word did she utter,
Zeus her father resenting, and gripped by a violent anger.
No such anger could Hera restrain in her breast, but she spoke out:
25   "Most dread scion of Kronos, and what is this word you have spoken!
How can you want to make idle and fruitless all of this labor,
all of the sweat I have sweated in toil, my horses exhausted,
gathering troops to bring evil to Priam as well as his children?
Do it: but not in the least we other gods all will approve it."
30   Mightily vexed, thus spoke to her then the cloud-gathering god Zeus:

"Most strange lady, and what now have Priam and Priam's children
done so evil to you that you strive in a furious haste to
ransack the well-built city of Ilion, utterly waste it?
If inside of the gates and the towering walls you could enter,
35 then you could eat raw Priam and Priam's children, as well as
all of the rest of the Trojans; at last your wrath would be sated.
Do it however you want to; but let this quarrel hereafter
never become an enormous cause of contention between us.
Something else I will tell you, and you keep this in your mind now:
40 when sometime I am eager myself to demolish a city,
ruin a town in which there are men most dear to you dwelling,
not in the least will you thwart my wrath, but allow me to do it,
since I have willingly granted you this, my spirit unwilling.
For of the cities that under the sun and the star-filled heaven,
45 all those many of them which earthbound people inhabit,
most by far in my spirit was sacred Ilion honored,
Priam as well, and the people of Priam the excellent spearman;
since there, never my altar was lacking a well-shared banquet,
savory smoke and libations: for these we get as our prizes."

50 Speaking to him then answered the ox-eyed queen, Lady Hera:
"There are indeed three cities that are most dear to my spirit—
Argos is one, then Sparta, and also wide-wayed Mykénè.
These do you ransack when to your heart they become too hateful;
I will not stand up before them against you nor at all grudge you,
55 since although I object and I would not let you destroy them,
nothing I gain by objecting, for you are indeed much stronger.
Nevertheless, my labor should not go quite unaccomplished,
since I too am a god, my lineage even what yours is—
I am the first of the daughters of Kronos of crooked devices,
60 both in respect of my birth and because of the name that I have as
bedmate to you, and you rule as the lord over all the immortals.
But as concerns these things, let us each give way to the other,
I to your will, you also to mine; and the other immortal
gods will accede to us both. Now quickly command that Athena
65 go down into the terrible strife of Achaians and Trojans;
there she will try to arrange that the Trojans will start violating
first those oaths they swore to the glorious noble Achaians."

She spoke, nor disobeyed her the father of gods and of mankind;
straightway he spoke to Athena—in these winged words he addressed her:
70 "Speedily go down now to the host of Achaians and Trojans;

there you will try to arrange that the Trojans will start violating
first those oaths they swore to the glorious noble Achaians."
    Thus he spoke, and Athena he roused, who already was eager;
speedily she came down from the summit of lofty Olympos.
75 Like some star that the scion of Kronos of crooked devices
hurls as an omen to sailors or widespread armies of soldiers
glittering brightly, and many a scintillant spark it discharges,
like that star as she rushed to the earth now Pallas Athena
leapt in the midst of the armies; and held by wonder observing
80 this were the Trojans, tamers of horses, and well-greaved Achaians;
thus someone would have said as he looked at another beside him:
"So once more there will be grim battle and terrible combat
here between us, or a peaceable friendship between the two sides now
Zeus will arrange, he who is for men the dispenser of battle."
85   So someone would have spoken among the Achaians and Trojans.
She in the guise of a man went into the Trojans' assembly,
like to Laódokos son of Anténor, a powerful spearman,
godlike Pándaros seeking, if somewhere there she could find him.
Soon she discovered the faultless and powerful son of Lykáon
90 standing; about him there were the powerful ranks of shield-bearing
troops who followed with him from the streams of the river Aisépos.
There then, standing beside him, in these winged words she addressed him:
"Will you obey what I tell you, the war-skilled son of Lykáon?
Then you would dare let fly a swift arrow at Lord Meneláos,
95 so as to win much glory and favor from all of the Trojans,
but among all of them, surely the most from Prince Alexander.
First indeed before all you would carry off glorious presents
were he to see warlike Meneláos, the scion of Atreus,
brought down under your missile, go onto the pyre of affliction.
100 But come, shoot off an arrow at glorious Lord Meneláos,
making a vow to Apollo the wolf-born glorious archer
that of the firstborn lambs you will offer a splendid oblation
once you have gone back home to the sacred city Zeleía."
    So did Athena address him; his senseless heart she persuaded;
105 quickly he stripped of its cover the bow well-polished of horn he
got from a fleet wild goat which he himself shot in the chest as
it came down from a rock to the place he was waiting to take it;
straight in its chest he struck, and it fell on its back in the boulders.
Sixteen palm-breadths long were the horns which grew from the goat's head;
110 these had a craftsman, a worker in horn, joined deftly together,

smoothed it all well, and a gold tip, notched for the string, set upon it.
Skillfully stretching the string to the bow, upright on the ground he
placed it; in front of him, noble companions were holding their shields up,
so that the warlike sons of Achaians would not be attacking
115 him before he struck Atreus' warlike son Meneláos.
Stripping the cover away from the quiver, he took out an arrow,
feathered, as yet unshot, the conveyor of black lamentations;
straightway onto the bowstring he fitted the sharp bitter arrow,
making a vow to Apollo the wolf-born glorious archer
120 that of the firstborn lambs he would offer a splendid oblation
once he had gone back home to the sacred city Zeleía.
Then he, pulling the notches and bowstring of sinew together,
drew to his nipple the string, to the bow thus bringing the iron.
Finally, when he had stretched the enormous bow to a circle,
125 twanging the bow, loud-screaming the string, sharp-pointed the arrow
leaping away from his hand flew furiously through the army.
      Now, Meneláos, of you were the fortunate gods, the immortals,
not forgetful, and first of them Zeus' spoil-plundering daughter—
standing in front of you she warded off that sharp-piercing arrow.
130 Only as much she kept it away from his skin as a mother
keeps some fly from her child who is lying at ease in a sweet sleep,
guiding the arrow herself to the spot where the war-belt's golden
buckles were clasped and the plates of the corselet met, overlapping.
Onto the well-fitted war-belt the sharp bitter arrow descended,
135 clear on through the elaborate war-belt then it was driven,
and the elaborate corselet too it struck, penetrating,
also the metal band worn as a skin-guard, keeping the spears off,
which protected him most—this too did the arrow go right through,
then was the skin of the man just grazed by the tip of the arrow;
140 straightway out of the wound a dark cloud of his blood began gushing.
      As when a woman, a Karian or a Maiónian, colors
ivory with a red stain to be used as a cheek-piece for horses—
there in her chamber it lies, though numerous charioteers are
longing to take it away; but it lies there to be a king's splendor,
145 both for his horses adornment and glorious pride for the driver—
thus indeed, Meneláos, with red blood now were your shapely
thighs deep-stained, and your legs, and the handsome ankles beneath them.
      Straightway shuddered in dread Agamemnon, lord of the people,
as he observed how out of the wound was the black blood gushing;
150 so too shuddered in dread Meneláos beloved of Ares.

83

But as he saw that the fastening thread and the barbs remained outside,
then once more back into his breast was the spirit collected.
Heavily groaning, among them spoke forth strong Agamemnon—
Lord Meneláos he held by the hand, as the comrades lamented:

155 "Oh dear brother, it seems for your death were the oaths that I swore to
set you alone there before the Achaians to battle the Trojans;
so have the Trojans struck you and trampled the oaths they had plighted.
Yet not fruitless will be those oaths and the blood of the lambs and
unmixed wine that we poured and the right hands' clasp that we trusted,

160 since even if just now the Olympian does not achieve them,
later on he will fulfill them. Enormous redress will they make us
first with their own heads, then with their women as well as their children,
since this thing I know very well in my mind and my spirit:
there will a day come when holy Ilion falls in destruction,

165 Priam as well, and the people of Priam the excellent spearman;
seated aloft, Zeus scion of Kronos, who dwells in the heavens,
brandishes over them all the dark gloom of his threatening aegis,
wrathful because of the falsehood; and not unaccomplished will this be.
But most terrible grief will I suffer for you, Meneláos,

170 should you perish and fill out the lifetime to which you are destined.
Most despicable I would arrive back in Argos the thirsty,
for the Achaians at once will remember the land of their fathers,
so as a trophy for Priam and all of the Trojans would we leave
Helen of Argos, and so this earth will be rotting your bones as

175 you lie dead here in Troy with the task you tried unaccomplished.
Thus somebody will utter among those arrogant Trojans,
as he cavorts on the grave-mound of glorious Lord Meneláos:
'Would it were so against all Agamemnon accomplished his anger,
as now he has in vain led hither a host of Achaians,

180 then he has gone back home to the much-loved land of his fathers
still with his ships quite empty, abandoning brave Meneláos.'
Thus somebody will say; may the broad earth then yawn to take me."

Cheering his heart spoke forth to him then light-haired Meneláos:
"Take heart, do not at all make fearful the host of Achaians.

185 Not in a place that is mortal is stuck the sharp arrow, but it was
warded away before that by the glittering war-belt, beneath it
also the waist-cloth, as well as the metal band made by the bronzesmiths."

Answering him in return then spoke forth strong Agamemnon:
"Would that it might be just as you say, dear Lord Meneláos!

190 Then will the healer examine and care for the wound and upon it

84

sprinkle remedial herbs, so putting a stop to the black pain."
    Thus; to the godlike herald Talthýbios he addressed these words:
"Quick as you can, Talthýbios, order Macháon to come here,
that man who is the son of Asklépios, faultless physician,
195 so he can see Meneláos the warlike scion of Atreus,
who has been shot with an arrow by someone skilled as an archer,
Trojan or Lykian, glory for him, but for us a great sorrow."
    So he spoke, and the herald did not disobey, having listened;
he set forth through the army of those bronze-armored Achaians,
200 looking about for the hero Macháon, and soon he perceived him
standing, and there about him were the powerful ranks of shield-bearing
troops who had followed along when he left horse-nourishing Trikkè.
There then, standing beside him, in these winged words he addressed him:
"Son of Asklépios, rise; you are summoned by strong Agamemnon,
205 so you can see Meneláos the warlike scion of Atreus,
who has been shot with an arrow by someone skilled as an archer,
Trojan or Lykian, glory for him, but for us a great sorrow."
    So he spoke, and in him he roused up the heart in his bosom;
they set forth in the throng through the widespread host of Achaians.
210 But then, when they arrived at the place light-haired Meneláos
had been wounded, and there in a circle were gathered about him
numerous nobles, the godlike man came right to the middle;
straightway he from the well-fitted war-belt pulled out the arrow;
backward the sharp barbs broke from the point as the arrow was pulled out.
215 Then on his body he loosened the glittering war-belt, beneath it
also the loincloth, as well as the metal band made by the bronzesmiths.
Soon as he saw that wound where the sharp bitter arrow had fallen,
skillfully sucking the blood out, the soothing remedial herbs he
sprinkled that Cheiron had once with a kind thought given his father.
220   While they attended upon the great crier of war Meneláos,
all that time were approaching the ranks of shield-carrying Trojans;
so they put on their armor again, took thought of their war-craft.
    Then you would not have seen drowsy the excellent lord Agamemnon,
neither in fear was he crouching nor was he reluctant to battle,
225 but most eager to hurry to battle that wins a man glory.
There did he leave his steeds and his chariot, gleaming with bronze-work;
snorting, the horses were kept from the battleground by a retainer,
noble Eurýmedon, son of Peiraíos' son Ptolemaíos,
for upon him he had laid a strong order to hold them, until his
230 limbs were seized with exhaustion from marshaling so many soldiers;

meanwhile he went on foot, and the ranks of the men he inspected.
Those he observed of the swift-horsed Dánaäns eager for battle,
them with his words as he stood at their side he cheered and encouraged:
"Argives, not in the least give up your impetuous valor,
235 since it will not be the liars to whom Zeus father is helper.
Rather the ones who first violated the oaths they had plighted,
theirs are the delicate bodies that vultures will soon be devouring,
then we will carry their much-loved wives and their innocent children
off in the galleys, as soon as we take their city and sack it."
240 But whomever he saw holding back from the odious warfare,
them with his angry and scornful words he rebuked and derided:
"Argives, shooters of arrows, disgraces, are you not embarrassed?
Why in bewilderment thus do you stand, in the manner of fawns that,
once they have grown exhausted from running across a great meadow,
245 stand there, and nothing at all of their prowess remains in their spirits;
so in bewilderment now do you stand here, nor are you fighting.
Or do you wait for the Trojans to come up close where the well-sterned
galleys have been dragged up on the shore of the silvery deep sea,
so as to learn if the hand of the scion of Kronos protects you?"
250 Thus he marshaled the host, and the ranks of the men he inspected.
Making his way through throngs of the men he came to the Cretans;
they were around war-skilled Idómeneus arming for battle;
there like a boar in his prowess Idómeneus stood in the vanguard,
Mérionés kept urging ahead the last ranks of the fighters.
255 Looking at them Agamemnon the lord of the people was gladdened;
so to Idómeneus he straightway spoke words of approval:
"You above all I honor, Idómeneus, out of the swift-horsed
Dánaäns, whether it be in war or in some other labor,
or in the banquet, whenever the noblest men of the Argives
260 mix in the mixing bowl the bright-glistening wine of the elders,
since in fact if the rest of the long-haired men, the Achaians,
drink up all of their share, your goblet is always standing
full in the way mine is, to be drunk as the spirit commands you.
Rise up and fight, like the man you have boasted to be from aforetime."
265 Speaking to him made answer Idómeneus, lord of the Cretans:
"Scion of Atreus, certain it is your trustworthy comrade
I will remain, as I first made promise and nodded agreement.
But go rouse up the rest of the long-haired men, the Achaians,
so that we quickly may fight, for in fact their oaths have the Trojans
270 made null and void; and for them this act will be death and disaster

afterward, since they first violated the oaths they had plighted."

He spoke, and Atreus' son passed onward, rejoicing in spirit.
Going ahead through the throng of the men he reached the Ajaxes
arming themselves, and along with them followed a cloud of foot soldiers.
275 As when a goatherd looks from a lookout place at a cloud which
comes at him over the seaway before the loud blast of the west wind,
though it is yet far off, it appears to him blacker than pitch as
it goes over the seaway and drives an enormous tempest—
looking at it he shudders and hurries his flocks to a cavern—
280 so now about the Ajaxes were moving ahead the compacted
ranks of the Zeus-reared vigorous youths to the violent battle,
dark as a cloud and with bucklers and spear-shafts fearfully bristling.
Looking at these men too the strong lord Agamemnon was gladdened,
raising his voice he spoke, and in these winged words he addressed them:
285 "Noble Ajaxes, commanders of all these bronze-armored Argives,
it is not seemly for me to urge you, and I give you no orders,
since of yourselves you exhort your men to do strenuous combat.
Oh Zeus, father of all, and Athena as well, and Apollo,
would that in every breast were a spirit as valiant as these are!
290 Then very quickly the city of great Lord Priam would bow down
under our conquering hands, be taken and utterly ransacked!"

So having spoken he left them there, and he went among others;
thereupon he found Nestor, the clear-voiced speaker of Pylos,
setting his comrades in order and urging them on to do battle,
295 there about him tall Pélagon, Chrómios too, and Alástor,
also powerful Haimon, and Bias, the shepherd of people.
First were the horsemen, along with the horses and chariots, which he
ranged on the field, and behind were the footmen, many and noble,
who were the bulwark of battle; the cowards he drove to the center,
300 so even though unwilling a man perforce would be fighting.
First on the charioteers he laid his commands, for he bade them
keep their horses in hand, nor among the melee be entangled;
"Let no man so confide in his horsemanship and his prowess
as to be eager alone, before others, to fight with the Trojans,
305 neither let any retreat, for in that case you will be feebler.
He who can reach to an enemy chariot out of his own car,
let him lunge with his spear, since that way will be much better.
So did the fighters of earlier times sack cities and ramparts,
those who held in their breasts this valorous purpose and spirit."
310 So did the old man urge who was long since learnèd in warfare.

Looking at him also the strong lord Agamemnon was gladdened;
raising his voice he spoke, and in these winged words he addressed him:
"Old man, would it were thus, as the spirit is great in your bosom,
so could your knees too follow, the strength be steady within you.

315 Common to all is the age that exhausts you; but would that another
one of the men had yours and that you were among the more youthful!"
       Speaking to him then answered the horseman Gerenian Nestor:
"Scion of Atreus, I could myself much wish that I might be
such as I was at the time I great Ereuthálion slaughtered;

320 but no way do the gods give all things to men at the same time.
If then I was a youth, in its turn now old age besets me.
Nevertheless there among those horsemen will I be, and give them
orders with counsel and speeches; for this is the right of the old men.
Younger are those who fight by hurling their spears, at a later

325 time than myself were they born, and their own might still they confide in."
       He spoke, and Atreus' son passed onward, rejoicing in spirit.
He found Péteos' scion Menéstheus, driver of horses,
standing, and there about him the Athenians, lords of the war cry;
close beside them was standing Odysseus of many devices;

330 there too the ranks of the Képhallénians, none of them feeble,
stood, for their forces were not yet hearing the clamor of battle,
but just recently started were moving the battle arrays of
Trojans, tamers of steeds, and Achaians; and so did they stand there
waiting until some other Achaians advancing in column

335 made onslaught on the Trojans and thereby opened the battle.
Looking at them Agamemnon the lord of the people reproached them;
raising his voice he spoke, and in these winged words he addressed them:
"Oh you scion of Péteos, a ruler belovèd of heaven,
you too, excelling in evil deceit, so greedy and guileful,

340 why do you cower and stand here idle and wait for the others?
It is more seemly for both of you now to be up with the foremost
standing and there take part in the blistering heat of the battle,
since you two are the first who hear of my banquet whenever
we make ready a feast, we Achaians, for all of the elders.

345 Then to you both it is pleasing to eat roast flesh and to drink down
cup upon cup of the honey-sweet wine for as long as you want to.
Now you would be most pleased if you saw ten troops of Achaians
going with pitiless bronze in front of you into the battle."
       Looking with lowering brows said Odysseus of many devices:

350 "Atreus' son, what a word has escaped from the fence of your teeth now!

How can you say we keep from the fight any time the Achaians
rouse at the Trojans, tamers of horses, the bitter god Ares?
You will be witnessing, should you desire to and should it concern you,
even Telémachos' father engaged in fight with the foremost
355 Trojans, tamers of horses: the words you utter are windy."
    Smiling at him thus spoke and addressed him strong Agamemnon,
as he perceived he was angry, and took back what he had uttered:
"Zeus-sprung son of Laërtes, Odysseus of many devices,
neither do I beyond measure reproach you nor do I command you,
360 since I know very well how the heart in your bosom is ever
skilled in benevolent counsel; for what you think, so do I think.
But come, later will I make up for it, should any bad word
now have been said; may the gods make all these things be as nothing."
    So having spoken he left them there, and he went among others.
365 Then he came upon Tydeus' son, high-souled Diomédes,
standing among his horses and chariots, skillfully jointed;
there too, standing beside him, was Sthénelos Kápaneus' scion.
So as he saw him too, thus scolded him strong Agamemnon—
raising his voice he spoke, and in these winged words he addressed him:
370 "Ah me, scion of Tydeus the war-skilled tamer of horses,
why do you cower, and why just gaze at the battle-embankments?
Never did Tydeus make it his habit to cower in terror,
rather, to fight with his foes far ahead of his own dear comrades.
So do they say who had seen him at labor, for I never either
375 met him or looked upon him; they say he was better than others.
Once in fact without fighting he came as a guest to Mykéne
bringing with him godlike Polyneíkes, assembling an army;
they at the sacred bulwark of Thebes were then mounting a campaign.
Much they entreated the people to furnish them glorious allies;
380 these were desiring to give them, assenting to what he requested;
but Zeus turned it aside by showing them signs of ill omen.
Those two, when they departed and went well ahead in their journey,
came to the river Asópos of deep rush-marshes and grass banks;
there the Achaians dispatched Lord Tydeus to carry a message.
385 He went forth, and arriving he found those many Kadmeíans
eating a feast in the house of Etéokles, mighty in prowess.
There though he was a stranger was Tydeus the chariot-driver
not at all frightened, alone as he was among many Kadmeíans;
rather he challenged the youths to contend with him—all he defeated
390 easily—so was Athena to him a supporter and helper.

But the Kadmeíans, goaders of horses, became very angry,
so as he went back home, they brought out and set a strong ambush,
fifty of them, all youthful, and two there were as the leaders,
Maion the scion of Haimon, a man most like the immortals,
395   also Autóphonos' son Polyphóntes, steadfast in battle.
But a most hideous fate did Tydeus loose upon these men
too, for he slaughtered them all; one only he sent to return home—
Maion he sent on his way, in obedience to the gods' portents.
Such a man was Aitolian Tydeus; but as for the son he
400   sired, he is worse in battle than he, though better at talking."
    So he spoke; not a word to him then said strong Diomédes,   ·
reverencing the reproach he had heard from the august ruler.
It was illustrious Kápaneus' scion who made him an answer:
"Atreus' son, do not lie, as you know well how to speak truly.
405   It is our boast to be men far better than ever our fathers;
we are the ones who took the foundation of Thebes of the seven
gates, though lesser the host we led at a wall that was stronger,
putting our trust in the signs of the gods and the aid of the lord Zeus;
those by their own mad recklessness were consigned to destruction.
410   Therefore do not assign the same honor to us and our fathers."
    Looking with lowering brows thus strong Diomédes addressed him:
"No, dear friend, keep silent; obey this word that I utter.
Not in the least do I blame Agamemnon, shepherd of people,
now that he urges to battle the well-greaved men, the Achaians;
415   for upon him great glory will follow, in case the Achaians
ever should slaughter the Trojans and sacred Ilion capture.
If the Achaians are killed, upon him great sorrow will follow.
But come, let us as well take thought of our furious valor."
    Thus, then he to the ground from his chariot leapt in his armor;
420   dreadfully clattered the bronze on the breast of the king as he started
rushing; and fear would have gripped any man, though steadfast of spirit.
    As at a time when the surf of the sea on the thundering seashore
rushes in rapid succession before the onset of the west wind,
out on the seaway first it collects to a crest, on the mainland
425   then it crashes and loudly resounds, and around the high headlands
arches aloft in a billowing breaker and spews the saltwater,
so then in rapid succession were moving the Dánaän forces,
ever unceasing, to battle; and each of the leaders commanded
his own men, and the others were silent, and you would have thought no
430   voice in their breasts those numerous troops who followed along had,

so were they silent for fear of their leaders; around all the men was
gleaming the elegant armor that while they marched they were wearing.
But for the Trojans, as sheep in the fold of a man of great substance
stand in a countless flock and await to be milked of their white milk,
435　bleating interminably while hearing the cries of their lambkins,
so did the clamor arise from the widespread host of the Trojans,
since not all of them used the same speech nor possessed one language—
mixed were the tongues of the men called thither from numerous countries.
These by Ares were roused, and their foes by bright-eyed Athena,
440　and by Terror and Panic and Conflict, ceaselessly raging,
who is the sister and comrade of dire man-slaughtering Ares,
rearing her crest at the start but a little, but shortly thereafter
fixing her head in the heavens as she on the earth keeps striding.
Equal for both was the strife she cast in the midst of the armies
445　now as she went through the throng and the men's groans ever augmented.

　　Finally, when they arrived in the same place, coming together,
shield upon shield they dashed, and their spears, and the furious might of
men well armored in bronze; and the shields made massive with bosses
clashed each one on another, and huge was the clamor that rose up.
450　There were the grief-filled groans and the triumph-shouts to be heard of
men who were killing and men who were killed; the earth streamed with their lifeblood.
As when rivers of winter, as they flow down from the mountains
into a meeting of gullies, unite their powerful waters
out of the great springs into the hollow ravine of the torrent—
455　far off up in the mountains a shepherd is hearing their thunder—
so from the meeting in battle of these came shouting and turmoil.

　　First Antílochos killed a strong-helmeted man of the Trojans,
noble, among the best fighters, Thalýsias' son Echepólos,
struck him first on the ridge of his helmet crested with horsehair;
460　into his forehead plunged the bronze spear-point, then penetrated
deep inside of the bone; and his eyes were enshrouded in darkness;
he fell down as a rampart does, in the violent combat.
Then by the foot as he fell he was seized by strong Elephénor,
Chálchodon's scion, the leader among the greathearted Abántes,
465　who from the missiles attempted to drag him in order to strip his
armor from him very quickly; but short-lived proved his endeavor,
for as he dragged that corpse, greathearted Agénor observed him,
then in the side that appeared from beneath his shield as he stooped, he
struck with his smooth spear pointed with bronze, and his limbs unloosened.
470　So did the spirit forsake him, and over his body a grievous

toil of Achaians and Trojans ensued—like wolves they were leaping
each of them onto another, and man against man was colliding.
　　Ajax Télamon's son then struck Anthémion's scion—
this Simoeísios, blooming with youth, his mother had once brought
475　forth by the banks of the Símoeis River, as she from Mount Ida
came down, where she had followed her parents to see to the sheep flocks;
him therefore they had named Simoeísios; never his much-loved
parents would he give quittance for rearing him: brief did his life span
prove—by the spear of the greathearted Ajax thus was he vanquished.
480　For as he first strode forth, he was struck on the breast by Ajax
near the right nipple; and right on through the whole shoulder the bronze spear
went, and he fell to the ground in the dust in the way a black poplar
topples that grows in the rich low land of a great water-meadow,
smooth-barked, yet from the top of its trunk sprout numerous branches;
485　this with his lustrous iron a chariot-maker has cut down,
so for a beautiful chariot he might bend a strong wheel-rim;
it lies drying and hardening there by the banks of a river.
Such Anthémion's son Simoeísios now was, subdued by
Zeus-sprung Ajax, at whom then Ántiphos, glittering-armored,
490　scion of Priam, a sharp spear hurled in the midst of the melee;
he missed Ajax but Leukos, Odysseus' illustrious comrade,
struck in the groin, as he dragged off a corpse to the other
side, and he fell upon it, from his hands thus dropping the body.
Then was Odysseus, for him who was killed, much angered in spirit;
495　he strode forth through the foremost, in bright bronze armor accoutered;
going to stand close by, he cast with his glittering spear while
warily glancing around, and the Trojans withdrew in the face of
that man casting at them. Nor in vain he let fly the spear but
straight at Demókoön struck, illegitimate scion of Priam,
500　who from Abýdos had come to his father, forsaking his swift mares.
Him with his spear did Odysseus strike, in his wrath for his comrade,
square on the temple, and then the bronze point right on through the other
temple as well penetrated; his eyes were enshrouded in darkness.
Falling he crashed to the ground, and around him clattered his armor.
505　Then did the foremost fighters retreat, and illustrious Hektor;
loudly the Argives shouted in triumph and dragged off the corpses,
afterward charging ahead much farther; Apollo was angered,
looking from Pérgamos downward; and shouting he called to the Trojans:
"Rise up, Trojans, tamers of horses, do not in the battle
510　yield to the Argives, for none of their flesh is of stone or of iron

so that it might hold off the flesh-severing bronze they are struck with.
Nor in fact is Achilles the scion of fair-haired Thetis
fighting, but there by his ships heart-anguishing wrath he is nursing."
     So from the citadel shouted the terrible god. The Achaians
515 glorious Trítogeneía the daughter of Zeus was arousing,
going among the melee, wherever she saw them relaxing.
     There doom caught in its snare Amarýngkeus' scion Dióres,
for with a boulder enormous and rough he was struck on the ankle
of his right leg; and the man who threw it was chief of the Thracians,
520 Peíroös, Ímbrasos' son, who had come to the fighting from Ainos;
both of the tendons as well as the bone by the pitiless stone were
utterly shattered and crushed, so that down on his back in the dust he
fell while both of his hands he stretched to his much-loved comrades,
gasping his life-breath out; and to him rushed he who had struck him,
525 Peíroös, stabbing at him with his spear by the navel, and all his
guts gushed out on the ground, and his eyes were enshrouded in darkness.
     Him, as he speeded away, with a spear Aitolian Thoas
struck on the breast by the nipple, impaling his lung with the bronze point.
Thoas approached him and stood at his side, and he pulled his
530 powerful spear from his chest, and his sharp sword drew from its scabbard,
then in the midst of his belly he jabbed, and of life he deprived him.
Yet he did not strip him of his armor; around him his Thracian
comrades with top-grown hair stood holding in hand their long spear-shafts;
they now, great as he was, and as powerful too, and as valiant,
535 thrust him away from themselves, and he gave way, staggering backward.
So those two lay stretched in the dust close by one another;
both men, one of the Thracians and one the bronze-armored Epeíans,
were the commanders; and numerous others around them were slaughtered.
     Then no more could a man make light of the toil he had entered
540 who was as yet unwounded, as yet unstruck by the sharp bronze,
though in its midst he was moving with Pallas Athena to guide him,
holding his hand, and away from him warding the volley of missiles;
for upon that one day there were many Achaians and Trojans
who lay stretched face down in the dust close by one another.

BOOK 5

To Diomédes the scion of Tydeus Pallas Athena
then gave courage and strength, so that he among all of the Argives
might prove most outstanding and win for himself noble glory.
Weariless flame she kindled to blaze from his shield and his helmet,
5   like that star which late in the summer above all the others
brilliantly shines as it comes up out of its bath in the Ocean;
such was the flame she kindled to blaze from his head and his shoulders,
rousing him into the middle, the place most fighters were struggling.
There was among those Trojans a Dares, wealthy and faultless,
10 who was a priest of Hephaistos; of two sons he was the father,
Phégeus one, and Idaíos, and both well skilled in all warfare.
Breaking away from the others, the two men charged Diomédes:
they from their chariots fought; on foot on the ground he assailed them.
When in coming together the men were close to each other,
15 Phégeus then was the first who hurled a long-shadowing spear-shaft;
over the strong left shoulder of Tydeus' scion the spear-point
passed, and it did not strike him; and after him Tydeus' scion
rushed with the bronze, nor in vain from his hand went flying the missile,
but in the midst of the breast it struck; from his horses it thrust him.
20 Straightway leaving his beautiful chariot, backward Idaíos
sprang, and he did not dare stand over the corpse of his brother.
Nevertheless he himself would not have escaped from a black fate
but that Hephaistos protected and saved him, hid him in darkness,
so that the old man might not be desolated entirely.
25 But his horses the great-souled scion of Tydeus drove off;
he gave them to his comrades to lead to the hollow galleys.
Soon as the great-souled Trojans observed of the scions of Dares
one who avoided his death, one there by his chariot slaughtered,
then in them all was the heart much troubled. And bright-eyed Athena
30 taking his hand spoke out in these words to impetuous Ares:

"Ares, man-slaying Ares, the bloodstained stormer of bulwarks,
is it not best that we leave the Achaians and Trojans to join in
battle, to whichever side Zeus father decides to grant glory?
But as for us two, let us withdraw and avoid Zeus's anger."

35   So having said, from the battle she led impetuous Ares.
When she had made him sit on the sand-strewn banks of Skamánder,
straightway the Dánaäns routed the Trojans, and each of the leaders
killed him a fighter; and first Agamemnon, lord of the people,
hurled from his chariot Ódios, the great Halizonian chieftain,

40   for as he just was turning, between his shoulders the hero
planted a spear in his back, and ahead through the chest he impelled it;
falling he crashed to the ground, and around him clattered his armor.
Then Idómeneus slaughtered the son of Maiónian Boros,
Phaistos, a fighter who came from the deep-soiled country of Tarnè;

45   he was the man spear-famed Idómeneus now with his long spear
pierced clear through the right shoulder, as he on his chariot mounted;
he from the chariot fell and was seized by odious darkness.
Him straightway Idómeneus' comrades stripped of his armor.
Meanwhile Strophios' scion Skamándrios, skilled in the chase, was

50   killed with a sharp-pointed spear by Atreus' son Meneláos—
he was an excellent hunter, for Artemis taught him herself to
strike down all the wild beasts to which mountainous woods provide nurture.
But no help to him then gave Artemis shooter of arrows,
nor did the archery skills in which he before was outstanding;

55   rather did Atreus' son Meneláos renowned as a spearman
stab him as he was fleeing—between his shoulders the hero
planted a spear in his back, and ahead through the chest he impelled it;
He fell flat on his face, and around him clattered his armor.
Thereupon Mérionés killed Phéreklos, scion of Tekton,

60   Harmon's son; all manner of exquisite things he was skilled to
make with his hands, since Pallas Athena especially loved him;
he also had constructed for Lord Alexander the balanced
ships, the beginning of bane, that for all of the Trojans were evil,
and for himself, for he knew not what the decrees of the gods were.

65   Him now Mérionés went after and, when he had caught him,
struck on the buttock, the right one, and straight on through unimpeded
under the bone penetrated the spear-point, into the bladder.
Down on his knees he fell; as he groaned, death covered him over.
Meges as well then slaughtered Pedaíos, the son of Anténor,

70   who in fact was a bastard, but noble Theáno had nursed him

carefully, like her own children, in order to please her dear husband.
Coming up close to him, Phyleus' scion, renowned as a spearman,
struck at the back of his head with his sharp spear, hitting the tendon;
then through the teeth straight onward the bronze point severed the tongue-root.
75 Down in the dust he dropped, with his teeth still biting the cold bronze.
     Then Eurýpylos, son of Euaímon, the noble Hypsénor
slaughtered, the scion of high-souled Dolópion, who of Skamánder
had been chosen as priest—as a god by the folk he was honored;
him Eurýpylos now, the illustrious son of Euaímon,
80 as he was fleeing before, ran after and struck on the shoulder,
thrusting at him with his sword, thus cutting his powerful arm off.
Bleeding the arm fell onto the ground; down over his eyes came
seizing him blood-red death and his own irresistible doomsday.
     So were they laboring there all over the violent combat;
85 nor as to Tydeus' son would you know which side he belonged to,
whether he battled along with the Trojans or with the Achaians.
For in the plain he was storming ahead like a torrent in winter
swollen in spate whose strong swift current destroys the embankments;
this no more the embankments, although strong-bulwarked, can hold back,
90 neither indeed do the walls of the flourishing gardens restrain its
sudden arrival in force, when rain of Zeus presses upon it;
many a beautiful work of the young men crumble before it.
So before Tydeus' son were the compact ranks of the Trojans
driven confused and did not stand up to him, though they were many.
95   Straightway, when the illustrious son of Lykáon observed him
storming along in the plain and the ranks all driven before him,
quickly his curved bow he began stretching at Tydeus' scion,
whom as he charged he shot at, and hit him upon the right shoulder,
just on the corselet-plate; clear through did the sharp bitter arrow
100 speed on its way straight onward; with blood was the corselet spattered.
Over him shouted aloud the illustrious son of Lykáon:
"Rise up now, you greathearted Trojans, goaders of horses,
seeing the best of the Achaians has been struck, nor do I think he
long will resist this powerful missile, if truly Apollo,
105 lord, son of Zeus, has aroused me from Lykia here to the battle."
     Boasting he spoke; the swift arrow had not brought down Diomédes,
but withdrawing, in front of his horses and chariot he stood;
speaking to Sthénelos, Kápaneus' son, these words he addressed him:
"Rise up, dear friend, Kápaneus' son, from the chariot come down,
110 so that you may pull out of my shoulder the sharp bitter arrow."

So he spoke; to the ground from the chariot Sthénelos leapt and,
standing beside him, pulled the sharp arrow out, clean through his shoulder;
up through the pliable cloth of his tunic the blood began spurting.
Then straightway thus prayed the great crier of war Diomédes:
115 "Hear me, offspring of Zeus of the aegis, unwearying goddess,
if in benevolent mind you have stood at the side of my father,
ever, in violent war, now befriend me also, Athena;
grant that I kill this man and to him I come within spear-cast
who struck me before I was aware of him; boasting he says that
120 not long I will be looking on Helios' radiant sunlight."
So he spoke as he prayed; he was heard by Pallas Athena,
who made nimble his limbs, his feet and his hands up above them;
there then, standing beside him, in these winged words she addressed him:
"Now take heart, Diomédes, and go on fighting the Trojans,
125 since inside of your breast I have put the great force of your father,
fearless and sure, that the wielder of shields had, Tydeus the horseman.
Off of your eyes I have taken the mist that before was upon them,
so that you may know well which one is a god and which human.
Therefore now, if a god comes hither and puts you to trial,
130 never against any gods, the immortals, should you do battle,
none of the other ones, but if the daughter of Zeus Aphrodítè
were to come into the combat, you should wound her with the sharp bronze."
Thus then when she had spoken departed the bright-eyed Athena;
Tydeus' son went back in the fray, with the champions mingled.
135 Though in his heart he before had been raging to fight with the Trojans,
now strength three times as great took hold of him, as of a lion
which in the pastures a shepherd attending his wool-fleeced sheep flock
grazes as it leaps over the wall of the fold, and he does not
kill it but rouses its strength; then he no longer defends them,
140 but in the steadings he hides, and the sheep, forsaken, are routed;
they throng closely together and pile up one on another;
mightily raging the lion again leaps out of the deep fold.
So now strong Diomédes was raging to mix with the Trojans.
There he Astýnoös killed and Hypeíron the shepherd of people;
145 one with his bronze-tipped spear he hit just over the nipple,
while on the collarbone close to the shoulder the other he struck with
his great sword—from the neck and the back he severed the shoulder.
Leaving them there, he went to pursue Polyḯdos and Abas,
sons of Eurýdamas, who was an old man skilled in dream-reading.
150 Never when they came back would their dreams be read by the old man;

rather indeed by strong Diomédes were both of them slaughtered.
Then after Xanthos and Thoön he went, two scions of Phainops,
both late-born, and with odious age their father was stricken;
no other son he begot to be left in charge of his treasures.

155 There he slaughtered the men and the dear life took from the breasts of
both of them; so to the father affliction and odious woes he
left, since never would he be greeting his sons yet alive when
they came home from the war, and his goods other kinsmen divided.

  There also did he take two sons of Dardánian Priam,
160 both men, Echémmon and Chrómios, in one chariot riding.
As among cattle a lion leaps onto and shatters the neck of
some fat heifer or bull of the herd which feeds in a coppice,
so from the chariot now did the scion of Tydeus bring down
both men, sorely unwilling, and both he stripped of their armor,
165 while their horses he gave to his comrades to drive to the galleys.

  Then Aineías observed him destroying the ranks of the fighters;
he set forth through the battle, among the confusion of spear-thrusts,
godlike Pándaros seeking, in hopes somewhere he could find him.
When he discovered the faultless and powerful son of Lykáon,
170 standing in front of him then he spoke; these words he addressed him:
"Pándaros, where indeed are your bow and your feather-winged arrows?
Where is your glory, in which no one now here is your rival?
Neither do any in Lykia claim to be better than you are.
But come, lifting your hands up to Zeus, fire an arrow at this man,
175 whosoever he is, so strong to do Trojans so many
evils, for those whose limbs he has loosened are many and noble,
if it is not some god enraged at the Trojans, resenting
offerings left unaccomplished; the wrath of a god is oppressive."
  Speaking to him made answer the glorious son of Lykáon:
180 "Noble Aineías, the counselor-lord of the bronze-clad Trojans,
it is to Tydeus' war-skilled son in all ways I compare him,
recognizing the look of his shield and his socketed helmet,
seeing his horses as well; whether he is a god, I am not sure.
If as I think he is human, the war-skilled scion of Tydeus,
185 not without god is he raging in this way, but an immortal
stands there close at his side, with a cloud enshrouding his shoulders,
who has diverted from him a swift missile of mine as it reached him.
For just now I fired off an arrow that on the right shoulder
struck him, and clear through the corselet-plate its shaft penetrated,
190 so that I told myself I would cast him away to Aidóneus;

yet I did not subdue him, and some god must be resentful.
Horses I do not have, nor a chariot which I could mount on;
yet in the house of Lykáon are chariots—there are eleven,
beautiful, new-made, freshly arrayed, and around them are covers
195   spread; and beside each chariot harnessed in pairs are the horses
standing, and fine white barley and oats they are munching as fodder.
Yes, and as I was departing, the elderly spearman Lykáon
charged me many and many a time, in the well-built palace,
giving me orders that I on a chariot mounted, and horses,
200   go forth leading the Trojans among these violent combats.
Yet I did not heed him, though that would have been much better,
sparing the horses instead, lest they lack fodder among these
multitudes here—they were used to consuming as much as they wanted.
Therefore I left them and came here to Ilion as a foot soldier,
205   putting my trust in my bow, which clearly would profit me nothing,
since I have shot already at two of the noblest among them,
Tydeus' scion and Atreus' scion, and both of them I have
struck unerringly, drawing their blood, but I only aroused them.
So to a terrible fate from its peg I took down the well-curved
210   bow on the day I parted for Ilion, lovely and charming,
leading my Trojans and carrying favor to glorious Hektor.
Should I ever return to my home and behold with my own eyes
my dear country and bedmate and my great high-roofed palace,
straightway then may the head be cut from my neck by a stranger,
215   if this bow I do not throw into the flames of a bright fire,
breaking it up with my hands; for a blustery nothing it serves me."
     Then in response Aineías, the chief of the Trojans, addressed him:
"Do not talk in that way; it will not be otherwise mended
ever until with our horses and chariot both of us going
220   out to that man make trial of him face to face in our armor.
But come, climb up onto my chariot, so that you see what
breed are the horses of Tros, most skillful in rapidly crossing
over the plain one way and another, pursuing and fleeing;
they will as well bring both of us safe to the city, if Zeus should
225   once more grant Diomédes the scion of Tydeus glory.
Nevertheless, you take up the whip and the glittering reins and
manage them; I will dismount from the chariot now to do battle;
otherwise you can await him, and I will take care of the horses."
     Speaking to him made answer the glorious son of Lykáon:
230   "Do you yourself, Aineías, keep holding the reins and your horses;

under their usual charioteer they better will draw this
well-curved chariot if we are fleeing from Tydeus' scion;
otherwise they would be frightened and restive and not at all willing
out of the battle to take us—for your voice they would be longing—
235   so that the great-souled scion of Tydeus, leaping on us, would
put us both to the slaughter and drive off the single-hoofed horses.
But as for these, your horses and chariot, you yourself drive them;
I will await that man with a sharp spear when he assails us."
      Soon as they said these words and the elegant chariot mounted,
240   eagerly straight against Tydeus' son they directed the horses.
Straightway Sthénelos, Kápaneus' glorious son, as he saw them,
spoke out to Tydeus' son, and in these winged words he addressed him:
"Tydeus' son Diomédes, in whom my heart is delighted,
two strong men I see who are eager to battle against you,
245   both having measureless strength, one of them with the bow most skillful,
Pándaros, boasting moreover that he is the son of Lykáon,
then Aineías, who boasts that as son of greathearted Anchíses
he was brought forth, and as well that his mother is Áphrodítè.
But come, let us withdraw in our chariot, nor in the foremost
250   fighters in this way charge, lest you chance losing your life-breath."
      Looking from lowering brows thus spoke to him strong Diomédes:
"Do not advise me to flee, for I think you will never persuade me,
since it would not be noble for me to go skulking in battle,
cowering down out of fear; and in me is the strength yet steadfast.
255   I hesitate to go onto the chariot but will confront them
just as I am, nor does Pallas Athena allow me to take flight.
Those men never their swift-hoofed horses will carry away from
us, not both of them, even if one might manage to flee us.
Something else I will tell you, and you keep this in your mind now:
260   if the deep-counseling goddess Athena should grant me the glory
both those fighters to kill, these swift-hoofed horses do you keep
back right here, to the rim of the chariot making the reins fast,
then be mindful to rush forth after the steeds of Aineías,
drive them away from the Trojans and back to the well-greaved Achaians.
265   For of that breed they are that to Tros wide-thundering Zeus once
gave, recompense for his son Ganymédes, because among horses,
all who exist beneath dawn and the sunlight, they are the finest;
stealing from that breed then, Anchíses the lord of the people
put his own mares under them, but without Laómedon knowing;
270   out of these unions were six foals born for the lord in the palace;

four of them he kept there for himself, at the manger he reared them,
while the two others, devisers of panic, he gave to Aineías.
Could we but take those two, we would win for ourselves noble glory."
    Such things then they spoke and addressed each one to the other;
275 driving the swift-hoofed horses the other two quickly approached them.
First to him then thus spoke the illustrious son of Lykáon:
"Powerful-hearted and war-skilled scion of glorious Tydeus,
plainly the swift shaft did not subdue you, the sharp bitter arrow;
now instead I will try with my spear to see whether I hit you."
280   So did he say, then brandished and threw his long-shadowing spear-shaft,
Tydeus' son he hit on the shield, and the spear-point of bronze went
speeding ahead straight through it and then on into the breastplate.
Over him shouted aloud the illustrious son of Lykáon:
"You have been struck clear through in the midriff—I do not think you
285 now much longer will last; you have granted to me a great glory."
    Then not frightened at all thus spoke to him strong Diomédes:
"Me you have missed, not struck, and I do not think that the two of
you will be leaving the fight until one or the other in falling
gluts with his blood fierce Ares, the warrior wielding a hide shield."
290   So having spoken, he threw; and Athena directed the weapon
right to the nose by the eye; through the white teeth it penetrated,
so that the obstinate bronze quite severed the root of the man's tongue;
close underneath it the point came out, by the base of the jawbone.
He from the chariot fell, and around him clattered his armor,
295 glittering brightly about, and his swift-hoofed horses, affrighted,
swerved to the side; right there were his life and his strength unloosened.
    Holding his shield and his great long spear then sprang out Aineías,
fearing that somehow the body would be dragged off by Achaians.
Over the man he stepped like a lion that trusts in its prowess,
300 holding his spear and his circular shield in front of his body,
eager to kill any fighter who might come forward against him,
shouting a terrible shout. In his hand then Tydeus' son took
up a huge stone—a great feat—which no two mortals could carry,
such as are men nowadays, but alone did he easily wield it;
305 throwing, he hit Aineías with it on the hip, where the thighbone
turns inside the hip-joint, at the place men call the cup-socket.
This cup-socket it smashed, and as well broke both of the sinews;
back from the muscle the rough stone tore the skin, so that the hero,
falling on one knee, stooped, and he leaned on the earth with his mighty
310 hand, while over his eyes black night came down to enshroud them.

Now right there would have died Aineías the lord of the people,
had not keenly observed Aphrodítè the daughter of Zeus, who
was his mother and who to Anchíses the oxherd had born him.
Quickly around that son so dear to her flinging her white arms,
315 she in front of him put a great fold of her shimmering robe as
shelter from missiles, lest some swift-horsed Dánaän fighter,
hurling a bronze spear into his chest, of his life should deprive him.
      Thus that goddess was bearing her dear son out of the battle;
Sthénelos, Kápaneus' scion, did not forget the injunctions
320 laid upon him by his lord, the great crier of war Diomédes;
but well apart from the roar of the battle the single-hoofed horses
he kept back, to the rim of the chariot making the reins fast;
then he at once rushed after the fair-maned steeds of Aineías,
drove them away from the Trojans and back to the well-greaved Achaians,
325 then to Deḯpylos gave them, the friend whom most among all his
youthful companions he prized, as a match to himself in his thinking,
so to the hollow ships he could drive them. Meanwhile the hero
mounted behind his own horses, and taking the shimmering reins he
guided the strong-hoofed horses at once to seek Tydeus' scion,
330 avidly. He however had gone with his pitiless bronze after Cypris,
knowing that she was a cowardly goddess and never among those
goddesses who in the battles of men are commanders and marshals;
neither Athena she was nor the sacker of cities Enýö.
But then, when he had reached her, pursuing her through the great tumult,
335 thereon the son of the great-souled Tydeus, aiming at her his
spear with a sharp point, wounded the base of her delicate hand by
lunging at her; and the spear penetrated her flesh as it went straight
through the ambrosial robe that the Graces themselves had fashioned,
over her palm, by the wrist. The ambrosial blood of the goddess
340 poured out, ichor, the sort which flows in the blessèd immortals,
since no food they consume, nor of glistening wine are they drinkers;
therefore they are without any blood and are called the immortals.
Loudly she shrieked, and her dear son she let fall from her bosom;
but with his own hands Phoibos Apollo removed him and rescued
345 him in a dark cloud, lest some swift-horsed Danaän fighter,
hurling a bronze spear into his chest, of his life should deprive him.
Over her shouted aloud the great crier of war Diomédes:
"Hold back, daughter of Zeus, from the battle and terrible combat.
Does it not satisfy you, the beguilement of cowardly women?
350 Yet if you will keep entering battle, I think you will surely

shudder at battle indeed, even if you hear it from elsewhere."
　　　So he spoke; in a frenzy she went away, sorely afflicted.
Then she was taken and led from the tumult by wind-footed Iris,
suffering terrible pain, with her beautiful flesh much darkened.

355　There to the left of the battle she found impetuous Ares
sitting and propping his spear on a cloud, and his two swift horses;
right there she fell onto her knees, and her much-loved brother
strongly imploring, she begged him for his gold-frontleted horses:
"My dear brother, assist me and rescue me—give me your horses,

360　so I can go to Olympos, on which the abode of the gods is.
I am in too much pain from a wound that a mortal inflicted,
Tydeus' scion, who now against Zeus himself would do battle."
　　　She spoke; Ares at once gave her the gold-frontleted horses.
Onto the chariot then she climbed, much troubled in spirit,

365　Iris mounted beside her, and taking the reins in her hands she
drove forth, lashing the steeds, nor against their wishes did they fly.
Straightway, when they arrived at the seat of the gods, steep Olympos,
there swift wind-footed Iris halted the horses and set them
loose from the chariot-yoke, and ambrosial fodder she gave them.

370　Quickly divine Aphrodíte fell onto the knees of Dióne,
her dear mother, and she, in her arms embracing her daughter,
gave her a pat with her hand and said these words, calling upon her:
"Who among Oúranos' offspring has done such things to you, dear child,
idly and rashly, as if you were openly working some evil?"

375　　　Answering her then spoke Aphrodíte the lover of laughter:
"I was wounded by Tydeus' son, great-souled Diomédes,
only because I was bearing my dear son out of the battle,
noble Aineías, who is far dearest to me among all men.
Now no longer between the Achaians and Trojans the dreadful

380　combat is, but against the immortals the Dánaäns battle."
　　　Speaking to her then answered Dióne the glorious goddess:
"Be of good heart, my child, and endure, although you are grieving,
since there are many of us with Olympian dwellings who suffer
sorrows from men, and as well inflict harsh grief on each other.

385　So suffered Ares, the time when strong Ephiáltes and Otos,
sons of Alóeus, bound him tightly in powerful bindings;
thirteen months in a great deep caldron of bronze he was tied up;
now indeed would have perished the battle-insatiate Ares
had not Alóeus' sons' stepmother, surpassingly lovely

390　Éériboía, reported to Hermes, who stole away Ares

when he was quite worn out, for the terrible bonds overcame him.
So suffered Hera, the time Amphítryon's powerful offspring
wounded her sorely upon the right breast by shooting a three-barbed
arrow at her; she too was then gripped by unbearable anguish.

395 So like them suffered monstrous Hades a sharp-pointed arrow,
when the same man, that scion of Zeus who carries the aegis,
struck him in Pylos among dead men and to agonies gave him.
But to the palace of Zeus he went, and to lofty Olympos,
grieved in his heart, transfixed with his pains, for the arrow was driven

400 into his huge stout shoulder, and he was afflicted in spirit.
Sprinkling upon it painkilling herbs, Paiëon the healer
cured it, for not in the least was his nature in any way mortal.
Pitiless violence-worker, who did not shrink to do evil,
who with his archery troubled the gods who dwell on Olympos.

405 This man was set against you by the goddess bright-eyed Athena;
simpleton, nor in his mind does the scion of Tydeus know how
not very long is alive any man who fights the immortals,
nor will his children about his knees be prattling to papa
once he arrives back home from the war and the terrible combat.

410 Therefore, powerful now though he is, let Tydeus' scion
keep it in mind, lest someone better than you are should fight him,
lest the sagacious child of Adréstos, Aígialeía,
wailing and moaning, awaken her dear house-servants from slumber,
in her desire for the husband she wedded, the best of the Achaians,

415 that proud-spirited wife of the tamer of steeds Diomédes."
    Thus, and with both of her hands from her wrist she wiped off the ichor,
so that the wrist grew well and the terrible pain was abated.
Then as they gazed at the conversation, Athena and Hera
tried with bantering words to provoke Zeus, scion of Kronos;

420 speaking among them opened the goddess bright-eyed Athena:
"Father Zeus, will you be angry at me for a thing I will tell you?
Surely the Cyprian goddess has eagerly urged an Achaian
woman to follow the Trojans, of whom she is now so enamored;
then she, while she caressed someone of the fair-robed Achaians,

425 injured her delicate hand, on the point of a gold brooch scratched it."
    So she spoke, and the father of men and of gods began smiling;
calling her over to him, he addressed Aphrodítè the golden:
"Not upon you, my child, are bestowed such labors of warfare,
rather are your concern the delectable labors of marriage;

430 all these things are for Ares the swift and Athena to care for."

Such things then they spoke and addressed each one to the other,
while at Aineías was charging the crier of war Diomédes,
though he perceived that above him Apollo was holding his arms up;
yet he did not shrink back from the great god: ever was he most
435   eager to kill Aineías and strip off his glorious armor.
Thrice he charged at the man, so strongly desiring to kill him;
thrice did Apollo repel him, his bright shield battering backward.
But then, when the fourth time he was rushing at him like a demon,
fearfully shouting aloud, far-working Apollo addressed him:
440   "Take care, Tydeus' scion, and give way, nor to the gods be
wishing to equal your thoughts, since not in the least the immortal
gods and the people who walk on the earth are of one and the same race."
So he spoke, and the scion of Tydeus drew back a little,
thereby avoiding the wrath of the god far-shooting Apollo.
445   Then well apart from the throng Aineías was set by Apollo,
inside sacred Pérgamos fort, where his temple had been built.
Him straightway then Leto and Artemis shooter of arrows
healed in the great inner room, and as well augmented his splendor.
But a phantasm Apollo the god of the silvery bow made
450   like Aineías himself, and resembling him also in armor,
so that around the phantasm the Trojans and noble Achaians
kept on fighting each other by smiting the circular oxhide
shields protecting their chests, and the fluttering shaggy-fringed bucklers.
Thus then Phoibos Apollo addressed impetuous Ares:
455   "Ares, man-slaying Ares, the bloodstained stormer of bulwarks,
will you at last not enter the battle and drag away this man,
Tydeus' son, who now against Zeus himself would do battle?
Cypris in close fight first he stabbed on the hand by the wrist-joint,
but then even against myself he rushed like a demon."
460   So having said, on the summit of Pérgamos fort he alighted.
Ares the baneful went to encourage the ranks of the Trojans,
seeming in looks much like swift Ákamas, chief of the Thracians.
There, exhorting the Zeus-loved scions of Priam, he shouted:
"Oh you fighters, the scions of Zeus-loved Priam the ruler,
465   how long will you allow the Achaians to slaughter the army?
Will it continue until by the well-built gates they are fighting?
There does a man lie whom like glorious Hektor we honored;
it is Aineías, the son of the lord greathearted Anchíses;
but come now, let us save from the tumult our excellent comrade."
470   So he spoke and aroused in each fighter the strength and the spirit.

Then Sarpédon severely upbraided illustrious Hektor:
"Hektor, where has the force disappeared which you until now had?
Once you expected, perhaps, without army or allies to hold this
city alone and with only your brothers-in-law and your brothers.
475 Now of those men not one am I able to see or to notice—
no, they cower the way hounds do when circling a lion;
we are the ones who fight, though we are mere allies among you,
since it is from a great distance that I have come as an ally—
Lykia lies far off by the eddying current of Xanthos;
480 there I left a dear bedmate behind and a son yet an infant,
also many possessions whoever is needy would wish for;
yet even so I stir up the Lykians; I am myself most
eager to battle my man, though nothing at all do I have here
such as would either be carried or driven away by Achaians.
485 You just stand here now, not even commanding the other
men of the army to stay and defend their wives in the battle;
take care lest, as if taken in meshes of flax that ensnares all,
you yourselves become booty and plunder for enemy fighters,
who then swiftly will ransack your well-inhabited city.
490 You should be thinking of all these things, both nighttime and daytime,
ever beseeching the lords of the far-famed allies to hold out
ceaselessly and so put from yourself this terrible censure."

So Sarpédon addressed him; the word stung Hektor in spirit.
Straightway he to the ground from his chariot leapt in his armor;
495 wielding his two sharp spears, he ranged all over the army,
urging the men to do battle, and roused up terrible combat.
They wheeled round in a rally and stood to confront the Achaians;
but in close order the Argives awaited them, nor did they take flight.
Just as a wind drives chaff all over the sacred threshing
500 floors among men who are winnowing grain, when fair-haired Deméter
separates chaff from the grain by the winds which bluster upon it—
under them heaped-up chaff starts whitening: so the Achaians
then grew whiter beneath a great dust-cloud which in the melee
up to the bronze-bright heaven the hooves of the horses were beating,
505 as again they joined battle; and backward the charioteers wheeled;
they brought forward the force of their hands; impetuous Ares
covered them over with night, so aiding the Trojans in battle,
ranging in every quarter, and bringing to pass the behest of
Phoibos Apollo the god of the gold sword, since he had bid him
510 rouse up the heart of the Trojans, on seeing that Pallas Athena

then had departed; for she had been giving the Dánaäns succor.
Out of the rich inner room Aineías was sent by the same great
god, who as well put strength in the breast of the shepherd of people.
There with his comrades stood Aineías, and they became joyful,
515   seeing that he was returning to join them living and healthy,
full of his glorious prowess; but nothing at all did they ask him—
other toil did not allow it, that he of the silvery bow had
roused, and man-slaughtering Ares, and Conflict ceaselessly raging.
     There were the two Ajaxes, Odysseus, and strong Diomédes
520   rousing the Dánaäns up to do battle; and they were themselves not
quavering under the might of the Trojans, nor under their onslaughts;
rather they stood their ground like clouds that the scion of Kronos
stations in windless weather aloft on the peaks of the mountains,
stilled, when are sleeping the forces of Boreas and of the other
525   violent blustering winds which scatter the shadowy clouds all
over the sky by blowing upon them in whistling storm blasts:
so at the Trojans the Dánaäns stood fast, nor did they take flight.
Through the whole throng ranged Atreus' scion with many an order:
"Now, dear friends, be men, keep hold of your valorous spirit,
530   feel shame, each on account of the rest in the violent combats;
more of the men who feel such shame live safely than perish,
while from the ones who flee no glory nor any defense springs."
     He spoke; swiftly he hurled his spear, and a champion fighter
struck, great-souled Aineías' companion Deïkoön, son of
535   Pérgasos, whom as much as the offspring of Priam the Trojans
honored, because he was swift to do battle along with the foremost.
Square on his shield with the spear he was struck by strong Agamemnon;
nor was the spear held off, but it passed right on through the bronze shield;
into the base of the belly he drove it ahead through the war-belt.
540   Falling he crashed to the ground, and around him clattered his armor.
     There Aineías in turn killed two of the Dánaäns' best men,
scions of Díokles: one Orsílochos, Krethon the other;
theirs was a father who lived in the well-built city of Phérai;
wealthy he was in substance, his family sprung from the river
545   Álpheios, who flows broad through the Pylians' country, and who had
sired Ortílochos there to be lord of a numerous people;
then in his turn Ortílochos great-souled Díokles fathered;
next in succession, begotten of Díokles, were the twin offspring,
Krethon and Orsílochos, well skilled in all manner of warfare.
550   These two, coming to manhood, had followed along with the Argive

host on the dark-hued galleys to Ilion, land of fine horses,
winning for Atreus' sons Agamemnon and Meneláos
honor; but there by death's finality both were enshrouded.
These men were like two lions aloft in the peaks of the mountains
555 which their mother has reared in the thickets within a deep forest;
both of them, snatching away as their provender cattle and fat sheep,
visit destruction on men's farmsteads, till they are themselves brought
into the hands of the men and with bronze swords put to the slaughter.
So did the two men now, brought down at the hands of Aineías,
560 fall to the ground with a crash, in the way tall fir trees topple.
    Pitying them as they fell Meneláos belovèd of Ares
strode forth then through the foremost, in bright bronze armor accoutered,
shaking the shaft of his spear, for his mettle was Ares arousing,
having in mind that he be brought down at the hands of Aineías.
565 But Antílochos saw him, the scion of greathearted Nestor;
he strode out through the foremost in fear for the shepherd of people,
lest he be injured and utterly disappoint them of their labor.
Now were the two foes holding their hands and their spears with the sharp points
out each one at the other, and both were eager for combat,
570 when Antílochos came up close to the shepherd of people.
Nor did Aineías remain, though he was a spirited fighter,
as the two men he observed there waiting beside one another.
After they dragged those bodies away to the host of Achaians,
both of the miserable men they laid in the arms of their comrades,
575 then themselves turned back to do battle among the best fighters.
    Thereon the two men killed Pylaímenes, equal to Ares,
who was the lord of the great-souled Páphlagónian shield-men;
him did Atreus' son Meneláos renowned as a spearman
pierce with his spear as he stood there firm, by the collarbone striking;
580 while Antílochos aimed at his charioteer and companion
Mydon, Atýmnios' valorous son, as the single-hoofed steeds he
turned, with a stone which struck mid-elbow; and out of his hands down
onto the ground in the dust did the ivory-glistening reins fall.
Leaping at him with his sword, Antílochos thrust at his temple;
585 straightway, gasping for breath, from the well-built chariot headlong
he fell into the dust, down onto his head and his shoulders.
There he stayed a long time, for the sand was deep where he landed,
till on the ground in the dust his horses had trampled and knocked him.
These Antílochos lashed and drove back to the host of Achaians.
590   Hektor indeed was observing the men through the ranks, and he rushed at

them with a shout; the battalions of Trojans were following after,
huge in strength; it was Ares and queenly Enÿö who led them—
she was attended by reckless Turmoil, shameless in carnage,
while in his hand an enormous spear fierce Ares was wielding,
595 sometimes ranging before great Hektor and sometimes behind him.
     Noticing him the great crier of war Diomédes was shaken.
As when a man who is crossing a great plain helplessly halts on
reaching the banks of a swift-flowing river that flows to the sea-brine
roaring and seething with foam—he sees it and starts away backward;
600 so now Tydeus' son gave ground, and he spoke to his people:
"Oh friends, how we have marveled, indeed, at the glorious Hektor,
seeing that he is skilled as a spearman and bold as a fighter,
yet at his side there is always a god who guards him from ruin,
just as beside him there now is Ares, resembling a mortal.
605 But toward Troy keep turning your faces as you ever backward
yield—let us not be eager with gods to do strenuous combat."
     So he spoke; very close to them now were advancing the Trojans;
then there were two men skillful in war-craft slaughtered by Hektor,
both in one chariot borne, Anchíalos, noble Menésthes.
610 Pitying them as they fell, the great scion of Télamon Ajax
came up beside them and stood, then hurling his glistening spear at
Ámphios, Sélagos' son, he struck him, a man who in Paiso
dwelt and was rich in substance and grainlands, but destiny led him
thither to Priam to serve as an ally to him and his children.
615 Now on the belt he was struck by the scion of Télamon Ajax,
so in the base of the belly was fixed the long-shadowing spear-shaft;
falling he crashed to the ground, and to him rushed glorious Ajax,
so as to strip off his armor; the Trojans were raining upon him
spears sharp-pointed and shining—his shield caught many a weapon.
620 Nevertheless on the corpse he planted his heel, and the brazen
spear drew out; but the rest of the beautiful armor he could not
seize and remove from the shoulders, for he was assaulted by missiles.
He feared being surrounded in force by the venturous Trojans
who stood many and noble against him, holding their spears up;
625 they now, great as he was, and as powerful too, and as valiant,
thrust him away from themselves, and he gave way, staggering backward.
     So were they laboring there all over the violent combat.
Then Tlepólemos Herakles' son, stout-bodied and valiant,
powerful Doom incited against Sarpédon the godlike.
630 When in coming together the men were close to each other

who were the grandson and son of the great cloud-gathering god Zeus,
first Tlepólemos spoke and addressed these words to the other:
"Well, Sarpédon, the Lykians' counselor, what is compelling
you to be skulking about, as a man unskillful in combat?
635　Liars are they who say that of Zeus who carries the aegis
you are the son, since you are inferior far to the fighting
men who of Zeus were begotten, among those living before us;
quite of another description was powerful Herakles, so they
say, my father, the stalwart and bold, with the soul of a lion,
640　who one time came here on account of Laómedon's horses—
six ships only he had, and with men far fewer than this he
captured and ransacked Ilion city, the streets desolated;
yours is a cowardly heart, your people are wasted and dying.
Nor do I think you ever will be a defense for the Trojans,
645　coming from Lykia thus, although you are mighty in prowess,
rather by me brought down you will enter the portals of Hades."
　　Answering him then spoke Sarpédon, the Lykians' leader:
"Yes, Tlepólemos, sacred Ilion he indeed laid waste
through the great folly of Lord Laómedon—he was the man who
650　scolded the hero with strong harsh words for the good he accomplished,
nor did he give him the horses for which from afar he had come here.
But as for you, I tell you that death and the darkness of doom will
come to you here at my hands, and that you, brought down by my spear, will
give to me fame, and your spirit to Hades of glorious horses."
655　So Sarpédon addressed him; Tlepólemos lifted his ash-wood
spear to the ready, and both of the long shafts sped at the same time
out of the hands of the men; in the midst of his neck Sarpédon
struck him, and straight on through the injurious point penetrated;
then down over his eyes came shadowy night to enshroud him.
660　Yet Tlepólemos had with his long spear smitten Sarpédon
on the left thigh; straight through it the furious point drove forward,
grazing the bone, but as yet his father was warding his death off.
　　Then by his noble companions at once Sarpédon the godlike
was borne out of the battle; the long spear dragging behind him
665　weighted him down; yet no one among them noticed or thought of
drawing the ash-wood spear from his thigh, so that he on his feet might
walk, so great was their haste, such labor they had to attend him.
　　So by the well-greaved Achaians Tlepólemos was on the other
side borne out of the battle; and noble Odysseus of steadfast
670　spirit at once took note, and the heart inside him was stirred up;

then he began to revolve his thoughts in his mind and his spirit,
whether to chase yet farther the son of loud-thundering Lord Zeus
or to deprive yet more of the Lykian men of their life-breath.
But it was not ordained greathearted Odysseus that he should
675 slaughter the powerful scion of Zeus with a sharp bronze weapon;
so to the Lykian host was his mind turned back by Athena.
Koíranos there he killed, then Chrómios too, and Alástor,
Hálios, then Alkándros, and Prýtanis too, and Noêmon.
Yet more Lykians now would the noble Odysseus have slaughtered
680 had not keenly observed great Hektor of glittering helmet.
He strode forth through the foremost, in bright bronze armor accoutered,
bringing the Dánaäns fear; Sarpédon the scion of Zeus felt
joy as he came up close, and a piteous word he addressed him:
"Scion of Priam, a prey for the Dánaäns do not allow me
685 now to lie here, but afford me protection; and then in your city
let my spirit forsake me, for I am not destined to go back
there to my home, back there to the much-loved land of my fathers,
so as to gladden the wife I love and my son yet an infant."
So he spoke; not a word said Hektor of glittering helmet,
690 but straight past him he rushed in his eagerness, so he could quickly
thrust back the Argive fighters and many deprive of their life-breath.
Then by his noble companions was laid Sarpédon the godlike
under the beautiful oak tree of Zeus who carries the aegis;
powerful Pélagon, who was the hero's belovèd companion,
695 thrust clear through and on out of his thigh that spear made of ash wood;
then did the life-breath leave him, and over his eyes was a mist poured;
yet he again caught breath as around him Boreas' breezes,
breathing on him, roused life in the soul so badly exhausted.
But before Ares and great bronze-helmeted Hektor the Argives
700 never at all either turned to the dark-hued ships and retreated,
nor did they ever in fight stand firm, but they always were yielding
backward, as they saw plainly that Ares was there with the Trojans.
There then who was the first, who last of the warriors killed by
Hektor the scion of Priam as well as by Ares the brazen?
705 Godlike Teuthras was one, and the driver of horses Orestes,
Trechos, Aitolian spearman, and then Oinómaös also,
Hélenos, scion of Oinops, Orésbios, glittering-belted,
who in Hylè had dwelt and was much concerned with his riches,
living beside the Kephisian lake, where close to him other
710 men of Boiótia dwelt, a most fertile country possessing.

When those two were observed by the goddess white-armed Hera
as they slaughtered the Argive troops in the violent combat,
quickly she spoke to Athena, in these winged words she addressed her:
"Well now, offspring of Zeus of the aegis, unwearying goddess,
715 fruitless indeed was the word we promised to Lord Meneláos—
after he ransacked strong-walled Ilion he would return home—
should we allow to keep thus rampaging the murderous Ares.
But come, let us as well take thought of our furious valor."
     She spoke, nor disobeyed her the goddess bright-eyed Athena.
720 Then got busy and harnessed the two gold-frontleted horses
Hera the august goddess, the daughter of powerful Kronos.
Speedily Hebè attached the curved wheels to the chariot, both sides,
eight-spoked, fashioned of bronze, set onto the axle of iron.
Golden are their indestructible felloes; to them on the outside
725 bronze-wrought tires are securely affixed, a great marvel to look at,
fashioned of silver the hubs that revolve one side and the other.
Then with strapwork of silver and gold is the chariot-body
plaited on all sides; there is a double rail running around it.
Silver the pole which jutted in front of it; right at the end she
730 fastened the beautiful gold-wrought yoke and attached to it breast-straps,
beautiful, fashioned of gold; then under the yoke at last Hera
guided the swift-hoofed horses, desirous of strife and the war cry.
     Meanwhile Athena, the daughter of Zeus who carries the aegis,
cast down there on her father's threshold the carefully woven
735 delicate robe which she had herself made, worked with her own hands;
donning the tunic of war of the great cloud-gathering god Zeus,
she then accoutered herself in his armor for dolorous battle;
over her shoulders she threw on the aegis, streaming with tassels,
terrible, all around which dread Panic is set as a garland;
740 on it is Conflict and Valor, and on it is blood-chilling Onslaught,
on it the head of the Gorgon, of that most terrible monster,
ugly and terrible image, a token of Zeus of the aegis.
Then on her head she set a great four-bossed double-ridged helmet,
gold-wrought; a hundred towns' foot soldiers were fitted upon it.
745 Into the fiery chariot stepping, she took up the spear-shaft,
heavy and huge and compact, that she uses to shatter the close-pressed
ranks of the fighters who rouse her wrath whose Father is mighty.
Speedily Hera began with the whip to lay into the horses;
moving themselves then grated the gates of the sky that the Seasons
750 keep, to whose care the great sky is entrusted, as well as Olympos,

whether to open the dense cloud-masses or rather to shut them.
Out through them they directed the horses enduring the whip-rod.
Sitting apart from the rest of the gods the great scion of Kronos
they found high on the loftiest summit of rocky Olympos;
755 there then halting the horses the goddess white-armed Hera
questioned supreme Zeus, scion of Kronos, and thus she addressed him:
"Father Zeus, now for his violent deeds do you not blame Ares,
who has slaughtered so great and so noble a host of Achaians
recklessly, not in due order, a sorrow to me, while at ease now
760 Cypris is glad, and Apollo the god of the silvery bow, at
having unloosed this madman who knows not anything lawful?
Father Zeus, would you indeed be angry with me, if at Ares
I should painfully strike, so driving him out of the battle?"
    Answering her in return spoke forth the cloud-gathering god Zeus:
765 "Go then, rouse up against him Athena the driver of plunder,
who above all is accustomed to bring to him evil afflictions."
    He spoke, nor disobeyed him the goddess white-armed Hera;
she began lashing the steeds, nor against their wishes did they fly
out in the space midway between earth and the star-filled heaven.
770 Far as a man with his eyes sees into the mist of the distance
sitting aloft on a crag to gaze over the wine-dark seaway,
just so far were the loud-neighing steeds of the gods overleaping.
But then, when they arrived at Troy and the eddying rivers,
where are united the streams of the Símoeis and the Skamánder,
775 there then halting the horses the goddess white-armed Hera
loose from the chariot set them and poured thick mist all around them;
Símoeis made ambrosia grow for the horses to graze on.
    Forward the goddesses walked, in their steps like timorous pigeons,
ready and eager to come to the aid of the Argive fighters.
780 But then, when they arrived at the place where the most and the noblest
men stood, close to the might of the tamer of steeds Diomédes
gathered together—and much like lions that feed upon raw flesh
or like fierce wild boars, whose power is not ineffective—
standing beside them cried out the goddess white-armed Hera,
785 making herself like Stentor, a lord greathearted and bronze-voiced,
one who was always shouting as loudly as shout fifty others:
"Shame on you Argives, base disgraces, admired for appearance!
During the time when noble Achilles would enter the battle,
never outside and beyond the Dardánian Gates were the Trojans
790 venturing forth, for they dreaded the powerful spear of that hero;

now by the hollow ships they are fighting, and far from the city."
      She spoke, rousing in each of the warriors valor and spirit.
Rushing to Tydeus' scion the goddess bright-eyed Athena
came upon that lord still by his horses and chariot standing,
795 cooling the wound which Pándaros had with his arrow inflicted.
For his sweat kept troubling him sorely beneath the wide strap which
carried his circular shield; it pained him; his arm was exhausted,
so he was holding the strap up and wiping the dark-clotted blood off.
Laying her hand on the yoke of his horses, the goddess addressed him:
800 "Little resembling himself is the son which Tydeus fathered!
Tydeus, truly, was small in stature, but he was a fighter;
even the time, in fact, that I did not allow him to battle
or to distinguish himself, when he without other Achaians
came with a message to Thebes and arrived among many Kadmeíans—
805 I had commanded him rather to dine at his ease in the palace—
yet with his powerful heart he then, as on former occasions,
challenged the young Kadmeíans and beat them in every contest
easily; so to your father was I a supporter and helper.
So also am I standing beside you, giving protection;
810 earnestly now I urge you to go on fighting the Trojans;
yet exhaustion has entered your limbs from your many encounters,
or else spiritless terror perhaps holds you—you are surely
then no offspring of Tydeus, the war-skilled scion of Oíneus."
      Answering her in return then spoke forth strong Diomédes:
815 "You I recognize, goddess and daughter of Zeus of the aegis;
therefore will I speak this word earnestly, nor will conceal it.
Not at all spiritless terror is holding me, nor any slackness,
but still mindful am I of the orders with which you charged me:
never against any fortunate gods you allowed me to battle,
820 none of the other ones, but if the daughter of Zeus Aphrodítè
were to come into the battle, I should wound her with the sharp bronze.
Therefore I have myself now yielded, and all of the other
Argives likewise have ordered to come here, gathered together,
since I recognize Ares as lording it over the battle."
825   Speaking to him then answered the goddess bright-eyed Athena:
"Tydeus' son Diomédes, in whom my heart is delighted,
neither should you fear Ares in this way, nor any other
deathless god—so am I now to you a supporter and helper.
But come, straightway at Ares direct your single-hoofed horses,
830 strike at close range and do not be in awe of impetuous Ares

thus rampaging, perfected in evil, a treacherous turncoat,
who just recently speaking to me and to Hera declared that
he would battle the Trojans and give his support to the Argives;
now he consorts with the Trojans; the promises he has forgotten."

835   She spoke; Sthénelos then from the chariot onto the ground she
pushed by drawing him back with her hand, and he speedily leapt out.
She on the chariot mounted beside Diomédes the noble,
eager for battle, the goddess, and loudly the axle of oak creaked
under the weight, for a terrible goddess it bore, and a great man.

840   Then were the reins and the whip picked up by Pallas Athena;
first against Ares she swiftly directed the single-hoofed horses.
He was just stripping the armor from Périphas, strong and enormous,
best of Aitolian fighters, Ochésios' glorious scion;
him then bloodstained Ares was stripping; the cap of the dark god

845   Hades Athena put on, so that Ares the strong would not see her.
        When man-slaughtering Ares perceived Diomédes the noble,
Périphas, strong and enormous, at once he left in the same place
lying, in which he before had killed him and taken his life-breath;
then straight onward he went for the tamer of steeds Diomédes.

850   When in coming together the two were close to each other,
Ares the first out over the yoke and the reins of his horses
lunged with his bronze-wrought spear, most eager of life to deprive him;
catching the spear in her hand then the goddess bright-eyed Athena
over the chariot pushed it to fly away fruitlessly onward.

855   Next came rushing at him the great crier of war Diomédes,
wielding his bronze-wrought spear; it was thrust by Pallas Athena
into the nethermost belly, where Ares was girt by his war-belt;
there he wounded him, striking, the beautiful flesh lacerated,
and again drew out the spear; then shrieked out Ares the brazen

860   loud as a war cry which nine thousand or yet ten thousand
warriors raise in a battle, in joining the conflict of Ares.
Shivering seized on the fighters, on both the Achaians and Trojans,
terrified, such was the shrieking of battle-insatiate Ares.
        Just as a darkening mist appears lowering out of the storm clouds

865   after the heat of the day, when a blustery wind is arising,
so appeared Ares the brazen to Tydeus' son Diomédes
now as among storm clouds he was going above to broad heaven.
Speedily then he arrived at the seat of the gods, steep Olympos;
sitting beside Zeus, scion of Kronos, in anguish of spirit,

870   he showed him the ambrosial blood from his wound still flowing.

Sorrowing then he spoke, and in these winged words he addressed him:
"Father Zeus, are you not angry at witnessing deeds so ferocious?
Always in fact we gods most harshly and cruelly suffer
each by the will of the others, conferring our favors on mortals.

875   All of us battle with you, for a mindless daughter you brought forth,
murderous too, who is always concerned with deeds of injustice.
For of the gods, all others of those who dwell on Olympos
listen to you and obey you, and we are each subject beneath you;
neither in word nor in action at all do you ever oppose her,

880   rather incite her, for you yourself got so baneful an offspring!
She now Tydeus' scion, the arrogant-souled Diomédes,
even at deathless gods has incited to go on a rampage.
Cypris in close fight first he stabbed on the hand by the wrist-joint,
but then even at me myself he rushed like a demon.

885   Now have my swift feet borne me away, since otherwise I would
long have remained there suffering pain among miserable corpses,
or be alive yet strengthless because of the strokes of a bronze blade."

    Looking from lowering brow spoke forth the cloud-gathering god Zeus:
"Treacherous turncoat, do not keep sitting beside me and whining.

890   You are most hateful to me of the gods who inhabit Olympos;
always conflict is dear to your spirit, and battles and warfare.
So ungoverned, unyielding in you is the rage of your mother,
Hera—and even myself, by my words, I can hardly control her—
so I suppose it is by her promptings that you endure these things.

895   Still, I will never permit you to be in pain for a long time,
since you are my offspring and to me you were born by your mother.
If of another god you had been born so baneful an offspring,
long since you would have been far lower than Oúranos' children."

    So he spoke, and he ordered the healer Paiëon to cure him.

900   Sprinkling upon him painkilling herbs, Paiëon the healer
cured him, for not in the least was his nature in any way mortal.
Just as the juice of the fig makes white milk thicken that has been
liquid, and it very quickly is curdled as somebody stirs it,
just so quickly did he now heal impetuous Ares.

905   Then he was washed by Hebè and dressed in delightful apparel;
there by Zeus son of Kronos he sat, in his glory exulting.

    Then those goddesses went back up to the palace of great Zeus—
Argive Hera the queen and the guardian-goddess Athena—
once they had halted the murderous toil of man-slaughtering Ares.

BOOK 6

To the Achaians and Trojans was left that terrible combat;
often the fight swayed over the plain one way and the other,
as each man at another the bronze-tipped spears they directed,
there between those two rivers, the Símoeis and the Skamánder.
5 First then Ajax Télamon's son, the Achaians' protector,
shattered the ranks of the Trojans and brought light to his companions,
striking a man who was clearly the noblest of all of the Thracians,
Ákamas, son of Eussóros, a man stout-bodied and valiant,
struck at him first on the ridge of his helmet crested with horsehair;
10 into his forehead plunged the bronze spear-point, then penetrated
deep inside of the bone; and his eyes were enshrouded in darkness.
    Áxylos next was killed by the crier of war Diomédes—
he was the scion of Teuthras and dwelt in well-built Arísbè;
wealthy he was in substance, as well as beloved of the people,
15 for in a house by the road as he dwelt, all men he befriended.
Yet now no one among them would guard him from wretched destruction,
standing before him; and both Diomédes bereft of their spirits,
him and his comrade Kalésios too, who guided his horses,
serving as charioteer; so under the earth the two men passed.
20 Drésos then and Ophéltios both did Eurýalos slaughter,
then he pursued Aisépos and Pédasos—them had the fountain
nymph Abarbárea once to the faultless Boukólion brought forth.
This Boukólion was the revered Laómedon's scion,
oldest he was in years, but his mother in stealth had conceived him.
25 Once while tending his sheep, he mingled in bed and affection
with that nymph of the spring, who conceived twin children and bore them.
Now of them both Eurýalos son of Mekísteus loosed their
might and their glorious limbs, and the armor he stripped from their shoulders.
By Polypoítes, steadfast in fight, was Astýalos slaughtered;
30 noble Odysseus disposed of a man of Perkótè, Pidýtes,

using a bronze spear; Teukros destroyed Aretáon the noble.
With a bright spear was Abléros killed by Antílochos, Nestor's
scion, and Élatos by Agamemnon, lord of the people—
he by the banks of the beautiful stream Satníoeis dwelt in
35 steep Pédasos. By the warrior Léïtos Phýlakos too was
killed as he fled; by Eurýpylos then was Melánthios slaughtered.
        Then by the crier of war Meneláos Adréstos was captured
living, for over the plain as they fled in terror his horses
got entangled in tamarisk bushes, and breaking the curving
40 chariot just at the end of the yoke-pole, they of themselves kept
on to the city, to which other horses were bolting in terror;
out of the chariot, down by the wheel, was Adréstos ejected
headlong onto his face in the dust; and above him was standing
Atreus' son Meneláos, who held a long-shadowing spear-shaft;
45 clinging to him by the knees then, Adréstos began to implore him:
"Take me alive, son of Atreus; accept an appropriate ransom.
Plenty of riches are stored in the house of my prosperous father,
treasures of bronze and of gold and of iron, laborious metal;
taking of them my father would please you with measureless ransom,
50 should he discover that I am alive at the ships of the Achaians."
        So he spoke, and in him persuaded the heart in his bosom;
he was about to entrust him to one of his comrades to take back
there to the swift ships of the Achaians; but then Agamemnon
came to encounter him, running, and spoke this word to rebuke him:
55 "Brother of mine, Meneláos, for these men why would you be so
caring? Have excellent things been accomplished for you by the Trojans
there in your house? Let none of them flee from a wretched destruction
under our hands, not even the young boy whom in her womb his
mother is carrying; not even he may escape, but from Ilion all must
60 utterly perish together and be unmourned and unmentioned."
        So having spoken, the hero persuaded the mind of his brother,
winning him over to do the right thing; from himself with his hand he
thrust that hero Adréstos, and him then strong Agamemnon
stabbed in the flank, so that he fell backward, and Atreus' scion
65 planted his foot on his chest, then drew out the spear made of ash wood.
        Nestor began exhorting the Argives; loudly he shouted:
"Oh friends, Dánaän heroes and noble attendants of Ares,
now let nobody, throwing himself on the plunder, remain back
out of the battle, to take the most loot as he goes to the galleys;
70 let us instead kill men, then afterward you at your ease from

dead men's bodies all over the plain shall strip off the armor."
      So he spoke and aroused in each fighter the strength and the spirit.
Then would the Trojans have been by the Ares-belovèd Achaians
back into Ilion driven, by their own cowardice vanquished,
75   had not Hélenos, scion of Priam, the best of diviners,
standing beside them, spoke these words to Aineías and Hektor:
"Both Aineías and Hektor, because upon you above others
rests this war-toil of Trojans and Lykians, since in our ventures,
all of them, you are the best, in fighting as well as in thinking,
80   hold ground here, and in front of the gates keep holding the army,
going around all over, before in the arms of their women,
once they have fled, they fall, so becoming a joy to our foemen.
But then afterward, once you have roused up all the battalions,
we will remain here facing the Dánaäns, giving them battle,
85   though we are quite worn out, for necessity drives us to do it.
But you, Hektor, return to the city, and when you arrive say
thus to your mother and mine: let her gather together the older
women above in the citadel-temple of bright-eyed Athena;
when with the key she has opened the doors of the sacred dwelling,
90   straightway the robe she thinks is the loveliest one and the amplest
there in the hall, that which to herself by far is the dearest,
this let her lay on the knees of Athena of beautiful tresses;
let her as well make promise to sacrifice twelve of the heifers,
yearlings as yet untamed, in the shrine to her, hoping that she will
95   pity the city and wives of the Trojans, and innocent children,
hoping from sacred Ilion she will keep Tydeus' scion,
that most savage of spearmen, the mighty deviser of panic,
who I say has become the most mighty among the Achaians.
Never we felt such fear of Achilles, the marshal of people,
100   who as they tell it was born to a goddess; but this is a man who
rages insanely, and none can rival him now in his fury."
      So he spoke, nor did Hektor at all disobey his own brother;
straightway he to the ground from his chariot leapt in his armor;
wielding his two sharp spears, he ranged all over the army,
105   urging the men to do battle, and roused up terrible combat.
They wheeled round in a rally and stood to confront the Achaians,
so that the Argives gave ground before them and ceased from the slaughter,
thinking that one of the deathless gods from the star-filled heaven
had come down to the Trojans to help them, so had they rallied.
110   Hektor began exhorting the Trojans, and loudly he shouted:

"All of you high-souled Trojans and far-famed allies in battle,
now be men, dear friends, and remember your furious valor,
while I go back up into Ilion, so as to tell those
elders sitting in council and our own bedmates to raise their
115   prayers to the gods in heaven and hecatombs promise to offer."
        So having said, great Hektor of glittering helmet departed;
striking against his ankles as well as his neck was the black hide
forming the rim that surrounded his shield made massive with bosses.
        Glaukos the child of Hippólochos, then, and the scion of Tydeus
120   met in the middle between the two hosts, both eager for battle.
When in coming together the men were close to each other,
first spoke out to his foe the great crier of war Diomédes:
"Who are you then, most excellent sir, among men who are mortal?
Since I have not seen you in the battle that wins a man honor
125   ever before; yet now you have stridden out far in advance of
all in your boldness, to stand against my long-shadowing spear-shaft.
Miserable are the men whose children contend with my fury.
If however you are an immortal descended from heaven,
certainly not against gods of the heaven will I enter battle,
130   no, since not even mighty Lykoúrgos, the scion of Dryas,
lived long, who against gods of the heaven attempted to quarrel,
who once harried the nurses of frenzy-possessed Dionýsos
down from the sacred mountain of Nysa; and they all together
scattered their wands on the ground, by the fierce man-slaying Lykoúrgos
135   struck with an ox-goad; driven to terrified flight, Dionýsos
plunged in the waves of the sea; in her lap then Thetis received him
frightened, for strong was the terror in which he was held by the man's threats.
Then against him grew angry the gods whose living is easy—
he was struck blind by the scion of Kronos, and no very long time
140   yet did he live, since he was so hated by all the immortals.
So against fortunate gods I would not be willing to battle;
but if of men you are, who feed on the fruit of the plowland,
come up closer, that sooner you enter the bonds of destruction."
        Speaking to him then answered Hippólochos' glorious scion:
145   "Tydeus' great-souled son, of my lineage why do you ask me?
Like generations of leaves are those of humanity also.
Just as a wind pours some leaves groundward, and others the forest,
burgeoning, sprouts at the coming of springtime, so in the same way
one generation of men grows up as another is fading.
150   Yet if you wish, hear this from me too, so that you may know well

what my lineage is—and the people who know it are many:
there is a city, Ephýra, remote in horse-nourishing Argos,
wherein Sísyphos lived, who was born the most crafty of mankind,
Sísyphos, Aíolos' son, and a son he too begot, Glaukos;
155   then in his turn did Glaukos the faultless Bellérophon father.
He was endowed by the gods with beauty as well as a pleasing
manliness; yet King Proítos devised in his heart for him evil—
since he was mightier far than Bellérophon, out of the Argives'
land he drove him, for Zeus had to Proítos' scepter subdued him.
160   Noble Anteía the consort of Proítos had madly desired to
mingle in passion with him clandestinely; nevertheless she
never persuaded the war-skilled Bellérophon, noble in thinking.
So these words she addressed King Proítos, speaking a falsehood:
"Either yourself die, Proítos, or slaughter Bellérophon, since he
165   wanted to mingled in passion with me, though I did not want to."
So as she spoke, wrath seized on the lord at the words he was hearing;
killing the man he shunned, for at heart he shrank from that action,
yet he to Lykia sent him, and baleful tokens he gave him;
onto a folding tablet he scratched them, many and deadly,
170   bidding him show them to his wife's father, so he would destroy him.
So he to Lykia went, with the gods' unfailing conveyance;
but then, when he to Lykia came, and the streams of the Xanthos,
zealous of heart broad Lykia's ruler accorded him honor—
nine days he entertained him, and nine bulls offered as victims.
175   But then, soon as the Dawn shone forth rose-fingered the tenth day,
he began making inquiry and asking to look at whatever
token Bellérophon carried to him from his son-in-law Proítos.
Then when he had received his son-in-law's token of evil,
first he ordered the hero to slaughter the raging Chimaíra,
180   who was a beast of divine generation and not at all human,
lion in front but a serpent behind, in the middle a she-goat,
breathing the terrible force of a bright-flamed fire from her nostrils.
Her then Bellérophon slaughtered, obeying the gods' clear portents.
Second, against the illustrious Sólymoi boldly he battled—
185   this was the mightiest battle of men, he said, he had entered.
Third in order, he slaughtered the Amazons, peers of the heroes.
As he returned, yet another insidious ruse the king wove him:
having selected the best of the men of broad Lykia, he set
them in an ambush; but those men never at all returned homeward,
190   since they all were in fact by the faultless Bellérophon slaughtered.

But then, when as the powerful son of a god the king knew him,
there in his house he detained him and also gave him his daughter,
even endowed him with half of the whole great honor of kingship
and an estate for him finer than others the Lykians marked off,
195 lovely in vineyard, orchard, and plowland, so he could settle.
Then to Bellérophon, skillful in warfare, the Lykian princess
bore three children: Isándros, Hippólochos, Láodameía.
When Zeus Counselor lay in desire beside Láodameía,
she to him bore godlike Sarpédon, the marshal of weapons;
200 but as in turn that hero was hated by all the immortals,
then all alone he wandered along on the plain of Aleíos
eating his heart out, shunning the pathways trodden by people.
As for Isándros his son, by battle-insatiate Ares
he was destroyed while against the illustrious Sólymoi fighting;
205 Artemis of the gold reins in her wrath killed Láodameía.
It was Hippólochos who begot me—I claim him as father.
He dispatched me to Troy, and he ordered me often and strongly
always to be outstanding, preeminent over the others,
not to dishonor the race of my fathers, the men who by far were
210 noblest-born in Ephýra and in broad Lykia also.
So it is such generation and blood I boast to be sprung from."
     So he spoke, and the crier of war Diomédes was gladdened;
in the much-nourishing earth he straightway planted his spear-shaft,
then in agreeable words he spoke to the shepherd of people:
215 "Certainly you are a family friend to me then, of long standing,
since once excellent Oíneus kept as a guest in his palace
faultless Bellérophon, there for a full twenty days entertained him;
beautiful guest-gifts too they exchanged, each one with the other—
Oíneus gave to his guest a fine war-belt shining with purple,
220 while Bellérophon gave him a goblet of gold, double-handled,
which I left back there in my house when I came on the voyage.
Tydeus now I cannot recall, for he left me when I was
still quite little, the time in Thebes the Achaian host perished.
Therefore am I a dear friend to you now in the center of Argos,
225 just as in Lykia you are to me, when I come to that country.
Even in close fight let us keep clear of the spears of each other,
since there are many for me to destroy, both Trojans and famous
allies, whomever a god gives me and I reach on my swift feet,
also many Achaians for you to kill, should you be able.
230 Let us exchange with each other our armor, in order that these men

too may know that we boast ourselves to be family guest-friends."

    After the two men spoke, from the chariots both of them leapt down,
then by the hand they grasped each other in mutual pledges.
There by Zeus son of Kronos the senses were taken from Glaukos,

235 who in exchange for the armor of Tydeus' son Diomédes,
brazen and worth nine oxen, returned gold arms worth a hundred.

    Now when Hektor arrived at the Skaian Gates and the oak tree,
there about him came running the daughters and wives of the Trojans,
making inquiry about their children and brothers and neighbors,

240 and of their husbands; and then he ordered them all in their turn to
raise their prayers to the gods; on many affliction was fastened.

    But then, when he arrived at the beautiful palace of Priam,
fashioned with colonnades polished to smoothness—and inside the dwelling
fifty in all were the chambers of stone smooth-polished and gleaming,

245 each of them built quite close to the others, and there were the sons of
Priam accustomed to sleep at the sides of the wives they had wedded;
facing them, inside the courtyard and opposite, stood twelve well-roofed
rooms of the daughters of Priam, of stone smooth-polished and gleaming,
each of them built quite close to the others, and therein did Priam's

250 sons-in-law go to sleep at the sides of their virtuous bedmates—
there his mother of bountiful gifts came out to meet Hektor,
leading Laódikè, who of her daughters was best in her beauty,
clasped his hand in her own and said these words, calling upon him:
"Why have you come here, child, forsaking the arduous battle?

255 Surely indeed those sons of Achaians so baneful of name are
wearing you down as they fight by the town, and your spirit has made you
come in to raise your hands up to Zeus from the peak of the city.
But now stay until I have brought honey-sweet wine, so that you may
pour libations to great Father Zeus and the other immortals

260 first, and if you then drink it, the benefit you will have also.
When someone is fatigued, wine greatly increases his power,
as now you are fatigued from defending your kinsmen and neighbors."

    Answering her then spoke great Hektor of glittering helmet:
"Do not offer me honey-souled wine, my lady and mother,

265 lest you cripple my strength and I care no longer for valor.
Surely with hands unwashed I shrink to pour glistening wine to
Zeus, for in no way possible is it for one who is fouled with
blood and defilement to pray to the dark-cloud scion of Kronos.
But you go to the shrine of Athena the driver of plunder

270 with burnt-offerings, having assembled the elderly women;

straightway the robe you think is the loveliest one and the largest
there in the hall, that which to yourself by far is the dearest,
this do you lay on the knees of Athena of beautiful tresses;
do you as well make promise to sacrifice twelve of the heifers,
275 yearlings as yet untamed, in the shrine to her, hoping that she will
pity the city and wives of the Trojans, and innocent children,
hoping from sacred Ilion she will keep Tydeus' scion,
that most savage of spearmen, the mighty deviser of panic.
But you go to the shrine of Athena the driver of plunder;
280 meanwhile I will go looking for Paris, in order to call him,
should he be willing to listen to anything. Would that the earth might
gape for him there! For a monstrous bane the Olympian reared him
both for the Trojans and great-souled Priam, as well as his children.
If that man I could see gone down to the palace of Hades,
285 then I would say my heart had entirely forgotten its sorrow."
     So he spoke, and she went back into the palace and called her
handmaids; they through the city assembled the elderly women.
As for herself, she went downstairs to a sweet-smelling chamber;
there were the robes, all brightly embroidered, the work of the women,
290 those Sidonians whom godlike Alexander himself had
taken from Sidon, as over the broad seaway he had voyaged,
that same journey on which he had brought back noble-born Helen.
One of these Hékabè lifted and took as a gift for Athena,
which was the loveliest in its adornment, as well as the largest—
295 it shone bright as a star; it had lain there under the others.
She set forth; many elderly women were hastening after.
     When they arrived at the peak of the city, the shrine of Athena,
there were the doors laid open to them by fair-cheeked Theáno,
daughter of Kisses and wife of Anténor the tamer of horses,
300 since it was she whom the Trojans had made priestess of Athena.
All of them raised their hands to Athena with loud ululations;
straightway from Hékabè taking the robe then, fair-cheeked Theáno
laid it down on the knees of Athena of beautiful tresses,
then she uttered a prayer, imploring the daughter of great Zeus:
305 "Lady Athena, the city-defender and glorious goddess,
shatter the spear of the strong Diomédes, and grant that the man fall
flat on his face in front of the Skaian Gates of the city,
so that at once we now may sacrifice twelve of the heifers,
yearlings as yet untamed, in the shrine to you, hoping that you will
310 pity the city and wives of the Trojans, and innocent children."

So in her prayer she addressed her, but Pallas Athena denied it.
　　So as the women addressed their prayers to the daughter of great Zeus,
Hektor had gone to the beautiful palace of Lord Alexander,
which he himself had built with the men who then were the finest
315　there in the fertile country of Troy, men skilled in construction;
they had erected for him a bedchamber, a hall, and a courtyard
close to the houses of Priam and Hektor above in the city.
Into it now went Zeus-loved Hektor; a spear of eleven
cubits' length he held in his hand, and before him the brazen
320　spear-point shone, with a gold-wrought ring-clasp running around it.
He found him in his room occupied with his beautiful armor,
both his shield and his corslet; his curved bow too he was handling.
Helen of Argos was sitting among her women-attendants
and was directing the glorious labor assigned to her handmaids.
325　Looking at him then Hektor rebuked him in words of derision:
"Strange man, it is not seemly to keep this wrath in your spirit.
People are dying around the whole city and on the steep ramparts
fighting the battle, and on your account are the tumult and warfare
blazing about this town; you surely would fight with another
330　whom you saw anywhere holding back from the odious warfare.
Up, lest soon this town be ablaze in a conflagration!"
　　Then in answer to him spoke forth godlike Alexander:
"Hektor, because you have justly rebuked me and not beyond justice,
therefore will I tell you; now you pay attention and hear me.
335　Not so much on account of resentment or wrath at the Trojans
did I sit in my room, but I wished to give way to my anguish.
But just now with her softening words my wife was persuading
me and exhorting me into the battle; and that is the course which
seems to me also the better; from man to man victory passes.
340　But come, wait for me now—my armor of war I will put on.
Or go; I will soon follow—I think that I can overtake you."
　　So he spoke; not a word said Hektor of glittering helmet;
Helen however addressed him in honey-sweet words of persuasion,
"Brother-in-law of the bitch I am, bane-scheming, abhorrent,
345　would that on that very day I was first brought forth by my mother,
I had been taken and borne by the baneful blast of a storm wind
onto a peak or a wave of the deep sea booming and roaring,
where some wave would have swept me away before these things happened.
Yet since such evil things were devised by the gods in this manner,
350　I could at least wish I had been wife of a man who was better,

one who would feel the resentment, the many insults, of the people.
But as for this one, no firm mind has he now nor will ever
have hereafter—of that, I think, he will gather the harvest.
But now come on into the chamber and sit on this armchair,
355 brother, for yours above all is the spirit oppressed by the trouble
caused by the bitch I am and by Lord Alexander's delusion,
us upon whom Zeus set evil destiny, so that hereafter
we be subject of song for the men who live in the future."
    Answering her then spoke great Hektor of glittering helmet:
360 "Helen, although you love me, do not ask me to sit down, for
you will not sway me; my heart already is eager that I should
succor the Trojans, who feel great longing for me in my absence.
Rather, arouse this man; let himself be hastened to action,
so that he may overtake me while I stay yet in the city.
365 For to my own house now I will set forth, so I can see my
household servants and much-loved wife and my son, yet an infant,
since I do not know whether to them any more I will come back
or if the gods will destroy me now at the hands of the Achaians."
    So having said, great Hektor of glittering helmet departed.
370 Straightway, when he arrived at his house well built as a dwelling,
not in the halls white-armed Andrómachè did he discover;
rather, along with her child and a fair-robed woman-attendant,
she was outside on the rampart standing, lamenting and weeping.
Hektor, as soon as he found that his faultless wife was not inside,
375 went to the threshold and stood and addressed these words to the handmaids:
"Come now, handmaids, report to me truthfully what I will ask you:
whither has gone white-armed Andrómachè out of the palace?
She to my sisters, perhaps, or the fair-robed wives of my brothers,
or to the shrine of Athena has gone, where also the other
380 fair-tressed women of Troy are imploring the terrible goddess?"
    Then these answering words the expert housekeeper addressed him:
"Hektor, because you have urgently asked that we truthfully tell you,
not to yours sisters and not to the fair-robed wives of your brothers
has she gone, nor the shrine of Athena, in which are the other
385 fair-tressed women of Troy imploring the terrible goddess,
but to the great high rampart of Ilion, since she had heard our
Trojans were quite worn down and in strength the Achaians were greater.
Therefore she has departed to go to the wall in a hurry,
like a madwoman, and with her a nursemaid carries the baby."
390   So did the housekeeper say; from the house went hastening Hektor,

taking the same way again back over the well-built roadways.
When he had passed through the whole great city and come to the Skaian
Gates, through which out onto the plain he was going to set forth,
there came running to meet him his bedmate, wealthy in bride-gifts,
395 fair Andrómachè, who was greathearted Eëtion's daughter;
this man, Eëtion, had his abode beneath forested Plakos,
Thébè the town beneath Plakos, and ruled the Kilíkian people;
his was the daughter the lord bronze-helmeted Hektor had wedded.
She encountered him there, and along with her came an attendant
400 holding the child in her bosom, an innocent, only a baby,
much-loved scion of Hektor—a beautiful star he resembled—
Hektor Skamándrios called him, but others, "the lord of the city"—
Ástyanáx—for of Ilion Hektor alone was defender.
Hektor was smiling as he in silence regarded his dear son;
405 close to his side Andrómachè stood, then, letting her tears fall,
clasped his hand in her own and said these words, calling upon him:
"My dear husband, your strength will destroy you, and neither your tender
child do you pity nor me, ill-fated, who soon am to be your
widow, because the Achaians will soon all rush to attack you
410 so as to put you to death; and for me it would be much better,
once I have lost you, to go down into the earth, for no other
comfort will ever be mine, when you have encountered your doomsday,
only despair; and I have no father or reverend mother.
For in fact my father was killed by noble Achilles,
415 who ransacked the Kilíkians' well-inhabited city,
Thébè of towering gates; and Eëtion then did he slaughter,
yet he did not strip him, for at heart he shrank from that action;
rather he burned his body with all his elaborate armor,
over it heaping a grave-mound; around it the nymphs of the mountains,
420 daughters of Zeus who carries the aegis, have planted their elm trees.
Seven as well there were who were brothers of mine in the palace—
all on the very same day went into the dwelling of Hades,
since they were all killed by swift-footed and noble Achilles
while they tended the white-fleeced sheep and the swing-pacing oxen.
425 As for my mother, who ruled as the queen beneath forested Plakos,
after he brought her hither along with the rest of his plunder,
then he, accepting a measureless ransom, released her, but she was
killed in the house of her father by Artemis shooter of arrows.
Hektor, you are to me both father and reverend mother,
430 you are as well my brother, and you are my vigorous husband.

127

But come now, take pity and stay right here on the rampart,
so that your child you not make an orphan, your woman a widow.
Station the army beside the wild fig tree—there where the city
most to invasion is open, the wall by attack may be taken.

435 For to that place three times have the best men come to attempt it,
those with the two Ajaxes, Idómeneus famous in glory,
and the two scions of Atreus, and Tydeus' valorous scion,
whether perhaps some man most skillful in prophecy told them,
whether instead it is their own spirit commanding and urging."

440   Answering her then spoke great Hektor of glittering helmet:
"All this worries me also, lady, but dreadfully I feel
shame in front of the Trojans and women of Troy of the long robes
if back here I skulk like a coward, avoiding the warfare,
neither does my heart let me, for I have learned to be valiant

445 always and ever to battle along with the foremost Trojans,
striving to win great fame for my father as well as my own self,
since this thing I know very well in my mind and my spirit:
there will a day come when holy Ilion falls in destruction,
Priam as well, and the people of Priam the excellent spearman.

450 Yet I am not so moved by the sorrow to come for the Trojans,
not by the anguish of Hékabè even nor that of Lord Priam,
not by the pains of my brothers, the many and valorous men who
shall drop into the dust at the hands of the enemy fighters,
as about you I am troubled, when some bronze-armored Achaian

455 leads you weeping away, robs you of the day of your freedom.
Then you will be in Argos and weave on the loom of another;
then you will carry the water from springs, Messeis, Hypereía—
quite unwilling, but mighty necessity then will compel you.
Then somebody will say as he sees you letting the tears fall:

460 'She is the consort of Hektor, who used to excel in the battle
all those horse-taming Trojans, when they around Ilion battled.'
So somebody will say, and to you it will be a fresh anguish,
lacking a man like me who could ward off the day of your bondage.
But then dead may I lie, may the heaped earth cover me over,

465 sooner than hear you shrieking as you are dragged off to enslavement."
    After he said these words, for his child reached glorious Hektor;
but back into the nursemaid's fair-girdled bosom the infant
shrank with a scream, terrified at the sight of his own dear father,
stricken with fright by the helmet of bronze and the crest made of horsehair,

470 as he beheld it fearfully nodding from high on the helmet.

Both of them laughed out loud, the dear father and reverend mother.
Taking the helmet at once from his head then, glorious Hektor
laid it down beside him on the ground there, glittering brightly;
after his much-loved son he had kissed, in his arms he had dandled,

475 straightway to Zeus and the rest of the gods he spoke and implored them:
"Zeus and the rest of the gods, now grant me that this my child may
be as I am myself, outstanding among all the Trojans,
noble as me in strength, over Ilion mightily ruling;
someday may a man say, 'He is better by far than his father,'

480 when he returns from a war; may he bring back bloody the armor
after he slaughters his foe; may his mother rejoice in her spirit."
     So having said, in the arms of his much-loved bedmate he placed his
dear son, and into her fragrant bosom his mother received him
weeping and laughing at once; her husband beheld her and pitied,

485 gave her a pat with his hand and said these words, calling upon her:
"Poor wife, do not lament too much over me in your spirit—
never beyond what is fated will any man hurl me to Hades;
never I think anyone among men has escaped from his own fate,
neither the base nor the noble, when once he is brought into being.

490 But go back to the house and devote more care to your own work,
weaving and spinning, the loom and the distaff, bidding your handmaids
busy themselves with their labor; the men will attend to the warfare,
all of them, I above all, who in Ilion city are living."
     Thus, and the helmet crested with horsehair glorious Hektor

495 took in his hand; but his much-loved wife set out to go homeward;
often she turned to look back, and she shed great tears in abundance.
Straightway, when she arrived at the house well-built as a dwelling,
that of man-slaughtering Hektor, and found inside it her many
women-attendants, among them all she aroused lamentation.

500 So in his house while he still was alive, they lamented for Hektor,
since in fact they believed he would never again from the battle
come back, having escaped from the force and the hands of the Achaians.
     Neither did Paris delay very long in his high-roofed palace—
soon as his glorious armor inlaid with bronze he had put on,

505 down through the city he rushed, on his swift feet ever relying.
Just as a horse in a stall that is fed at the manger on barley,
breaking his rope, runs over the plain with thundering hoofbeat—
he is accustomed to bathe in the stream of a fair-running river—
proud in his strength, with his head held high, while over his shoulders

510 streaming his mane floats back; he exults in his glorious splendor;

nimbly his limbs bear him to the pastures and haunts of the horses;
so now from Pérgamos' height did Paris the scion of Priam,
brilliantly shining in armor as bright as the sun, stride downward
laughing aloud, and his swift feet bore him, and rapidly moving
515 he overtook noble Hektor his brother, as he was about to
turn from the place where he and his wife had been fondly conversing.
First spoke out and addressed him then godlike Alexander:
"Brother, undoubtedly I have been holding you back in your hurry,
lingering, not at the right time coming along, as you told me."
520   Answering him in return spoke Hektor of glittering helmet:
"Strange man, never a person there is who, thinking aright, can
disrespect your performance in battle, for you are courageous.
Yet you choose to be slack, unwilling you are, and at that my
heart in my breast is disturbed as I hear about you the reproachful
525 words of the Trojans, who have for your sake such terrible trouble.
Still, let us go; these things we will put right later, if ever
Zeus should grant that the wine bowl of liberty here in the palace
we be able to set for the heavenly gods who live always,
once we have finally driven from Troy those well-greaved Achaians."

BOOK 7

So having talked to him, out of the gates rushed glorious Hektor,
following him, Alexander his brother; and both of the men were
ready and eager in spirit to join in the fight and do battle.
As at a time when a god gives sailors who strongly desire them
5 following winds, since they are exhausted at beating the sea with
well-polished fir-wood oars—by fatigue their limbs have been loosened—
so now these two appeared to the Trojans who strongly desired them.
There Alexander slaughtered the son of Lord Áreïthóös
who had inhabited Arnè, Menésthios; him the mace-fighter
10 Áreïthóös engendered, and ox-eyed Phýlomedoúsa;
Hektor struck Eïóneus then with a sharp-pointed spear-shaft,
under his helmet of bronze, on the neck, and his limbs he unloosened.
Glaukos the son of Hippólochos, lord of the Lykian men, struck
Dexios' scion Iphínoös then, with a spear to the shoulder,
15 there in the violent combat, as he a swift chariot mounted;
he from the chariot fell to the ground, and his limbs were unloosened.
When these men were observed by the goddess bright-eyed Athena
as they slaughtered the Argive troops in the violent combat,
speedily she came down from the peak of Olympos and entered
20 sacred Ilion; thither to meet with her hastened Apollo,
having from Pérgamos seen her—he wanted the Trojans to triumph.
So just there by the oak tree the two gods met one another;
then, first speaking, the lord Zeus' scion Apollo addressed her:
"Why have you once more now so eagerly, daughter of great Zeus,
25 come down here from Olympos, and why has your great heart sent you?
Is it to grant to the Dánaän fighters a battle-reversing
triumph? For not in the least you pity the perishing Trojans.
But if at all you would heed me—indeed, much better would that be—
now let us bring to a halt this battle and terrible combat
30 just for the day, and tomorrow again they will fight till they find out

Ilion's limit of doom, since so to the hearts of you deathless
goddesses now it is pleasing that this great city be ransacked."
        Speaking to him made answer the goddess bright-eyed Athena:
"So let it be, Far-worker; in this thought I have myself now
35   come down here from Olympos among the Achaians and Trojans.
But come, how are you minded to stop this strife of the fighters?"
        Speaking to her made answer the lord, Zeus' scion Apollo:
"Let us arouse the strong spirit of Hektor the tamer of horses,
so that he might give challenge to one of the Dánaän heroes
40   now to do battle with him man-to-man in terrible combat;
straightway, admiring him, grudging him glory, the bronze-greaved Achaians
then will arouse somebody to fight with illustrious Hektor."
        He spoke, nor disobeyed him the goddess bright-eyed Athena.
Hélenos then, the dear scion of Priam, received in his heart this
45   counsel of theirs that the gods when talking together had favored.
Going to Hektor, he stood at his side, and a word he addressed him:
"Hektor the scion of Priam, the equal of Zeus in devices,
will you at all now listen and heed me? For I am your brother.
Order the others, the Trojans and all the Achaians, to sit down;
50   you give challenge yourself to whatever Achaian is best that
he do battle with you man-to-man in terrible combat,
since not yet are you fated to die and encounter your doomsday,
since thus now have I heard from the voice of the gods who live always."
        So did he say; much Hektor rejoiced at his word as he listened;
55   into the middle he went, and the ranks of the Trojans he held back,
holding his spear by the middle, and all of them quickly were seated.
Then Agamemnon ordered the well-greaved Achaians to sit down.
Thereat Athena herself and Apollo of silvery bow by
taking the semblance of birds, great vultures, were sitting above them,
60   high on top of the oak of Zeus Father who carries the aegis,
taking delight in the men whose ranks sat crowded together,
all with their shields, their helmets and spear-shafts fearfully bristling.
As when over the seaway the rustle of Zephyr the west wind
newly arisen is spreading and under it darkens the seaway,
65   so dark now were the ranks who were sitting, Achaians and Trojans,
there in the plain; and between the two sides thus Hektor addressed them:
"Listen to me now, Trojans and all you well-greaved Achaians,
so I can say such things as the heart in my breast is demanding.
Kronos' son, seated aloft, our oaths did not bring to fulfillment,
70   but with a cruel intention ordains both armies a limit,

either until you capture and ransack Troy of the strong walls
or yourselves you are vanquished beside your seafaring galleys.
Seeing that there among you are the best men of all the Achaians,
now among them let him whose spirit commands him to fight me
75   come from you all to be champion here against glorious Hektor.
Thus I declare my intent, and to this let Zeus be the witness:
should that man take away my life with a sharp-pointed bronze blade,
stripping the armor from me, to the hollow ships let him bear it,
giving my body to take back home, so that I in my death am
80   granted a funeral fire by the Trojans and wives of the Trojans.
Should I take away his, and Apollo accord me the glory,
stripping his armor, to sacred Ilion I will convey it;
there I will hang it in front of the shrine of far-shooting Apollo;
as for the man's corpse, back to the well-benched ships I will give it,
85   so he may get death-rites from the long-haired men, the Achaians,
and a grave-mound they will heap by the broad Hellespont in his honor.
Then some day someone among men born later may say when
sailing the wine-dark sea in a galley of numerous oarlocks,
'That is the funeral mound of a man who long ago perished,
90   who, once noblest in prowess, was killed by illustrious Hektor.'
So one day will say someone; and never my glory will perish."
    So did he say; then all of the people were hushed in silence;
they were ashamed to refuse him but feared undertaking the challenge.
Finally then Meneláos arose to his feet and addressed them,
95   scolding the men with reproaches; at heart he sorely was groaning:
"Ah me! Braggarts, the daughters, no longer the sons, of Achaians!
Shame outrageous will this be, certainly, baleful and baneful,
if not one of the Dánaäns now goes out to meet Hektor.
No, may you all be changed in nature to earth and to water,
100   every man who is sitting here spiritless, wholly dishonored.
I will myself don armor against him. But from above are
wielded the victory-cables, among the high gods who live always."
    So having spoken, he dressed himself in his beautiful armor.
There would the end of your life, Meneláos, have come to you surely
105   under the hands of great Hektor, for he was indeed much stronger,
had not leapt up and held you the princes among the Achaians;
Atreus' scion himself, wide-governing Lord Agamemnon,
then by the right hand caught you and spoke thus, calling upon you:
"You are insane, Zeus-loved Meneláos, and not at all have you
110   need of this madness—restrain yourself, in spite of your anguish,

133

nor in mere rivalry wish to combat one better than you are,
Hektor the scion of Priam, at whom most others are frightened.
Even Achilles with him, in the battle that wins a man glory,
shudders to meet and contend, though he is far better than you are.
115 But now you go and sit down there with the throng of your comrades—
some other champion will the Achaians put forward against him.
Then, although he is fearless and never is sated with fighting,
he will be happy, I think, to relax his limbs, if he even
makes his escape from the violent battle and terrible combat."

120   So having spoken, the hero persuaded the mind of his brother,
winning him over to do the right thing; Meneláos obeyed him;
joyfully then his attendants removed from his shoulders the armor.
Nestor among them rose to his feet, and he spoke to the Argives:
"Oh shame! What a great sorrow has come on the land of Achaia!
125 Loudly indeed would groan old Peleus the chariot-driver,
excellent counselor he of the Mýrmidons, excellent speaker,
who in his house once, questioning me, most greatly rejoiced in
talking about the descent and the offspring of all of the Argives.
If now he were to hear that all these before Hektor are cringing,
130 to the immortals would he very often be lifting his hands up
that from his limbs his spirit would go to the palace of Hades.
Oh Zeus, father of all, and Athena as well, and Apollo,
would I were youthful, as when by the Kéladon, rapidly flowing,
Pylians gathered to fight Arkádians, passionate spearmen,
135 there around Pheia's walls, by the streams of the river Iardános.
Then as their champion stood Ereuthálion, godlike in manhood,
wearing the armor of Áreïthóös, the king, on his shoulders,
Áreïthóös the noble, to whom was the name mace-fighter
often assigned by the men and the women with beautiful girdles,
140 since with a bow or a long spear never he went into battle;
rather it was with an iron-wrought mace that he shattered battalions.
Him did Lykoúrgos kill by a trick, not at all by his prowess,
when in a narrow defile of the road that iron-wrought mace could
not ward off his destruction; Lykoúrgos was quicker at stabbing
145 him with his spear in the middle, and he to the ground fell backward;
he stripped him of the armor that Ares the brazen had given.
This was the armor that he himself wore in the struggle of Ares;
but then, soon as Lykoúrgos became an old man in his palace,
he to his dear comrade Ereuthálion gave it to put on.
150 Wearing this armor was he now challenging all of the nobles.

They were all dreadfully trembling and fearful, and nobody dared it;
but inside me the heart, much-daring, aroused me to fight him,
bold as I was, although of them all in age I was youngest.
So with the hero I fought, and Athena accorded me glory.
155 He was the tallest and mightiest man I ever have slaughtered,
for an enormous bulk was he sprawled one way and the other.
How I wish I were young and my strength yet steady within me;
soon would encounter a fight great Hektor of glittering helmet.
Although here among you are the best men of all the Achaians,
160 you are not willing and eager to go man-to-man against Hektor."
      So did the old man scold, and in all nine warriors stood up.
First by far then arose Agamemnon, lord of the people;
after him rose up the scion of Tydeus, strong Diomédes;
after them, both the Ajaxes, appareled in furious valor;
165 after those heroes, Idómeneus stood, and Idómeneus' comrade
Mérionés, that peer of Enyálios, killer of fighters;
next, Eurýpylos stood, the illustrious son of Euaímon;
up rose Thoas, the son of Andraímon, and noble Odysseus;
all these heroes were willing to battle the noble lord Hektor.
170 Once more spoke out among them the horseman Gerenian Nestor:
"Now let the lots be thoroughly shaken, to see who is chosen;
certainly he will obtain benefit for the well-greaved Achaians,
then in his heart will himself gain benefit, if in the end he
makes his escape from the violent battle and terrible combat."
175   So he spoke, and a shard they each one marked as his own lot,
throwing it into the helmet of Atreus' son Agamemnon.
Then prayed all of the host; to the gods they lifted their hands up;
so would one of them utter as he looked up to broad heaven:
"Father Zeus, grant that the lot choose Ajax or Tydeus' scion
180 or else the king himself of the gold-rich city Mykénè."
      So they spoke; by the horseman Gerenian Nestor the lots were
shaken, and out of the helmet the lot which they were desiring
leapt, that of Ajax, and through the whole throng it was borne by the herald,
shown from the left to the right among all of the noble Achaians;
185 none of them recognized it, so each of the heroes denied it.
But when, bearing it through the whole throng, he came to the man who
marked it and cast it into the helmet—illustrious Ajax
holding his hand out—the lot he dropped in it, standing beside him;
seeing the lot, he recognized it and rejoiced in his spirit.
190 Down to the ground by his feet he threw it, and thus he addressed them:

135

"Oh friends, this is indeed my lot—I am gladdened myself in
spirit, for I am quite sure I will vanquish glorious Hektor.
But come, while I am putting upon me the armor of warfare,
you meanwhile begin praying to Lord Zeus scion of Kronos,
195 silently, all to yourselves, so as not to be heard by the Trojans,
or out loud in the open, for we fear nothing in this case,
since by his will and with force nobody could drive me unwilling,
nor in the least by his skill, for I think it was not without skill that
I in Salamis Island was born and brought up to adulthood."
200   He spoke; they began praying to Lord Zeus scion of Kronos;
so would one of them utter as he looked up to broad heaven:
"Father Zeus, ruling from Ida, the lord most honored and mighty,
grant this triumph to Ajax, to win him glory resplendent;
even in fact if Hektor as well you cherish and care for,
205 grant that for both these heroes the strength and the honor be equal."
       So did they say; then Ajax accoutered himself in his bright bronze.
But then, when he had clothed his body in all of his armor,
swiftly he rushed forth, just as enormous Ares advances
when to a battle he goes, among men whom the scion of Kronos
210 causes to fight with the fury of strife, the devourer of spirits.
So was attacking enormous Ajax, the Achaians' protector,
wearing a smile on his menacing face, on his feet underneath in
great strides rushing, and brandishing high a long-shadowing spear-shaft.
On the one side were the Argives gladdened at looking upon him;
215 as for the Trojans, on each man's limbs crept terror and trembling.
Even in Hektor himself did the heart in his breast beat harder;
nevertheless, no way could he now take flight or retreat back
into the throng of the army, for his was the challenge to combat.
Ajax came up close to him bearing a shield like a tower,
220 brazen, of sevenfold hides, which Týchios made by his labor,
far best he of all workers in leather; his home was in Hylè;
he had made him this glittering shield out of sevenfold hides from
well-fed bulls and upon them an eighth bronze layer had hammered.
Bearing this shield in front of his chest now Télamon's scion
225 Ajax stood near Hektor, and threatening words he addressed him:
"Hektor, indeed you will surely discover in man-to-man fashion
now what manner of men are among these Dánaän nobles
after Achilles himself, the rank-breaker with soul of a lion.
He however is now at his well-curved seafaring galleys
230 lying, and raging against Agamemnon, shepherd of people;

136

nevertheless, such fighters are we as can stand up against you—
many in fact we are; so begin this battle and combat."
    Answering him then spoke great Hektor of glittering helmet:
"Ajax the Zeus-sprung scion of Télamon, marshal of people,
235 not in the least be testing me now like a powerless stripling,
nor like a woman who does not know any labors of warfare;
well I know about battles and men being slaughtered in combat;
I know too how to wield to the right and the left hand a shield of
well-tanned oxhide, and so I am bold with the shield in a battle;
240 I know how to assail the melee of swift chariot-horses;
I know too how to dance in close combat for violent Ares.
Yet now, such as you are, I do not want to attack you
stealthily, eyeing your weakness, but openly, hoping to hit you."
    So did he say, then brandished and threw his long-shadowing spear-shaft
245 so that it struck Ajax's tremendous sevenfold oxhide
shield on the outermost bronze that on it was the eighth of the layers.
Through six folds went tearing the inexhaustible bronze point,
but on the seventh hide it was halted, and then in his own turn
Ajax descended of Zeus let fly his long-shadowing spear-shaft,
250 square on the circular shield thus striking the scion of Priam.
Straight through the glittering shield penetrated the powerful spear-shaft,
thrusting its way on through the elaborate work of the breastplate;
grazing his flank very closely the spear-point then through the tunic
pierced; and he swerved to the side and avoided the blackest of doomsdays.
255 Both of the men with their hands drew out the long spears at the same time,
then they fell on each other like lions that feed upon raw flesh
or like fierce wild boars whose power is not ineffective.
Square on the shield with his spear did Priam's son then strike Ajax,
nor did the bronze break through, but the point of the spear bent backward;
260 leaping upon him, Ajax thrust at his shield, and the spear went
right on through it, and caused him to reel in his furious onset,
wounding his neck as it went, and the dark blood started to gush up.
Not even so from the fight went Hektor of glittering helmet;
yielding some ground, in his powerful hand he picked up a boulder,
265 which on the plain was lying, a black one, enormous and jagged,
then with it struck Ajax's tremendous sevenfold oxhide
shield on the boss in the center—the bronze rang loudly around it.
After him Ajax lifted another stone even more massive;
whirling about he threw it, and measureless strength he exerted—
270 inward the shield he shattered by hurling the rock like a millstone,

pounding the knees underneath him, and he on his back lay sprawling,
stretched out under his shield; but at once he was raised by Apollo.
Now with their swords in a close combat they would have been thrusting
had not heralds, the messengers both of Lord Zeus and of mortals,
275   come out, one from the Trojans and one from the bronze-clad Achaians;
thoughtful were both, Talthýbios one and Idaíos the other.
There between them they held their staves, and the herald Idaíos,
skillful in thoughtful advising, addressed them, speaking in these words:
"No more now, dear children, continue to fight or to struggle;
280   since you are both very dear to the great cloud-gathering god Zeus;
both moreover are spearmen, and that we certainly all know.
Night already is here—it is good to pay heed to the nighttime."
       Answering him in return spoke Ajax, Télamon's scion:
"Now give order to Hektor, Idaíos, to speak about these things,
285   since it was he who challenged the best of us all to the combat.
Let him begin—I will gladly assent to whatever he urges."
       Answering him then spoke great Hektor of glittering helmet:
"Ajax, seeing a god endowed you with stature and power,
wisdom as well—with a spear you are strongest among the Achaians—
290   now let us bring to a halt this battle and violent combat
just for the day, and tomorrow again we will fight till a god has
chosen between us and gives triumph to one side or the other.
Night already is here—it is good to pay heed to the nighttime,
so that beside their galleys you make glad all the Achaians,
295   and above all, your kinsmen and comrades who are with you here;
meanwhile I, all through the great city of Priam the lord, will
gladden the Trojans and women of Troy with their trailing apparel,
who for my sake will pray when they enter the sacred assembly.
Come, let us both give glorious gifts, each one to the other,
300   so that among the Achaians and Trojans alike may a man say,
'These two fought each other in strife, the devourer of spirits,
then, having joined in harmonious friendship, they separated.'"
       So having spoken, he gave him a sword all studded with silver,
bringing it over to him with its scabbard and well-cut baldric;
305   Ajax in turn gave him a fine war-belt shining with purple.
Then those two separated, and one to the host of Achaians
went, and the other the throng of the Trojans, and these became joyful,
seeing that he was returning to join them living and healthy,
after escaping the might and invincible hands of great Ajax;
310   they led him to the town, having been in despair of his safety.

But on the other side Ajax was led by well-greaved Achaians
over to great Agamemnon, as he in his triumph exulted.
    Then when they had arrived at the cabins of Atreus' scion,
there a fat bull of five years Agamemnon, lord of the people,
315 offered as victim to Zeus, the all-powerful scion of Kronos.
This they flayed and prepared, dismembering all of the carcass;
skillfully cutting it up, on stakes they spitted the pieces;
carefully roasting the meat, they drew off all of the morsels.
Then when they had completed the work and had readied the dinner,
320 they dined, nor of the well-shared meal were their hearts at all wanting.
But with the whole long cut from the chine of the victim was Ajax
honored by Atreus' son, wide-governing Lord Agamemnon.
When they had quite satisfied their appetites, drinking and eating,
first of them all who started to weave plans then was the old man
325 Nestor—before this too his advice had been seen to be noblest;
he with benevolent wisdom addressed them, giving them counsel:
"Atreus' son and you others, the noblest of all the Achaians,
since so many have died of the long-haired men, the Achaians,
those whose dark blood now by the beautiful-flowing Skamánder
330 Ares the savage has spilled and whose souls have descended to Hades,
therefore you in the morning should stop the combat of Achaians;
we will assemble the corpses and wheel them here on our wagons
pulled by oxen and mules, and the dead men then we will burn up
somewhat apart from the ships, so that each may carry the bones back
335 home to the children, whenever we part for the land of our fathers.
Close to the pyre let us heap one mound for the corpses together,
dragging the dirt down here from the plain, then quickly beside it
build a high-towering wall as defense for ourselves and our galleys;
gates close-fitting and strong let us also make in the rampart,
340 so as to furnish a road through it for the chariot-horses.
Then on the outside, close to the wall, let us dig out a deep trench,
which will encircle the camp to hold off their horses and army,
so that we never are crushed by the strife of the venturous Trojans."
    So he spoke, and the other kings too all gave their approval.
345 High in the city of Ilion also assembled the Trojans,
fiercely tumultuous, there in front of the portals of Priam;
speaking among them thoughtful Anténor began the discussion:
"Listen to me now, Trojans, Dardánians also, and allies,
so I can say such things as the heart in my breast is demanding.
350 Come then: Helen of Argos, along with her all her possessions,

let us give Atreus' scions to take back; now as we battle,
those firm pledges of ours prove falsehoods; therefore I do not
hope any good for us will be accomplished if we do not do that."
So having spoken he sat back down, and among them stood up
355 Lord Alexander, the husband of Helen of beautiful tresses,
who now gave him an answer—in these winged words he addressed him:
"Pleasing to me no longer, Anténor, is what you are saying—
you know how to devise some other speech better than this one.
But if indeed such things you truly are speaking in earnest,
360 then have the gods themselves most certainly ruined your senses.
Now I too will address these Trojans, tamers of horses;
outright I will declare: I will not give back that woman.
As for the treasures that I brought here to our palace from Argos,
all am I willing to give and to add yet more from my own goods."
365 So having spoken he sat back down, and among them stood up
Dárdanos' son King Priam, the peer of the gods as adviser;
he with benevolent wisdom addressed them, giving them counsel:
"Listen to me now, Trojans, Dardánians also, and allies,
so I can say such things as the heart in my breast is demanding.
370 Now take supper all over the city, as you have before done;
keep in remembrance the night-watch, and every man remain wakeful;
early at dawn let Idaíos go down to the hollow ships and
there tell Atreus' sons Agamemnon and Meneláos
what now says Alexander, for whose sake strife has arisen;
375 let him as well give this wise message to them, in the hope that
they will be willing to cease from the dolorous battle until we
burn up the bodies; and later again we will fight till a god has
chosen between us and gives triumph to one side or the other."
So did he say; they carefully listened to him and obeyed him,
380 then took supper all over the army, in ordered divisions.
Early at dawn Idaíos went down to the hollow ships and
there in assembly discovered the Dánaäns, Ares' companions,
near Agamemnon's ship, at the stern; then standing among them
right in the middle, the loud-voiced herald began to address them:
385 "Atreus' sons and you others, the noblest of all the Achaians,
Priam as well as the other illustrious Trojans have ordered
me to declare, in the hope it will be to you welcome and pleasant,
what now says Alexander, for whose sake strife has arisen.
As for the treasures that Lord Alexander in hollow galleys
390 brought back homeward to Troy—I wish he had perished before that!—

all is he willing to give and to add yet more from his own goods.
But for the lawful wife of the glorious lord Meneláos,
her he declares he will not give, in spite of the Trojans who urge it.
I am as well to convey this message to you, in the hope that
395   you will be willing to cease from the dolorous battle until we
burn up the bodies; and later again we will fight till a god has
chosen between us and gives triumph to one side or the other."

So did he say; then all of the people were hushed in silence;
finally spoke out among them the crier of war Diomédes:
400   "Now those treasures from Lord Alexander or Helen herself let
no one accept, since even to childish fools it is well known
that on the Trojans already the grim death-bindings are fastened."

So he spoke, and the sons of Achaians all shouted approval,
marveling much at the words of the tamer of steeds Diomédes.
405   Then to Idaíos at once spoke forth the strong lord Agamemnon:
"You are yourself now hearing, Idaíos, the words of the Achaians,
how they are answering you; and to me too, so is it pleasing.
As for the dead men, not in the least I grudge that you burn them,
since no grudging can there ever be to the bodies of those who
410   perish, as soon as they die to console them quickly with burning.
Witness to this be Zeus, the loud-thundering husband of Hera."

So having spoken, to all of the gods he lifted his scepter;
back to the sacred city of Ilion parted Idaíos.
In the assembly the Trojans sat, the Dardánians also,
415   all of them gathered together, awaiting Idaíos, until he
came back there; and as soon as he came, he spoke out the message
as in their midst he stood. They quickly prepared for the twofold
task, some gathering corpses and others collecting the firewood.
While on the opposite side, the Argives from the well-benched galleys
420   rushed, some gathering corpses and others collecting the firewood.

Helios then was beginning to strike at the plowlands, arisen
out of the silently gliding abysmal stream of the Ocean,
climbing above to the sky; and the hosts encountered each other.
There most difficult was it to recognize each of the dead men;
425   but first washing with water the blood and the gore from the bodies,
letting the hot tears fall, they lifted them onto the wagons.
Nor did great Priam allow them to wail—they rather in silence
piled up the dead men there on the pyre, much grieving in spirit,
then burned them in the fire and to sacred Ilion parted.
430   So on the other side in the same manner the well-greaved Achaians

piled up the dead men there on the pyre, much grieving in spirit,
then burned them in the fire and returned to the hollow galleys.
    While it was not yet morning, but night was still in its twilight,
gathered about that pyre, a picked company of the Achaians
435 started to make about it one mound for the corpses together,
dragging the dirt down there from the plain, then quickly beside it
built a high-towering wall as defense for themselves and their galleys;
gates close-fitting and strong they also made in the rampart,
so as to furnish a road through it for the chariot-horses.
440 Then on the outside, close to the wall, they dug out a deep trench,
making it broad and enormous, and stakes they planted within it.
    Thus then kept on toiling the long-haired men, the Achaians;
meanwhile the gods were sitting with Zeus the great thunderbolt-wielder
marveling at the huge labor of those bronze-armored Achaians.
445 Speaking among them opened the great earth-shaker Poseidon:
"Zeus our father, is there on the measureless earth among mortals
anyone who will yet tell the immortals his mind and intention?
Do you not see how the long-haired men, the Achaians, have just now
built that wall in defense of their ships, and about it a trench have
450 driven, but have not given the gods any splendid oblations?
Surely the deed will have glory as long and as far as the dawn spreads;
men will forget that wall which Phoibos Apollo and I once
labored to build for defending the hero Laómedon's city."
    Mightily vexed, thus spoke to him then the cloud-gathering god Zeus:
455 "Well, Earth-shaker of widespread strength, what word do you utter!
Somebody else of the gods would perhaps be frightened at that thought,
one who is weaker than you by far in his hands and his power.
Certainly yours will be glory as long and as far as the dawn spreads.
Come now, as soon as again those long-haired men, the Achaians,
460 leave with their galleys to go to the much-loved land of their fathers,
break that wall into pieces and sweep it all into the sea-brine,
cover the great beach over again with sand to conceal it,
so that indeed the great wall the Achaians erected is leveled."
    Such things then they spoke and addressed each one to the other;
465 then did the sun go down, and the work of the Achaians was finished;
slaughtering oxen among their cabins, they readied their supper.
Galleys conveying them wine now arrived nearby, out of Lemnos,
many of them sent there by the scion of Jason Eunéos,
whom Hypsípylè brought forth to Jason, the shepherd of people.
470 Solely on Atreus' sons Agamemnon and Meneláos

Jason's son bestowed wine to be brought them, a thousand containers.
Wine was obtained from the ships by the long-haired men, the Achaians,
some of them paying with bronze, yet others with glittering iron;
others with hides made payment, and others with whole live cattle,
475 others with captives of war; and a sumptuous dinner they readied.
Then for the whole night through were the long-haired men, the Achaians,
feasting, as were in the city the Trojans along with their allies.
But for the whole night through Zeus Counselor plotted afflictions,
thundering terribly down on the armies, and green fear seized them;
480 wine they poured on the ground from the goblets, and nobody dared to
drink before making libation to Kronos' all-powerful scion.
Then they lay down to rest and accepted the present of slumber.

BOOK 8

Now all over the earth Dawn saffron-appareled was spreading,
when an assembly of gods Lord Zeus the great thunderbolt-hurler
called high up on the loftiest summit of rocky Olympos.
There he addressed them himself, and the gods all carefully listened:
5   "All of the gods and the goddesses all, now listen and heed me,
so I can say such things as the heart in my breast is demanding.
Let not one of the gods, no male among you and no female,
make any effort to thwart this word of mine—rather together
all give assent, so that I may quickly accomplish these actions.
10 Anyone I may observe who apart from the gods is desiring
either to go to the aid of the Dánaäns or of the Trojans,
lightning-stricken will he come shamefully back to Olympos,
or into Tártaros, misty and dark, I will snatch up and hurl him,
far, very far, where under the earth is the deepest abysm,
15 where its gates are constructed of iron, of bronze is the threshold,
just so far beneath Hades' domain as the sky is above earth;
then you will know how much among all of the gods I am strongest.
But come, give it a try, you gods, so that all of you know this:
taking a cord made of gold, then fastening it from the heavens,
20 all of the gods and the goddesses all, lay hold of it firmly;
never would you be able to pull to the ground out of heaven
Counselor Zeus most high, even if you toiled to exhaustion.
But whenever I wanted to pull and I strongly was minded,
then with the earth itself I would pull up the cord, and the sea too.
25 Then I would fasten the cord around some huge spur of Olympos—
all those things in the middle of space thereafter would dangle.
So much I to the gods am superior, so much to mortals."
    So did he say; then all the immortals were hushed in silence,
marveling much at his words; for indeed he had strongly addressed them.
30 Finally spoke out among them the goddess bright-eyed Athena:

"Father of all of us, scion of Kronos and sovereign ruler,
we are aware already of your irresistible power;
but even so we are sorrowing over the Dánaän spearmen,
who are indeed to accomplish a fate most evil and perish.

35   Nevertheless, we will keep from the battle, as you are commanding,
yet to the Argives we will give counsel, whatever will help them,
so that they not all perish because of your wrath and resentment."
        Smiling at her thus uttered the great cloud-gathering god Zeus:
"Take heart, Trítogeneía, my dear child—not in the least I

40   speak with a serious mind, but to you I want to be kindly."
        So did he say, then under his chariot harnessed the bronze-hoofed
horses of swift strong flight, with their manes all golden and flowing;
golden the armor he put on his body, and skillfully wrought of
gold was the whip he grasped; then onto the chariot mounting,

45   he drove, lashing the steeds, nor against their wishes did they fly
out in the space midway between earth and the star-filled heaven.
Ida of numerous springs he came to, the mother of wild beasts,
even to Gárgaros, where are his precinct and odorous altar.
There the great father of gods and of mankind halted his horses,

50   then from the chariot loosed them and poured thick mist all around them;
he himself sat down there amid peaks, in his glory exulting,
while on the city of Trojans he gazed, and the ships of Achaians.
        Meanwhile, the long-haired men, the Achaians, had hastily taken
dinner among their cabins, and then they put on their armor.

55   So on their side did the Trojans array themselves in the city,
fewer indeed, yet ready and eager to fight in the combat
under necessity's force, to defend their wives and their children.
Then were the gates all opened, and out of them hurried the army,
both foot soldiers and horsemen; and huge was the clamor that rose up.

60   Finally, when they arrived in the same place, coming together,
shield upon shield they dashed, and their spears, and the furious might of
men well armored in bronze; and the shields made massive with bosses
clashed each one on another, and huge was the clamor that rose up.
There were the grief-filled groans and the triumph-shouts to be heard of

65   men who were killing and men who were killed; the earth streamed with their lifeblood.
        While it was morning as yet and the sacred daylight was waxing,
missiles of both sides sped to their targets, and people were falling;
soon as the sun while coursing the sky stood high in mid-heaven,
then by the Father were balanced the gold-wrought scales, and he set in

70   them two destiny-portions of death so long in the mourning,

those of the horse-taming Trojans and of the bronze-armored Achaians;
grasping the middle, he poised it; and down sank the Achaians' doomsday.
To the much-nourishing earth thus settled the destiny-portions
of the Achaians, and those of the Trojans arose to the broad sky.
75 Then he himself loud-thundered from Ida and scintillant lightning
hurled down into the host of Achaians; and when they observed it,
greatly they marveled, and all of the people were gripped by a green fear.
    Neither Idómeneus dared to remain then, nor Agamemnon,
nor did the two Ajaxes remain, the companions of Ares;
80 only Gerenian Nestor remained, the Achaians' protector,
not of his own will—rather his horse had been hurt when the noble
lord Alexander, the husband of Helen of beautiful tresses,
struck with an arrow the crown of its head, where the first of a horse's
hairs grow out of its skull, the most fatal of spots to be wounded.
85 Stricken with anguish, it reared as the missile entered the brainpan,
putting the horses in panic—about the bronze barb it was writhing.
Then as the old man sprang from his chariot, cutting the traces
free from the horse with his sword, meanwhile the swift horses of Hektor
came through the tumult; bold was the charioteer they were bringing,
90 Hektor, and now in fact the old man would have forfeited life-breath
had not keenly observed the great crier of war Diomédes.
Shouting a terrible shout, he at once exhorted Odysseus:
"Zeus-sprung son of Laërtes, Odysseus of many devices,
where are you fleeing and turning your back on the throng like a coward?
95 Let not somebody plant his spear in your back as you take flight,
but stay, so we can beat the wild fighter away from the old man."
    So did he say; much-suffering noble Odysseus did not hear,
rather he rushed past him to the hollow ships of the Achaians.
Tydeus' scion, alone as he was, with the champions mingled,
100 standing in front of the steeds of the old man, Neleus' scion;
raising his voice he spoke, and in these winged words he addressed him:
"Old man, these young fighters are certainly making you weary,
loosened is all your strength, and a harsh old age is upon you;
now is your comrade too but a weakling, and slow are your horses.
105 But come, climb up onto my chariot, so that you see what
breed are the horses of Tros, most skillful in rapidly crossing
over the plain one way and the other, pursuing and fleeing,
those I recently took from Ainéas, devisers of panic.
Let the companions attend to your horses, and we will keep driving
110 these two straight at the Trojans, the tamers of horses, that Hektor

know well whether in my hands too my spear is rampaging."
    He spoke, nor disobeyed him the horseman Gerenian Nestor.
Then to the horses of Nestor the two companions attended,
powerful Sthénelos one, and Eurýmedon, kindly and thoughtful.
115 Onto the chariot of Diomédes the other two mounted.
Into his hands were the glittering reins then taken by Nestor;
he began lashing the steeds, and they speedily came near Hektor.
Him as he rushed straight onward the scion of Tydeus aimed at;
missing his mark, he struck his companion, the chariot-driver
120 Éniopeús, offspring of the powerful-hearted Thebaíos,
who stood holding the reins—on his chest by the nipple he hit him.
He from the chariot fell, and his swift-hoofed horses, affrighted,
swerved to the side; right there were his life and his strength unloosened.
Terrible grief in his mind for his charioteer engulfed Hektor;
125 yet even so, although he mourned for his comrade, he left him
lying to go seek out a bold charioteer; nor a long time
yet were his horses in want of a master; for quickly he found bold
Árcheptólemos, Íphitos' scion, and bade him behind his
swift-hoofed horses to mount; and the reins to his hands he delivered.
130   There then would have been ruin and deeds incurably baneful,
now like sheep within Ilion city would they have been penned up,
had not keenly observed it the father of gods and of mankind.
Thundering terribly, he threw down white-glittering lightning,
hurled it to earth in front of the horses of Lord Diomédes;
135 terrible flames rose up from the sulphurous conflagration;
under the chariot, both of the horses were cringing in terror.
Quickly the shimmering reins slipped out of the hands of Lord Nestor;
he was afraid in his spirit, and thus he addressed Diomédes:
"Tydeus' son, come, turn in retreat your single-hoofed horses.
140 Do you not see how triumph from Zeus no longer attends you?
For to that man now Zeus son of Kronos is giving the glory
this day; but later again upon us too, should he be minded,
he will bestow it; the purpose of Zeus a man never can frustrate,
not even one very brave, for the god by far is the stronger."
145   Speaking to him then answered the crier of war Diomédes:
"Yes, of all this, old sir, you speak as is fitting and proper.
Yet this terrible grief comes over my heart and my spirit,
since some day as he talks to the Trojans will Hektor be saying,
'Tydeus' scion was driven in flight before me to the galleys.'
150 So one day he will boast; may the broad earth then yawn to take me."

Speaking to him then answered the horseman Gerenian Nestor:
"Ah me, scion of war-skilled Tydeus, what are you saying—
since even if Lord Hektor declares you a coward and weakling,
yet the Dardánians never will be convinced, nor the Trojans,
155 nor indeed will the wives of the great-souled shield-bearing Trojans,
women of whom you have thrown in the dust the young vigorous bedmates."
So he spoke, and he turned in retreat those single-hoofed horses
back through the tumult of fighters; upon them the Trojans and Hektor,
raising a marvelous din, poured down their maleficent missiles.
160 Over them shouted aloud great Hektor of glittering helmet:
"Tydeus' son, above all have the swift-horsed Dánaäns honored
you with the seat you hold, with meat and with ever-full goblets;
now they will scorn you; for you I see are no more than a woman.
Off with you, cowardly puppet, for never will you be climbing
165 onto our ramparts because I yielded, nor ever will take our
women away in the ships: before that, your doom I will grant you."
So he spoke, and the scion of Tydeus doubtfully pondered
whether to turn his horses around and do battle against him.
Thrice indeed he pondered the question in mind and in spirit;
170 thrice Zeus Counselor thundered aloft from the summits of Ida,
giving the Trojans an omen of victory, battle-reversing.
Hektor began exhorting the Trojans, and loudly he shouted:
"Trojans and Lykians all, Dardánians, hand-to-hand fighters,
now be men, dear friends, and remember your furious valor;
175 I know the scion of Kronos has nodded his head and accorded
triumph to me, great glory, but woe to the Dánaän army,
childish fools, who indeed have devised these fortifications
frail, unworthy of note, that will never withstand our prowess;
easily over the trench they dug will be leaping the horses.
180 But when finally I have arrived at the hollow galleys,
then of the ravening fire let someone remember to take thought,
so with the fire I can burn up the galleys and slaughter the men, those
Argives panicked because of the smoke there close to the galleys."
So having said, he called to his horses, and thus he addressed them:
185 "Xanthos and you, Podárgos, and Aithon and Lampos the noble,
now is the time to repay the provisioning that in abundant
heaps greathearted Eëtion's daughter Andrómachè set there
close to you, ever the first of the horses—the wheat, honey-hearted,
mingling with it some wine to be drunk, when her spirit commanded,
190 even before me, who, as I boast, am her vigorous husband.

But come follow me closely and hasten, in order that we may
capture the shield of Lord Nestor—to heaven its fame now reaches,
how it is all gold, the shield itself and the strengthening cross-rods—
then from the shoulders of Lord Diomédes the tamer of horses
195   take the elaborate breastplate wrought by the toil of Hephaistos.
If these two we could seize, then I might hope the Achaians
this same night we would cause to embark on the swift-sailing galleys."
     So he spoke as he boasted, but Hera the queen was indignant;
there in her seat she shuddered, and lofty Olympos was shaken,
200   and to Poseidon the powerful god she spoke out directly:
"Well, Earth-shaker of widespread strength, not even in you is
grieving the heart in your breast for the Dánaän men who are dying,
yet they carry to Hélikè presents for you, and to Aigai,
offerings many and pleasing; and you did want them to triumph.
205   For if we all who are aiding the Dánaäns made up our minds to
drive those Trojans away and to hold wide-thundering Zeus back,
there then he would be grieving and sitting alone upon Ida."
     Then in his great vexation the strong earth-shaker addressed her:
"Hera, of speech so reckless, and what word now have you spoken!
210   I would not wish for the others of us against Zeus son of Kronos
ever to join in battle, for he is much stronger than we are."
     Such words then they spoke and addressed each one to the other.
Now was the space that the trench enclosed, in front of the wall which
guarded the ships, filled full of the horses and shield-bearing fighters
215   penned up together; for they were penned in by the equal of Ares,
Hektor the scion of Priam, as Zeus kept granting him glory.
He would have burned those balanced ships with a fiery blaze had
Hera the queen not put in the spirit of Lord Agamemnon
now to exert himself so as quickly to rouse the Achaians.
220   He went passing along the Achaians' cabins and galleys
holding in his stout hand a voluminous mantle of purple;
then he stood by the hollow and huge black ship of Odysseus
which in the midmost lay, so his shout might reach to the two sides,
both to the far-off cabins of Ajax, Télamon's son, and
225   those of Achilles, for theirs were the balanced ships that were drawn up
farthest away—they trusted their powerful hands and their valor.
Piercingly then he yelled to the Dánaäns; loudly he shouted:
"Shame on you, Argives, base disgraces, admired for appearance!
Where have the boasts gone, when we declared ourselves to be bravest—
230   empty and vain, those boasts you uttered when you were in Lemnos

eating the plentiful savory flesh of the cattle with straight horns,
drinking the wine from the mixing bowls all filled up and brimming,
saying that each of you might stand up face-to-face with a hundred
Trojans in fight, or two hundred; but now we cannot match one man,
235   Hektor, who soon with a fiery blaze will be burning the galleys.
Zeus our father, have you before now ever blinded a mighty
ruler with such dark blindness and taken away his great glory?
Never, I say, I slighted a beautiful altar of yours while
cursedly voyaging here in a galley of numerous oarlocks;
240   rather on all I burned the rich fat and the thighbones of oxen,
eagerly hoping to capture and ransack Troy of the strong walls.
But Zeus, do you at least fulfill this wish that I utter:
let us at least ourselves get away and escape from the battle—
do not allow the Achaians to be thus quelled by the Trojans."
245   So he spoke, and the Father had pity on him as he shed tears;
then he nodded assent that the host be safe and not perish.
Straightway an eagle he sent, among winged birds surest of omens,
holding a fawn, the offspring of a swift-paced hind, in its talons;
there by the beautiful altar of Zeus it let the fawn drop down,
250   where the Achaians to Zeus of All Prophesies offered their victims.
Seeing the bird, they knew that from Zeus it had come and were yet more
eager to leap at the Trojans, recalling their ardor for battle.
     Thereupon nobody else of the Dánaäns, though they were many,
boasted that sooner than Tydeus' son he had driven his swift steeds,
255   guiding them over the trench, or engaged in man-to-man combat;
rather, the first by far, he slaughtered a well-armored Trojan,
Phradmon's son Ageláos—in flight he was turning his horses;
but as around he was wheeling, between his shoulders the hero
planted a spear in his back, and ahead through the chest he impelled it.
260   He from the chariot fell, and around him clattered his armor.
     After him Atreus' sons, Agamemnon and Meneláos,
after them, both the Ajaxes, appareled in furious valor,
after those heroes, Idómeneus came, and Idómeneus' comrade
Mérionés, that peer of Enyálios, slayer of fighters,
265   then Eurýpylos came, the illustrious son of Euaímon.
Teukros arrived as the ninth—his back-curved bow he was stretching;
he stood under the shield of the scion of Télamon Ajax.
Ajax then would remove his shield from him, so that the hero,
looking around for his mark, then shooting an arrow, would strike some
270   man in the throng, who would fall right there, so losing his life-breath;

back once more he would run, as a child to his mother, and take his
shelter with Ajax, who with his glittering shield would conceal him.
　　Then who first of the Trojans was killed by Teukros the faultless?
First Orsílochos perished and Órmenos and Ophiléstes,
275　Daítora, Chrómios too, and as well godlike Lykophóntes,
then Polyaímon's son Amopáon, and then Melaníppos—
all to the nourishing earth he brought in rapid succession.
Looking at him Agamemnon the lord of the people was gladdened,
as with the powerful bow he destroyed the battalions of Trojans;
280　going to him, he stood at his side, and a word he addressed him:
"Teukros, dear friend, scion of Télamon, marshal of people,
shoot thus, so that a light to the Dánaäns you may become, to
Télamon also, your father, who nurtured you while you were little—
although you were a bastard—and cared for you there in his own house.
285　Now faraway as he is, exalt him and bring him to glory.
Thus I say to you plainly, and this thing will be accomplished:
Should great Zeus who carries the aegis as well as Athena
grant to me well-built Ilion city to capture and ransack,
first, just after my own, will I place in your hand an award of
290　honor, a tripod, or else with a chariot two of the horses,
even a woman who into your own bed then would be going."
　　Then in answer to him thus spoke forth Teukros the faultless:
"Glorious scion of Atreus, and why exhort me when I am
eager myself? Not at all, so far as the might is within me,
295　have I stopped, but as we toward Ilion started to drive them,
since then, lying in wait with my bow, I have slaughtered the fighters.
Eight of my long-barbed arrows have I already dispatched them,
all struck home in bodies of young men swift in the battle;
that man I am unable to strike, that furious mad dog."
300　　So he spoke, and he shot from the string of his bow yet another
arrow directly at Hektor—his spirit was eager to strike him.
Him he missed; Gorgýthion rather, the faultless and valiant
scion of Priam, did he strike square on the chest with the arrow.
He to a mother was born who was taken as wife from Aisýmè,
305　beautiful Kástianeíra, in stature resembling a goddess.
Off to one side his head he let drop, like a poppy that in some
garden is heavy with its own seed and the showers of springtime—
so to one side did his head incline, weighed down by his helmet.
　　Straightway Teukros shot from the string of his bow yet another
310　arrow directly at Hektor—his spirit was eager to strike him.

Yet he missed him again, for Apollo deflected the arrow;
Árcheptólemos then, the bold charioteer of Lord Hektor,
hastening into the battle, he hit on the chest by the nipple.
He from the chariot fell, and his swift-hoofed horses, affrighted,

315   swerved to the side; right there were his life and his strength unloosened.
Terrible grief in his mind for his charioteer engulfed Hektor;
yet even so, although he mourned for his comrade, he left him;
then he ordered his brother Kebríones who was nearby to
take up the reins of the horses; he heard and did not disobey him.

320   Onto the ground from the glittering chariot he himself leapt down
shouting a terrible shout; in his hand then taking a huge stone,
straight toward Teukros he went, for his heart enjoined him to strike him.
He at the moment had drawn from his quiver a sharp bitter arrow,
placing it onto the string; as he pulled it back, by his shoulder

325   Hektor of glittering helm struck him in a spot very deadly,
where by the collarbone are separated the neck and the chestbone—
there, as he eagerly aimed, he was struck by the huge rough boulder
so that the bowstring broke, and his hand at the wrist was deadened;
onto his knees he dropped and remained; from his hand the great bow fell.

330   Ajax was not unmindful that his own brother had fallen,
but ran up and bestrode him, and so with his shield he concealed him.
Stooping to take up Teukros, a pair of the trustworthy comrades,
valiant Mekísteus, Échios' son, and the noble Alástor,
carried him heavily groaning away to the hollow galleys.

335   Now in the Trojans again the Olympian roused up the spirit;
so straight back to the deep-delved trench they thrust the Achaians;
Hektor, advancing among the foremost, in his strength was exulting.
As at a time when a hound in pursuit of a lion or wild boar
snatches at it from behind, on his swift feet rushing toward it,

340   snapping at buttocks and flanks, and he watches as it keeps swerving,
so now Hektor was pressing the long-haired men, the Achaians,
always killing the man who was hindmost—they were all routed.
But then, when the defensive stakes they had passed, and the deep trench,
fleeing, and many had been brought down at the hands of the Trojans,

345   finally close to the ships they came to a stop and remained there;
each to the others the men called out, and to all of the gods then
raising their hands up high, they fervently, loudly implored them;
Hektor was wheeling his fair-maned horses in every direction—
his were the eyes of a Gorgon or of man-slaughtering Ares.

350   Seeing the men, great pity the goddess white-armed Hera

felt, and at once to Athena in these winged words began speaking:
"Well then, daughter of Zeus of the aegis, so not any longer
are we to care for the perishing Dánaäns, even this last time?
Evil indeed is the doom they will now fulfill as they perish

355 by the assault of one man: no more to be borne in his rage is
Priam's son Hektor, and he has indeed wrought many an evil."
    Speaking to her made answer the goddess bright-eyed Athena:
"I could indeed wish strongly that he lose spirit and life-breath,
killed at the hands of the Argive troops in the land of his fathers;

360 now however with spirit malign my father is raging,
stubborn and always oppressive, a thwarter of anything I want.
Not in the least he remembers the numerous times that I rescued
Herakles, his own son, worn down by Eurýstheus' labors—
he would be making lament toward heaven, and I was the one whom

365 Zeus sent down out of heaven to bring him aid and protection—
since if indeed I had known this then in shrewdness of mind, when
he was dispatched to the dwelling of Hades the strong gatekeeper
so that from Érebos he might bring up the hound of detested
Hades, he would not then have escaped the steep Stygian waters.

370 Now Zeus hates me, and he has accomplished the scheming of Thetis,
who once, kissing his knees and caressing his chin with her soft hand,
strongly implored him to honor Achilles the sacker of cities.
Yet will the day again come that he calls me his bright-eyed darling.
But now you make ready for us our single-hoofed horses,

375 while going into the palace of Zeus who carries the aegis,
I will accouter myself in armor for battle, that I may
see whether Hektor of glittering helmet, the scion of Priam,
will be rejoicing as we appear there on the battle embankments,
whether the dogs and the carrion-birds some Trojan instead will

380 glut with his fat and his flesh when he falls by the ships of the Achaians."
    She spoke, nor disobeyed her the goddess white-armed Hera.
Then got busy and harnessed the two gold-frontleted horses
Hera the august goddess, the daughter of powerful Kronos;
meanwhile Athena the daughter of Zeus who carries the aegis

385 cast down there on the floor of her father the richly embroidered
delicate robe which she had herself made, worked with her own hands;
donning the tunic of war of the great cloud-gathering god Zeus,
she then accoutered herself in his armor for dolorous battle.
Into the fiery chariot stepping, she took up the spear-shaft,

390 heavy and huge and compact, that she uses to shatter the close-pressed

ranks of the fighters who rouse her wrath whose Father is mighty.
Speedily Hera began with the whip to lay into the horses;
moving themselves then grated the gates of the sky that the Seasons
keep, to whose care the great sky is entrusted, as well as Olympos,
395 whether to open the dense cloud-masses or rather to shut them.
Out through them they directed the horses enduring the whip-rod.
    Then, as from Ida he looked, Zeus Father was dreadfully angered;
so he aroused up gold-winged Iris to carry a message:
"Go there at once, swift Iris, and turn them back—do not let them
400 come against me—for it is not seemly for us to join battle.
For I say to you plainly, and this thing will be accomplished:
under their chariot first I will cripple the swift-running horses;
hurling themselves from the chariot then, I will smash it to pieces;
never till ten long years turn round in the circle of seasons
405 they will be healed of the wounds that my lightning will have inflicted,
so that the bright-eyed maid knows when she has fought with her father.
But against Hera I do not feel such wrath or resentment,
since it is always her habit to thwart me, whatever I tell her."
    He spoke; storm-footed Iris arose to go carry the message;
410 then from the summits of Ida she parted, to lofty Olympos.
There at the outermost gates of Olympos of many ravines she
met them and held them back, and the words Zeus spoke she addressed them:
"Where do you hasten? And why do the hearts rage so in your bosoms?
Kronos' scion does not let you give aid to the Argives;
415 for thus threatens the offspring of Kronos, and he will fulfill it:
under your chariot first he will cripple the swift-running horses;
hurling yourselves from the chariot then, he will smash it to pieces;
never till ten long years turn round in the circle of seasons
you will be healed of the wounds that his lightning will have inflicted,
420 so that you, bright-eyed maid, know when you have fought with your father.
But against Hera he does not feel such wrath or resentment,
since it is always her habit to thwart him, whatever he tells her.
Most audacious you are, you foolhardy bitch, if in truth you
venture to raise your enormous spear in defiance of great Zeus."
425   So having spoken her message, the swift-footed Iris departed;
straightway Hera addressed these words to the goddess Athena:
"Well now, daughter of Zeus who carries the aegis, I can no
longer allow us to fight against Zeus for the sake of those mortals.
Now among them one man is to die and another to live whose
430 fortune it is; as for him, in his heart let him meditate these things,

judging between those Trojans and Dánaäns—so is it fitting."
      Soon as she said these words, she turned back the single-hoofed horses
Them did the Seasons attend, unyoking the fair-maned horses,
which they tethered for feeding at their ambrosial mangers,
435   leaning the chariot there on the shimmering wall of the entrance.
They themselves straightway, as they sat on their gold-wrought couches,
joined with the rest of the gods, in their hearts much troubled and grieving.
      Meanwhile his horses and well-wheeled chariot Father Zeus drove from
Ida and back to Olympos, and came to the gods in assembly.
440   There the renowned earth-shaker for him unharnessed the horses,
onto its stand set the chariot, over it spreading the cover;
then on a throne well-fashioned of gold the wide-thundering god Zeus
sat down; under his feet began quaking enormous Olympos.
There then only Athena and Hera were sitting apart from
445   Zeus, and they did not say anything, nor ask any questions;
but in his mind he knew of the matter, and thus he addressed them:
"Why are you so much troubled and grieving, Athena and Hera?
Surely you are not weary, in battle that wins a man glory,
killing the Trojans, at whom you feel such terrible rancor.
450   Certain it is, so great is my strength, my hands so resistless,
never would turn me back all the gods who live on Olympos;
as for the two of you, sooner did shivering grip your resplendent
limbs before you saw combat or combat's horrible actions.
For I say to you plainly, and this thing would have been compassed:
455   not on your chariot, once you were struck by the lightning, would you have
come back here to Olympos, on which the immortals are dwelling."
      So he spoke, and against him muttered Athena and Hera;
they sat next to each other and planned great banes for the Trojans.
Then in silence Athena remained; not a word did she utter,
460   Zeus her father resenting, and gripped by a violent anger.
No such anger could Hera restrain in her breast, but she spoke out:
"Most dread scion of Kronos, and what is this word you have spoken!
We are aware already of your irresistible power;
but even so we are sorrowing over the Dánaän spearmen,
465   who are indeed to accomplish a fate most evil and perish.
Nevertheless, we will keep from the battle, as you are commanding,
yet to the Argives we will give counsel, whatever will help them,
so that they not all perish because of your wrath and resentment."
      Answering her in return spoke forth the cloud-gathering god Zeus:
470   "Surely indeed in the morning will you, ox-eyed Lady Hera,

155

should you desire it, behold the all-powerful scion of Kronos
kill yet more of the numerous army of Argive spearmen,
since no sooner will powerful Hektor be stayed from the battle
till is aroused by his galleys the swift-footed scion of Peleus,
475 on that day when they at the sterns of the galleys are fighting
in the most terrible straits, in defence of the perished Patróklos,
since that way is it destined. About you now and your anger
I care not, even if you go to the nethermost limits
both of the earth and the sea, where Iápetos sits, and Lord Kronos—
480 never do they have pleasure at all in the rays of the High Lord
Helios, nor in the breezes, but Tártaros' depth is around them;
even if you came there in your wandering, not in the least I
care for your wrath, since nobody else is more currish than you are."
     So he spoke, but to him not a word spoke Hera of white arms.
485 Helios' radiant sunlight then fell into the Ocean,
drawing the black night over the grain-giving land, and against their
will did the light sink down on the Trojans; for the Achaians
welcome indeed, thrice prayed for, the dark night settled upon them.
     Then an assembly of Trojans was called by glorious Hektor,
490 who led them from the galleys, away by the eddying river,
where in a place now vacant the ground showed clear of all corpses.
They stepped onto the ground from their chariots, so as to hear what
word to them Hektor, belovèd of Zeus, would speak—of eleven
cubits the spear he held in his hand, and before him the brazen
495 spear-point shone, with a gold-wrought ring-clasp running around it.
Leaning upon this now, these words he addressed to the Trojans:
"Listen to me now, Trojans, Dardánians also, and allies,
I thought after destroying the galleys and all the Achaians,
we were to go back homeward to windswept Ilion city;
500 but before that came darkness, and this above all has now saved those
Argives as well as the ships which lie by the surf of the deep sea.
Nevertheless let us now pay heed to the darkness of nighttime—
let us prepare our dinner; the fair-maned horses as well set
loose from the chariot-harness, and throw down fodder before them;
505 then for the meal bring here from the city the cattle and fat sheep,
going in haste, and provide enough wine, honey-hearted, for drinking,
out of your houses, and victuals, and pile up plentiful firewood,
so that the whole night through till the dawn shows, early at daybreak,
many a fire we burn, and the glow goes up to the heavens,
510 lest perchance in the nighttime the long-haired men, the Achaians,

hastily set forth fleeing across the broad back of the deep sea;
not at their ease, without struggling, should they get onto the galleys,
but so even at home some of them brood over a missile,
struck in their flesh by an arrow or else by a spear with a sharp point
515 as on the ship they were leaping, that many another may shrink from
bringing a dolorous war on the Trojans, tamers of horses.
Then let heralds belovèd of Zeus go through the whole city
giving command that the stripling boys and the gray-templed elders
make their camp on the god-built ramparts surrounding the city;
520 as for the females, within our houses let each of the women
kindle a great bright fire; let the watch be steadily maintained,
lest as the army is absent, an ambush enter the city.
So let it be, you great-souled Trojans, the way that I tell you;
let this word that I say to our profit for now be sufficient;
525 further at dawn I will counsel the Trojans, tamers of horses.
Praying to Zeus and the rest of the gods, I hope and expect to
drive those dogs brought here by the death-fates out of the country,
all of the men that the fates brought here on their dark-hued galleys.
But for ourselves in the night we will maintain watch and defenses;
530 early at dawn in the morning, accoutered in armor, will we down
there by the hollow galleys arouse the sharp warfare of Ares.
I will discover if strong Diomédes the scion of Tydeus
back to the wall from the galleys will thrust me, or whether instead I
will kill him with the bronze and will carry off bloodstained plunder.
535 He will discover his prowess tomorrow, if he can abide my
spear as it comes to attack him; but he I believe in the foremost
stricken and wounded will lie, and around him many companions,
when on the morrow the sun comes up. As for me, I could wish that
I might be as immortal and ageless forever and ever,
540 honored the way that Athena is honored, and lordly Apollo,
as now certain it is, this day brings bane to the Argives."
     So among them spoke Hektor; the Trojans shouted approval.
First, unhitching the sweat-drenched horses from under the harness,
close to his chariot each man tethered his team by their halters;
545 then for the meal they brought from the city the cattle and fat sheep,
going in haste, and provided the wine, honey-hearted, for drinking,
out of their houses, and victuals, and piled up plentiful firewood.
To the immortals they offered up hecatombs full and effective;
up from the plain to the sky their savor was borne by the breezes;
550 sweet were the fumes; yet nothing of them did the fortunate gods share,

nor were they minded, for sacred Ilion so they detested,
Priam as well, and the people of Priam the excellent spearman.
     Pondering mighty resolve, right there by the battle embankments
all through the night they sat, and their fires burned many and brilliant.
555 As at a time that the stars in heaven surrounding the shining
moon are themselves bright shining, when high in the air it is windless,
so that the lookout places appear, and the lofty escarpments,
and the ravines, and the measureless air breaks open from heaven—
all of the stars can be seen; in his spirit the shepherd rejoices—
560 just so now were, between those ships and the streams of the Xanthos
there before Ilion, shining the fires that the Trojans had kindled.
Over the plain were a thousand fires now burning, and fifty
Trojans were sitting beside each one in the glow of the firelight.
There too, feeding upon white barley and oats, were the horses
565 close to the chariots standing; the fair-throned Dawn they awaited.

BOOK 9

So were the Trojans holding their watch; meanwhile the Achaians
marvelous Panic was holding, the comrade of shivering Terror;
with an unbearable sorrow were all of the best men stricken.
Just as the fish-thronged seaway is stirred to commotion as two winds
5 blowing from Thrace, both Zephyr and Boreas, west wind and north wind,
suddenly come down hard in a squall, and at once is a black wave
reared to a crest, and it scatters the seaweed out on the seashore,
so in the breasts of the Achaians the spirits were now lacerated.
    Stricken at heart with enormous anguish the scion of Atreus
10 went about giving command to the clear-voiced heralds that they should
summon the host to assembly and call each man by his own name,
not with a loud outcry; then he himself toiled with the foremost.
They sat down in assembly, dispirited; then Agamemnon
stood among them, and he poured out tears like a dark-water fountain
15 which pours down a precipitous rock its shadowy water;
heavily groaning, he spoke and addressed these words to the Argives:
"Oh dear friends and companions, the Argives' leaders and princes,
Zeus son of Kronos has mightily bound me in grievous derangement,
cruel and harsh—he before made promise and nodded agreement
20 after I ransacked strong-walled Ilion I would return home;
now instead he has plotted an evil deception and bids me
go back to Argos dishonored when I have lost many people.
Thus no doubt to all-powerful Zeus it will be very pleasing,
who already has ruined the citadels in many cities—
25 yes, and yet more will he ruin, for his is the mightiest power.
But come, just as I say, let all of us heed and obey it:
let us take flight with our ships to the much-loved land of our fathers,
since there is hope no longer that wide-wayed Troy we will capture."
    So did he say; then all of the people were hushed in silence.
30 Now a long time the dispirited sons of Achaians were voiceless;

finally spoke out among them the crier of war Diomédes:
"Scion of Atreus, first will I fight against you in your folly—
so is it right, Lord, here in assembly—be not at all angered.
Mine was the valor you slighted the first among Dánaän fighters,
35 saying I am unwarlike and valorless—all of these things are
known to the Argives, both to the young men and to the elders;
halfway the scion of Kronos of crooked devices endowed you,
granted to you to be honored beyond all men with the scepter;
valor he did not grant you, the might that is finest and greatest.
40 Strange man, do you suppose in fact that the sons of Achaians
really are such unwarlike and valorless men as you call them?
If in yourself your heart is so eager to go back homeward,
go, for the road is before you, and down by the sea are your galleys
standing, the many that followed along with you here from Mykénè.
45 Nevertheless, these others will stay, these long-haired Achaians,
right to the time we have ransacked Troy; nay, even if they should
now take flight with their ships to the much-loved land of their fathers,
we two will wage war, I and Lord Sthénelos, till we discover
Ilion's limit of doom, for we came here with a god's favor."
50   So he spoke, and the sons of Achaians all shouted approval,
marveling much at the words of the tamer of steeds Diomédes.
Standing among them, thus spoke out to them Nestor the horseman:
"Tydeus' son, beyond others are you most mighty in battle,
and among all of the men your age you are best in the council;
55 surely will no one of all the Achaians belittle the word you
speak or gainsay it; but you have not come to your speech's conclusion.
You are indeed quite young, and a child of my own you could even
be, and the latest in birth; yet thoughtful advice you address these
kings of the Argives, since you have said what is fitting and proper.
60 But come, I who declare myself to be older than you will
speak out now and review the whole matter, and nobody here will
scorn what I say, not even the powerful lord Agamemnon.
Out of his clan and an outlaw without any hearth is a man who
longs for the brute chill horror of battle among his own people.
65 Nevertheless, let us now pay heed to the darkness of nighttime—
let us prepare our dinner, and let each band of the guards take
stations along the wide trench that we dug outside of the rampart.
This is the charge I lay on the young men; but in the next place,
Atreus' son, you take the command, since you are most kingly.
70 Furnish the elders a feast—it is fitting and never unseemly.

Surely your cabins are full of the wine that the ships of Achaians
carry to you each day out of Thrace and across the wide seaway;
all hospitality you have at hand—you are lord over many.
In an assembly of many, the one you will heed is the man who
75 counsels the shrewdest advice; very much now all the Achaians
need what is soundest and best, for the enemies close to the ships are
kindling numerous fires, and at that what man would be gladdened?
This is the night that will either destroy our army or save it."
     So did he say; they carefully listened to him and obeyed him;
80 straightway out of assembly the sentinels rushed in their armor,
some around Nestor's son Thrasymédes the shepherd of people,
some with Askálaphos and with Iálmenos, scions of Ares,
some with Deïpyros, others with Mérionés and Aphàreus,
some around Kreion's scion, the excellent lord Lykomédes.
85 Seven in all were the sentinels' leaders; with each were a hundred
young men striding along, in their hands all carrying long spears;
out between rampart and trench they went to the middle and sat down;
there they kindled a fire, and they each made ready their supper.
     Atreus' son then led the Achaians' cohort of elders
90 into his cabin and set before them a heart-gladdening dinner.
They put forth eager hands to partake of the food lying ready.
When they had quite satisfied their appetites, drinking and eating,
first of them all who started to weave plans then was the old man
Nestor—before this too his advice had been seen to be noblest;
95 he with benevolent wisdom addressed them, giving them counsel:
"Atreus' glorious son Agamemnon, lord of the people,
it is with you I will end and with you will begin, for to many
people are you their lord, and to you Zeus granted the royal
scepter and power of judgment, that you take counsel for their sake.
100 So too you above all must utter your words and must listen,
also achieve for another whatever his heart should demand that
he speak out for the good, for on you will depend what he broaches.
Therefore will I now speak in the way I think is the best one.
No man else will devise any thought that is better than this is,
105 which in mind I have had long since and indeed even now have,
ever since, Zeus-sprung lord, that maiden, the daughter of Bríseus,
you went after and seized from the cabin of angry Achilles,
not in accordance with our wills at all. For indeed I attempted
strongly to talk you around; but you, to your greathearted temper
110 yielding, dishonored the mightiest man, whom the very immortals

honor, by taking and keeping his prize; yet nevertheless now
still let us take thought how to conciliate him and persuade him,
giving him generous gifts and addressing him words of appeasement."
    Answering him then spoke Agamemnon, lord of the people:
115 "Old sir, not at all false is your story about my delusion.
I was deluded—I cannot deny it myself now, for many
people is that man worth whom Zeus in his heart loves deeply,
just as he honors him now, and the host of Achaians he beats down.
But since I was deluded by trusting to miserable passion,
120 now I want to redress it and give unmeasured requital.
Here in the midst of you all, these glorious gifts I will name off:
tripods, seven unsmirched by the fire, ten talents of fine gold,
glittering cauldrons, twenty in all, and as well twelve horses,
strong prizewinners who gain with their swift feet prizes for racing.
125 Certainly not without riches would be any man who had that much,
nor would he be at all lacking in gold much-honored and cherished,
such great prizes for me have been won by the single-hoofed horses.
I will give women of Lesbos, in faultless handiwork skilled, those
seven whom I, at the time he himself took well-built Lesbos,
130 chose for myself, in their beauty surpassing the races of women.
These will I give, and among them the girl that I then took away from
him, that daughter of Bríseus; a great oath too I will swear him,
never did I get into her bed, nor with her did I mingle,
as is the natural custom of people, of men and of women.
135 All these things will be his straightway; but again if the gods should
grant us later to capture and sack the great city of Priam,
then let him heap in his galleys the gold and the bronze in abundance,
entering in at the time the Achaians are sharing the plunder,
then also for himself twenty women of Troy let him choose out,
140 those who are all the most beautiful ones after Helen of Argos.
Should we return to Achaian Argos, the bounteous land, my
son-in-law he may be—I will honor him then like Orestes,
who as my late-born son has been reared in the greatest abundance.
Three are the daughters I have in the well-built halls of my palace,
145 first Chrysóthemis, next Laódikè, Íphianássa
last; and of them let him lead whichever he likes without bride-price
homeward to Peleus' house; then too I will give him a dowry,
such great presents as no man yet ever gave with a daughter.
Seven in all are the well-inhabited towns I will give him,
150 Kárdamylè, then Énopè also, and Hirè the grassy,

sacred Phérai as well, Antheía of deep rich meadows,
lovely Aipeía, and finally Pédasos, wealthy in vineyards.
All these lie near the sea, at the limits of sandy-soiled Pylos;
therein do men live wealthy in cattle and wealthy in sheep flocks,
155   so with their offerings as to a god they will render him honor,
under his scepter will they bring prosperous laws to fulfillment.
These things I will accomplish for him, if he ceases from anger.
Let him but yield—ungentle and ever unyielding is Hades;
therefore of all of the gods is he the most hated by mortals—
160   let him be subject to me, inasmuch as I am the more kingly,
then also as I claim to be older than he in my birth date."
        Speaking to him then answered the horseman Gerenian Nestor:
"Atreus' glorious son Agamemnon, lord of the people,
not to be scorned any more are the gifts you give Lord Achilles;
165   but come, let us select and dispatch men so that they quickly
make their way to the cabin of Peleus' scion Achilles.
Rather, the ones whom I will select, let them be persuaded.
First of them all, let Phoinix belovèd of Zeus be the leader,
going along with him then, great Ajax and noble Odysseus,
170   then as the heralds let Odios follow them, and Eurybátes.
Bring us the water for washing our hands; bid all to be silent,
so that we may pray Zeus son of Kronos, if he will have pity."
        So did he say, and the word he spoke pleased all of the nobles.
Heralds at once poured over their hands clean water for washing;
175   young men filled to the brim great wine bowls, ready for drinking,
then poured wine into all of the cups to begin the observance.
When they had made libation and drunk whatever their hearts wished,
they set forth from the cabin of Atreus' son Agamemnon.
Many a charge they heard from the horseman Gerenian Nestor,
180   who looked closely at each, at Odysseus more than the others,
bidding them try to win over the faultless scion of Peleus.
        Those two went by the shore of the deep sea booming and roaring,
uttering many a prayer to the holder and shaker of earth that
easily they would persuade the great spirit of Aíakos' scion.
185   Then when they had arrived at the Mýrmidons' cabins and galleys,
there they found him pleasing his heart by playing a clear-toned
lyre of elaborate beauty, upon it a bridge made of silver,
which he took from the spoil when he ruined Eëtion's city;
pleasing his spirit with this he sang of men's glorious actions.
190   Opposite him was Patróklos alone there, sitting in silence,

waiting for Aíakos' scion, until he should leave off singing.
Both of the men came forward, and noble Odysseus was leading,
then they stood before him; in astonishment leapt up Achilles
holding the lyre still, leaving the seat where he had been sitting.
195 So in the same way Patróklos, when he too saw the men, stood up.
Greeting the two men, thus spoke forth swift-footed Achilles:
"Welcome! As friends indeed you have come here—great must the need be—
who even now in my wrath are the dearest among the Achaians."
     So he addressed them, and then they were led by noble Achilles
200 into the cabin and seated on couches and covers of purple;
straightway then he spoke to Patróklos, who was beside him:
"Son of Menoítios, set out a mixing bowl that is larger,
mix up drink that is stronger, and pour it in each of the goblets,
since these men who are under my roof are to me far the dearest."
205   So he spoke, and Patróklos obeyed his belovèd companion.
There in the light of the fire he at once threw down a great wood-block,
then laid upon it the back of a sheep and the back of a fat goat,
also upon it the chine of a huge hog, mottled with rich lard.
These Autómedon held; they were carved by noble Achilles;
210 after he skillfully sliced them, on spits he skewered the pieces;
quickly the godlike son of Menoítios made the fire blaze up.
But then, after the fire burned down and the flame was abated,
spreading apart the hot embers, the spits he extended above them,
onto the andirons set them, and sprinkled the meat with divine salt.
215 But then, after he roasted the morsels and heaped them on platters,
taking the bread, on the table Patróklos set out the portions
piled in beautiful baskets; the meat was served by Achilles.
He was himself then seated across from the godlike Odysseus,
next to the opposite wall; his comrade Patróklos he bade to
220 make sacrifice to the gods; on the fire he cast the first morsels.
They put forth eager hands to partake of the food lying ready.
When they had quite satisfied their appetites, drinking and eating,
Ajax nodded to Phoinix, and noble Odysseus observed it;
filling a goblet with wine, he lifted it, pledging Achilles:
225 "Greetings, Achilles! Of equally shared feasts we are not lacking
either indeed in the cabin of Atreus' son Agamemnon
or right now in your own, since here there is much heart-pleasing
food for a feast; but delightful feasting is not our concern now
but the enormous affliction, belovèd of Zeus, that we look on
230 and are afraid: it is doubtful if we will be able to save our

well-benched ships or will lose them, unless you put on your valor.
For quite close to the ships and the cabins have set their encampment
all of the high-souled Trojans and far-famed allies in battle,
kindling many a fire on the plain; they are saying that they not
235 yet any longer will be held off but will fall on the black ships.
Zeus son of Kronos is showing his omens for them on the right hand,
hurling his lightning; and Hektor is hugely exulting in strength and
furiously rampaging, confiding in Zeus, and he shows no
honor to men or to gods, for the powerful rage is upon him.
240 He now prays that the glorious Dawn will appear very quickly,
since he threatens to cut off the high sternposts of our galleys,
burn up the ships themselves with a violent fire, and beside them
kill the Achaians as we by the smoke have been stricken to panic.
All these things I dreadfully fear in my heart, that the threats he
245 utters the gods may achieve, that for us our destiny be to
perish at once in Troy, faraway from horse-nourishing Argos.
Up then, should you perhaps be inclined, even though it is late, to
rescue the sons of Achaians fatigued by the tumult of Trojans.
Later, on you yourself the affliction will come—no relief by
250 healing is found for an evil inflicted; but rather before that
take thought how you may keep from the Dánaäns that day of evil.
Dear friend, such was the charge that your own father Peleus gave you,
that same day that from Phthia to join Agamemnon he sent you:
'My dear son, invincible might will Athena and Hera
255 give you, if they be willing; but you hold back the greathearted
temper inside of your breast, for benevolent kindness is better.
Keep from contention, deviser of evil, in order that you be
honored the more by the Argives, the young men as well as the elders.'
So the old man charged—you have forgotten; but even now do you
260 bring to a halt, let go of heart-anguishing wrath; Agamemnon
offers you valuable presents if you will but cease from your anger.
Come now, listen to me if you will; I will tell you the whole tale,
all of the gifts Agamemnon promised to you in his cabin:
tripods, seven unsmirched by the fire, ten talents of fine gold,
265 glittering cauldrons, twenty in all, and as well twelve horses,
strong prizewinners who gain with their swift feet prizes for racing.
Certainly not without riches would be any man who had that much,
nor would he be at all lacking in gold much-honored and cherished,
prizes so great Agamemnon's horses have won with their swift feet.
270 He will give women of Lesbos, in faultless handiwork skilled, those

seven whom he, at the time you yourself took well-built Lesbos,
chose for himself, in their beauty surpassing the races of women.
These he will give, and among them the girl that he then took away from
you, that daughter of Bríseus; a great oath too he will swear you,

275 never did he get into her bed, nor with her did he mingle,
as, lord, it is the natural custom of men and of women.
All these things will be yours straightway; but again if the gods should
grant us later to capture and sack the great city of Priam,
then you may heap in your galleys the gold and the bronze in abundance,

280 entering in at the time the Achaians are sharing the plunder,
then also for yourself twenty women of Troy you may choose out,
those who are all the most beautiful ones after Helen of Argos.
Should we return to Achaian Argos, the bounteous land, his
son-in-law you may be—he will honor you then like Orestes,

285 who as his late-born son has been reared in the greatest abundance.
Three are the daughters he has in the well-built halls of his palace,
first Chrysóthemis, next Laódikè, Íphianássa
last—and of them you may lead whichever you like without bride-price
homeward to Peleus' house; then too he will give you a dowry,

290 such great presents as no man yet ever gave with a daughter.
Seven in all are the well-inhabited towns he will give you,
Kárdamylè, then Énopè also, and Hirè the grassy,
sacred Phérai as well, Antheía of deep rich meadows,
lovely Aipeía, and finally Pédasos, wealthy in vineyards.

295 All these lie near the sea, at the limits of sandy-soiled Pylos;
therein do men live wealthy in cattle and wealthy in sheep flocks,
so with their offerings as to a god they will render you honor,
under your scepter will they bring prosperous laws to fulfillment.
These things he will accomplish for you, if you cease from your anger.

300 But if the scion of Atreus is hated too much in your spirit,
both himself and his presents, then all of the other Achaians
pity as they are worn down, the whole army of them: they will honor
you as a god; for among them would you win very great glory.
Hektor you might now kill, since he would approach very near you,

305 gripped by a rage so destructive, for he says no one at all is
equal to him among Dánaän men brought here in the galleys."
        Answering him in return spoke forth swift-footed Achilles:
"Zeus-sprung son of Laértes, Odysseus of many devices,
now indeed unsparingly I must speak out my purpose,

310 what in fact I am thinking and how it will come to fulfillment,

166

lest you wheedle me, sitting by me one side or the other.
Equally hateful to me as are Hades' gates is the man who
keeps one thing concealed in his mind while saying another.
Therefore will I now speak in the way I think is the best one:
315   I do not think Agamemnon, Atreus' son, will persuade me,
nor will the rest of the Dánaäns here, since there was no thanks for
fighting against those enemy men incessantly, always.
Equal the portion for one who holds back and for one who fights boldly;
one same honor is given the cowardly man and the noble;
320   both alike perish, the man who does much and the man who does nothing.
Profit remains for me none, when pains in my heart I have suffered,
always setting my life at hazard in fighting a battle.
Just as a mother bird brings back home to her unfledged nestlings
mouthfuls whenever she finds them, although for herself it goes badly,
325   so for myself: there was many a night I passed without sleeping,
bloody with gore were the days I spent then, fighting in battle,
waging a war with the enemy host for the sake of their women.
Twelve are the cities of people that I ransacked with my galleys,
then on the land I claim in the soil-rich Troäd eleven;
330   out of them all, their treasures of wealth so many and noble
I stripped; then I would bring all those here to give Agamemnon,
Atreus' son; he, staying behind by the swift-sailing galleys,
took them, and then he would share out a few, while he would keep many.
Some, it is true, he granted as prizes to nobles and princes;
335   they remain firm for those men; and among the Achaians, he took mine
only and holds my affectionate bedmate—let him rejoice in
lying beside her! But why do the Argives need to be fighting
Trojans? And why did he gather together and lead here an army,
Atreus' son? Was it not for the sake of the fair-haired Helen?
340   Are they alone among men who are mortal in loving their bedmates,
Atreus' sons? Since whatever man is both noble and thoughtful
loves her who is his own, and he cherishes her, so did I too
love her deep in my heart, though she of my spear was a captive.
Now, since out of my hands he has taken my prize and deceived me,
345   let him not try me who know him so well—he will never persuade me.
Rather, Odysseus, together with you and the rest of the princes,
let him take thought of the way to keep ravening fire from the galleys.
Much hard labor, indeed, has he done while I have been absent—
ramparts he has constructed, a trench he has driven about them
350   broad and enormous, and there within it sharp stakes he has planted;

but not thus is he able to hold man-slaughtering Hektor's
strength back. During the time I battled among the Achaians,
never did Hektor desire so far from his walls to rouse battle,
only as far would he come as the Skaian Gates and the oak tree;
355   there he met me alone once and barely escaped from my onslaught.
Now then, as I do not want to do battle with excellent Hektor,
victims to Zeus and to all of the gods I will offer tomorrow;
well I will load my galleys when I drag them to the sea-brine;
you will be witnessing, should you desire to and should it concern you,
360   all of my ships set sail on the Hellespont teeming with fishes
early at dawn, with the men on board most eager to row them.
So if the glorious shaker of earth grants me a good voyage,
soon, on the third day, I will arrive in Phthia the fertile.
Much I have that I left to come hither, a cursèd adventure;
365   yet more riches from here, fine gold, red-glistening bronzes,
women as well, fair-girdled, and silver-gray iron, will I take
home that I got as my portion; and as for my prize, he who gave it
has outrageously taken it back now, strong Agamemnon,
Atreus' son. So report to him all this, just as I tell you,
370   openly, so that the other Achaians as well may be angry,
should he perhaps hope some other Dánaän he may deceive yet,
he who is always appareled in shamelessness; but he would not,
currish indeed though he is, endure to look me in the face now;
neither will I share counsel with him at all, nor any action,
375   since he deceived me sorely and injured me. Never again may
he with his speeches beguile me; enough for him; but of his own will
let him be damned, for his mind Zeus Counselor wholly has stolen.
Hateful to me are his presents—the worth of a hair I esteem them.
Not if he gave ten times, not twenty, as much are all those
380   goods which now he possesses, and others he added from elsewhere,
even such riches as come to Orchómenos, or to Egyptian
Thebes, where enormous treasures of wealth lie stored in the houses,
whose gates number a hundred, and out of each one of the gates two
hundred men with their horses and chariots sally to battle,
385   not if he gave me as many as sand and as many as dust are,
not even so Agamemnon would touch my heart or persuade it,
till the full measure he pays me back of heart-anguishing outrage.
Nor will I marry the daughter of Atreus' son Agamemnon,
not even if Aphrodítè the golden she rival in beauty,
390   or in the work of her hands she be equal to bright-eyed Athena,

not even so will I wed her; another Achaian let him choose,
one who befits him better and who is more kingly than I am.
For if the gods should save me and I should arrive in my homeland,
Peleus then will himself start seeking a wife for me, surely.

395   Many Achaian women there are throughout Hellas and Pthia,
daughters of noblemen who of the citadels are the defenders;
any of them, whichever I choose, I will make my dear bedmate.
There very often my valorous heart kept urging me on to
take in marriage a bedmate, a wife who suited my fancy,

400   and to enjoy the possessions that old man Peleus gathered,
for to my thought not equal the value of life are the riches
they say Ilion gathered, the well-inhabited city,
formerly, during the peace, before sons of Achaians had come here,
nor those that are enclosed by the stone threshold of the archer

405   Phoibos Apollo, within his precincts in rock-strewn Pytho.
For by pillage are cattle and fine fat sheep to be gotten,
tripods are won by trading, and so too tawny-maned horses;
neither by pillage or trade will a man's life ever be coming
back any more, once over the fence of his teeth it has left him.

410   For my own mother, the goddess Thetis of silvery feet, has
told me that twofold fates to my death's finality bear me:
should I remain here fighting against this city of Trojans,
lost is my homeward return, but never will perish my glory;
should I return back home to the much-loved land of my fathers,

415   lost is my excellent glory, but then long years of a lifetime
I will enjoy, nor will death's finality come to me quickly.
Then moreover, to all of the others would I give counsel
now to sail back home, since you will not be discovering steep-built
Ilion's limit of doom; for indeed wide-thundering Zeus holds

420   over the city his hand, and the people are greatly emboldened.
But now you, going back, to the noblest among the Achaians
tell this message of mine—since such is the right of the elders—
so in their minds they may then take thought of another and better
scheme that would save their galleys as well as the host of Achaians

425   here by the hollow galleys, for useless to them has proved this one
which now they have devised on account of my wrathful resentment.
Yet let Phoinix remain beside us, lie down to his sleep here,
so that tomorrow with me to the much-loved fatherland he may
go in the ships, if he wishes, but not by force will I take him."

430   So did he say; then all of the nobles were hushed in silence,

marveling much at his words; for indeed he had strongly refused them.
Finally spoke among them old Phoinix the chariot-driver;
tears burst forth from his eyes, as he feared for the ships of the Achaians:
"If in your mind you truly are pondering, brilliant Achilles,
435 going back home, nor at all are you willing to keep the destructive
fire from the swift ships, since on your heart such anger has fallen,
how without you, dear child, shall I then be left in this country
all by myself? For with you old Peleus the chariot-driver
sent me the day that from Phthia to Lord Agamemnon he sent you
440 still but a child, not yet very skilled in the leveling combat,
neither as yet in the council, in which men come to distinction.
Therefore did he send me to instruct you in all of these matters;
you were to be both a speaker of words and a doer of actions.
So without you, dear child, I would not want now to be left back
445 here all alone, even if some god were to promise himself that,
scraping away old age, he would make me a vigorous stripling,
as at the time that I first left Hellas of beautiful women,
fleeing from strife with my father Amýntor, Órmenos' scion;
he was then angry at me on account of a fair-haired mistress   .
450 whom he himself made love to, and thus dishonored his bedmate,
my own mother, who always was clasping my knees and imploring
me with the mistress to lie, so the old man she would find loathsome.
Her I obeyed, and I did it; at once my father, suspecting,
cursed me strongly, the hateful Erínyes calling upon me,
455 praying that he on his knees would never be setting a dear child
who by me was begotten; the gods have accomplished the curses,
Zeus of the regions beneath and Perséphone honored and dreaded.
I with myself took counsel to murder him then with the sharp bronze,
nevertheless an immortal restrained my wrath, in my spirit
460 putting the voice of the people, the many reproaches of mankind,
so that a parricide men would not call me among the Achaians.
Then no way would the heart in my breast yet longer be kept back
still to be tarrying there in the halls of a father so angry.
Many a plea, indeed, did the kinsmen and cousins about me
465 utter in supplication to keep me there in the palace;
many the fine fat sheep and the swing-paced crooked-horned cattle
they then slaughtered, and many the swine too, swelling with rich fat,
they stretched over the fire of Hephaistos, singeing the hair off.
Much moreover was drunk of the wine from the jars of the old man.
470 Nine nights there around me they kept on sleeping the whole night,

changing about in the watches they kept, so that never the fires were
quenched, one under the portico out in the well-walled courtyard,
there in the forecourt another, in front of the doors of my chamber.
Nevertheless, when the tenth night murky and dark came upon me,
475 finally then, having broken the close-fitted doors of the chamber,
I got out and at once jumped over the wall of the courtyard
easily, quite unseen by the guards and the women-attendants.
Then I fled faraway, through the great broad spaces of Hellas,
finally coming to Phthia the fertile, the mother of sheep flocks,
480 into Lord Peleus' house; he received me gladly and kindly,
even his love he gave me, as much as a father would love his
only and late-born son who was heir to his many possessions;
wealthy indeed he made me, and numerous people he gave me;
out at the limits of Phthia I dwelt, the Dolopians' ruler.
485 Such as you are, I reared you to manhood, godlike Achilles,
loving you deep in my heart, since neither with anyone else you
wanted to go to a feast nor to eat any meal in the palace
ever, until on my knees I sat you and gave you your fill of
morsels of meat I cut for you first, and the wine I presented.
490 Many a time you wetted the tunic I wore on my chest when
you in your mischievous childishness would sputter the wine out.
Thus for your sake I have suffered so much and have labored so greatly,
mindful of this, that the gods would in no way bring into being
offspring from me; but I wanted to make you, godlike Achilles,
495 my child, so you may someday guard me from shameful destruction.
Come then, Achilles, subdue your great spirit—a pitiless heart is
not what you should be holding; the gods themselves can be altered,
greater indeed as they are in excellence, honor, and power;
yes, even them, with the fragrance of incense and prayers of appeasement,
500 with libations and offering-smoke, men turn from their anger,
raising their supplications, when someone errs and transgresses.
Then too there are the Prayers, those daughters of Zeus almighty,
halting of foot, with their visages wrinkled, askance in their glances,
who take care to be following after accursèd Delusion.
505 Strong is Delusion, and swift on her feet; therefore she can outrun
all of the others by far; all over the world in advance she
baffles and injures the people; the Prayers bring remedy later.
He who reveres those daughters of Zeus whenever they come near,
him they benefit much, and they heed him when he is praying;
510 he who denies those Prayers and who stiffly refuses to hear them,

going to Kronos' son Zeus, they plead that accursèd Delusion
follow the man, so that he, soon baffled, will pay his requital.
You too, Achilles, allow to attend those daughters of Zeus such
honor as bends the intentions of others as well who are noble.
515 For if he did not proffer you gifts and name others for later,
Atreus' son, but were always swollen with violent rancor,
not even I would be bidding you now to get rid of your anger
and to defend these Argives, although they needed you sorely.
Many he offers at once now, and more he has promised for later,
520 then too he has sent here to implore you the best of the men whom
he from the host of Achaians selected, and who to yourself are
dearest among the Argives: so do not dishonor their speeches
nor their journey—before, not at all you were blamed, being angry.
So from an earlier time we have heard of the glorious deeds of
525 men who were heroes, whenever on one of them violent wrath came—
gifts those men would accept, by speeches would they be persuaded.
This is a deed I remember myself—it is old and not recent—
just how it was: and among you all who are friends, I will tell it.
Once Kourétes were fighting Aitolians, staunch in the battle,
530 close around Kálydon city, and they were destroying each other;
pleasant Kálydon were the Aitolians hotly defending,
while the Kourétes were eager to ransack the city in battle.
For a great evil had gold-throned Artemis roused at the people,
angry that Oíneus did not offer to her in his plentiful orchard
535 firstfruits, whereas the rest of the gods on a hecatomb feasted;
only to her, that daughter of great Zeus, nothing he offered,
either forgetting or never intending, deluded in spirit.
Then in her anger the offspring of Zeus, that shooter of arrows,
roused up against him a white-tusked boar, a wild dweller of grassland,
540 which wrought many an evil by ravaging Oíneus' orchard,
many the great tall trees, uprooted, it threw to the ground there,
scattering out fruit-blossoms, the roots themselves and the branches.
This wild boar Meleágros the scion of Oíneus slaughtered,
gathering hunters together from many a city, the men as
545 well as their hounds, since not with a few men he would have killed it,
so was it massive, and many it placed on the pyre of affliction.
There about it she caused much clamor and many an outcry
when the Kourétes against the Aitolians, mighty of spirit,
wrangled about the boar's head and its hide all shaggy and bristling.
550 While Meleágros belovèd of Ares was fighting against them,

so long for the Kourétes it went ill, nor were they even
able to stand firm outside the wall, although they were many;
then when upon Meleágros had come such anger as causes
minds in other men too, though thoughtful, to swell in their bosoms,
555 then he, angry at heart with his mother, belovèd Althaía,
lay at the side of the wife he had courted, the fair Kleopatra,
daughter of Euénos' child, Marpéssa of beautiful ankles,
also of Idas, the man who of all on earth was the strongest
those days, who on account of the maiden with beautiful ankles,
560 going against Lord Phoibos Apollo, had taken his bow up.
Then in the palace her father and august mother had nicknamed
her Alkýonè after a bird; for the mother herself had
shared in the plight of the sorrowful shrill kingfisher and wept when
Phoibos Apollo the great far-worker had taken her daughter.
565 With Kleopatra he lay; heart-anguishing anger he nourished,
angry because of the curses his mother had uttered in praying
many a time to the gods in grief for the death of her brother;
many a time with her hands the much-nurturing earth she had beaten,
calling on Hades and on Perséphonè honored and dreaded,
570 kneeling to them, with her tears bedrenching the folds of her bosom,
that to her son they would soon give death; and a mother's Erínys
walking in shadows, relentless in spirit, from Érebos heard her.
Quickly around their gates did a tumult arise, and the noise of
ramparts battered and smashed; straightway the Aitolian elders,
575 sending the noblest priests of the gods, implored Meleágros
quickly to come out and aid them; and great was the present they promised:
where in delightful Kálydon's plain its soil was the fattest,
there they bade him to choose the most beautiful place for his holdings—
fifty his measures of land, and of these one half would be vineyard,
580 half would be cleared, cut out of the plain to be arable farmland.
Many a time old Oíneus the chariot-driver implored him,
going to stand on the threshold of his high-vaulted apartment,
shaking the doors, well jointed, and his own son supplicating;
many a time his sisters implored him, and so did his august
585 mother, and yet much more he refused them, and many a time his
comrades who among all were devoted the most, were the dearest;
nevertheless, not that way the heart in his breast they persuaded,
not till his chamber was fiercely attacked, the Kourétes were climbing
up on the towers and setting the whole great city to burning.
590 Finally then his bedmate of beautiful girdle began with

173

sorrowing tears to implore Meleágros, and all the afflictions
which come over a people whose city is taken she reckoned:
they then slaughter the men, fire burns the whole city to ashes,
foreigners lead away captive the children and deep-girdled women.
595   Then was his heart stirred up as he heard about such evildoings;
he set forth, and he put on his body his glittering armor.
From the Aitolians thus he warded the day of affliction,
yielding to his own heart; no more those gifts they would give him
many and pleasing, and yet even so he warded off evil.
600   But in your mind do not think such things, and do not let a god turn
you into that path, my dear friend; it would be even harder
warding them off when the galleys are burning; but now for the gifts go
forth straightway—then you like a god the Achaians will honor;
but if the battle, destroyer of men, you enter without gifts,
605   you will no longer be honored the same, though warding off battle."
        Answering him in return spoke forth swift-footed Achilles:
"Phoinix, my dear old papa, belovèd of Zeus, I do not need
honor like this; I think by the purpose of Zeus I am honored,
which by the well-curved galleys will hold me as long as the life-breath
610   keeps its strength in my breast and my knees have vigor for action.
Something else I will tell you, and you keep this in your mind now:
do not confound the resolve of my heart by lamenting and grieving,
doing a favor for Atreus' scion, the hero; you must not
love him at all, so as not to be hated by me who love you.
615   Good it is rather with me to afflict someone who afflicts me.
Equal to me be king, and partake of the half of my honor;
these will deliver my message, but you stay here for your slumber
now in a soft warm bed; and together, at earliest daybreak,
we will decide whether we should return to our country or stay here."
620   So he spoke; with his brows, to Patróklos he silently nodded
thick soft bedding to spread out for Phoinix, that quickly the men would
take thought to go back home from his cabin; but uttering these words
Ajax the godlike scion of Télamon spoke and addressed them:
"Zeus-sprung son of Laërtes, Odysseus of many devices,
625   let us depart, for I think that the aim of our speeches and journey
hither will not be accomplished; and we must carry the message
back to the Dánaäns quickly—although it is certainly not good—
who I suppose are now sitting and waiting for it. But Achilles
has inside of his breast made savage the greathearted temper,
630   obstinate man, and he does not care for the love of his comrades,

174

that with which beyond others we honored him there by the galleys,
pitiless one!—since often a man will accept from his brother's
killer a blood-price, or even indeed for a son who was murdered,
then in his country the killer remains, a great penalty paying,
635 while in the other are bridled the heart and the valorous temper
once he has taken the blood-price. But evil and obdurate is this
temper the gods put into your breast on account of a single
maiden, but we now offer you seven, the noblest selection,
many another gift too; make gracious the temper within you,
640 show your respect for your house, since under your roof we have come here
out of the Dánaäns' host, and are eager beyond any others
to be the nearest to you and the dearest of all the Achaians."
    Answering him in return spoke forth swift-footed Achilles:
"Ajax the Zeus-sprung scion of Télamon, marshal of people,
645 all these things you seem to have said in accord with my spirit,
yet my heart becomes swollen with anger whenever I think of
this, among Argives what an indignity I have been done by
Atreus' son, as if I were a person dishonored and outcast.
But now you go back there and plainly deliver my message,
650 since no sooner will I take thought of the bloody encounter
ever, until noble Hektor the son of the war-skilled Priam
finally shall have arrived at the Mýrmidons' cabins and galleys,
killing the Argive host, and with fire have burned up the galleys.
There then around my cabin and my black galley I think that
655 Hektor will be held back, though eager he be for the battle."
    He spoke; they, having each one taken a two-handled cup and
poured a libation, returned by the galleys; Odysseus was leading.
Meanwhile Patróklos directed the comrades and women-attendants
quickly as possible thick soft bedding to spread out for Phoinix.
660 They in obedience spread out the bedding the way he had told them,
fleeces beneath, and a rug, and a fine soft cover of linen.
There the old man lay down and awaited the glorious morning.
But in a nook of his well-built cabin Achilles was sleeping,
lying beside him there was a woman whom he had from Lesbos
665 taken away, fair-cheeked Diomédè the daughter of Phorbas.
But on the other side lay down Patróklos, and likewise beside him
fair-girdled Iphis, a girl whom noble Achilles had given
him upon capturing steep-built Skyros, Enýeus' city.
    But then, when they arrived at the cabins of Atreus' scion,
670 there straightway with the gold-wrought goblets the sons of Achaians

stood one side and the other and pledged them, asking them questions;
first then questioned the men Agamemnon, lord of the people:
"Come, tell me, the Achaians' renown, much-honored Odysseus,
whether to ward off ravening fire from the ships he is minded,
675 or he refuses, and wrath is still holding his greathearted spirit."
    Then spoke answering him much-suffering noble Odysseus:
"Atreus' glorious son Agamemnon, lord of the people,
no, that man is not minded to quench his wrath, but is yet more
filled with his rage than before, and rejects both you and your presents.
680 As for yourself, he bids you to take thought now with the Argives
how you may save our galleys as well as the host of Achaians;
but as for him, he threatens, tomorrow at earliest daybreak
down to the sea he will drag his well-benched tractable galleys.
Then he declared that to all of the others would he give counsel
685 now to sail back home, since you will not be discovering steep-built
Ilion's limit of doom, for indeed wide-thundering Zeus holds
over the city his hand, and the people are greatly emboldened.
So he spoke; there are these men also to tell it who went with
me there, Ajax and our two heralds, the both of them thoughtful.
690 There old Phoinix is resting, for thus did Achilles command him,
so that tomorrow with him to the much-loved fatherland he may
go in the ships if he wishes; but not by force will he take him."
    So did he say, then all of the people were hushed in silence,
marveling much at his words; for indeed he had strongly addressed them.
695 Now a long time the dispirited sons of Achaians were voiceless;
finally spoke out among them the crier of war Diomédes:
"Atreus' glorious son Agamemnon, lord of the people,
would you had not supplicated the faultless scion of Peleus,
giving him numberless gifts; even otherwise he is most haughty;
700 yet much further have you now into his haughtiness thrust him.
Nevertheless, let us leave him alone now, whether he goes or
whether he stays; and again sometime he will battle, whenever
deep in his breast his spirit commands him and some god stirs him.
But come, just as I say, let all of us heed and obey it:
705 now lie down to your rest, once we have delighted our hearts with
victuals and wine, for in them there is vigorous spirit and valor.
But then, soon as the Dawn shines forth, rose-fingered and lovely,
straightway in front of the galleys array both people and horses,
urging them on, and yourself with the foremost enter the battle."
710   So he spoke, and the rest of the kings all gave their approval,

marveling much at the words of the tamer of steeds Diomédes.
Then having poured libations they went each one to his cabin;
there they lay down to rest and accepted the present of slumber.

BOOK 10

There by the ships were the others, the noblest of all the Achaians,
sleeping the whole night through, and subdued in a soft mild slumber;
but upon Atreus' son Agamemnon, shepherd of people,
no sweet slumber had seized—many things in his spirit he pondered.
5 As at a time that the husband of fair-tressed Hera is flashing
lightning to ready a great unspeakable rain or a hailstorm,
or a fierce blizzard of snow, when snowflakes sprinkle the plowlands,
or somewhere the huge jaws of a bitter and virulent battle,
so inside of his breast Agamemnon was bitterly groaning,
10 deep down, out of his heart, and the spirit within him was trembling.
Then would the lord, as he gazed out over the plain of the Troäd,
marvel at how many fires there were before Ilion burning,
and at the sounds of the flutes and the pipes and the din of the people;
but then, when he would look at the ships and the host of Achaians
15 many a hair from his head he pulled by the root in appeal to
Zeus on high; in his glorious heart he was mightily groaning.
This is the plan which seemed to him then in his spirit the best one:
first of the men to go look for the scion of Neleus, Nestor,
hoping that he might work out with him some faultless contrivance,
20 one that for all of the Dánaäns there might ward off affliction.
So he arose, and about his chest he put on a tunic;
under his glistening feet he bound his beautiful sandals,
then he appareled himself in the tawny-haired pelt of a lion,
fire-bright, enormous, reaching his feet, and he took up a great spear.
25   Likewise shuddering seized Meneláos—for not on his eyelids
either did sleep come settling to stay—in his fear that the Argives
suffer in some way, men who across much water had come to
Troy on account of himself, and had roused bold warfare against it.
First he covered his great broad back with the skin of a leopard
30 mottled with spots, and a helmet of bronze he lifted, and placed it

onto his head; in his large strong hand he picked up a spear and
then set forth to awaken his brother, who over the Argives,
all of them, mightily ruled—as a god by the folk he was honored.
He found him putting onto his shoulders the beautiful armor
35   there by the stern of his galley, and welcome to him was his coming.
First spoke out to him then the great crier of war Meneláos:
"Why do you take arms, brother, in this way? One of your comrades
will you arouse as a spy on the Trojans? But dreadfully do I
fear that for you nobody will take on himself this action,
40   going alone against enemy fighters and spying upon them
through the ambrosial night—he will need to be most bold-hearted."
      Answering him in return then spoke forth strong Agamemnon:
"Both you and I now need, Meneláos belovèd of great Zeus,
cunning of counsel, if anyone is to preserve and defend these
45   Argives as well as the ships, for from us Zeus' heart is averted.
More upon Hektor's oblations than ours he has settled his spirit,
since not once have I seen nor have heard from another man's telling
how one man has devised in a day so many afflictions
as those Zeus-loved Hektor has wrought on the sons of Achaians
50   singly, although he is not the dear son of a god or a goddess.
Deeds he has done that I think will be sorrowful cares for the Argives
many long days—so many the evils he wrought the Achaians.
But now at once go summon Idómeneus hither, and Ajax—
rapidly run by the galleys—while I go after the noble
55   Nestor and rouse him to get out of bed, in hopes he is willing
now to go out to the sacred post of the guards and give orders.
For above all they would listen to him best, since by his own dear
son those guards are commanded, and by Idómeneus' comrade
Mérionés, for to them above all we entrusted the mission."
60   Answering him then spoke the great crier of war Meneláos:
"Well, in your words what charge do you lay upon me, and what bid me?
Shall I remain there waiting among those men until you come,
or run back after you, when well I have given the orders?"
      Answering him then spoke Agamemnon, lord of the people:
65   "Do you remain there, lest somehow we should miss one another
while we are going; for numerous paths run through the encampment.
Speak out loudly wherever you go and command them to wake up,
calling the men, each one, by the name of his clan and his father,
giving them all due honor; do not be haughty in spirit;
70   rather ourselves let us toil at the labor, for so I suppose did

Zeus upon us at our birth send down such heavy affliction."
    He spoke, sending his brother away after giving him orders.
He set forth to go out after Nestor the shepherd of people,
whom he came upon there by his cabin and near his black galley
75 in a soft bed, and beside him elaborate armor was lying;
there were the shield and as well two spears and the glittering helmet;
there lay also the shimmering belt with which the old man was
girded whenever for war, the destroyer of men, he was armored,
leading his troops, since he had not yielded to odious old age.
80 Raising himself, he leaned on an elbow, lifting his head up;
Atreus' son he addressed and in these words made his inquiry:
"Who are you, coming alone by the ships and about the encampment
through the obscure night-gloom, at a time other mortals are sleeping?
Is it for one of your mules you search, or for one of your comrades?
85 Speak, and do not come upon me silently—what do you need here?"
    Answering him then spoke Agamemnon, lord of the people:
"Nestor Neleus' son, the Achaians' preeminent glory,
you will know Atreus' son Agamemnon, whom beyond all men
Zeus has set among labors incessant, as long as the life-breath
90 keeps its strength in my breast and my knees have vigor for action.
Thus I wander because on my eyes no sweetness of slumber
settles, but I am perplexed by the war, the Achaians' distresses.
Dreadfully I am afraid for the Dánaäns, nor is my spirit
steadfast—rather am I most troubled, and out of my breast is
95 leaping my heart, and the glorious limbs are aquiver beneath me.
But if you want to do something, as neither upon you has sleep come,
let us at once go out to the sentinels, so we may see them,
lest they, quite worn out with the labor and drowsiness, have now
fallen asleep and have wholly forgotten their sentinel-duty;
100 close to us here sit men who are enemies, nor do we know if
even at night they might not eagerly wish to do battle."
    Speaking to him then answered the horseman Gerenian Nestor:
"Atreus' glorious son Agamemnon, lord of the people,
never for Hektor, in fact, Zeus Counselor will be achieving
105 all his intentions, as much as he hopes for now, but I think that
he will be striving with yet more troubles, if only Achilles
ever should turn his heart once more from its ruinous anger.
Gladly with you will I go—let us also rouse up the others,
Tydeus' scion renowned as a spearman, as well as Odysseus,
110 swift Ajax, and the valorous scion of Phyleus, Meges.

It would as well be good if a man went after and summoned
those men, the godlike Ajax, Idómeneus, lord of the Cretans,
since their ships are the farthest of all and are not at all nearby.
Yet though he is most dear and respected, the lord Meneláos
115   I will reproach, even if you will blame me—I will not hide it—
how he sleeps and has left it to you alone, doing this labor.
Now among all of the noblest should he be doing this labor,
begging them, since no more to be borne is the need that has risen."
　　Answering him then spoke Agamemnon, lord of the people:
120   "Old sir, I would myself at another time bid you rebuke him,
since he often relaxes and is not minded to labor,
not through yielding to sloth or to heedlessness in his thinking,
but through looking to me and awaiting my word of incitement;
this time, well before me he awakened and stood at my bedside;
125   I have myself just sent him to summon the men you inquire of.
Rather, let us go now; in front of the gates we will find them,
out with the sentries, for there I directed them all to assemble."
　　Speaking to him then answered the horseman Gerenian Nestor:
"Certainly thus nobody will blame him or fail to obey him,
130   none of the Argives, whenever he rouses a man and commands him."
　　So did he say, and around his chest he put on a tunic,
under his glistening feet he bound his beautiful sandals,
then with a brooch he fastened about him a mantle of purple
folded in two and capacious, the wool-nap shaggy upon it;
135   straightway, taking his powerful spear, well pointed with sharp bronze,
he set forth to the galleys of those bronze-armored Achaians.
First then it was Odysseus the equal of Zeus in devices
who was awakened from sleep by the horseman Gerenian Nestor
calling him loudly, as quickly the sound penetrated his spirit;
140   he came out of his cabin and with these words he addressed them:
"Why are you ranging alone by the ships and about the encampment
through the ambrosial night—what need so urgent has risen?"
　　Speaking to him then answered the horseman Gerenian Nestor:
"Zeus-sprung son of Laërtes, Odysseus of many devices,
145   do not blame me, for such great grief has beset the Achaians.
But now follow, that we may awaken another to whom is
fitting the consultation of whether to flee or do battle."
　　Thus; going into his cabin Odysseus of many devices
put his elaborate shield on his shoulders and went with the others.
150   They all went after Tydeus' son Diomédes and found him

181

outside his cabin, along with his arms, and around him his comrades
slumbered, with shields underneath their heads; their spear-shafts were driven
upright, butt-end, into the ground; far distant the bronze was
flashing, as lightning of Father Zeus flashes; but still was the hero
155   sleeping—beneath him was spread the great hide of an ox of the pasture,
while underneath his head was extended a glistening blanket.
Standing beside him, the horseman Gerenian Nestor awoke him,
stirring him up with his heel; to his face he roused him and scolded:
"Wake up, Tydeus' son; why pass the whole nighttime in slumber?
160   Do you not hear how the Trojans are now on the rise of the flatland
sitting so close to the ships, what a scant space holds them away still?"
      So he spoke; from his sleep Diomédes awoke very quickly;
raising his voice he spoke, and in these winged words he addressed him:
"Old sir, you are relentless and never do you stop toiling.
165   Are there at hand not other and younger men, sons of Achaians,
who might therefore arouse from his sleep each one of the princes,
going all over the camp? You are truly impossible, old sir!"
      Speaking to him made answer the horseman Gerenian Nestor:
"Certainly all this, friend, you speak as is fitting and proper.
170   Yes, there are my own excellent sons, and as well there are many
troops; and of them anyone might go around summoning others.
But very great is the need that has now come upon the Achaians,
since on the edge of a razor for all these matters are standing,
either a shameful destruction or for the Achaians to live on.
175   But go now, and arouse swift Ajax and Phyleus' scion
Meges to waken, for younger you are—if you pity me that much."
      Thus; and around his shoulders he put on the pelt of a lion,
fire-bright, enormous, reaching his feet, and he took up a great spear.
Then setting forth that hero awakened the others and brought them.
180   These men, soon as they joined those sentinels gathered together,
did not find as they came that the sentinels' leaders were sleeping,
rather that they were all wakeful and sat there holding their weapons.
Just as the dogs around sheep in a fold keep painful surveillance,
hearing a wild beast, powerful-hearted, that crosses a woodland
185   as among mountains it comes, then huge is the noise that about it
rises, of men and of dogs, and at once their slumber is ruined,
so on the lids of the watchers the sweet soft slumber was ruined
as in the night of affliction they watched there, since they were always
turned to the plain, in case they should hear any Trojans advancing.
190   So as he saw them the old man rejoiced; with a speech he encouraged

them as he raised his voice, and in these winged words he addressed them:
"So do you now, dear children, remain on guard, and do not let
sleep seize anyone, lest to our foes we are cause for rejoicing."
   So as he said, through the trench he hastened; along with him went those
195 kings of the Argives, as many as had been summoned to council.
Mérionés too followed, and Nestor's illustrious scion
went, for the kings themselves called them to take part in the council.
When they had crossed out over the trench they had dug, they sat down
in a clean space, where the ground showed clear of the bodies of fighters
200 fallen in battle, the place where powerful Hektor had turned back
from the destruction of Argives, when finally night had concealed them.
There then seating themselves, they uttered their words to each other.
Speaking among them opened the horseman Gerenian Nestor:
"Dear friends, is there indeed no man who would trust to his own strong
205 venturous spirit to set forth boldly among the greathearted
Trojans, if he might take someone of the enemy who was
straggling, or hear some rumor, perhaps, in the midst of the Trojans:
what are they planning among themselves now—are they intending
here to remain by the ships, faraway from the walls, or to draw back
210 into the city again, since they have subdued the Achaians?
All this he could discover, and back to us here he would then come
quite uninjured, and great would his fame be under the heavens
then among all mankind, and the gift he gets will be noble—
all of the highborn chieftains who lord it over the galleys,
215 every man among all those nobles will give him a black sheep,
female, nursing a lamb; no treasure is equal to this one.
Always with us will he be at our dinners and festival banquets."
   So did he say; then all of the people were hushed in silence.
Also among them spoke the great crier of war Diomédes:
220 "Nestor, indeed my heart and my valorous spirit arouse me
now to go into the camp of the enemy men who are nearby,
Trojans—but if some other man also would follow me thither,
then it will be a more comfortable, more confident mission.
With two going together, of them one sooner discerns just
225 where the advantage may lie; but a lone man, should he discern it,
still his discernment is shorter, and feeble as well his devices."
   He spoke; many were willing to follow with Lord Diomédes;
willing were both the Ajaxes, the mighty attendants of Ares;
willing was Mérionés, most willing the scion of Nestor;
230 willing was Atreus' son Meneláos renowned as a spearman;

183

willing as well was the daring Odysseus to enter the throng of
Trojans, for always inside of his breast his spirit was steadfast.
Then spoke also to them Agamemnon, lord of the people:
"Tydeus' son Diomédes, in whom my heart is delighted,

235 you will now choose, indeed, whomever you wish as your comrade,
him who is best among those who offer, as many are eager.
Not for respect you feel in your heart do you leave here the better
man and the worse as your comrade take, giving way to respect and
looking to birth, even if some other should be the more kingly."

240   So he spoke; he was fearful about light-haired Meneláos.
Then once more to them spoke the great crier of war Diomédes:
"If in fact you are ordering me to select a companion,
how could I ever indeed be forgetful of godlike Odysseus,
who has a heart and a valorous spirit distinguished for zeal in

245 every labor, and who is belovèd of Pallas Athena.
If it were he who followed with me, even out of a blazing
fire we both would return, since he is most skilled in devices."

     Then spoke answering him much-suffering noble Odysseus:
"Tydeus' son, do not praise me overmuch, neither reproach me,

250 for to the Argives who are informed of these things you are speaking.
Let us go then, for the night wanes quickly, the dawn is approaching,
onward the stars have advanced; of the nighttime more than two watches
now have gone by, so that only the third of the watches is left us."

     So they spoke, and accoutered themselves in terrible armor:

255 then Thrasymédes, steadfast in battle, to Tydeus' scion
proffered a double-edged sword, for his own he had left by the galley,
also a shield; and about his head he put on a helmet,
oxhide, without any bosses or horsehair crest, of the sort called
skullcap, which is for guarding the heads of the vigorous young men.

260 Mérionés then gave to Odysseus a bow and a quiver,
also a sword, and about his head he put on a helmet
fashioned of leather; within, reinforcement of numerous sinews
were stretched rigid and tight; on the outside surface the gleaming
teeth of a white-tusked boar were attached one way and the other

265 thickly, with cunning and craft; felt lining was sewn to the inside.
This out of Éleon once Autólykos stole from Amýntor,
Órmenos' son, when into his strong-built house he had broken;
he Kytheréan Amphídamas gave it to take to Skandeía;
then Amphídamas, making a guest-gift, gave it to Molos,

270 who to his own son, Mérionés, then gave it to be worn;

now it was set on the head of Odysseus and covered it closely.
     When those two had accoutered themselves in terrible armor,
they set forth, and they left in the same place all of the nobles.
Then for the men on their right hand, close to the way, was a heron
275 sent by Pallas Athena; and not with their eyes they discerned it
through the obscure night-gloom, but instead they heard its sharp outcry.
So at the bird-sign Odysseus rejoiced, and he prayed to Athena:
"Hear me, offspring of Zeus of the aegis, who always, in all my
labors and woes, stand right at my side, who never forget me
280 once I am roused—so again, even more now, befriend me, Athena,
grant us to come back here to the galleys with glorious honor
once we have done a great deed that will cause much grief to the Trojans."
     After him prayed in his turn the great crier of war Diomédes:
"Hear me as well now, offspring of Zeus, unwearying goddess:
285 follow with me, as you followed to Thebes with my father the noble
Tydeus, when in advance he went as a messenger of the Achaians.
Those bronze-armored Achaians he left by the river Asópos,
while he brought the Kadmeíans a word of benevolent mildness
there, but as he went back he was scheming maleficent actions
290 with you, goddess divine—you were zealously standing beside him.
So now also be minded to stand beside me and protect me;
I will make offer to you then, a heifer, a broad-browed yearling
not yet broken, that no man has ever led under the plow-yoke;
her I will offer to you with her horns all covered with gold leaf."
295   So they spoke as they prayed; they were heard by Pallas Athena.
Those two, when they had made their prayer to the daughter of great Zeus,
like two lions began to go forth in the gloom of the nighttime
passing the carnage and corpses, among the war-gear and the black blood.
     Nor in the least did Hektor allow that the valorous Trojans
300 go on sleeping, but all of the noblest he summoned together,
all those many who served as the Trojans' leaders and princes;
these men calling together, he framed shrewd counsel among them:
"Who would take on himself this action for me and achieve it
for an enormous gift? The reward he gets will suffice him,
305 since I will offer a chariot and two mighty-necked horses
which are the best among those by the swift ships of the Achaians,
to whoever should dare, who would thus for himself win glory,
now to go close to the swift-sailing galleys to spy and discover
whether the swift ships, yet as before, are carefully guarded,
310 whether instead those men that were brought down under our hands are

185

planning among themselves for their flight, no longer desiring
still to keep watch in the night, worn out with a dreadful exhaustion."
　　So did he say; then all of the people were hushed in silence.
There was among those Trojans a Dolon, the son of the godlike
315　herald Eumédes, and wealthy in gold, most wealthy in bronzeware.
Ugly indeed he was in his figure, but he was swift-footed;
then too, he was the one sole brother among five sisters.
He it was then who addressed this word to the Trojans and Hektor:
"Hektor, indeed my heart and my valorous spirit arouse me
320　now to go close to the swift-sailing galleys to spy and discover.
But come, hold up the scepter for me, then swear me an oath that
you will in fact give me those steeds and the bronze-ornamented
chariot which now carry the faultless scion of Peleus.
No vain spy will I be for you then, nor at all disappointing,
325　since I will go straight on in the army until Agamemnon's
ship I have reached, where, so I imagine, the nobles will now be
gathered and pondering counsel on whether to flee or do battle."
　　So he spoke; in his hands the lord took up the scepter and swore him:
"Zeus be witness himself, the loud-thundering husband of Hera,
330　never upon those horses will any man else of the Trojans
mount, but I say you only will glory in them without ceasing."
　　So he spoke, and he swore him a vain oath, stirring the man up.
Straightway then a curved bow he threw on, over his shoulders,
and as a cloak he put on a gray wolf's pelt, and a polecat's
335　pelt was the cap on his head; a sharp javelin also he took up,
then set forth to the ships from the army; but never would he be
coming again from the galleys to carry a message to Hektor.
But then, when he had left that throng of the men and the horses,
eagerly forth on his way he ran; as he went he was seen by
340　Zeus-descended Odysseus, who spoke and addressed Diomédes:
"There some man, Diomédes, is coming away from the army;
I know not whether he comes here as a spy on our galleys
or is intending to strip some corpse among those who have perished.
But first let us allow him to pass by over the plain some
345　distance, and then straightway by rushing at him we will take him
suddenly; should he be able on his swift feet to outstrip us,
always away from the army toward our galleys confine him,
rushing at him with your spear, lest he should escape to the city."
　　So having spoken, away from the path and among the dead bodies
350　they crouched down; in his folly he ran past them very quickly.

But then, when he was distant from them as the length of a mule-team's
furrow in plowing—for mules are indeed more suited than oxen
are for dragging a well-jointed plowshare through the deep fallow—
after him both men ran, and he stood still, hearing the footsteps;
355   for in his heart he hoped that his comrades had come from the Trojans
so as to turn him back and that Hektor commanded returning.
But then, when at a spear-throw's distance they were, or a bit less,
he knew they were his foes, and his knees he rapidly plied in
fleeing from them; they quickly bestirred themselves to pursue him.
360   As at a time two sharp-fanged hounds that are skilled at the hunt are
charging at either a fawn or a hare, incessantly eager,
through some forested place, and it runs in front of them screaming,
so now Tydeus' son and the sacker of cities Odysseus,
cutting him off from the army, pursued, incessantly eager.
365   But then, when with the sentries the man was about to be mingling,
as to the ships he fled, into Tydeus' scion Athena
put great might, so that no one among the bronze-armored Achaians
ever would claim to have struck before he did and he would come second.
Rushing at him with his spear, thus strong Diomédes addressed him:
370   "Stand there, or I with my spear will catch you, nor do I think that
you will escape very long from an utter destruction at my hands."
      Thus, and his spear he hurled, but he purposely missed hitting Dolon—
over the man's right shoulder the point of the well-polished spear-shaft
passed and was fixed in the ground; and he stood there stricken with terror,
375   stuttering so that the chattering teeth in his mouth were aclatter,
greenish because of his fear; and the two men panting for breath came
up to him, seizing his hands; then weeping, a word he addressed them:
"Take me alive—I will ransom myself, since there in our house are
treasures of bronze and of gold and of iron, laborious metal;
380   taking of them my father would please you with measureless ransom
should he discover that I am alive at the ships of the Achaians."
      Speaking to him then answered Odysseus of many devices:
"Take heart, and let not death be at all a concern to your spirit.
But come now, tell me this and recount it exactly and fully:
385   where are you going alone, to the ships and away from the army,
through the obscure night-gloom, at a time other mortals are sleeping?
Are you intending to strip some corpse among those who have perished,
or were you sent by Hektor to spy out all and discover
things by the hollow ships? Or did your own spirit impel you?"
390   Answering him spoke Dolon—his knees were aquiver beneath him:

187

"Out of my mind by many bewilderments Hektor misled me,
promising I would be given the single-hoofed horses of Peleus'
excellent scion, as well as his chariot, bronze-ornamented,
giving me orders to go, in the swift black shadows of nighttime,
395   close to the enemy fighters in order to spy and discover
whether the swift ships, yet as before, are carefully guarded,
whether instead your men, having been brought down by our hands, are
planning among themselves for your flight, no longer desiring
still to keep watch in the night, worn out by a dreadful exhaustion."
400   Smiling at him then answered Odysseus of many devices:
"Those are indeed great gifts that your spirit was eager to have, those
steeds of the war-skilled scion of Aíakos—difficult steeds for
men who are mortal to tame or in front of a chariot drive them,
save for Achilles alone, who was born to a mother immortal.
405   But come now, tell me this and recount it exactly and fully:
Where as you came here did you leave Hektor the shepherd of people?
Where are his battle accouterments lying, and where are his horses?
How are the guards and the bivouacs of the rest of the Trojans?
What are they planning among themselves now—are they intending
410   here to remain by the ships, faraway from the town, or to draw back
into the city again, since they have subdued the Achaians?"
      Then in answer to him spoke Dolon the son of Eumédes:
"These things I will indeed now tell you exactly and fully.
Hektor, among those who are his counselors, is at the moment
415   holding a council beside the grave-mound of the godlike Ilos,
far from the tumult; and as to the guards you ask about, hero,
there is no chosen detail which watches the army or guards it.
Those of the Trojans with family hearth-fires, to whom it is needful,
keep on lying awake and incite each other to maintain
420   sentinel-duty; but as to the allies, summoned from many
lands, they are sleeping, for they leave keeping the watch to the Trojans,
since no children of theirs lie near at hand, nor do their women."
      Speaking to him then answered Odysseus of many devices:
"How is it now—do they sleep with the Trojans, the tamers of horses,
425   mingled, or lying apart? Tell me all this, so that I know it."
      Then in answer to him spoke Dolon the son of Eumédes:
"These things I will indeed now tell you exactly and fully.
Karians lie by the sea, and Paiónians, they of the curved bows,
Léleges, noble Pelásgians too, Kaukónians also;
430   Lykians camp near Thymbrè, and venturous Mysians too, and

Phrygians, fighters on steeds, and Maiónians, chariot-fighters.
But now why do ask me in such detail about these things?
For if indeed you are eager to enter the throng of the Trojans,
Thracians are there, newcomers and separate, far from the others,
435 there too among them Rhesos the king, Eióneus' offspring.
His are the handsomest horses that ever I saw, and the greatest,
whiter than snow, and resembling the winds in swiftness of running.
He has a chariot skillfully fashioned with silver- and gold-work;
also of gold is the armor, prodigious, a marvel to look on,
440 which he arrived here bringing, and not at all suited for mortal
men to be wearing, but rather indeed for the gods undying.
But now you will dispatch me to go to the swift-sailing galleys—
or else tie me up here in a pitiless binding and leave me,
so that the two of you might go onward and put to the proof this
445 word, see whether or not I have truthfully told you of these things."
        Looking with lowering brows spoke out to him strong Diomédes:
"Dolon, do not put into your heart any thought of escaping,
excellent though your report is, as into our hands you have fallen.
For if indeed we release you now or allow you to leave us,
450 later will you come back to the swift ships of the Achaians
either to spy upon us or to fight in a battle against us.
But if beneath my hands you are brought down, losing your life-breath,
never again will you then be trouble and bane to the Argives."
        Thus, and the man was about to reach up to his chin with his stout hand
455 so as to supplicate him; but he struck at his neck in the middle,
leaping at him with his sword, and he cut through both of the tendons,
so that his head lay mingled with dust even while he was speaking.
Then from his head they stripped off the polecat's pelt of his helmet,
taking the wolf's pelt too, and the back-bent bow and the long spear;
460 these to Athena dispenser of spoil did noble Odysseus
hold up high in his hand, and he spoke this word to her, praying:
"Goddess, rejoice in these; for to you now first of the deathless
gods on Olympos shall we cry out for your aid; but direct us
yet again now to the horses and bivouacs of the Thracians."
465   So did he say, then, raising the spoil on high from himself, set
it on a tamarisk there, and beside it set a clear marker,
making a bundle of reeds and luxuriant tamarisk branches,
lest they forget, coming back in the swift black shadows of nighttime.
Both of the men went forward among the war-gear and the black blood;
470 rapidly making their way they came to the Thracians' position.

They were asleep, worn down by fatigue; their beautiful battle
gear lay there on the ground near them, most carefully ordered,
in three rows; and beside them each was a team of two horses.
Rhesos was sleeping among them, and there at his side the swift horses
475 stood—by the reins to the chariot's topmost rail they were tethered.
To Diomédes Odysseus, the soonest to notice him, showed him:
"This is the man indeed, Diomédes, and these are the horses,
those of which we were informed by Dolon, the man that we slaughtered.
But come now and exert your mightiest strength; you should not be
480 standing in idleness here with your arms, but unfasten the horses;
or else you kill the fighters, and I will attend to the horses."
     Thus; and the hero, as bright-eyed Athena inspired him with power,
killed one after another; and miserable was the groan that
rose from the sword-slain fighters; the earth grew red with their life-blood.
485 Just as a lion at coming upon unshepherded flocks of
goats or of sheep jumps into their midst, intending them evil,
so now Tydeus' son went after the Thracian fighters,
till he had killed twelve men; but Odysseus of many devices—
anyone Tydeus' son stood over and struck with his bronze sword,
490 seizing the man from behind by the foot, to the side would Odysseus
drag him away, as he thought in his heart that the fair-maned horses
then might easily pass, nor would they in their hearts be affrighted
treading upon dead men; for to them they were still unaccustomed.
But when finally then to the king came Tydeus' scion,
495 him thirteenth of the men he robbed of his honey-sweet life as
he lay panting; for over his head in the night did an evil
dream stand—the scion of Oíneus' son—by Athena's contrivance.
Meanwhile daring Odysseus unloosened the single-hoofed horses,
bound them together with reins, and away from the army he drove them,
500 striking at them with his bow, since he had not noticed and taken
up in his hands that elegant chariot's glittering whip-rod.
Then he whistled to signal the excellent lord Diomédes.
Staying instead, he weighed the audacity he could accomplish
seizing the chariot, wherein elaborate armor was lying,
505 drawing it off by the yoke-pole, or lifting it up to remove it,
or else taking the lives of yet more of the Thracian fighters.
As in his mind he was pondering these things, meanwhile Athena,
standing beside him, spoke to the excellent lord Diomédes:
"Great-souled Tydeus' son, take thought straightway of returning
510 back to the hollow ships, that you not go utterly routed,

should there perhaps be some other god who rouses the Trojans."
    So she said, and he heeded the words that the goddess had spoken;
hastily then he mounted the horses; Odysseus at once struck
them with his bow, and they sped to the swift ships of the Achaians.
515   Nor was Apollo of silvery bow maintaining a blind watch,
so that he saw how Athena was caring for Tydeus' scion;
wrathful at her he entered the great multitude of the Trojans,
rousing Hippókoön, who was a man of the Thracian council
and was an excellent cousin of Rhesos; he sprang from his slumber;
520 when he beheld the place empty in which had stood the swift horses,
men too, gasping for breath in the horrible gore of the slaughter,
loudly he groaned, and he called by name his belovèd companion.
Clamor arose from the Trojans, and measureless panic, as they came
rushing together; and there they witnessed the horrible work those
525 men had achieved before they had gone back to the hollow galleys.
    When these came to the place where Hektor's spy had been slaughtered,
there did Odysseus belovèd of Zeus rein in the swift horses;
Tydeus' son leapt down to the ground, and the bloodstained war-gear
placed in the hands of Odysseus, and once more mounted the horses.
530 He began lashing the steeds, nor against their wishes did they speed
forth to the hollow galleys, for that was the way their hearts longed for.
Nestor was first in hearing the clatter and spoke to his comrades:
"Oh dear friends and companions, the Argives' leaders and princes,
will it be error I speak, or the truth? For my spirit commands me.
535 Onto my ears is striking the clatter of swift-hoofed horses;
how I hope that Odysseus and strong Diomédes have driven
hither so quickly away from the Trojans the single-hoofed horses!
But in my heart I dreadfully fear that the best of the Argives
might in the tumult and strife of the Trojans have suffered some evil."
540 All of his words he had not yet said when they themselves came up.
Then they leapt down onto the ground, and the others, rejoicing,
made them welcome with handclasps and honey-sweet words of affection.
First then questioning them was the horseman Gerenian Nestor:
"Come, tell me, the Achaians' renown, much-honored Odysseus,
545 how did the two of you take these steeds—going into the throng of
Trojans? Or was it instead some god who met you and gave them?
They are indeed most dreadfully like to the radiant sunbeams.
Always with Trojans have I been mingling, and never at all I
stay by the ships, I say, even though I am old as a fighter;
550 yet I never have seen or imagined any such horses.

No, I suppose it was one of the gods who met you and gave them,
since you are both very dear to the great cloud-gathering god Zeus
and to the daughter of Zeus of the aegis, bright-eyed Athena."
　　Speaking to him then answered Odysseus of many devices:
555 "Nestor, Neleus' son, the Achaians' preeminent glory,
easily one of the gods, if he wished, could bestow even better
horses than these two are, since they are in fact far stronger.
These fine horses of which you ask, old sir, are but newly
come here from Thrace; their lord was a man whom brave Diomédes
560 killed, and beside him twelve of his comrades, all of them noble.
Then as the thirteenth man we killed a scout close to the galleys,
one whom hither to be their spy on our troops and encampment
Hektor himself had sent, and the other illustrious Trojans."
　　He spoke; over the trench he guided the single-hoofed horses,
565 laughing aloud, and rejoicing with him went the other Achaians.
When they arrived at the well-built cabin of Tydeus' scion,
then they fastened the horses with straps well crafted of leather
there at the manger for horses, at which also Diomédes'
swift-hoofed horses were standing, and honey-sweet grain they were eating;
570 but on the stern of his ship was the bloodstained war-gear of Dolon
set by Odysseus, till they for Athena could ready oblations.
They themselves, going into the sea, washed off the abundant
sweat which covered their shins, their necks, their thighs, and their shoulders.
But then, soon as the surf of the sea had washed the abundant
575 sweat well off of their skin, and the hearts inside them were freshened,
they stepped into the well-polished tubs and were given a washing.
When they had bathed and anointed themselves with the oil of the olive,
they sat down to a dinner, and out of the full wine bowl they
drew off honey-sweet wine and an offering poured to Athena.

BOOK 11

Dawn rose out of her bed, from beside resplendent Tithónos,
so that she might bring light to the deathless gods and to mortals;
down to the swift ships of the Achaians Zeus sent Conflict,
cruel and harsh—in her hands she was holding a portent of battle.
5   There she stood by the hollow and huge black ship of Odysseus,
which in the midmost lay, so her shout might reach to the two sides,
both to the far-off cabins of Ajax, Télamon's son, and
those of Achilles, for theirs were the balanced ships that were drawn up
farthest away—they trusted their powerful hands and their valor.
10 There then standing, a war cry mighty and fearful the goddess
shouted, and mighty the strength she cast into every Achaian's
heart inside him to battle implacably, fight without ceasing.
Quickly the battle became much sweeter to them than to go back
home in the hollow ships to the much-loved land of their fathers.
15 Atreus' son called loudly and gave his command that the Argives
gird themselves, and himself in glittering bronze he accoutered.
First, strong greaves on the calves of his legs he carefully fastened,
fine ones skillfully fitted with silver-wrought ankle-protectors;
second in order, about his chest he put on the breastplate
20 which had been given to him as a guest-gift once by Kinýres,
for in Cyprus he heard a loud rumor of how the Achaians
soon were to set sail out on the sea toward Troy in their galleys;
therefore he had presented the king this gift as a favor.
Ten of its ornament-courses were fashioned of cobalt enamel,
25 twelve were of gold, and of tin there were twenty; of cobalt enamel
also were fashioned the serpents that stretched to the neck on the breastplate,
three on both of its sides, like rainbows the scion of Kronos
fixes above in the clouds to be omens for men who are mortal.
Over his shoulders he threw on his sword, and upon it were gleaming
30 brightly its studs, all golden; about it there was a silver

scabbard, and fastened to this was a sword-strap, gold-ornamented.
Then his elaborate furious shield, the man-covering shelter,
beautiful work, he grasped; there were ten bronze circles upon it.
Also scattered across it were twenty raised bosses of tin that
35 gleamed white; one in the middle was fashioned of cobalt enamel—
grim in her visage, a Gorgon was set as a garland upon it,
glaring her terrible stare, and about her were Terror and Panic.
Fixed to the shield was a baldric of silver, upon it a serpent
writhing, of cobalt enamel, on which there were three heads twisted,
40 two of them circling the third, but from one neck all generated.
Then on his head he set a great four-bossed double-ridged helmet,
crested with horsehair—the plume on top of it fearfully nodded.
Two stout valorous spears he picked up, headed with sharp bronze
points; and the bronze of his armor was flashing afar from himself right
45 up to the heavens; and over him thundered Athena and Hera
so as to honor the king of the gold-rich city Mykénè.

    Then to his charioteer each man gave orders that he should
rein in the horses alongside the trench in an orderly manner;
they themselves were advancing on foot and accoutered in armor,
50 rushing ahead; and a shout unquenchable rose in the morning.
There in advance of the charioteers at the trench they were marshaled;
slightly behind them the charioteers came. Evil the uproar
then that the scion of Kronos aroused, while down from aloft he
cast dew dripping with blood from the heavens, because very shortly
55 many a powerful head he would send to the dwelling of Hades.

    So on the other side too, on the plain's high ground, were the Trojans
marshaled about great Hektor and faultless Polýdamas, also
Lord Aineías, revered like a god in the land of the Trojans,
then three sons of Anténor: Pólybos, noble Agénor,
60 Ákamas third, in his youthful prime most like the immortals.
Hektor was wielding his circular shield in the midst of the foremost.
As at a time that a murderous star gleams out among dark clouds
glittering bright, then again sinks into the shadowy cloud-mass,
so now Hektor was sometimes showing himself in the foremost,
65 then in the hindmost, giving commands, and entirely in bronze he
flashed like lightning of Zeus the great father who carries the aegis.

    Then, like reapers on opposite sides who, facing each other,
drive their swaths through the field of a prosperous man as they cut his
barley or wheat, and the armfuls are falling in rapid succession—
70 so the Achaians and Trojans against each other were leaping,

slaughtering, nor about ruinous panic was either side thinking.
Equal the battle was holding the heads of both sides as they raged like
wolves, so that baleful dolorous Conflict rejoiced to behold them,
for of the gods she only was taking a part with the fighters—
75 none of the rest of the gods were among them; rather untroubled
they in their chambers were seated apart, in the places in which for
each had a beautiful house been built in the folds of Olympos.
All cast blame on the scion of Kronos, the lord of the dark cloud,
seeing that he was intending to give great fame to the Trojans.
80 Nor was the Father concerned about them; he, turning aside, was
sitting apart from the other gods now, in his glory exulting,
while on the town of the Trojans he gazed, and the ships of Achaians,
and the bright flashing of bronze, men slaying and men being slaughtered.
    While it was morning as yet and the sacred daylight was waxing,
85 missiles of both sides sped to their targets, and people were falling;
but at the time that a cutter of wood makes ready his breakfast
high in the folds of a mountain, fatigued in his arms and his hands from
cutting the tall trees down, so that weariness comes on his spirit
and a desire for delectable food takes hold of his senses,
90 then by their excellent valor the Dánaäns smashed the battalions,
calling across their ranks to their comrades. First Agamemnon
rushed forth and slaughtered a fighter, Biénor the shepherd of people,
both himself and his comrade Oïleus, driver of horses.
Down from his chariot leaping, the man stood face-to-face, charging
95 straight at him, furious; he with his sharp spear struck at his forehead
mightily, nor was the spear held off by the bronze-heavy helmet;
rather it passed through it and the bone, so that all of his brain was
spattered about inside—so furiously he subdued him.
There Agamemnon the lord of the people abandoned the two men
100 gleaming with chests all bare, since he had stripped them of their tunics;
then he advanced toward Isos and Ántiphos, aiming to kill them,
two of the sons of King Priam—a bastard and one born in wedlock,
both in one chariot riding. The reins were held by the bastard;
glorious Ántiphos rode at his side; them once had Achilles
105 seized in the spurs of Mount Ida and bound with flexible withies
while they tended their sheep, and he set them free for a ransom.
But now Atreus' son, wide-governing Lord Agamemnon,
struck one of them with his spear in the chest just over the nipple;
Ántiphos close to the ear he hit, from his chariot threw him.
110 Hastily off of them both he stripped their beautiful armor,

knowing them well; for before by the hollow ships he had seen those
two, at the time swift-footed Achilles had brought them from Ida.
Just as a lion who meets with a swift deer's innocent offspring
easily tears them apart, with his powerful teeth having seized them,
115 entering into their lair, and of delicate life he deprives them,
even if she should happen to be close by them, the mother
doe cannot save them, for over her too comes terrible trembling—
speedily darting along in the dense underbrush and the woodland
sweating she rushes away from the powerful wild beast's onslaught—
120 so now none of the Trojans was able to help or to save these
two men; rather themselves they were fleeing in front of the Argives.
     Then Peisándros he took, and Hippólochos steadfast in battle,
sons of Antímachos, skillful in warfare, who above others,
hoping for glorious presents of gold Alexander had promised,
125 back to light-haired Meneláos would never agree to give Helen.
His were the two sons who were now taken by strong Agamemnon
both in one chariot; they were attempting to hold the swift horses,
since their glittering reins had escaped from their hands, and the horses
both were in panic confusion. Against them rushed like a lion
130 Atreus' scion; and him from the chariot they entreated:
"Take us alive, son of Atreus; accept an appropriate ransom.
Plenty of riches are stored inside Antímachos' palace,
treasures of bronze and of gold and of iron, laborious metal;
taking of them our father would please you with measureless ransom
135 should he discover that we are alive at the ships of the Achaians."
     Thus then weeping and wailing the two men spoke to the king in
gentle and supplicant words; but the voice they heard was not gentle:
"If in fact you are sons of Antímachos, skillful in warfare,
him who once in the Trojans' assembly, the time Meneláos
140 came on an embassy hither along with godlike Odysseus,
urged that he be killed there and not go back to the Achaians,
you will indeed now pay for your father's despicable outrage!"
     Thus; Peisándros he thrust to the ground from the chariot then by
striking his chest with his spear; on his back on the earth he was stretched out,
145 while Hippólochos leapt from the car; on the ground he destroyed him,
cutting away his arms with his sword, then hewing his neck off,
then like a log he set him to rolling along through the army.
Leaving them there, he rushed to the place the battalions in greatest
numbers were routed, and others with him went, well-greaved Achaians.
150 Footmen were slaughtering footmen who under compulsion were fleeing,

horsemen horsemen were killing—beneath them, up from the plain was
rising the dust that the thundering hooves of their horses were raising—
slaying with weapons of bronze. Meanwhile the strong lord Agamemnon,
slaughtering always, followed, and shouted commands to the Argives.

155　Just as a ruinous fire falls onto a thick-wooded forest—
whirling in every direction a wind bears it, and the bushes
fall uprooted, assailed by the rush of the conflagration—
so before Atreus' son Agamemnon were falling the heads of
Trojans attempting to flee, while numerous mighty-necked horses

160　rattled the chariots empty of men on the battle embankments,
longing for faultless charioteers, who now on the earth were
lying and loved far more by the vultures than by their bedmates.
　　Out of the missiles and out of the dust now Zeus drew Hektor,
out of the manslaughter, out of the bloodshed, out of the tumult;

165　Atreus' son came after, the Dánaäns fiercely exhorting.
Passing the barrow of Ilos of old times, Dárdanos' scion,
they rushed over the plain, through the middle, and passing the fig tree
eagerly sped to the city, and always followed them, yelling,
Atreus' son, his invincible hands with battle-gore spattered.

170　But then, when they arrived at the Skaian Gates and the oak tree,
there they halted and stood and on both sides awaited the others.
Over the plain, through the middle, were some still fleeing like cattle
which in the dead of the night some lion has driven in stampede,
all of them; but to one only appears her utter destruction:

175　first he shatters her neck, in his powerful teeth having seized it,
then her blood he greedily swallows, and all of her innards.
So now followed the scion of Atreus, strong Agamemnon,
always slaughtering those who were hindmost; thus were they routed.
Many from chariots fell on their faces or backs at the hands of

180　Atreus' scion, for he with his spear kept rushing against them.
But when under the city and its steep wall he would soon be
coming, at that same moment the father of gods and of mankind
sat on the summits of Ida of bounteous fountains, descending
out of the sky; in his hands he was holding a bolt of his lightning.

185　Then he aroused up gold-winged Iris to carry a message:
"Go there at once, swift Iris, and say this counsel to Hektor:
just so long as he sees Agamemnon, shepherd of people,
there with the foremost raging, destroying battalions of fighters,
so long let him hold back and command that the rest of the army

190　go on fighting the enemy host in the violent combat.

197

But when he, by a spear being wounded, or struck by an arrow,
into his chariot leaps, upon Hektor will I bestow power
so he can slaughter until he arrives at the well-benched galleys
just as the sun goes down and upon him comes holy darkness."
195   So did he say; swift wind-footed Iris did not disobey, but
down into sacred Ilion went from the summits of Ida.
There she found noble Hektor the scion of war-skilled Priam
standing among his horses and chariots, skillfully jointed;
thus then, standing beside him, addressed him swift-footed Iris:
200   "Hektor the scion of Priam, the equal of Zeus in devices,
Zeus our father has sent me to you, this counsel to tell you:
just so long as you see Agamemnon, shepherd of people,
here with the foremost raging, destroying battalions of fighters,
so long keep from the fight and command that the rest of the army
205   go on fighting the enemy host in the violent combat.
But when he, by a spear being wounded, or struck by an arrow,
into his chariot leaps, upon you will Zeus bestow power
so you can slaughter until you arrive at the well-benched galleys
just as the sun goes down and upon you comes holy darkness."
210   So having spoken her message the swift-footed Iris departed.
Hektor at once to the ground from his chariot leapt in his armor,
wielding his two sharp spears, and he ranged all over the army,
urging the men to do battle, and roused up terrible combat.
They wheeled round in a rally and stood to confront the Achaians,
215   while on the opposite side the Argives reinforced their battalions,
readying battle, and facing them stood; Agamemnon among them
rushed forth first, as he wanted to fight far ahead of all others.

Now speak out to me, Muses who live in Olympian dwellings;
tell which one was the first who came against Lord Agamemnon,
220   either among those Trojans themselves or the glorious allies.
It was Iphídamas, son of Anténor, stout-bodied and valiant,
who had been nurtured in fertile Thrace, that mother of sheep flocks;
Kisses had nurtured him in his house while he was yet little—
he was his mother's father, begetter of fair-cheeked Theáno—   ·
225   but then, once he had come to the measure of glorious manhood,
there in his house he detained him, and his own daughter he gave him.
Soon as he married, from their bedchamber he went to seek glory
from the Achaians, and following him were his twelve curved galleys.
Once he had reached Perkótè the balanced galleys he left there,
230   while he himself on foot went onward to Ilion city;

he it was now who came against Atreus' son Agamemnon.
When in coming together the men were close to each other,
Atreus' son missed him, and his spear turned, passing its target;
into his war-belt under the breastplate Iphídamas quickly
235 struck, and himself thrust hard—in his ponderous hand he confided;
still he did not penetrate that glittering belt, but before that,
hitting the silver, the point of the spear like lead bent backward.
Seizing the spear with his hand, wide-governing Lord Agamemnon
dragged it to him as he raged like a lion, and out of his hand he
240 pulled it; striking the neck with his sword, his limbs he unloosened.
There he thus fell, and he lay in a deep bronze sleep, the unhappy
youth who, aiding his townsmen, was far from the wife he had wedded,
far from his bride—no delight had he known of her; much had he given;
cattle he first gave, a hundred, and then he had promised a thousand—
245 goats and as well fine sheep that for him beyond number were pastured.
Straightway then Agamemnon the scion of Atreus stripped him;
bearing the beautiful armor he went through the throng of Achaians.

   Then when he was observed by Koön, distinguished among men,
who was the firstborn son of Anténor, a powerful sorrow
250 came down over his eyes on account of the fall of his brother.
Sideways he stood with a spear, unseen by great Agamemnon,
then as he struck his arm in the middle and under the elbow,
right on through it the point of the glittering spear penetrated.
Straightway shuddered in dread Agamemnon, lord of the people;
255 not even so did he cease from the battle and leave off the combat,
but with a spear wind-nurtured to toughness leapt upon Koön.
He by the foot was eagerly dragging Iphídamas, his own
brother by one same father, and calling to all of the nobles;
as in the throng he dragged him, beneath the bossed shield Agamemnon
260 struck with his smooth spear pointed with bronze, and his limbs unloosened,
then stood beside him and over Iphídamas, cutting his head off.
There beneath Atreus' scion the king, those sons of Anténor,
filling their measures of fate, went into the palace of Hades.

   Then he continued ranging about in the ranks of the others,
265 using as weapons his spear and his sword and enormous boulders,
just so long as the blood still ran warm out of the spear-wound;
but then, soon as the wound dried up and the flow of the blood stopped,
sharp were the pains that invaded the spirit of Atreus' scion.
Just as a woman in labor is gripped by a bitter and piercing
270 pain-dart the Eíleithúia, the childbirth-goddesses, send her—

daughters of Hera who have in their keeping the sharp bitter birth-pangs—
such sharp pains now invaded the spirit of Atreus' scion.
Into his chariot leaping, the charioteer he commanded
quickly to drive to the hollow ships; for his spirit was heavy.
275   Piercingly then he yelled to the Dánaäns; loudly he shouted:
"Oh dear friends and companions, the Argives' leaders and princes,
now do you keep on holding away from the seafaring galleys
grievous and wearisome combat, because Zeus Counselor does not
let me continue the whole day long to make war on the Trojans."
280   So he spoke, and the fair-maned horses the charioteer lashed
on to the hollow ships, nor against their wishes did they speed;
flecked with foam were their chests, with dust underneath were they spattered,
as they carried away from the battle the king who was worn out.
    Hektor, as soon as he noticed that Lord Agamemnon was absent,
285   called to the Trojan and Lykian warriors; loudly he shouted:
"Trojans and Lykians all, Dardánians, hand-to-hand fighters,
now be men, dear friends, and remember your furious valor;
gone is the best of their men, and to me has Zeus son of Kronos
granted a mighty renown; drive onward the single-hoofed horses
290   at the strong Dánaän fighters, to win a renown yet greater."
    So he spoke and aroused in each fighter the strength and the spirit.
As at a time when a hunter is setting his hounds with their gleaming
teeth at a beast of the country, a fierce wild boar or a lion,
so now was setting the great-souled Trojans against the Achaians
295   Hektor the scion of Priam, the peer of man-slaughtering Ares.
He with enormous resolve was himself in the foremost striding;
onto the battle he fell in the way that a blustering stormwind
swoops down onto the violet seaway and raises its fury.
    There then who was the first, who last of the warriors killed by
300   Hektor the scion of Priam as Zeus kept granting him glory?
First was Asaíos killed, Autónoös too, and Opítes,
Dolops, Klytios' scion, Ophéltios, and Ageláos,
Oros and Aísymnos and Hippónoös, steadfast in battle.
These of the Dánaäns' leaders he slaughtered, and then in addition
305   multitudes, as when Zephyr the west wind thrashes the clouds of
glittering Notos the south wind and strikes in a fathomless tempest;
many a billow is swollen and rolling, and high up above is
wave-spume scattered about by the blast of the wandering stormwind.
Such were the numerous heads of the men there slaughtered by Hektor.
310   There then would have been ruin and deeds incurably baneful,

so would the fleeing Achaians have fallen in rout on the galleys,
had not Odysseus shouted to Tydeus' son Diomédes:
"Tydeus' son, what happens that we forget furious valor?
But come, friend, stand here beside me, for a shame it will surely
315   be if the galleys are taken by Hektor of glittering helmet."
        Answering him in return then spoke forth strong Diomédes:
"I will indeed stay here and endure this; yet very briefly
shall we gain any profit, because the cloud-gathering god Zeus
wishes to grant might now to the Trojans instead of to our side."
320   Thus, and Thymbraíos he hurled from his chariot onto the ground by
striking his chest with his spear on the left side; so did Odysseus
bring down Mólion, who was the godlike comrade of that lord.
There these men they abandoned as soon as they ended their fighting;
ranging about in the throng, both men raised havoc, as when two
325   boars of enormous resolve fall onto the hounds of a huntsman;
so they, roused at the Trojans again, killed them; the Achaians
gladly recovered their breath from fleeing before noble Hektor.
        There they a chariot took and the two best men of their country,
both of them sons of Perkósian Mérops, who was beyond all
330   men in prophetic endowment, nor did he allow that his children
go into battle, destroyer of men; yet not in the least they
listened to him; for the spirits of black death guided them onward.
Them did Tydeus' scion renowned for his spear, Diomédes,
rob of their spirit and life-breath and strip of their glorious armor.
335   Then were Hippódamos and Hypeírochos killed by Odysseus.
        Thereat the scion of Kronos for them stretched equal the combat
as he observed it from Ida; and they kept killing each other.
Tydeus' son with his spear then wounded Agástrophos, who was
Paion's warrior son, on the hip bone, nor were his horses
340   nearby for him to take flight—in his mind he was greatly deluded,
since well apart was his comrade holding them; he on his feet was
raging among the foremost, till the time he lost his dear life-breath.
Hektor was keenly observing the men through the ranks, and he rushed at
them with a shout; the battalions of Trojans were following after.
345   Noticing him the great crier of war Diomédes was shaken;
hastily then to Odysseus he spoke out, seeing him nearby:
"Such an affliction is rolling on both of us—powerful Hektor!
Come then, here let us stand to defend ourselves and await him."
        So did he say, then brandished and threw his long-shadowing spear-shaft
350   so that it struck him and did not miss—at his head he had aimed it—

right on top of the helmet; but back from the bronze was the bronze turned,
nor did it reach the fair flesh—it was kept from its mark by the helmet,
threefold, socketed, he had been given by Phoibos Apollo.
Hektor at once sprang away to a distance and mixed with the throng and,
355   falling on one knee, stooped, and he leaned on the earth with his mighty
hand, while over his eyes black night came down to enshroud them.
Then while Tydeus' son went after the cast of his spear-shaft
far through the foremost fighters to where on the earth it had speeded,
Hektor recovered his breath, then back in his chariot leaping
360   drove it away to the throng and avoided the blackest of doomsdays;
rushing at him with his spear then spoke to him strong Diomédes:
"Now you again, you hound, have escaped death, though very near you
evil had come; now again you were saved by Phoibos Apollo,
whom you must supplicate as you enter the din of the spear-fight.
365   Later on I will eliminate you, whenever I meet you,
should there be for me also a god who serves as a helpmate;
now will I go in pursuit of the others, whomever I come to."
     Thus, and he set about stripping the spear-famed scion of Paíon.
Then Alexander, the husband of Helen of beautiful tresses,
370   stretched his bow against Tydeus' scion, the shepherd of people,
leaning against the gravestone on the man-made funeral mound of
Ilos Dárdanos' son, of the old-time people an elder.
So as the one was stripping from valiant Agástrophos' chest his
shimmering breastplate then, and removing the shield from his shoulders,
375   also his massive helmet, the other man drew his bow's handgrip
back, and let fly—nor in vain from his hand flew forward the missile—
striking the flat of his right upper foot; clean through it the arrow
passed and was stuck in the ground; Alexander, delightedly laughing,
leapt from his place of concealment and spoke this word to him, boasting:
380   "You have been struck, nor in vain flew the missile! How I could wish that
I in the nethermost belly had struck you and taken your life out.
So would the Trojans again have recovered their breath from affliction,
those who shudder at you like loud-bleating goats at a lion."
     Then not frightened at all spoke forth to him strong Diomédes:
385   "Archer, insulter, resplendent in hairstyle, ogler of maidens,
should you indeed against me make man-to-man trial with weapons,
then no advantage would be your bow or your thick-flying arrows;
now just grazing the flat of my foot, even so are you boasting.
Nor do I care, as if struck by a witless child or a woman;
390   for of a man without valor, of no account, blunt is the missile.

Differently from myself, though slightly it touches the target,
passes the keen-edged weapon, and quickly it lays him lifeless;
then indeed are the cheeks of his wife, both sides, lacerated;
fatherless too are his children; and staining the earth with his blood he
395 rots, and at once more birds are around his body than women."
　　So he spoke, and Odysseus renowned as a spearman approached and
stood before him; he, sitting behind him, drew the sharp missile
out of his foot, and a harrowing pain came over his body.
Into his chariot leaping, the charioteer he commanded
400 quickly to drive to the hollow ships; for his spirit was heavy.
　　Only Odysseus renowned as a spearman remained, and no other
Argives stayed with him there, since fear gripped all of the fighters;
deeply disturbed, he spoke to his own magnanimous spirit:
"Ah me, what will befall me? The evil is great if in fear of
405 men so many I flee, yet viler if I should alone be
taken—the rest of the Dánaäns here has Kronos' son routed.
Yet why now is it dear to my heart to debate about these things,
since I know that the cowards at once walk out of the warfare,
while for whoever would be distinguished in battle, the great need
410 is to stand strong, whether he be struck or he strike down another."
As he was pondering over these things in his mind and his spirit,
all that time were approaching the ranks of shield-carrying Trojans,
hemming him up in their midst, on themselves thus bringing disaster.
Just as against a wild boar young vigorous men and their hounds are
415 pressing from every direction, and out of the depths of a thicket
it runs, whetting the tusks which gleam white out of its curved jaw,
they come charging around, and the clatter of tusks is resounding
loud, but without hesitation they stand there, though it is dreadful,
so now surrounding Odysseus belovèd of Zeus were the Trojans
420 pressing; and first he struck at the faultless Déïopítes,
leaping on him from above with a sharp spear, wounding his shoulder;
then straightway both Thoön and Énnomos he did away with,
then as Chersídamas leapt from his chariot onto the ground, he
thrust with his spear at him, under his shield made massive with bosses,
425 into his navel; he fell in the dust, with his hand the earth clutching.
Leaving them there, he struck with a spear-thrust Híppasos' scion
Charops, who was the brother of wealthy and well-born Sokos.
Then to his rescue at once came Sokos, godlike in manhood;
he stood close to Odysseus and spoke this word to address him:
430 "Oh much honored Odysseus, insatiably guileful and toiling,

this day above both scions of Híppasos you will be boasting,
having in fact killed two such fighters and stripped them of armor;
otherwise, struck down under my spear, your life you will forfeit."
    So having spoken, he struck at the circular shield of Odysseus;
435 straight through the glittering shield penetrated the powerful spear-shaft,
thrusting its way on through the elaborate work of the breastplate;
all of the flesh from the ribs it severed, but Pallas Athena
did not allow it to penetrate further the warrior's innards.
Then was Odysseus aware that the spear had not fatally reached him,
440 quickly he drew himself back, and in these words spoke out to Sokos:
"Ah, wretch! Surely indeed now comes to you sheerest destruction!
Yes, it is true you have caused me to leave off fighting the Trojans;
but as for you, I tell you that death and the darkness of doom will
come to you here this day, and that you, brought down by my spear, will
445 give to me fame, and your spirit to Hades of glorious horses."
    Thus he spoke, and the other man turned back, trying to flee him;
but then, as he was turning, between his shoulders the hero
planted the spear in his back, and ahead through the chest he impelled it.
Falling he crashed to the ground; thus noble Odysseus exulted:
450 "Sokos, the scion of war-skilled Híppasos, tamer of horses,
sooner to you came death's finality, nor could you flee it.
Ah wretch, never for you will your father and reverend mother
close your eyes at the moment of dying, but rather the vultures,
carrion-eaters, will rend you with wings fast-beating about you;
455 funeral rites, if I perish, the noble Achaians will give me."
    So he spoke, and the powerful spear of the war-skilled Sokos
he pulled out of his flesh and his great shield, massive with bosses;
once it was drawn out, blood gushed up, and his heart was afflicted.
But as the great-souled Trojans observed that blood of Odysseus,
460 loud in the throng they shouted, and all began charging against him.
Back he at once drew, yielding some ground, and he called to his comrades.
Thrice then a yell he shouted as loud as the head of a man holds;
thrice heard him as he yelled Meneláos belovèd of Ares;
straightway then he spoke out to Ajax, since he was nearby:
465 "Ajax the Zeus-sprung scion of Télamon, marshal of people,
round me is ringing the outcry of steadfast-hearted Odysseus,
sounding as if he is all by himself, and the Trojans have cut him
off and are bringing him down by force in the violent combat.
Through the melee let us go, since better it is to defend him.
470 I fear he will be injured, as he is alone among Trojans,

brave though he is—then greatly indeed will the Dánaäns miss him."

So having spoken he led, and the godlike man followed after.
Then they found Zeus-cherished Odysseus; and there about him were
Trojans besetting him, as in the mountains tawny-haired jackals
475 swarm at a horned stag which has been stricken—a man with an arrow
fired from a string struck him; and escaping the man, on his feet he
took his flight while his blood stayed warm and his knees were in motion;
but then, when the sharp arrow has finally broken and quelled him,
high in the mountains the ravening jackals begin to devour him
480 there in a shadowy grove; and against them a ravaging lion
some god brings, and the jackals are scattered; the quarry he eats up.
So then about ingenious various-minded Odysseus
Trojans beset him, many and valorous, while with his spear that
hero was rushing at them and averting a pitiless doomsday.
485 Ajax, coming up close to him, bearing a shield like a tower,
stood there beside him; the Trojans were scattering hither and thither.
Out of the throng warlike Meneláos escorted the hero,
holding his hand, till his horses were driven up by his attendant.

Ajax leapt on the Trojans and brought down noble Doryklos,
490 scion of Priam, a bastard, and thrusting at Pándokos, killed him,
killed Lysánder as well, then Pýrasos too, and Pylártes.
As at a time that a river in flood runs down to the flatland
out of the mountains, by Zeus' rain driven, a torrent of winter—
many a dried-out oak it carries, and many a pine tree,
495 rushing ahead, and it hurls much driftwood into the sea-brine—
so then charged on the plain, rampaging, illustrious Ajax,
killing the horses as well as the fighters; but Hektor as yet knew
nothing, because at the left of the whole combat he was fighting,
close to the banks of the river Skamánder, the place where the heads of
500 fighters were falling the most, and a noise unquenchable, rising
round great Nestor and warlike Idómeneus, now was resounding.
Hektor among these mingled, and grim were the deeds that he wrought with
spear and with horsemanship to destroy the battalions of young men.
Not even so from his path would the noble Achaians have yielded
505 had Alexander, the husband of Helen of beautiful tresses,
not stopped short in his prowess Macháon, the shepherd of people,
firing a three-barbed arrow at him which struck his right shoulder.
Thereat greatly were frightened the furious-breathing Achaians,
lest as the battle was turning, perhaps those fighters would kill him.
510 Straightway Idómeneus thus spoke out and addressed noble Nestor:

"Nestor Neleus' son, the Achaians' preeminent glory,
come, climb onto your chariot now, and beside you Macháon
also must mount; to the ships drive swiftly the single-hoofed horses;
for a man who is a healer is worth many others in knowing
515   how to cut arrows from wounds and to sprinkle on herbs that are soothing."
      He spoke, nor disobeyed him the horseman Gerenian Nestor.
Onto his chariot quickly he climbed, and beside him Macháon
mounted as well, that son of Asklépios, faultless physician;
he began lashing the steeds, nor against their wishes did they speed
520   forth to the hollow galleys; for that was the way their hearts longed for.
      Then did Kebríones notice the way that the Trojans were driven
as beside Hektor he stood, and he spoke this word and addressed him:
"Hektor, indeed with the Dánaän troops we mingle in strife out
here at the edge of the dolorous warfare; meanwhile the other
525   Trojans are driven to flee in confusion, themselves and their horses.
Ajax, Télamon's scion, is driving them—well do I know him,
for a broad shield he bears on his shoulders; but now let us also
drive over there our horses and chariot, where above all are
fighters on horse and on foot engaging in terrible conflict,
530   putting each other to death, and a noise unquenchable rises."
      Soon as he said these words, his fair-maned horses he lashed on,
wielding the whistling whip; they, hearing and feeling the whip-stroke,
bore the swift chariot lightly toward the Achaians and Trojans,
trampling upon dead bodies and shields; bespattered with blood were
535   all of the axle below and the rim that surrounded the car-box,
fouled by drops of the gore thrown up from the hooves of the horses
and from the rims of the wheels. He was eager to enter the throng of
fighters and smash them by leaping on them, and a baneful confusion
he at the Dánaäns sent; from his spear he rested but little.
540   Thus did he go on ranging about in the ranks of the others,
using as weapons his spear and his sword and enormous boulders,
yet he avoided a battle with Ajax, Télamon's scion,
[since Zeus ever begrudged it when he fought somebody stronger.]
      Father Zeus, seated aloft, now roused up Ajax to take flight;
545   he stood dazed and his sevenfold oxhide shield put behind him;
fearfully glancing about, he withdrew to the throng like a wild beast,
constantly turning around, while leg passed leg very slowly.
Just as a tawny-haired lion is driven away from the farmyard
pens and the cattle in them by hounds and the men of the country,
550   nor do they ever allow him to seize from the cattle a fat one,

staying awake all night—he, greedily longing for flesh, keeps
forging ahead, but accomplishes nothing, for javelins flying
swiftly and thickly from bold stout hands keep rushing against him,
fiery torches as well, and he quails at them, though he is eager;
555   early at dawn he goes on his way, in his spirit disgruntled—
thus went Ajax, his heart disgruntled, away from the Trojans,
much unwilling, for sorely he feared for the ships of the Achaians.
Just as a donkey that passes a field outpowers the boys who
lead him, an obstinate ass on which many sticks have been broken—
560   going inside, he gobbles the deep grain-crop, as the boys keep
striking at him with their sticks; their power is childishly puny;
only with toil is he driven away when glutted with fodder—
so were the high-souled Trojans and allies collected from many
lands then striking the great lord Ajax, Télamon's scion,
565   square on his shield in the middle with spears, incessantly pressing.
Ajax then for a time would remember his furious valor—
wheeling at them, the battalions of Trojans, the tamers of horses,
he would awhile hold back; then turning again, he would take flight.
All those foes he prevented from making their way to the swift ships;
570   standing himself in the middle, between the Achaians and Trojans,
he kept struggling alone; and from bold stout hands were the spears that,
some of them, stuck in his huge broad shield as ahead they were driven;
many, before they grazed white flesh, stood there in the middle,
upright, fixed in the earth, and desiring on flesh to be glutted.
575   Soon as the glorious son of Euaímon, Eurýpylos, noticed
how by the dense swift missiles the hero was thus overpowered,
going to stand close by, he cast with his glittering spear and
so struck Phaúsias' son Apisáon, the shepherd of people,
under the chest in the liver—at once his knees he unloosened;
580   leaping on him, his armor Eurýpylos stripped from his shoulders.
But then, soon as the lord godlike Alexander observed him
stripping the armor from bold Apisáon, at once with his bow he
aimed at Eurýpylos, shooting and striking the man with an arrow
in the right thigh, and the shaft broke off, and his thigh became heavy.
585   He shrank back to the band of his comrades, avoiding destruction.
Piercingly then he yelled to the Dánaäns; loudly he shouted:
"Oh dear friends and companions, the Argives' leaders and princes,
turn around, stand firm now, and from Ajax a pitiless doomsday
ward off—he by the missiles is quite overpowered, nor do I
590   think he will flee from the dolorous warfare; yet do you stand firm

facing the fighters, around great Ajax, Télamon's scion."
    So then addressed them the wounded Eurýpylos; many of them came,
taking a stand there beside him and leaning their shields on their shoulders,
holding their spears outstretched; then Ajax came to rejoin them;
595 turning around he stood, when he came to the band of his comrades.
    So as the two sides fought like the blaze of a conflagration,
dripping with sweat Lord Neleus' mares took out of the combat
Nestor, and also carried Machâon the shepherd of people.
Looking at him took note swift-footed and noble Achilles,
600 for on the stern of his huge-hulled galley the hero was standing,
watching the sheer war-toil and the tearful pursuits and the onslaughts.
Then he at once spoke out and addressed his comrade Patróklos,
calling to him from the galley; and hearing him, out of the cabin
he came much like Ares—for him, the beginning of evil.
605 First spoke out and addressed him Menoítios' valorous scion:
"Why do you call me, Achilles, and now what need of me have you?"
Answering him in return spoke forth swift-foot Achilles:
"Noble Menoítios' scion, in whom my heart is delighted,
now I think the Achaians about my knees will be standing,
610 begging me, since no more to be borne is the need that has risen.
But go now, Zeus-cherished Patróklos, inquiring of Nestor
which of the men he is carrying wounded away from the battle.
Truly indeed, from behind in all ways he resembles Machâon,
noble Asklépios' son, but the face of the man I did not see,
615 since right past me the horses were eagerly hastening forward."
    So he spoke, and Patróklos obeyed his belovèd companion;
he went running along the Achaians' cabins and galleys.
    Now when the others arrived at the cabin of Neleus' scion,
on the much-nourishing earth from the chariot they dismounted,
620 and the retainer Eurýmedon loosened the old man's horses
then from the chariot; both men dried off the sweat from their tunics,
standing and facing the wind by the shore of the sea; but at last they
went on into the cabin, and there on chairs they were seated.
Then for the men fair-haired Hekamédè concocted a potion—
625 her had the old man taken from Ténedos once when Achilles
sacked it; she was great-souled Arsínoös' daughter, selected
by the Achaians for Nestor, for he excelled all in his counsel.
First, in front of the men she drew out forward a table,
well carved, lovely, with dark blue feet, and upon it a brazen
630 basket she set, inside it an onion, a relish for drinking,

pale green honey and meal of the sacred barley she set there
too, and a beautiful cup brought thither from home by the old man,
brilliantly studded with nails all golden, and four were the earlike
handles for holding the goblet; about each handle were fashioned
635 two doves feeding, in gold; there were double supports underneath it.
This cup even with effort another would hardly have lifted
when it was full—old Nestor could raise it without any effort.
Therein the woman resembling the goddesses mixed them a potion—
Prámneian wine she used, and upon it grated some goat cheese
640 with a bronze grater, and fine white barley meal sprinkled upon it.
Then she urged them to drink, once she had made ready the potion.
When with the drinking the two had sated the thirst that had parched them,
taking delight in their words, they spoke each one to the other;
then did Patróklos the godlike man stand there in the doorway.
645 Soon as he saw him the old man sprang from his glistening armchair;
taking his hand he led him inside, and he made him be seated.
Yet from his own side Patróklos refused, and a word he addressed him:
"I cannot sit, Zeus-cherished old sir, nor can you persuade me.
He is irascible, dreaded, who sent me forth to discover
650 which of the men you were carrying wounded away; but I know it
clearly myself as I look at Macháon the shepherd of people.
Now this message, when I go back, I will say to Achilles.
You know well, Zeus-cherished old sir, what sort of a man he
is, most terrible; quickly would he blame even the blameless."
655   Speaking to him then answered the horseman Gerenian Nestor:
"Why does Achilles indeed so pity the sons of Achaians,
all those who have been struck by missiles? Nothing he knows what
grief has arisen throughout the encampment, for those who are best are
lying among our ships—they were struck by missiles and wounded.
660 So has been struck Lord Tydeus' powerful son Diomédes;
wounded as well is Odysseus renowned for his spear, Agamemnon
too, and Eurýpylos has been struck in the thigh with an arrow;
this other man I have just been carrying out of the combat,
struck with an arrow that flew from a bowstring. Meanwhile Achilles,
665 brave as he is, cares not for the Dánaäns, feels no compassion.
Is he to go on waiting until the swift ships by the sea are
burnt in the blistering fire in spite of the toil of the Argives,
till we ourselves one after another are killed? For indeed no
longer the force in my flexible limbs is such as it once was.
670 How I wish I were young and my strength yet steady within me,

as at the time that a quarrel between the Eleíans and us rose
over the stealing of cattle, when I Hypeírochos' noble
scion Itýmoneus slaughtered—he made his dwelling in Elis—
as in reprisal I drove off stock; while defending his cattle,
675 he by a spear from my hand was among the front ranks of the smitten,
so that he fell, and around him the countrymen fled in terror.
Plunder in ample abundance we drove from the pastures together—
fifty in all were the herds of the cattle, as many the sheep flocks,
also the droves of fat swine, and as many the wandering goat flocks.
680 Chestnut horses as well we took, one hundred and fifty,
all of them mares—under many of them were foals at the nipple.
This loot then we drove into Neleus' citadel, Pylos,
up to the town, by night; in his spirit was Neleus gladdened,
since so much had I won as a young man going to battle.
685 Loudly and clearly at earliest daybreak heralds proclaimed that
those to whom debts were owing in sacred Elis should come there;
so then gathered together the men who were leaders in Pylos,
splitting the loot; for to many were debts owed by the Epeíans,
so few people in Pylos we were—we had suffered oppression,
690 since strong Herakles' power had come upon us and oppressed us,
once in earlier years, and the noblest among us had been killed,
since in fact of the twelve of us faultless scions of Neleus
I was alone of them left, while all of the others had perished.
Wanton and arrogant over these things, the bronze-armored Epeíans
695 started to outrage us and devised deeds reckless and wicked.
Then for himself the old man took one herd of cattle, a large flock
too of the sheep, for he chose three hundred along with the shepherds.
For a great debt they owed the old man in Elis the sacred:
four prize-garnering horses along with the chariot they drew,
700 which to the games had gone—they were going to run for a tripod
in competition, but there had Augeías, the lord of the people,
kept them, and sent their driver away much grieved for the horses.
Angry because of these things, both speeches and actions, the old man
took unlimited loot, and the rest he gave to the people
705 to be divided, that no one would leave there deprived of his portion.
Everything we disposed for the best, and all over the city
wrought sacrifice to the gods; on the third day all the Epeíans
gathered together, themselves and as well their single-hoofed horses,
acting in haste, and among them the two Molíones were armored,
710 though they were boys yet, not very skillful in furious valor.

There is a town Thryoëssa, a steep hill far at a distance
close to the Álpheios, outermost region of sandy-soiled Pylos;
this their army besieged, most eager to seize and destroy it.
But then, when they had scoured the whole flatland, to us did Athena
715 come as a messenger, hastening down in the night from Olympos,
bidding us arm—not averse was the host she gathered in Pylos,
rather most eager to mingle in battle; but Neleus would not
let me accouter myself—in fact, he had hidden my horses—
since he thought that as yet I was not at all skillful in war-deeds.
720 Nevertheless, I was most outstanding among our horsemen,
even though I was on foot, for Athena so guided the fighting.
Into the sea-brine there flows forth the Minyéïos River
close to Arénè; we Pylian horsemen awaited the sacred
morning in that place; then came streaming the bands of foot soldiers.
725 Moving in haste from the river, accoutered with armor and weapons,
we to the sacred stream of the Álpheios came in the noontide.
There to all-powerful Zeus we sacrificed beautiful victims,
also to Álpheios offered a bull, and a bull to Poseidon,
offered a cow of the herd, moreover, to bright-eyed Athena,
730 then took supper all over the army, in ordered divisions,
finally lay down to sleep, each man still wearing his armor,
there by the streams of the river. But those greathearted Epeíans
stood surrounding the town, most eager to seize and destroy it.
But before that could happen appeared a great action of Ares;
735 for when above earth radiant Helios started ascending,
then in the battle we joined, while praying to Zeus and Athena.
But then, during the strife of the Pylians and the Epeíans,
I first slaughtered a man, and I took his single-hoofed horses—
Moúlios was he, a spearman, the son-in-law of Augeías,
740 having the eldest daughter as wife, fair-haired Agamédè,
who knew all the medicinal herbs that the broad earth nurtures.
Him with a bronze-tipped spear I struck as he came to attack me;
down in the dust he dropped; I, onto his chariot leaping,
took a stand there with the foremost; but those greathearted Epeíans
745 fled one way or another, as soon as they saw the man fallen
who was the horsemen's leader, the best among them in the battle.
Charging upon them then like a whirlwind black and ferocious,
I took chariots, fifty of them, and by each at its sides were
two men taking the soil in their teeth, brought down by my spear-thrust.
750 Aktor's scions would I have destroyed now, both Moliónes,

had their genuine sire, the wide-governing shaker of earth, not
rescued them from the battle, enveloping them in a thick mist.
Thereupon great was the might Zeus granted the Pylian fighters,
since so long we followed them over the breadth of the flatland,

755 killing the men themselves and collecting their beautiful armor,
till to Bouprásion, rich in wheat, we had driven our horses,
and the Olénian Rock and the Hill of Alésion, so-called
there in the land, where the host was again turned back by Athena.
Killing my last man there, I left him; and then the Achaians

760 back from Bouprásion drove their swift-running horses to Pylos;
Zeus among gods they were all glorifying, and Nestor among men.
    "Such I was among men—if ever I was—but advantage
only Achilles will have from his valor; indeed I believe that
he will lament very much, too late, when the army has perished.

765 Dear friend, such was the charge indeed that Menoítios gave you,
that same day that from Phthia to join Agamemnon he sent you.
Both of us then were within, myself and the noble Odysseus;
everything we heard in the halls, what charges he gave you;
there we had come to the palace of Peleus, pleasant to dwell in,

770 gathering soldiers throughout the much-nourishing land of Achaia.
There in the palace the hero Menoítios then we discovered,
you and Achilles as well; old Peleus the chariot-driver
fat ox-thighs was just burning to Zeus the great thunderbolt-hurler
out in the well-walled courtyard; a goblet of gold he was holding,

775 pouring the glistening wine out over the burning oblations.
You two were busy preparing the flesh of the ox, and as we two
stood in the doorway there, in astonishment leapt up Achilles,
grasped our hands, led us in, and invited us both to be seated;
generous welcome he set before us, as is fitting for strangers.

780 When we had quite satisfied our appetites, eating and drinking,
I then started to talk, and to follow along with us bade you.
You both strongly desired to, and those two gave many charges.
Thus old Peleus laid this charge on his offspring Achilles,
always to be outstanding, preeminent over all others;

785 this was the charge on you of Menoítios, scion of Aktor:
'My child, true that in birth and in blood is Achilles above you;
you are the elder indeed, but in strength he is greatly the better.
Yet speak serious words to him wisely, and furnish him counsel,
give him sagacious guidance; and he will obey to his own good.'

790 So the old man charged—you have forgotten. But even now might you

speak of these matters to war-skilled Achilles, in case he would heed you.
Who knows whether you might with a god's aid, rousing his spirit,
talk him around? For an excellent thing is a comrade's persuasion.
Should he in fact be shunning a prophecy known to his own heart,
795   something from Zeus put into his mind by the lady his mother,
yet let him send you out, and as well let the rest of his army,
Mýrmidons, follow, that you for the Dánaäns might be a beacon;
let him as well give you his fine armor to wear into battle,
so that the Trojans perhaps might think you are he and refrain from
800   combat, and then these warlike sons of Achaians could take breath,
tired as they are; very scant is the time to take breath in a battle.
Easily you, unwearied, could drive those men who are now so
weary with strife, toward town and away from the galleys and cabins."
    So he spoke, and in him he roused up the heart in his bosom;
805   running, he went by the galleys to Aíakos' scion Achilles.
But then, when by the galleys of godlike Odysseus Patróklos
came in his running, the place of the people's assembly and judgments,
where also for the gods their altars had all been erected,
there did the Zeus-sprung son of Euaímon, Eurýpylos, meet him—
810   that man recently wounded when struck in the thigh by an arrow—
limping away from the battle; and down from his head and his shoulders
sweat kept running in streams, while out of his terrible wound was
oozing the thick black blood, but his mind was as steady as ever.
Looking at him felt pity Menoítios' valorous scion;
815   sorrowing then he spoke, and in these winged words he addressed him:
"Oh you miserable wretches, the Dánaäns' leaders and princes,
then were you destined, far from your friends and the land of your fathers,
here in Troy to be glutting the swift dogs thus with your white fat?
But come now, tell me this, Zeus-cherished Eurýpylos, hero,
820   whether somehow the Achaians will yet hold back huge Hektor,
whether instead they will die now and under his spear will be vanquished."
    Wounded Eurýpylos then spoke out to him, giving an answer:
"No more, Zeus-descended Patróklos, will the Achaians
make a defense—instead they will hurl themselves on the black ships,
825   since those men who before were the noblest in fighting are all now
lying among our ships—they were struck by missiles and wounded
under the hands of the Trojans, whose strength keeps ever increasing.
But now save me and take me with you back there to the black ship;
out of my thigh cut the arrow; the dark blood coating the wound then
830   clean off well in warm water, and sprinkle on herbs that are soothing,

excellent ones that are said to have been taught you by Achilles,
whom first Cheiron instructed, the most upright of the Centaurs.
For of the healers indeed, Podaleírios, noble Macháon,
one of the two, I believe, has a wound, so he at the cabins
835   lies now, being himself in need of an excellent healer,
while on the flatland the other awaits the fierce strife of the Trojans."
     Speaking to him made answer Menoítios' valorous scion:
"How can these things be? What shall we do, Eurýpylos, hero?
I am now going to carry a message to war-skilled Achilles
840   as the Achaians' protector, Gerenian Nestor, commanded;
yet even so, I will not, in your pain and exhaustion, neglect you."
     Thus, and he grasped by the chest that shepherd of people and led him
into the cabin; his comrade saw them and spread out some oxhides.
There, first stretching him out, from his thigh with a dagger Patróklos
845   cut the sharp arrow that pierced it; the dark blood coating the wound he
cleaned off well in warm water; upon it he scattered a bitter
root he crumbled apart in his hand, a painkiller, and it stopped
all of his pains, and the wound dried out, and the blood stopped flowing.

BOOK 12

So inside of the cabin Menoítios' valorous scion
kept on tending the wounded Eurýpylos. Meanwhile the others,
Argives and Trojans, were fighting in close throngs. Not very long that
trench of the Dánaän army would hold, and above it the wide wall
5   which they had built in defense of the ships, and about it a trench had
driven—but had not given the gods any splendid oblation—
so it would hold the swift ships and the masses of plunder inside it,
thereby keeping them safe; however, against the immortal
gods' wills it had been built; so for no long time it remained firm.
10   While yet Hektor was living, as long as Achilles was angry,
while that city of Priam the lord was untaken and unsacked,
so long also the great wall of the Achaians remained firm.
Finally, after the bravest and best of the Trojans had perished,
and of the many Argives some brought down, others surviving,
15   when in the tenth year taken and sacked was the city of Priam,
back to their own dear country the Argives went in the galleys;
then did Poseidon the lord and Apollo decide on a scheme for
wrecking the wall by bringing against it the might of the rivers,
all those which flow down to the sea from the summits of Ida,
20   Rhesos and Heptáporos and Karésos and Rhodios River,
Grénikos and Aisépos as well, and the noble Skamánder,
Símoeis too, where many an oxhide shield and a four-horned
helmet had dropped in the dust, and the race of the demigod-heroes;
all of their mouths then Phoibos Apollo diverted together,
25   nine days throwing the stream at the wall; incessantly Zeus was
raining, that he more swiftly could deluge the wall in the sea-brine.
Holding his trident aloft in his hands the earth-shaker himself was
leading, and into the billows he sent forth all the foundations,
whether of logs or of stones, the Achaians had labored to put down,
30   making the shore quite smooth by the Hellespont's powerful current.

Then with sand the great beach of the sea he again covered over,
once he had wrecked that wall, and diverted the rivers to those same
channels in which they had earlier poured their fair-flowing water.
    Such were the things that Poseidon the lord and Apollo would later
35 bring to fulfillment; but then was the clamor of battle ignited
there by the well-built wall, and the beams of the towers were clanging
loud when struck; and the Argives, quelled by the lash of great Zeus, were
penned in close to the hollow galleys and crowded together,
checked by terror of Hektor, the mighty deviser of panic.
40 Meanwhile he, as before he had done, fought on like a whirlwind.
As at a time that among hounds thronging together with huntsmen
either a boar or a lion is wheeling, exulting in vigor,
so that against it the hunters array themselves like a bastion,
stand there facing the quarry, and javelins thick and incessant
45 hurl from their hands, yet never in it does the glorious spirit
tremble or quail in fear—its courage indeed is what kills it—
over and over it wheels at the ranks of the hunters to try them;
then wherever it charges retire those ranks of the hunters—
just so Hektor was wheeling about in the throng, and his comrades
50 urging ahead to cross over the trench. But his own swift-footed
horses did not dare do it, but whinnying loud, on the very
brink they stood in affright, for the broad trench there before them was
scaring them off, nor would either to overleap it or to drive through
be at all easy, for banks overhanging along its whole circuit
55 stood on both of its sides; it was fitted above on the banks with
palisades pointed and sharp that the sons of Achaians had planted,
close-set, many and huge, a defense against enemy fighters.
There any horse, at a well-wheeled chariot straining, would not go
easily in, but if men were on foot they were eager to do so.
60 Thereat Polýdamas, standing beside bold Hektor, addressed him:
"Hektor and others, the chiefs of the Trojans as well as the allies,
foolishly over the trench we are trying to drive the swift horses.
It is most difficult going across it, for sharp palisades are
planted within it, and close by them is the wall of the Achaians;
65 no way possible is it to go with the chariots down there,
neither to fight—it is narrow and I think we will be beaten.
For if intending them ill now Zeus who thunders above is
wholly destroying the foe while sending his aid to the Trojans,
then I would want this too, that immediately it would happen
70 that the Achaians should die here nameless and distant from Argos;

216

but if instead they turn against us and at once we are driven
back from the galleys and there in the deep-dug trench are entangled,
then I believe no longer would anyone go with a message
back to the city, if once the Achaians have rallied against us.

75　But come, just as I say, let all of us heed and obey it:
there by the trench now let the attendants rein in the horses,
let us ourselves, advancing on foot and accoutered in armor,
follow along in a body with Hektor; and then the Achaians
will not stay, if upon them the grim death-bindings are fastened."

80　　So said Polýdamas; Hektor was pleased by his counsel of prudence;
straightway he to the ground from his chariot leapt in his armor.
Nor did the rest of the Trojans remain on chariots gathered,
rather they all leapt out, as they saw noble Hektor had done so.
Then to his charioteer each man gave orders that he should

85　rein in the horses alongside the trench in an orderly manner;
meanwhile the fighters, dividing, arranged themselves in a body,
so that in five well-ordered battalions they followed the leaders.
Those who were going with Hektor, and faultless Polýdamas also,
they were the greatest in number, the noblest, and eager beyond all

90　others to shatter the wall and to fight by the hollow galleys.
Also with them as a third did Kebríones follow—a lesser
man than Kebríones there with his chariot Hektor was leaving.
Leading the second were Paris, Alkáthoös too, and Agénor.
Hélenos then and the godlike Deíphobos headed the third, both

95　scions of Priam; as third did the hero Ásios join them—
Ásios, Hýrtakos' son, whom there from Arísbè his horses
tawny and mighty had taken, away from the river Selléëis.
Then of the fourth Ainéas, the powerful son of Anchíses,
served as the chief, and along with him went two sons of Anténor,

100　Ákamas and Archélochos, skilled in all manner of battle.
Then Sarpédon was leading the band of the glorious allies;
he as well chose out Glaukos and warlike Ásteropaíos,
since those two were the ones he believed to be clearly the best of
other men after himself; but among all he was outstanding.

105　Once they had fenced each other by joining the shields made of oxhide,
they charged avidly straight at the Dánaäns, nor did they think that
those any longer would hold, but would fall back into the black ships.
Then did the rest of the Trojans and far-famed allies in battle,
heeding the counsel of faultless Polýdamas, quickly obey it,

110　but not Ásios, Hýrtakos' scion, the marshal of men, was

willing to leave there his steeds and the charioteer his attendant;
rather with them he went up close to the swift-faring galleys,
childish fool, who was not to escape from a baneful destruction,
nor in his horses and chariot glorying there by the galleys
115 ever to go back homeward to windswept Ilion city,
for before that, by the spear of Deukálion's glorious scion,
Lord Idómeneus, banefully named doom shrouded him over.
For to the left of the galleys he headed, to where the Achaians
often were going with horses and chariots out of the flatland;
120 thither he drove his own horses and chariot, nor at the gate he
found its leaves had been shut and the long bar fixed in the sockets;
rather the men kept holding them open, that some of their comrades
might be saved as they fled to the galleys away from the battle.
There with unfaltering mind he headed his horses; his men came
125 after him, stridently shouting, nor did they think the Achaians
there any longer would hold, but would fall back into the black ships,
childish fools! At the gates they found two men of the noblest,
both of them high-souled scions of Lapiths, illustrious spearmen,
one, Peiríthoös' scion, the powerful lord Polypoítes,
130 noble Leónteus the other, a peer of man-slaughtering Ares.
These were the two who stationed themselves in front of the high-built
gates, stood there like oaks high-crested with leaves in the mountains—
all of their days they endure, withstanding the wind and the rainfall,
planted and fixed as they are by their roots long-reaching and mighty.
135 So did the two men, putting their trust in their hands and their power,
stay to endure the assault of great Ásios, nor did they take flight.
Straight on up to the well-built rampart, raising on high their
shields of dried oxhide, now were advancing with clamor enormous
those Lord Ásios led and Iámenos too, and Orestes,
140 Ádamas Ásios' son, Oinámaös also, and Thoön.
Those two men who were inside the rampart had now for a time been
rousing the well-greaved Achaians to fight in defense of the galleys;
but then, when they observed that the Trojans were charging against that
rampart, and how on the Dánaäns clamor and panic had fallen,
145 out of the gate then both of them rushed and in front of it started
fighting, the way that a couple of wild boars high in the mountains
stand to await some rabble of hunters and hounds that assails them,
slantwise charging to every side they shatter the forest,
cutting the trees at the root, and the clatter of tusks is resounding
150 loud till somebody strikes them and takes life out of their bodies.

So then clattered the glittering bronze on the chests of the two men
struck by foes near at hand, since both of them mightily battled,
putting their trust in the men above them and as well in their own strength.
Those up above kept hurling enormous stones from the well-built
155   bastions to fight in defense of their own lives and of the cabins
and of the swift-faring ships. To the earth like snow did the boulders
fall, like flakes that a fierce wind driving the shadowy clouds pours
on the much-nourishing earth in a snowstorm dense and incessant;
so from their hands were the missiles pouring, from both the Achaians'
160   hands and the hands of the Trojans; about them helmets were clanging
harshly, and strong-bossed shields, being struck by the rocks like millstones.
Finally striking his thighs both sides, in his agony groaning,
these words Ásios Hýrtakos' son spoke forth in resentment:
"Father Zeus, now it is clear you too are a lover of falsehood,
165   utterly so; for I did not think that the hero-Achaians
would be able to hold our might and invincible hands back;
yet these men, as the wasps with flexible waists or the bees that
make their dwelling upon some highway rugged and rocky
never forsake their hollow abode, but are always remaining
170   there to protect their offspring and ward off men who are hunting,
so from the gate these men, though they are but two, are unwilling
ever to give ground now, till either they kill or are taken."
    So he spoke, but he did not sway Zeus' mind as he said it,
for in his heart Zeus wished to bestow great glory on Hektor.
175   Others about other gates kept fighting and joining in battle;
it would be hard, though I were a god, to recount them all fully.
Everywhere by the stone-built wall was the ravenous wildfire
rising; the Argives, pained as they were, of necessity kept on
fighting, defending the ships. In their spirits the gods were dejected,
180   all those who had been helping the Dánaän troops in the battle.
    So did the Lapiths continue the struggle and join in the combat.
Casting his spear again, strong Polypoítes, Peiríthoös' scion,
struck bold Dámasos square on his helmet with bronze cheek-pieces,
nor was the bronze point stopped by the helmet of bronze, but it broke clean
185   through it and utterly shattered the bone, so that all of his brain was
spattered about inside—so furiously he subdued him.
Then straightway both Pylon and Órmenos he did away with.
Meanwhile the scion of Ares, Leónteus, letting his spear fly,
struck Antímachos' scion Hippómachos square on the war-belt.
190   Then again, drawing his sword with the sharp point out of its scabbard,

he rushed straight through the melee against Antíphates first and
struck him in close combat; to the earth he was thrown down backward.
Then he at once killed Menon, Iámenos too, and Orestes—
all to the nourishing earth he brought in rapid succession.

195   While those Lapiths were stripping the corpses of glittering armor,
meanwhile the young men who with Polýdamas followed, and Hektor—
who were the greatest in number, the noblest, and eager beyond all
others to shatter the wall and to hurl fire into the galleys—
these men there by the trench yet stood to consider the matter.

200 For to the host so eager to cross had the sign of a bird come;
it was a high-flying eagle that skirted the left of the people,
holding a monstrous and blood red serpent aloft in his talons,
one still living and panting, its war-craft not yet forgotten;
for at the eagle who held it, with head back-twisted it struck and

205 hit on the chest by the neck; then, stung with the pain, to the ground he
threw it from him; in the midst of the throng he allowed it to fall down,
while he himself with a scream flew away on the breath of the stormwind.
Then did the Trojans shudder, at seeing the glistening serpent
where in their midst it lay as an omen of Zeus of the aegis.

210 Thereat Polýdamas, standing beside bold Hektor, addressed him:
"Hektor, in some way always do you chide me in assemblies,
even if I speak nobly, for not at all seemly is it for
one of the people to counsel against you, not in the council
nor in the warfare, ever, but always to strengthen your power;

215 nevertheless I will now speak out what seems to me wisest.
Let us indeed not go for the Dánaäns, fight by the galleys.
For it is so, I believe, that the issue will be, if the bird-sign
which just came to the Trojans so eager to cross is a true one—
it was a high-flying eagle that skirted the left of the people,

220 holding a monstrous and blood red serpent aloft in his talons,
living, but suddenly dropped it before he arrived at his dear home,
nor did he finish the labor, to take it to give to his offspring.
So for ourselves—even if those gates and the wall of the Achaians
we by our great might shatter, and if the Achaians should give way,

225 not in good order will we go back from the ships on the same road;
many a Trojan will we be leaving, the ones the Achaians
will with the bronze bring down in the battle, defending the galleys.
So would a prophet interpret the omen, a man who in spirit
had clear knowledge of signs and by whom were persuaded the people."

230   Looking from lowering brows spoke Hektor of glittering helmet:

"Pleasing to me no longer, Polýdamas, what you are saying—
you know how to devise some other speech better than this one.
But if indeed such things you truly are speaking in earnest,
then have the gods themselves most certainly ruined your senses,
235   you who bid me forget the advice of loud-thundering Zeus that
he himself gave me, making a promise and nodding agreement.
Do you indeed then bid me to take such heed of the long-winged
birds, about which I am neither concerned nor in any way troubled,
whether they go to the right, the direction of dawn and the sunrise,
240   whether instead to the left and toward the night-murk and the shadows?
Rather indeed let us now take heed of the counsel of great Zeus,
who is the lord over all us mortals and all the immortals.
One bird-sign is the best one—to fight in defense of the country.
Why are you thus so frightened of battle and violent combat?
245   For even if we others are all of us utterly slaughtered
here by the ships of the Argives, for you is no fear that you perish,
since inside you the heart is not steady in battle nor warlike.
Now if you hold yourself from the combat, or if with your words you
win some other man over and turn him away from the battle,
250   straightway, struck down under my spear, your life you will forfeit."
      So having spoken to him, he started ahead, and they followed
raising a marvelous din; then Zeus the great thunderbolt-hurler
roused over them from the summits of Ida a blast of the stormwinds
carrying dust straight on at the galleys, and thus the Achaians'
255   minds he amazed, and the glory he gave to the Trojans and Hektor.
Therefore, putting their trust in the portents as well as their own might,
they kept trying to shatter the great wall of the Achaians.
They dragged off of the bastions the copings; the breastworks they threw
down, then pried up the posts projecting, the ones the Achaians
260   first in the earth had planted as buttresses holding the bastions;
these they tried to pull out, and expected to breach the Achaians'
rampart; but not yet out of their way did the Dánaäns give ground;
rather with oxhides closing the breastworks, out of them they kept
casting at enemy troops who were coming up under the rampart.
265   Meanwhile both the Ajaxes were giving out orders and ranging
everywhere by the bastions and rousing the might of the Achaians,
one with the mildest of words, but another with speeches unyielding
they would rebuke, whomever they saw shrink back from the battle:
"Friends, you who of the Argives are leaders, and you who are middling,
270   you also who are lower—because in no manner are all men

equal in fighting—for all there is now much work to accomplish;
this, I suppose, of yourself you recognize. Back to the galleys
let not anyone turn as he hears a foe shouting to battle;
no, charge forward instead and exhort each other to do so,
275 hoping that Zeus, the Olympian lord of the lightning, may grant us
both to repel the assault and to drive our foes to the city."
    So in front the two, shouting, aroused the Achaians to battle.
But from the others—as thick and incessant the snowflakes are falling
all of a wintery day, at a time Zeus Counselor rouses
280 snow to descend, so showing to men what missiles he uses,
lulling the winds to a slumber, he pours out snow until he has
shrouded the peaks of the towering mountains, the lofty escarpments,
and the luxuriant grasslands and fertile labors of farmers;
down on the silvery sea it is poured, and the shores and the harbors;
285 plashing upon it the breaker is quieted; every other
thing it enshrouds from above, when snow of Zeus presses upon it—
so both sides from the fighters the stones flew thick and incessant,
some at the Trojans and some from the Trojans against the Achaians,
so were they throwing; above the whole wall their clamor was rising.
290   Not even then, in fact, would the Trojans and glorious Hektor
ever have shattered the gates of the rampart and broken the long bar,
had Zeus Counselor not roused up Sarpédon, his own son,
now at the Argive troops, like a lion at crooked-horned cattle.
Quickly in front of his body he lifted his circular shield up,
295 beautiful, fashioned of hammered-out bronze that a worker of bronze had
hammered, and then on the inward side he had stitched thick-folded
oxhides with stitches of gold, a continuous circuit about it;
this then holding in front of his body, and brandishing two spears,
he set forth like a mountain-bred lion who has for a long time
300 been quite lacking in meat, and his valorous spirit commands him
even to try for the flocks by approaching a strong-built homestead,
since even though he should find inside of it shepherds, the men who
there with dogs and with spears maintain guard over the sheep flock,
he is not minded to flee from the fold without making a trial;
305 rather, he either will seize one, jumping inside, or himself be
struck at his first onset by a javelin out of a quick hand;
so it was then that his spirit aroused Sarpédon the godlike
strongly to charge at the wall and to break right into the breastworks.
Quickly a word he uttered to Glaukos, Hippólochos' offspring:
310 "Glaukos, why is it then that we two are especially honored

with the high seats we hold, with meat and with ever-full goblets
back in the Lykian land, and as gods all the people regard us?
And an enormous estate we possess on the banks of the Xanthos,
lovely in vineyard, orchard, and rich wheat-nourishing plowland.
315 Therefore now with the foremost Lykians must we indeed keep
standing and ever engaged in the blistering heat of the battle,
so that a man of the mail-clad Lykians speak thus about us:
'Certainly not without glory are leading the Lykian country
those two rulers of ours—as the sheep they eat are the fattest,
320 choicest the honey-sweet wine they drink, so also their might is
noblest, for they with the foremost Lykians enter the combat.'
Ah friend, were we indeed to escape this battle, and were we
going to live as immortal and ageless forever and ever,
neither would I myself with the foremost enter the combat,
325 nor would I urge you into the battle that wins a man glory;
but now, since over us anyway stand spirits of death in
myriads, which no mortal can either evade or escape from,
let us go, either to give a man glory or win it from someone."
    He spoke; Glaukos did not turn away nor at all disobey him;
330 straight on both of them went, the great tribe of the Lykians leading.
As he observed them Menéstheus the scion of Péteos shuddered,
for it was toward his bastion the two came bringing disaster.
Over the bastion he scanned the Achaians, in hopes that he might see
one of the leaders to keep the disaster away from his comrades;
335 then he noticed the two Ajaxes, insatiate of warfare,
standing, and Teukros, who had just recently come from his cabin,
close to their side; but in no way could he have shouted to reach them,
since so great was the tumult—the noise went up to the sky of
shields being struck and of four-horned helmets crested with horsehair,
340 and of the gates, since all had been closed, and before them were standing
fighters attempting to break them open by force and to enter.
Straightway to Ajax then he dispatched his herald Thoötes;
"Go on the run now, noble Thoötes, and summon here Ajax,
both of them preferably, since that by far would be best of
345 all, for a sheer destruction will very soon here be accomplished,
since so press us the Lykian leaders, the ones who before have
proven to be most formidable in the violent combats.
If among them there too war-labor and strife have arisen,
then by himself let valorous Ajax Télamon's son come,
350 and let follow him Teukros, the man well skilled as an archer."

So he spoke; having listened the herald did not disobey him.
He went running along by the wall of the bronze-clad Achaians,
reached the Ajaxes, and standing beside them, at once he addressed them:
"Both Ajaxes, commanders in war of the bronze-shirted Argives,
355   now the dear son of the Zeus-sprung Péteos wants me to bid you
come over there so that you, though briefly, encounter the war-toil,
both of you preferably, since that by far would be best of
all, for a sheer destruction will very soon there be accomplished,
since so press them the Lykian leaders, the ones who before have
360   proven to be most formidable in the violent combats.
If among you here too war-labor and strife have arisen,
then by himself let valorous Ajax Télamon's son come,
and let follow him Teukros, the man well skilled as an archer."
He spoke, nor disobeyed the great scion of Télamon Ajax.
365   Straightway in these winged words he spoke to Oïleus' scion:
"Ajax, here do you both, yourself and the strong Lykomédes,
stand fast, rousing the Dánaäns up to do strenuous combat;
meanwhile I will go over, and there I will join in the fighting.
Quickly will I come back when well I have come to their rescue."
370   So having spoken departed the scion of Télamon Ajax;
following him went Teukros, his brother by one same father;
Pándion went with them also to bear the curved bow of Lord Teukros.
Just at the time they reached greathearted Menéstheus' bastion,
walking inside of the rampart, and reached those men who were hard-pressed,
375   onto the breastworks like a black threatening tempest were mounting
powerful enemy fighters, the Lykians' leaders and princes;
they charged forward to fight against them, and the battle cry rose up.
Ajax Télamon's son was the first who slaughtered a fighter—
it was the comrade of Lord Sarpédon, the great-souled Epíkles—
380   striking at him with a huge rough boulder that inside the wall was
lying, the uppermost piled by the breastwork, nor could a man have
easily held it in both of his hands, not even a strong man,
such as are men nowadays; but aloft he raised it and hurled it,
shattered his four-horned helmet and instantly battered together
385   all of the bones of his head, and at once he dropped like a tumbler
down from the bastion above, and his spirit abandoned the bone-frame.
Teukros then, as the powerful son of Hippólochos, Glaukos,
rushed at the high-built wall, let fly at the man with an arrow,
where he observed his arm was uncovered, and halted his combat.
390   Back from the wall he stealthily leapt, so that none of the Achaians

might see how he was wounded and boast about him in their speeches.
Sorrow descended upon Sarpédon that Glaukos was leaving,
soon as he knew it, and yet he never forgot his own war-craft;
rather he thrust with his spear at Alkmáon the scion of Thestor,
395   struck him, and drew out the blade; he followed the spear as he fell down
flat on his face, and around him clattered his bronze-adorned armor.
Grasping the breastwork then in his ponderous hands Sarpédon
pulled it, and all of it came down, the whole length, so that the rampart
stood uncovered above, and a path he had opened for many.
400   Now against him came Ajax and Teukros together, and Teukros
struck with an arrow the glistening baldric surrounding his chest to
hold the man-sheltering shield; yet Zeus kept warding the doomsday
off of his son, so that not by the ships' sterns he would be vanquished;
leaping upon him, Ajax struck at his shield, but the spear did
405   not go through it but caused him to reel in his furious onset.
He from the breastwork yielded a little, but not altogether
did he withdraw, for at heart he was hoping to win himself glory.
Wheeling about he called to the godlike Lykian fighters:
"Lykians, why are you slackening so from your furious valor?
410   Difficult is it for me, indeed, although I am mighty,
breaking the wall single-handed to open a path to the galleys.
Now come along, for the more who labor, the better the work is."
     So he spoke, and his men, terrified of their lord's disapproval,
started to press more strongly around that lord of the counsels,
415   while on the opposite side the Argives reinforced their battalions
there inside of the rampart; to all then appeared a great labor,
since now neither were those strong Lykians able at all to
shatter the Dánaäns' rampart and open a path to the galleys,
nor were the Dánaän spearmen in turn ever able at all to
420   thrust those Lykians back from the rampart, once they had neared it.
Just in the way two men might fight around boundary-markers,
holding their measuring-rods in their hands, in a communal plowland,
on a minute bit of ground they wrangle for equal allotments,
so did the breastworks hold these foes apart; over them, both sides
425   kept on fighting each other by smiting the circular oxhide
shields protecting their chests, and the fluttering shaggy-fringed bucklers.
There by the pitiless bronze in their flesh were many men wounded,
both when somebody twisted away and his back was laid bare while
fighting, and straight through the shield itself were struck many others.
430   Everywhere were the bastions and breastworks spattered with blood from

fighters on both sides, alike from the Trojans and from the Achaiäns.
Yet even so they could not raise panic among the Achaians;
rather they held, like scales that a woman, an honest handworker,
holds, and upon the two pans she raises the weight and the wool up,
435   making them equal, to garner a pitiful wage for her children;
equally so for the fighters the battle was stretched, and the warfare,
up to the time Zeus granted superior glory to Hektor
scion of Priam, the first to leap inside the wall of the Achaians.
Piercingly then he yelled to the Trojans, and loudly he shouted:
440   "Rise up, Trojans, tamers of horses, and shatter the Argives'
rampart and hurl right into the galleys the ravenous wildfire!"
    So he spoke to exhort them; they all gave ear to him, heeding;
straight at the wall they rushed in a body, and onto the copings
then they at once climbed up, while gripping their spears with the sharp points.
445   Hektor snatched up and carried a stone that in front of the gates was
standing, a ponderous mass in its lower part, while it was sharp up
higher; and this not even the two best men of the people
easily off of the ground could have heaved up onto a wagon,
such as are men nowadays; but alone did he easily wield it—
450   it was made light by the scion of Kronos of crooked devices.
Just as a shepherd easily carries the fleece of a huge ram,
picking it up in one hand, and upon him the load weighs little,
so now Hektor was lifting and bearing the rock to the door-leaves
which protected the gates close-fitted and strongly constructed,
455   double gates, loftily built; and the bars inside them were double,
held by crossing each other, with one bolt fixing them firmly.
Nearing them, he stood bracing himself, struck them in the middle,
setting his feet wide so that his missile would not be weakened,
breaking the hinges on both of the door-leaves; inward the stone fell
460   ponderously, and the gates groaned loud both sides, and the bar did
not hold firm, but the doors one way and the other were sundered
under the force of the stone. Inside lunged glorious Hektor,
dark in his face as a night come suddenly, brightly agleam with
terrible bronze that he wore on his body, and two were the spears he
465   held in his hands; nobody who met him except for the gods could
hold him back when he leapt in the gates, eyes blazing with wildfire.
Wheeling around in the throng he called to the Trojans and bade them
climb up over the rampart, and they at his urging obeyed him.
Straightway some climbed over the rampart, as others were pouring
470   in at the strong-built gates, and the Dánaäns scattered in panic
there by the hollow galleys; the tumult arose unabated.

BOOK 13

Now Zeus, once he had brought to the galleys the Trojans and Hektor,
left them there by the ships to endure war-labor and hardship
ceaselessly, and himself his glittering eyes he averted,
gazing afar, out over the land of the Thracian horsemen
and of the Mysians, hand-to-hand fighters, renowned Hippemólgoi,
mare's-milk-drinkers, and Ábioi, who of all men are most righteous.
No more at all toward Troy his glittering eyes he directed,
since in his heart he did not expect anyone of the deathless
gods to come down to the aid of the Dánaäns or of the Trojans.
Nor was the powerful shaker of earth maintaining a blind watch,
since he in fact sat marveling over the battle and warfare
high on the topmost peak of the forested island of Samos,
Thracian domain; for from there all Ida appeared to his vision,
so did the city of Priam appear, and the ships of the Achaians—
thither he came from the sea-brine and sat; the Achaians he pitied,
how they were quelled by the Trojans, and Zeus he strongly resented.
Straightway he went down from the mountaintop rugged and rocky,
striding on swift feet forth; the tall peaks and the forest were trembling
under the deathless feet of Poseidon as he was advancing.
Thrice he strode as he went, and arrived at his goal with the fourth step,
Aigai; there in the depths of the sea had his glorious palace
been constructed aglitter with gold, unfailing forever.
Thither he came, then under his chariot harnessed his bronze-hoofed
horses of swift strong flight, with their manes all golden and flowing;
golden the armor he put on his body, and skillfully wrought of
gold was the whip he grasped; on his chariot mounting he set forth
driving ahead on the waves; and the seabeasts gamboled beneath on
all sides out of the depths, nor did they ignore their own master;
gladly the sea-brine parted before him; the horses were flying
rapidly, nor underneath was the axle of bronze at all wetted.

Him to the ships of the Achaians the light-hoofed horses were taking.
 There is a great broad cave in the depths of the deep sea-chasms
halfway from Ténedos island to Imbros, rugged and rocky.
Therein Poseidon the shaker of earth now halted his horses,
35 then from the chariot loosed them and cast ambrosial fodder
near them to eat, and around their feet he cast golden hobbles
not to be broken or loosed, so they would be safely awaiting
there the return of their lord, and he went to the host of Achaians.
 Meanwhile the Trojans in one great throng, like a blaze or a stormwind,
40 wildly insatiable, followed with Hektor the scion of Priam,
roaring and shouting as one; they were hoping to seize the Achaians'
galleys at last and beside them to slaughter the best of the fighters.
Now however Poseidon the holder and shaker of earth was
urging the Argives on, having come from the depths of the sea-brine,
45 making himself in his form and his weariless voice like Kalchas.
First to the two Ajaxes he spoke, themselves very eager:
"Both of you now, Ajaxes, will save this host of Achaians,
keeping in mind your valor, and not chill terror and panic.
For it is true, elsewhere the invincible hands of the Trojans
50 I do not fear, those who in a throng climbed over the great wall,
since they all will be kept in check by the well-greaved Achaians;
but in this place I dreadfully fear we may suffer affliction,
where one raging with war like a conflagration is leading,
Hektor, who boasts himself to be offspring of Zeus Almighty.
55 So in the hearts of you both may some god bring it to pass that
you stand strongly yourselves and exhort these others to do so;
thereby, hard though he charges, may you from the swift-sailing galleys
drive him away, even if the Olympian rouses him onward."
 So having said, with his trident the holder and shaker of earth struck
60 both of the men, and he filled them both with a powerful valor,
made them nimble of limb, their feet and the hands up above them.
Then he himself, as a swift-winged falcon arises to fly up,
lifting herself from the lofty precipitous rock of her aerie,
then speeds forth in pursuit of another bird over the flatland,
65 so from the men now darted the great earth-shaker Poseidon.
First of the two, swift Ajax, Oïleus' son, recognized him;
then he at once spoke out to the scion of Télamon Ajax:
"Ajax, since now one of the gods who inhabit Olympos
likens himself to the prophet and tells us to fight by the galleys—
70 this is in truth not Kalchas the soothsayer, reader of bird-signs,

since from behind, as from us he parted, the forms of his feet and
legs I easily knew; conspicuous ever the gods are—
then moreover in my own self is the heart in my breast now
rousing me up more strongly to enter the fight and do battle,
75   also are eager beneath me the feet, and the hands up above them."
      Speaking to him then answered the scion of Télamon Ajax:
"Thus now also in me the invincible hands on my spear are
eager, and so my spirit is roused, my feet underneath are
both impatient to move; I am eager for even a single
80   combat with Hektor, the wildly insatiable scion of Priam."
      Such things then they spoke and addressed each one to the other,
glad with the ardor for battle the god put into their spirits.
Meanwhile the shaker of earth roused up the Achaians behind them,
who were recovering strength in their spirits beside the swift galleys.
85   Long had their limbs been loosened by grievous and wearisome war-toil,
then moreover the sorrow arose in their hearts as they saw those
Trojans and how in a mass they had climbed up over the great wall.
Seeing them there, they were letting the tears flow under their eyebrows,
since they thought they would not escape evil; but now the earth-shaker,
90   nimbly advancing among them, was rousing the mighty battalions.
Teukros the first he came to, and Léïtos, urging them onward,
valiant Penéleos too, and Deîpyros also, and Thoas,
Mérionés and as well Antílochos, lords of the war cry;
them he exhorted to battle; in these winged words he addressed them:
95   "Shame, you Argives, greenest of striplings! In you I have trusted
fully that you would be able to save our ships by your fighting;
but if indeed you slacken yourselves from the sorrowful warfare,
now it appears this day we will be brought down by the Trojans.
Well then! Immense is the marvel that I with my eyes am beholding,
100   this dread thing I never imagined would come to fulfillment,
Trojans advancing against our galleys, the men who before were
like deer timid and given to panicking, which in the woodland
furnish the beasts, fierce jackals and leopards and wolves, with their quarry,
skulking in cowardice vainly, in them no ardor for battle.
105   So with the Trojans before: with the might and the hands of the Achaians
they were unwilling to stand face-to-face, not even a little;
now at the hollow ships they are fighting, and far from the city,
since our leader has proven so base and the people are slackers—
they from wrangling with him no longer are minded to guard our
110   swift-sailing galleys at all; instead they are slaughtered among them.

Yet if indeed it really and wholly is true that the cause is
valorous Atreus' son, wide-governing lord Agamemnon,
seeing that he dishonored the swift-footed scion of Peleus,
still for ourselves no way is it proper to slacken from battle;
115   quickly instead let us heal it—a healable heart has a good man.
You would do well no longer to slacken your furious valor,
all you who are the best of the army; and as for myself I
never would quarrel against some man who slackened from battle
were he of no account; but against you in my heart I am wrathful.
120   Oh you weaklings, you soon will accomplish a bane even greater
through this slackness of yours. Yet each of you put in your spirit
shame and the fear of rebuke, for indeed great strife has arisen.
Hektor the lord of the war cry is there at the ships and is fighting,
mighty in strength, and the gates and the long bar now he has shattered."
125   So did the shaker of earth exhort and arouse the Achaians.
There with the two Ajaxes were taking a stand the battalions,
mighty in strength, which neither would Ares have slighted if he had
come among them, nor Athena the rouser of hosts, for the best men,
marshaled apart, were awaiting the Trojans and excellent Hektor;
130   spear by spear was protected, and shield by shield overlapping;
buckler on buckler and helmet on helmet and man against man pressed,
even the helmets with horsehair plumed on the glittering ridges
touched as they nodded their heads, they stood so close to each other;
so did the spears in the bold hands bend back under the strain when
135   brandished, as they with their thoughts unswerving were eager to battle.
       Then in a throng charged forward the Trojans, and Hektor was leading,
avidly pressing ahead, as a rock rolls down from a cliff, thrust
off of the crest of a hill when a river with winter rains swollen
breaks with a marvelous deluge the pitiless cliff's foundation;
140   bounding aloft it is flying along, and beneath it the woods are
crashing, and it speeds ever unswerving until at the level
plain it arrives, then rolls no longer for all of its onrush;
so for a time now Hektor was threatening clear to the seashore
nimbly to go down through the Achaians' cabins and galleys
145   slaughtering; but then, when he encountered the clustered battalions,
there he stood, having come quite close; and the sons of Achaians
faced him and, striking at him with their swords and their double-edged spear-blades,
thrust him away from themselves; and he gave way, staggering backward.
Piercingly then he yelled to the Trojans, and loudly he shouted:
150   "Trojans and Lykians all, Dardánians, hand-to-hand fighters,

stay here beside me; not very long the Achaians will hold me;
even if they have arrayed themselves as a bastion against me,
still I think they will yield to my sword, if in truth I have been roused
up by the greatest of gods, the loud-thundering husband of Hera."
155   So he spoke and aroused in each fighter the strength and the spirit.
There with enormous resolve Deïphobos, scion of Priam,
strode among them; his circular shield he was holding before him,
striding on light foot forth as beneath his shield he went forward.
Mérionés then, aiming a blow with his glittering spear at
160 him, struck square, not missing his aim, on the circular shield of
oxhide, yet not through did he drive it, but well in advance of
that the long spear-shaft broke in the socket; Deïphobos quickly
held from himself his shield made of oxhide, as in his heart he
dreaded the spear of the war-skilled Mérionés, but the hero
165 shrank back into the band of his comrades, terribly angry
both for the victory missed and the spear which he had just broken.
He went passing along the Achaians' cabins and galleys,
so as to fetch for himself a long spear he had left in his cabin.
    Meanwhile the rest fought on, and a noise unquenchable rose up.
170 First then, Teukros the scion of Télamon slaughtered the spearman
Ímbrios, scion of Mentor of numerous horses; before those
sons of Achaians had come he dwelt in Pedaíos and had as
bedmate Médesikástè, a bastard daughter of Priam;
then when the Dánaäns' tractable galleys had come, he returned to
175 Ilion, where among all of the Trojans he was outstanding;
there he abode near Priam, who honored him like his own children.
Him now under the ear with his long spear Télamon's scion
struck, and he drew out the spear; and at once he fell like an ash tree
which on top of a mountain, observed all sides from a distance,
180 hewed by the bronze, brings down to the ground its burgeoning leafage.
So did he fall, and around him clattered his bronze-adorned armor.
Teukros was eager to strip his armor from him, and he rushed out;
but as he rushed up Hektor let fly with his glittering spear-shaft;
he however, observing him closely, avoided the bronze spear
185 barely; Amphímachos, scion of Ktéatos scion of Aktor,
coming to battle, was struck in the chest by the spear of the Trojan;
falling he crashed to the ground, and around him clattered his armor.
Hektor at once charged forward to tear from the head of the great-souled
fighter Amphímachos his strong helmet that fitted his temples;
190 Ajax then with his glittering spear lunged straight at the charging

Hektor, but nowhere he reached his body, as he was entirely
covered in terrible bronze; but he did strike square on the shield-boss,
thrusting him off with his powerful strength, and he gave ground backward
from the two dead men; these the Achaians dragged from the fighting.
195 It was Amphímachos whom noble Stíchios then and Menéstheus,
they the Athenians' lords, bore off to the host of Achaians;
Ímbrios both the Ajaxes, with eager and furious valor,
carried, and like two lions who, snatching a goat from the hounds with
sharp teeth, go off carrying it through thick heavy brushwood—
200 high up over the ground in their jaws they are holding the quarry—
so high up now the two Ajaxes, commanders, were holding
him as his armor they stripped, and his head from the delicate neck was
hewed by Oïleus' son in his wrath at Amphímachos' slaughter;
swinging about, he threw it to spin like a ball through the fighters;
205 down in the dust it fell in front of the feet of Lord Hektor.
      Straightway deep in his heart was Poseidon aroused to a rage at
how that son of his son had fallen in terrible combat.
He went passing along the Achaians' cabins and galleys,
rousing the Dánaäns up, while woe for the Trojans he fashioned.
210 There Idómeneus, famed as a spearman, encountered the god while
coming away from a comrade who out of the battle had come just
recently, struck in the hollow behind his knee by a sharp spear.
Him had his comrades carried away; to the healers the lord gave
charge, then left for his cabin, for he was still eager to enter
215 battle. The powerful shaker of earth now spoke to the hero,
making himself in his voice like Thoas the son of Andraímon,
who in all Pleuron as well as in Kálydon's mountainous uplands
ruled the Aitolians—there as a god by the folk he was honored:
"Where, Idómeneus, counselor-lord of the Cretans, have those threats
220 vanished with which by the sons of Achaians were threatened the Trojans?"
      Speaking to him made answer Idómeneus, lord of the Cretans:
"Thoas, indeed there is no man now blameworthy, as far as
I can perceive, since all of us know well how to do battle.
Neither does spiritless fear hold anyone, nor is there any,
225 yielding to dread, who withdraws from the baneful battle; but thus no
doubt, I suppose, it will please the all-powerful scion of Kronos
that the Achaians should die here nameless and distant from Argos.
But as before this, Thoas, you ever were steady in battle,
rousing another man also, whenever you saw any slacker,
230 therefore do not stop now, but to each man shout and exhort him."

Speaking to him then answered the great earth-shaker Poseidon:
"No, Idómeneus, never may that man go any more back
home out of Troy, but a mere plaything for the hounds let him stay here,
any who this day willfully slackens from fighting the battle.
235　But come—taking your arms, come hither; together we must keep
speeding the toil, in hopes we can help, though we are but two men.
Even to no-account men comes prowess when acting together;
we two know how to fight against even the men who are bravest."
　　　So having spoken the god went back to the toil of the fighters.
240　Soon as Idómeneus came back there to his well-built cabin,
beautiful armor he put on his body, and took up his two spears,
then he set forth to go like lightning the scion of Kronos
takes in his hand, and he brandishes it from resplendent Olympos,
showing a portent to mortals; the rays flash brightly about it—
245　so on his breast as he ran shone brightly Idómeneus' bronze arms.
Mérionés, his mighty retainer, encountered the lord while
he was yet close to his cabin, for after a bronze spear he was
coming, to take it; and mighty Idómeneus spoke and addressed him:
"Molos' son Mérionés, fleet-footed, the dearest of comrades,
250　why have you come here, leaving the battle and terrible combat?
Are you wounded, perhaps, worn down by the point of a missile?
Or do you come on account of a message to me? For myself I
do not desire in the cabin to sit, but to enter the battle."
　　　Thoughtful Mérionés spoke out to him, giving an answer:
255　"Now, Idómeneus, counselor-lord of the bronze-clad Cretans,
I go after a spear, if you have one left in the cabin,
so I can take it—the one I earlier carried was broken
when at the shield of Deïphobos, reckless and haughty, I cast it."
　　　Speaking to him made answer Idómeneus, lord of the Cretans:
260　"Spears indeed, if you want, you will find, be it one, be it twenty;
they in the cabin are standing against the bright wall by the entrance—
Trojan spears that I take from the men I kill; for I am not
minded to stand faraway from the enemy men to do battle;
therefore spears I possess, and as well shields massive with bosses,
265　also helmets and breastplates of polished and glittering brilliance."
　　　Thoughtful Mérionés spoke out to him, giving an answer:
"Yes, in my cabin as well and my black ship many a weapon
do I have of the Trojans, but they are not near to be taken,
since not at all, I say, have I ever forgotten my valor,
270　but with the foremost men in the battle that wins a man glory

I stand always, whenever the wrangling of warfare arises.
No doubt some of the others among the bronze-armored Achaians
are unaware of my fighting, but you, I know, have observed it."
    Speaking to him made answer Idómeneus, lord of the Cretans:
275 "I know you and your prowess—so why do you need to say these things?
For if the best of the men by the galleys were all to be chosen
now for a foray, in which men's prowess is clearly distinguished—
there it is shown which man is a coward and which is courageous,
for of the base man the skin turns color to this or to that hue,
280 nor in his breast does the heart restrain him to sit without moving;
rather he shifts between haunches and sits in turn upon both feet;
also within him the heart pounds violently in his breast as
he is imagining deaths, and his teeth incessantly chatter;
but of the brave man neither the skin-hue changes nor is he
285 terrified once he has taken his place in the ambush of fighters;
rather he prays very soon to be mingling in dolorous battle—
there no man would disparage the might of your hands or your spirit,
since if in war-toil you should be struck by a missile or spear-thrust,
not from behind on the neck or the back that weapon would hit you,
290 but on the chest or perhaps on the belly it rather would meet you
eagerly pressing ahead to the champions' ardent encounter.
But come now, let us talk no longer of this like children,
standing around, lest someone perhaps impatiently blame us;
rather do you go on to the cabin and pick out a strong spear."
295   He spoke; Mériones, that equal of Ares in swiftness,
rapidly went; from the cabin a bronze-tipped spear he selected,
then with Idómeneus followed, his mind set strongly on battle.
Just in the way man-slaughtering Ares advances to battle,
after him Panic, his much-loved son, both mighty and fearless,
300 follows, who causes a fighter though steadfast-hearted to panic;
arming themselves, these two out of Thrace join with the Ephýroi
or with the great-souled Phlégyan warriors; never indeed they
listen to both sides, but give glory to one or the other;
so did Mériones and Idómeneus, leaders of men, now
305 go forth into the battle, in bright bronze armor accoutered.
Mériones first spoke to Idómeneus, uttering these words:
"Son of Deukálion, where are you eager to enter the melee?
Is it to be on the right of the whole host, or in the center,
or on the left side rather? For nowhere else, I believe, so
310 lacking in strength for the fight are the long-haired men, the Achaians."

234

Speaking to him made answer Idómeneus, lord of the Cretans:
"There with the ships in the middle are others indeed who protect them,
both Ajaxes and Teukros, who is among all the Achaians
best in his archery, excellent also in hand-to-hand fighting.
315 Eager to fight as he is, to satiety they will be driving
Hektor the scion of Priam, although he is mighty in power.
Sheer hard work it will be, even if he is avid for battle,
winning against the invincible hands and the power of those men,
then setting fire to the galleys, unless Kronos' scion himself should
320 hurl down into the swift-sailing galleys a firebrand blazing.
Not to a man would yield mighty Ajax Télamon's scion,
anyone who is a mortal, consuming the grain of Deméter,
who can be broken apart by bronze or enormous boulders.
Even to strong rank-breaking Achilles would he not give ground
325 in a close fight—but on foot nobody can rival Achilles.
So, as for us two, drive to the left of the army, that quickly
we know whether we give a man glory or win it from someone."
He spoke; Mériones, that equal of Ares in swiftness,
led them until they arrived at the army, as he had been bidden.
330 Then, as Idómeneus they observed, like a blaze in his valor,
him and as well his retainer, in finely elaborate armor,
all of them, shouting throughout that melee, were going against him;
there by the sterns of the galleys arose their mutual combat.
Just as the gusts of a whistling wind blow swift and ferocious
335 on some day when the dust all over the roads is the thickest,
ever the blast keeps raising a turmoil of dust in a great cloud,
so their battle was clashing together, and they in their hearts were
eager to kill each other with sharp bronze swords in the melee.
Battle in which men perish was bristling there in the long spears,
340 piercers of flesh, that the warriors wielded; the bronze coruscation
blinded their eyes as it glanced bright off of the glittering helmets,
off of the breastplates, burnished anew, and the glistening shields as
they in the turmoil met; stouthearted indeed would a person
be who rejoiced as he saw the war-toil and was not grief-stricken.
345 Thus with divided intent the two powerful scions of Kronos
fashioned for all those heroes and warriors woeful afflictions:
Zeus was desiring the victory now for the Trojans and Hektor,
honoring thus fleet-footed Achilles; but not in the least he
wished that the host of Achaians at Ilion wholly should perish;
350 rather, to Thetis and her strong-spirited son he gave glory.

It was the Argives Poseidon was going among to arouse them,
stealthily issuing out of the silvery sea—he was vexed at
how they were quelled by the Trojans, and Zeus he strongly resented.
Both gods were, to be sure, of the same generation and parents;
355   Zeus however in birth was the elder, in knowledge the greater.
Therefore Poseidon avoided defending the troops in the open;
stealthily always, in semblance a man, he roused the whole army.
Those two, looping between both armies the cable of mighty
conflict and leveling combat, were straining to tighten the cable,
360   not to be broken or loosened, that loosened the knees of the many.
      There, half-gray though he was, Idómeneus yelled to exhort those
Dánaäns; into the Trojans he charged and aroused them to panic;
Óthryoneús he slaughtered, a man who had come from Kabésos.
Recently he, having heard a report of the war, had arrived there
365   seeking in marriage the noblest in form of the daughters of Priam,
lovely Kassandra, without bride-gift, but he promised a great deed—
thrusting from Troy, however unwilling, the sons of Achaians.
So old Priam to him made promise and nodded agreement,
giving the girl; he, trusting the promises, entered the battle.
370   It was at him that Idómeneus aimed with his glittering spear and
threw it and hit him as he strode haughtily, nor did the brazen
breastplate he wore protect him—the spear stuck square in his belly.
Falling he crashed to the ground, and the other, exulting, addressed him:
"Óthryoneús, now beyond all mortals indeed I commend you,
375   should you in fact bring all to fulfillment, as much as you promised
Dárdanos' son, Lord Priam, who promised to give you his daughter.
Such are the things we also would promise and bring to fulfillment,
give you the noblest in form of the daughters of Atreus' scion,
bringing her hither from Argos to wed you, if joining us you will
380   capture and ransack Ilion's well-inhabited city.
But now follow, that we may agree by the seafaring galleys
over a marriage, for we are not paltry in dealing with bride-gifts."
      So having spoken the hero Idómeneus, seizing his foot, dragged
him through the violent combat; but Ásios came to his rescue,
385   striding in front of the horses the charioteer, his attendant,
always held at his shoulders and breathing on him; in his heart he
wanted to strike at Idómeneus, who, too quick with his spear, struck
under the chin on his neck, then drove the bronze point straight through it.
He fell, as at a time that an oak tree falls, or a poplar,
390   or a tall pine tree, which on a mountainside men who are shipwrights

cut with their new-whetted axes to use as the beam of a galley;
so in front of his horses and chariot Ásios now lay
stretched out, roaring with pain; at the blood-soaked dust he was clutching.
Out of the charioteer were the wits quite stricken that he had
395 earlier had, and he did not dare to escape from the enemy's hands by
turning his horses around; Antílochos, steadfast in battle,
lunged with his spear, in the middle impaled him, nor did the brazen
breastplate protect him—the spear he wore stuck square in the belly.
Quickly he fell from the well-built chariot, gasping his life out;
400 as for the steeds, Antílochos, son of the great-souled Nestor,
drove them away from the Trojans and back to the well-greaved Achaians.
    Meanwhile close to Idómeneus came up Deḯphobos, grieving
sorely for Ásios' death, and he cast with his glittering spear at
him, but Idómeneus, sharply observing, avoided the bronze spear,
405 since underneath his circular shield he was covered and hidden—
this, ornamented with oxhide circles and glittering bronze and
fitted with two cross-rods, he would always carry to battle.
Under it he was all crouched, while over him speeded the bronze spear;
harshly and loudly the shield resounded as it by the spear was
410 grazed—yet not in vain from his ponderous hand did he throw it,
but struck Híppasos' son Hypsénor, the shepherd of people,
under the chest in the liver—at once his knees he unloosened.
Vehemently Deḯphobos vaunted, and loudly he shouted:
"Not in the least unavenged lies Ásios—rather I think that
415 now as he enters the dwelling of Hades the strong gatekeeper
he will rejoice in his heart, since I have dispatched him an escort."
    He spoke; grief came over the Argives as he was exulting,
but in war-minded Antílochos most he stirred up the spirit.
Yet although he was grieved, not at all he neglected his comrade,
420 but ran up and bestrode him, and so with his shield he concealed him.
Stooping to take Hypsénor, a pair of the trustworthy comrades,
valiant Mekísteus, Échios' son, and the noble Alástor,
carried him heavily groaning away to the hollow galleys.
    Never Idómeneus slackened his great rage; always he wanted
425 either to shroud in the shadowy night someone of the Trojans
or in his own death fall as he kept bane from the Achaians.
It was the own dear son of the Zeus-sprung lord Aisyétes,
brave Alkáthoös—he was the son-in-law of Anchíses
and of his daughters had wedded the eldest, Híppodameía,
430 whom above all in the house her father and reverend mother

loved in their hearts, since every girl of her age she excelled in
beauty, in skill at her work, and in wisdom; and therefore the noblest
man among those of the broad Troäd took her as his consort—
he was the man that Poseidon subdued at Idómeneus' hands by

435   casting a spell on his glittering eyes, and he fettered his bright limbs;
therefore neither could he take flight to the rear nor evade him;
rather he stood like a pillar of stone or a lofty and leafy
tree unmoved, and the hero Idómeneus struck with his spear his
chest in the middle and thereby shattered the tunic of bronze he

440   wore about him, which had until then kept death from his body,
but now, rent by the spear, it harshly and loudly resounded.
Falling he crashed to the ground; in his heart was the spear firm-planted,
yet still throbbing, the heart set even the butt of the spear to
quivering; finally powerful Ares abated its fury.

445   Vehemently Idómeneus vaunted, and loudly he shouted:
"Maybe, Deïphobos, we can suppose the requital is worthy,
three men slaughtered for one, since you so loudly have boasted?
Strange man! Nevertheless, you stand up yourself to confront me,
so you may know what sort of a scion of Zeus I have come here,

450   even of Zeus, who first as a warder for Crete begot Minos,
then was a faultless son Deukálion fathered by Minos;
next Deukálion fathered myself to be lord over many
people in broad Crete; hither have I been brought by the galleys
now as a bane for your father and you and the rest of the Trojans."

455   So he spoke, and Deïphobos two ways pondered the matter,
whether as comrade to seek someone of the greathearted Trojans,
yielding the ground for the moment, or whether alone to make trial.
So as he pondered the matter, the best course seemed to be this one,
going to seek Aineías; the farthest away in the throng he

460   found him standing—against noble Priam he always was angry,
seeing that, brave as he was among men, not at all was he honored.
There then, standing beside him, in these winged words he addressed him:
"Now, Aineías, the counselor-lord of the Trojans, you must give
aid to your brother-in-law, if on you comes grief for a kinsman.

465   Yes, follow me, let us aid Alkáthoös, who was your sister's
husband and nurtured you in his house, while you were yet little.
Him, I tell you, Idómeneus famed as a spearman has slaughtered."
    So he spoke, and in him he roused up the heart in his bosom;
he for Idómeneus went, with his mind set strongly on battle;

470   yet no panic took hold of Idómeneus, as of a stripling,

but he awaited, as when some mountain boar, trusting his valor,
stands and awaits a great rabble of men which comes to assail him
off in a desolate place, and the top of his back is abristle,
both of his eyes flash brilliant as fire, and his teeth he is whetting
475 noisily, eagerly holding at bay both the hounds and the hunters;
so there waited Idómeneus famed as a spearman and did not
yield as Aineías arrived to give succor, but called to his comrades,
looked to Askálaphos and to Deḯpyros and to Apháreus,
Mérionés and as well Antílochos, lords of the war cry;
480 so exhorting them forward, in these winged words he addressed them:
"Come to my aid, friends; I am alone here; dreadfully do I
fear fleet-footed Aineías' assault—he is coming against me;
he is exceedingly mighty at slaughtering men in the battle;
also the flower of youth he possesses, the strength that is greatest.
485 For if in age we two were the same, and in this same spirit,
either would he soon win a great triumph, or else I would win it."
　　So he spoke, and they all, in their breasts having one strong spirit,
stood close by one another; their shields they leaned on their shoulders.
Then from the opposite side Aineías called to his comrades,
490 looked to Deḯphobos, Paris as well, and to noble Agénor,
who were the leaders, with him, of the Trojans; and then did the army
follow as well, as a sheep flock follows a ram from the pasture
down to the water to drink; in his spirit the shepherd is gladdened;
just so now in Aineías the heart in his breast was rejoicing,
495 as he beheld there following him that band of the army.
　　Over Alkáthoös then they fought in a hand-to-hand combat
wielding their long smooth spears; and about their chests was the brazen
armor resounding in terrible clashes as they in the melee
aimed at each other; surpassing the rest, two fighters, the warlike
500 equals of Ares, Idómeneus one, and Aineías, were each most
eager to hack with the pitiless bronze at the flesh of the other.
Then at Idómeneus first was a missile thrown by Aineías,
but Idómeneus, sharply observing, avoided the bronze spear;
onto the ground then landed the sharp spear-shaft of Aineías
505 quivering, since from his powerful hand in vain it had speeded.
Then Idómeneus, hitting Oinómaös square in the belly,
shattered the plate of his corslet; the bronze spear hollowed his bowels
out, and the earth he clutched in his hand as he fell in the dust there.
Straightway then Idómeneus drew the long-shadowing spear-shaft
510 out of the corpse; but the rest of the beautiful armor he could not

seize and remove from the shoulders, for he was assaulted by missiles,
since no longer the joints of his feet were as steady for charging,
either to rush after his own throw or avoid any other's.
So in a hand-to-hand fight he held off the pitiless doomsday,
515   yet for a flight his feet were not nimble to bear him from battle.
So as he went back step after step, Deḯphobos cast at
him a bright spear; for the grudge he bore him was ever unceasing.
But again he missed him, and Askálaphos then with his spear he
struck, Enyálios' son; and the powerful spear through the shoulder
520   passed, and the earth he clutched in his hand as he fell in the dust there.
Not yet powerful Ares of huge loud voice had at all heard
how that son of his own had fallen in violent combat,
but on the topmost peak of Olympos he sat, beneath golden
clouds, restrained by the will of great Zeus; and the other immortal
525   gods were in that place also, prevented from joining the battle.
       Over Askálaphos then they fought in a hand-to-hand combat;
just as Deḯphobos was from Askálaphos snatching the shining
helmet, Mérionés, that equal of Ares in swiftness,
leaping upon him, struck with his spear at his arm, and the helmet,
530   crested and socketed, fell from his hand to the earth with a clatter.
Thereupon Mérionés once more leapt forth like a vulture;
drawing the powerful spear from the top of his enemy's arm he
shrank back into the band of his comrades; the Trojan was gathered
into both arms by his brother Polítes, embraced at the midriff—
535   out of the dolorous battle he led him, until to the swift-hoofed
horses he came, at the rear of the battle and combat, as they stood
there with the charioteer and the elegant chariot waiting;
these then carried him off to the citadel, heavily groaning,
badly distressed; blood flowed from the arm just recently wounded.
540   Meanwhile the rest fought on, and a noise unquenchable rose up.
Thereat Aineías leapt on Áphareus, son of Kalétor,
who had just turned toward him, so hitting the throat with his sharp spear;
down to the side was the head bent over, his shield and his helmet
crashed upon him, and around him was poured death, spirit-destroying.
545   Watching for Thoön to turn his back, Antílochos wounded
him by lunging at him, and he utterly severed the vessel
running along the whole length of the back till it reaches the neck-bone;
this he utterly severed; and down on his back in the dust he
fell while both of his hands he stretched to his much-loved comrades.
550   On him Antílochos leapt, from his shoulders was stripping the armor,

240

warily looking about, and on all sides Trojans around him
pounded his broad bright-glittering shield, but Antílochos' tender
flesh inside with their pitiless bronze blades they were unable
even to graze, for securely Poseidon the shaker of earth was
555 guarding the scion of Nestor amid such numerous missiles,
since not ever was he without enemies, but among them was
ranging, nor ever his spear held motionless, but he was always
shaking and brandishing it; in his mind he was aiming at either
striking a man with a spear-cast or charging in hand-to-hand combat.
560   But in the melee as he kept aiming, he soon was observed by
Ádamas, Ásios' son, who struck midshield with the sharp bronze,
charging at him near at hand; but the point by Poseidon the dark-haired
god was deprived of its force—Antílochos' life he begrudged it.
Then of the spear one part, like a stake which burning has sharpened,
565 stayed in Antílochos' shield, and the other part lay on the ground there;
he shrank back to the band of his comrades, avoiding destruction;
Mérionés, as he went, came following, then with his spear struck
halfway between his navel and genitals, just at the spot where
Ares is ever especially painful to miserable mortals.
570 There he planted the spear; to the spear which pierced him he yielded,
struggling the way that an ox does when in the mountains the oxherds
bind it with ropes they have plaited and forcibly lead it unwilling;
so being struck he struggled a little, but not for a long time,
only until from his body the warrior Mérionés had
575 drawn that spear, coming close, and his eyes were enshrouded in darkness.
        Hélenos struck Deḯpyros' temple in hand-to-hand combat
with a huge Thracian sword; on his head he shattered the helmet,
which thus broken away fell onto the earth; an Achaian
grabbed it as it went rolling about through the feet of the fighters;
580 then down over his eyes came shadowy night to enshroud him.
        Grief seized Atreus' son, the great crier of war Meneláos;
uttering threats he strode against Hélenos, hero and leader,
wielding a sharp spear; Hélenos too drew back his bow's handgrip.
Both at the same time started the action, the one with the sharp spear
585 making his cast, and the other the arrow he shot from the bowstring.
Then on the chest struck him with his arrow the scion of Priam
square on the corselet-plate, but away flew the sharp bitter arrow.
As when away from a broad flat shovel, along a great threshing
floor, are the black-skinned beans or the chickpeas leaping and bouncing
590 under the whistling wind and the swing of the winnower's labor,

so from the corselet-plate of the glorious lord Meneláos
glancing away flew far to a distance the sharp bitter arrow.
Him then Atreus' son, the great crier of war Meneláos,
struck on the hand that was holding the well-polished bow, and the brazen
595 spear right into the bow and as well through the hand was driven.
He shrank back to the band of his comrades, avoiding destruction,
dangling his hand at his side; and the ash wood shaft it was dragging.
Out of his hand was the spear-point drawn by great-souled Agénor,
who then bandaged the hand with a strip well-twisted of sheep's wool
600 into a sling his attendant haď brought to the shepherd of people.
      Then Peisándros straight for the glorious lord Meneláos
went, but a baneful fate to the limit of death was conducting
him to be slain by you, Meneláos, in terrible combat.
When in coming together the men were close to each other,
605 Atreus' son missed him, and aside his spear was diverted,
while Peisándros struck at the glorious lord Meneláos
square on his shield, but the bronze he could not drive onward and through it,
for the broad shield held strong against it; in the socket the spear-shaft
broke, yet he in his heart was rejoicing and hoping to triumph.
610 Atreus' son, first drawing his sword all studded with silver,
leapt on the lord Peisándros, and he then, under his shield, took
hold of his beautiful ax, well-fashioned of bronze on a haft of
olive wood, long and well-polished, and as they came at each other,
he struck square on the ridge of the helmet crested with horsehair
615 under the plume, at the top, but as he was advancing, the other
struck on his forehead above the nose-root, and the bones cracked open—
bloodily onto the earth in the dust by his feet fell his eyeballs;
doubled in death, he fell; and his feet on his chest he planted,
then he stripped off his armor and spoke this word to him, boasting:
620 "Certainly this is the way you will leave these ships of the swift-horsed
Dánaäns, arrogant Trojans, insatiate of terrible war-din;
nor do you lack that other insult, that shameful disgrace with
which you insulted me, you foul curs, nor at all in your spirit
are you afraid of the terrible wrath of loud-thundering Zeus, that
625 warder of guests, who will someday ruin your steep-built city,
you who lawlessly carried away as you parted my wedded
bedmate and many possessions, when she as a friend had received you;
now once more you are raging among these seafaring ships to
cast in them ruinous fire and to slaughter the hero-Achaians.
630 Yet I am sure you will be kept back, though avid for battle.

Father Zeus, men say you are beyond all others in wisdom,
mortals and gods, yet it is from you all this is accomplished;
such is the way you favor the doers of outrage, the Trojans,
whose might always is foolish and reckless, nor are they able
635　ever to be satiated with strife and the leveling combat.
There is satiety surely of all things, of sleep, of lovemaking,
and of the sweetness of song and the blameless pleasure of dancing;
surely of these anyone would rather desire satisfaction
than of a war; but the Trojans are still unsated of battle."
640　So he spoke; from the body the faultless lord Meneláos
stripping the bloodstained armor, at once gave it to his comrades;
then he himself, going back once more, joined strife with the foremost.
There Harpálion, scion of King Pylaímenes, straightway
leapt against him; he had followed his much-loved father to Troy to
645　enter the war but was not to return to the land of his fathers;
now he struck at the scion of Atreus square on his shield in
close combat, but the bronze he could not drive onward and through it;
he shrank back to the band of his comrades, avoiding destruction,
glancing to all sides, lest with the bronze his body be injured.
650　Then as he drew back, Mérionés shot a bronze-tipped arrow,
striking his right side square on the buttock; and quickly the arrow
passed through under the bone straight onward and into the bladder.
He sank down on the spot in the arms of his much-loved comrades,
gasping his life-breath out; then there on the earth like a worm he
655　lay stretched out, and the earth by the black blood flowing was moistened.
Then were the great-souled Páphlagónians busied about him—
they in a chariot laid him and sorrowing took him to sacred
Ilion; so did his father with them go, pouring his tears out;
no blood-price would he ever receive for his child who had perished.
660　Over the man thus slaughtered was Paris enraged in his spirit,
for among numerous Páphlagónians he was a guest-friend,
so for his sake, in his anger, a bronze-tipped arrow he let fly.
There was a man, Euchénor, the son of the seer Polyídos—
wealthy he was and a good man—who had his dwelling in Korinth;
665　he well aware of his ruinous fate had embarked on a galley,
since very often the good old man Polyídos had told him
he was to die by a grievous and wasting disease in his own house
or by the ships of the Achaians to be brought down by the Trojans.
By the one act he avoided the grievous fine the Achaians
670　asked and the hateful disease, so that pain in his heart he would not feel.

Under the jaw and the ear he was struck by Paris; the life-breath
swiftly abandoned his limbs—he was seized by odious darkness.
    So as the two sides fought like the blaze of a conflagration,
Hektor belovèd of Zeus heard nothing about it and did not
675 know in the least that his men on the left of the galleys were being
killed by the Argive fighters—and soon indeed the Achaians
would have won glory, for so was the holder and shaker of earth now
urging the Argives on; with his own strength too he was helping—
rather, he held where first he had leapt at the gates and the rampart,
680 where he had broken the close-pressed ranks of the Dánaän shield-men;
in that place were the galleys of Ajax and Prótesiláos
hauled out onto the shore of the silvery sea, and above them
there was the wall built lowest of all; and especially savage
there were the men themselves and their horses in waging the battle.
685   There the Boiótians and the Iónians, wearers of long robes,
also the Lókrians, Pthíans, and glorious noble Epeíans,
hardly could hold him away from the ships as he charged nor at all were
able to thrust from themselves that man like a blaze, noble Hektor.
There also were the chosen Athenians; leading among them
690 Péteos' scion Menéstheus came, then following him were
Pheídas and excellent Bías and Stíchios; of the Epeíans
Ámphion, Drákios, Meges Phýleus' son were commanders;
Medon the Pthians led, and Podárkes, steadfast in battle.
One of the two in fact was the godlike Oïleus' bastard
695 son and the brother of Ajax, Medon—but Phýlakè he was
then inhabiting, far from his country; a man he had murdered,
kin of his own stepmother, Oïleus' wife Eriópis—
while Podárkes was scion of Íphiklos, Phýlakos' offspring.
These at the front of the great-souled Phthians, accoutered in armor,
700 there in defense of the galleys were fighting beside the Boiótians.
Now no longer at all swift Ajax, son of Oïleus,
stood even slightly apart from the scion of Télamon Ajax,
but in the way two wine-dark oxen will strain in the fallow
land at a well-joined plow with equivalent force, and abundant
705 sweat from the roots of their horns keeps oozing and drenching their faces—
only the yoke, well-polished, is holding apart the two oxen
laboring through those furrows and reaching the edge of the plowland—
so now coming together the two stood close to each other.
But indeed with the scion of Télamon, many and noble
710 men his companions followed, attendants receiving his shield from

him whenever the sweat came over his limbs, and exhaustion.
None of the Lokrians followed the great-souled son of Oïleus,
since not steadfast remained their hearts in a hand-to-hand combat,
since they possessed no helmets of bronze well-crested with horsehair,
715   neither did they have circular shields nor spears made of ash wood;
rather confiding in bows and in slings well-twisted of sheep's wool
they had to Ilion followed, and it was with them they were shooting
thickly, repeatedly, trying to break the battalions of Trojans.
So indeed were the ones in front, with elaborate war-gear,
720   fighting against those Trojans, against bronze-helmeted Hektor;
those who shot from behind were invisible; nor were the Trojans
mindful of ardor for war, for the arrows were causing confusion.

There most miserably from the galleys and cabins the Trojans
then would have yielded the ground toward windswept Ilion city,
725   had not Polýdamas, standing beside bold Hektor, addressed him:
"You are a difficult man to convince with words of persuasion,
Hektor—because some god gave you war-deeds beyond others,
therefore in counsel as well beyond others you wish to have wisdom.
But no way by yourself can you possibly have all together.
730   For it is true that the god gives war-deeds mainly to one man,
and to another the dance, to another the song and lyre-playing,
while in another man's bosom the lord wide-thundering Zeus puts
excellent wisdom, from which many people derive the advantage—
numerous men he saves, but himself best knows of its value.
735   Therefore will I now speak in the way I think is the best one,
for around you all over is blazing a circle of battle;
now that the great-souled Trojans have made way over the rampart,
some are just standing aside with their war-gear, others are fighting,
fewer themselves against many and scattered about through the galleys.
740   But do you now draw back and the best men all summon hither;
thereupon we will indeed take thought of all manner of counsel,
whether we should now fall on the galleys of numerous oarlocks,
see if the god might wish to grant victory—otherwise we might
go unscathed from the galleys; for I am myself most
745   fearful lest the Achaians for yesterday's debt will requite us,
since by the galleys is staying a man insatiate of warfare
who I believe no more will be utterly held from the battle."

So said Polýdamas; Hektor was pleased by his counsel of prudence;
straightway he to the ground from his chariot leapt in his armor.
750   Raising his voice he spoke, and in these winged words he addressed him:

"Do you, Polýdamas, hold back here all those who are noblest;
meanwhile I will go there and take part with the men who are fighting;
quickly again will I come, when well I have given them orders."
    So he spoke, and he started to go like a snow-clad mountain,
755 yelling, and speeded ahead through the Trojans as well as the allies.
Straightway to Pánthoös' scion Polýdamas, kindly and thoughtful,
they all started to rush when they heard what Hektor was saying.
He for Deḯphobos searched, and for Hélenos, lordly in power,
Ádamas Ásios' scion, and Ásios Hýrtakos' offspring,
760 ranging about in the foremost fighters, in hopes he could find them.
These he found no longer entirely unscathed or unslaughtered;
rather indeed at the sterns of the Achaians' galleys were lying
some who had lost their lives at the hands of the Argives, and others
had inside of the wall been struck by missiles and wounded.
765 Quickly he found on the left of the tearful battle the noble
lord Alexander, the husband of Helen of beautiful tresses,
cheering the hearts of his comrades and rousing them up to the combat;
there then, standing beside him, he spoke in words of derision:
"Paris the bane, best-seeming, you woman-mad cheat and deceiver,
770 where is Deḯphobos gone, where Hélenos, lordly in power,
Ádamas Ásios' scion, and Ásios Hýrtakos' offspring?
Where is Othrýoneus gone? Now wholly destroyed from the top down
steep-built Ilion is; now assured is your sheer destruction."
    Then in answer to him spoke forth godlike Alexander:
775 "Hektor, because you are minded to blame someone who is blameless,
some other time, not now, would I draw back out of the battle,
since not wholly a coward was I brought forth by my mother,
for from the time by the ships you roused up the battle of comrades,
since then we have encountered the Dánaäns, staying among them
780 ceaselessly; but the comrades of whom you ask have been slaughtered.
Only Deḯphobos and Prince Hélenos, lordly in power,
now have departed from here, both having been struck in the arms by
long spears—they were defended from death by the scion of Kronos.
Now lead forward, wherever your heart and your spirit command you;
785 we will be eagerly following you, for I do not imagine
we will lack courage at all, so far as we have any power;
no man, even if eager , beyond his power can battle."
    So having spoken the hero prevailed on the heart of his brother;
they set forth to the place where the battle and strife were the greatest;
790 there was Kebríones fighting and faultless Polýdamas also,

Phálkes as well, Orthaíos, and brave godlike Polyphétes,
also Hippótion's sons, Askánios, Palmys, and Morys,
who had arrived from fertile Askánia as a relief force
only the morning before; now Zeus roused them to do battle.
795   They came onward, resembling a blast of the violent stormwinds
which comes down on the earth beneath thunder of Zeus the great father—
wondrously whistling it joins with the sea-brine; many a wave goes
surging and crashing along in the deep sea booming and roaring,
arching aloft into white-foamed crests, some ahead, others after.
800   So did the Trojans in close ranks now, some ahead, others after,
follow along with their leaders, in brazen accouterments flashing.
Hektor the scion of Priam, the peer of man-slaughtering Ares,
led in the fight; his circular shield he was holding before him,
well-compacted of hides into which much bronze had been beaten;
805   shaken about on his temples was his bright-glittering helmet.
Everywhere the battalions he tested as he edged forward,
whether they might give ground as he strode forth under his shield there;
yet he could not confuse any heart in the breasts of the Achaians.
Ajax then was the first who challenged him, coming in long strides:
810   "Madman, come up close—why now of the Argives are you so
frightened? Indeed we are not in the least unskillful in warfare,
but by the baneful whiplash of Zeus the Achaians were brought down.
Now is your heart, no doubt, expecting to seize and destroy our
galleys; but hands we also possess, strong enough to defend them.
815   No, much sooner than that your well-inhabited city
under our hands is to be both taken and utterly ransacked.
As for yourself, I say that the time comes closer in which when
taking to flight you will pray Father Zeus and the other immortals
that much swifter than falcons your horses with beautiful manes are,
820   those that will carry you, raising the dust of the plain, to the city."
      As these words he was speaking, a bird flew by on his right hand,
it was a high-flying eagle; the host of Achaians, encouraged
thus by the bird-sign, shouted; but glorious Hektor responded:
"Ajax, bumbling in speech, ox-braggart, what are you speaking!
825   How I wish that as surely the offspring of Zeus of the aegis,
all of my days, I were, and that august Hera had borne me,
honored the way that Athena is honored, and lordly Apollo,
as now certain it is, this day brings bane to the Argives,
all of them; you among them will be slaughtered, if you can endure to
830   stand against my long spear that will bite your lily-white body.

Straightway you will be glutting the dogs and the birds of the Trojans
then with your fat and your flesh, when you fall by the ships of the Achaians."
    So having spoken to him, he started ahead and they followed,
raising a marvelous din, and the host all shouted behind him.
835 So on the other side shouted the Argives, nor were forgetful
now of their valor, but stood the assault of the best of the Trojans.
Up to the splendor of Zeus, to the ether, the clamor of both rose.

BOOK 14

Nestor, although he was drinking, was not unaware of the uproar,
but to Asklépios' son he spoke, winged words he addressed him:
"Take thought, noble Macháon, of how these matters will happen—
louder resounds by the galleys the war cry of vigorous young men.
5   Nevertheless you sit here drinking the glistening wine now,
till Hekamédè of beautiful tresses has heated the water
for a hot bath and has washed off the blood-caked gore from your body;
meanwhile I will go out to a lookout-place and survey things."
    So he spoke, and he took up the well-made shield that was lying
10   there in the hut, of his son Thrasymédes the tamer of horses,
glittering brightly with bronze; for the son had the shield of his father.
Then he took up a powerful spear, well pointed with sharp bronze;
outside the cabin he stood, and the shameful action he witnessed—
men being driven in flight, and behind them men who were driving,
15   high-souled Trojans; and quite overthrown was the wall of the Achaians.
As at a time that the great sea quietly seethes in a ground-swell,
thus foreboding the swift sharp passage of whistling stormwinds
silently, nor one way or the other the billows are rolling,
till Zeus chooses a wind to blow steadily, sending it downward,
20   so did the old man ponder, revolving the question in spirit
two ways, whether to go to the swift-horsed Dánaäns' melee,
whether to Atreus' son Agamemnon, shepherd of people.
So as he pondered the matter the best course seemed to be this one,
going to Atreus' son. But the rest of them kept on fighting,
25   killing each other; about their bodies the weariless bronze was
clanging as they were struck with the swords and the double-edged spear-blades.
    There then Nestor encountered the kings, Zeus-nourished, as they were
coming along by the ships, those who had been struck with the bronze blades,
Tydeus' son and Odysseus and Atreus' son Agamemnon—
30   since their galleys had been drawn up far out of the battle,

down on the shore of the sea, for the first ones they to the plain had
drawn out, then at the sterns of the ships had erected the rampart,
since, although it was broad, that beach was unable in any
way to accommodate all those ships, and the people were cooped up,
35 so they had drawn them out into rows, and had filled up the lengthy
mouth of the whole seashore, so much as the headlands encompassed.
Therefore, wishing to look at the clamor and combat, the kings were
going together, supported on spear-shafts; grieved was the spirit
deep inside of their breasts; it was there that the old man Nestor
40 met them and caused dismay to the hearts in the breasts of the Achaians.
Raising his voice then spoke and addressed him strong Agamemnon:
"Nestor Neleus' son, the Achaians' preeminent glory,
why now, leaving the battle, destroyer of men, do you come here?
I fear powerful Hektor will bring that word to fulfillment
45 just as once he threatened as he among Trojans was speaking—
never to Ilion would he return from the ships before he had
set these galleys on fire and the men themselves he had slaughtered.
So at the time he spoke; now this is all being accomplished.
Well then, certain it is that the rest of the well-greaved Achaians
50 lay up wrath in their hearts against me, as Achilles is doing,
nor do they wish any longer to fight by the sterns of the galleys."
     Speaking to him made answer the horseman Gerenian Nestor:
"Yes, these things have been brought to fulfillment; not otherwise could
Zeus who thunders above himself have devised the achievement,
55 since overthrown indeed is the rampart in which we were trusting
that for ourselves and the ships it would be an unbreakable bulwark.
They at the swift ships now maintain combat unabated,
ceaseless, and you would not know, although you looked very closely,
from which side the Achaians are driven in panic and routed,
60 slaughtered in such confusion; the clamor is reaching the heavens.
Let us ourselves take thought of the way these matters will happen,
if thought does anything. But I urge that the battle we do not
enter; for there is no way that a man can fight who is wounded."
     Answering him then spoke Agamemnon, lord of the people:
65 "Nestor, because indeed by the sterns of the ships they are fighting,
neither the well-built wall nor the trench has availed to protect us,
where our Dánaäns much have endured—they hoped in their spirits
that for ourselves and the ships it would be an unbreakable bulwark.
Thus no doubt to all-powerful Zeus it will be very pleasing
70 that the Achaians should die here nameless and distant from Argos.

This I knew when he zealously came to the Dánaäns' succor;
now I know when he honors the others as much as the blessèd
gods, so that now instead our power and hands he has trammeled.
But come, just as I say, let all of us heed and obey it.
75   Those of the ships that are drawn up close to the sea in the first rank,
down let us drag them, drawing them all to the luminous sea-brine;
there let us moor them afloat with the anchors, until the immortal
night comes upon us, if even at that time the Trojans refrain from
battle; and finally then we could draw down all of the galleys,
80   since there is no blame, fleeing from evil, not even at nighttime—
better if one flees evil, escaping, than if he is taken."
     Looking from lowering brows said Odysseus of many devices:
"Atreus' son, what a word has escaped from the fence of your teeth now!
Ruinous king! I wish that another and cowardly army
85   you were commanding, and never were lord over us, to whom Zeus has
granted from our young years right up to old age to accomplish
painful and difficult warfare, until we, each of us, perish.
Are you in fact so eager the broad-wayed city of Trojans
now to abandon, for which such manifold evils we suffer?
90   Keep your silence, for fear some other Achaian should hear this
word, which never at all through his mouth would a man let pass who
had in his mind understanding to speak such things as are fitting,
who was a king with a scepter, and who was obeyed by as many
people as are these Argives among whom you are the ruler.
95   Utterly now I despise your mind, such things you have spoken,
you who command us, when we are joined in the battle and clamor,
down to the sea-brine to drag these well-benched ships, so that even
more will the Trojans exult, though they are already triumphant,
so that on us sheer ruin may crash down. For the Achaians
100   never will maintain war as the galleys are dragged to the sea-brine—
rather will they keep looking away and withdraw from the fighting.
Then your advice will have caused a catastrophe, marshal of people."
     Answering him then spoke Agamemnon, lord of the people:
"Sorely, Odysseus, have you reached deep in my heart with a speech so
105   bitter and harsh; but I do not urge that the sons of Achaians
should unwillingly drag these well-benched ships to the sea-brine.
Now let somebody speak whose counsel is better than this was,
either a young or an old man; to me it would be very welcome."
     Then spoke also among them the crier of war Diomédes:
110   "Near is the man, nor in vain will we seek him, should you indeed be

251

willing to heed him, and each of you not indignant or grudging
simply because, as to birth date, among you I am the youngest;
I too boast that I have my birth from an excellent father,
Tydeus, whom in Thebes heaped earth is now covering over.

115   For by the faultless Portheus were three male children begotten
who inhabited Pleuron and steep-built Kálydon city—
Ágrios, Melas the second, and third was Oíneus the horseman,
father of my own father, in prowess distinguished among them.
There he remained, while wandering off, my father in Argos

120   settled, for so I suppose did Zeus and the other gods wish it.
There he married Adréstos' daughter and lived in a palace
rich in the substance of life; an abundance of wheat-bearing plowlands
also were his, and about him were numerous orchards of fruit trees;
numerous sheep he possessed; he excelled over all the Achaians,

125   wielding a spear—you must have heard this, as indeed it is truthful.
Therefore would you not say that in birth I am base or a coward,
so to dishonor the word I speak, whatever I speak well.
Come, let us go into battle—we must—although we are wounded;
there then let us restrain ourselves from the violent combat,

130   out of the shooting, so wound upon wound now none of us suffers;
urging the others, ahead we will send them, those who before this,
yielding to anger, were standing about, not entering battle."
      So did he say; they carefully listened to him and obeyed him.
They set forth; Agamemnon the lord of the people was leading.

135   Nor was the glorious shaker of earth maintaining a blind watch,
but in their company went, in appearance resembling an old man;
he by the right hand took Agamemnon, Atreus' scion;
raising his voice he spoke, and in these winged words he addressed him:
"Atreus' son, now doubtless the baleful heart of Achilles

140   feels great joy in his breast, as the slaughter and rout of Achaians
he is observing, for there is no sense in him, even the slightest.
Yet even so may he die, may a god strike him to perdition,
while against you are the fortunate gods not utterly wrathful,
yet even now, I believe, will the Trojans' leaders and princes

145   raise up the dust on the great broad plain—you will see it yourself as
they take flight to the city, away from the galleys and cabins."
      He spoke, mightily shouting, as over the plain he was speeding.
Loud as the war cry which nine thousand or yet ten thousand
warriors raise in a fight while joining the conflict of Ares,

150   just so loud was the shout that the powerful shaker of earth now

sent from his breast; great strength he planted in every Achaian's
heart to engage in battle and join implacable combat.
Gold-throned Hera herself with her own eyes then was observing
him from the spur of Olympos on which she stood, and at once knew
155　him as he busied himself in the battle that wins a man glory—
it was her brother and brother-in-law—and rejoiced in her spirit;
then she observed Zeus sitting away on the loftiest peak of
Ida of numerous springs; most hateful he was to her spirit.
Straightway started to ponder the ox-eyed queen, Lady Hera,
160　how she could cozen the senses of Zeus who carries the aegis.
This is the plan which seemed to her then in her spirit the best one—
she would to Ida depart, once she was arrayed in her beauty,
seeing if he would perhaps feel longing to lie in affection
next to her body, and she would shed sleep, unharmful and balmy,
165　over him, onto his eyelids and his ingenious spirit.
She set forth to the chamber constructed for her by Hephaistos,
her dear son, and the strong tight doors he had fixed to the doorposts,
using a secret door-bolt that no other god ever opened.
There after entering into the chamber, the glittering doors she
170　shut fast; first with ambrosia then she cleansed her delightful
body of every stain, and she richly anointed her robe with
sweet ambrosial oil that she had there, pleasantly scented;
this when shaken about in the bronze-floored palace of Zeus sent
fragrance wafting below to the earth and around to the heavens.
175　Then, when she had anointed her beautiful body with this and
combed her hair, with her hands she plaited the shimmering tresses,
lovely ambrosial braids on the deathless head of the goddess.
Then she put on herself the ambrosial robe that Athena
finely had fashioned for her and had put on much decoration;
180　this with her gold-wrought brooches she pinned on over her bosom.
Then she belted her waist with a belt of a hundred tassels;
onto the well-pierced lobes of her ears she fastened her earrings,
each three clustering droplets, from which great glamour was shining.
Over her head that splendor of goddesses put on a head-scarf,
185　beautiful, recently woven, its color as white as the sun is;
under her glistening feet she fastened her beautiful sandals.
But then, having appareled her body with all its adornments,
she set forth from her chamber and, calling upon Aphrodítè,
spoke, and apart from the rest of the gods these words she addressed her:
190　"Now will you listen to me, dear child, and obey what I tell you,

or will you rather refuse it, resentful of me in your spirit,
since to the Dánaäns I grant succor, and you to the Trojans?"
       Speaking to her then answered the daughter of Zeus Aphrodítè:
"Hera the august goddess, the daughter of powerful Kronos,
195 speak what you have in your mind, for my heart bids me to achieve it,
if I am able to do it and if it can well be accomplished."
       Then in cunning of spirit addressed her the queen, Lady Hera:
"Grant to me now to arouse the desire and affection with which you
vanquish all the immortals as well as all men who are mortal,
200 since to the ends of the nourishing earth I am going, to visit
Ocean, the gods' ancestor, as well as Tethys the mother,
those who lovingly nursed me within their palace and reared me,
having received me from Rheia, the time loud-thundering Zeus had
under the earth thrust Kronos, and under the desolate sea-brine.
205 Them I am going to see, to resolve their endless contention,
since for a long time they have been holding aloof from each other
now, and from bed and affection, for into their hearts fell anger;
if by talking to them I prevailed on both of their dear hearts,
so as to bring them to bed to be joined in love and affection,
210 always belovèd would I be called by them, and respected."
       Answering her then spoke Aphrodítè the lover of laughter:
"Now to refuse your word is not possible, nor is it seemly,
since you lie at your ease in the arms of the mightiest god Zeus."
       She spoke, then from her breasts unloosened the pierced and embroidered
215 strap on which all sorts of allurements are brightly emblazoned;
there upon it is affection, upon it desire and seductive
dalliance which robs even a sensible person of wisdom.
This she put in her hands and spoke these words, calling upon her:
"There now, here is a strap which you put into your bosom,
220 well-embroidered, on which all things are emblazoned; I do not
think you will come back here with the wish in your heart unaccomplished."
       So she spoke, and the ox-eyed queen, Lady Hera, was smiling;
still she smiled as she took it and put it away in her bosom.
       Then to her palace departed the daughter of Zeus Aphrodítè,
225 Hera as well rushed off, so leaving the spur of Olympos;
down to Piéria then and to lovely Emáthia coming,
she sped over the snow-clad range of the Thracian horsemen,
over their topmost peaks, not touching the ground with her two feet;
then clear down to the billowing sea she descended from Athos;
230 next she arrived in Lemnos, the city of Thoas the godlike.

There then Slumber, the brother of Death, she encountered, and quickly
clasped his hand in her own and said these words, calling upon him:
"Slumber, the lord above all of the gods and above all mortals,
if you ever have listened to my word, now again also
235 heed me; and all of my days my gratitude I will acknowledge.
Lull to a sleep the bright eyes of the lord Zeus under his eyebrows,
straightway, as soon as I lie at his side in affectionate love-play.
Gifts I will give you, a beautiful throne, unfailing forever,
fashioned of gold, that Hephaistos the twice-lame child of my own will
240 skillfully make for you, setting a stool for your feet underneath it,
then upon it you can rest your glistening feet as you revel."
　　Speaking to her in return made answer delectable Slumber:
"Hera the august goddess, the daughter of powerful Kronos,
I would indeed quite easily lull to a slumber another
245 one of the gods who live always, though it were the streams of the river
Ocean himself, the divine ancestor of all in existence;
nowhere near would I come to the lord Zeus, scion of Kronos,
neither would lull him to sleep unless he himself should command it.
For before now a command you gave me has taught me a lesson,
250 on that day when the high-souled Herakles scion of Zeus was
sailing from Ilion, after he sacked that city of Trojans.
I then lulled to a slumber the senses of Zeus of the aegis,
pleasantly drifted around him, and you in your heart devised evil,
stirred up blasts of the violent stormwinds over the sea and
255 carried the hero to Kos, that well-inhabited island,
distant from all of his friends. Zeus, waking, in wrath began flinging
gods all over his halls, and for me above all he was looking;
down from the sky to the sea out of sight he then would have hurled me,
had not Night the subduer of gods and of mortals preserved me;
260 her I reached as I fled, and he left off, though he was angry,
since he shrank to perform anything displeasing to swift Night.
Now this other impossible task you bid me accomplish!"
　　Speaking to him made answer the ox-eyed queen, Lady Hera:
"Why now, Slumber, do you in your heart keep pondering these things?
265 Do you suppose wide-thundering Zeus will succor the Trojans
quite in the way he raged about Herakles, who is his own son?
But come, do me the favor, and one of the youthful Graces
I will present you to marry, and so to be known as your bedmate—
even Pasíthea, whom you have wanted forever and always."
270 　　So she spoke; then Slumber rejoiced and addressed her an answer:

"Come now, swear me an oath by Styx's inviolate water,
while with one of your hands the much-nourishing earth you are holding,
and with the other the shimmering sea, so that all of the gods with
Kronos beneath are the witnesses now to our mutual compact:
275   you will present me to marry the one of the youthful Graces,
even Pasíthea, whom I have wanted forever and always."
     He spoke, nor disobeyed him the goddess white-armed Hera;
she swore just as he ordered, and named out all of the gods who
dwell down under the chasm of Tártaros, who are called Titans.
280   But then, when she had sworn and had brought her oath to completion,
both of them went away, leaving the cities of Lemnos and Imbros;
mantling themselves in a mist, they swiftly accomplished the journey.
Ida of numerous springs they came to, the mother of wild beasts,
Lekton, at which they arrived when leaving the sea; on the land they
285   went, and the top of the forest was quivering under their footsteps.
There then Slumber awaited, before Zeus' eyes could observe him,
climbing aloft on a towering fir tree, which was the tallest
tree then growing in Ida—it reached through mist up to heaven.
There he was sitting, concealed by the branches and leaves of the fir tree,
290   seeming in form like the clear-toned bird which high in the mountains
gods call *chalkis* the brazen and which men call the *kymíndis*.
     Rapidly Hera ascended to Gárgaros, high on the peak of
towering Ida, and there the cloud-gathering god Zeus saw her.
Soon as he saw her, desire enveloped his resolute spirit,
295   as at the time they first had joined in affectionate love-play,
going together to bed unbeknownst to their much-loved parents.
Standing before her, a word he addressed her, calling upon her:
"Where are you hurrying, Hera, to come this way from Olympos?
There are no horses and chariot here with which you could travel."
300   Then in cunning of spirit addressed him the queen, Lady Hera:
"Now to the ends of the nourishing earth I am going, to visit
Ocean, the gods' ancestor, as well as Tethys the mother,
those who lovingly nursed me within their palace and reared me.
Them I am going to see, to resolve their endless contention,
305   since for a long time they have been holding aloof from each other
now, and from bed and affection, for into their hearts fell anger.
Down in the foothills of Ida of numerous springs are the horses
standing that over the dry land and over the water will bear me.
It is because of you now that I come here, down from Olympos,
310   lest you should in the future, perhaps, be angry with me if

I were in silence to go to the palace of deep-flowing Ocean."
    Answering her in return spoke forth the cloud-gathering god Zeus:
"Hera, it surely will be quite possible later to go there;
let us instead go now to our bed to enjoy our affection,
315   since not ever before has desire for a goddess or woman,
pouring itself all over the heart in my breast, so quelled me—
not at the time when I was enamored of Ixion's bedmate,
who Peiríthoös bore, that peer of the gods as adviser;
neither when Dánaë lovely of ankle, Akrísios' daughter,
320   I was desiring, the mother of Perseus, famed among all men;
neither when I was in love with the daughter of far-renowned Phoinix,
who bore Minos to me, and as well godlike Rhadamánthys;
not when of Sémelè I was the lover in Thebes, or Alkménè,
who as her offspring brought forth Herakles, powerful-hearted,
325   while fair Sémelè bore Dionýsos, gladdening mortals;
not when I courted the lady Deméter of beautiful tresses;
not when glorious Leto I loved; not you yourself even—
never, as now I love you and sweetest desire for you grips me."
    Then in cunning of spirit addressed him the queen, Lady Hera:
330   "Most dread scion of Kronos, and what is this word you have spoken!
If now you are desirous of mingling in bed and affection
here on the summit of Ida, and all is revealed for the viewing,
how would it be, should one of the gods who live always observe us
here as we lie in slumber, and going to all of the other
335   gods tell them? Then not to your palace would I be returning
after arising from bed; it would be an affair most shameful!
But if indeed you wish it, and it is so dear to your spirit,
certainly there is a chamber constructed for you by Hephaistos,
our dear son, and the strong tight doors he fixed to the doorposts—
340   there let us go lie down, since bed is the pleasure you long for."
    Answering her in return spoke forth the cloud-gathering god Zeus:
"Hera, do not be fearful that either of gods or of men will
anyone see—so well I will hide us around with a golden
cloud, not Helios even could look through it to discern us,
345   not though his is the radiant sight that is keenest at seeing."
    Speaking, the scion of Kronos embraced in his arms his dear bedmate;
under the two the divine earth bore fresh-burgeoning grasses;
lotuses sprang, dew-moistened, and crocus and hyacinth flowers
thickly and softly beneath them, and held them away from the hard earth.
350   So upon them they reclined; there they by a beautiful golden

cloud were appareled about, and from it fell glistening dewdrops.
　　Peacefully thus did the Father on topmost Gárgaros slumber;
quelled by sleep and affection, he held in his arms his dear bedmate,
while to the ships of the Achaians delectable Sleep went running,
355　bearing a message to say to the great earth-holder and -shaker.
There then, standing beside him, in these winged words he addressed him:
"Eagerly now be of aid to the Dánaäns, lordly Poseidon;
grant them glory, though it be briefly, as long as is sleeping
Zeus, since soft is the slumber in which I covered and hid him.
360　Hera indeed has beguiled him to lie in affection beside her."
　　So he spoke, and he left for the glorious nations of mankind;
yet even more to give aid to the Dánaäns he had aroused him.
Straightway leaping ahead to the foremost, loudly he shouted:
"Argives, shall we to Hektor the scion of Priam surrender
365　triumph again, so he takes our galleys and garners the glory?
Yet it is thus he is saying and boasting, because Lord Achilles
stays back here by the hollow ships and is angry in spirit—
not much longing for him there will be anyway, if the rest of
us start rousing ourselves to defend and assist one another.
370　But come, just as I say, let all of us heed and obey it:
such of the shields as are best in the army, as well as the largest,
now let us put on ourselves; our heads let us cover with helmets
gleaming all over, and take in our hands those spears that are longest;
then let us go; myself I will lead you, and not any longer
375　Priam's son Hektor will stay, I think, no matter how zealous.
Let a man steadfast in battle who has on his shoulder a small shield
give it to one who is lesser and put on a shield that is larger."
　　So did he say; they carefully listened to him and obeyed him;
it was the kings themselves, though wounded, who marshaled the fighters,
380　Tydeus' son and Odysseus and Atreus' son Agamemnon;
going among them all, they made them exchange battle-armor—
good did the good put on, and the worse they gave to the worse men.
Straightway, when in the glittering bronze their bodies were covered,
they set forth, and the great earth-shaker Poseidon was leading.
385　Dreadful in his huge hand was the sharp-edged sword he was holding,
bright as a lightning bolt; no fighter may ever encounter
it in the horrible strife—sheer dread keeps men at a distance.
　　Opposite them did illustrious Hektor marshal the Trojans.
Thus so tightly were stretching the terrible conflict of battle
390　mighty Poseidon the dark-haired god and illustrious Hektor,

who was assisting the Trojans; the other was helping the Argives.
Then was the sea right up to the Argives' cabins and galleys
surging, and they with a huge war cry came clashing together.
Not so mighty the roar of a breaker that batters the seashore,
395   driven along from the sea by a harrowing blast of the north wind,
not so mightily thunder the flames of a conflagration
deep in a mountain's ravine when it roars up, burning the forest,
not so mighty the wind that among oaks lofty and leafy
shrieks out, even a tempest that thunders the loudest and rages,
400   not so mighty as was the war cry of Achaians and Trojans
raising a terrible tumult as each man charged at another.
   It was at Ajax first of the fighters that glorious Hektor
cast with his spear, as he turned straight toward him, nor did he miss him—
he struck him where across his chest were stretched the two baldrics,
405   one from his shield and the other his sword, all studded with silver;
these two guarded his delicate flesh, so that Hektor was angered
since so fruitlessly out of his hand had flown the swift missile;
he shrank back to the band of his comrades, avoiding destruction.
Him as he drew back then the great scion of Télamon Ajax
410   struck with a boulder, among those many, the props of the swift ships,
which rolled under their feet as they fought—he raised one of these and
struck him square on the chest by the neck well over the shield-rim,
whirled him about like a top with the blow, and around he was spinning.
As at a time when under the stroke of Zeus Father an oak tree
415   falls uprooted, and terrible then is the sulphurous odor
rising from it—no boldness possesses a man who is close by
looking at it, so cruel and harsh is the lightning of great Zeus—
suddenly so to the ground in the dust fell powerful Hektor,
out of his hand he let the spear drop, and his shield and his helmet
420   crashed upon him, and around him clattered his bronze-adorned armor.
Then ran up to him shouting aloud those sons of Achaians,
hoping to drag him away; spears dense and incessant did they keep
hurling, but straight at the shepherd of people was nobody able
either to stab or to strike, for before that, nobles around him
425   came, Aineías, Polýdamas also, and noble Agénor,
then Sarpédon, the Lykians' leader, and Glaukos the faultless.
None of the others neglected to care for him; rather they held their
circular shields in front of him closely; the comrades, lifting
him in their arms, from the war-toil bore him, until to the swift-hoofed
430   horses they came, at the rear of the battle and combat, as they stood

there with the charioteer and the elegant chariot waiting;
these then carried him off to the citadel, heavily groaning.
　　But then, when they arrived at the ford of the beautiful-flowing
river, the eddying Xanthos that deathless Zeus had begotten,
435　they put him on the ground from the chariot, over him pouring
water, and he was revived; with his eyes he started to look up,
then as he knelt on his knees he vomited blood, black-clouded;
there he again fell backward and sank to the ground, with the black night
covering both of his eyes, and the blow still quelling his spirit.
440　　Now as they saw Lord Hektor withdrawing, the Argives were yet more
eager to leap at the Trojans, recalling their ardor for battle.
There then the first by far swift Ajax, son of Oïleus,
leapt with a sharp spear so that he wounded the scion of Énops,
Sátnios, who had been born by a Naiad, a faultless nymph, to
445　Énops as he by the river Satníoeis tended his cattle.
It was to him that the spear-famed son of Oïleus came up
close, in the flank he stabbed him, and he fell backward; about him
Trojan and Dánaän fighters collided in violent combat.
In his defense spear-wielding Polýdamas, Pánthoös' scion,
450　came to his side, and he struck Areïlochos' son Prothoënor
on the right shoulder; the powerful spear drove on through the shoulder;
down in the dust he fell, and he clutched at the earth with his fingers.
Vehemently Polýdamas vaunted, and loudly he shouted:
"Certainly not in vain has the spear leapt out of the massive
455　hand of the great-souled scion of Pánthoös now, I imagine;
one of the Argives rather is carrying it in his body—
leaning on it, I believe, he will go to the palace of Hades."
　　So he spoke; as he vaunted the grief came over the Argives,
but above all in the war-skilled scion of Télamon Ajax
460　he was arousing the spirit, for closest to him did the man fall.
Swiftly he cast at the other, as he drew back, with a bright spear;
still was Polýdamas able himself to escape from a black fate,
jumping away to the side; Archélochos, son of Anténor,
rather, received it, for his was the ruin the gods had determined.
465　It struck him at the place where the head and the neck are together
joined, on the top spine-bone, and it cut through both of the sinews.
Then, as he fell, much sooner his head and his neck and his nostrils
dropped down onto the ground than his knees and the shins of his legs did.
So in his turn to the faultless Polýdamas cried out Ajax:
470　"Well then, Polýdamas, think this over and truthfully tell me:

is not this man worth being killed to requite Prothoënor's
slaughter? For no base man does he seem to me, nor of base fathers,
rather a brother of Lord Anténor the tamer of horses,
maybe a son; for he seems quite close in descent and appearance."

475   He spoke knowing him well; grief seized on the hearts of the Trojans.
Over his brother as Ákamas stood he stabbed the Boiótian
Prómachos then with his spear—by the foot he was dragging the body.
Vehemently thus Ákamas vaunted, and loudly he shouted:
"Argives, shooters of arrows, insatiably uttering menace,

480 not, it appears, will the toil and the sorrow of battle be only
ours, but instead sometimes in this way you too will be slaughtered.
Take good thought of your Prómachos now, how quelled by my spear he
lies here asleep, so that not very long will the price of my brother's
killing remain unpaid. Therefore a man prays that a kinsman

485 may be left in his dwelling to ward off harm and avenge him."
So he spoke; as he vaunted the grief came over the Argives;
he above all in the war-skilled Penéleos roused up the spirit;
he toward Ákamas rushed, nor at all did the fighter remain there
under the onset, and lordly Penéleos stabbed Ilióneus,

490 scion of Phorbas of numerous sheep flocks, whom of the Trojans
Hermes especially loved and had made him rich in possessions;
but Ilióneus alone his mother had born to his father.
Him now under the eyebrow Penéleos stabbed, in the eye-root,
thrusting his eyeball out; and the spear went straight through the eye and

495 on through the tendon, and he sank backward, stretching his two hands
out; and Penéleos, drawing his sharp sword out of its scabbard,
lunged at the neck in the middle and hewed off onto the ground his
head with the helmet he wore; even yet that powerful spear was
stuck in his eye; he, lifting it up like the head of a poppy,

500 pointed it out to the Trojans and thus exulting addressed them:
"Trojans, from me say this to the much-loved father and mother,
there in the halls, of renowned Ilióneus—raise lamentation;
neither indeed will the bedmate of Prómachos, Lord Alegénor's
scion, rejoice when her much-loved husband arrives, on the day we

505 sons of Achaians return to our country from Troy with the galleys."
So did he say; on them all fell shivering, seizing their bodies;
each looked round for a place to escape from a sheer destruction.
Now speak out to me, Muses who live in Olympian dwellings,
tell which one was the first of the Achaians to strip off the bloodstained

510 spoils of a man when the famed earth-shaker had shifted the battle.

Ajax scion of Télamon first stabbed Gyrtios' scion
Hyrtios, who of the stout-souled Mysian men was the leader;
next Antílochos struck dead Phalkes, and Mérmeros also;
Mériones killed Morys and noble Hippótion also;
515 Teukros in turn stripped Próthoön off, and as well Periphétes;
Atreus' son then stabbed Hyperénor, the shepherd of people,
striking at him in the flank, and the bronze spear hollowed his bowels
out by cutting the flesh; then speedily out of the stricken
stab-wound hurried his soul, and his eyes were enshrouded in darkness.
520 But the most warriors Ajax killed, the swift son of Oïleus,
since no other was equal to him on foot at pursuing
men who were running away, when Zeus roused panic among them.

BOOK 15

After the Trojans had gone back through the sharp stakes and the trench in
fleeing, and under the hands of the Dánaäns many were vanquished,
there they finally came to a halt by the chariots, waiting,
green with panic and utterly terrified; Zeus was awakened
5 where beside gold-throned Hera he lay on the summit of Ida.
Rising, he stood upright, and he saw the Achaians and Trojans,
these being driven in flight, and behind them, those who were driving,
Argive fighters; and also with them was the lordly Poseidon;
Hektor he saw on the flatland lying, his comrades about him
10 sitting, as he with a heart insensible, painfully gasping,
vomited blood, since not the most feeble Achaian had struck him.
Then, as he saw him, the father of men and of gods felt pity;
terribly scowling at Hera from lowering brows, he addressed her:
"So has your treacherous baneful contrivance, obstinate Hera,
15 halted from warfare excellent Hektor and routed the people.
I do not know but again you first may be reaping the fruit of
such an iniquitous painful plot—with blows I will whip you.
Are you not mindful of when you were hung from on high, and I fastened
anvils to both of your feet and around both hands put a golden
20 chain unbreakably strong? There you in the clouds and the air were
hanging; on lofty Olympos the gods were indignant, but none were
able to get near you and release you; anyone whom I
caught I picked up and threw from the threshold until he arrived on
earth with his strength all spent; yet not even so did the constant
25 pain I felt over godlike Herakles part from my spirit,
him whom you with the aid of the north wind, swaying the storm-blasts,
sent forth over the desolate seaway, devising him evil,
then to the well-inhabited island of Kos you drove him.
It was from there I saved him and back to horse-nourishing Argos
30 brought him again, though many indeed were the toils he had suffered.

Shall I remind you again about this, so you stop your deceptions,
so that you see if in fact lovemaking protects you, the bed in
which you mingled with me when you came from the gods and deceived me?"
    So he spoke, and she shuddered, the ox-eyed queen, Lady Hera;
35   raising her voice she spoke, and in these winged words she addressed him:
"Now earth witness to this, and the wide sky stretching above us,
so too the water of Styx, down-flowing, for this is the greatest
oath and the oath most dreadful among us blessèd immortals,
also your head, most sacred, and that same bed of the wedded
40   love of us both, by which I never would swear an oath vainly:
not on account of my will does the great earth-shaker Poseidon
do such harm to the Trojans and Hektor, assisting the others.
Rather his own heart surely it is that arouses and bids him—
there at the galleys he sees the Achaians exhausted, and pities.
45   Nevertheless, him too I would counsel and try to persuade him
ever to go in the way that you lead us, lord of the dark cloud."
    So she spoke, and the father of men and of gods began smiling;
answering her he spoke, and in these winged words he addressed her:
"Should it be so hereafter, my ox-eyed queen, Lady Hera,
50   that you, sitting among the immortals, were minded as I am,
even Poseidon himself, though strongly he otherwise wishes,
straightway to follow your heart and my own would alter his purpose.
But if indeed it is truth you are speaking, exactly and fully,
now go straight to the tribes of the gods, there summoning hither
55   messenger Iris to come, and Apollo the glorious archer,
so to the army of those bronze-armored Achaians the goddess
may go down and deliver a message to lordly Poseidon,
tell him to leave off fighting and go back now to his own house;
then let Phoibos Apollo arouse up Hektor to battle,
60   let him again breathe strength into him to forget the afflictions
that are distressing him now in his spirit, and let him again turn
back the Achaians, arousing a cowardly panic, so they will
take flight, flinging themselves on the galleys of numerous oars of
Peleus' scion Achilles; and he will arouse his companion,
65   noble Patróklos, and him with a spear will illustrious Hektor
kill before Ilion, after Patróklos has killed many other
vigorous fighters, among them my own son, noble Sarpédon.
Noble Achilles will then kill Hektor, in wrath for Patróklos.
Then thereafter the Trojans' retreat from the galleys will I be
70   bringing about, incessantly, always, until the Achaians

take steep Ilion, through the advice that Athena will give them.
Never before will I put any stop to my anger, nor will I
suffer to aid those Dánaäns there any other immortal,
never until is accomplished the wish of the scion of Peleus,
75 just as I promised at first—with my head I nodded agreement—
that day Thetis the goddess in supplication embraced my
knees and implored me to honor Achilles the sacker of cities."

He spoke, nor disobeyed him the goddess white-armed Hera;
then from the summits of Ida she parted, to lofty Olympos.
80 Just so swiftly as rushes the mind of a man who has journeyed
far, through many a land, and he thinks with ingenious spirit,
"Would I were this place, or that"—he wishes for many arrivals—
so now eagerly, swiftly, was speeding the queen, Lady Hera;
she soon reached steep Olympos, and there she found the immortal
85 gods in the palace of Zeus all gathered, and soon as they saw her,
they all sprang to their feet and with wine cups gave her a welcome.
Others of them she passed, but a cup she took from the goddess
Themis of beautiful cheeks, who the first came running to meet her;
raising her voice she spoke, and in these winged words she addressed her:
90 "Why have you come now, Hera? You look like one who is frightened.
Surely the scion of Kronos has terrified you, your own husband!"

Speaking to her then answered the goddess white-armed Hera:
"Question me not about these things, Themis divine, for yourself you
know what sort of a spirit is his, overproud and unbending.
95 Rather do you now start the shared feast for the gods in the palace;
certainly then these things you will hear among all the immortals,
what evil deeds great Zeus is revealing, and I do not think that
it will alike be pleasing to all hearts, either to men or
gods, if indeed even now anyone is still merrily feasting."
100 So having spoken, the august queen, Lady Hera, was seated.
There in the palace of Zeus were troubled the gods, and the goddess
smiled with her lips, but above dark brows no smoother became her
forehead; among them all she spoke in her indignation:
"Simpletons, who in our thoughtlessness are resentful of great Zeus!
105 We are most eager to come near him even yet and to thwart him
either by word or by force; he, sitting apart, cares nothing,
nor is he worried; for thus he declares, that among the immortal
gods far greatest he is, beyond doubt, in strength and in power.
Therefore you have, each one, whatever he sends you of evil,
110 since I expect already for Ares has sorrow been fashioned,

for in the battle has perished the son who to him was the dearest
man, Askálaphos, whom strong Ares declares is his offspring."
　　So she spoke; in response, with the palms of his hands the lord Ares
struck at his vigorous thighs, and he said these words in his anguish:

115 "Now do not blame me, you who inhabit Olympian dwellings,
going for vengeance for my son's death to the ships of the Achaians,
even if my fate be by the lightning of Zeus to be stricken
so that I lie down there in the blood and the dust with the corpses."
　　So he spoke, and he bade that his comrades Terror and Panic

120 harness his horses, and dressed himself in his glittering armor.
There then would have been fashioned against the immortals another
wrath yet greater from Zeus and a yet more violent anger,
had not Athena, enormously fearful for all of the gods, not
sprung from the chair she was sitting upon, rushed out of the doorway,

125 taken the helmet off of his head and the shield from his shoulders,
taken as well his bronze-wrought spear from his powerful hand and
stood it aside, and in these words scolded the furious Ares:
"Madman, crazy at heart, you are ruined, and useless for hearing
now are your ears, and your mind is destroyed, and as well your discretion.

130 Do you not hear what is said by the goddess white-armed Hera,
who just now from the side of Olympian Zeus has arrived here?
Or do you wish for yourself to fill up a huge measure of evil,
then come back to Olympos, though painfully, under compulsion,
and to have planted a terrible evil for all of the others—

135 since he will straightway leave the Achaians as well as the high-souled
Trojans and come to Olympos to wreak great havoc among us;
each in turn he will seize on, the guiltless as well as the guilty.
Therefore your wrath for your son do I now ask you to abandon,
since already have some who are greater in hands and in strength than

140 he been killed or will yet be killed, and a difficult thing it
is to preserve the descent and the offspring of all of the people."
　　She spoke, then in his chair caused furious Ares to sit down.
Hera requested Apollo to go with her out of the palace,
Iris as well, who among the immortals is messenger-goddess;

145 raising her voice she spoke, and in these winged words she addressed them:
"Zeus bids both of you, swiftly as possible, travel to Ida;
once you have reached that place and the visage of Zeus you have looked on,
you are to do anything he demands and whatever he orders."
　　So having spoken, the august queen, Lady Hera, returning,

150 sat back down on her chair; and the two sprang up and went speeding.

Ida of numerous springs they came to, the mother of wild beasts;
there upon Gárgaros' height the wide-thundering scion of Kronos
they found sitting, and he by a fragrant cloud was enveloped.
Both of the gods then, coming before the cloud-gathering god Zeus,
155   stood there, nor in his heart as he looked upon them was he angry,
seeing that they so swiftly had heeded the words of his dear wife;
Iris the first he greeted—in these winged words he addressed her:
"Go there at once, swift Iris; a message to lordly Poseidon
carry about all this, and do not be false in reporting.
160   Give him my order that he is to cease from the battle and warfare,
go to the tribes of the gods or else down in the luminous sea-brine.
If to my words he will not be obedient, but disregards them,
let him indeed then think about this in his mind and his spirit:
never would he, although he is mighty, endure or withstand me
165   coming at him, for in might, I say, I am greater than he by
far, and the eldest in birth; but his spirit does not hesitate at
calling himself my equal, though other gods tremble before me."
      So did he say; swift wind-footed Iris did not disobey him;
down from the summits of Ida to sacred Ilion she went.
170   As at a time when out of the clouds fly snowflakes or frozen
hailstones under the blast of the north wind born in the bright air,
just so nimbly and eagerly now swift Iris was speeding;
then by the glorious shaker of earth she stood, and addressed him:
"Bearing a message for you, dark-haired upholder of earth, have
175   I come here on an errand from Zeus who carries the aegis.
He sends order that you are to cease from the battle and warfare,
go to the tribe of the gods or else down in the luminous sea-brine.
If to his words you will not be obedient, but disregard them,
then he threatens that he will himself come here and engage in
180   battle with you, face-to-face; and to keep well away from his hands he
strongly suggests, for in might, he says, he is greater than you by
far, and the eldest in birth; but your spirit does not hesitate at
calling yourself his equal, though other gods tremble before him."
      Mightily vexed, thus spoke to her then the renowned earth-shaker:
185   "Well now, noble and great as he is, he has haughtily spoken,
if by force he restrains me against my will, his own equal,
since three brothers we are who were born by Rhea to Kronos,
Zeus, myself, and third Hades, the lord over those who have perished.
All the domains were divided in three; we each had a portion—
190   I when the lots were cast was allotted the silvery sea to

267

dwell in forever; the shadowy murk was allotted to Hades;
Zeus was allotted, above in the air and the clouds, broad heaven;
still to us all is the earth held common, and lofty Olympos.
Therefore will I not live in the way Zeus wills it; but let him
195 peacefully stay in his own third share, although he is mighty.
Nor with his hands let him try, as if I were a coward, to scare me;
better for them would it be if he scolded with vehement words those
daughters and sons of his own, those offspring he himself fathered,
who of necessity will take heed of whatever he urges."
200   Giving an answer to him then spoke swift wind-footed Iris:
"Is it indeed your thought, dark-haired upholder of earth, that
I now carry to Zeus this word unyielding and forceful,
or will you change it a little? The minds of the noble are pliant.
You know how the Erínyes are always attending the elder."
205   Speaking to her made answer the great earth-shaker Poseidon:
"Iris divine, this word you have spoken is fitting and proper.
It is an excellent thing when a messenger knows the right measure.
Yet this terrible grief comes over the heart and the spirit
when somebody desires to revile with speeches of anger
210 one who is equal in portion, to whom a like share is allotted.
Nevertheless I yield to you now, though I am resentful;
something else I will tell you and make this threat in my spirit:
if in despite of myself and Athena the driver of plunder,
also of Hera and Hermes as well as of lordly Hephaistos,
215 he takes mercy on steep-built Ilion, nor does he want to
capture and sack it, and thus a great victory give to the Argives,
let him know this, that between us will be unappeasable anger."
     So having said, from the host of Achaians the earth-shaker parted,
went to the sea, and plunged in; he was missed by the hero-Achaians.
220 Then to Apollo addressed these words the cloud-gathering god Zeus:
"Now do you go, dear Phoibos, to great bronze-helmeted Hektor,
since in fact the great holder and shaker of earth has departed
now and gone down in the luminous sea-brine, shunning my dreaded
anger; for others have had an experience too of our fighting,
225 those who are gods of the regions beneath and accompany Kronos.
Yet far better it was for the two of us, both for myself and
him, that before that happened, despite his resentment, he yielded
under my hands, since not without sweat would the matter have ended.
But now take in your hands the great aegis, streaming with tassels,
230 savagely shake it to frighten the hero-Achaians to panic;

also concern yourself, Far-shooter, with glorious Hektor,
so long rousing in him a great temper until the Achaians
fleeing from him come down to the Hellespont and to the galleys;
then thereafter will I contrive it, in word and in action,
235　so that again the Achaians recover their breath from their labor."
　　So he spoke; to his father Apollo did not fail to listen;
he went down from the mountains of Ida, resembling a speedy
killer of pigeons, a falcon, of all winged creatures the swiftest.
There he found noble Hektor, the scion of war-skilled Priam,
240　sitting—he lay no longer; his mind just now had recovered—
recognizing the comrades around him; the panting and sweat had
stopped, since he had been roused by the purpose of Zeus of the aegis.
Standing beside him, thus spoke out far-working Apollo:
"Why now, Hektor the scion of Priam, apart from the others,
245　are you sitting so feebly? Has pain somehow overcome you?"
　　Feebly in answer to him spoke Hektor of glittering helmet:
"Which of the gods are you, mightiest one, who face-to-face ask this?
Do you not know how Ajax the crier of battle, as I was
killing his comrades there by the sterns of the Achaians' ships, struck
250　me on the chest with a boulder and halted my furious valor?
I felt certain that I would be viewing the dead and the house of
Hades on this very day, when the dear life-breath I had gasped out."
　　Speaking to him then answered the lord far-working Apollo:
"Now take heart, so mighty a helper the scion of Kronos
255　has dispatched you from Ida to stand beside you and protect you—
Phoibos Apollo the god of the gold sword, who have before this
kept you from harm; both you and the steep citadel I have guarded.
But come now and arouse your numerous charioteers to
drive their swift-running horses ahead at the hollow galleys;
260　meanwhile I will be going before them and making the whole way
smooth for the horses, and turning in flight those hero-Achaians."
　　So he spoke and inspired great strength in the shepherd of people.
Just as a horse in a stall that is fed at the manger on barley,
breaking his rope, runs over the plain with thundering hoofbeat—
265　he is accustomed to bathe in the stream of a fair-running river—
proud in his strength, with his head held high, while over his shoulders
streaming his mane floats back; he exults in his glorious splendor;
nimbly his limbs bear him to the pastures and haunts of the horses;
so now Hektor was agilely plying his feet and his legs and
270　urging his charioteers, for the voice of the god he was heeding.

They then, as at a time when hounds and the men of the country
hasten ahead in pursuit of a full-horned stag or a wild goat—
him however a towering rock or a shadowy woodland
rescues from them—it was not their portion allotted to reach him;
275 then at their clamor, a well-bearded lion appears on the pathway
there, and at once he turns them all back in spite of their ardor;
so for a time was a throng of the Dánaäns following closely,
always thrusting and striking with swords and with double-edged spear-blades;
but then, seeing that Hektor was ranging the ranks of the fighters,
280 they took fright, and the hearts of them all sank down to their ankles.
       Straightway among them then spoke Thoas the son of Andraímon,
of the Aitolians best by far, at the javelin skillful,
brave in the close combat, and whenever the youths were contending
in the assembly with speeches, but few of the Achaians surpassed him;
285 he with benevolent wisdom addressed them, giving them counsel:
"Well then! Immense is the marvel that I with my eyes am beholding—
such is the man—once more has Hektor recovered, avoiding
fate now; surely the hearts in us each hoped strongly that he had
died here under the hands of the scion of Télamon Ajax.
290 Nevertheless, once more some god has delivered and rescued
Hektor—the knees under many a Dánaän he has unloosened;
so I believe he will do now also, for not without Zeus who
thunders abroad he stands as the champion, eager for battle.
But come, just as I say, let all of us heed and obey it.
295 Let us command that the multitude now go back to the galleys,
while we all who declare ourselves to be best in the army
stand here hoping that we can oppose him first and protect them,
raising our spears; although he is eager, I think in his spirit
he will be fearful to enter the melee of Dánaän fighters."
300   So did he say; they carefully listened to him and obeyed him.
Those who accompanied Ajax, and lordly Idómeneus also,
Teukros and Mérionés, with Meges the equal of Ares,
marshaled the violent combat and called on the best of the fighters
there to face Hektor and all those Trojans; and meanwhile behind them
305 back once more to the ships of the Achaians the multitude hastened.
       Then in a throng charged forward the Trojans, and Hektor was leading,
moving in long strides; Phoibos Apollo was going before him,
wearing a cloud on his shoulders and holding the furious aegis,
terrible, shaggily-fringed, bright-glittering, which had been given
310 Zeus by Hephaistos the bronzesmith to carry and terrify fighters;

this now holding aloft in his hands he was leading the army.

　　There in a throng were awaiting the Argives; rising from both sides
sounded a shrill war cry; from the bowstrings arrows were leaping
swiftly away, and from bold stout hands were the numerous spears that,
315　some of them, lodged in the flesh of the young men swift in the battle;
many, before they grazed white flesh, stood there in the middle,
upright, fixed in the earth, and desiring on flesh to be glutted.
While unmoving the aegis was held by Phoibos Apollo,
missiles of both sides sped to their targets, and people were falling;
320　but then, when in the swift-horsed Dánaäns' faces he looked and
shook it, and yelled out loudly himself, their hearts he enchanted
deep in their bosoms, and so they forgot their furious valor.
As when a pair of wild beasts drive into disorder a cattle
herd or a great sheep flock in the deep black shadows of nighttime,
325　suddenly coming on them at a time no herdsman is nearby,
so the Achaians were panicked, bereft of their valor—Apollo
sent them panic; the glory he gave to the Trojans and Hektor.

　　There then man killed man as the violent battle was scattered.
Hektor himself killed Stíchios first, and bold Árkesiláos;
330　one was a leader among the bronze-armored Boiótian fighters,
while of greathearted Menéstheus the other was trustworthy comrade.
Medon and Íasos both were then slaughtered and stripped by Aineías;
one of the two in fact was the godlike Oïleus' bastard
son and the brother of Ajax, Medon, but Phýlakè he was
335　then inhabiting, far from his country—a man he had murdered,
kin of his own stepmother, Oïleus' wife Eriópis.
Of the Athenians Íasos came to the war as a leader;
him they called the own son of the scion of Boúkolos, Sphelos.
Then was Mekísteus killed by Polýdamas, Échios, fighting
340　in the first line, by Polítes, and Klónios by noble Agénor.
Then from behind, as Deïphobos fled with the foremost, Paris
struck on the base of his shoulder and drove the bronze blade right through him.

　　While from the men their armor was stripped, meanwhile the Achaians
there in the trench they had dug and the sharp palisades were entangled,
345　fleeing one way or the other and forced inside of the rampart.
Hektor began exhorting the Trojans, and loudly he shouted:
"Now charge straight at the ships and abandon the bloodstained armor;
anyone whom I notice away from the galleys and elsewhere,
I will devise for him death right there—then never will kinsmen
350　nor kinswomen provide any funeral fire for the dead man;

rather the dogs shall tear him to pieces in front of our city."

 Speaking, his horses he drove with a whip-stroke down from the shoulder,
yelling across those ranks of the Trojans; together with him they
all then shouted for action and guided the chariot-drawing

355 steeds with a marvelous din; and before them Phoibos Apollo
easily kicked with his feet at the banks of the deep-dug trench and
threw them down in the middle and thus bridged over a pathway,
great in length and in breadth, so far as the distance a spear is
thrown when a man hurls it while making a trial of prowess.

360 Over it they poured forward in ranks, and before them Apollo
lifted the priceless aegis; the wall of the Achaians he tore down
easily, just as a child might do with the sand on the seashore,
who in his childishness first makes sand castles to play in,
then with his feet and his hands, still playing, confounds and destroys them.

365 Thus you, glorious Phoibos, confounded the mighty and painful
work of the Argive fighters and roused up panic among them.

 So now, close to the galleys, the Dánaäns halted and stayed there;
each to the others the men called out, and to all of the gods then
raising their hands up high, they fervently, loudly implored them;

370 most of them all the Achaians' protector, Gerenian Nestor,
prayed while stretching his hands on high to the star-filled heaven:
"Zeus our father, if anyone ever in grain-rich Argos
burnt in your honor the fat thigh pieces of sheep or of heifers
praying to go back home, and you promised and nodded agreement,

375 call them to mind now, Olympian, ward off the pitiless doomsday,
do not allow the Achaians to be thus quelled by the Trojans."

 So he spoke in his prayer; Zeus Counselor mightily thundered,
soon as he heard that plea of the old man, Neleus' scion.

 Hearing the thunder of Zeus of the aegis, the Trojans were yet more

380 eager to leap at the Argives, recalling their ardor for battle.
As at a time that a wave on the great broad path of the deep sea
sweeps up over the sides of a galley whenever a mighty
stormwind pounds it and raises a mountainous swell in the billows,
so with a great shout over the wall those Trojans were coming,

385 driving the chariots; then they fought at the sterns of the ships in
close combat with their double-edged spears—from the chariots they were
fighting; the Argives fought from the black ships, climbing aloft and
wielding the long-staffed pikes that were lying at hand on the galleys,
powerful-jointed, with tips bronze-covered, for naval encounters.

390 As for Patróklos, as long as the others, Achaians and Trojans,

kept on fighting about that rampart, away from the swift ships,
so long he was inside kindhearted Eurýpylos' cabin,
sitting, and he entertained him with talking, and over his painful
wound he was spreading the herbs as a cure and relief for his black pain;
395   but then, when he observed how Trojans were charging across that
rampart and how on the Dánaäns clamor and panic had fallen,
then straightway he uttered a groan; with the palms of his hands he
struck at his thighs, both sides, and in these words made lamentation:
"Even although you need me, Eurýpylos, I can no longer
400   stay here beside you, for great indeed is the strife that has risen;
let your attendant instead entertain you—I will myself go
hastily back to Achilles, that I may exhort him to battle.
Who knows whether I might with a god's aid, rousing his spirit,
talk him around? For an excellent thing is a comrade's persuasion."
405   When he had spoken, his feet soon carried him off; the Achaians
firmly awaited the Trojans as they came onward, but were not
able to thrust them away from the ships, though they were the fewer,
nor yet through the battalions of Dánaäns there were the Trojans
able to break, to join battle among their cabins and galleys.
410   Just as the beams of a galley are cut to a tight-stretched chalk-line
held in the hands of an expert worker, a man who is skilled in
every manner of craft by the help and advice of Athena,
so were the battle and warfare of both sides equally tight-stretched.
Some around some of the galleys were fighting, and some around others;
415   meanwhile Hektor himself went straight for illustrious Ajax.
These two around one ship kept toiling, and neither was able,
Hektor to drive back Ajax and then set fire to the galley,
Ajax to thrust him away, for a god to the galley had brought him.
Then at Kalétor the scion of Klýtios glorious Ajax
420   struck on the chest with his spear, as he brought fire there to the galley;
falling he crashed to the ground; from his hand went flying the firebrand.
Hektor, as soon as he took good note with his eyes that his cousin
there in the dust in front of the dark-hued galley had fallen,
called to the Trojan and Lykian warriors; loudly he shouted:
425   "Trojans and Lykians all, Dardánians, hand-to-hand fighters,
never in this tight place yield even a little from battle,
but now rescue the scion of Klýtios, lest the Achaians
strip his armor from him who fell where the galleys are gathered."
       So having spoken, at Ajax he cast with his glittering spear-shaft.
430   Him he missed, but the spear struck Lýkophron scion of Mastor,

that Kytheréan attendant of Ajax who with the hero
dwelt, for a man in sacred Kýthera once he had slaughtered—
him on the head just over the ear he struck with his sharp bronze
sword as he stood by Ajax; and he to the ground in the dust fell

435 down from the stern of the ship on his back, and his limbs were unloosened.
Ajax shuddered to see it, and thus he spoke to his brother:
"Look, dear Teukros, at how has been killed our trustworthy comrade,
Mastor's son, who, coming from Kýthera, there in our house was
dwelling, and whom we honored as much as our own dear parents.

440 That man great-souled Hektor has killed. Where now are the arrows,
swift death-bringers, and bow that to you gave Phoibos Apollo?"
    He spoke; Teukros had heard him and ran to stand next to his brother,
holding his back-curved bow in his hand and his arrow-containing
quiver; and swift were the missiles that he let fly at the Trojans.

445 Kleitos the first he struck, the illustrious son of Peisénor—
he of Polýdamas, Pánthoös' glorious son, was a comrade—
while in his hands he was holding the reins, engaged with his horses,
for to the place the battalions were most being routed he drove them,
doing a favor to Hektor and all those Trojans; but swiftly

450 came to him evil that no one, no matter how eager, could ward off,
since on his neck in back fell an arrow of measureless sorrow;
he from the chariot fell; to the side then swerving, the horses
rattled the car, now empty. The lordly Polýdamas quickly
noticed, and he was the first who came in front of the horses;

455 to Protiáön's son Astýnoös handing them over,
strongly he urged him to hold them there nearby and to watch him;
then he himself went back, with the foremost fighters to mingle.
    Teukros against bronze-helmeted Hektor drew out another
arrow and there at the Achaians' ships would have halted his combat,

460 had he but struck him in his rampaging and taken his life-breath.
But the shrewd notice of Zeus this did not escape—he was watching
Hektor; the glory he took from the scion of Télamon Teukros,
who on the faultless bow quite shattered the string, well-twisted,
just as he drew it at Hektor; the bronze-heavy arrow was driven

465 swerving away to the side; from his hand went flying the great bow.
Teukros shuddered to see it, and thus he spoke to his brother:
"Oh, what a shame! Our battle-intent some god is entirely
cutting to nothing—the bow he has struck from my hands, and the bowstring,
recently twisted, has broken, that I in the morning had bound on

470 so it would stand the incessantly springing succession of arrows."

Answering him then spoke the great scion of Télamon Ajax:
"Yes, dear brother, but let that bow and the showering arrows
lie there, because some god with a grudge at the Dánaäns wrecked them;
taking instead in your hands a long spear, and a shield on your shoulder,

475 keep on fighting the Trojans and rouse up the rest of the army.
May they not, even if they have beaten us, capture the well-benched
galleys without any struggle, but let us remember our war-craft."
    So he spoke, and his brother returned his bow to the cabin.
Then he placed on his shoulders a shield four-layered of oxhide;

480 onto his powerful head he fitted a well-made helmet
crested with horsehair; the plume on top of it fearfully nodded;
straightway taking his powerful spear, well-pointed with sharp bronze,
he set forth, very speedily running to stand beside Ajax.
    Hektor, as soon as he saw that the arrows of Teukros were thwarted,

485 called to the Trojan and Lykian warriors; loudly he shouted:
"Trojans and Lykians all, Dardánians, hand-to-hand fighters,
now be men, dear friends, and remember your furious valor
here by the hollow ships, for in fact I have seen with my own eyes
how by Zeus were disabled the arrows of one of the best men.

490 Easily known is the valor of Zeus that appears among fighters,
whether among those whom he endows with superior glory
or among those he weakens and does not want to assist them—
so now the Argives' might he weakens, and us he is helping.
Fight on then by the galleys together—whoever among you,

495 hit by a missile or struck with a spear, meets death and his doomsday,
let him die; no dishonor for him who fights for his country
is it to die, but his wife is safe, and his children who follow,
also unharmed are his house and his property, should the Achaians
go back home with their ships to the much-loved land of their fathers."

500 So he spoke and aroused in each fighter the strength and the spirit.
Then from the opposite side great Ajax called to his comrades:
"Shame on you, Argives! Now it is sure, we either will perish
or will be saved and will thrust this evil away from the galleys.
Or do you hope that if Hektor of glittering helmet should take these

505 ships you will go on foot, each one, to the land of your fathers?
Do you not hear how Hektor is rousing up all of his people,
how in fact he is raging to set our galleys to burning?
Certainly not to a dance he calls them to come, but to battle.
Nor is there any device, any scheme for us better than this one—

510 now with our hands and our power to mingle in hand-to-hand combat.

Better the one time either to perish or, winning, to live on,
than to be pressed so long to exhaustion in terrible combat
thus in vain at our galleys by such inferior fighters."
      So he spoke and aroused in each fighter the strength and the spirit.
515   Then by Hektor was Schédios killed, Perimédes' scion,
one of the Phokians' lords, while Ajax slaughtered a leader
of the foot soldiers, Laódamas, glorious son of Anténor;
also Polýdamas slaughtered and stripped the Kyllénian Otos,
comrade of Phýleus' son and a chief of the great-souled Epeíans.
520   Meges, observing it, leapt upon him, but Polýdamas swerved from
under his onset, and he missed him, for Apollo would not let
Pánthoös' son be vanquished among those champion fighters;
Kroismos it was whom square on the chest he struck with a spear-thrust;
falling he crashed to the ground, and the armor he stripped from his shoulders.
525   Meanwhile rushing at him came Dolops, skilled as a spearman,
scion of Lampos, the mightiest son Laómedon's scion
Lampos had fathered, the one most skillful in furious valor;
square on the shield he struck with a spear-thrust Phýleus' scion,
rushing from nearby; yet he was saved by the corselet he was
530   wearing, a solid one fitted with bronze plates, which from Ephýra
Phýleus once had carried away, from the river Selléïis.
This did his guest-friend there, Euphétes the lord of the people,
give him to wear into war as protection from enemy fighters;
it now guarded the body of his dear son from destruction.
535   Meges in turn with a keen-edged spear struck high on the topmost
socket of Dolops' helmet of bronze, well-crested with horsehair,
shearing the horsehair plume from the helmet, and groundward it all then
fell down into the dust, still shining with new sea-purple.
Still he remained there fighting with him, still hoping to beat him,
540   while warlike Meneláos arrived to defend him and stood there
unobserved off to the side with his spear; from behind at his shoulder
he struck; furiously did the point speed straight through the breastbone,
eagerly rushing ahead; and he slumped to the ground face forward.
Both of the men were desiring to strip from his shoulders the brazen
545   armor; but Hektor began to call out to his brothers and cousins,
all of them; yet Hiketáon's son was the first that he scolded,
strong Melaníppos; before, his swing-paced cattle had he been
pasturing in Perkótè, as long as the foemen were far off,
then when the Dánaäns' tractable galleys had come, he returned to
550   Ilion, where among all of the Trojans he was outstanding;

there he abode near Priam, who honored him like his own children.
Him now Hektor rebuked and said these words, calling upon him:
"Thus, Melaníppos, are we to be slackening? Does it in fact not
matter to you in your own dear heart that your cousin is slaughtered?
555   Do you not see how busied they are with the armor of Dolops?
But come, follow; for we no longer can fight with the Argives
standing away at a distance, till either we kill them or they have
utterly seized steep Ilion city and slaughtered the townsmen."
So having said he led, and the godlike man followed after.
560   Rousing the Argives spoke the great scion of Télamon Ajax:
"Now, dear friends, be men, in your hearts put fear of dishonor,
feel shame, each on account of the rest in the violent combats;
more of the men who feel such shame live safely than perish,
while from the ones who flee no renown springs, nor any valor."
565   So he spoke; and themselves that foe they were raging to ward off;
into their hearts they put his command; with a rampart of bronze they
fenced in the galleys, and Zeus was arousing the Trojans against them.
Urging Antílochos spoke the great crier of war Meneláos:
"There is no other Achaian, Antílochos, younger than you here,
570   none more rapid of foot or as valiant as you to do battle;
doubtless you could leap forward and strike some man of the Trojans."
He spoke; back to the battle he sped—he had stirred up the other,
who sprang forth from the foremost and cast with his glittering spear while
warily glancing around, and the Trojans withdrew in the face of
575   that man casting at them; nor in vain he let fly the weapon,
but Hiketáon's son, high-souled Melaníppos, as he was
coming again to the battle, he struck in the chest by the nipple;
falling he crashed to the ground, and his eyes were enshrouded in darkness.
Then Antílochos sprang upon him like a hound that upon some
580   fawn leaps which has been wounded in breaking away from its covert;
certain of aim was the hunter who loosened its limbs when he struck it.
So, Melaníppos, on you Antílochos steadfast in fight was
leaping to strip you of armor; but excellent Hektor observed him;
he came running to meet him across that violent combat.
585   Nor did Antílochos stay, though speedy he was as a fighter;
rather he fled as a wild beast flees that has been doing evil,
one that has slaughtered a dog or a herdsman out with his cattle,
then starts fleeing before any posse of men can be gathered;
so fled the scion of Nestor; upon him the Trojans and Hektor,
590   raising a marvelous din, poured down their maleficent missiles;

turning around he stood, when he came to the band of his comrades.

Still, like ravening lions that eat raw flesh, were the Trojans
rushing ahead at the ships, and the orders of Zeus they accomplished—
always in them he aroused huge might, and he trammeled the Argives'
595   spirits and took their glory away as he stirred up the others,
for in his heart Zeus wished to bestow great glory on Hektor
scion of Priam, so ravenous fire, unwearying, he might
throw on the well-curved galleys and thereby fully accomplish
Thetis' immoderate prayer, and for this Zeus Counselor waited,
600   till with his eyes he could look on the blaze as a galley was burning,
since thereafter would he start causing the Trojans to go back,
driven away from the ships, thus giving the Dánaäns glory.
Thinking of these things now he aroused at the hollow galleys
Hektor the scion of Priam, though avid indeed he himself was.
605   Raging he battled, as when spear-brandishing Ares or deadly
fire among peaks in the dense underbrush of a deep wood rages;
foam encircled his mouth as he slavered, and both of his eyes were
glittering under his terrible eyebrows; the helmet around his
temples was horribly shaken and clattering loudly as Hektor
610   kept on fighting, for Zeus himself out of heaven was helping
him and, alone as he was among numerous warriors, showed him
honor and granted him glory; for brief was the span of his lifetime
going to be, for the day of his doom was Pallas Athena
speeding already ahead by the power of Peleus' scion.
615   He kept wanting to shatter the ranks of the fighters and made his
trial wherever he saw the most thronging, the best of the armor;
yet not thus could he shatter the troops, though greatly he rampaged,
since firm-fixed they held like a rampart, the way an enormous
towering sea-cliff holds steadfast by the silvery sea-brine,
620   which withstands swift-rushing assaults of the whistling winds and
blows of the billowing breakers that belch forth roaring against it;
so did the Dánaäns stoutly withstand those Trojans and fled not.
Yet he, flashing his fire to all sides, leapt into the melee,
falling on them in the way that a wave falls onto a swift ship,
625   violent, raised from the clouds by a stormwind, so that the ship is
wholly concealed by the spume, and the terrible blast of the tempest
thunders against her sail; in their hearts then shudder the sailors,
terrified, since no more than a little from death they are carried;
so in the breasts of the Achaians the spirits were now lacerated.
630   Yet he—just as a murderous-spirited lion approaches

cattle that graze on the rich low land of a great water-meadow,
myriads, nor is the herdsman among them skillful as yet in
fighting a wild beast over the corpse of a crooked-horned heifer,
yet there, now by the foremost and then by the hindmost cattle,
635   always he keeps on pacing, but into the middle it leaps and
eats some cow, and they all flee terrified—so the Achaians
then by Hektor and Zeus the great father were wondrously routed,
all, though he slaughtered but one, Periphétes, a man of Mykénè,
much-loved scion of Kópreus, who often from Lord Eurýstheus
640   went on an errand to powerful Herakles bearing a message.
So of a sire much baser an excellent son was begotten,
better in prowess of every sort, on his feet and in battle,
also in thinking among the foremost of the men of Mykénè;
he it was who bestowed the superior glory on Hektor.
645   For as he turned to go back he tripped on the rim of the shield he
carried himself, one reaching his feet as a wall against spear-casts;
stumbling on this he fell down backward; the helmet around his
temples was clattering loudly about him as down he was falling.
Hektor was quick to observe, and he ran up, standing beside him;
650   planting a spear in his chest, by his own dear comrades he killed him;
these, though mourning their comrade, were quite unable to give him
succor, for they themselves much dreaded the noble lord Hektor.
     Now they were facing the ships, and encircling them were the outmost
ships they had dragged up first, but the Trojans continued to stream in.
655   Thus did the Argives yield of necessity, back from the galleys,
those that were outmost; there on the shore they stayed by the cabins
thronging and did not scatter about the encampment; for shame and
fear held them, as incessantly they called out to each other.
Most of them all, the Achaians' protector, Gerenian Nestor,
660   begged and implored each warrior there for the sake of his parents:
"Now, dear friends, be men, in your hearts put fear of dishonor
others indeed might show you, and each of you call to remembrance
now your children and bedmates, your property too, and your parents,
whether a man's own kinsmen are living or rather have perished;
665   now for the sake of the ones not present do I supplicate you
here most strongly to stand and not turn back, fleeing in panic."
     So he spoke and aroused in each fighter the strength and the spirit.
Then from the eyes of the fighters the marvelous cloud of a mist was
thrust by Athena; and brightly from both sides light was appearing,
670   both on the side of the ships and on that of the leveling combat.

They knew Hektor himself, of the great war cry, and his comrades,
both those who in the rear stood away, not entering battle,
and those who were engaged in the battle beside the swift galleys.
   Then no longer the spirit of great-souled Ajax was pleased with

675 standing aside where the rest of the sons of Achaians were standing;
rather with great strides he kept walking the decks of the galleys,
brandishing high in his hands an enormous pike for sea-fighting,
one well jointed with clamps and in length full twenty-two cubits.
As at a time when a man well skilled in riding on horseback,

680 who four horses selected from many has harnessed together,
drives them speeding away from the flatland toward a great city
over a road much traveled, and numerous people, admiring,
watch him, the men and the women, and steadily, always securely,
passing from one to another he leaps, while onward they gallop,

685 so now over the numerous decks of the swift ships Ajax
ranged with his great long strides, and his voice went up to the heavens;
always the Dánaäns he kept urging with terrible outcry
still to defend their galleys and cabins. But Hektor himself did
not stay back in the throng of the sturdily mail-clad Trojans,

690 but as a dark red eagle descends in a swoop on a flock of
winged fowl scratching for food on the banks of a river, a gaggle
either of geese or of cranes or of long-necked swans of the meadow,
so now Hektor directed his course at a dark-prowed galley,
rushing against it, while from behind Zeus thrust him ahead with

695 powerful hand, and to follow with him he roused up the army.
   Then once more was a bitter combat fought there by the galleys.
You might well have imagined that they untamed and unwearied
faced each other in war, so violently they were fighting.
This is the way they were thinking as they fought on: the Achaians

700 did not think to escape from the evil, but rather to perish;
as for the Trojans, the heart in the bosom of each was expecting
soon to set fire to the galleys and slaughter the hero-Achaians.
Such were the things they thought as they stood there fighting each other;
Hektor himself laid hold of the stern of the seafaring galley,

705 beautiful, swift on the sea-brine, that had brought Prótesiláos
thither to Troy, but it did not carry him back to his country.
It was around that galley that now the Achaians and Trojans
killed each other in hand-to-hand combat; not at a distance
were they awaiting the volleys from bows or the javelins rushing;

710 rather beside one another they stood with a single intention;

there they fought with their keen-edged hatchets and strong battle-axes,
waging the fight with their huge swords too and their double-edged spear-blades.
Many a beautiful sword, well-hilted and bound with a black thong,
fell to the ground, some out of their hands, some off of their shoulders,
715 as those men were contending; the black earth streamed with their lifeblood.
Hektor did not let go of the ship's stern, once he had seized it;
holding the sternpost firmly in hand, he yelled to the Trojans:
"Bring me fire, and together at once raise clamor of battle;
Zeus has indeed now granted a day to us worth all the others,
720 letting us capture the ships that against the gods' will came hither,
causing for us by our old men's cowardice many afflictions—
they at the time I wanted to fight by the sterns of the galleys
kept me away myself, and as well they held back the army.
But if indeed wide-thundering Zeus then thwarted the judgments
725 we ourselves made, now he of himself stirs up and commands us."
      So he spoke, and at that even more they rushed at the Argives.
Firm no longer did Ajax remain; he was pressed by the missiles,
rather, to give ground slightly—believing that he was to perish—
back on the seven-foot bench, so leaving the deck of the balanced
730 ship, and he stood expectant; away from the ships with his spear he
always warded the Trojans who brought unwearying fire there;
always the Dánaäns he kept urging with terrible outcry:
"Oh friends, Dánaän heroes and noble attendants of Ares,
now be men, dear friends, and remember your furious valor.
735 Are we perhaps to suppose there are others behind who will help us,
maybe a wall yet stronger to ward off death from the fighters?
Not anywhere nearby is a city constructed with walls in
which to defend ourselves, with people to add to our valor;
no, since here in the plain of the sturdily mail-clad Trojans
740 we now sit with our backs to the sea, faraway from our country,
so in our hands is our safety, and not in slackness in battle."
      Thus he spoke, and he avidly drove at the foe with his sharp spear.
Then whoever among those Trojans would rush at the hollow
ships with a firebrand's flame, for the favor of Hektor who urged it,
745 Ajax there would await him and give him a wound with his long spear;
twelve in front of the ships he wounded in hand-to-hand fighting.

BOOK 16

So for the well-benched galley were both sides fighting around it;
meanwhile Patróklos, approaching Achilles the shepherd of people,
stood beside him, and he shed hot tears like a dark-water fountain
which pours down a precipitous rock its shadowy water.
5 There fleet-footed and noble Achilles observed him and pitied;
raising his voice he spoke, and in these winged words he addressed him:
"Why now, Patróklos, do you shed tears in the way that an infant
girl does who with her mother is running and begs her to pick her
up as she clutches her dress and prevents her from hurrying onward?
10 Shedding her tears she looks at her mother until she is picked up.
Like that infant, Patróklos, the soft tears now you are shedding.
Have you something to say to the Mýrmidons or to myself now,
or a report you only have heard, some message from Phthía?
Still, they tell us, is living Menoítios, scion of Aktor;
15 still with the Mýrmidons lives Lord Peleus, Aíakos' scion—
certainly over them both we greatly would mourn if they perished.
Or do you grieve on account of the Argives, how they are dying
there by the hollow galleys because of their arrogant conduct?
Speak out, hiding it not in your mind, so that both of us know it."
20 Heavily groaning, you gave him an answer, Patróklos the horseman:
"Peleus' scion Achilles, far greatest among the Achaians,
do not reproach me, for such great grief has beset the Achaians,
since those men who before were the noblest in fighting are all now
lying among our ships; they were struck by missiles and wounded.
25 So has been struck Lord Tydeus' powerful son Diomédes;
wounded as well is Odysseus renowned with the spear, Agamemnon
too; and Eurýpylos has been struck in the thigh with an arrow.
Over these men are the healers expert in medicines busied,
seeking to cure their wounds; yet you are unyielding, Achilles.
30 Never on me let such wrath seize as the anger you cherish,

baneful in prowess!—From you who else born later will profit,
should you indeed not ward from the Argives shameful destruction?
Pitiless man, your father cannot be Peleus the horseman,
neither was Thetis your mother; the gray sea rather it was that
35 bore you, and towering cliffs, your mind is so harshly unbending.
Should you in fact be shunning an oracle known to your own heart,
something from Zeus put into your mind by the lady your mother,
quickly at least send me, and as well let the rest of the host of
Mýrmidons follow, that I for the Dánaäns might be a beacon.
40 Give me as well that armor of yours to be worn on my shoulders,
so that the Trojans perhaps might think I am you and refrain from
combat, and then these warlike sons of Achaians could take breath,
tired as they are; very scant is the time to take breath in a battle.
Easily we, unwearied, could thrust those men who are now so
45 weary with strife, toward town and away from the galleys and cabins."
       So imploring he spoke, great fool that he was, for an evil
death it would be for himself, his own doom which he was beseeching.
Mightily vexed, thus spoke to him then swift-footed Achilles:
"Ah me, Zeus-descended Patróklos, what are you saying!
50 There is no oracle I am concerned with, none that I know of,
nothing from Zeus put into my mind by the lady my mother;
yet this terrible grief comes over the heart and the spirit
when some man has a mind to despoil one who is his equal
and of his prize to deprive him, because he surpasses in power.
55 This is my terrible grief, since pains in my heart I have suffered.
That girl chosen for me as a prize by the sons of Achaians,
won by my own spear after I captured a well-walled city,
her from my arms has taken the powerful lord Agamemnon,
Atreus' son, as if I were a person dishonored and outcast.
60 Yet let us leave these things that are done with; never would I be
able to keep in my heart such furious anger; indeed I
said I would never desist from my wrath till the time that
finally came to my galleys the clamor and tumult of warfare.
But now you put over your shoulders my glorious armor,
65 lead these Mýrmidons, lovers of warfare, out to do battle,
if in fact the dark cloud of the Trojans has come to the galleys,
strongly surrounding them there, and the men on the shore of the deep sea
stand with their backs to it, hold but a small part now of the land, those
Argives; and all of the city of Trojans has come out against them
70 boldly, because they are not now seeing the face of my helmet

close to them, brightly ablaze; they would soon be filling the channels
up with their dead while fleeing, if powerful Lord Agamemnon
thought of me kindly; but now they battle about the encampment,
since in the hands of the scion of Tydeus, Lord Diomédes,
75 no spear rages to ward from the Dánaäns utter destruction,
neither as yet have I heard the loud voice of the scion of Atreus
shout from his odious head, while that of man-slaughtering Hektor
echoes around as he urges the Trojans, and they with a war cry
hold the entire plain as in the battle they beat the Achaians.
80 Yet even so, from the galleys, Patróklos, ward off destruction,
mightily fall upon them, lest they with the blistering flames set
fire to the ships, so taking away our desired homecoming.
Do you obey as I put in your mind this word of conclusion,
so that you might win even for me great honor and glory
85 from the whole Dánaän army, and that most beautiful maiden
they send back to me then, and as well give glorious presents.
When from the ships you have thrust them, return here; even if you are
given to win fame by the loud-thundering husband of Hera,
do not without me avidly enter the battle against those
90 Trojans, lovers of war—then you will diminish my honor.
Neither do you, exulting in battle and terrible combat,
fighting and killing the Trojans, lead onward to Ilion city,
lest someone of the gods who live always descend from Olympos
into the battle—Apollo who works from afar much loves them.
95 Rather return again, once you have planted a beacon among those
galleys, and leave to the others to fight there over the flatland.
Oh Zeus, father of all, and Athena as well, and Apollo,
I wish none of the Trojans, of all there are, would escape death,
nor anyone of the Argives, but we might shun our destruction,
100 so that alone we could loose Troy's sacred circlet of towers."
　　Such things then they spoke and addressed each one to the other.
Firm no longer did Ajax remain—he was pressed by the missiles;
he was subdued by the purpose of Zeus and the glorious Trojans
striking at him; and around his temples the glittering helmet
105 terribly clattered as it was struck—it was constantly being
struck on its well-made plates; his shoulder was weary, the left one,
always holding his bright shield steadfast, nor were they able,
hard as they pressed with their missiles, to beat it back from around him.
Always painful and hard was his breathing, and down from his limbs all
110 over his body the sweat flowed copious, nor was he able

even to breathe; all around him evil was heaped upon evil.

Now speak out to me, Muses who live in Olympian dwellings,
tell how first was the fire thrown onto the ships of the Achaians.

Hektor, advancing to stand near Ajax, struck at the ash-wood
115 shaft with his great sword under the spear-point close to the socket,
utterly cutting it off, and the scion of Télamon Ajax
futilely shook in his hand that stump of the spear, and the brazen
spear-point onto the ground faraway from him plummeted clanging.
Ajax knew in his faultless spirit, and shuddered, that these were
120 acts of a god—their battle-intent high-thundering Zeus was
cutting to nothing, desiring a victory now for the Trojans;
he gave ground from the missiles. The weariless fire they at once cast
on the swift ship; unquenchable flame streamed over it quickly.
So did the fire take care of the ship's stern. Meanwhile Achilles,
125 striking his thighs, both sides, spoke out in these words to Patróklos:
"Rise up, Zeus-descended Patróklos, illustrious horseman;
surely I see the onrush of a ravening fire by the galleys;
let them not take the ships so that we no more could escape them!
Hastily put on the armor, and I will assemble the fighters."

130 So he spoke, and Patróklos in glittering bronze was accoutered.
First, strong greaves on the calves of his legs he carefully fastened,
fine ones skillfully fitted with silver-wrought ankle-protectors;
second in order, around his chest he put on the breastplate,
intricate work, star-spangled, of Aíakos' swift-footed scion.
135 Over his shoulders he slung on the sword, all studded with silver,
fashioned of bronze, then also the great shield, massive and heavy.
Onto his powerful head he fitted the well-made helmet
crested with horsehair; the plume on top of it fearfully nodded.
Then he took up two powerful spears which fitted his handgrip.
140 Only the spear of the scion of Aíakos he did not take up,
heavy and huge and compact, which none of the other Achaians
ever could wield, but Achilles alone was skillful to wield it,
it was of Pélian ash, and to his dear father had Cheiron
brought it from Pélion's summit to use for the slaughter of heroes.
145 Then he commanded Autómedon swiftly to harness the horses—
him he above all honored except rank-breaking Achilles;
most trustworthy he was to await his command in a battle.
Under the harness for him Autómedon led the swift horses,
Xanthos and Balios, who flew speeding along with the stormwinds;
150 they to the west wind Zephyr were born by stormy Podárgè

while she grazed on the meadow beside the great stream of the Ocean.
Faultless Pédasos then in the traces beside them he fastened,
him from Eëtion's city Achilles had led, when he took it;
he though only a mortal was following immortal horses.

155 Meanwhile Achilles, among those Mýrmidons there in the cabins
going about, was arraying them all in armor; and they like
wolves, flesh-eaters who have in their hearts unspeakable fury,
who in the mountains have slaughtered a great horned stag and devour it,
tearing it up, and the jaws of them all gleam ruddy with bloodstains,
160 then in a pack they go to get drink from a dark-water fountain,
avidly lapping with long thin tongues on the surface of its dark
water, and belching the blood and the gore—unflinching the spirits
are inside of their breasts, their stomachs are glutted and growling—
such indeed was the way that the Mýrmidons' leaders and princes
165 after the noble attendant of swift-footed Aíakos' scion
speeded away; and among them warlike Achilles was standing,
urging the horses ahead and as well the shield-carrying fighters.

 Fifty the swift ships were that Achilles belovèd of Zeus had
led transporting his army to Troy, and in each of the galleys
170 fifty in all were the men, the companions who sat at the oarlocks;
five were the captains that he had appointed, to whom he entrusted
leadership; he was himself in his great strength lord of the army.
One of the lines was led by Menésthios of glittering breastplate,
scion of Spercheios, that river descended from heaven;
175 this son Peleus' daughter, the fair Polydóra, had borne to
weariless Spercheios—by a god had the woman been bedded—
but in name it appeared Periéres' son Boros had sired him,
openly marrying her, first giving a measureless bride-price.
Then of the next ship-line warlike Eudóros was leader,
180 son of an unwed girl—Polymélè, fair in the dance, had
borne him, the daughter of Phylas: the powerful slayer of Argos
loved her when with his eyes he beheld her among maids dancing
once in the chorus of Artemis, clamorous huntress with gold darts.
Straightway Hermes the healer went up to her room and in secret
185 lay with her there, and a glorious son, Eudóros, she gave him,
swift beyond others in running, distinguished too as a fighter.
Then when Eíleithúia, the goddess of difficult childbirth,
brought him forth to the light and he looked on Helios' sunbeams,
straightway stalwart and mighty Echékles, the scion of Aktor,
190 brought that girl to his house, when a huge bride-price he had given;

as for her son, old Phylas himself well nourished and reared him,
tenderly loving the boy as if he were raising his own son.
Then of the third ship-line warlike Peisándros was leader,
Maímalos' son, who among all Mýrmidons there was distinguished,

195   after the comrade of Peleus' son, in waging a spear-fight.
Of the fourth line old Phoinix the chariot-driver was leader,
and of the fifth Alkímedon, faultless son of Laërkes.
Finally, after Achilles had stationed them all with their leaders,
having divided them well, upon them he laid a strong order:

200   "Mýrmidons, now of your threats let none of you all be forgetful,
those with which by the swift-sailing ships you threatened the Trojans,
all that time of my anger, and each of you often reproached me:
'Peleus' obstinate son, with bile you were nursed by your mother,
pitiless one, who keep by the ships the unwilling companions.

205   Let us indeed go homeward again with the seafaring galleys,
such is the baneful anger that over your spirit has fallen.'
Often together you said to me these things; now has the mighty
labor of battle appeared, of which formerly you were enamored.
Then with a valorous heart let each man battle the Trojans."

210   So he spoke and aroused in each fighter the strength and the spirit.
Yet more closely the ranks, as they heard their king, were compacted.
Just as a builder compacts with stones set closely together
walls for a high-roofed dwelling, resisting the might of the stormwinds,
so were compacted the helmets and shields made massive with bosses;

215   buckler on buckler and helmet on helmet and man against man pressed;
even the helmets with horsehair plumed on the glittering ridges
touched as they nodded their heads, they stood so close to each other.
There in front of them all were the two men dressing themselves in
armor, Patróklos and bold Autómedon, both with the same fierce

220   mind to do battle in front of the Mýrmidons. Meanwhile Achilles
went back into his cabin and opened the lid of a chest of
fine and elaborate beauty that Thetis of silvery feet had
put on his galley to bring, when well she had filled it with tunics,
also with mantles and blankets of wool for protection from stormwinds.

225   Inside there was a well-made goblet, and neither did any
other man drink from it glistening wine, nor did he to another
god ever pour libations, but only to Zeus the great father.
This cup then he took from the coffer and cleaned it with sulfur
first, then carefully washed it in beautiful currents of water,

230   also washing his hands, and the glistening wine he drew off.

Standing in mid-court then he prayed, and he looked at the sky and
poured out the wine; nor did Zeus the great thunderbolt-hurler ignore him:
"Great Zeus, Lord of Dodóna, Pelasgian, dwelling afar off,
you who rule over wintry Dodóna—about you the Selloi
235 dwell, your prophets with feet unwashed who sleep on the ground there—
just as before one time you listened to what I was praying,
honoring me when strongly you struck at the host of Achaians,
so once more for me now do you grant this boon that I pray for,
seeing that I will myself stay here where the galleys are gathered,
240 but a companion with numerous Mýrmidons now I am sending
forth to do battle; with him, wide-thundering Zeus, send glory,
making the heart inside of his breast bold, so even Hektor
might find out whether even alone my henchman in fact is
skilled in battle, or whether his hands rampage unvanquished
245 only when I myself go into the turmoil of Ares.
Finally, when from the ships he has driven the battle and clamor,
quite unscathed may he then come back to me here at the swift ships,
still with the armor entire and his comrades, hand-to-hand fighters."
So he spoke as he prayed; Zeus Counselor heard him and heeded;
250 one of his wishes the father bestowed, but refused him the other,
granted Patróklos to thrust from the galleys the battle and combat,
while he refused that he come back safe to him out of the battle.
After he poured libation, appealing to Zeus the great father,
back in the cabin he went, and the goblet he laid in the coffer;
255 coming to stand in front of the cabin, he still in his heart was
eager to look on the terrible strife of Achaians and Trojans.

Now those who were accoutered along with greathearted Patróklos
marched forth till with enormous resolve they lunged at the Trojans.
Speedily they poured out of the ships like wasps that are living
260 close to a road and that children are often arousing to anger,
always teasing them out of the nests they have at the roadside,
foolish boys, and a common distress they bring upon many.
Then if perchance some wayfaring man who passes arouses
them unwittingly, all of the wasps with valorous spirit
265 fly, each one from its place, to do battle defending their children.
Theirs was the heart and the temper with which those Mýrmidons swiftly
poured forth out of the ships, and a shout unquenchable rose up.
Thus did Patróklos exhort the companions, and loudly he shouted:
"Mýrmidons, comrades in battle of Peleus' scion Achilles,
270 now be men, dear friends, and remember your furious valor,

so that we honor the scion of Peleus—who of the Argives
far is the best by the ships—and his comrades, hand-to-to hand fighters,
also that Atreus' son, wide-governing Lord Agamemnon,
know his delusion in not honoring that best of the Achaians."
275   So he spoke and aroused in each fighter the strength and the spirit;
then in a throng they fell on the Trojans; about them the galleys
dreadfully echoed around to the clamorous sound of Achaians.
Then as the Trojans witnessed Menoítios' valorous scion,
him and as well his attendant accoutered in glittering armor,
280   stirred was the heart in them all, their ranks were aroused to commotion;
there by the ships they supposed that the swift-footed scion of Peleus
had now thrown his anger away and had taken up friendship;
each looked round for a place to escape from a sheer destruction.
It was Patróklos who first let fly with a glittering spear-shaft
285   straight out into the middle, the place where the most men crowded,
close to the stern of the galley of great-souled Prótesiláos,
striking Pyraíchmes, who led the Paiónians, chariot-marshals,
thither from Ámydon town, from the Áxios, broad in its current;
him he struck on his shoulder, the right one; backward he fell down
290   there in the dust as he groaned; the Paiónian comrades around him
panicked and fled, since panic had been thrown into them all by
noble Patróklos in killing their lord, who was best in the battle.
Then from the ships he drove them and put out the fire that was blazing.
Half-burnt thus was the ship left there, and the Trojans were driven,
295   panicked and raising a marvelous din, as the Dánaäns poured back
into the hollow ships; incessant the clamor was rising.
Just as when from the topmost crest of a towering mountain
Zeus who gathers the lightning is moving away a dense storm-cloud,
so that the lookout places appear, and the lofty escarpments,
300   and the ravines, and the measureless air breaks open from heaven,
so those Dánaäns, ravening fire having thrust from the galleys,
briefly were taking a breath; yet there was no pause from the battle,
since not yet by Achaians belovèd of Ares the Trojans
had been panicked and turned in a headlong rout from the black ships,
305   but were resisting as yet, though yielding perforce from the galleys.
Thereupon man killed man as the battle-encounter of leaders
scattered apart; and the first did Menoítios' valorous scion
strike Areílochos' thigh with his sharp spear just at the moment
he turned fleeing; the bronze he drove straight onward, the spear passed
310   clear through, breaking the bone, and he fell headlong on his face down

onto the ground. Meanwhile warlike Meneláos at Thoas
struck, on his bare chest next to his shield, and his limbs he unloosened.
Phýleus' son, having seen Amphíklos rushing upon him,
struck more quickly than he at the top of his leg where a man has
315   muscle the greatest in thickness; around the sharp point of the spear his
sinews were cloven asunder; his eyes were enshrouded in darkness.
As for the scions of Nestor, Antílochos thrust with his sharp spear,
hitting Atýmnios, then drove on through his flank the bronze spear-head,
so that he fell down forward. But Maris, enraged for his brother,
320   straight at Antílochos rushed with his spear for a hand-to-hand combat,
standing in front of the dead man; but then godlike Thrasymédes
struck more quickly—before he could stab; nor at all did he miss him—
right on the shoulder; the base of the arm by the point of the spear was
sheared from the muscular chest, and the bone was utterly shattered.
325   Falling he crashed to the ground, and his eyes were enshrouded in darkness.
So those two, having been brought down at the hands of two brothers,
went into Érebos, both of them brave comrades of Sarpédon,
hurlers of javelins, scions of Ámisodáros, the man who
nurtured the raging Chimaíra, an evil for many of mankind.
330   Then too Ajax, Oïleus' son, at Kleóboulos charging,
took him alive, impeded by panic confusion; but there he
loosened his might by striking his neck with a well-hilted sword-blade,
and the whole blade grew warm with his blood; down over his eyes came
seizing him blood red death and his own irresistible doomsday.
335   Lykon charged, and Penéleos, running together, for they had
missed one another with spears—in vain both fighters had cast them;
therefore together they ran with their swords; at the ridge of the helmet
crested with horsehair, Lykon drove, and upon it his sword-blade
broke at the socketed hilt, and Penéleos struck at his neck just
340   under the ear, and the sword sank all the way in so that only
skin still held, and his head hung aside, and his limbs were unloosened.
Mérionés on his swift feet overtook Ákamas then and
struck at his shoulder, the right one, as he on his chariot mounted.
He from the chariot fell; down over his eyes was a mist poured.
345   Square on the mouth Idómeneus struck Érymas with the cruel
bronze, so that straight on through it the bronze spear passed, penetrating
under the brain, and the white skull-bones it shattered asunder;
out of their sockets the teeth were ejected, and both of the eyes were
filled with blood, while up through the gullet and down through the nostrils,
350   gaping, he spewed blood; death in a dark cloud shrouded him over.

Such were the Dánaän leaders who each one slaughtered a fighter.
Just as ravening wolves wreak havoc on lambs or on young goats,
choosing them out of the flocks that are scattered abroad in the mountains
through the neglect of a careless shepherd—the wolves, upon seeing,
355 suddenly snatch those young that are weak and of cowardly spirit—
such was the havoc the Dánaäns wrought on the Trojans, and panic,
baneful of sound, they recalled, but forgot their furious valor.
     Ajax the great was desiring to strike bronze-helmeted Hektor,
always, with his huge spear; yet he with his knowledge of warfare,
360 covering his broad shoulders about with a shield made of oxhide,
carefully watched for the crashing of spears and the whistle of arrows.
He in fact recognized the reverse in the course of the battle,
yet even so he remained there to save his trustworthy comrades.
     As when down from Olympos a cloud comes out of the shining
365 ether and into the sky, at a time Zeus causes a tempest,
just so out of the galleys arose their clamor and panic,
nor in good order did they cross back; with his armor was Hektor
taken away by his swift-hoofed horses, forsaking the Trojan
host, whom all unwilling the well-dug trench was restraining.
370 Many the swift steeds, chariot-pullers, that there in the trench were
breaking the pole at the end and their masters' chariots leaving;
following after, Patróklos was calling the Dánaäns fiercely,
wishing the Trojans affliction; and they in their shouting and panic
filled all the ways, since they were so scattered apart, and the dust-storm
375 spread high up to the clouds, as the single-hoofed horses were straining
back to the city again and away from the galleys and cabins.
Then wherever Patróklos could see the most men being routed,
there with a shout he would drive, and the men fell under the axles
out of their chariots headlong; the chariots overturned, rattling.
380 Finally straight on over the trench then leapt the swift horses,
deathless ones that the gods gave Peleus, glorious presents,
hurrying on; against Hektor Patróklos' temper aroused him,
eager to strike as he was, but the swift steeds bore away Hektor.
As at a time that the whole black earth is oppressed by a tempest
385 on some late summer day when Zeus pours down the torrential
water, when he is indignant and feels great anger at men who
violently in assembly delivering crooked decisions
drive out justice without any care for the gods' supervision—
these are the men whose rivers are all of them flowing and filled up;
390 many the hillsides then that the torrents are cutting to gullies;

down to the dark blue sea they are rushing in thunderous tumult
headlong out of the mountains; the farms of the people are ruined—
so those steeds of the Trojans were running in thunderous tumult.

    Soon as Patróklos had cut off the foremost Trojan battalions,
395 back once more by the galleys he hemmed them, nor would he let them
go to the city, as much as they wished to, but there in the middle
space between river and ships and the high-built wall of the city,
rushing among them, killed them, exacting requital for many.
Then it was Prónoös first that he hit with a glittering spear-shaft,
400 striking his bare chest next to his shield, and his limbs he unloosened;
falling he crashed to the ground. It was Thestor the scion of Énops
next that Patróklos charged as he sat, crouched down, in his polished
chariot, since his mind had been driven from him, and the reins had
slipped from his hands; with a spear while standing beside him Patróklos
405 stabbed at his lower right jaw, and ahead through the teeth he drove it;
seizing the spear he dragged him over the rail, like a man who
sits on a rock out-jutting and drags from the sea-brine a sacred
fish by using a flax fish-line and a glittering bronze hook;
so from the chariot, gaping, was he now dragged by the bright spear,
410 then thrust onto his face; and his life left him as he fell down.
As Eryláos was charging at him then, square on his head he
struck with a stone, and the head entirely was cloven asunder
inside the ponderous helmet; he fell down there face forward
onto the ground, and about him was poured death, spirit-destroying.
415 Thereupon, Érymas fell, Amphóteros too, and Epáltes,
Échios too, Tlepólemos son of Damástor, and Pyris,
Ípheus also, Euíppos, and Árgeas' son Polymélos,
all to the nourishing earth he brought in rapid succession.

    Now Sarpédon, observing his comrades of tunic unbelted
420 brought down under the hands of Menoítios' scion Patróklos,
shouting reproach, called out to the godlike Lykian fighters:
"Shame, you Lykians—where are you fleeing to? Fierce you must now be,
since this man I am going to meet with, so that I find out
who of such prowess he is, so strong to do Trojans so many
425 evils, for those whose limbs he has loosened are many and noble."

    Thus, then he to the ground from his chariot leapt in his armor.
Opposite, seeing him there, from his chariot sprang out Patróklos.
Then those fighters, as eagles with strong-curved talons and hooked beaks,
stridently screaming, aloft on a high rock fight with each other,
430 so were the two men screaming and charging against one another.

Pitying saw them the scion of Kronos of crooked devices;
thus he spoke out to Hera, his sister as well as his consort:
"Oh, woe is me, that my own Sarpédon the dearest of men is
destined to be brought down by Menoítios' scion Patróklos!

435   So my heart is divided in thought, as in spirit I ponder
whether to snatch him away while he is alive from the tearful
battle and set him down in the Lykians' fertile domain, or
let him be brought down now at the hands of Menoítios' scion."
      Speaking to him then answered the ox-eyed queen, Lady Hera:

440   "Most dread scion of Kronos, and what is this word you have spoken!
This man, who is a mortal and long since doomed by his destined
fate, are you minded to take from a dolorous death and release him?
Do it: but not in the least we other gods all will approve it.
Something else I will tell you, and you keep this in your mind now:

445   should you in fact send back Sarpédon alive to his homeland,
take thought lest some other god also then should desire it,
sending his own dear son faraway from the violent combat,
since there fighting around the great city of Priam are many
sons of immortals among whom you will set terrible rancor.

450   But if to you he is dear, and your doleful heart is lamenting,
then hold off and allow him to be, in the violent combat,
brought down under the hands of Menoítios' scion Patróklos;
afterward, soon as the soul and the life-breath finally leave him,
then do you send down Death and delectable Slumber to carry

455   him until they have arrived in Lykia's spacious dominion;
burial there will be given to him by his brothers and kinsmen,
with a grave-mound and a pillar; for this is the prize of the perished."
      She spoke, nor disobeyed her the father of gods and of mankind;
bloody the raindrops were that he let fall onto the ground in

460   honor of his dear son, whom noble Patróklos was going
soon to destroy in the deep-soiled Troäd and far from his country.
      When in coming together the two were close to each other,
then did Patróklos strike Thrasymélos, the glorious fighter
who was the mighty attendant of noble and lordly Sarpédon;

465   his were the limbs he loosened by striking the base of his belly.
Then with his glittering spear as in turn he attacked, Sarpédon
missed hitting him, but the trace-horse Pédasos rather on his right
shoulder he struck with his spear; he, screaming and gasping his life-breath
out, fell groaning beneath to the dust, and away flew the spirit.

470   Wheeling apart, yoke creaking, the other two steeds were entangled

293

there in the reins, since low in the dust was the trace-horse lying;
yet Autómedon, famed as a spearman, found a solution:
drawing the keen-edged sword from its sheath on his powerful thigh he
leapt out—quickly he cut loose the trace-horse, nor did he falter,
475 so that the other two horses were righted and pulled at the guide-reins;
once more the warriors met in strife, the devourer of spirits.

        Then Sarpédon again missed him with his glittering spear-shaft;
over Patróklos' shoulder, the left one, the point of the spear went
flying, and did not strike him; Patróklos in turn with his brazen
480 spear charged him, nor in vain from his hand went flying the missile;
rather it struck where the lungs hold close the dense heart, in the midriff.
Down he fell, in the way some oak tree falls, or a poplar,
or a tall pine tree, which on a mountainside men who are shipwrights
cut with their new-whetted axes to use as the beam of a galley;
485 so in front of his horses and chariot lay Sarpédon,
stretched out, roaring with pain; at the blood-soaked dust he was clutching.
Just as a lion that comes on a cattle herd slaughters a great bull,
tawny and mighty of spirit, among those swing-pacing oxen,
groaning, it perishes under the huge strong jaws of the lion,
490 so now under Patróklos the chief of the Lykian shield-men
struggled in rage as he died, and he called his belovèd companion:
"Glaukos my friend, you fighter among men, now it is yet more
needful that you be skilled as a spearman and bold as a fighter;
now let the baleful war be your wish, if indeed you are still keen.
495 First then, going about among all of the Lykians' leaders
everywhere, do you rouse them to fight on behalf of Sarpédon;
then with your bronze spear you must yourself fight hard to defend me.
For to yourself also a disgrace and an infamy later,
all of your days, I will be unceasingly, should the Achaians
500 strip my armor from me, brought down where the galleys are gathered.
Hold then, strongly and steadfast, and rouse up all of the army."

        So as he uttered, his death's finality came to enfold his
nostrils and eyes, and Patróklos, setting a heel on his chest, dragged
out of the body his spear, and the lungs came following after;
505 so at the same time then drawn out were the soul and the spear-point.
There were the Mýrmidons holding the steeds, loud-snorting, that now were
eager to flee, since their lords' chariot they had abandoned.

        Terrible grief, as he heard that voice, then came over Glaukos;
stirred was the heart in his breast—he was quite unable to help him.
510 Grasping his arm with his hand, he squeezed it tight, for the wound was

wearing him down where Teukros, defending his comrades from ruin,
had struck him with an arrow as he was assailing the high wall.
Raising his voice in prayer he addressed far-shooting Apollo:
"Hear me, lord, who perhaps are in Lykia's fertile dominion,

515 or are perhaps in Troy! Wherever you are you can listen
well to a sorrowful man, as upon me now has come sorrow,
since this wound that I have is a terrible one, and my arm is
pierced all about with a sharp strong agony, nor am I able
even to dry off the blood—by the wound my shoulder is weighted.

520 Neither can I hold firmly a spear-shaft, nor can I go forth
so as to battle the foe, and the best of the fighters has perished,
Zeus' own son Sarpédon—for even his child he does not help.
But at the least for me, Lord, do you heal this terrible wound now,
soothing the pains, then grant to me strength so that I to my comrade

525 Lykians may call out exhorting them into the battle,
also that I may fight for the body of him who has perished."
      So did he speak in prayer; he was heard by Phoibos Apollo.
Straightway he put a stop to his pains, then dried the black blood that
flowed from his burdensome wound, and he put might into his spirit.

530 Glaukos recognized this in his mind, and at once he was gladdened
that the great god so quickly had listened to what he was praying.
First then, going about among all of the Lykians' leaders
everywhere, he aroused them to fight on behalf of Sarpédon;
then he proceeded with long strides forward to go to the Trojans,

535 Pánthoös' scion Polýdamas first, and the noble Agénor;
also he went to Aineías and great bronze-helmeted Hektor;
there then standing beside them, in these winged words he addressed them:
"Hektor, you certainly now have forgotten your allies in battle,
who are for your sake, far from their friends and the land of their fathers,

540 wasting their spirits away, while you are not minded to help them.
There Sarpédon is lying, the lord of the Lykian shield-men,
he who Lykia guarded with his own strength and with justice;
Ares the brazen has brought him down by the spear of Patróklos.
Yet, friends, stand beside him, and consider the shame in your spirit,

545 lest those Mýrmidons strip him of armor and mangle his body,
do it dishonor, enraged for the Dánaäns, all who have perished,
those whom we with our spears at the swift-sailing galleys have slaughtered."
      So he spoke, and the Trojans were utterly gripped by a sorrow
uncontrollable, not to be borne, since he was the city's

550 buttress, though he was a foreigner there, for along with him many

people had followed, among whom he was the best in the battle;
eagerly they went straight for the Dánaäns; Hektor was leading
them, enraged on account of Sarpédon; and quickly the savage
heart of Patróklos the son of Menoítios roused the Achaians;
555   first to the two Ajaxes he spoke, themselves very eager:
"Both Ajaxes, in you the desire must be to defend us
now, and be such as before you were among men, or yet braver.
There lies the man who was first to leap inside the wall of the Achaians,
Lord Sarpédon; but now let us seize him and mangle his body,
560   stripping his armor away from his shoulders, and some of his comrades
who are defending him there, with our pitiless bronze let us vanquish."
     He spoke; they were themselves most eager to offer resistance.
Soon as they had on both of the sides reinforced the battalions,
Trojan and Lykian fighters and Mýrmidon troops and Achaians,
565   they joined battle to fight for the body of him who had perished,
dreadfully shouting, and loudly were clashing the arms of the fighters.
Zeus spread ruinous night out over the violent combat,
so that surrounding his own dear child would be ruinous war-toil.
     It was the Trojans who first pushed back the quick-glancing Achaians,
570   since not worst of the Mýrmidons there was the man who was smitten—
he was the son of the great-souled Ágakles, noble Epeígeus,
who in the well-inhabited town Boudeíon had ruled as the lord in
earlier times; then, since he had slaughtered a noble-born kinsman,
came supplicating to Peleus and Thetis the silvery-footed;
575   they then sent him to follow along with rank-breaking Achilles
over to Ilion, land of fine horses, to battle the Trojans.
Him, as his hands on the corpse he was laying, illustrious Hektor
struck with a stone to the head, which all, inside of the heavy
helmet, was broken in two, and he fell down there face forward
580   onto the corpse, and about him was poured death, spirit-destroying.
Then for his comrade slain, great grief came over Patróklos;
straight through the foremost fighters he charged—he resembled a swift-winged
falcon that frightens the birds to a panic, the starlings and jackdaws;
so at the Lykian fighters, Patróklos, illustrious horseman,
585   straight you charged, and the Trojans, enraged in your heart for your comrade.
Then with a stone he struck Stheneláos, Ithaímenes' dear son,
hitting his neck, thus breaking the sinews away from around it.
Quickly the foremost fighters withdrew, and illustrious Hektor.
Just so far as the range in its flight of a long light spear is,
590   which some man casts either when trying his strength in a contest

or in a battle when pressed by his enemies, spirit-destroying,
so far now did the Trojans withdraw—the Achaians were driving.
First among them did Glaukos, the lord of the Lykian shield-men,
turn back; it was the great-souled Báthykles then that he slaughtered,
595 much-loved scion of Chalkon, who had his dwelling in Hellas;
he among Mýrmidons was outstanding in wealth and possessions.
He was the man whom Glaukos in midchest struck with a spear-thrust,
suddenly turning upon him as he in pursuit overtook him;
falling he crashed to the ground, and a dense grief seized the Achaians,
600 such a good man had fallen; but greatly the Trojans were gladdened,
they came thronging and stood around him, nor did the Achaians
cease to be mindful of valor, but carried their might straight toward them.
Mérionés then slaughtered a well-armed chief of the Trojans,
bold Laógonos son of Onétor, who of Idaían
605 Zeus had served as the priest; he was honored as god by the people.
Under the jaw and the ear he was struck by the hero; the life-breath
swiftly departed his limbs—he was seized by odious darkness.
Then Aineías at Mérionés let fly with his bronze spear,
since he was hoping to hit him as under his shield he was coming;
610 he however, observing him closely, avoided the bronze spear,
for as he stooped down forward, behind his back the long spear-shaft
planted itself in the ground, and above it the butt of the spear was
quivering; finally powerful Ares abated its fury.
[Onto the ground thus landed the sharp spear-shaft of Aineías
615 quivering, since from his powerful hand in vain it had speeded.]
Then in his heart Aineías was angry, and thus he addressed him:
"Mérionés, very soon, though you are an excellent dancer,
that spear of mine would have stopped you forever, if I could have struck you."
Spear-famed Mérionés spoke out to him, giving an answer:
620 "Strong as you are, Aineías, a difficult thing you would find it,
quenching the temper of every fighter who came to confront you,
making defense of himself; you too, I suppose, are a mortal,
so that if I struck you with a bronze spear, hitting you squarely,
straightway you, although you are mighty and trust in your hands, would
625 give to me fame, and your spirit to Hades of glorious horses."
So he spoke, and Menoítios' valorous scion rebuked him:
"Mérionés, why, brave as you are, do you speak in this manner?
Dear friend, not in the least for your words of abuse will the Trojans
yield from the corpse, but before that, many of us will the earth hold,
630 since in our hands is the issue of war, that of words in the council;

therefore speech we should not be swelling, but rather should battle."
So having spoken he led, and the godlike man followed after.
Then from the hosts, as a tumult arises from woodcutters working
in the ravines of a mountain, a din heard far at a distance,
635 so from the fighters arose loud noise from the earth of the broad ways,
made by the bronze and the leather, the shields well-fashioned of oxhide,
as at each other they struck with their swords and their double-edged spear-blades.
Now no longer a man would have recognized, even a shrewd one,
noble Sarpédon, for he with the blood and the dust and the missiles
640 clear from his head to the tips of his feet entirely was covered.
Always about his corpse they crowded, as when in a farmstead
flies come swarming and buzzing around milk pails overflowing
when in the springtime season the milk pours into the buckets;
so now about his corpse they crowded, and never at all did
645 Zeus turn away his glittering eyes from the violent combat,
but kept always looking at them; in his heart he was thinking,
pondering many a matter concerning the death of Patróklos,
whether at that very time, right there in the violent combat,
over Sarpédon the godlike fighter, illustrious Hektor
650 should with a spear kill him, then strip from his shoulders the armor,
whether he should increase for yet more of the men the sheer war-toil.
So as he pondered the matter, the best course seemed to be this one,
that the intrepid attendant of Peleus' scion Achilles
now should impel those Trojans and great bronze-helmeted Hektor
655 back once more to the city, and many deprive of their life-breath.
Hektor it was whom first he endued with a cowardly spirit;
mounting his chariot, he turned fleeing and called to the other
Trojans to flee, for the sacred balance of Zeus he had noticed.
Nor did the powerful Lykians stay there—rather they all were
660 panicked, as they saw how in his heart their king had been smitten,
how in a pile of the dead he was lying, for many had fallen
over him, when fierce conflict the scion of Kronos had stretched out.
Then from the shoulders of Lord Sarpédon they stripped off the armor,
brazen and brightly agleam, and Menoítios' valorous scion
665 handed it to his companions to take to the hollow galleys.
Then spoke forth to Apollo the great cloud-gathering god Zeus:
"Come, dear Phoibos, and cleanse Sarpédon of dark-clotted bloodstains;
go now, carry him out of the missiles' range, and remove him
far to a distance and give him a bath in the streams of the river,
670 then with ambrosia rub him, in raiment ambrosial dress him,

give him to carry away with them then to the nimble conveyers
Slumber and Death, twin brothers, and those two swiftly will lay him
down in his own dear land, broad Lykia's fertile dominion;
burial there will be given to him by his brothers and kinsmen,
675 with a grave-mound and a tombstone; for this is the prize of the perished."
     So he spoke, and Apollo did not disobey his dear father.
Down from the summits of Ida he went, to the terrible combat,
raised up noble Sarpédon and quickly away from the missiles
bore him a distance and gave him a bath in the streams of the river,
680 then with ambrosia rubbed him, in raiment ambrosial dressed him,
gave him to carry away with them then to the nimble conveyers
Slumber and Death, twin brothers, and those two speedily laid him
down in his own dear land, broad Lykia's fertile dominion.
     Calling upon Autómedon then, and the horses, Patróklos
685 went straight after the Trojans and Lykians; blind was his fury,
poor fool! Could he have kept the commandment of Peleus' scion,
he might well have escaped from the baneful fate of a black death.
Always greater than men's, however, the purpose of Zeus is;
even a valorous man he panics and robs of his triumph
690 easily, after himself he has roused him up to do battle;
now it was he who put such rage in the breast of Patróklos.
     There then who was the first, who last of the warriors whom you
slaughtered, Patróklos, the time that the gods were calling you deathward?
First was Adréstos killed, Autónoos too, and Echéklos,
695 Périmos scion of Mégas, Epístor, and then Melaníppos;
then too Élasos, Moúlios also, as well as Pylártes—
these he killed; and the rest took thought, each one, of escaping.
     Then Troy, lofty of gate, would the sons of Achaians have taken
under the hands of Patróklos, for he with his spear rushed forward,
700 had not Phoibos Apollo aloft on a well-built tower
stood, intending him ruin and giving the Trojans his succor.
Thrice did Patróklos attempt to climb onto a corner of that high
rampart, and thrice did Apollo repel him, beating him backward,
pushing at him on his glittering shield with his hands undying.
705 Then at his fourth try, when like a god he was rushing against him,
terribly he cried out, and in these winged words he addressed him:
"Zeus-descended Patróklos, retreat—not fated it is that
now by your spear will be sacked this city of venturous Trojans,
nor by that of Achilles, a man far better than you are."
710 So he spoke, and Patróklos at once drew back a good distance,

thereby avoiding the wrath of the god far-shooting Apollo.
     Hektor was holding his single-hoofed steeds inside of the Skaian
Gates, for he wondered if he should again fight, into the turmoil
drive them, or call to his army to gather inside of the ramparts.
715 As these things he was thinking, by him stood Phoibos Apollo,
taking the form of a man most mighty, abounding in vigor,
Ásios, who was the uncle of Hektor the tamer of horses,
Hékabè's own womb-brother he was, and the son of Lord Dymas,
who in Phrygia dwelt by the river Sangários' current;
720 making himself like him spoke forth Zeus' scion Apollo:
"Hektor, why do you cease from the warfare? That you must not do.
Would that I were as much stronger than you as in fact I am weaker!
Quickly to your own grief you would then draw back from the battle.
But come, direct your horses with powerful hooves at Patróklos,
725 hoping you might kill him, and Apollo accord you the glory."
     So having spoken the god went back to the toil of the fighters;
glorious Hektor commanded Kebríones, skillful in warfare,
quickly to lash into battle his horses; and meanwhile Apollo
set forth, entered the melee, and there threw onto the Argives
730 baneful confusion; the glory he gave to the Trojans and Hektor.
Hektor neglected the rest of the Dánaäns, nor would he kill them,
rather he drove his horses with powerful hooves at Patróklos.
Opposite him, to the ground from his chariot leapt down Patróklos,
holding a spear in his left hand; a stone he grasped in the other,
735 glittering, jagged and hard, that his hand held closely and firmly;
bracing himself, he threw it, nor far from the man did it fall short;
neither was fruitless the missile, but Hektor's charioteer he
wounded, Kebríones, bastard son of illustrious Priam,
with the sharp rock on the brow as he wielded the reins of the horses;
740 into each other the stone smashed both brows, nor did the skull-bone
hold steadfast, but the eyes fell onto the earth in the dust right
there in front of his feet, and at once he dropped like a tumbler
down from the well-made car-box; his spirit abandoned the bone-frame.
Mocking and jeering at him you spoke to him, horseman Patróklos:
745 "Well now! How very nimble a man, how lightly he tumbles!
Were he indeed, I suppose, to go into the fish-thronged seaway,
many the men this diver would satisfy, seeking for oysters,
plummeting down from a ship, even in tempestuous weather—
down to the ground from the chariot now so lightly he tumbles.
750 Certainly also among these Trojans are excellent tumblers."

So he spoke, and he went at the hero Kebríones fiercely,
with the onrush of a lion who while he ravages farmsteads
has been struck in the chest, and his own great valor destroys him;
eagerly so at Kebríones you leapt, noble Patróklos.
755 Opposite him, to the ground from his chariot leapt down Hektor.
Over Kebríones then did the two fight fiercely as lions
which on the peaks of a mountain about some doe that is slaughtered
join strife, both of them famished and both stronghearted and haughty;
over Kebríones thus were the two great lords of the war cry,
760 noble Menoítios' scion Patróklos and glorious Hektor,
eager to hack with the pitiless bronze at the flesh of each other.
Hektor did not let go of the man's head, once he had seized it;
opposite him was the foot held fast by Patróklos; the other
Trojan and Dánaän fighters collided in violent combat.
765   Just as against each other the east and the south winds wrangle
in the ravines of a mountain to set a deep forest to tossing,
shaking the oaks and the ash trees there, and the smooth-barked cornels,
which each one at the others are hurling their boughs with the sharp points,
raising a marvelous din and a clatter of shattering branches,
770 so the Achaians and Trojans against each other were leaping,
slaughtering; nor about ruinous panic was either side thinking.
Many a sharp spear then was around Kebríones planted,
many the well-winged arrows that darted away from the bowstring,
many the huge rough boulders that struck on the shields of the fighters
775 as around him they battled; but he in the turbulent dust lay
mighty and mightily fallen, his skill as a horseman forgotten.
    Now as the sun while coursing the sky stood high in midheaven,
missiles of both sides sped to their targets, and people were falling;
but as the sun turned downward, the time when oxen are unyoked,
780 even beyond what was fated for them the Achaians were stronger.
Then the Achaians heroic Kebríones dragged from the missiles'
range, from the clamor of Trojans, and stripped from his shoulders the armor;
onto the Trojans, intending them harm, leapt noble Patróklos.
Three times then did he leap upon them, that peer of swift Ares,
785 shouting a terrible shout; nine men three times did he slaughter.
Finally, when for the fourth time he like a god was attacking,
then was the end of your life shown forth to you, noble Patróklos,
since great Phoibos encountered you there in the violent combat,
terrible god; but Patróklos did not know him in the turmoil
790 striding, for he met him all shrouded about in a thick mist;

standing behind him there, he struck at his back and broad shoulders
using the flat of his hand, and his eyes whirled round in their sockets;
off of his head his helmet was knocked by Phoibos Apollo;
under the feet of the horses was rolling the socketed four-horned
795 helmet with clattering din, and the plumes on it were defiled with
blood and with dust; before this, indeed, it had not been permitted
ever with dust to be dirtied the helmet crested with horsehair;
rather it guarded the head and the beautiful brow of the godlike
fighter and hero Achilles; but then Zeus gave it to Hektor
800 so on his head he could wear it; but near him too was destruction.
Then in his hands quite shattered was his long-shadowing spear-shaft,
heavy and huge and compact, bronze-headed, and down from his shoulders
onto the ground his shield with the tassels dropped, and the baldric.
Then was the breastplate loosed by the lord, Zeus' scion Apollo.
805 Blindness seized on his mind, and beneath him the glorious limbs were
loosened as he stood dazed; from behind a Dardánian man close
by with a sharp spear struck at his back and between his shoulders—
Pánthoös' son Euphórbos, a man who surpassed his age-mates in
throwing a spear and in horsemanship and in running on swift feet.
810 Out of their chariots he already had struck down twenty
fighters when first he arrived with his chariot, learning of warfare;
he first cast at you now with a missile, horseman Patróklos,
nor did he quell you, but he ran back again, joining the melee,
once he had taken the ash-wood spear from the flesh, and he did not
815 stay to encounter Patróklos, unarmed though he was, in the combat.
Overcome both by the blow of the god and the spear-thrust, Patróklos
tried to retreat to the band of his comrades, and so to avoid fate.
    Hektor, as soon as he witnessed the way greathearted Patróklos
drew back out of the strife, by the sharp bronze smitten and wounded,
820 came up close to him, crossing the ranks, and he thrust with his spear right
into the base of the belly and drove the bronze point straight through it;
falling he crashed to the ground; most grieved was the host of Achaians.
Just as a weariless boar is defeated in strife by a lion
when in the peaks of a mountain the two beasts haughty of spirit
825 fight over some small spring which both are desiring to drink from,
then as the boar pants sorely the lion by might overcomes it,
so after slaughtering many, Menoítios' valorous son was
robbed of his life close at hand with a spear by Priam's son Hektor.
    Over him Hektor exulted; in these winged words he addressed him:
830 "Doubtless, Patróklos, you thought this city of ours you would ravage,

then first robbing the women of Troy of the day of their freedom,
you in the ships to the much-loved land of your fathers would take them.
Childish fool! In front of them still the swift horses of Hektor
stride on their light feet into the battle, and I with a spear am
835   finest among all Trojans, the lovers of war, and I keep their
day of compulsion from them, while right here vultures will eat you.
Poor wretch! Nor did Achilles for all of his valor defend you,
who as he stayed there, doubtless, was strict to command as you left him:
'Come not back to me ever, Patróklos the master of horses,
840   here at the hollow galleys, until man-slaughtering Hektor's
tunic around his chest you have torn into bloodstained tatters.'
So to you doubtless he spoke, and your senseless heart he persuaded."
    Feebly in answer to him you spoke thus, horseman Patróklos:
"Right now, Hektor, can you boast loudly, for Zeus son of Kronos
845   gave you the victory now, and Apollo, and they overcame me
easily, since from my shoulders themselves they took off the armor.
Even if twenty of those like you had encountered me fighting,
they would have all been ruined and brought down under my spear-thrust.
It was a ruinous fate and the offspring of Leto that killed me,
850   then among men Euphórbos, and third you strip me of armor.
Something else I will tell you, and you keep this in your mind now:
not very long, it is certain, will you be alive, but already
standing beside you is death and your own irresistible doom to
die at the hands of the scion of Aíakos, faultless Achilles."
855   So as he uttered, his death's finality covered him over.
Flitting away from the limbs his soul went down into Hades,
sorrowing over its fate and forsaking its vigor and manhood.
Even as he lay dead, thus spoke to him glorious Hektor:
"Why now, Patróklos, are you foretelling for me sheer ruin?
860   Who knows whether Achilles, the offspring of fair-haired Thetis,
might before that be struck by my spear, so losing his life-breath?"
    So did he say, then out of the wound he drew the bronze spear by
planting his heel on the body and thrusting it back from the spear-head.
Then with the spear in his hand he went for Autómedon quickly—
865   he was the godlike attendant of Aíakos' swift-footed scion—
since he was eager to strike him; away he was borne by the swift steeds,
deathless ones that the gods gave Péleus, glorious presents.

BOOK 17

Nor ignored Atreus' son Meneláos belovèd of Ares
that in the battle Patróklos had been brought down by the Trojans.
He strode forth through the foremost, in bright bronze armor accoutered,
then he bestrode that hero, as over the calf that she first brought
5   forth stands lowing its mother, who knew no birthing before it.
So now over Patróklos bestrode light-haired Meneláos,
holding his spear and his circular shield in front of his body,
eager to kill any fighter who might come forward against him.
Neither unheedful was Pánthoös' son, of the fine ash spear, that
10   faultless Patróklos had fallen in battle, but close to him there he
stood, and a word he addressed Meneláos belovèd of Ares:
"Atreus' son Zeus-loved Meneláos, the marshal of people,
give way, go from the corpse and abandon the bloodstained armor,
for before me no man of the Trojans or glorious allies
15   struck with a spear at Patróklos in all this violent combat;
therefore allow me to garner a noble renown among Trojans,
lest I strike you and strip from your body the honey-sweet spirit."
    Mightily vexed, thus spoke to him then light-haired Meneláos:
"Father Zeus! No good comes of excessively, recklessly boasting.
20   Not such, surely, the rage of the leopard, nor yet of the lion,
nor of the wild boar, murderous-minded, in which is the greatest
spirit inside of its breast to exult in its strength and its vigor,
never, as Pánthoös' sons, of the fine ash spear, are exalted.
No, not even the strong Hyperénor, the tamer of horses,
25   profited much from his youth when he scorned me, stood to confront me,
said moreover that I of the Dánaäns here am the weakest
warrior—yet I am certain that not on his feet will he go back
homeward to gladden his much-loved wife and his reverend parents.
So, I am sure, your strength will I slacken as well if you keep on
30   standing against me—rather I urge you, withdraw and retreat back

into the multitude, not keep standing to face me, before you
suffer some harm—for a done deed even a fool recognizes."
    So did he say, yet did not persuade him; in answer he spoke out:
"Certainly now, Zeus-loved Meneláos, the penalty you will
35   pay for my brother you slaughtered, of whom you speak in derision,
making his wife in the depth of the new bride-chamber a widow;
you on his parents have brought unspeakable wailing and sorrow.
To the unhappy ones I would afford some pause from lamenting
should I indeed be able to bring your head and your armor
40   back and in Pánthoös' hands put them, and in those of bright Phrontis.
Certainly now no longer will go untested the struggle,
neither unfought will it be, whether it shows valor or terror."
    So having said, on the circular shield he struck at the fighter,
nor did the bronze break through, but the point of the spear bent backward
45   there in the strong round shield. Then next to attack with the bronze was
Atreus' son Meneláos, while praying to Zeus the great father;
just as the man drew back, at the base of his throat Meneláos
struck, and himself thrust hard—in his ponderous hand he confided;
into the delicate neck and on through it the point penetrated;
50   falling he crashed to the ground, and around him clattered his armor.
Drenched in blood were his tresses resembling the hair of the Graces,
locks in braids that were twisted with spirals of gold and of silver.
Just as a man takes care of the burgeoning shoot of an olive
tree someplace by itself, which plenty of water has moistened—
55   finely it flourishes there as the breezes of all of the winds are
setting aquiver its leaves, and it breaks out white with its blossoms—
then of a sudden a wind comes up in a terrible tempest,
wrenches it out of its hollow and stretches it out on the ground there,
thus now Pánthoös' son, of the fine ash spear, Euphórbos,
60   Atreus' son Meneláos had killed and was stripping his armor.
Just in the way some mountain-bred lion that trusts in his valor
snatches from out of a herd as it grazes the best of the cattle—
first he shatters her neck, in his powerful teeth having seized it,
then her blood he greedily swallows, and all of her entrails,
65   tearing at her—and around him there are the hounds and the herdsmen
clamoring loudly from off at a distance, and they are unwilling
even to come up and face him, for green fear mightily grips them,
so in none of the Trojans the heart in his breast was emboldened
even to come up and face that glorious lord Meneláos.
70   Easily then would Atreus' scion have taken the splendid

armor of Pánthoös' son, but that Phoibos Apollo begrudged it,
so he aroused up Hektor, the equal of Ares in swiftness,
making himself like Mentes, the noble Kikonians' leader;
raising his voice he spoke, and in these winged words he addressed him:
75 "Hektor, as you go running to seek unattainable horses,
those of the war-skilled scion of Aíakos—difficult steeds for
men who are mortal to tame or in front of a chariot drive them,
save for Achilles alone, who was born to a mother immortal—
meanwhile Lord Meneláos, the warlike scion of Atreus,
80 stood there over Patróklos and slaughtered the best of the Trojans,
Pánthoös' son Euphórbos, and stopped his furious valor."
     So having spoken, the god went back to the toil of the fighters.
Terrible grief overclouded the grim black spirit of Hektor;
then, as along through the ranks of the fighters he looked, he at once took
85 note of the one who was seizing the glorious arms, and the one who
lay on the ground, and the blood flowed down from the wound of the spear-stroke.
He strode forth through the foremost, in bright bronze armor accoutered,
stridently uttering cries, and resembling the blaze of Hephaistos
ever unquenched, nor did Atreus' son miss hearing the shrill cry;
90 deeply disturbed, he spoke to his own magnanimous spirit:
"Oh, woe is me! If indeed I abandon the beautiful armor,
leaving Patróklos, who here for the sake of my honor is lying,
some of the Dánaäns surely would blame me, whoever may see me.
Yet if alone I fight against Hektor as well as the Trojans,
95 fearing the shame, then they would surround me, many against one;
Hektor of glittering helmet is leading here all of the Trojans.
Yet why now is it dear to my heart to debate about these things?
When a man wishes against a god's will to contend with another
warrior whom the god honors, at once great woe rolls upon him.
100 Therefore will none of the Dánaäns blame me, whoever may see me
yielding the ground before Hektor, for he makes war with a god's help.
If somewhere I discovered the crier of war, the lord Ajax,
then could the two of us, coming again, take thought of our war-craft
even against the gods' will, that for Peleus' scion Achilles
105 we might rescue the dead man: the best among evils would that be."
     As he was pondering over these things in his mind and his spirit,
meanwhile the ranks of the Trojans approached him, and Hektor was leading.
Backward he went, so yielding the ground, and abandoned the dead man,
always turning about on his way, like a well-bearded lion
110 which both herders and sheepdogs are chasing away from a steading,

wielding their spears and their voices; the valorous heart in his breast is
chilled, so that he albeit unwillingly goes from the farmstead;
so from Patróklos now light-haired Meneláos retreated.
Turning around he stood, when he came to the band of his comrades,
115 glancing about for the powerful Ajax, Télamon's scion.
Him very quickly he saw on the left of the whole great battle,
cheering the hearts of his comrades and rousing them up to the combat—
into them Phoibos Apollo had cast unspeakable terror;
he went running and straightway stood close by and addressed him:
120 "Ajax, friend, come here, let us hurry to fallen Patróklos,
save him to carry him out to Achilles, if only his body—
naked, as Hektor of glittering helmet has taken the armor."
      So did he say, and in war-skilled Ajax roused up the spirit;
he set forth through the foremost, with him light-haired Meneláos.
125 Hektor, as soon as he stripped from Patróklos the glorious armor,
dragged him to sever his head with a sharp bronze blade from his shoulders—
drawing his corpse off then, to the Trojans' dogs he would give it.
Ajax came up close to him bearing a shield like a tower;
Hektor at once gave ground, withdrew to the throng of his comrades,
130 into his chariot leapt, and the beautiful armor he gave those
Trojans to take to the city to be for himself a great glory.
Ajax covered Menoítios' scion about with his broad shield,
standing above him, much as a lioness over her offspring,
one whom men on a hunt encounter as she in the woods is
135 leading her helpless whelps—in her might she stands there defiant,
drawing her whole wide brow down over her eyes to conceal them;
so now over the hero Patróklos was Ajax standing.
Close to him, Atreus' son, Meneláos belovèd of Ares,
stood there; deep in his breast he was nourishing terrible sorrow.
140   Glaukos Hippólochos' scion, the chief of the Lykian fighters,
looking at Hektor from lowering brows, with a harsh word scolded:
"Hektor, the noblest in beauty, in warfare much are you lacking.
Vainly an excellent fame holds you who flee like a woman.
Take thought how you may save your citadel now and the city
145 all by yourself, and with only the men born in Ilion aiding,
since of the Lykians here nobody will go out to fight those
Dánaäns over the city, for no thanks ever would come for
fighting against those enemy men incessantly, always.
How is it now you would save an inferior man in the melee,
150 hard heart, when Sarpédon, at once your guest and your comrade,

you to the Argives abandoned to be their prey and their plunder,
who was of such great profit to you, to yourself and the city,
while yet alive; now you lacked courage for keeping the dogs off.
So now, should any man of the Lykian fighters obey me,
155 home will we go, and for Troy will be manifest utter destruction,
since, if now in the Trojans were such bold valor of spirit,
dauntless, as comes on men who fight for the sake of their country,
raising up toil and contention against all enemy fighters,
then into Ilion quickly would we be dragging Patróklos.
160 Should this man come, though but a corpse, to the great citadel of
Priam the lord, and if we were to drag him away from the warfare,
then would the Argives quickly relinquish the lord Sarpédon's
beautiful armor, and we would to Ilion carry his body—
such is the man whose henchman is slaughtered, the best of the Argives
165 here at the ships by far, and his henchmen, hand-to-hand fighters.
You however did not have courage to stand against great-souled
Ajax and look at him straight in the eyes in the violent combat,
nor to do battle direct, since he is far better than you are."
     Looking from lowering brows spoke Hektor of glittering helmet:
170 "Glaukos, a man like you—why have you with such arrogance spoken?
What shame! I thought you were beyond all others in wisdom,
all those people who dwell in Lykia, fertile in farmland;
utterly now I despise your mind, such things you have spoken,
saying I did not stand to encounter enormous Ajax.
175 Not at the battle I shudder, and not at the thunder of horses;
always greater than men's, however, the purpose of Zeus is;
even a valorous man he panics and robs of his triumph
easily, after himself he has roused him up to do battle.
Yet come hither, my friend; stand near me and witness my labor,
180 whether the whole day I will be cowardly, as you declare me,
whether instead I will stop some Dánaän, even if he be
avid in valor to fight in defense of the fallen Patróklos."
     So having said, he called to the Trojans, and loudly he shouted:
"Trojans and Lykians all, Dardánians, hand-to-hand fighters,
185 now be men, dear friends, and remember your furious valor,
while I put on the beautiful armor of faultless Achilles,
which I stripped off after I slaughtered the might of Patróklos."
     Soon as he said these things, great Hektor of glittering helmet
went from the furious battle, and running, he came to his comrades
190 quickly, as they were not far, on his swift feet following those who

carried the glorious armor of Peleus' son to the city.
Standing apart from the dolorous battle and changing his armor,
he gave his to the lovers of battle, the Trojans, to take to
sacred Ilion city, and put on himself the immortal
195   armor of Peleus' scion Achilles the heavenly gods had
given his much-loved father; in turn, grown old, to his son he
gave it; but not in the arms of the father the son was to grow old.
     When from afar the cloud-gathering god Zeus noticed the hero
arming himself in the sacred armor of Peleus' scion,
200   shaking his head he spoke these words to himself in his spirit:
"Ah poor wretch, not at all in your mind is a thought of the death that
certainly now comes near you; but you put on the immortal
armor of that great fighter before whom other men tremble.
His is the comrade, kindly and strong, whom you have just slaughtered;
205   then improperly you from his head and his shoulders have stripped his
armor; but I will bestow on you now great might in amends for
this: Andrómachè never will take from your hands, as you come back
home from the battle, the glorious armor of Peleus' scion."
     Thus did Kronos' son speak, and he nodded his head with its dark brows;
210   onto the body of Hektor he fitted the armor; and Ares,
dread Enyálios, entered him then, and within were his limbs made
full of great valor and strength; with the glorious allies in battle
he went shouting aloud, and to all of the fighters he showed forth
glittering bright in the armor of great-souled Peleus' scion.
215   Ranging the ranks, he aroused each man to the battle with speeches,
Mesthles and Glaukos he roused, Thersílochos also, and Medon,
Ásteropaíos as well, Hippólochos too, and Deisénor,
Phorkys and Chrómios also, and Énnomos, reader of bird-signs;
them he aroused to do battle—in these winged words he addressed them:
220   "Listen to me now, numberless tribes of our neighboring allies:
not because I was in search or in need of a multitude did I
summon you here, each man from your various cities, together—
rather that you in the zeal of your hearts might rescue the Trojans'
bedmates and innocent children from those war-loving Achaians.
225   Thinking of this, with the gifts and the food I give I am wearing
down my people, but thus in each of you strengthen the spirit.
Therefore now let a man turn straight to the fighting, to perish
or to survive, since such is the ardent encounter of battle.
As for Patróklos, although he is dead, whoever can drag him
230   back among horse-taming Trojans and cause great Ajax to give ground,

half of the plunder will I share out to him, half of it I will
keep for myself, and the glory he gets will be such as my own is."
   He spoke; they in full force charged straight at the Dánaän fighters,
stretching their spears out forward; the hearts inside them were strongly

235   hoping to drag that corpse from the scion of Télamon Ajax.
Fools! For above it he robbed of their life-breath many a fighter.
Thereupon Ajax addressed the great crier of war Meneláos:
"Friend, Meneláos belovèd of Zeus, no longer do I have
hope that the two of us even alone will return from the battle.

240   It is not just that I fear so much for the corpse of Patróklos,
that it will soon be glutting the dogs and the birds of the Trojans,
as for my own head I am afraid, lest something befall it,
also for yours, since everything is engulfed by the war-cloud
Hektor; for us also is appearing our utter destruction.

245   But come, call on the best of the Dánaäns, should any hear you."
   He spoke, nor disobeyed him the crier of war Meneláos;
piercingly then he yelled to the Dánaäns, loudly he shouted:
"Oh dear friends and companions, the Argives' leaders and princes,
who beside Atreus' sons, Agamemnon and Lord Meneláos,

250   drink at the communal bowl and who each give out to your men their
orders, bestowed by Zeus are the honor and fame that attend you.
Difficult is it for me to discern each leader among our
chief men, since so hotly the struggle of battle has blazed up;
yet of himself let each man move, feel shame in his heart lest

255   noble Patróklos become a plaything for the dogs of the Trojans."
   He spoke; keenly did Ajax the son of Oïleus hear him;
he was the first who ran up to meet him, along through the combat;
following him Idómeneus came and Idómeneus' comrade
Mérionés, that peer of Enyálios, killer of fighters.

260   But of the rest, what man from his own mind ever could name them,
all who followed and roused up battle among the Achaians?
   Then in a throng charged forward the Trojans, and Hektor was leading.
As at the mouth of a river descended from heaven the mighty
surf rolls thundering into the outflow—loudly the coastal

265   headlands on both sides roar, and beyond them belches the sea-brine—
with such clamor the Trojans were coming; and yet the Achaians
stood there surrounding Menoítios' son, all single in spirit,
fencing themselves with their bronze-wrought shields, while over their shining
helmets the scion of Kronos was pouring around them a thick mist,

270   since not ever before had he hated Menoítios' scion,

while he yet was alive and the henchman of Aíakos' scion;
now Zeus hated that he should become for the dogs of the hostile
Trojans the prey, so his comrades he roused up to defend him.
    It was the Trojans who first pushed back the quick-glancing Achaians;
275 leaving the corpse they took flight, terrified; nor did the high-souled
Trojans, as much as they wished to, with spears take any among them,
but began dragging the body, from which the Achaians would be held
off for a short time only, for they very swiftly were turned back
thither by Ajax, who in his looks and his deeds outrivaled
280 all of the Dánaäns other than Peleus' excellent scion.
He charged straight through the foremost, in valor resembling a savage
wild boar high in the mountains that easily scatters the hounds and
vigorous youths, by turning at them, through gullies and woodlands;
so now the son of illustrious Télamon, glorious Ajax,
285 speeding against them, easily scattered the ranks of the Trojans,
who were bestriding Patróklos, and who most strongly were minded
now to drag him up into their city to garner them glory.
    Now was Hippóthoös, glorious son of Pelasgian Lethos,
dragging the dead man off by the foot through the violent combat,
290 having his baldric attached to the tendons of both of the ankles,
giving delight to the Trojans and Hektor; but swiftly upon him
came an affliction that no one, as much as he wished to, could ward off.
Rushing at him through the melee the scion of Télamon struck from
close to his side, and he thrust through the bronze cheek-piece of his helmet;
295 shattered around the spear-point was the helmet crested with horsehair,
mightily struck as it was by a huge long spear and a strong hand;
out of the deep wound spurted the brain, and along the spear-socket,
mingled with blood; there then was his strength loosed; out of his hands he
let fall downward the foot of greathearted Patróklos to lie right
300 there on the ground, and he fell face down nearby on the body,
far from the fertile land of Laríssa, and never his much-loved
parents would he give quittance for rearing him: brief did his life span
prove—by the spear of the great-souled Ajax thus was he vanquished.
Hektor at Ajax cast in turn with his glittering spear-shaft;
305 he however, observing him closely, avoided the bronze spear
slightly; but it struck Schédios, great-souled Íphitos' scion,
best by far of the Phokians there, who lived in his house in
famous Panópeus, ruling as lord of a numerous people—
him he struck square under the collarbone; onward the brazen
310 spear-point pierced, and it came out under the base of the shoulder;

falling he crashed to the ground, and around him clattered his armor.
Ajax in turn struck Phorkys, the war-skilled scion of Phainops,
square in the belly as over Hippóthoös' corpse he was standing,
breaking the plate of his corslet; the bronze spear hollowed his bowels
315   out, and the earth he clutched in his hand as he fell in the dust there.
Then did the foremost fighters retreat, and illustrious Hektor;
loudly the Argives shouted in triumph and dragged off the corpses,
Phorkys and Hippóthoös, and the armor they loosed from their shoulders.
     Then would the Trojans have been by the Ares-belovèd Achaians
320   back into Ilion driven, by their own cowardice vanquished—
fame would the Argives have garnered, beyond what Zeus had apportioned
them, by their own great might and their strength—but Apollo himself then
roused Aineías, in form like Périphas, who was a herald,
Épytos' son; in the house of Aineías' old father Anchíses
325   he as a herald had grown old, skilled in benevolent wisdom.
Making himself like him spoke forth Zeus' scion Apollo:
"How, Aineías, could you men defend steep Ilion city
even against a god's will, as indeed I have seen other men do,
trusting in their own might and their strength and their valorous manhood,
330   and in superior forces, with even a land less peopled?
It is much rather for us than the Dánaäns Zeus is desiring
victory; yet you are terribly fearful, and you do not fight them."
     So he spoke; as he looked at him straight in the face, Aineías
knew far-shooting Apollo and called out, speaking to Hektor:
335   "Hektor and others, the chiefs of the Trojans as well as the allies,
this is a shame, to be driven by Ares-belovèd Achaians
back into Ilion now, by our own weak cowardice vanquished!
One of the gods, however, has stood at my side and declared that
Counselor Zeus most high is as yet our helper in battle—
340   therefore straight at the Dánaäns let us advance, so that they may
not at their ease take back to their galleys the fallen Patróklos."
     So he spoke, and he leapt far ahead of the foremost and stood there;
turning around they rallied and stood to confront the Achaians.
Then Leiókritos, son of Arísbas, the lord Lykomédes'
345   noble companion, was stabbed right through by the spear of Aineías;
pitying him as he fell, Lykomédes belovèd of Ares,
going to stand close by, let fly with his glittering spear and
so struck Híppasos' son Apisáon, the shepherd of people,
under the chest in the liver—at once his limbs he unloosened.
350   This Apisáon had come from Paiónia, fertile of farmland;

he after Ásteropaíos was most outstanding in battle;
pitying him as he fell there, the warlike Ásteropaíos
also charged straight on at the Dánaäns, eager to fight them,
yet no way could he do it, for they all about with their shields were
355   bulwarked, surrounding Patróklos, and stood firm, holding their spears out—
Ajax among them all kept ranging, and much he exhorted:
no one, so he commanded, should yield ground, back from the body,
neither should go forth fighting in front of the other Achaians,
rather should stand right over the corpse in a hand-to-hand combat.
360   So was enormous Ajax commanding the men, and the earth was
drenched with the crimson blood; there one by another were dropping
bodies alike of the Trojans and powerful allies in battle
and of the Dánaäns too, since these fought not without bloodshed,
though far fewer of them then perished, for they in the melee
365   ever were thinking to guard each other from utter destruction.
      So they fought like a conflagration, and you would not think that
either the sun or the moon could still be secure in the heavens,
since in a mist were enclosed all those who were noblest in battle,
standing around that son of Menoítios, him who had perished.
370   Still however the rest of the Trojans and well-greaved Achaians
under a clear sky fought unimpeded, and sharply the sunbeams
scattered abroad upon them; over all of the earth and the mountains
no cloud ever appeared; they kept intermittently fighting;
each side shunned the maleficent missiles of those who opposed them,
375   standing apart some distance. But those in the middle were feeling
pain from the mist and the fight, and with pitiless bronze were exhausted,
all those who were the noblest; but two of the glorious fighting
men, Thrasymédes and bold Antílochos, never had learned that
faultless Patróklos was dead already, but thought that he still was
380   living and fighting the Trojans among the forefront of the tumult.
Those two, keeping a watch on the death and the rout of their comrades,
fought at a distance apart, since thus had Nestor commanded,
when to the battle he roused them to go from the dark-hued galleys.
      All day long among them a huge struggle of combat was raging,
385   cruel and harsh; incessantly, always, with sweat and fatigue were
spattered the knees and the calves and the feet of each fighter, beneath him,
also the hands and the eyes of the men, both sides, who were battling
over the excellent henchman of Aíakos' swift-footed scion.
      As to his people a master delivers the hide of a mighty
390   bullock to be stretched out, once it has been drenched in the deep fat,

313

taking it, they stand there in a circle about it and stretch it
tautly, and quickly its moisture is forced out, so that the fat can
enter, as many are tugging, and it all over is stretched out,
so to one side and the other were both sides trying to drag that
395 corpse in a space quite small, and the hearts inside them were strongly
hoping to drag it, the Trojans to Ilion, but the Achaians
back to the hollow ships, and around it the struggle was raging
savagely; not even Ares the rouser of hosts or Athena,
witnessing this, would have scorned it, no matter how much they were angered.
400   Such was the terrible warfare-toil of the men and the horses
Zeus that day stretched over Patróklos; but not in the least had
noble Achilles as yet found out that Patróklos had perished,
since faraway from the swift ships now they were waging the battle
under the wall of the Trojans; at heart he did not expect that
405 he would be slaughtered, but having arrived at the gates he would come back
living to him, for he did not at all expect that Patróklos
would try sacking the city without him, and not even with him,
since from his mother, apart from the others, he often had heard this,
when a report she would bring him of Zeus Almighty's intention.
410 Never indeed such evil as this that had happened his mother
then told him, that the comrade he loved most dearly had perished.
        Ever around that body with sharp-pointed spears in their hands they
kept incessantly pressing, the two hosts killing each other.
Thus would speak some fighter among those bronze-clad Achaians:
415 "Oh friends, no fine glory for us there would be in returning
back to the hollow galleys, but here on the spot let the black earth
gape for us all—that quickly would be much better for us if
we are to yield this man to the Trojans, the tamers of horses,
now to be dragged up into their city and garner them glory."
420   Thus in turn would declare some man of the greathearted Trojans:
"Oh friends, should it be destined that all of us over this man be
slaughtered together, at least let no one retreat from the combat."
        Thus then someone would speak and in each man rouse up the spirit.
Thus were they waging the battle; the hard loud din as of iron
425 went through the desolate air and above to the bronze-bright heaven;
then were the horses of Aíakos' scion, apart from the battle,
weeping, as soon as they first found out that their charioteer had
fallen and lay in the dust at the hands of man-slaughtering Hektor.
As for Autómedon, who was the valorous son of Dióres,
430 often did he with a sharp whiplash lay into them, striking;

often with soft mild words he called to them, often with curses—
those two neither were minded to go back down to the galleys,
down to the broad Hellespont, nor to battle among the Achaians,
but in the way that a gravestone remains steadfast that is standing
435 over the funeral mound of a dead man or of a woman,
so they, holding the beautiful chariot motionless, stayed there,
letting their heads bow downward and rest on the earth, and the hot tears
flowed down onto the ground from their eyelids, so were they weeping,
missing their charioteer, and their long thick manes were befouled as
440 they streamed out, both sides of the yoke and from under the yoke-pad.
So as they mourned him the scion of Kronos observed them and pitied;
shaking his head he spoke this word to himself in his spirit:
"Oh unhappy ones, why did we give you at all to a mortal
man, Lord Peleus, while you two are immortal and ageless?
445 Was it that you among men ill-fated would suffer afflictions?
Since more miserable than a man, I am certain, is nothing
even among all creatures on earth both breathing and creeping.
Yet most certainly Hektor the scion of Priam will not be
mounted on you and the elegant chariot—I will not let him.
450 Is he not satisfied, having the armor and boasting about it?
Into you now I will put great might, in your knees and your spirit,
so that the two of you bring Autómedon safe from the battle
back to the hollow galleys; for still to the Trojans will I grant
glory to slaughter, until they arrive at the well-benched galleys
455 just as the sun goes down and upon them comes holy darkness."
      So he spoke and inspired great strength in both of the horses.
Straightway shaking the dust from their manes off onto the ground, they
bore the swift chariot lightly toward the Achaians and Trojans,
while behind them Autómedon fought, though he mourned for his comrade;
460 much as a vulture swoops upon geese, he charged with the horses,
since he would easily flee from the battle-tumult of the Trojans,
then he would easily charge and pursue them across the great melee.
Yet no men did he slaughter as he went rushing to chase them—
being alone in the sacred chariot he was in no way
465 able to lunge with his spear while keeping in hand the swift horses.
One of the fighters at last saw him with his eyes, his own comrade
noble Alkímedon, son of Laërkes the scion of Haimon;
he to Autómedon spoke, in back of his chariot standing:
"Tell me, which of the gods, Autómedon, into your breast has
470 put such profitless counsel and taken your excellent senses,

315

so that alone as you are in the foremost melee you fight these
Trojans? Your comrade has just been slaughtered, and Hektor himself now
wears on his shoulders, exulting, the armor of Aíakos' scion."
    Answering him then spoke Autómedon, son of Dióres:
475   "Well, Alkímedon, what man else of the Achaians is equal
to the control, to restraining the might, of the deathless horses,
save for Patróklos, the peer of the gods in counsel, as long as
he was yet living? But now have his death and his doom overcome him.
Nevertheless, you take up the whip and the glittering reins and
480   manage them; I will dismount from the chariot now to do battle."
    So did he say; then onto the chariot, swift in the battle,
leapt Alkímedon; quickly the whip and the reins in his hands he
grasped; Autómedon leapt to the ground, and illustrious Hektor
noticed and straightway spoke to Aineías, who stood there beside him:
485   "Noble Aineías, the counselor-lord of the bronze-clad Trojans,
here I notice the horses of Aíakos' swift-footed scion
showing themselves in the battle with charioteers who are feeble.
Therefore would I be hopeful of seizing them, if in your spirit
you are so minded, for neither of them would dare to await us
490   charging at them, or to stand and engage in a battle against us."
    He spoke, nor disobeyed him the powerful son of Anchíses.
Both of them went straight forward, concealing their shoulders in shields of
oxhide, tough and well-tanned, into which much bronze had been beaten.
Chrómios too went forward with them, and the godlike Arétos—
495   both men followed along, and the hearts inside them were strongly
hoping to slaughter the men and to drive off the mighty-necked horses,
fools that they were, since not without bloodshed they would be going
back from Autómedon later; and praying to Zeus the great father,
he in his grim dark heart was replenished with vigor and courage;
500   straightway he to Alkímedon spoke, his trustworthy comrade:
"Now, Alkímedon, be not far from me holding the horses—
let them instead breathe right on my back—since I do not think that
Hektor the scion of Priam will cease from his vehement passion,
ever, until he has mounted behind the two fair-maned horses,
505   once he has slaughtered us both and has routed the ranks of the Argive
fighters—or he may himself be killed among those in the forefront."
    Thus, and he called to the two Ajaxes and Lord Meneláos:
"Both Ajaxes, the Argives' leaders, and Lord Meneláos,
this dead body entrust to the care of the men who are bravest,
510   who will bestride and surround it and ward off the ranks of the fighters;

but from us two yet alive you ward off a pitiless doomsday,
since in the dolorous battle are now hard-pressing against us
Hektor and Lord Aineías, the men who are best of the Trojans.
Nevertheless, on the knees of the gods these matters are resting;
515 I will myself throw a spear, for in all things Zeus is decisive."
        So did he say, then brandished and threw his long-shadowing spear-shaft,
square on the circular shield thus striking the noble Arétos;
nor was the spear held off, but it passed right on through the bronze shield;
into the base of the belly he drove it ahead through the war-belt.
520 As at a time that a vigorous man who is holding a sharp ax
strikes at an ox of the pastures behind its neck, and the weapon
cuts through all of the sinews, and it leaps forward and topples,
so leapt forward Arétos and fell on his back; and the sharp spear
loosened his limbs as it stood there quivering deep in his entrails.
525 Hektor in turn at Autómedon cast with his glittering spear-shaft;
he however, observing him closely, avoided the bronze spear,
for as he stooped down forward, behind his back the long spear-shaft
planted itself in the ground, and above it the butt of the spear was
quivering; finally powerful Ares abated its fury.
530 Now with their swords they would have engaged in a hand-to-hand combat,
had not the two Ajaxes divided the men who were rushing—
they at the call of their comrade had now come up through the melee.
Terrified by their appearance, the Trojans yielded the ground back—
Hektor and Lord Aineías and godlike Chrómios also.
535 Thus on the spot they abandoned Arétos and left him to lie there
stricken to death; Autómedon, equal to Ares in swiftness,
stripped from his body the armor and spoke out vaunting above him:
"Surely, if only a little, the pain for Menoítios' scion's
death I have put from my heart, though lesser the man I have slaughtered."
540   So he spoke, and he took up the gore-stained armor and put it
onto the chariot, mounting; his feet and his hands up above were
bloodstained, just as a lion would be who had eaten a bullock.
        Once more over Patróklos was stretched out violent combat
painful and laden with tears, and Athena awoke the contention,
545 having descended from heaven; for her wide-thundering Zeus sent
rousing the Dánaäns up; for in fact his purpose had shifted.
As at a time Zeus stretches for mortals a shimmering rainbow
out of the heavens to serve as a portent either of warfare
or of a wintery tempest that makes men cease from the farmwork
550 which they do on the face of the earth, and that troubles the cattle,

so now wrapping herself in a shimmering cloud did Athena
enter the band of Achaians and stir up each of the fighters.
First then Atreus' son she addressed and aroused him to action,
strong Meneláos—for he was the one who was standing beside her—
555   making herself in her form and her weariless voice like Phoinix:
"Now, Meneláos, for you a disgrace and an infamy, surely,
it will become if the trustworthy comrade of lordly Achilles
under the walls of the Trojans is torn piecemeal by the swift dogs.
But do you hold steadfast and arouse up all of the army."
560   Then spoke answering her the great crier of war Meneláos:
"Phoinix, my dear old papa of ancient birth, if Athena
only would grant me strength and would ward off the volley of missiles!
So then I would be minded to stand steadfast by Patróklos,
giving protection, for deep in my heart his dying has touched me.
565   But the dread force of a fire now Hektor possesses, and does not
leave off raging with bronze, for to him is Zeus giving the glory."
    So he spoke, and the goddess bright-eyed Athena was gladdened
that it was she among all of the gods whom first he entreated.
Into his knees she put great power, and into his shoulders;
570   into his breast, moreover, the courage she put of a fly that,
often though it be driven away from the flesh of a person,
keeps on trying to bite him, so much is a man's blood pleasing;
such was the courage with which his grim dark heart she replenished.
Over Patróklos he stood, and he cast with his glittering spear-shaft.
575   There was among those Trojans the son of Eëtion, Podes;
wealthy he was, and a good man, and Hektor especially honored
him of the people, because he was dear as a dining companion.
He was the one whom now on the belt light-haired Meneláos
struck as he started to flee, and he drove the bronze point right through it;
580   falling he crashed to the ground; then Atreus' son Meneláos
dragged off the corpse from the Trojans and back to the band of his comrades.
    Coming to stand near Hektor, Apollo began to arouse him,
much like Phainops the scion of Ásios, who was of all his
guest-friends dearest to him and who lived in a house at Abýdos;
585   making himself like him spoke forth far-working Apollo:
"Hektor, among the Achaians what other will yet terrify you,
so are you fleeing before Meneláos, who was in the past quite
feeble and soft as a spearman? But now all alone he has gone off
taking a corpse from the Trojans—he killed your trustworthy comrade,
590   valiant among your foremost, the son of Eëtion, Podes."

So he spoke; a black cloud of distress enshrouded the hero;
he strode forth through the foremost, in bright bronze armor accoutered.
Then straightway did the scion of Kronos take up the aegis,
streaming with tassels and flashing, and Ida in clouds he enshrouded;
595 hurling his lightning he mightily thundered and brandished the aegis,
granted the Trojans the triumph, and drove in rout the Achaians.
    First a Boiótian fighter Penéleos started the fleeing,
since with a spear his shoulder was struck, as he ever was turning
toward the attack, a slight blow on top; but Polýdamas' spear-point
600 pierced right through to the bone—he had come up near him and thrown it.
Hektor in close fight then stabbed Léïtos square by the wrist-joint—
he was greathearted Aléktryon's scion—and halted his combat;
fearfully glancing about he withdrew, since he in his heart could
hope no more with a spear in his hand to do battle with Trojans.
605 Rushing at Léïtos, Hektor was struck by Idómeneus squarely
over his breast on the corselet-plate quite close to the nipple.
But at the socket was broken the long spear-shaft, and the Trojans
shouted aloud; at Idómeneus, son of Deukálion, standing
there on his chariot, Hektor cast, and he missed but a little;
610 rather the charioteer and attendant of Mérionés, bold
Koíranos, who had accompanied him out of well-built Lyktos—
since first, leaving the tractable galleys, Idómeneus came on
foot, and he would have afforded a great triumph to the Trojans,
had not Koíranos speedily driven up swift-hoofed horses;
615 so as a beacon he came, warding off his pitiless doomsday,
while he himself lost life at the hands of man-slaughtering Hektor—
under the jaw and the ear he was struck by Hektor; his teeth were
dashed from the roots by the spear, and his tongue cut through in the middle;
he from the chariot fell, on the ground there letting the reins fall.
620 These in his own hands Mérionés caught up as he leaned down,
gathering them from the plain; to Idómeneus thus did he speak out:
"Lash them now, until you have arrived back down at the swift ships;
you yourself see that the strength no longer is with the Achaians."
    So he spoke, and Idómeneus lashed up the fair-maned horses
625 back to the hollow galleys, for fear came over his spirit.
    Great-souled Ajax and Lord Meneláos were not unaware that
Zeus to the Trojans was giving the victory, battle-reversing.
First of the two spoke out the great scion of Télamon Ajax:
"Well then! Anyone now, no matter how childish a fool, can
630 reckon that Zeus the great father himself is assisting the Trojans,

since their missiles are all of them striking, whoever may hurl them,
whether a base or a good man; and all alike Zeus is directing;
while to the ground are the weapons of all of us plummeting useless.
But come, let us ourselves take thought of what counsel is wisest,
635 both so that we may drag off the body and so that ourselves we
gladden our much-loved comrades as we go back there among them—
they no doubt are alarmed as they look at us, nor are they thinking
that the great might and invincible hands of man-slaughtering Hektor
yet any longer will be held off, but will fall on the black ships.
640 How I wish there were some comrade who could carry a message
swiftly to Peleus' son, for I think he has not even now heard
any heart-sickening message that his dear comrade has perished.
Yet nowhere can I see such a man here among the Achaians,
for in a mist they all are enshrouded, themselves and their horses.
645 Oh Father Zeus, from the mist now rescue the sons of Achaians,
make it a clear bright sky, with our own eyes grant us to see things;
even destroy us in daylight, for such is surely your pleasure."
    So he spoke, and the father had pity on him as he shed tears;
quickly he scattered the mist, and the gloom he drove from the fighters,
650 so that the sun blazed out and the whole great battle was showing;
then did Ajax address the great crier of war Meneláos:
"Now, Meneláos belovèd of Zeus, look well in the hope you
see Antílochos, scion of great-souled Nestor, alive yet;
urge him to go very quickly to war-skilled Achilles and give this
655 message to him, that the comrade he loves most dearly has perished."
    He spoke, nor disobeyed him the crier of war Meneláos;
he set forth on the errand as out of a farmyard a lion
goes that has grown exhausted provoking the hounds and the herdsmen,
nor have they ever allowed him to seize from the cattle a fat one,
660 staying awake all night; he, greedily longing for flesh, keeps
forging ahead, but accomplishes nothing, for javelins flying
swiftly and thickly from bold stout hands keep rushing against him,
fiery torches as well, and he quails at them, though he is eager;
early at dawn he goes on his way, in his spirit disgruntled;
665 so from Patróklos departed the crier of war Meneláos,
much unwilling, for sorely did he fear lest the Achaians
might in the perilous rout leave him to be enemy plunder.
Strongly he charged bold Mériones and the two Ajaxes:
"Mériones and the two Ajaxes, the Argives' leaders,
670 now let each of his comrades the kindness of wretched Patróklos

keep in his mind, since he was inclined to be gentle to all while
he was yet living; but now have his death and his doom overcome him."
    Soon as he said these things, light-haired Meneláos departed,
glancing to all sides, much like an eagle, the bird that as men say
675 sees most sharply of all of the winged things under the heavens,
whom, high up though he be, not even the fleet-footed hare can
ever elude as it crouches beneath a dense bush, but the eagle,
swooping upon it, seizes it swiftly and robs it of life-breath.
Just so then, Meneláos belovèd of Zeus, were your bright eyes
680 turning to all sides over the band of your many companions,
hoping that they might see still living the scion of Nestor.
Him very quickly he saw on the left of the whole great battle,
cheering the hearts of his comrades and rousing them up to the combat;
going to stand near him spoke forth light-haired Meneláos:
685 "Come, Antílochos, hither, belovèd of Zeus, so that you may
hear a heart-sickening message of what should never have happened.
You I suppose of yourself already, as you are observing,
know that a god is indeed on the Dánaäns rolling affliction,
giving the Trojans the triumph; the best of the Achaians is slaughtered,
690 noble Patróklos, and great is the loss that the Dánaäns suffer.
Hurry at once to the ships of the Achaians, and there to Achilles
tell it, that he very soon to his ship might rescue the body—
naked, as Hektor of glittering helmet has taken the armor."
    So did he say; Antílochos hated the word as he heard it;
695 speechlessness for a long time gripped him, and both of his eyes were
filled with the tears he shed, and the flow of his voice was arrested.
Not even so he neglected the charge Meneláos had given;
rather he ran off; his armor he gave to the faultless companion,
noble Laódokos, who brought near him the single-hoofed horses.
700   So as he wept, on his feet he was carried away from the battle,
bearing to Peleus' scion Achilles a message of evil.
Nor was your heart, Meneláos belovèd of Zeus, at all minded
now to assist and defend the exhausted companions from whom had
gone Antílochos—great was the longing the Pylians suffered.
705 Rather he sent to them brave Thrasymédes the scion of Nestor,
while he himself went back to bestride that hero Patróklos;
running, he stood by the two Ajaxes and straightway addressed them:
"That man I have dispatched back there to the swift-sailing galleys—
he is to go to fleet-footed Achilles; but I do not think that
710 he will come now, despite his great wrath at the noble lord Hektor,

since no way, unarmed as he is, would he fight with the Trojans.
Meanwhile, let us ourselves take thought of what counsel is wisest,
both so that we may drag off the body and so that ourselves we
may escape death and the day of our doom from the tumult of Trojans."

715   Answering him then spoke the great scion of Télamon Ajax:
"All you have spoken is fitting and proper, renowned Meneláos;
hastily Mérionés and yourself get under the body,
raise it and carry it out of the war-toil; meanwhile behind you
we two will keep on fighting the Trojans and excellent Hektor,

720   having the same name, so too the same heart, as in the past we
stayed in a bitter combat by standing beside one another."
       So did he say; then taking the corpse from the ground in their arms they
lifted it up with great effort; behind them shouted the Trojan
army, as soon as they saw the Achaians were lifting the body.

725   Straight against them they charged, as the hounds pursuing a wounded
boar go savagely rushing ahead of the youthful huntsmen—
they for a time keep running, desiring to tear him to pieces,
then, whenever he wheels to confront them, trusting his valor,
they yield backward and scatter in flight, one here, there another.

730   So for a time that throng of the Trojans was following closely,
always thrusting and striking with swords and with double-edged spear-blades,
then whenever the two Ajaxes would turn back against them,
taking a stand, their color would change; no longer would any
dare rush forward to join in a combat about the dead body.

735   So were the two men straining to carry the corpse from the battle
back to the hollow ships, and against them battle was stretched out
fierce as a conflagration that falls on a city of people,
suddenly rushing, and sets it aflame, and the houses are ruined
in the enormous blaze, and the wind's might sets it to roaring;

740   so upon those two men as they went on their way the incessant
thunder of horses and chariots came, and of strong spear-fighters.
They like mules that, exerting their powerful spirit on both sides,
drag down out of the peaks on a pathway rugged and rocky
either a beam or a huge ship's timber—the spirit inside them

745   gets worn out with the sweat and exhaustion as they keep striving—
so were they straining to carry the corpse, and behind them the foe was
held by the two Ajaxes, as water is held by a rocky
forested ridge which stretches without any break through a flatland,
one which holds back even the ruinous currents of mighty

750   rivers—at once to the plain it forces the streams of them all to

wander, and never do they break through it, though mightily surging;
always thus the Ajaxes were holding the battle of Trojans
back; yet follow they did, and especially two were among them,
Lord Aineías the son of Anchíses and glorious Hektor.

755   Then they, just as arises a bird-cloud, starlings or jackdaws,
dreadfully shrieking as they see coming upon them a falcon,
one which carries along for the small birds death and destruction,
so before Hektor and Lord Aineías the youthful Achaians,
dreadfully shrieking, were running, and war-craft they had forgotten.

760   Many fine pieces of armor of Dánaäns fleeing were dropping
round and about that trench; yet there was no pause in the battle.

BOOK 18

So as the two sides fought like the blaze of a conflagration,
swift on his feet with the message Antílochos came to Achilles.
Him he discovered in front of the ships with their horns uplifted,
pondering still in his heart on the things that had come to fulfillment;
5 deeply disturbed he spoke to his own magnanimous spirit:
"Ah me, how does it happen again that the long-haired Achaians
over the plain clear back to the galleys are driven in panic?
Now for my heart may the gods not achieve such evil afflictions
as on a time my mother imparted to me, and declared that
10 while I still was alive the best man of the Mýrmidons would be
made to abandon the light of the sun at the hands of the Trojans.
Certainly now has perished Menoítios' valorous scion,
rash man, though I commanded that once he had thrust the fierce fire off,
he should return to the ships, not mightily battle with Hektor."
15 As he was pondering over these things in his mind and his spirit,
then came up and approached him the scion of excellent Nestor,
pouring the hot tears out, and the sorrowful message he told him:
"Ah me, war-skilled Peleus' son, a heart-sickening message
you are to hear, of a thing I wish might never have happened!
20 Fallen in death is Patróklos, and they fight over his body—
naked, as Hektor of glittering helmet has taken the armor."
So he spoke, and a black cloud of grief enshrouded Achilles;
taking the grimy and ash-gray dust into both of his hands, he
poured it over his head, and his handsome face he disfigured;
25 onto his fragrant tunic the black ash settled and stained it.
There stretched out in the dust, in his mightiness mighty, Achilles
lay, and with his own hands he tore at his hair and defiled it.
There were the maids that Achilles and noble Patróklos had captured
shrieking aloud in anguish of spirit as out of the door they
30 ran to surround war-minded Achilles, and all of the maids were

beating their breasts with their hands; under each were the knees unloosened.
So on the other side wailed Antílochos, pouring his tears out,
holding the hands of Achilles, who groaned in his glorious spirit,
since he feared that the hero would cut his own throat with a knife-blade.

35   Dreadfully, loudly he moaned; he was heard by the lady his mother,
who in the depths of the sea-brine was sitting beside her old father;
shrilly she started to cry, and the goddesses gathered about her,
all of them Néreus' daughters, below in the depths of the sea-brine:
there then Glaukè was sitting and Kýmodoké and Thaleía,

40   Speío, Nesaíë, and ox-eyed Hálië also, and Thóë,
Kýmothoë and as well Aktaíë and Límnoreía,
Mélitè too and Iaíra, Amphíthoë too and Agaúë,
Dýnamené and Pheroúsa, as well as Doto and Proto,
Déxamené, Amphínomè also, and Kállianeíra,

45   Doris and Pánopè too, and the glorious nymph Galateía,
Némertés and as well Apseúdes and Kállianássa;
there too Klýmenè was, Ianeíra as well, Ianássa,
Maíra and Óreithuía, the fair-tressed nymph Amatheía,
others of Néreus' daughters as well, in the depths of the sea-brine.

50   Filled was the silvery cave with the goddesses; all were together
beating their breasts, and the leader in lamentation was Thetis:
"Hear me, sisters, the daughters of Néreus, so that you all may
know well, once you have heard, what sorrows I have in my spirit.
Oh unhappy me! Oh me, the mother accursed of the best man,

55   seeing that I gave birth to a son so faultless and mighty,
brilliant among all heroes; and he shot up like a sapling;
then after nurturing him like a tree on the slope of an orchard,
over to Ilion I sent him with the well-curved galleys,
there with the Trojans to battle; but never again will I give him

60   welcome when he comes home, back there to the palace of Peleus.
While he yet is alive and is looking on Helios' sunlight,
he is in anguish, and I can in no way succor him, even if I go.
Yet I will go, so that I may see the dear child—I will hear what
sorrow has come upon him while staying away from the battle."

65   So having spoken, she left that cave, and the others along with
her went dolefully weeping; around them the waves of the sea were
broken apart; and as soon as they came to the fertile Troäd,
one by one on the shore they stepped, in the place where the close-ranked
ships of the Mýrmidons had been drawn out around swift Achilles.

70   There as he heavily groaned stood near him the lady his mother;

shrilly she started to cry, embracing the head of her dear son;
sorrowing then she spoke, and in these winged words she addressed him:
"Why do you weep, my child? What grief has come over your spirit?
Speak out, do not conceal it—by Zeus those things are accomplished
75 just in the way you earlier prayed for, lifting your hands up—
all of the sons of Achaians to be penned in at the ships' sterns,
sorely in need of you, and to endure disgraceful afflictions."
        Heavily groaning, to her spoke forth swift-footed Achilles:
"Mother, indeed these things the Olympian now has accomplished;
80 yet what pleasure have I? For my own dear comrade has perished,
noble Patróklos, the man I honored above all the comrades,
even as much as myself. I have lost him. The armor has Hektor
stripped off after he killed him—enormous, a marvel to look on,
beautiful armor the gods gave Peleus, a glorious present,
85 that day they placed you in the bed of a man who was mortal.
How I wish you had kept on living below with the deathless
maids of the sea, and a mortal bedmate had Peleus wedded!
Now it is so, that at heart you too have measureless sorrow
over a son who has perished, and never again will you give him
90 welcome when he comes home, since now my spirit commands me
neither to live nor to stay among mortals, unless great Hektor
under my spear gets struck down first, and he loses his life-breath,
paying the price for despoiling Menoítios' scion Patróklos."
        Answering him, thus Thetis addressed him, pouring her tears out:
95 "Doomed to a quick death, child, you will be, from what you are saying,
since very soon after Hektor's is your fate ready to take you."
        Deeply disturbed, thus spoke to her then swift-footed Achilles:
"Soon may I die then, since I was not, as my comrade was being
slaughtered, to come to his rescue, and far from his fatherland has he
100 died—he needed me sorely to be his defender from ruin.
Now, as I will not return to the much-loved land of my fathers,
nor to Patróklos could I be a torchlight, nor to the other
comrades, all those many that noble Lord Hektor has vanquished—
rather I sit by the ships, on the earth so useless a burden,
105 I who am such as no other among bronze-armored Achaians
here in a battle, although there are other men better in counsel—
may strife vanish away from among gods and from among men,
also the wrath that arouses a man, though prudent, to raging,
anger that, sweeter by far than the honey from honeycombs dripping,
110 waxes to rage like smoke from a blaze inside of a man's breast;

so just now Agamemnon, the lord of the people, enraged me.
Yet let us leave these things that are done with, though we are grieving,
out of necessity quelling the heart inside of our bosoms;
now I go, so that I catch Hektor, the killer of that dear
115 comrade; and then my death will I welcome whenever in fact Zeus
wishes, along with the rest of the deathless gods, to achieve it,
since not even evaded his death great Herakles' power,
though he was greatly belovèd of Lord Zeus scion of Kronos—
still he was quelled by his fate and the baleful anger of Hera.
120 So for myself, if indeed for me too a like fate has been fashioned,
I will be lying in death; but a glorious fame let me now win;
many a deep-bosomed woman of Troy or Dardánia shall I
give good reason to wipe disconsolate tears from her tender
cheeks with both of her hands and to keep incessantly moaning—
125 then may they know I have long stayed out of the combat. And do not
keep me from battle, though loving me so; you will never persuade me."
      Thetis the goddess of silvery feet then gave him an answer:
"Certainly what you have spoken is true, child; it is no coward's
act to ward off from your worn-out comrades utter destruction.
130 Yet now there among Trojans is held your beautiful armor,
brazen and brightly agleam; great Hektor of glittering helmet
wears it himself on his shoulders, exulting; and yet I am certain
not long he will take glory in it: near him is his own death.
Nevertheless, not yet do you enter the turmoil of Ares,
135 ever, before with your eyes you see me again coming hither;
for in the morning will I come back to you, when the sun rises,
then will I bring you beautiful armor from lordly Hephaistos."
      These words when she had spoken, away from her son she again turned;
after she turned, she spoke to her sisters, the maids of the sea-brine:
140 "You now plunge down under the great broad breast of the deep sea,
visiting there the old man of the sea and the house of our father—
tell him about all this; but to lofty Olympos will I go
now, to Hephaistos the glorious craftsman, to see if he might be
willing to give my son resplendent and glorious armor."
145 So she spoke, and at once they plunged down under the sea-waves;
meanwhile the goddess Thetis of silvery feet to Olympos
went, so that she might bring to her dear son glorious armor.
      Thus to Olympos her feet bore her; meanwhile the Achaians,
fleeing in marvelous tumult before man-slaughtering Hektor,
150 finally came clear down to the Hellespont and to the galleys,

327

nor from among those missiles at all were the well-greaved Achaians
able to drag off the corpse of Achilles' henchman Patróklos,
since once more upon him were the fighters and chariots coming,
Hektor the scion of Priam as well, like a fire in his valor.

155   Three times then from behind by the feet did glorious Hektor
seize him, eager to drag him, and loudly he called on the Trojans;
three times both the Ajaxes, appareled in furious valor,
beat him away from the body; but he, in his valor confiding
ever, would sometimes rush upon them in the melee and sometimes

160   stand there mightily shouting, but not at all backward he yielded.
Just as the countrymen keeping their flocks are unable at all to
drive from a carcass a tawny-haired lion who sorely is famished,
so from the body the two Ajaxes, the marshals of men, were
quite unable to frighten off Hektor the scion of Priam.

165   He would have dragged it away now and won unspeakable glory
had not come from Olympos at once swift wind-footed Iris
running, and bearing a message to Peleus' scion to take arms,
hidden from Zeus and the rest of the gods, since Hera had sent her.
There then, standing beside him, in these winged words she addressed him:

170   "Rise up, Peleus' son, the most marvelous man among all men;
rescue Patróklos, defend him, for whose sake terrible strife has
risen in front of the galleys, and they are destroying each other,
some of them striving to rescue the body of him who has perished,
while toward windswept Ilion city the Trojans are ever

175   struggling to draw him away, and especially glorious Hektor
eagerly wishes to drag him; his spirit commands him to cut his
head from the delicate neck and on sharp palisades to impale it.
Up now, lie here no longer, but let shame come on your heart lest
noble Patróklos become a plaything for the dogs of the Trojans;

180   yours is the blame if at all his corpse comes back mutilated."
        Answering her then spoke swift-footed and noble Achilles:
"Iris divine, which god dispatched you to me with the message?"
        Once more spoke forth, answering him, swift wind-footed Iris:
"Hera the goddess dispatched me, the glorious bedmate of great Zeus;

185   Kronos' son seated aloft knows nothing of this, nor the other
deathless gods who inhabit the snow-clad peak of Olympos."
        Answering her in return spoke forth swift-footed Achilles:
"How can I enter the melee? For they have hold of my armor;
nor does my own dear mother allow me to arm for the battle,

190   ever, before with my eyes I see her again coming hither;

beautiful armor, she says, she will bring me then from Hephaistos.
Nor any other I know whose glorious arms I could put on,
only excepting the shield of the scion of Télamon Ajax.
Yet I suppose he himself is among the foremost in the melee,

195   slaughtering foes with a spear in defense of the perished Patróklos."
Once more spoke forth, answering him, swift wind-footed Iris:
"We are already aware that they hold your glorious armor;
yet go just as you are to the trench and appear to the Trojans;
possibly then in their terror of you those Trojans will hold back

200   out of the battle, allowing the sons of Achaians to take breath,
tired as they are; very scant is the time to take breath in a battle."
So having spoken her message, the swift-footed Iris departed.
Meanwhile Achilles belovèd of Zeus rose up; with the aegis
streaming with tassels Athena surrounded his powerful shoulders;

205   then with a bright gold cloud that splendor of goddesses wreathed his
head, and a radiant flame she made blaze out of the hero.
Just as smoke goes up from a city and reaches the heavens
from afar off, from an island that enemy forces beleaguer—
all day long they contend in the warfare of odious Ares,

210   fighting the combat right from the city—and then at the sunset
blaze one after another the beacons, and high up above goes
rushing the glare to be seen by men who are dwelling around them,
so that they might come over in ships as defenders from ruin,
so did the blaze rise up to the sky from the head of Achilles.

215   Then from the wall he went to the trench, and he stood there and did not
join the Achaians, for he respected his mother's astute charge.
There was he standing and shouting; afar off Pallas Athena
yelled out, thus in the Trojans arousing unspeakable turmoil.
Clear to be heard as the clarion voice of a trumpet resounding

220   when some city is being beleaguered by murderous foemen,
so clear then to be heard was the voice of Lord Aíakos' scion.
Then as they listened to that bronze voice of Lord Aíakos' scion,
deep in them all their hearts were alarmed, and the fair-maned horses
turned their chariots back, for they saw great grief in their spirits.

225   Stricken with fear were the charioteers as the weariless fire they
saw blaze over the head of the great-souled scion of Peleus
dreadfully, caused to blaze up by the goddess bright-eyed Athena.
Three times over the trench yelled mightily noble Achilles;
three times stricken with dread were the Trojans and glorious allies.

230   There and at that time twelve of the best of their warriors perished

right among their own spears and their chariots. But the Achaians
happily picked up Patróklos and drew him from under the missiles,
then placed him on a litter; around him stood his belovèd
comrades, weeping; among them went swift-footed Achilles
235 pouring the hot tears out, as he looked at his trustworthy comrade
lying upon that bier, by the sharp bronze blade mutilated.
Him indeed with his horses and chariot once he had sent out
into the battle, but never received him again when he came back.
    Into the streams of the Ocean the ox-eyed queen, Lady Hera,
240 now sent weariless Helios, though unwilling, to enter;
straightway Helios then went down, and the noble Achaians
brought to a halt that violent battle and leveling combat.
    So on the other side too gave way from the violent battle
all of the Trojans, and loosed from the chariots their swift horses,
245 then in assembly they gathered, before they thought of their dinner.
In the assembly they stood on their feet; not one of them dared to
sit down, since on them all dread fastened because of Achilles
showing himself—he had long held off from the dolorous combat.
Speaking among them thoughtful Polýdamas, Pánthoös' scion,
250 started the talking, for he alone saw the before and the after;
he was a comrade of Hektor, and both were born on the same night;
one was the better by far in speeches, the other in spear-fights.
He with benevolent wisdom addressed them, giving them counsel:
"Take thought, friends, of both choices we have; myself I exhort you
255 now to the city to go, not wait for the sacred morning
here in the plain by the galleys, for we are quite far from the ramparts.
While that fighter was raging against noble Lord Agamemnon,
all that time the Achaians were much more easy to fight with,
since I too was rejoicing to sleep there next to the swift ships,
260 hoping that we might finally capture the tractable galleys.
Dreadfully now do I fear Lord Peleus' swift-footed scion;
so overbearing a temper he has, he will never be minded
just to remain in the plain, in the middle of which are the Trojans
and the Achaians partaking the fury of Ares, on both sides;
265 over the city instead he will battle, and over the women.
No, let us go to the city, obey me, for thus will it happen:
now the ambrosial night has brought to a halt the swift-footed
scion of Peleus; but if tomorrow, when he in his armor
starts his attack, he comes upon us here, then will a man know
270 him very well, and to sacred Ilion gladly will any

come who escape, but the dogs and the vultures will feed on
many a Trojan—but far from my ears let such a tale keep off!
If in spite of our pain we obey these words I am speaking,
during the night we will keep our strength in the place of assembly,
275 while to the city the ramparts and towering gates and the polished
tall doors fitted and bolted in them will be giving protection.
Early at dawn in the morning, accoutered in armor, will we go
stand on the ramparts; and it will be painful for him if he wishes
then to come out of the ships and do battle with us for the ramparts.
280 Back to the ships he will go, when his mighty-necked mares he has sated,
aimlessly wandering under the city in every direction;
but to burst into the city his spirit will never allow him,
neither will he ransack it; before, swift dogs will devour him."
      Looking from lowering brows spoke Hektor of glittering helmet:
285 "Pleasing to me no longer, Polýdamas, what you are saying—
urging that we go back to the city again to be penned in.
Have you indeed not enough being cooped up inside the ramparts?
For of the city of Priam before would every mortal
man speak often as wealthy in gold-work, wealthy in bronze-work,
290 yet those beautiful treasures are now quite lost from the houses;
many indeed of our riches have been sold off and have gone to
Phrygia and lovely Maiónia since great Zeus became angry.
Now, when the scion of Kronos of crooked devices has granted
me by the ships to win fame, by the sea to entrap the Achaians,
295 childish fool, no longer propose such schemes to the people,
since no man of the Trojans will heed you, for I will not let them.
But come, just as I say, let all of us heed and obey it.
Now take supper all over the army, in ordered divisions;
keep in remembrance the night-watch, and every man remain wakeful;
300 but of the Trojans, whoever is hugely distressed for his riches,
let him collect them to give to the people for communal feasting—
better that they be getting the benefit than the Achaians.
Early at dawn in the morning, accoutered in armor, will we down
there by the hollow galleys arouse sharp warfare of Ares.
305 Then if in truth by the galleys is roused up noble Achilles,
worse will it be for him, should he desire to fight; I will indeed not
flee him, away from the dolorous warfare; no, I will stand firm
facing him, whether he wins a great triumph or whether I win it.
Common to all Enyálios is, and the slayer he slaughters."
310   So among them spoke Hektor; the Trojans shouted approval,

331

fools, for their senses were taken from them by Pallas Athena,
since it was Hektor of whom they approved, though he advised evil—
no one Polýdamas praised, who devised them excellent counsel.
Then throughout the encampment a meal they took. The Achaians
315   over Patróklos the whole night long were lamenting and wailing.
Peleus' scion among them was leading the vehement wailing,
laying his own man-slaughtering hands on the chest of his comrade,
deeply, incessantly moaning, the way some well-bearded lion
moans whose whelps have been taken away by a man on a stag-hunt
320   out of a deep thick wood, and she comes back late and is anguished;
tracking the man's footsteps, through many a valley she ranges,
somewhere hoping to find them, for sharp is the anger that grips her;
so to the Mýrmidons now he spoke forth, heavily groaning:
"Ah me! Fruitless indeed was the word I uttered on that day,
325   saying to hearten the hero Menoítios there in the house that,
Ilion once ransacked, his illustrious son I would bring him
back to Opóeis, along with his share of the plunder allotted.
But not all the intentions of men Zeus brings to fulfillment,
since we are both of us destined to redden the self-same earth with
330   blood right here in the Troäd, for never will give me a welcome,
when to his halls I return, old Peleus the chariot-driver,
neither will Thetis my mother, but this earth here will enshroud me.
Now, since I will go under the earth after you do, Patróklos,
I will not give you burial rites till I have brought hither
335   Hektor's armor and head, since he was your great-souled killer;
then will I bring twelve glorious sons of the Trojans and slit their
throats in front of your pyre, enraged as I am at your slaughter.
But until then you will lie here just as you are by the curved ships;
meanwhile deep-bosomed women of Troy and Dardánia will be
340   pouring out tears by night and by day and lamenting around you,
those whom we ourselves labored to get with our strength and our long spears
during the times we ransacked the prosperous cities of mortals."
    So these words having spoken, at once did noble Achilles
order the comrades to set a great tripod over the fireplace,
345   so that the blood-caked gore they quickly could wash from Patróklos.
Then in the blaze of the fire first setting a bathwater cauldron,
into it they poured water, and put wood under, and lit it.
Over the cauldron's belly the fire spread, heating the water;
when in the shimmering cauldron the water was heated to boiling,
350   then they bathed him and rubbed him richly with oil of the olive;

all of his wounds they filled with an unguent seasoned for nine years;
laying him out on a bed, with delicate linen they covered
him from his head to his feet; on top they put a white mantle.
Then for the whole night through there around fleet-footed Achilles
355 over Patróklos the Mýrmidons all were lamenting and wailing.
Zeus then spoke out to Hera, his sister as well as his bedmate:
"This you at last have accomplished, my ox-eyed queen, Lady Hera—
you have aroused fleet-footed Achilles; and now it is clear that
out of your own womb issued the long-haired men, the Achaians."
360   Speaking to him then answered the ox-eyed queen, Lady Hera:
"Most dread scion of Kronos, and what is this word you have spoken!
Even a man, I suppose, would achieve his intent for another,
though he is mortal and knows no counsel as crafty as mine is.
How then was I—who assert that of goddesses I am the highest
365 both in respect my birth and because of the name that I have as
bedmate to you, and you rule as the lord over all the immortals—
not in my angry resentment to weave great banes for the Trojans?"
     Such things then they spoke and addressed each one to the other.
Thetis of silvery feet came then to the house of Hephaistos,
370 indestructible, starry, distinguished among the immortals,
bronze-wrought, which that clubfooted god himself had erected.
Him she came upon sweating and hurrying, wheeling among his
bellows, for tripods, twenty in all, he was making, so he could
stand them next to the wall of the well-built hall of his palace;
375 gold-wrought wheels he had fastened beneath each foot of the tripods,
so of themselves at command the assembly of gods they could enter,
then could again go back to the palace—a marvel to look on.
Thus far they were complete; the elaborate handles were not yet
set upon them—he now was preparing them, forging the rivets.
380 While at this task he labored with his ingenious cunning,
coming beside him the goddess Thetis of silvery feet stood.
Charis of shimmering head-scarf observed her there and approached her—
Charis the fair, whom the glorious twice-lame cripple had wedded—
clasped her hand in her own and said these words, calling upon her:
385 "Why now, long-robed Thetis, have you come here to our dwelling,
honored and welcome? For you have not visited often before now.
Follow me in, so that I may provide you a guest's entertainment."
     So having spoken the splendor of goddesses guided her forward.
Then she gave her a seat on an armchair studded with silver,
390 beautiful, skillfully made; underneath for her feet was a footstool;

calling, she spoke these words to Hephaistos the glorious craftsman:
"Come to me hither, Hephaistos—your help is Thetis in need of."
Speaking to her then answered the glorious twice-lame cripple:
"Well now, here in my house is a dreaded and reverend goddess,

395 she who preserved me the time pain came upon me as I fell far
down through the will of my bitch-faced mother, who wanted to hide me,
lame as I am; much woe in my heart then I would have suffered,
had not Thetis received me, Eurýnomè too, in their bosoms,
that Eurýnomè who of the back-flowing Ocean is daughter.

400 Nine years then I was forging for them much elegant handwork,
brooches and spiraling hairpins and necklaces also and bracelets,
there in the hollow cave; and around me the stream of the Ocean
flowed with its foam, ineffably murmuring; neither was any
other of gods or of men who were mortal aware of my presence;

405 Thetis alone and Eurýnomè knew it, the ones who had saved me.
Now to our house she has come, so surely a full recompense I
must give Thetis of beautiful tresses for saving my life then.
But now you put before her an excellent guest's entertainment,
while I put to the side my bellows and all of the hand-tools."

410   So having said, from the anvil-block the enormous and panting
god stood, limping; beneath him his thin legs nimbly were moving.
Out of the fire he set the great bellows, and all of the hand-tools
used in his work he gathered and laid in a toolbox of silver;
then with a sponge his visage and both of his hands he wiped off,

415 also his huge strong neck and his breast all shaggy with hair, then
put on a tunic, and taking his ponderous staff, to the doorway
limping he went; to support their lord then ran up his handmaids
fashioned of gold and resembling in form young girls who are living;
understanding they have in their minds; speech too they possess, and

420 strength, and as well from the deathless gods have knowledge of handcrafts.
They now busied themselves to support their master, and limping
closer to Thetis, he sat down there on a shimmering armchair,
clasped her hand in his own, and said these words, calling upon her:
"Why now, long-robed Thetis, have you come here to our dwelling,

425 honored and welcome? For you have not visited often before now.
Speak what you have in your mind, for my heart bids me to achieve it,
if I am able to do it and if it can well be accomplished."
    Then in answer to him spoke Thetis, pouring her tears out:
"Is there, Hephaistos, of all of the goddesses up on Olympos,

430 any who suffers in heart such hateful afflictions as are these

pains Zeus scion of Kronos has given to me beyond others?
For of the maids of the sea I alone to a man he subjected,
Peleus, Aíakos' son, and I suffered the bed of a mortal,
though I was much unwilling; and he in detestable old age
435 lies overcome in his palace; but I have other afflictions,
since he gave me a son to be born, to be reared to adulthood,
brilliant among all heroes; and he shot up like a sapling;
then after nurturing him like a tree on the slope of an orchard,
over to Ilion I sent him with the well-curved galleys,
440 there with the Trojans to battle; but never again will I give him
welcome when he comes home, back there to the palace of Peleus.
While he yet is alive and is looking on Helios' sunlight,
he is in anguish, and I can in no way succor him, even if I go.
That girl chosen for him as a prize by the sons of Achaians—
445 her from his arms has the powerful lord Agamemnon taken.
Grieving for her he wasted his spirit, and meanwhile the Trojans
kept the Achaians enclosed by the galleys and would not allow them
ever to go outside; and the Argive elders entreated
him then, naming the many and glorious gifts they would give him.
450 Thereupon he had refused himself to ward off the destruction;
nevertheless, on Patróklos he put his own armor and sent him
out to the fight and to follow with him dispatched a large cohort.
Then for the whole day long by the Skaian Gates they were battling;
that same day would the city have been ransacked, had Apollo,
455 after Menoítios' valorous scion had wrought many evils,
not in the foremost killed him and granted the glory to Hektor.
Therefore have I come here to your knees now, hoping you might be
willing to give my son, quick-dying, a shield and a helmet,
also beautiful greaves well fitted with ankle-protectors,
460 and a breastplate; for the others his trustworthy comrade lost when
quelled by the Trojans; and he on the ground lies grieving in spirit."
   Speaking to her then answered the glorious twice-lame cripple:
"Take heart—do not allow these matters to trouble your spirit.
How I wish I were able as surely to hide him away from
465 dolorous death, at the time his terrible fate overcomes him,
as now beautiful armor will be his, such as hereafter
many a mortal will wonder to look at, whoever beholds it."
   So having spoken he left her there and returned to his bellows;
these to the fire he turned and commanded that they start working.
470 Then did the bellows, twenty in all, blow into the nozzles,

blasting out air at all levels of force for the fire that was needed,
sometimes to one place where he was working and sometimes another,
just as Hephaistos desired and as he could accomplish the labor.
Into the crucibles over the fires, unwearying bronze he
475   threw, tin also, and silver and precious gold; and he then set
onto the anvil-block a huge anvil; in one of his hands he
took up a massive hammer; the tongs he took in the other.
     It was a shield then first that he fashioned, enormous and heavy,
well ornamented in every part, and around it a glittering rim he
480   set, three-banded and gleaming, and put on a baldric of silver.
Five full layers the shield itself was, and upon it he fashioned
many elaborate scenes with ingenious craft and adroitness.
     There upon it he fashioned the earth and the sea and the heavens;
on it as well were the weariless sun and the moon at its fullest.
485   On it were all of the constellations the heavens are crowned with:
there were the Pleíades, Hýades also, and mighty Oríon,
and the Great Bear—men call it another name also, the Wagon—
which turns round in position and keeps its eye on Oríon
and is alone in not having a share in the baths of the Ocean.
490   There upon it he made two beautiful cities of mortal
men. Inside of the one there were weddings and festival banquets;
out of their chambers the brides they led by the light of the blazing
torches along though the city, and loud hymeneals were rising.
Young men, dancers, were whirling about in a circle; among them
495   kept on sounding the lyres and the oboes, and all of the women
marveled at what they were seeing as each one stood in her doorway.
But in the place of assembly the people were gathered: contention
there had arisen, with two men quarreling over the blood-price
paid for a man who was murdered, and one claimed he had paid fully,
500   stating his case to the people; the other refused to take any;
both men sought for an arbitrator, to get a decision.
People were cheering them both and to both sides giving assistance;
heralds were holding the people in hand, and the elders were sitting
there on the polished stones in the sacred circle of justice,
505   keeping their hands on the staves of the heralds with high-raised voices.
Then with the staves they rose, and in turn they delivered their judgments.
There in their midst two talents of gold lay; they would be given
him among them who would utter the judgment straightest and wisest.
     But two armies of fighters were stationed surrounding the other
510   city, resplendent in arms; two plans found favor among them,

whether to sack it, or whether instead to divide with the townsmen
all the possessions contained inside the delectable city;
not yet they were persuaded, but armed themselves for an ambush.
There on the wall were the dear bedmates and the innocent children
515 standing and guarding the town, and with them men trammeled by old age;
out did the rest go, led by Ares and Pallas Athena,
both of them fashioned of gold; gold too were the clothes they were wearing;
beautiful were they, and great in their armor, the way that the gods are,
clear to the view from afar, and the people beneath them were smaller.
520 When they arrived at the place they thought to be good for an ambush
down at a river, in which was a watering place for all cattle,
there they seated themselves, in their bright bronze armor enveloped.
Then there were two scouts whom they posted apart from the army,
waiting until they sighted the sheep and the crooked-horned cattle.
525 These soon made their appearance; with them two herdsmen were coming,
pleasing themselves with their pipes, not at all foreseeing deception.
Then as they saw them, the ambushers ran out against them and swiftly
cut off the herds of the cattle as well as the beautiful flocks of
sheep with shimmering fleeces, and also slaughtered the herdsmen.
530 As the besiegers perceived the tumultuous din from the cattle,
where in the place of assembly they sat, they mounted behind their
high-paced horses at once and went after them, swiftly arriving.
Taking a stand they engaged combat on the banks of the river,
each of the two sides striking with bronze-tipped spears at the other.
535 There among them joined Conflict and Tumult; among them destructive
Fate took one man alive new-wounded, another unwounded,
while yet another she dragged off dead by the feet through the carnage;
ruddy with blood of the men were the clothes she wore on her shoulders.
Just like men who are living, they joined in the melee and battled,
540 each of them dragging away dead bodies the others had slaughtered.
     There upon it he set soft fallowland, fertile for planting,
spacious and three times plowed, and upon it numerous plowmen
who kept wheeling their teams as they drove them in either direction.
When in making the turn they came to the edge of the plowland,
545 then would a man come up and a flagon of honey-sweet wine would
give to the hands of each one; they would turn back over the furrows,
eager to come once more to the edge of the deep-soiled fallow.
This grew blacker behind them and looked like earth that has been plowed,
even though it was of gold—so wondrous the work he accomplished.
550   There upon it he set the estate of a king, upon which were

laborers reaping with sharp-edged sickles in hand; of the armfuls,
some fell onto the ground in swaths, one after another,
while sheaf-binders were binding the others together with sheaf-ties.
Three sheaf-binders were standing at hand there; meanwhile behind them
555   boys kept gathering armfuls, and carrying them in their arms, they
brought them continually to the binders; the king with his scepter
stood among them at the swath in silence, rejoicing in spirit.
Under an oak tree heralds apart made ready a banquet,
busy about a great ox they had slaughtered; the women were sprinkling
560   much white barley in wine as a noontide meal for the workers.
     There upon it he set a great vineyard laden with clusters,
beautiful, fashioned of gold, while black its bunches of grapes were,
fashioned of silver the poles upon which throughout were the vines held.
All around it was a ditch in cobalt enamel; a fence of
565   tin he drove about that, and to it there was one path only,
which grape-gatherers followed whenever they gathered the vintage.
Maidens and young men, feeling the innocent pleasure of childhood,
gathered and carried the honey-sweet fruit in wickerwork baskets.
There among them in the middle a boy with a clear-toned lyre was
570   playing delightfully; sweetly to it he was singing the Linos
song in a delicate voice; and along with it beating the time and
dancing and shouting and sporting on feet high-skipping they followed.
     There upon it he fashioned a herd of fat cattle with straight horns;
skillfully modeled of gold and of tin were the cattle he set there;
575   lowing, away from the farmyard dung they hurried to pasture
down by a murmuring river, by thickets of reeds in the marshland.
Modeled of gold were the herdsmen advancing along with the cattle,
four of them; nine were the hounds, swift-footed, that after them followed.
There were two terrible lions among the foremost of the cattle,
580   gripping a bellowing bull, who, mightily lowing, was being
dragged off; after him hastily followed the hounds and the young men.
Having ripped open the hide of the huge bull, both of the beasts were
gulping the black blood down, and the entrails; meanwhile the herdsmen
vainly were trying to rouse the swift hounds, set them at the lions;
585   they from the lions were turning aside, unwilling to bite them,
yet very near they would take their stand, then leap away barking.
     There upon it also did the glorious twice-lame cripple
fashion a great broad pasture of white-fleeced sheep in a lovely
valley, and farmyards also and well-roofed cabins and sheepfolds.
590   There upon it also did the glorious twice-lame cripple

model a place for the dance, like the one that in spacious Knosos
Daídalos fashioned of old for the fair-tressed girl Ariádnè.
There did the youths and the maids worth numerous cattle as bride-price
enter the dance—by the wrists of their hands they held one another.
595 They were appareled, the maids in delicate linen, the youths in
tunics of fine-wove cloth, soft-gleaming with oil of the olive.
All of the maids wore beautiful diadems; all of the youths were
carrying daggers of gold suspended from baldrics of silver.
Sometimes they with the skill of their feet ran round in a circle
600 easily, as by a wheel well-fitted for gripping, a potter
sits while making a trial to find out whether it functions;
sometimes they would be running in rows and toward one another.
Great was the company standing around the delectable dance and
taking delight, and among them was singing a godlike singer,
605 playing the lyre; and as well two tumblers were dancing about them—
they had begun with the song and were whirling around in the middle.

   There upon it he set the great might of the river of Ocean,
right on the outmost rim of the strong-built shield, all around it.

   Next, when at last he had finished the fine shield, massive and sturdy,
610 then he made him a corselet brighter than light from a bonfire;
also he made him a massive helmet that fitted his temples,
beautiful, elegant work, and a gold-wrought crest set upon it;
finally then, out of pliable tin, leg-armor he made him.

   Soon as the glorious twice-lame cripple had made all the armor,
615 taking it up, in front of Achilles' mother he laid it;
she then swooped like a hawk from the snow-clad peak of Olympos,
carrying down from the hands of Hephaistos the glittering armor.

BOOK 19

Now from the streams of the Ocean arose Dawn, saffron-appareled,
so that she might bring light to the deathless gods and to mortals;
bringing the gifts of the god then Thetis arrived at the galleys.
There she found her dear son as he lay embracing Patróklos,
5 piercingly, loudly lamenting; around him were many companions
weeping; among them the splendor of goddesses came up beside him,
clasped his hand in her own, and said these words, calling upon him:
"My child, though we are grieving for this man, now let us leave him
lying, for he has indeed by the will of the gods been vanquished.
10 Rather receive this gift of Hephaistos, the glorious armor,
such in beauty as never a man yet wore on his shoulders."
When she had said these words, in front of Achilles the goddess
set on the ground that armor, and all its splendor was clanging.
Trembling at once seized all of the Mýrmidons; none of them even
15 dared to behold it directly, but shrank in fear; as Achilles
looked at it, so upon him came still more anger—his eyes were
terribly flashing in beams like lightning from under his eyelids;
yet he rejoiced as he held in his hands the god's glittering presents.
Then, when he had rejoiced in his mind as he looked at the splendor,
20 he at once spoke to his mother, and these winged words he addressed her:
"Mother of mine, these arms that the god has given are such as
works of immortals should be; no man who is mortal could make them.
Now therefore I will arm for the battle; but dreadfully do I
fear lest into the corpse of Menoítios' valorous scion
25 flies in the meantime go through the wounds that the bronze inflicted;
maggots would they engender and so disfigure the body—
out of it life has been stricken—and all his flesh would be rotted."
Thetis the goddess of silvery feet then gave him an answer:
"My child, do not allow these matters to trouble your spirit.
30 I will endeavor to keep from his body the pitiless savage

340

nations of flies, which always consume men slaughtered in battle;
then, even if he lies there until a whole year is completed,
always his flesh will continue as sound as it is, or yet better.
You now call to assembly the hero-Achaians; renouncing
35 there your wrath against Lord Agamemnon, shepherd of people,
hastily arm yourself for the battle and put on your valor."
     Soon as she said these words, she put bold strength in his spirit,
then for Patróklos she dripped ambrosial ichor and ruddy
nectar within through his nostrils, that ever his flesh would remain sound.
40   Striding along by the shore of the sea went noble Achilles,
shouting a terrible shout and arousing the hero-Achaians.
Even the men who had earlier stayed where the galleys were gathered,
those who were helmsmen and wielded the steering-oars of the galleys,
those also in the ships who were stewards, dispensers of victuals,
45 this time they too came to assembly, because of Achilles
showing himself—he had long held off from the dolorous combat.
Two among them came there still limping, attendants of Ares,
Tydeus' son, steadfast in the battle, and noble Odysseus,
both men leaning on spears, for the pain of their wounds was yet grievous;
50 when they arrived, they took their seats at the front of the meeting.
Then came last of them all Agamemnon, lord of the people,
nursing a wound; for indeed him too in the violent combat,
wielding a bronze spear, Koön the son of Anténor had wounded.
Finally, when the Achaians were all there, gathered together,
55 rising to stand among them spoke forth swift-footed Achilles:
"Atreus' son, this course we took—for us both was it better,
whether for you or for me, that because of the grief in our hearts we
raged in strife, the devourer of souls, for the sake of a maiden?
Would that she in the ships had been killed by Artemis' arrow
60 that same day that I chose her, when I had destroyed Lyrnéssos!
Then so many Achaians would not have taken the boundless
earth in their teeth at the enemy's hands on account of my raging.
Better it was for the Trojans and Hektor, but long the Achaians,
so I believe, this quarrel between you and me will remember.
65 Yet let us leave these things that are done with, though we are grieving,
out of necessity quelling the hearts inside of our bosoms.
Now I am putting an end to my wrath—no way can I keep on
raging forever and unrelentingly. Come then and swiftly
rouse up into the battle the long-haired men, the Achaians,
70 so that against those Trojans I may again go and make trial

whether in truth they wish by the galleys to sleep; but I think that
many of them to relax their limbs will be happy, whoever
makes his escape from the violent battle, from under my spear-thrust."
     So he spoke, and the well-greaved Achaians rejoiced at the words of
75 Peleus' great-souled son, that his wrath now he was renouncing.
Also among them spoke Agamemnon, lord of the people,
right from the chair where he sat, not taking a stand in the middle:
"Oh friends, Dánaän heroes and noble attendants of Ares,
good it is, surely, to listen to one who stands speaking, nor is it
80 seemly to interrupt, since that troubles him, though he is skillful.
How in the manifold clamor of men could anyone listen,
how could he talk? Then even a clear-voiced speaker is baffled.
I will declare this to Peleus' son, but the rest of the Argives
listen to me, to my word each man pay careful attention.
85 Often indeed this word the Achaians have spoken against me,
censuring, making reproach, but it is not I who am blameful—
no, Zeus rather, and Fate, and Erínys, walking in shadows,
who cast onto my mind in assembly a savage delusion,
that day when of myself I took his prize from Achilles.
90 Yet what else could I do? For the god brings all to fulfillment.
Eldest daughter of Zeus is Delusion, the one who deludes all,
ruinous goddess, and tender of foot, since never the earth she
touches, but ever she strides in the air—men's heads are beneath her—
baffling and injuring people; another as well she has shackled.
95 For on a time even Zeus she deluded, the one they declare is
greatest among all men and all gods; yet even on him did
Hera, a female, practice deception with cunning of spirit
that same day that in Thebes of the beautiful circlet of towers
fair Alkméné was going to bring forth Herakles' power.
100 Then among all of the gods Zeus spoke forth boasting about it:
'All of the gods and the goddesses all, now listen and heed me,
so I can say such things as the heart in my breast is demanding.
This day a man shall Eíleithúia the goddess of childbirth
bring to the light, who will rule over all those dwelling about him—
105 one of the race of the men who of my own blood are engendered.'
Then in cunning of spirit addressed him the queen, Lady Hera:
'You will deceive, and again to your word not bring its fulfillment.
Come now, Olympian, swear me an oath unbreakably potent,
saying the man is to rule over all those dwelling about him
110 who this day will have fallen between the two feet of a woman,

one of the race of the men who of your own blood are engendered.'
She spoke; not at all Zeus was aware of her cunning of spirit,
but a great oath he swore and was therein greatly deluded.
Hera at once rushed forth, so leaving the peak of Olympos;
115 swiftly she came to Achaian Argos, in which as she knew was
dwelling the reverend bedmate of Sthénelos, Perseus' scion;
with a dear son she was pregnant—the seventh month was upon her.
Him she brought to the light although he was lacking his term and
halted the birth to Alkméne, restraining the Eíleithúia.
120 Bearing the message herself, she addressed Zeus scion of Kronos:
'Father Zeus, bright in the lightning, a word I will put in your spirit:
now has the excellent man been born to rule over the Argives—
he is Eurýstheus, offspring of Sthénelos, Perseus' scion,
your descendant, and he will not shame you, ruling the Argives.'
125 So she spoke; with a sharp pain deep in his mind he was stricken;
then by her bright-tressed head he at once laid hold of Delusion;
raging in mind, he swore a great oath unbreakably potent,
not to Olympos again and aloft to the star-strewn heaven
ever Delusion would come, who deludes all people and all gods.
130 He spoke; whirling the goddess about with his hand, from the star-strewn
heaven he flung her, and quickly she came to the farmlands of mankind.
Always then he would groan over her as he witnessed his dear son
doing the shameful toil of the trials Eurýstheus set him.
Neither could I, at the time great Hektor of glittering helmet
135 kept on destroying the Argive troops by the sterns of the galleys,
ever forget Delusion, by whom I first was deluded.
But since I was deluded and Zeus robbed me of my senses,
now I want to redress it and give unmeasured requital.
But come, rise for the battle and rouse up the rest of your people.
140 Here am I offering all of the gifts, those many that when he
yesterday came to your cabin were promised by noble Odysseus.
Or if you wish to, wait for a while, though ardent for warfare;
then my attendants will take those gifts from my galley and bring them
here to you, so that you see I will give what pleases your spirit."
145   Answering him in return spoke forth swift-footed Achilles:
"Atreus' glorious son Agamemnon, lord of the people,
as for the gifts, give them if you wish, as is fitting and proper;
otherwise, keep them yourself. Now let us take thought of our war-craft
quickly, at once, for we must not stay here chattering idly,
150 neither should we waste time, for as yet undone is a great work.

So now as each man looks on Achilles again in the foremost
wielding a bronze-tipped spear to destroy the battalions of Trojans,
let each one of you take good thought of the man that he battles."
Speaking to him then answered Odysseus of many devices:
155 "Even as brave as you are, not in this way, godlike Achilles,
rouse up the sons of Achaians to go against Ilion fasting,
so as to fight with the Trojans; for no short time will the battle
last when once the battalions of men encounter each other
fighting, and into the armies on both sides a god breathes fury.
160 Rather, command the Achaians beside our galleys to feed on
victuals and wine, for in them there is vigorous spirit and valor,
since no man will be able the whole day long till the sunset
always to battle the foe unfed, all sustenance lacking,
since although in his heart he is ardent for entering combat,
165 yet unawares do his limbs grow heavy, and hunger and thirst are
always coming upon him, and while he is going his knees ache.
As for the man who has taken his fill of his wine and his victuals,
he for the whole day long against enemy fighters is battling—
then is the heart in his breast both cheerful and bold, and his limbs are
170 never exhausted until all the men withdraw from the combat.
Come then, make your army disperse, tell them to prepare their
dinner; and then those gifts Agamemnon, lord of the people,
must bring here to the midst of the meeting, that all the Achaians
see them with their own eyes, and that you in your spirit are gladdened.
175 Let him arise in the midst of the Argives and swear you an oath that
never did he get into her bed, nor with her did he mingle,
as, lord, it is the natural custom of men and of women;
so in your own breast then let the heart be kindly and gracious.
Let him as well then make you amends with a feast in his cabin,
180 sumptuously, that you do not lack anything that is due you.
Atreus' son, hereafter as well to another will you be
much more just, since not at all blame is assigned when a king makes
proper amends to a man, when himself he first became angry."
Answering him then spoke Agamemnon, lord of the people:
185 "Son of Laërtes, I have great joy of your words as I listen,
since you rightly have gone through all these matters and told them.
This oath now I am minded to swear, and my spirit commands it,
neither will I forswear myself, before God. Let Achilles
stay right here for the time, though ardent he is for the warfare;
190 all you others remain here together as well, till the gifts have

been brought here from my cabin and we swear oaths that are trusty.
But upon you yourself this charge do I lay, and I bid you,
having selected the best young men out of all the Achaians,
here from my ship now carry the presents, the many I promised
195   yesterday I would give to Achilles, and lead here the women.
Let Talthýbios quickly, amid the broad host of Achaians,
ready a boar, which I will to Zeus and to Helios offer."

        Answering him in return spoke forth swift-footed Achilles:
"Atreus' glorious son Agamemnon, lord of the people,
200   rather another time it would be better to see to these matters,
sometime when in the course of the battle a pause is occurring,
when too the fury within my breast is not so ferocious.
Now as it is they lie mutilated, the men who were killed by
Hektor the scion of Priam as Zeus was granting him glory,
205   while you two urge us to be eating! But I for my part would
now at once order to go into battle the sons of Achaians
fasting and quite unfed, then later, the time that the sun sets,
ready for them a great feast, once we have requited the outrage.
Never before then, at least through my throat, either the drink or
210   food will be going, because it is my comrade who has perished,
who with the sharp bronze sword mutilated is now in my cabin
lying, his feet turned out to the doorway; around him the comrades
weep for him; not in the least those things are a care to my spirit,
no, but the slaughter and bloodshed and agonized groaning of fighters."
215   Speaking to him then answered Odysseus of many devices:
"Peleus' scion Achilles, far greatest among the Achaians,
stronger you are than myself, far greater, and not by a little,
wielding a spear, while I in counsel would surely excel you
greatly, because I was born before you were, so I have learned more.
220   Therefore constrain your heart to endure my words as you listen.
Quickly do men have more than enough of a violent combat
when bronze scatters the stalks on the ground in enormous abundance
though very scant is the harvest, whenever the scale is inclined by
Zeus, who for mankind is the dispenser of fortunes in battle.
225   But no way the Achaians can mourn their dead with the belly,
since one after another and day by day are too many
falling, and when would a man find respite from toil and affliction?
No, it is rather for us to be burying him who has perished,
making our hearts hard, shedding our tears over him but the one day;
230   then all those who survive from the painful and wearisome battle

must be mindful of drinking and eating, that we even more may
keep on fighting the enemy men incessantly, always,
clothing our bodies in bronze unwearying. Neither must any
man of the host hold back, still waiting for some other summons,

235 since this now is the summons—a bane it will be for whoever
stays at the ships of the Argives. But let us, arising together,
waken against those horse-taming Trojans the bitter god Ares."
        He spoke; taking along both sons of illustrious Nestor,
Mérionés too, Thoas, and Meges, Phýleus' scion,

240 also Kreion's son Lykomédes and Lord Melaníppos,
he set out to the cabin of Atreus' son Agamemnon.
Then straightway as the word was spoken the deed was accomplished:
they bore out of the cabin the seven tripods he had promised,
glittering cauldrons, twenty in all, and as well twelve horses;

245 quickly they led out the women in faultless handiwork skilled, all
seven of them, and the eighth was the fair-cheeked daughter of Bríseus.
Then having weighed out gold to a full ten talents, Odysseus
led, and the other Achaian young men came bringing the presents.
They placed them in the midst of the meeting, and Lord Agamemnon

250 rose; Talthýbios then, who resembled a god in his speaking,
holding a boar in his hands, stood there by the shepherd of people.
Atreus' son in his hands then seizing and drawing his knife from
where it was always hanging beside the great sheath of his sword-blade
cut off the offering hairs from the boar, then lifted his hands up

255 praying to Zeus, and the Argives all sat there in their places
silently, as it was right, to the king all listening closely.
Thus in his prayer he uttered as he looked up to broad heaven:
"Zeus be witness the first—of the gods, he is highest and greatest—
also the earth and the sun, the Erínyës too that beneath earth

260 give the requital to men, to whoever has sworn to a false oath,
never have I laid hand on the maiden, the daughter of Bríseus,
neither desiring her, thinking of bed, nor for anything other;
rather, unsought and untouched she ever remained in my cabin.
Should any part of this oath be false, may the gods give many

265 woes to me, such as they give to whoever offends them in swearing."
        Thus, and the throat of the boar he cut with the pitiless bronze blade.
Whirling the boar, Talthýbios hurled it into the great broad
gulf of the silvery sea for the fishes to eat; but Achilles,
meanwhile, stood up and spoke to the Argives, lovers of combat:

270 "Father Zeus, mighty delusions indeed you send upon people;

otherwise, never so sorely the scion of Atreus would have
stirred up the heart in my breast, nor stubbornly taken away that
maiden against my will and intention; but certainly Zeus was
minded that death be visited here on many Achaians.

275　Now let us go to our dinner, that we may engage in the battle."
　　　So to the people he spoke, then quickly dismissed the assembly.
Most of the men dispersed, each one went away to his galley;
meanwhile the great-souled Mýrmidons busied themselves with the presents—
carrying them they went to the galley of godlike Achilles.

280　They put them in the cabins, and there they seated the women;
driving the horses away to the herd went noble attendants.
　　　Brìseus' daughter, in form like Áphrodítè the golden,
when she saw, mutilated with sharp bronze, noble Patróklos,
throwing herself upon him, cried piercingly as with her hands she

285　tore at her breasts and her delicate neck and her beautiful visage.
So as she wailed was the woman resembling the goddesses saying:
"Noble Patróklos, the dearest of men to my miserable spirit,
you were alive as I left you when I went out of the cabin;
now I discover you dead as I come back, marshal of people;

290　so is it always for me that affliction follows affliction.
So that husband to whom my father and reverend mother
gave me I saw mutilated in front of the city with sharp bronze,
then all three of the brothers that my own mother had brought forth,
dear to my heart, those all encountered the day of destruction.

295　Not even then would you let me weep when rapid Achilles
killed my husband and ransacked the city of godlike Mynes,
not even mourn, but declared you would make me the lawful wife of
godlike Achilles and take me away in the galleys to Phthía,
then with the Mýrmidons you would arrange us a feast for the marriage.

300　So without cease I wail for you dead who were always so gentle."
　　　So she spoke as she wailed, and the women as well were lamenting,
thinking indeed of Patróklos, but each also of her own woes.
Then the Achaians' elders together surrounded Achilles,
begging that he eat dinner; but raising a groan, he refused them:

305　"Now I beg you, if any of my dear comrades will heed me,
do not sooner exhort me to sate my heart by partaking
either of food or of drink, since terrible grief is upon me—
no, till the sun goes down I will stay as I am and be steadfast."
　　　So he spoke, and the rest of the kings he sent from the cabin;

310　Atreus' sons both stayed there, and noble Odysseus, and Nestor,

also Idómeneus and the old driver of chariots, Phoinix,
trying to cheer him as he grieved steadily; but in his heart no
cheer would he feel till he entered the jaws of the bloody encounter.
Then as he thought of his friend he fervently sighed and addressed him:
315 "There was a time when you, ill-fated one, dearest of comrades,
here in the cabin, yourself set out for me savory dinner
quickly and dexterously, any time the Achaians were rushing,
bringing the dolorous war on the Trojans, tamers of horses.
Now do you lie here thus mutilated; the spirit in me is
320 utterly starving of food and of drink, though they are at hand, through
yearning for you, since no other thing any worse could I suffer,
no, not even if I found out that my father had perished,
who now doubtless in Phthia a soft tear sheds from his eyelids,
missing a son like me—in a country of alien people
325 I for the sake of detestable Helen am battling the Trojans;
neither if it were the much-loved son who in Skyros is being
reared for me—should godlike Neoptólemos still be alive now—
for it is true that the heart in my breast had earlier hoped that
I would alone be perishing far from horse-nourishing Argos
330 here in the country of Troy, while you would be going to Phthia,
so you would take my child in your swift black galley away from
Skyros with you; then you would be showing him everything that
I am possessed of, the slaves and the spacious and high roofed palace,
since I imagine that either by now has Peleus entirely
335 perished, or else, though perhaps yet barely alive, he is sorely
troubled with odious age and is always expecting a painful
message about me, awaiting the time he hears I have perished."
     So he spoke as he wailed, and the old men too were lamenting,
having in mind each one what he in his halls had forsaken.
340 So as they mourned him, the scion of Kronos observed them and pitied;
quickly he spoke to Athena, and these winged words he addressed her:
"So, my child, that fighter of yours you have wholly abandoned.
Now no more do you have any care in your heart for Achilles?
There is he sitting in front of his ships with the horns uplifted;
345 he is lamenting his much-loved comrade; the others indeed have
left him to go to their dinner, but he stays fasting and unfed.
But now go to him—nectar and pleasant ambrosia do you
let drip into his breast, so that hunger may not come upon him."
     So he spoke, and Athena he roused, who already was eager;
350 then in the form of a long-winged shrill-voiced falcon she leapt down

348

out of the sky and along through the air. Meanwhile the Achaians
straightway armed themselves in the camp. Then into Achilles
she dripped nectar and pleasant ambrosia, into his bosom,
so that upon his limbs there would come no burdensome hunger;

355   she herself went to the strong-built house of her powerful father.
Meanwhile, out of the swift-faring ships the Achaians were pouring.
As when aflutter from Zeus fall snowflakes, thick and incessant,
chilled by the thunderous blast of the north wind, born in the bright sky,
so then thick and incessant the helmets, aglitter and brilliant,

360   out of the galleys were borne, and the shields made massive with bosses,
also the breastplates, riveted firm, and the spears made of ash wood.
Up to the sky the gleam went, and the earth was all laughing about them
under the glitter of bronze, and from under the feet of the men rose
thunder; and there in their midst donned armor the noble Achilles.

365   Clattering came from his teeth as he gnashed them; both of his eyes were
flashing as bright as a fiery thunderbolt; into his spirit
entered unbearable grief; thus he in his rage at the Trojans
put on the gifts of the god that Hephaistos had labored to make him.
First, strong greaves on the calves of his legs he carefully fastened,

370   fine ones skillfully fitted with silver-wrought ankle-protectors;
second in order, around his chest he put on the breastplate.
Over his shoulders he slung on the sword, all studded with silver,
fashioned of bronze, then also the great shield, massive and heavy,
he grasped; faraway shone its gleam like that from a full moon.

375   As at a time when over the sea is appearing to sailors
light of a fire, bright-blazing—it burns far up in the mountains
high in a desolate steading; against their will are the stormwinds
bearing them over the fish-thronged seaway and far from their loved ones—
so did the gleam rise up to the sky from the shield of Achilles,

380   beautiful, skillfully wrought; and his massive helmet he lifted,
putting it onto his head; then bright as a star did the helmet
shine forth, crested with horsehair; around it nodded the golden
plumes that had been set thickly along the whole crest by Hephaistos.
Noble Achilles tested himself in his armor, to find out

385   whether it fitted and whether his glorious limbs moved freely;
then it became like wings, uplifting the shepherd of people.
Out of the spear-case then he drew the great spear of his father,
heavy and huge and compact, which none of the other Achaians
ever could wield, but Achilles alone was skillful to wield it—

390   it was of Pélian ash, and to his dear father had Cheiron

brought it from Pélion's summit to use for the slaughter of heroes.
Then both Álkimos and Autómedon busied themselves with
yoking the horses, about them putting the beautiful breast-straps,
thrusting the snaffle-bits into their jaws, and the reins they drew right
395 back to the strong-joined chariot-box; and the glittering whip-rod,
fitted so well to his hand, Autómedon grasped, and he leapt up
onto the chariot; after him stepped up the armored Achilles,
brilliantly shining in armor as bright as the radiant High Lord;
terribly, loudly he called to the horses of his dear father:
400 "Xanthos and Balios, far-famed children of noble Podárgè,
now in another way think to deliver the charioteer back
safe to the Dánaäns' host, once we have been sated with battle;
do not forsake him to lie there dead, as you did to Patróklos."
     Speaking from under the harness addressed him the glittering-hoofed horse
405 Xanthos, suddenly bowing his head so that all of his mane was
streaming away to the ground by the yoke and from under the yoke-pad;
he had been given a voice by the goddess white-armed Hera:
"We will indeed for the time yet save you, mighty Achilles;
nevertheless near you is the day of destruction, and we will
410 not be the cause, but a great god rather, and Fate almighty,
since it was not through slackness of ours, through careless behavior,
then, that the Trojans stripped from Patróklos' shoulders the armor;
rather, the best of the gods, whom Leto of beautiful hair bore,
there in the foremost killed him and granted the glory to Hektor.
415 But as for us, we would both run fast as the breath of the west wind,
which they say is the swiftest of all winds; as for yourself, your
fate is to be brought down by a god and a powerful fighter."
     Once he had said these words, the Erínyës stopped him from speaking.
Mightily vexed, thus spoke to him then swift-footed Achilles:
420 "Xanthos, why do you prophesy death for me? You do not need to.
I of myself know well that my destiny is to be killed here,
far from my much-loved father and mother, and yet I will not leave
off before driving the Trojans to get their fill of the warfare."
     Thus; with the foremost, yelling, he drove his single-hoofed horses.

BOOK 20

So the Achaians beside the curved galleys were arming themselves for
battle around you, Peleus' son insatiate of combat;
likewise, opposite them on the swell of the plain, were the Trojans.
Then from the peak of Olympos of many ravines Zeus ordered
5 Themis to summon the gods to assembly, and everywhere she
hastened about, and to come to the palace of Zeus she enjoined them.
There was no river who did not come but the river of Ocean,
nor anyone of the nymphs who dwell in beautiful copses,
nor those dwelling in sources of rivers or grass-clad meadows.
10 When they arrived at the house of the great cloud-gathering god Zeus,
they sat down in the colonnades, polished and smooth, that Hephaistos
had for his father erected with masterful craft and adroitness.
    Thus in the palace of Zeus they gathered; the shaker of earth did
not fail heeding the goddess, but came from the sea-brine to join them;
15 there in the midst he sat, and of Zeus he asked his intention:
"Why again, Thunderbolt-lord, do you summon the gods to assembly?
Are you pondering something about the Achaians and Trojans—
since now closely indeed their battle and combat is blazing?"
    Answering him in return spoke forth the cloud-gathering god Zeus:
20 "Shaker of Earth, you know the intent I have in my mind for
which I gathered you: though they perish I care for the armies.
Nevertheless in a fold of Olympos I will myself stay
seated, and watching from here I will please my heart, but the others,
all of you, go; then, coming among the Achaians and Trojans,
25 furnish assistance to both sides there, as the mind of each wishes.
For if Achilles is left by himself to contend with the Trojans,
no time at all will they hold off Peleus' swift-footed scion.
Even before this, they would be trembling in fear if they saw him;
now, when his heart so dreadfully rages because of his comrade,
30 I fear he will destroy their rampart beyond what is fated."

So said the scion of Kronos and roused up war unabated.
Then did the gods start out to the battle, divided in counsel—
Hera to where all the galleys were gathered, and Pallas Athena,
earth-upholding Poseidon as well, and the powerful runner
35　Hermes, the god who excels them all for ingenious spirit;
also Hephaistos accompanied them, in his power exulting,
limping along, but the thin legs under him rapidly moving.
Ares of glittering helmet the Trojans approached, and with him went
Phoibos of unshorn tresses and Artemis shooter of arrows,
40　Leto and Xanthos and Áphrodítè the lover of laughter.
　　Just so long as the gods were apart from the men who were mortal,
then the Achaians were greatly triumphant because of Achilles
showing himself—he had long held off from the dolorous combat;
but on the limbs of the Trojans, on each man, terrible trembling
45　came as they looked in fear upon Peleus' swift-footed scion
glittering bright in his armor, the peer of man-slaughtering Ares.
When the Olympian gods came into the melee of fighters,
Conflict the powerful rouser of hosts leapt up, and Athena
shouted—at times by the trench they had dug outside of the rampart;
50　sometimes too she shouted aloud on the thundering seashore.
There like a black windstorm on the other side Ares was shouting,
shrilly exhorting the Trojans from high on top of the city,
then as he ran by the Símoeis' shore toward Kállikolónè.
　　Thus did the fortunate gods rouse both of the armies to join in
55　battle, among them causing the hateful conflict to break out;
loudly and fearfully thundered the father of gods and of mankind
high up above, while down underneath them Poseidon was making
quake the immeasurable earth and the steep high peaks of the mountains.
Every foothill of Ida of numerous fountains was shaken;
60　so were the summits, the city of Troy, and the ships of the Achaians.
Down in the depths Aïdóneus, lord of the shades, felt fear and
leapt from his throne—he shouted aloud in his fear that above him
great earth-shaking Poseidon would make earth shatter asunder,
so that to mortals and to the immortals would plainly appear his
65　dreadful and moldering house, which even the gods find loathsome.
Such was the clamor that rose as the gods engaged in the conflict,
since now there in the battle opposing the lordly Poseidon
Phoibos Apollo was standing and holding his feather-winged arrows;
bright-eyed Athena the goddess against Enyálios stood there,
70　while against Hera was standing the clamorous huntress with gold darts,

Artemis, shooter of arrows, the great far-shooter's own sister,
while against Leto was standing the powerful messenger Hermes;
there stood opposing Hephaistos the great deep-eddying river
called Xanthos by the gods, and by men on earth the Skamánder.

75　So against gods were the gods all going, and meanwhile Achilles
wanted to enter the throng and especially fight against Hektor,
Priam's son, with whose blood his heart was especially bidding
him that he satiate Ares, the warrior wielding a hide-shield.
But then Apollo the rouser of hosts urged noble Aineías

80　straight against Peleus' son, and he put great power within him.
Making his voice like that of Lykáon, the offspring of Priam,
like him as well in his form, spoke forth Zeus' scion Apollo:
"Noble Aineías, the counselor-lord of the Trojans, I wonder
where are the threats which, drinking, you vowed to the kings of the Trojans,

85　promising man-to-man fight against Peleus' scion Achilles?"
　　Then in return made answer Aineías, and thus he addressed him:
"Priam's son, why thus do you urge me, if I am not minded
now to engage in battle with Peleus' high-hearted scion?
Not for the first time now will I face swift-footed Achilles,

90　taking a stand; with his spear he once already from Ida
drove me—that was the time he had come there after our cattle,
sacking as well Lyrnéssos and Pédasos; then it was Zeus who
saved me, rousing the strength inside me and making my knees quick.
Under the hands of Achilles I would have been killed, and Athena's—

95　she was going before him and giving him aid, and she bade that
he with a bronze sword slaughter the Léleges there, and the Trojans.
So not possible is it that any man battle Achilles,
since at his side there is always a god who wards off his ruin.
Then moreover his spear flies straight to the target and never

100　ceases until it pierces a man's flesh. Yet if a god should
stretch out equal the issue of war, not easily would he
win over me, not though to be wholly of bronze he is boasting."
　　Speaking to him then answered the lord, Zeus' scion Apollo:
"Come now, hero, and you too pray to the gods who live always.

105　Men do say Aphrodítè the daughter of Zeus was the one who
bore you, and that man had an inferior goddess as mother—
yours is of Zeus, but of his the Old Man of the Sea is the father.
Then do you bear straight onward the obstinate bronze, and do not let
him turn you from the mark by words of derision and menace."

110　So he spoke and inspired great strength in the shepherd of people;

he strode forth through the foremost, in bright bronze armor accoutered.
Not unaware of the son of Anchíses was white-armed Hera
as against Peleus' son he went through the throng of the fighters.
Calling together the gods, she spoke these words and addressed them:
115 "Now take counsel between you, Poseidon and Pallas Athena,
deep inside of your minds, of the way these matters will happen.
Here has advanced Aineías, in bright bronze armor accoutered,
out against Peleus' son—he was sent by Phoibos Apollo.
But come, let us immediately now turn him away from
120 there to go back, or let one of us then stand close to Achilles
also and give great strength to him too—in his heart let him not lack
anything, so that he knows that among the immortals the noblest
love him, and that those gods are as worthless as wind who before now
warded away from the Trojans the battle and violent combat.
125 We have all come down here from Olympos intending to join this
battle, in order that he should suffer no harm at the Trojans'
hands this day; later on he will suffer whatever was spun for
him with her thread by Fate on the day he was born to his mother.
But if Achilles does not hear this from the voice of the gods, he
130 surely will take fright when against him in the battle a god is
coming, for harsh to encounter are gods who appear in their own shape."
    Speaking to her then answered the great earth-shaker Poseidon:
"Hera, do not be angry beyond all reason—you need not.
Certainly I would not wish that the gods be driven to conflict,
135 our side fighting the others, for we are much stronger than they are.
Let us instead then, going away from the road to a lookout
place, sit down there together; the men will take care of the warfare.
But should Ares engage in the battle, or Phoibos Apollo,
or if Achilles they hold in check, not letting him battle,
140 quickly from us also against them will the struggle of combat
then be aroused; very soon I think they, parting from us, will
go to Olympos again, where the rest of the gods are assembled,
once they are vanquished under our hands by mighty compulsion."
    So having spoken the god of the dark hair guided them onward,
145 coming to godlike Herakles' heaped-up bastion, the lofty
rampart erected for him by the Trojans and Pallas Athena,
so that he might take flight and escape from the deep-sea monster
when to the plain it started him running, away from the seashore.
Straightway Poseidon as well as the rest of the gods sat down there,
150 then with a dense impervious cloud they covered their shoulders;

those on the other side sat on the brow of fair Kállikolónè,
glorious Phoibos, around you and Ares the sacker of cities.
    So were the gods then sitting on opposite sides and devising
counsels, and nevertheless from beginning the dolorous warfare
155 both sides shrank, even though Zeus sitting aloft had enjoined it.
That whole plain was filled with the fighters, aflame with the bronze of
men and of horses; beneath their feet as they charged to collision
shuddered and thundered the earth. Two men, far best of the fighters,
met in the middle between the two hosts, both eager for battle,
160 Lord Aineías the son of Anchíses and noble Achilles.
Uttering threats, Aineías the first stalked out to the middle,
tossing his head with its ponderous helmet; his furious shield he
held in front of his chest, and his bronze-tipped spear he was shaking.
Peleus' son on the other side rushed against him like a lion
165 ravening, one which hunters are eagerly trying to slaughter,
all the community gathered together; at first he is heedless,
going along, but as one of the young men swift in the fight strikes
him with a spear, he crouches, his jaws gape, over his teeth foam
flows out, deep in his heart his valorous spirit is groaning,
170 whipping his tail over both of his sides he lashes his ribs and
buttocks and fiercely arouses himself to do battle; with eyes bright
glaring he drives in his rage straight forward, whether to slaughter
one of the men or himself to be killed at the start of the onslaught;
so in Achilles the rage and the valorous spirit were rousing
175 him to go out and engage in fight with greathearted Aineías.
When in coming together the men were close to each other,
first of the two spoke forth swift-footed and noble Achilles:
"Why have you come so far from the throng, Aineías, to stand and
face me? Is it indeed that your spirit commands you to fight me,
180 hoping to lord it among those Trojans, tamers of horses,
over the power of Priam? But should you happen to kill me,
never for that will Priam deliver the prize into your hands,
seeing that he has sons and is sound, not at all light-minded.
Or an estate do the Trojans reserve for you finer than others,
185 lovely in vineyard, orchard, and plowland, so you can settle,
should you kill me? But this, I expect, will be hard to accomplish.
I with my spear, I say, on another day set you to running.
Or do you have no mind of when you were alone and I chased you
down from the highlands of Ida, away from the cattle, on swift feet
190 rapidly running? And then as you fled, not once did you turn back.

Fleeing from there you went to Lyrnéssos, the city I ransacked,
making assault with the aid of Athena and Zeus the great father.
Then their women I robbed of the day of their freedom and led them
captive; but you yourself did Zeus and the other gods rescue.

195 Yet not now, I suppose, will they save you, as in your heart you
nourish the thought; I urge you instead to retreat and to go back
into the multitude, not keep standing to face me, before you
suffer some harm—for a done deed even a fool recognizes."
    Then in return made answer Aineías, and thus he addressed him:

200 "Peleus' scion, do not with words, as if I were a child, be
hoping to make me frightened, for I know clearly myself how
withering insults are uttered, and all injurious speeches.
Each of us knows of the birth of the other and knows of our parents,
having from old times heard those stories from men who are mortal;

205 yet with your eyes you never have seen mine, neither have I yours.
You they say were to faultless Peleus born as his offspring,
while your mother was Thetis, a fair-tressed queen of the sea-brine;
then as for me, I boast that as son of great-souled Anchíses
I was brought forth, and as well that my mother is Áphrodítè.

210 One pair now or the other of these will lament for a dear son
this very day, since not, I imagine, with babyish speeches
shall be parted the two of us now to go back from the battle.
Yet if you wish, hear this from me too, so that you may know well
what my lineage is—and the people who know it are many:

215 Dárdanos first was sired by the great cloud-gathering god Zeus;
he Dardánia founded, for not yet Ilion's sacred
town in the plain was settled to be a great city for mortals—
still they dwelt in the foothills of Ida of numerous fountains.
Dárdanos sired King Érichthónios then as successor,

220 him in fact who became, among men who are mortal, the richest—
his were the horses that grazed on the marshland, a full three thousand,
all of them females, mares that in fresh young foals were exulting;
then was the north wind enamored of them as they foraged the meadow;
making himself like a dark-maned stallion, he coupled with them there;

225 they of the north wind having conceived brought forth twelve fillies.
These while playfully bounding along on the grain-giving plowland
ever would run on the topmost ears of the grain and not break them,
then while playfully bounding along the broad back of the deep sea
ever would run on the topmost surf of the silvery sea-brine.

230 Érichthónios then sired Tros to be lord of the Trojans;

356

then by Tros in his turn three faultess children were fathered,
Ilos the first and Assárakos and Ganymédes the godlike,
he who was born the most beautiful child among men who are mortal,
so the gods snatched him and took him to be wine-pourer to great Zeus,
235   only because of his beauty, to dwell there among the immortals.
Then was a faultless son, Laómedon, fathered by Ilos;
next in turn Laómedon fathered Tithónos and Priam,
Lampos and Klýtios and Hiketáon, offshoot of Ares,
while to Assárakos Kápys was born; his child was Anchíses;
240   me Anchíses begot, while Priam begot noble Hektor.
This is the lineage, this is the blood, I boast to be sprung from.
Yet it is Zeus who in men augments and diminishes prowess,
just as he wishes to do, for of all gods he is the strongest.
But come now, let us talk no longer of this like children,
245   standing around as we are in the midst of a violent combat,
since in fact for us both there are withering insults to utter,
many—not even a ship of a hundred benches would bear them.
Pliant and glib is the tongue men have, and the speeches in it are
many and various—far do the words range hither and thither;
250   such as the word you speak is the word which you will be hearing.
But what need have the two of us now of such quarrels and conflicts,
facing each other with struggles of words, in the manner of women,
who in the furious wrath of a conflict, spirit-devouring,
go in the road, to the middle, and face each other with many
255   insults, true and untrue—this too is their anger demanding.
Not with words will you turn my ardor away from its valor
ever, until with the bronze man-to-man we have battled; but come now,
quickly with bronze-tipped spears let us each make proof of the other."
      Thus, and he drove with his powerful spear at the daunting and dreadful
260   shield, so that loudly about the sharp point of the spear the shield sounded.
Peleus' son with his ponderous hand held out from himself his
shield in terror, because he thought the long-shadowing spear-shaft
which greathearted Aineías had thrown would easily pierce it,
fool that he was, for he did not know in his heart and his spirit
265   that not easy at all are the glorious gifts of the gods for
men who are mortal to vanquish, nor easy at yielding before them.
Nor at that time did the powerful spear of war-minded Aineías
break through the shield, since it was held off by the gold, the god's present;
rather it went through two of the layers, but still there were three left,
270   since five layers the clubfooted god had welded upon it,

357

two of them fashioned of bronze, and of tin were the two on the inside;
one was a layer of gold by which was stopped the ash spear-shaft.
    After him then did Achilles let fly a long-shadowing spear-shaft
so that it struck on the circular shield of the noble Aineías
275 under the outermost rim, where the bronze ran thinnest upon it;
thinnest as well was the backing of oxhide. The Pélian ash-wood
spear rushed straight on through it, and under the blow the shield rang out.
Downward Aineías crouched, and his shield he held from his body,
frightened; above him the spear passed over his back and was planted
280 there in the earth in its rage, but it broke through two of the circles
of the man-sheltering shield; he, having evaded the long spear,
stood up—and over his eyes was poured down measureless anguish—
terrified that so near him was planted the spear. But Achilles,
drawing his sharp sword out of its sheath, leapt fiercely upon him,
285 shouting a terrible shout; in his hand Aineías at once took
up a huge stone—a great feat—which no two mortals could carry,
such as are men nowadays, but alone did he easily wield it.
Then would Aineías have struck his foe with the stone on the helmet
or on the shield that had warded from him his wretched destruction,
290 Peleus' son nearby with his sword would have taken his life-breath,
had not keenly observed it the great earth-shaker Poseidon.
Straightway among the immortals he spoke this word and addressed them:
"Well then! Anguish is heavy in me for greathearted Aineías,
who soon, vanquished by Peleus' son, will be going to Hades'
295 palace, because he heeded the words of far-shooting Apollo,
fool, nor at all will the god keep him from a wretched destruction.
Why then is this quite innocent man now suffering sorrows
vainly because of the woes of another, although he is always
giving agreeable gifts to the gods who hold the broad heaven?
300 Come then, let us ourselves now lead him away from the slaughter,
lest the great scion of Kronos be angry, if ever Achilles
managed to kill him, because his destiny is to escape him,
so that not without seed, disappearing, will perish the stock of
Dárdanos, whom above all of his offspring Kronos' son cherished,
305 all of his sons brought forth by the women he loved who were mortal,
since now Kronos' son holds in hatred the race of King Priam;
now indeed will the might of Aineías be lord of the Trojans,
so will the sons of his sons, all those to be born in the future."
    Speaking to him then answered the ox-eyed queen, Lady Hera:
310 "Shaker of Earth, then you take counsel yourself in your own mind

now of Aineías, if you are to save him or rather to leave him,
brave as he is, to be vanquished by Peleus' scion Achilles.
For it is true that the two of us, Pallas Athena and I, have
vowed in the numerous oaths we swore among all the immortals
315 never will we ward off from the Trojans the day of affliction,
no, not even when Troy is entirely consumed in the blazing
fire and the warlike sons of Achaians are burning the city."
       But then, soon as Poseidon the great earth-shaker had heard this,
he set forth through the battle, among the confusion of spear-thrusts,
320 coming to where Aineías was standing, and famous Achilles.
Straightway then he poured a thick mist down over the eyes of
Peleus' scion Achilles; the ash-wood spear with the bronze point
he drew out of the shield of the great-souled noble Aineías;
this he set on the ground in front of the feet of Achilles;
325 high from the ground he lifted Aineías and mightily hurled him.
Many the ranks of the heroes and many the horses that soaring
out of the hand of the god Aineías was sent overleaping,
then at the outermost edge of the turbulent battle he landed,
where the Kaukónian allies were arming themselves for the combat.
330 Close to his side then approached him the great earth-shaker Poseidon,
raising his voice he spoke, and in these winged words he addressed him:
"Which of the gods, Aineías, exhorts you with such a deluded
mind to engage in battle with Peleus' high-hearted scion,
who is both stronger than you are and more loved by the immortals?
335 Do you instead draw back, should ever you meet him in battle,
lest you, even beyond fate, enter the palace of Hades.
But then, soon as Achilles has met his death and his doomsday,
then indeed you may take good courage to fight with the foremost,
since no other Achaian will ever be able to kill you."
340   So having spoken he left him there, once he had revealed all.
Straightway then from the eyes of Achilles he scattered the wondrous
thick mist away, then he with his eyes stared widely about him;
deeply disturbed, he spoke to his own magnanimous spirit:
"Well then! Immense is the marvel that I with my eyes am beholding!
345 Here on the ground this spear of mine lies, yet nowhere do I now
see that fighter at whom I had hurled it, raging to kill him.
Surely Aineías as well to the deathless gods is belovèd,
even if I thought then that he vainly and idly was boasting.
Let him begone; no more to make trial of me will the spirit
350 be in his breast—even now to escape from his death he is happy.

359

But come, after exhorting the Dánaäns, lovers of battle,
I will myself go facing the rest of the Trojans and test them."
     Thus, and he leapt back into the ranks; each man he exhorted:
"Now no more stand far from the Trojans, noble Achaians,
355 but come, man against man go out and be avid to fight them.
Difficult is it for me, indeed, although I am mighty,
dealing with such great numbers of men and with all of them battling;
neither could Ares, a deathless god though he is, nor Athena,
deal with the jaws of a fight so fierce and accomplish the labor;
360 yet so much as with hands and with feet I can do, and as well with
strength, I am sure I will not slack off, not even a little;
no, I will go straight on through the enemy ranks, and I think no
Trojan will feel any gladness, should one come close to my spear-point."
     He spoke, rousing them up; to the Trojans illustrious Hektor
365 called out loudly and said he would go out facing Achilles:
"High-souled Trojans, do not be frightened of Peleus' scion.
I would myself with words fight even against the immortals;
but with a spear it is harder, for they are much stronger than we are.
Nor will Achilles himself bring all that he says to fulfillment—
370 part of it he will fulfill, and a part he will leave half-finished.
Now against him I will go, even though his hands are like wildfire,
though his hands are like wildfire, his passion like iron that blazes."
     So he spoke to arouse them; the Trojans lifted their spears up
facing the foe; their turbulent fury was joined, and a shout rose.
375 Thus then, standing by Hektor, did Phoibos Apollo address him:
"Hektor, do not go forth any longer to challenge Achilles;
rather await him back in the multitude, out of the war-din,
lest with a spear he hit you or strike near at hand with a sword-thrust."
     He spoke; Hektor again went back in the throng of the fighters,
380 frightened, as soon as he heard that voice of the god who was speaking.
Clothing his spirit in valor, Achilles leapt on the Trojans
shouting a terrible shout, and Iphítion first he slaughtered,
who was Otrýnteus' powerful son and the leader of many,
born by a Naiad nymph to Otrýnteus, sacker of cities,
385 there beneath snow-clad Tmolos in Hydè's fertile dominion.
Square on his head as he eagerly charged did noble Achilles
strike with his spear, and the head entirely was cloven asunder.
Falling he crashed to the ground; thus noble Achilles exulted:
"Low are you lying, Otrýnteus' son, most fearsome of all men;
390 here in this country you meet your death, though beside the Gygaían

Lake did you have your birth, where is found the estate of your fathers,
there by the fish-thronged Hyllos and eddying streams of the Hermos."
    Boasting he spoke, but the eyes of the other were shrouded in darkness.
Him with their wheels the Achaians' chariots tore into pieces
395 there at the front of the battle; above him he struck Anténor's
scion Demóleon, one who excelled in warding off combat,
right at the temple, upon his helmet with bronze cheek-pieces.
Nor was the spear-point stopped by the helmet of bronze, but it sped right
through it and utterly shattered the bone, so that all of the brain was
400 spattered about inside—so furiously he subdued him.
Then as Hippódamas leapt from his chariot onto the ground and
started to flee before him, he struck at his back with a spear-thrust.
Gasping his life-breath out, he bellowed, the way that a bull is
bellowing when he is dragged for Poseidon, Hélikè's patron—
405 young men drag him; by them is the great earth-shaker delighted.
So as he bellowed his valorous spirit abandoned the bone-frame.
Then with his spear he went in pursuit of godlike Polydóros,
offspring of Priam; his father would not let him go to battle,
seeing that he was the youngest in birth among all of his children—
410 he was the dearest to him, and surpassed them all on his swift feet;
then in his childish folly, displaying his prowess in running,
he rushed out through the foremost until he lost his dear life-breath.
Him now as he ran past swift-footed and noble Achilles
struck with a spear-cast square on the back, where the war-belt's golden
415 buckles were clasped and the plates of the corselet met, overlapping;
straight on through penetrated the point of the spear, by the navel;
groaning he fell to his knees, and a dark cloud shrouded him over;
slumping aside to the ground, with his hands he clutched at his bowels.
    Now when Hektor observed that a brother of his, Polydóros,
420 holding in hand his bowels and slumping aside on the earth there,
over his eyes was a thick mist poured down, nor could he longer
bear to be ranging apart, but he went face-to-face at Achilles
wielding a sharp spear bright as a wildfire; then as Achilles
saw him, forward he bounded and spoke out boasting in these words:
425 "Here close by is the man who above all wounded my spirit,
he who slaughtered the comrade I honored; but not very long yet
we on the battle embankments will cower away from each other."
Thus, then looking from lowering brows he addressed noble Hektor:
"Come up closer, that sooner you enter the bonds of destruction."
430   Then not terrified spoke to him Hektor of glittering helmet:

"Peleus' scion, do not with your words, as if I were a child, be
hoping to make me frightened, for I know clearly myself how
withering insults are uttered, and all injurious speeches.
I know well you are noble and I far weaker than you are.

435 Nevertheless, on the knees of the gods these matters are resting,
whether, although I am weaker, I rob you of life with a spear-thrust,
since before now my weapon as well has been found sharp-pointed."
      So he spoke, and the spear he brandished and threw, and Athena
turned it away with her breath from the glorious hero Achilles,

440 blowing at it very lightly, and back it returned to the noble
Hektor, and there it fell in front of his feet; but Achilles
leapt forth, fervently rushing against him and raging to kill him,
shouting a terrible shout, but away he was snatched by Apollo,
easily, just as a god can, and shrouded about by a great mist.

445 Three times then rushed forth swift-footed and noble Achilles
wielding his sharp bronze spear; three times he struck at the thick mist.
But then, when like a god he had rushed at the man for the fourth time,
terribly he cried out, and in these winged words he addressed him:
"Now you again, you hound, have escaped death, though very near you

450 evil had come; now again you were saved by Phoibos Apollo,
whom you must supplicate as you enter the din of the spear-fight.
Later on I will eliminate you, whenever I meet you,
should there be for me also a god who serves as a helpmate;
now I will go in pursuit of the others, whomever I come to."

455   He spoke and then struck Drýops square on the neck with a spear-thrust;
there in front of his feet he fell to the ground, and he left him;
hitting Demoúchos, Philétor's son stout-bodied and valiant,
square on the knee with his spear, he checked his attack and, at once then
striking at him with his great bronze sword, robbed him of his life-breath.

460 Straightway at Dárdanos and Laógonos, scions of Bias,
charging ahead, he thrust them both from their chariot groundward;
one he struck with a spear-cast and one with a sword at close quarters.
Then Tros, son of Alástor, who came to his knees to beseech him,
hoping that he might spare him and take him and let him go, living,

465 nor would he kill him, but show compassion for one of his own age—
fool that he was, not knowing that he would not be persuaded,
since not gentle of heart was the man, nor at all mild-minded,
rather exceedingly fierce—he grabbed with his hands at Achilles'
knees then, wishing to beg him; he struck with his sword in the liver;

470 outward the liver was driven; the dark blood spurted around it,

utterly drenching his tunic; his eyes were enshrouded in darkness,
as of his life he was robbed. By Moúlios standing, he struck him
square on the ear with his spear, and the bronze spear-point through the other
ear penetrated; and then at Echéklos the son of Agénor
475 driving, he struck him square on the head with his well-hilted sword-blade,
so that the whole blade smoked with the blood; down over his eyes came
seizing him blood red death and his own irresistible doomsday.
It was Deukálion next he struck—at the place where the elbow's
sinews are joined, there he with the bronze spear-point penetrated
480 right through his arm; he awaited his onset, the arm a mere burden,
seeing in front of him death; on his neck with the sword-blade the hero
struck, and the head with the helmet he hurled far away as the marrow
gushed up out of the spine, and he lay stretched out on the ground there.
Quickly he started to go for the faultless scion of Peires,
485 Rhigmos, a fighter who came from the deep-soiled Thracian dominions;
him in the waist he hit, and the bronze spear stuck in his belly;
he from the chariot fell; and his henchman Áreïthóös,
turning the horses around, he struck in the back with a sharp spear,
thrusting him out of the chariot there, and the horses were panicked.
490   As when rages the ravenous flame of a fire in the deep-carved
glens of a dry hot mountain and sets the deep timber to burning,
lashing it onward the wind whirls blazes in every direction,
so with a spear like a god he was rushing in every direction,
charging the men he slaughtered; the black earth streamed with their lifeblood.
495 As when a man yokes oxen, his big males broad in the forehead,
then on the strong-built floor they tread white barley to thresh it,
quickly it gets husked under the feet of the bellowing oxen,
so now beneath greathearted Achilles the single-hoofed horses
trampled alike dead bodies and shields; bespattered with blood were
500 all of the axle below and the rims that surrounded the car-box,
fouled by drops of the gore thrown up from the hooves of the horses
and from the rims of the wheels; and the scion of Peleus kept on
straining for glory; with gore his invincible hands were bespattered.

BOOK 21

Then, when the warriors came to the ford of the beautiful-flowing
river, the eddying Xanthos that deathless Zeus had begotten,
there did Achilles divide them, and some he chased to the plain that
led to the city, to where on the previous day the Achaians
5   had been fleeing in panic, when glorious Hektor was raging;
thither were Trojans streaming in flight—in front of them Hera
spread dense mist to impede their escape—while half of the troops were
crowded toward the deep-flowing and silvery-eddying river,
then with a huge din fell into it; the steep stream was resounding,
10 loudly around were the riverbanks ringing, and shouting the men were
swimming about one way or another and whirled in the eddies.
Just as before the onrush of a wildfire locusts arise and
swarm in flight to a river, and suddenly starting, the tireless
wildfire blazes as they go cowering into the water,
15 so in front of Achilles the thundering stream of the Xanthos,
eddying deep, filled full with the men and the horses commingled.
      There on the bank his spear did the hero descended of Zeus leave
leaning against tamarisks; like a god he leapt in the river,
brandishing only his sword; he devised evil deeds in his mind and
20 struck one after another, and miserable was the groan that
rose from the sword-slain fighters; the water was red with their lifeblood.
Just as in front of a monstrous dolphin the rest of the fishes
take flight, crowding the coves of a harbor of excellent moorage,
terrified, since he greedily eats up any he catches,
25 so now there in the stream of the terrible river the Trojans
cowered beneath the steep banks. When his hands grew weary of killing,
twelve of the youths he chose to be taken alive from the river
as a blood-price for the perished Patróklos, Menoítios' scion.
These men, bewildered with fear like fawns, he led from the water;
30 there he fastened their hands behind them with thongs made of leather,

those which they had been wearing about their pliable tunics,
and to his comrades gave them to lead to the hollow galleys.
Then he again leapt into the fray, still raging for slaughter.
      There he encountered a son of King Priam, Dárdanos' scion,
35   as he escaped from the river—Lykáon, whom he had himself once
captured and brought unwilling away from his father's orchard,
having approached by night. With a sharp bronze blade he was cutting
young shoots from a fig tree for the rails of a chariot-body;
then upon him came unforeseen evil, the noble Achilles,
40   who that time took him on a galley and sold him in well-built
Lemnos as slave; it was Jason's son who had given the payment;
thence had a guest-friend from Imbros, Eëtion, ransomed Lykáon—
great was the price he gave—and he sent him to noble Arísbè;
secretly fleeing from there he had come to the house of his fathers.
45   Having from Lemnos arrived, he delighted his heart for eleven
days right there with his friends; on the twelfth, however, a god cast
him again into the hands of Achilles, who now was about to
send him to Hades' dominion, as loath as he was to be going.
When swift-footed and noble Achilles perceived that the man was
50   naked, with neither a helmet or shield, nor a spear was he holding—
but to the ground he had thrown all those, for the sweat had fatigued him
as from the river he fled, and the knees were weary beneath him—
deeply disturbed, he spoke to his own magnanimous spirit:
"Well then! Immense is the marvel that I with my eyes am beholding!
55   Certainly even the great-souled Trojans that I have been killing
will again soon be arising from under the murk and the shadows,
like this man who has come here, escaping a pitiless doomsday,
though he was sold into sacred Lemnos: the silvery seaway's
water did not keep him, though against their will it holds many.
60   But come then, of the point of my spear he surely will now be
getting a taste, so that I in my mind may know and discover
whether from there too he will be coming, or whether the earth will
hold him, the giver of life which holds down even the mighty."
      So he thought as he waited; the other approached him, bewildered,
65   eagerly reaching for him at his knees; in his heart he was strongly
wishing to flee from a baneful death and the blackest of doomsdays.
High above him was the long spear lifted by noble Achilles,
eager to strike as he was; but the man ran under and stooped down,
clutching his knees; and the spear passed over his back and was planted
70   there in the earth as it raged to be glutted on flesh of a fighter.

Quickly with one of his hands he caught at his knees and beseeched him,
while with the other he held to the sharp spear, nor would he let go;
raising his voice he spoke, and in these winged words he addressed him:
"Now I implore you, Achilles, respect me and show me your mercy;
75   I in your sight, Zeus-loved, am a suppliant worthy of honor,
since it was at your table I first ate grain of Deméter
that day you in the well-planned orchard took me as captive,
then having led me away from my father and friends, into sacred
Lemnos you sold me as slave, and a hundred oxen I got you.
80   Now am I freed, having paid three times the amount; and the morning
now is the twelfth since I came back into Ilion city,
suffering much; now again has a ruinous destiny put me
into your hands, and I must be hateful to Zeus the great father,
since he has once more given you me: I was born to the briefest
85   life by my mother Laothoë, daughter of elderly Altes,
Altes who rules as the lord of the Léleges, lovers of battle;
steep-built Pédasos on the Satníoeis too he possesses.
His was the daughter that Priam espoused, with many another;
two were the sons she bore; now both of us you will have butchered.
90   One of us you brought down in the foremost ranks of the fighters,
that godlike Polydóros, when you with a sharp spear struck him;
now, right here, will the evil be coming to me, for I do not
think to escape your hands, as a god has driven me near them.
Something else I will tell you, and you put this in your mind now:
95   do not kill me, because I am not from the same womb as Hektor,
he who killed that comrade of yours most kindly and mighty."

So spoke then to Achilles the glorious offspring of Priam,
uttering supplicant words; but the voice he heard was not gentle:
"Childish fool, speak not to me now of a ransom, nor argue.
100   Always until my comrade Patróklos encountered his doomsday,
up to that time it pleased my mind to be sparing of Trojans—
many of them, in fact, I captured living and sold them.
Now there is nobody who will flee death, whomever a god may
happen to throw in my hands in front of great Ilion city,
105   even of all of the Trojans, especially sons of King Priam.
No, friend, you die also—and why in this way are you moaning?
Even Patróklos has perished, a man far better than you are.
Do you not see what a man I am, how handsome and mighty,
sprung of an excellent father, a goddess the mother who bore me?
110   Yet over me also hangs death, irresistible doomsday.

Either a dawn will arrive, or a shadowy dusk, or a noontime,
when some fighter from me also takes life in the battle,
whether he strikes with a spear or an arrow he shoots from a bowstring."
    So he spoke, and the knees and the heart of the other were loosened;
115 he let go of the spear and sank back on the ground with his two hands
outstretched; drawing his sharp sword out of its scabbard, Achilles
struck on the collarbone close to the neck, and the whole of the two-edged
sword plunged into the flesh; headlong on the ground he was lying
spread out; the black blood flowed from the wound, so drenching the earth there.
120 Seizing his foot, in the river Achilles threw him to be borne
off, then, boasting above him, in these winged words he addressed him:
"Now then, lie down there with the fishes; the blood from your wound will
they lick off, not caring at all for you; nor will your mother
moan as she lays you out on your bier; instead to the great broad
125 gulf of the seaway the eddying river Skamánder will bear you.
Then from beneath the dark ripple of billows will many a fish be
leaping, that it might feed on the rich white fat of Lykáon.
Perish you all, until we have arrived at the city of sacred
Ilion, you in flight, I behind you strewing destruction.
130 Nor will the river of silvery eddies and powerful currents
save you, in spite of the numerous bulls you offered as victims
and of the single-hoofed steeds you hurled alive into his eddies.
No: even thus by a terrible fate you will die, until all have
paid for the death of Patróklos and for the Achaians' destruction,
135 those whom you by the swift ships slaughtered the while I was absent."
    So he spoke, and the river was yet more vexed in his spirit,
pondering deep in his heart on the way he could halt from his labors
noble Achilles and ward off disaster and death from the Trojans.
Meanwhile Peleus' scion with his long-shadowing spear-shaft,
140 avid for slaughtering, leapt upon Ásteropaíos the son of
Pélegon, who by the Áxios, broad in his current, was gotten;
fair Periboía had born him, her sire Akessámenos' eldest
daughter, for it was with her the deep-eddying river had mingled.
Now upon him rushed Achilles, and he came out of the river,
145 standing with two spears facing him there; in his spirit the Xanthos
put strength, since he was angry because of the youths who had perished,
those whom Achilles had killed by the stream, not pitying any.
When in coming together the two were close to each other,
first spoke forth to the man swift-footed and noble Achilles:
150 "Who of men are you, from where, that you dare come out and oppose me?

Most unhappy are those whose children encounter my fury."
    Pélegon's glorious son thus spoke to him, giving an answer:
"Peleus' great-souled son, of my lineage why do you ask me?
I from Paiónia came here, a fertile and faraway country,
155 leading Paiónian men with their long spears; now the eleventh
morning is this I have seen since coming to Ilion city.
As to my lineage, it is from Áxios, broad in his current,
Áxios, who sends over the earth the most beautiful water—
he sired Pélegon, famed with the spear, who then, as they say, was
160 father to me; now let us do battle, renownèd Achilles!"
    So he spoke as he threatened; the Pélian spear made of ash wood
noble Achilles raised; but the warrior Ásteropaíos,
being in both hands strong, let fly two spears at the same time.
Square on the shield with one of the spears he struck, but it did not
165 break through the shield, since it was held off by the gold, the god's present,
while with the other he struck on the right forearm of Achilles,
grazing it; blood gushed out in a black cloud; over him passed that
spear and was fixed in the earth, still raging on flesh to be glutted.
Quickly Achilles in turn let fly with his missile of ash wood,
170 straight in flying, at Ásteropaía, desiring to kill him;
missing the man himself, he struck the high bank of the river;
half of its length in the bank he planted the ash-wood spear-shaft.
Peleus' son then, drawing his keen sword out of its thigh sheath,
avidly leapt upon him, and the other could not with his massive
175 hand pull out of the bank that ash-wood spear of Achilles.
Thrice he set it to shaking in eagerly trying to pull it;
thrice he gave up the effort; the fourth time, bending it back, he
wished in his spirit to break the ash spear-shaft of Aíakos' scion;
sooner Achilles approached and bereft him of life with a sword-thrust.
180 For in the belly he struck him, beside his navel, and all his
guts poured out on the ground, and his eyes were enshrouded in darkness
there as he gasped out life; then onto his midriff Achilles
leapt, and he stripped him of armor and spoke this word to him, vaunting:
"Lie thus—difficult is it to strive with the scions of Kronos'
185 powerful son, yes, even for one who is sprung from a river.
You told how in your birth you are sprung from a broad-flowing river;
I however can claim as the head of my lineage great Zeus.
Over the numerous Mýrmidons lorded the man who begot me,
Peleus, Aíakos' son, and of Zeus was Aíakos gotten.
190 So as Zeus mightier is than the rivers that flow to the sea-brine,

mightier too is the offspring of Zeus than a river's descendant.
For a great river is near you, if he can in any way help you,
but not possible is it to fight Zeus scion of Kronos;
never with him vies even the strong Achelóïos River,
195 neither indeed the enormous might of the deep-flowing Ocean,
though out of him flow all of the rivers and all of the seaway,
also from him spring all of the fountains and all of the deep wells;
nevertheless, he too is afraid of the lightning of great Zeus
and of his terrible thunder, when out of the heavens it crashes."
200   So he spoke, and he drew from the bank of the river the bronze spear;
him right there he abandoned, when he of his life had bereft him,
lying below in the sands, in a place dark water bedrenched him.
It was the eels and the fishes that busied themselves with his body,
tearing away and devouring the fat that surrounded his kidneys;
205 meanwhile Achilles against the Paiónians, chariot-masters,
went, who were scattering yet by the side of the eddying river,
since they had seen that best of their men in the violent combat
beaten by force at the hands and the sword of the scion of Peleus.
There he Thersílochos killed, Astýpylos also, and Mydon,
210 Mnésos and Thrásios also and Aínios and Opheléstes;
more Paiónians yet would rapid Achilles have slaughtered
had not angrily spoken to him the deep-eddying river,
calling to him in a voice like a man's from the depth of his eddies:
"You are outstanding, Achilles, in might, outstanding in doing
215 violent deeds, for the gods themselves take care of you always.
If then Kronos' son grants you to kill off all of the Trojans,
drive them out of me onto the plain, there wreaking your havoc,
since my delightful streams are in fact crammed full of dead bodies—
there is no way I can pour my waters along to the bright sea,
220 clogged as I am with the corpses as you keep ruthlessly killing.
But come now and leave off—awe grips me, lord of the people."
    Answering him in return spoke forth swift-footed Achilles:
"So shall it be, Zeus-nurtured Skamánder, the way you have ordered.
Yet I will not stop killing the arrogant Trojans until I
225 pen them up in the town and a man-to-man trial I make of
Hektor, to see whether he will subdue me or I will subdue him."
    These things when he had said, like a god he charged at the Trojans;
then spoke forth to Apollo the great deep-eddying river:
"Well now, god of the silvery bow, Zeus' child, you have not been
230 keeping the plans of the scion of Kronos, who earnestly bade you

stand at the side of the Trojans and guard them, until at the sunset
finally evening comes and the fertile plowlands are shadowed."
　　Thus, and Achilles renowned for his spear leapt into the middle,
springing away from the bank; but the god rushed surging upon him,
235　rousing the tumult of all of his currents and sweeping the many
corpses that lay in abundance below, that Achilles had slaughtered;
bellowing loud as a bull he cast these out of the river
onto the land, but the living he saved in his beautiful currents,
hiding them under the great wide depths of his eddying waters.
240　Dreadful surrounding Achilles arose the tumultuous billow,
so as the stream beat onto his shield it pounded him backward,
nor on his feet could he stand; but he grabbed with his hands at an elm tree,
well grown, shapely, and tall; but it fell uprooted and ripped off
all of the riverbank there; with its huge dense tangle of roots it
245　held back the beautiful currents and dammed up the river itself by
falling at full length across it; and he, as he leapt from the eddy,
started to fly on his nimble and swift feet over the flatland,
terrified; nor did the great god stop, but kept rushing upon him,
black in the surge of his wave, so that he might halt from his labor
250　noble Achilles and ward off hideous death from the Trojans.
Peleus' son rushed back from the river the length of a spear-cast,
speeding as fast as a great black eagle, a powerful hunter,
which among winged things is at the same time strongest and swiftest;
like that bird he was darting; upon his chest was the brazen
255　breastplate fearfully clashing, and swerving from under the onset
he ran fleeing; the god streamed after him, mightily roaring.
Just as a man irrigating conducts from a dark-water fountain
over the ground to his crops and his gardens a stream of the water—
holding a mattock in hand he throws dams out of the channel,
260　then as the stream flows onward the pebbles are all sent rolling
up from beneath, and it goes on gushing and rapidly streaming
down some slope of the land, outstripping the farmer who leads it—
always thus was the flood of the stream overtaking Achilles,
nimble of foot though he was, for the gods are stronger than mortals.
265　Every time swift-footed and noble Achilles attempted
taking a stand against it to discover if all the immortal
gods were intending to rout him—the gods who hold the broad heaven—
each time then would the powerful flood of the heaven-fed river
beat from above on his shoulders, and he in affliction of heart would
270　leap with his feet, high up; but the river was wearing his limbs out,

savagely streaming beneath him, from underfoot ripping the ground up.
Peleus' son spoke groaning as he looked up at the broad sky:
"Father Zeus, thus no god undertakes from the river to rescue
pitiful me; once saved, I would suffer whatever might happen.
275   None of the rest of the heavenly gods is so much blameworthy—
only my own dear mother, the one who beguiled me with false words
when she assured me that under the walls of the armor-clad Trojans
I was to be destroyed by the swift sharp darts of Apollo.
Would that Hektor had killed me, the best among those who were bred here!
280   Then would the slayer be noble, and noble the man he would slaughter.
Now instead it is doomed that a death most wretched should take me,
trapped in a powerful river, as when in the winter a swineherd
boy when trying to cross gets carried away by a torrent."
     So did he say; then quickly Poseidon and Pallas Athena
285   came nearby him and stood, and their forms they likened to mortals;
taking his hands in theirs, with their words they gave him assurance;
first then spoke out among them the great earth-shaker Poseidon:
"Peleus' son, do not so much tremble nor be at all frightened,
since such helpers are both of us gods who are standing beside you
290   with the approval of Zeus—myself and Pallas Athena,
since you have not been fated to be brought down by a river.
No, he will soon give over, and you yourself will perceive it.
Meanwhile, to you we will give this counsel, if you will obey us:
never allow your hands to desist from the leveling combat
295   till within Ilion's glorious walls you have penned up the Trojan
army, whoever escapes, and when Hektor's life you have taken,
go back down to the ships: we grant you to win a great glory."
     So having spoken, the two gods went back to the immortals;
meanwhile he went ahead—for the gods' charge greatly had stirred him—
300   into the plain, which wholly was filled with the outflow of water;
many and beautiful weapons of young men slain in the battle
tumbled upon it, and corpses; but he leapt high on his legs in
rushing against that stream, straight onward, nor could the river,
flowing abroad, hold him, for Athena in him put immense might.
305   Nor did Skamánder abate his strength, but was yet more greatly
angered at Peleus' son, and a wave of his current he marshaled,
raising it high in a crest, and he called to the Símoeis, shouting:
"Brother of mine, let us both now join in restraining the might of
this man, since very soon he will capture and ransack the mighty
310   city of Priam—the Trojans will not withstand him in battle.

Quick as you can, give aid to me now, and replenish your stream with
water from out of your sources, and stir up all of your torrents;
raise up high a huge wave and arouse an enormous commotion,
whether of timbers or stones, so that we may restrain the fierce fighter

315   who is so strong, and to equal the gods themselves he is eager,
since I am certain that neither his might nor his beauty will save him,
nor will the beautiful armor that somewhere deep underwater
covered in slime will be lying concealed; and the hero himself in
sands I will wrap, and will pour over him an abundance of gravel,

320   measureless, so the Achaians will not know where to collect his
bones for the rites—so deep I will cover him over with rubble.
So right there will his tomb be fashioned, and never will he have
need of a grave-mound when the Achaians would offer him death-rites."
    Thus; in a tumult he rushed at Achilles; aloft he was seething,

325   roaring in billows of foam and in blood and in bodies of dead men.
Purple and surging the wave of the river descended from heaven
towering stood and began overpowering Peleus' scion;
but then Hera exclaimed out loud, terrified for Achilles,
fearing the great deep-eddying river would sweep him away now;

330   straightway she spoke out to her dear son, mighty Hephaistos:
"Rise up, clubfooted god, my child, since it was against you,
so we supposed, that the eddying Xanthos was matched in the battle;
quick as you can give help to Achilles, and make a great fire blaze;
meanwhile I will go swiftly to rouse from the sea-brine a savage

335   blast of the west wind Zephyr and bright clear Notos the south wind,
which will consume by burning the bodies and gear of the Trojans,
bringing the blaze of affliction; and you on the banks of the Xanthos
burn up the trees, hurl fire into him, nor at all do you let him
turn you away with words of persuasion or threatening curses;

340   nor do you ever restrain your might, but exert it until I
call to you, raising a shout; then hold back the weariless blazing."
    So she spoke, and Hephaistos prepared fire, ravenous-blazing.
First on the plain that fire was ignited and burned up the many
corpses that lay thick there of the fighters Achilles had slaughtered;

345   all of the plain dried off, and the glittering water was held back.
As in the season of harvest the north wind rapidly dries some
orchard recently watered—the farmer who tills it rejoices—
rapidly so was the whole plain dried, and the bodies of dead men
burned up; then he diverted his radiant blaze to the river.

350   Burned up there were the elms and the tamarisk bushes and willows;

burned also were the lotus, the galingale plants, and the rushes,
which in abundance grew by the beautiful streams of the river;
down in the eddies the eels and the fishes were worn to exhaustion;
there in the beautiful streams they were tumbling hither and thither,
355   quite worn out by the blast of Hephaistos of many devices.
Burned was the might of the river, who called to the god and addressed him:
"No other god could against you, Hephaistos, strive in a quarrel;
neither would I now fight you, ablaze as you are with a wildfire.
Cease this conflict; the Trojans at once let noble Achilles
360   drive from the city—for why should I care about conflict and succor?"
        He spoke, blazing with fire, and his beautiful currents were seething.
Just as a cauldron is boiling inside, impelled by a great fire,
melting the lard of a hog that has been well-fatted for slaughter,
bubbling in every part, with the dry wood laid underneath it,
365   so in the fire his beautiful streams burned, water was boiling,
nor would he keep on flowing, but stopped, for the blast of the might of
skillful Hephaistos had wearied him utterly. Straightway to Hera
earnestly praying, he spoke, and in these winged words he addressed her:
"Hera, now why has your son so harried my stream as to vex me
370   more than the rest? I am not so much blameworthy to you as
all those others, the gods and the men who are aiding the Trojans.
Yet I will leave off now, if indeed you bid me to do so;
let him as well leave off; moreover, this oath I will swear you,
never will I ward off from the Trojans the day of affliction,
375   no, not even when Troy is entirely consumed in the blazing
fire and the warlike sons of Achaians are burning the city."
        When to his plea had listened the goddess white-armed Hera,
straightway she spoke out to her dear son, mighty Hephaistos:
"Hold off, Hephaistos, illustrious child, since it is not fitting
380   thus to maltreat an immortal, a god, for the sake of mere mortals."
        So she spoke, and Hephaistos extinguished the ravenous blazing;
back once more in the beautiful currents the billows were rolling.
        Soon as the might of the Xanthos was held back, both the contenders
stopped, since Hera restrained them from combat, though she was angry.
385   But then onto the rest of the gods fell burdensome conflict,
cruel and harsh, and the hearts in their breasts were blasted asunder.
With an enormous din they collided; the wide earth resounded;
round them the whole great heaven was trumpeting. Zeus on Olympos
sitting aloft, heard it, and the heart inside him was laughing,
390   since he rejoiced as he saw how the gods were joining in conflict.

Then no longer they stood there separate, for it was Ares
piercer of shields who started, and first he rushed at Athena,
holding in hand a bronze spear, and he spoke this word of revilement:
"Why again, dog-fly, are you arousing the gods to a conflict
395 with this vehement rashness, your great heart driving you onward?
Are you not mindful of when you made Diomédes the son of
Tydeus wound me, and grasping the spear yourself as all looked you
drove it directly at me and my beautiful flesh lacerated?
Therefore now, I am sure, I will pay back all you have done me."
400   So having spoken he struck on the aegis, streaming with tassels,
dreadful and grim—not even the lightning of Zeus can subdue it;
yet upon it with his long spear now struck bloodstained Ares.
Yielding some ground, in her powerful hand she picked up a boulder
which on the plain was lying, a black one, enormous and jagged;
405 this as a field's bound-marker had men of a former time set there.
Ares she struck on the neck with the stone, and his limbs she unloosened;
he fell, covering seven full measures; his hair became dusty;
crashing, his armor resounded, and Pallas Athena was laughing
as above him she exulted; in these winged words she addressed him:
410 "Fool, you have not yet learned how much more warlike than you I
boast myself, for against me now you are matching your fury.
So would you pay back in full the Erínyës sent by your mother,
who in her anger devises you evil, because the Achaians
you have forsaken and given your aid to the arrogant Trojans."
415   So having spoken, from him her glittering eyes she averted;
him as he sorely lamented the daughter of Zeus, Aphrodítè,
took by the hand and conducted; his breath he had hardly recovered.
Thereat, as soon as the goddess white-armed Hera observed her,
quickly she spoke to Athena; in these winged words she addressed her:
420 "Well now, offspring of Zeus of the aegis, unwearying goddess,
there once more does the dog-fly lead man-slaughtering Ares
out of the violent fight through the melee; but hurry and catch her!"
       So she spoke, and Athena, rejoicing in spirit, pursued her;
speeding along to her there, she struck at her breasts with her massive
425 hand, and the knees of the goddess collapsed, and the spirit within her.
So on the earth which nourishes many were both of them lying;
over them there she exulted, and these winged words did she utter:
"So may they all, whoever are giving their aid to the Trojans,
be now, when they would battle against the illustrious Argives—
430 just as courageous and daring, exactly the way Aphrodítè

374

came to the succor of Ares and stood to encounter my fury;
thereby we long ago would have brought this war to a finish,
having the well-built city of Ilion taken and ransacked."
 So she spoke, and the goddess white-armed Hera was smiling.
435 Meanwhile the strong earth-shaker addressed these words to Apollo:
"Phoibos, why here apart do we both stand? It is not right when
others have started, and shameful indeed would it be without fighting
back to Olympos to go, to the bronze-floored palace of great Zeus.
Start then, for you in birth are the younger, and it is not good for
440 me, since, being the earlier born, I am wiser than you are.
Fool, how senseless a mind you have! Do you never remember
now those many afflictions that we around Ilion suffered,
we two, alone of the gods, when the lordly Laómedon we were
serving, the time we came, at the orders of Zeus, for a full year,
445 working for wages agreed? That master was giving us orders!
I then built for the Trojans a wall that surrounded the city,
broad, very fine, so the city would never be broken and entered;
while you, Phoibos, were herding the swing-paced crooked-horned cattle
there upon forested Ida of many ravines, in the foothills.
450 But then, when the much-gladdening seasons were bringing the final
term of our hire, outrageous Laómedon cheated us, stealing
all our wages, and uttering threats, sent us from the city—
he indeed threatened to fasten together our feet, and our arms up
over our heads, then sell us to people in faraway islands;
455 vaunting, he promised to lop off the ears of us both with a bronze blade.
We then left him and went back home in a rancorous spirit,
angry because of the wages he promised but never delivered.
His are the people on whom you bestow your grace, and you are not
seeking with us that the arrogant Trojans be utterly ruined,
460 miserably, and along with their children and reverend bedmates."
 Speaking to him then answered the lord far-working Apollo:
"Shaker of earth, you never would call me prudent of mind if
I should indeed do battle with you for the sake of unhappy
mortals, who are like leaves and are sometimes full of the blazing
465 power of life while they are consuming the fruit of the plowland,
while other times they are wasted and perishing. No, let us quickly
cease from the battle, and let them go on fighting their own fights."
 So as he spoke he was turning away, for he felt it a shame to
join in a hand-to-hand fight with the brother of his own father.
470 Then his sister began to rebuke him, the queen of the wild beasts,

Artemis, roamer of fields; she spoke this word of revilement:
"So do you flee, Far-worker? The victory have you entirely
yielded Poseidon and given him glory with nothing accomplished?
Fool, why still are you holding a bow of less worth than the wind is?
475 Now no longer must I hear you in the halls of our father
boast as before you vaunted among us gods, the immortals,
how you would even engage in a man-to-man fight with Poseidon."
    So she spoke, but Apollo who works from afar did not answer;
it was the reverend bedmate of Zeus instead who in anger
480 scolded the goddess, the shooter of arrows, with words of revilement:
"How then, shameless bitch, are you now so eager to stand and
face me? I am for you a most difficult rival to match in
strength, though you carry a bow, for a lion to women did Zeus make
you, and of them he gave you to kill whomever you wanted.
485 Certainly better for you to be killing the beasts and the wild deer
high on the peaks than to battle with might those stronger than you are.
Yet if you wish, learn now about warfare, so that you know well
how much better I am, for in strength you are trying to match me."
    She spoke; both of her hands at the wrist she grasped with her left hand,
490 while with her right she stripped from her shoulder the bow and the quiver;
then she smiled as she beat her about her ears with the weapons;
Artemis twisted and turned—swift arrows fell out of her quiver.
Weeping, the goddess began to take flight before her like a dove that
flies in front of a falcon and into a hollow, a gaping
495 cleft in a rock—it is not her destiny yet to be taken.
So while weeping she fled, and her bow right there she abandoned.
Thus then spoke out to Leto the messenger, slayer of Argos:
"Leto, with you I will not do battle, for it is a hard thing
bandying blows with the wives of the great cloud-gathering god Zeus.
500 But speak boldly and freely in boasting among the immortal
gods now, telling them how by your great strength I was defeated."
    So did he say; then Leto collected the arrows and curved bow,
which in the turbulent dust one way or another had fallen.
Taking the bow and the arrows she went back after her daughter,
505 who to Olympos had gone, to the bronze-floored palace of great Zeus,
where at the knees of her father the maiden was sitting and weeping;
round her the fragrant robe was aquiver. Her father the son of
Kronos drew her toward him and questioned her, merrily laughing:
"Who among Oúranos' offspring has done such things to you, dear child,
510 idly and rashly, as if you were openly working some evil?"

Speaking to him made answer the fair-wreathed clamorous huntress:
"It was your own wife, father, who battered me, white-armed Hera,
from whom conflict and strife have fastened upon the immortals."
Such things then they spoke and addressed each one to the other.
515 Into the sacred city of Ilion Phoibos Apollo
went, since he was concerned for the wall of the well-built city,
lest beyond fate that day should the Dánaäns storm and destroy it.
Back to Olympos proceeded the rest of the gods who live always;
some among them were enraged, while others were greatly exulting;
520 they sat down by the father, the dark-cloud lord. But Achilles
meanwhile was killing the Trojans as well as their single-hoofed horses.
Just as the smoke goes upward and reaches the breadth of the heavens
out of a town that is burning—the gods' wrath driving it onward—
toil it inflicts on all, and on many it fastens afflictions,
525 so both toil and afflictions Achilles inflicted on Trojans.
     Up on the sacred bastion the old man Priam was standing;
looking, he noticed enormous Achilles and saw that the Trojans,
stricken with panic, were routed before him, nor was there any
rescue, and groaning he went back down to the ground from the bastion,
530 then by the wall he roused the illustrious guards of the gateway:
"Hold wide open the gates with your hands, till into the city,
routed, the army has entered, for there nearby is Achilles
making them panic, and now I think there will be a disaster.
But then, once they are crowded inside of the wall and regain breath,
535 straightway again shut tightly the double doors, carefully fitted,
since I fear lest the murderous man leap inside the rampart."
     So he spoke, and the gates they opened and thrust back the door-bars;
spread apart thus, the gates offered deliverance; meanwhile Apollo
leapt out to meet them, to keep destruction away from the Trojans.
540 They kept fleeing directly ahead to the city and right to the lofty
ramparts, parched with thirst and begrimed with dust from the flatland;
fiercely Achilles pursued with his spear, and the powerful madness
ever possessed his heart: he was eager to garner the glory.
     Then Troy, lofty of gates, would the sons of Achaians have taken,
545 had not Phoibos Apollo aroused up noble Agénor,
who was the son of Anténor and faultless and strong as a fighter.
Confidence he cast into his heart, and as well at his side he
stood himself, so that he might keep death's ponderous hand off;
there on the oak he leaned; in a great dense mist he was shrouded.
550 Then as the man caught sight of Achilles the sacker of cities,

he stopped; there as he waited, in him was the heart much troubled;
deeply disturbed, he spoke to his own magnanimous spirit:
     "Oh, woe is me! If in front of the might of Achilles I take flight
that same way where the others are stricken to panic and driven,
555 then even so he will catch me, a coward, and hack me to pieces.
But if I leave these men to be driven in panic in front of
Peleus' scion Achilles and flee on my feet in another
way from the walls to the flatland of Ilion, till I have reached those
spurs of Mount Ida and found refuge in the copses and thickets,
560 so in the evening, once I have bathed in the river to clean this
sweat off and dried myself, toward Ilion then would I go back.
Yet why now is it dear to my heart to debate about these things?
What if he saw me stealing away to the plain from the city,
rushed to pursue me, and so with his swiftness of foot overtook me?
565 Then no longer will I escape from my death and my doomsday,
since above all mankind he is far and away the most mighty.
But if I go encounter him here in front of the city,
his flesh too, I am certain, is vulnerable to the sharp bronze,
one life only he has in his body, and people report that
570 he is a mortal; but Zeus son of Kronos is granting him glory."
     So having said, he crouched and awaited Achilles; the valiant
heart inside him was stirred to engage in battle and combat.
Just as a leopard goes from the depths of a thicketed woodland
out to encounter the man who hunts her, and neither at heart she
575 feels any fear nor panics at hearing the hunting-hounds baying,
even if he anticipates her with a throw or a spear-thrust,
nevertheless, pierced through with a spear she never forsakes her
valor, until she engages her foe or is slaughtered and brought down,
so was the valorous son of Anténor, the noble Agénor,
580 now not minded to flee until he made proof of Achilles;
rather, his circular shield he held in front of his body,
then with his spear he aimed at the other, and loudly he shouted:
"Doubtless you in your spirit had great hopes, brilliant Achilles,
this same day to be sacking the city of venturous Trojans.
585 Fool! For on her account yet there are many afflictions to happen,
since inside her we are, we many and valorous fighters,
who will in front of our much-loved parents, our wives, and our children
watch over Ilion, while you here will encounter your doomsday,
dangerous man though you are and a warrior bold and defiant."
590   Thus did he say, and his sharp spear he let fly from his heavy

hand, and it struck on the shin right under the knee, and it did not
miss him, so that the shin-guard of tin just recently fashioned
dreadfully clattered about him; but backward it bounded, away from
where it had struck and did not pierce through, and the god's gift stopped it.
595 Next in his turn then, Peleus' scion at godlike Agénor
started to rush; but Apollo did not let him win the glory;
rather Agénor he snatched and in dense mist shrouded him over,
then he sent him away, to go quietly out of the battle.
Meanwhile he by a trick kept Peleus' son from the army;
600 making himself like Agénor in every way, the far-worker
stood in front of his feet, and he rushed on foot to pursue him.
Then, as Achilles was chasing him over the wheat-bearing flatland,
he kept turning toward the deep-eddying river Skamánder,
running a little ahead—by his cunning Apollo deceived him—
605 so with his swift feet always he hoped that he might overtake him;
meanwhile the rest of the Trojans had fled in panic and gladly
came in a mob to the town, and the city was filled as they thronged in;
neither at all they dared any more to await one another
outside the city and wall and to find out who had escaped or
610 who had been killed in battle, but eagerly into the city
streamed, whoever of them by his feet and his knees had been rescued.

BOOK 22

So having fled like fawns all over the city, the Trojan
fighters were drying the sweat off and drinking and slaking their thirst while
leaning against the magnificent battlements; but the Achaians
came up close to the wall, and they leaned their shields on their shoulders.
5 Hektor, however, a ruinous fate ensnared to remain right
there in front of the Skaian Gates and of Ilion city.
But to the scion of Peleus spoke forth Phoibos Apollo:
"Peleus' son, why thus on your swift feet do you pursue me—
being a mortal, while I am a deathless god? You do not yet
10 recognize me as a god—you are still unquenchably raging.
Nor do you care for your toil with the Trojans, the fighters you routed,
who even now throng into the city as you turn aside here.
You will not kill me, because I am not one fated to perish."
Mightily vexed, thus spoke to him then swift-footed Achilles:
15 "You have foiled me, Far-worker, the most destructive of all gods,
now by turning me here from the rampart, for otherwise many
yet would have bitten the earth before entering Ilion city.
Now you have stolen from me great glory, and them you have rescued
easily, since you did not fear any requital hereafter;
20 otherwise I would requite it, if I were endowed with the power."
So having spoken, with mighty resolve he strode to the city,
speeding the way some prizewinning horse with a chariot rushes,
running at full stride, easily galloping over the flatland—
just so agilely plying his feet and his legs was Achilles.
25 It was the old man Priam who noticed him first with his own eyes
speeding along on the flatland and glittering bright as the star that
comes at the season of harvest, the most outstanding of all those
numerous stars whose rays shine out in the gloom of the nighttime—
that same star to which people refer as the Dog of Oríon.
30 It is the brightest of all but appears as a sign of affliction,

bringing with it much feverish illness for miserable mortals.
So on his breast as he ran shone brightly the bronze of Achilles.
Sorely the old man groaned, and he beat at his head with his hands while
lifting them up on high, and he groaned out loudly and shouted,
35 begging his much-loved son, who there in front of the gates had
taken a stand and was savagely eager to battle Achilles;
piteously the old man thus called to him, stretching his arms out:
     "Hektor, my dear child, do not remain there alone to await that
man without others, for quickly you might encounter your doomsday,
40 quelled by Peleus' son, since he is far stronger than you are,
cruel and harsh; I wish he could be as beloved to the gods as
he is to me! Then swiftly the dogs and the vultures would eat him
up as he lay dead—out of my breast would depart dread sorrow—
he who has stolen from me my sons so many and noble,
45 slaughtering some of them, selling the others in faraway islands,
since even now two sons, Polydóros and noble Lykáon,
I cannot see among those in the town where Trojans are thronging.
They are the sons Laothoë bore me, a princess of women.
But should they be alive in the enemy camp, we will then be
50 able to free them with bronze and with gold—inside there is plenty,
since old Altes of glorious name gave much to his daughter.
Should they instead already be dead, in the palace of Hades,
sorrow it is to my heart and their mother's, the parents who bore them;
but to the rest of the people the sorrow will certainly be much
55 briefer if you do not perish as well, brought down by Achilles.
But now come inside of the walls, my child, so that you may
rescue the Trojans and women of Troy, not offer enormous
glory to Peleus' son and yourself be robbed of your dear life.
Pity as well my miserable self, still living but luckless;
60 by a harsh fate will the father, the scion of Kronos, destroy me
on the threshold of old age, once I have seen many afflictions—
sons brought down in destruction and daughters captured and dragged off,
chambers and halls ransacked and demolished, and innocent children
taken and dashed to the ground in the cruel and terrible combat,
65 daughters-in-law dragged off by the murderous hands of Achaians.
Last of them all, myself will the dogs in front of my doorway,
raw-flesh-eaters, be tearing asunder, when someone has taken
life from my limbs by striking with sharp bronze or with a spear-cast—
dogs I reared in my halls at my table as guards of the doorways—
70 then, having drunk my blood in madness of spirit, will they be

lying in front of the door. For a young man it is entirely
fitting when killed in a battle to lie lacerated by sharp bronze;
though he is dead, his body is all still lovely to look at.
But when upon the gray head of an old man slain, and the gray beard,
75   even the privates, the dogs wreak ugly and shameful defilement,
that is the one most piteous ending for miserable mortals."
      He spoke; taking some gray hairs into his hands, the old man tore
them from his head, but he did not persuade the bold spirit in Hektor.
So for her part his mother was moaning and letting her tears fall,
80   loosing the fold of her robe, with the other hand holding her breast out;
shedding her tears she·spoke, and in these winged words she addressed him:
"Hektor my own child, reverence this, take pity upon me
now, if ever I gave you the breast to assuage your affliction;
think, dear child, upon these things, and ward off the enemy fighter
85   staying inside of the ramparts—do not stand forth to confront him,
cruel and harsh; for if he kills you, then never will I be
wailing for you on your bier, dear offshoot to whom I gave birth,
nor will your bedmate, wealthy in bride-gifts; far from us, rather,
down by the Argives' ships will the swift dogs wholly devour you."
90   Wailing, the two spoke thus to their dear son, loudly imploring
him to relent; but they did not persuade the bold spirit in Hektor;
rather he waited for mighty Achilles as he was approaching.
Just as a serpent awaits some man at his lair in the mountains,
having consumed evil herbs, and a baneful gall is within him—
95   dreadfully coiling about his lair he glares at his victim—
so now Hektor with might unquenchable never retreated,
leaning his glittering shield on the bastion where it was jutting;
deeply disturbed, he spoke to his own magnanimous spirit:
"Ah, woe is me! If I enter inside these gates and the ramparts,
100   then a reproach will Polýdamas first be putting upon me,
since he told me to lead back into the city the Trojans
during the ruinous night when noble Achilles had risen;
yet I did not heed him, though that would have been far better.
Now since I in my obstinate folly have ruined the army,
105   I feel shame among Trojans and women of Troy of the long robes,
lest some other man baser than I sometime will be saying,
'Hektor, confiding in his own strength, has ruined the army.'
So will they say; and for me it would now be better by far to
go man-to-man with Achilles and kill him and come back homeward
110   or for myself to be killed in front of the city, in glory.

Or if instead I lay on the ground the shield massive with bosses,
also the ponderous helmet, and leaning the spear on the rampart,
going alone, set forth to encounter the faultless Achilles,
then I make him a promise that Helen along with the treasures,
115   all those many that once in his hollow ships Alexander
brought back homeward to Troy—that deed was the start of the conflict—
we will give Atreus' scions to take, and among the Achaians,
furthermore, share out the rest of the wealth this city possesses,
straightway then I will take from the Trojans an oath of the elders
120   not to conceal anything—instead, to distribute the treasures
equally, all that inside the delightful city are hoarded.
Yet why now is it dear to my heart to debate about these things?
I am afraid that if pleading I go to him, he will not pity
me nor at all respect me but rather will slaughter me unarmed,
125   just as I am, like a woman, when I have stripped off the armor.
Nor any way is it possible, surely, from rock or from oak tree
now to start fondly conversing with him as a maid and a youth do—
just as a maid and a youth might fondly converse with each other.
Better as quickly as possible now to be joining in conflict;
130   then we will see to which one the Olympian proffers the glory."
      So he pondered, awaiting; and near him then came Achilles,
peer of Enyálios, warrior-god of the glittering helmet,
shaking above his right shoulder the terrible Pélian ash-wood
spear-shaft; and there all around him his bronze arms' flashing resembled
135   either a wildfire's blaze or the beams of the sun as it rises.
Seeing him, Hektor was seized by shivering, nor did he dare stay
there any longer, but leaving the gate, in terror he took flight;
Peleus' son rushed after—in swiftness of foot he confided.
Just as a hawk high up in the mountains, the nimblest of winged things,
140   easily swoops down after a timorous fluttering pigeon—
she takes flight before him, while he near at hand with a shrill cry
darts at her over and over; his spirit commands him to seize her—
so in his eagerness he sped straight for him; Hektor retreated
under the wall of the Trojans, and nimbly his limbs he was plying.
145   Passing the lookout place and the fig tree bent by the stormwinds,
ever away from the wall they sped on the road for the wagons,
reaching the two springs, beautiful-flowing, in which there are fountains,
both of them gushing to nourish the eddying river Skamánder.
Water in one of the springs flows warm, and around it a vapor
150   rises above it as if it were smoke from a fire that is blazing;

even in summer the other is flowing as cold as a hailstorm
or as the frigid snow or as ice hard-frozen from water.
There to be found just next to the streams are the fine broad wash-troughs
fashioned of stone; and the beautiful daughters and wives of the Trojans
155 often would come out thither to wash their shimmering garments
formerly, during the peace, before sons of Achaians had come there.
Passing the place they ran, one fleeing, the other pursuing—
noble the man at the front who fled, far better the one who
swiftly pursued—since not for a sacrifice victim or bull's hide
160 they were contending, the prizes for men who run in a footrace;
no, they ran for the life of great Hektor the tamer of horses.
As when single-hoofed steeds, prizewinners, are nimbly and swiftly
running around the turn-posts, with a great prize set for the contest,
either a tripod or woman, to honor a warrior slaughtered,
165 so three times those two now circled the city of Priam,
running on swift feet forward, the gods all gazing upon them;
speaking among them opened the father of gods and of mankind:
"Well then! There with my own eyes I am beholding a dear man
being pursued all around those walls, and my heart is lamenting
170 Hektor—for me he has burned up many a thighbone of oxen
high on the ridges of Ida of many ravines, and at other
times in the topmost city—but now is the noble Achilles
chasing him on swift feet all around that city of Priam.
But come now and consider, you gods, take counsel together,
175 whether from death we will save him, or whether, as noble as he is,
now by Achilles the scion of Peleus we will subdue him."
     Speaking to him then answered the goddess bright-eyed Athena:
"Father, the lord of the lightning and black clouds, what are you saying!
This man who is a mortal, and long since doomed by his destined
180 fate, are you minded to take from a dolorous death and release him?
Do it: but not in the least we other gods all will approve it."
     Answering her in return spoke forth the cloud-gathering god Zeus:
"Take heart, Trítogeneía, my dear child—not in the least I
speak with a serious mind, but to you I want to be kindly;
185 do it however your mind tells you—no longer be held back."
     Thus he spoke, and Athena he roused, who already was eager;
speedily she came down from the summit of lofty Olympos.
     Rapid Achilles incessantly pressed on, driving at Hektor.
As when high in the mountains a dog is pursuing a deer's fawn,
190 rousing it out of its covert and through the ravines and the copses,

though it eludes him awhile by cowering under a thicket,
steadily he keeps running and tracks it down till he finds it,
so now Hektor did not elude Peleus' swift-footed scion.
Every time he attempted to reach the Dardánian gateways,
195 rushing directly at them to get under the strong-built ramparts,
hoping the fighters above might somehow protect him with missiles,
straightway Achilles would go in front of him, turning him backward
into the plain, and himself kept speeding along by the city.
As in a dream somebody cannot chase one who is fleeing—
200 neither is one of them able to flee, nor the other to chase him—
so on his feet he could not catch Hektor, nor Hektor elude him.
How could it be that the fate of his death then Hektor evaded,
had it not been that Apollo, although for the latest and last time,
came up close to him, rousing his spirit, and made his legs nimble?
205 Noble Achilles was shaking his head as a sign to his people—
he would not let them hurl any sharp bitter missiles at Hektor,
lest one, striking him, garner the glory, and he would come second.
Finally, when they arrived for the fourth time back at the fountains,
then by the Father were balanced the gold-wrought scales, and he set in
210 them two destiny-portions of death so long in the mourning,
one for Achilles, the other for Hektor the tamer of horses;
grasping the middle, he poised it; and down sank the doomsday of Hektor,
falling to Hades' dominion, and Phoibos Apollo forsook him.
Meanwhile, to Peleus' son came bright-eyed Athena the goddess;
215 there then, standing beside him, in these winged words she addressed him:
"Finally now I expect, Zeus-cherished and brilliant Achilles,
we to the galleys will take great glory among the Achaians,
once we have brought down Hektor, though he is insatiate of battle.
Now not possible is it that he any longer escape us,
220 not even though much pain far-working Apollo should suffer,
groveling even before Father Zeus who carries the aegis.
Now as for you, stand here and take breath, while I will myself go
over to him and persuade him to face you in man-to-man combat."
So said Athena, and he was obedient, joyful in spirit;
225 there he stood, and he leaned on his bronze-barbed spear made of ash wood.
She then parted from him to go after the noble lord Hektor,
like to Deïphobos both in her weariless voice and her body.
There then, standing beside him, in these winged words she addressed him:
"Brother, indeed now rapid Achilles is pressing you sorely,
230 chasing you on swift feet all around this city of Priam;

come then, here let us stand to defend ourselves and await him."
    Answering him then spoke great Hektor of glittering helmet:
"Noble Deïphobos, you were before far dearest to me of
all my brothers, the children that Priam and Hékabè brought forth;
235 yet I am still more minded to honor you now in my spirit,
you who for my sake dared, when you with your eyes had observed me,
outside the ramparts to come, while the others remain inside them."
    Speaking to him then answered the goddess bright-eyed Athena:
"Brother, in fact our father and reverend mother implored me
240 often, in turn, and the comrades around me, begging that I would
stay there within—so sorely are all of them quaking in terror.
Yet inside me the heart was afflicted with odious sorrow.
Straight to the fight let us now go eagerly, nor any sparing
let there be of the spears, so that we find out if Achilles,
245 once he has slaughtered us both, will carry our bloodstained armor
back to the hollow galleys or by your spear will be vanquished."
    So having spoken, Athena with crafty duplicity led him;
when in coming together the men were close to each other,
first spoke out to his foe great Hektor of glittering helmet:
250 "No more, Peleus' son, will I flee you, though I before was
three times running around the great city of Priam and never
dared stay waiting your onslaught; but now my spirit is making
me stand here against you, whether I slay you or am slaughtered.
But come here, let us give as our witness the gods, for the best of
255 witnesses, surely, will they be, and guardians of our agreements:
I will not do to you brutal defilement if Zeus should bestow on
me endurance and strength and if I rob you of your life-breath;
rather, as soon as I strip you of glorious armor, Achilles,
to the Achaians your corpse will I give back, and you do likewise."
260   Looking from lowering brows spoke forth swift-footed Achilles:
"Hektor, accursed, unforgiven, to me speak not of agreements.
Just as there are no trustworthy oaths between lions and people,
nor do the wolves and the lambs have hearts harmonious-thinking—
always instead they ponder afflictions, the ones for the others—
265 so you and I cannot love each other, and neither between us
will there be any oaths, until one or the other by falling
gluts with his blood fierce Ares, the warrior wielding a hide-shield.
Keep in your mind all manner of prowess: now is the need most
urgent that you be proven a spearman and valorous fighter.
270 Nor any longer is there an escape for you: Pallas Athena

386

under my spear will kill you, and now you will pay back together
all my woes for the comrades that you with your spear killed, raging."
      So did he say, then brandished and threw his long-shadowing spear-shaft;
glorious Hektor, observing him closely, avoided the missile—
275 seeing it come, he crouched, so that flying above him, the bronze spear
planted itself in the earth; then snatching it Pallas Athena
gave it to Achilles, unnoticed by Hektor the shepherd of people.
Hektor at once spoke forth to the faultless scion of Peleus:
"You missed, neither have you in any way, godlike Achilles,
280 ever discovered from Zeus my destiny, though you believed so;
rather you talked as a man who is glib-tongued, crafty in speaking,
so that in fear of you I would forget my spirit and valor.
Nor will you plant your spear in my back midriff as I flee you;
drive it instead straight into my chest as I eagerly charge you,
285 if a god grants you to do it; but you in your turn now avoid my
bronze spear—would that you might take all of it into your body!
Then would the battle become much lighter to bear for the Trojans,
once you were dead, since you are to them their greatest affliction."
      So did he say, then brandished and threw his long-shadowing spear-shaft,
290 striking the scion of Peleus square on the shield and not missing;
far from the shield that spear-shaft rebounded, and Hektor was angered,
since so fruitlessly out of his hand had flown the swift missile;
downcast he stood, for he had no other spear fashioned of ash wood.
Then to the white-shield-bearer Deïphobos loudly he shouted,
295 asking for his long spear; but he was not anywhere near him;
Hektor at once in his mind realized it; thus did he utter:
"Well now, surely the gods to my death have finally called me,
since I thought that the hero Deïphobos stood at my side here;
rather is he still inside the walls, and Athena has tricked me.
300 Near to me now is a baneful death; no more is it far off,
nor is there any escape—for a long time this must have been more
pleasing to Zeus and Zeus' son, the far-shooter, the gods who before were
eager at heart to protect me, but now has my doom overcome me.
Let me at least not die without making a fight, without glory,
305 but a great deed having done for the men of the future to hear of."
      Soon as he said these words, he drew his sharp sword from the scabbard
which at his flank was hanging, a weapon enormous and strong, and
gathered himself, then swooped upon him as a high-flying eagle
darts down onto the plain through shadowy clouds as it rushes
310 straight at a soft young lamb or a cowering hare that it snatches;

so now, wielding his keen-edged sword, swooped Hektor upon him.
But against him rushed Achilles, his heart filled full of a savage
fury; in front of his chest was the shield which covered and hid it,
beautiful, fashioned with care; he nodded his glittering helmet,

315 four-horn-crested; about it were waving the beautiful golden
plumes that had been set thickly along the whole crest by Hephaistos.
Just as a star comes out among stars in the gloom of the nighttime,
Hesper the evening star, the most beautiful set in the heavens,
so shone light from the keen-edged spear that Achilles was wielding

320 now in his right hand, planning affliction for noble Lord Hektor,
eyeing his beautiful body for where it least would resist him.
Now of his body the rest was held in the beautiful brazen
armor he stripped off after he slaughtered the might of Patróklos;
but it appeared where the collarbones parted the neck from the shoulders,

325 just in the gullet, the place where a life's destruction is swiftest;
there now, charging at him with his spear, struck noble Achilles,
into the delicate neck and on through it the point penetrated.
But the great ash spear, heavy with bronze, did not sever the windpipe,
so with his words still he could address him, giving an answer;

330 he in the dust dropped; over him noble Achilles exulted:
"Doubtless, Hektor, you thought, while killing and stripping Patróklos,
you would be safe, and you took no heed of me since I was absent,
childish fool; an avenger for him, far stronger than he was,
even myself, he had left back there at the hollow galleys;

335 I have now loosened your knees, and the dogs and the birds will be tearing
you most vilely, but burial rites the Achaians will give him."
     Feebly in answer to him spoke Hektor of glittering helmet:
"I beseech you, by your life and your knees and the parents who bore you,
not to allow, by the ships of the Achaians, the dogs to devour me;

340 rather receive those treasures of gold and of bronze in abundance,
all of the gifts my father and reverend mother will give you,
giving my body to take back home, so that I in my death am
granted a funeral fire by the Trojans and wives of the Trojans."
     Looking from lowering brows spoke forth swift-footed Achilles:

345 "Do not implore me, hound, by my knees or the parents who bore me.
I wish rather that somehow my spirit and fury would make me
butcher your flesh and devour it raw for the deeds you committed—
so no man is alive who could ward off dogs from your head now,
not even if those treasures were ten times greater, or twenty,

350 which they brought to me here, weighed out, and then promised me others,

not even if Lord Priam the scion of Dárdanos bade me
weigh your body for gold. Not thus will your reverend mother
moan as she lays you out on your bier, that mother who bore you;
rather the dogs and the carrion birds will entirely devour you."

355 So in dying replied to him Hektor of glittering helmet:
"Surely I know you well and was clearly aware I would not be
able to sway you; the heart in your breast indeed is of iron.
Now take thought, lest I be the cause of the wrath that the gods will
feel against you, on the day when Paris and Phoibos Apollo

360 slaughter you there at the Skaian Gates, in spite of your valor."
So as he uttered, his death's finality covered him over.
Flitting away from the limbs, his soul went down into Hades,
sorrowing over its fate and forsaking its vigor and manhood.
Even as he lay dead, thus spoke to him noble Achilles:

365 "Die now, and then my death will I welcome whenever in fact Zeus
wishes, along with the rest of the deathless gods, to achieve it."
So having said, he drew the great bronze spear out of the body,
then he placed it aside, and he stripped from his shoulders the bloody
armor; and running about him, the others, the sons of Achaians,

370 wondering, gazed at the face and the marvelous beauty of Hektor,
nor was he left unstabbed by anyone standing about him.
So would one of them say as he looked at another beside him:
"Well now! Certainly Hektor is milder and softer to handle
than at the time with the fiery blaze he was burning the galleys."

375 Thus would one of them say as he stabbed at him, standing beside him.
When swift-footed and noble Achilles had stripped him of armor,
standing among the Achaians, in these winged words he addressed them:
"Oh dear friends and companions, the Argives' leaders and princes,
since this man have the gods now granted to us to be brought down,

380 him who has wrought much evil beyond all others together,
come, let us go make trial in armor around the whole city,
so that we know yet more the intent in the minds of the Trojans,
whether with this man fallen the steep-built city they now will
leave, or will want to remain though Hektor no longer is living.

385 Yet why now is it dear to my heart to debate about these things?
There by the galleys is lying a corpse unwept and unburied,
noble Patróklos; of him I will not be forgetful, as long as
I am among the alive and my knees have vigor for action;
even if people forget their dead in the palace of Hades,

390 even in that place I will remember my dearest of comrades.

But come, singing a paean of triumph, sons of Achaians,
let us go down to the hollow ships now, carrying this man.
We a great glory have won; we have slaughtered the noble lord Hektor,
who as a god was invoked by the Trojans there in the city."

395   Thus he spoke and devised foul deeds for the noble lord Hektor.
Straightway the tendons behind both feet he pierced with a knife-point
right from the heels to the ankles, and fixed to them thongs made of oxhide,
these to his chariot tied, and the head left dragging behind it.
Mounting the chariot, into it lifting the glorious armor,
400   he drove, lashing the steeds, nor against their wishes did they speed.
Dust rose up from the body as Hektor was dragged, and to either
side did the dark hair flutter as all of the head that before had
been so beautiful lay in the dust—now Zeus to his foes had
given him over to be defiled in the land of his fathers.

405   So was the head of the man all fouled with the dust, and his mother
tore at her hair, and she hurled faraway from herself her resplendent
headdress, raising a loud shrill cry at the sight of her dear child;
piteous too were the groans of his father; the people around all
over the city were held in the grip of lamenting and groaning.
410   This it was that it most resembled, as if from the top down
beetling Ilion city were wholly consumed with a wildfire.
Hardly the people could hold the old man, impatient and chafing,
eager to go out through the Dardánian Gates of the city.
All of his men he begged while rolling about in the ordure;
415   calling on every man by name, he pleading addressed them:
"Hold off, friends, and allow me, in spite of your worries, to set forth
now by myself from the city and go to the ships of the Achaians;
let me beseech that man so reckless and violence-wreaking
whether in some way he may respect my years and may pity
420   old age, since I suppose he too has a father of this kind,
Peleus, he who begot him and reared him to be for the Trojans
such an affliction; to me has he brought woe more than all others,
such is the number of flourishing children of mine he has slaughtered;
though I lament for them all, I mourn over none of the others
425   as for the one over whom sharp sorrow will bring me to Hades,
Hektor—and how I wish that in my own arms he had perished,
thereby we would have taken our fill of lamenting and weeping,
both of us, I myself and the ill-starred mother who bore him."
So he spoke as he wailed; townspeople as well were lamenting,
430   Hékabè leading the women of Troy in the vehement wailing:

"Child, I am miserable! Why suffering sorely shall I yet
stay alive, now you have perished? For me in the day and the nighttime
you were my pride all over the town, and a blessing as well to
all of the Trojans and women of Troy in the city, who welcomed
435   you as a god, since you for them too were the greatest of glories
while yet living, but now have your death and your doom overcome you."
　　So she spoke as she wailed; but the bedmate of Hektor as yet knew
nothing about it, for no sure messenger yet had arrived to
make the report that her husband remained outside of the gateway,
440   but in a room of the high-built palace a cloak she was weaving,
purple, to wear double-folded, inweaving elaborate flowers.
She called out through the house to her maidens with beautiful tresses,
bidding them set on the fire a great tripod, so that the water
might be hot for his bath when Hektor returned from the battle—
445   innocent one, not knowing that, distant from waters for bathing,
bright-eyed Athena had brought him down at the hands of Achilles.
Then as she heard the outcries of distress and the groans from the bastion,
all of her limbs reeled, out of her hand to the ground fell the shuttle.
Then she again spoke out to her maidens with beautiful tresses:
450   "Come, two of you, follow me, so that I can observe what has happened.
That was the voice of my mother-in-law I heard, and within my
bosom the heart leaps up to my mouth, my limbs underneath are
frozen, and surely some evil is near for the children of Priam.
May the report stay far from this ear of mine; yet I am very
455   fearful that noble Achilles has cut off valorous Hektor
all by himself and has chased him away to the plain from the city,
even that he might have made him abandon the dangerous valor
that has possessed him, for never he stayed in the throng of the fighters,
but charged far in the front—in his courage he yielded to no one."
460   　　So having spoken, her heart loud-throbbing, she rushed through the palace
like some woman in frenzy; along with her followed her handmaids.
But then, when she arrived at the wall and the throng of the people,
standing above on the bastion and looking around, she observed him
there being dragged in front of the city; and harshly the swift-paced
465   horses were dragging him down to the hollow ships of the Achaians.
Then down over her eyes came shadowy night to enshroud her;
backward she fell down onto the ground, and her spirit she gasped out.
Then faraway from her head she cast off the shimmering headdress
made of a frontlet, a snood for the hair, and an interlaced headband,
470   and of the headscarf which Aphrodítè the golden had given

391

her on the same day Hektor of glittering helmet had led her
out of Eëtion's house, when a huge bride-price he had given.
Thronging around were her husband's sisters as well as his brothers'
wives—in their midst they held her, distraught now even to dying.
475 But then, when she revived and the strength came back to her spirit,
lifting her voice to the women of Troy, she spoke out wailing:
"Hektor, how wretched am I! To the same hard destiny we were
both of us born, you inside Troy in the palace of Priam,
while in Thébè, the town beneath forested Plakos, was I brought
480 forth in Eëtion's house; and he nurtured me while I was little,
he ill-starred and I doomed—how I wish he never had sired me!
Now have you gone down under the depths of the earth to the house of
Hades, but you have abandoned me to an odious sorrow
here in the palace, a widow, the boy a mere baby, the son whom
485 you and I both brought forth to be ill-starred: him you will never
benefit, Hektor, because you are dead, nor will he benefit you.
Even if he should escape from the dolorous war of the Achaians,
afterward, always for him there will be hard labor and sorrows,
surely, for others will soon take away from him all of his farmlands.
490 Then too, a child is bereft of all friends that day he is orphaned,
everywhere is his head bowed down, and his cheeks are tear-moistened.
In his bereavement a child goes up to his father's companions—
one he tugs by the cloak; of another he clutches the tunic.
One of those who take pity extends him his cup for a moment,
495 so that it moistens his lips, but it does not moisten his palate.
Someone who has both parents alive drives him from the feasting,
striking at him with his hands and reviling him, speaking abuses:
'Off with you now! Your father is not our dinner companion.'
Tearfully then back here to his mother the widow the child comes,
500 young Astýanax, who had before on the knees of his father
only partaken of rich white fat of a sheep and of marrow;
then when a slumber would take him, and he stopped playing his childish
games, he would sleep in a bed, in the arms of the nurse who attends him,
yes, in a soft warm bed, with his heart all full of glad feelings;
505 now that his own dear father is lost to him, much will he suffer,
young Astýanax, named by the Trojans 'the lord of the city,'
since it was you alone, Hektor, who guarded the gates and the long walls.
Now down there by the well-curved galleys and far from your parents,
after the dogs have been glutted, the glistening maggots will eat you
510 naked, in spite of the garments awaiting you here in the palace,

graceful and delicate, carefully wrought by the hands of the women.
But in a fiery blaze all those I will certainly burn up,
nothing at all for your good, since never in them will you lie here,
yet will they be from the Trojans and women of Troy to your glory."
515   So she spoke as she wailed, and the women as well were lamenting.

BOOK 23

So all over the city they wailed. Meanwhile the Achaians,
once they had made their way to the Hellespont and to the galleys,
most of them scattered apart; each man went onto his own ship;
as for Achilles, he did not permit that the Mýrmidons scatter—
5 rather he spoke these words to his comrades, lovers of warfare:
"Mýrmidons, you of swift horses, my own trustworthy companions,
not from the chariots yet let us loose our single-hoofed horses,
but as we are, with the horses and chariots coming up closer,
let us lament for Patróklos, for this is the prize of the perished.
10 Finally, when we have taken our pleasure in dire lamentation,
then we will loose our horses, and here we will all eat supper."
So he spoke, and together they wailed, with Achilles as leader.
Three times around the dead body the fair-maned horses they drove in
mourning, and Thetis aroused among them a desire for lamenting.
15 Drenched with tears were the sands, drenched too were the warriors' armor,
such deep longing they felt for the mighty deviser of panic.
Peleus' scion among them was leading the vehement wailing,
laying his own man-slaughtering hands on the breast of his comrade:
"Even in Hades' abode, farewell to you, noble Patróklos—
20 since I now am accomplishing all that I earlier promised,
said I would drag here Hektor to give to the dogs to devour raw,
then I would bring twelve glorious sons of the Trojans and slit their
throats in front of your pyre, enraged as I am at your slaughter."
Thus he spoke and devised foul deeds for the noble lord Hektor,
25 stretching him out on his face by the bier of Menoítios' scion,
down in the dust; and the men, each one, then took off their armor,
brazen and brightly agleam, and they loosed their loud-neighing horses,
then sat down by the galley of Aíakos' swift-footed scion,
thousands of them, and he gave them a banquet consoling their spirits.
30 Many the glistening bulls that were bellowing under the iron

knife, being slaughtered, and many the sheep and the goats, loud-bleating;
many the white-tusked swine for the offering, swelling with rich fat,
they stretched over the fire of Hephaistos, singeing the hair off;
all around that dead body the blood ran, caught by the cupful.

35   Now did the kings of the Achaians conduct swift-footed Achilles,
Aíakos' scion, the lord, to the excellent King Agamemnon,
barely persuading the man still raging in heart for his comrade.
They set forth and arrived at the cabin of Lord Agamemnon;
straightway then they commanded the clear-voiced heralds to set up

40   over the fire a great tripod and cauldron, in hopes of persuading
Peleus' scion to cleanse himself of the gore and the bloodstains.
He steadfastly refused, and an oath he swore them upon it:
"No, by Zeus, who among all gods is the highest and greatest,
it is not fitting that water should near my head until I have

45   laid out Patróklos over the fire and a mound I have heaped for
him and have cut my hair, since never again will a second
such grief reach my heart for as long as I stay with the living.
Nevertheless, let us now pay heed to the loathsome dinner.
Early at dawn rouse men, Agamemnon, lord of the people;

50   tell them to gather and lay wood here, and the things that are fitting
for a dead man to possess going under the murk and the shadows,
so that a weariless fire may consume this body and take it
quickly away from our eyes, and the army may turn to its labors."
So did he say; they carefully listened to him and obeyed him.

55   Eagerly, soon as the men, each one, made ready their supper,
they dined, nor of the well-shared meal were their hearts at all wanting.
When they had quite satisfied their appetites, drinking and eating,
then they departed to rest for the night, each one to his cabin;
Peleus' son on the beach of the deep sea rumbling and booming

60   lay down among his numerous Mýrmidons, heavily groaning,
out in the open, a place where the waves splashed over the seashore.
While he was held by slumber, releasing the cares from his spirit,
pouring around him sweetly—for greatly his glorious limbs were
wearied from rushing at windswept Ilion, harrying Hektor—

65   then came up and approached him the spirit of wretched Patróklos,
like him in every way, in his beautiful eyes and his stature,
even his voice; like too were the clothes he wore on his body.
Standing above his head, he spoke this word and addressed him:
"You are asleep and of me have become forgetful, Achilles;

70   never of me when I lived were you careless as now when I lie dead!

395

Bury me quickly, that I may pass through the portals of Hades.
Far off the spirits detain me, the phantoms of men who are worn out;
not yet do they allow me to join them, crossing the river;
vainly instead I roam at the broad-gated palace of Hades.
75 Here I implore you, give me your hand, since never again from
Hades will I come once my funeral fire you have granted.
Never again we two yet alive will apart from our much-loved
comrades sit and take counsel together—the hideous fate has
gaped to engulf me that I at my birth was allotted to suffer;
80 yes, and for you also it is destined, godlike Achilles,
under the walls of the well-born Trojans to come to destruction.
Something else I will tell you and charge you, if you will obey me:
never apart from your own lay my bones, noble Achilles;
rather together, the way I was brought up back in your palace,
85 when as a small lad still, from Opóeis Menoítios brought me
there to your home, on account of a miserable manslaughter
which took place on the day I killed Amphídamas' son, young
fool that I was, not wishing it, angry because of a dice game.
There in his palace the horseman Peleus warmly received me,
90 kindly he nurtured me, and he named me to be your attendant;
so too let the same urn envelop the bones of us both, that
vessel of gold, two-handled, the lady your mother once gave you."
    Answering him in return spoke forth swift-footed Achilles:
"Wherefore, dearest of comrades, have you now come to me hither;
95 why about each thing thus do you charge me? I am fulfilling
all of these things, in fact; I will heed you, just as you bid me.
But come closer and stand here, and let us embrace each other,
though but a short time, taking our pleasure in dire lamentation."
    Soon as he said these words, with his hands he reached for his comrade,
100 yet he did not clasp him—like smoke that spirit was gone down
twittering under the earth; in astonishment leapt up Achilles;
straightway clapping his hands, he spoke this word of dejection:
"Well now! Even in Hades' abode, I see, there is something—
spirit and phantom—and yet not at all does it have any substance,
105 since for the whole night through was the spirit of wretched Patróklos
standing above me weeping and wailing and laying upon me
charges about each thing; most marvelously it was like him."
    So he spoke; in them all he aroused a desire for lamenting;
coming upon them the Dawn shone forth, rose-fingered, as they were
110 weeping around that pitiful body; but strong Agamemnon

roused up men to assemble with mules from the cabins on all sides
so as to go fetch wood; and a good man set them in order,
Mérionés, who of kindly Idómeneus was the attendant.
They went holding in hand sharp axes for cutting the wood and
115 ropes well plaited and strong, and the mules went forward before them.
Much were they traveling upward and downward and crossward and slantwise;
when they arrived at the spurs of Mount Ida of numerous fountains,
oak trees, lofty and leafy, at once they eagerly started
felling with long-edged bronze, and the trees kept falling and crashing
120 loudly; and then, first splitting to pieces the logs, the Achaians
bound them behind their mules; with their hooves these tore up the earth in
straining ahead to the flatland and through dense copses and thickets.
All the woodcutters were carrying timbers, for so had commanded
Mérionés, who of kindly Idómeneus was the attendant.
125 These in a row they threw on the shore, in the place that Achilles
had for Patróklos as well as himself been planning a great mound.
Finally, when on all sides they had thrown down plentiful timber,
then they remained there sitting together, and straightway Achilles
gave the command to the Mýrmidons, lovers of battle, that they should
130 gird their bodies with bronze and should each to his chariot yoke their
horses; and they rose up and appareled themselves in their armor;
onto the chariots mounted the charioteers and the fighters;
first were the chariots moving, behind them a cloud of foot soldiers,
thousands; and there in the midst were his comrades bearing Patróklos.
135 All of his body was covered with hair they were cutting and throwing
over it; noble Achilles behind them was clasping his head and
sorrowing, since he was sending his faultless comrade to Hades.
　　　Finally, when they arrived at the place that Achilles had shown them,
setting him down, they rapidly piled up wood in abundance.
140 Then other things were devised by swift-footed noble Achilles:
standing away from the pyre, he cut off a tress of the yellow
hair whose flourishing growth he had nursed for the river Spercheios;
deeply disturbed, he looked on the wine-dark sea and said these words:
"Never for this, Spercheios, the promise to you that my father
145 Peleus vowed, that when I came back to the land of my fathers,
hair I would cut off for you and a sacred hecatomb make you—
fifty uncastrated rams would I offer as victims and throw them
into the springs at the spot of your sacred altar and precinct.
So did the old man vow, but his hope you did not accomplish.
150 Now, since never will I go back to the land of my fathers,

let me bestow this hair on the hero Patróklos to carry."
      So he spoke, and he placed his hair in the hands of his much-loved
comrade; so in them all he aroused a desire for lamenting.
Now would the light of the sun have gone down on the lamentation,
155   had not Achilles at once stood near Agamemnon and spoken:
"Atreus' son—for to you and your words will the host of Achaians
best be obedient—certainly one can be satisfied, wailing;
but now make them disperse from the pyre, tell them to prepare their
dinner; and we for whom this dead body is kin to be mourned will
160   labor around it, and let the commanders remain with us also."
      Straightway, when Agamemnon the lord of the people had heard this,
he made all of the army disperse to the balanced galleys;
those who were kindred mourners remained there piling the wood up,
making a pyre of a hundred feet one way and the other;
165   grieving at heart, on top of the pyre they set the dead body.
Many the fine fat sheep and the swing-paced crooked-horned cattle
there in front of the pyre they flayed and prepared, and the fat from
all greathearted Achilles collected, and wrapping the corpse in
it from the head to the feet, he piled the flayed bodies around him.
170   Onto it he set jars, two-handled, of oil and of honey,
leaning them all on the bier, and as well four mighty-necked horses
quickly he threw up onto the pyre while mightily groaning.
There were as well nine hounds that the lord had fed by his table;
two of them he threw onto the pyre, first slitting their gullets.
175   Those twelve excellent sons of the great-souled Trojans he also
killed with the bronze; most evil the work he devised in his spirit—
iron in might was the fire he threw on the pyre to devour them.
Then he groaned as he called by name on his dearest of comrades:
"Even in Hades' abode, farewell to you, noble Patróklos,
180   since I now am accomplishing all that I earlier promised—
these twelve excellent sons of the great-souled Trojans along with
you are all being devoured by the fire, but the scion of Priam
Hektor I will not give to the fire but to dogs to be eaten."
      So he threatening spoke; but the dogs were not busy about him;
185   rather the daughter of Zeus Aphrodítè was keeping the dogs from
him by day and by night, and with rosy ambrosial oil she
rubbed him so that Achilles would not tear him as he dragged him.
Over him Phoibos Apollo extended a darkening storm-cloud
onto the plain from the sky, entirely concealing the place in
190   which the dead body was stretched, so the sun's strength not before time would

wither and shrivel the flesh that covered the limbs and the sinews.
     But that pyre of the perished Patróklos would not be ignited;
then other things were devised by swift-footed noble Achilles.
Standing away from the pyre, he prayed to two winds, to the west wind
195 Zephyr and north wind Boreas, promising beautiful victims;
out of a gold cup pouring libations, he strongly implored them
both to come, so that with fire those corpses would rapidly burn up,
soon as the timber ignited and blazed forth. Speedily Iris,
hearing the prayer he raised, to the winds came bearing the message.
200 They in the dwelling of blustery Zephyr were gathered together,
eating a meal at a banquet, and once she had run there, Iris
stood on the stone-carved threshold; and when with their eyes they observed her,
all of the winds sprang up; to himself each one of them called her;
she however refused to sit down, but a word she addressed them:
205 "I cannot sit, for I go back soon to the stream of the Ocean,
to the Ethiopians' country, in which they are offering sacred
hecatombs to the immortals, so I too share in the victims.
Now is Achilles imploring that Boreas come, and resounding
Zephyr the west wind too, and he promises beautiful victims,
210 so that you may set burning the pyre upon which is Patróklos
lying, and all the Achaians are loudly lamenting around him."
     So having said, she departed from them; they sprang to obey her,
raising a marvelous din, in front of them driving the storm-clouds.
Swiftly they came to the seaway to blow on it—billows were swelling
215 under the whistling blast—and arrived at the deep-soiled Troäd;
there on the pyre they fell, then fiercely the ravening fire roared.
All night long they were beating the blaze to a conflagration,
piercingly blowing, and all night long was the rapid Achilles
holding a cup, two-handled, and drawing the wine from a golden
220 bowl, then pouring it out on the ground, so drenching the earth there,
calling again and again on the spirit of wretched Patróklos.
Just as a father laments for a son while burning his bones up,
one newly wed whose dying has grieved his miserable parents,
so did Achilles lament for his comrade, burning his bones up,
225 heavily pacing beside his pyre and incessantly groaning.
     Just when the dawn-star rises, and light to the earth it announces—
after it, saffron-appareled, the Dawn spreads over the sea-brine—
that was the time that the funeral pyre died down and the flame stopped.
Then did the winds set out to return once more to their dwelling
230 over the Thracian sea—with the swell of the billows it thundered.

Turning away from the funeral pyre then, Peleus' scion
lay down, worn to the bones, and upon him rushed sweet slumber.
Now in a throng those leaders with Atreus' scion assembled,
and the commotion and noise as they came there wakened Achilles,

235 so that he sat upright and in these words spoke and addressed them:
"Atreus' son and you others, the noblest of all the Achaians,
first, with glistening wine extinguish the flames of the whole great
pyre, wherever the might of the fire has extended, and straightway
then let us gather the bones of Patróklos Menoítios' scion,

240 carefully singling them out—distinguishing them will be easy,
for in the midst of the pyre he lay, and apart were the others
burned, at the edges, the horses and men all mingled together.
Those bones then let us place in a gold-wrought bowl and a double
layer of fat, until I am myself enshrouded in Hades.

245 No very large mound now do I bid you labor to build, but
such as is fitting and proper; and later on let the Achaians
raise it and make it lofty and broad, whoever of you are
left to survive me after my death by the well-benched galleys."
    So did he say; they heeded the swift-footed scion of Peleus.

250 First, with glistening wine they extinguished the flames of the whole great
pyre wherever the fire had spread and deep ashes had fallen;
then as they wept, they gathered their kindly and powerful comrade's
white bones into the gold-wrought bowl and the fat, double-layered;
putting it into the cabin, in delicate linen they wrapped it.

255 Then for the tomb they marked off a circle and set the retaining
wall surrounding the pyre, and at once heaped earth as a grave-mound;
soon as they heaped up the tomb, they began to return. But Achilles
kept there all of the people and made the broad gathering sit down,
then from his ships he brought out the prizes, the cauldrons and tripods,

260 also the horses and mules he brought, and the powerful oxen,
women as well, fair-girdled, and also silver-gray iron.
    For the swift charioteers were the glorious prizes that first he
set out, a woman to lead away, faultless in excellent handcraft,
also a tripod with ears, in capacity twenty-two measures,

265 both for the first prize; then for the second a mare did he set out,
six years old, unbroken, and pregnant as well with a mule-foal;
then for the third-prize winner he set out a beautiful cauldron
yet unsmirched by the fire and still bright, four measures containing;
then for the fourth-prize winner he set two talents of gold there,

270 while for the fifth he set out a bowl, unsmirched, double-handled.

There among them he stood, and a word he spoke to the Argives:
"Atreus' son and you others, the rest of the well-greaved Achaians,
in the assembly are set these prizes for chariot-racing.
If now it were another for whom we Achaians contended,
275 winning the first prize, surely, would I take it to my cabin;
for as you know, my horses are so outstanding in prowess,
seeing that they are immortal, and it was Poseidon who granted
them to my father, Peleus; on me in turn he bestowed them.
Nevertheless, I will stay here, and so will the single-hoofed horses,
280 such was the glorious might of the charioteer they have lost now,
one so gentle, who many a time poured over their manes soft
oil of the olive, whenever he washed them in shimmering water.
Therefore do they stand mourning for him—their manes on the ground are
trailing along as the two of them stand there grieving in spirit.
285 Yet in the host you others prepare, whichever Achaians
have good trust in their horses and chariots, skillfully jointed."
    Peleus' son spoke; quickly the charioteers were assembled.
First by far to arise was Eumélos, the lord of the people,
much-loved son of Admétos, a man most skilled as a horseman.
290 After him rose up Tydeus' scion, the strong Diomédes;
under the yoke he led those horses of Tros he had taken
once from Aineías—the man himself had been saved by Apollo.
After him Atreus' son rose up, light-haired Meneláos,
Zeus-descended, and under the yoke he led the swift horses,
295 Aithè, a mare Agamemnon possessed, and his own horse Podárgos.
Her as a gift Echepólos the son of Anchíses had given
Lord Agamemnon, that not toward windswept Ilion he should
follow, but stay and take pleasure at home, since Zeus had bestowed on
him great wealth, and he lived in Sikyon's spacious dominion;
300 under the yoke she was led; most eager she was to be running.
Fourth in order, his fair-maned horses Antílochos readied—
he was the glorious scion of Nestor, the high-souled lord and
scion of Neleus; drawing his chariot now were his swift-hoofed
steeds that were Pylos-bred; then standing beside him, his father
305 spoke to him, wisely advising a man who himself was discerning:
"Youthful indeed as you are, Antílochos, Zeus and Poseidon
both have befriended you; horsemanship of all kinds they have taught you;
therefore now there is no great need to instruct you, because you
know very well how to double the turn-post. Yet as to horses,
310 yours are the slowest to run, so I think this race will be rough work.

401

Swifter indeed are the horses of others, but none of the men are
any more skillful than you are yourself in devising your tactics.
Come then, dear son, into your mind put cunning devices,
all sorts, so that the prizes do not slip away or elude you.
315 More by cunning devices than strength is a woodcutter better;
better by cunning devices a helmsman out on the wine-dark
sea keeps steering the course of a swift ship tossed by the stormwinds;
better by cunning a charioteer than a charioteer is.
Somebody else who trusts in his horses and chariot keeps on
320 thoughtlessly swerving about, far off to one side and the other;
over the course his horses are roaming, nor does he control them.
He who is skilled in his craft, though worse are the steeds he is driving,
always eyeing the post, wheels close to it, never forgetting
how at the start with the oxhide reins to keep taut the two horses,
325 rather he steadily holds them and watches the man who is leading.
This unmistakable sign I will tell you, nor will you miss it:
up from the ground there stands to about one fathom a dry stump,
whether of oak or of pine; by the rain it never is rotted—
two white boulders are set on either side firmly against it
330 where the two legs of the track meet, smooth for the horse race around it—
either a grave-mark, maybe, of someone who long ago perished,
or as the post for a race set there by the people before us;
now as his post swift-footed and noble Achilles has marked it.
Press on it hard by driving your chariot close, and your horses;
335 you meanwhile in the well-plaited chariot lean a bit over
off to the left of the pair while goading the horse on the right hand,
calling on him with a shout, from your hand now giving him free rein.
Right in close to the turn-post then let the left-hand horse draw,
so that the hub of the well-made wheel seems almost to graze its
340 surface, but take great care to avoid quite touching the boulder,
lest you injure the horses, the chariot shatter to pieces—
that for the others will be a delight, a rebuke it will be for
you yourself; but indeed, dear son, be thoughtful to watch out,
since, should you at the post drive past those you are pursuing,
345 there is no one who would catch you by putting on speed or would pass you,
not even if in pursuit he were driving the noble Aríon,
that swift horse of Adréstos, from stock of a heavenly breeding,
or Laómedon's horses, the noble ones raised in this country."
So spoke Nestor, Neleus' son, and again in his place he
350 sat down, when he had talked to his son of each thing to accomplish.

Mérionés was the fifth to make ready his fair-maned horses.
Onto the chariots mounting, they threw lots into a helmet;
it was Achilles who shook them; the lot of Antílochos, Nestor's
son, leapt out, then after him strong Eumélos was chosen;

355 after him, Atreus' son Meneláos renowned as a spearman;
after him, Mérionés was allotted to drive, and the last place
Tydeus' son, far the best, was allotted for driving his horses.
They stood there in a row, and Achilles showed them the turn-post
far off over the smooth flat plain; and beside it he stationed

360 godlike Phoinix as umpire, his father's retainer and comrade,
so he could view and remember the running, and truly announce it.
      All of them lifted their whips at the same time over the pairs of
horses and then struck them with the lashes and eagerly called on
them in the words they yelled, and the plain they crossed very swiftly,

365 quickly away from the ships; and beneath their breasts did the dust rise
billowing up in the air, resembling a cloud or a whirlwind,
while on the breath of the wind the long manes of the horses were streaming.
Sometimes touching the nourishing earth were the chariots running,
then other times they bounded aloft, and the charioteers were

370 all in the chariots standing, the heart of each one of them throbbing,
eagerly striving to win; and they called out, each to his horses,
who as they flew on forward were raising the dust of the flatland.
      Finally, when the last leg of the race the swift horses were running
back to the silvery sea, most clearly the prowess of each man

375 showed as at once they ran at full stretch with the horses, and quickly
then raced forward the swift-hoofed mares of the scion of Pheres;
after them came on forward the stallions of strong Diomédes,
horses of Tros, not at all far after him, but very near him,
since on his chariot they seemed always about to be mounting,

380 so with their breath was the back of Eumélos and his broad shoulders
heated, for close to him they kept putting their heads as they flew on.
He would have passed him now or at least would have made it a dead heat,
had not Phoibos Apollo begrudged it for Tydeus' scion,
so that he struck down out of his hands his glittering whip-rod.

385 Straightway out of his eyes tears started to flow in his anger,
since he could see that the mares more swiftly than ever were moving,
while his own horses without any whip were hampered in running.
Not unaware was Athena of this, how Apollo was cheating
Tydeus' son; she, swiftly pursuing the shepherd of people,

390 gave him his whip-rod back, and she put strength into his horses.

Then in her rancor she went straight after the son of Admétos;
straightway the goddess shattered the chariot-yoke, so the two mares
swerved to the sides of the track; to the ground did the chariot-pole slip.
Out of the chariot, down by the wheel, was Eumélos ejected;
395   there were his elbows both lacerated, his mouth and his nostrils;
bruised was his forehead over his eyebrows; both of his eyes were
filled with the tears he shed, and the flow of his voice was arrested.
Turning his single-hoofed horses around him, Tydeus' son drove
forward and sped out far from the others, for now had Athena
400   put strength into his horses and granted to him to win glory.
After him Atreus' son, light-haired Meneláos, was driving.
Then to the horses of his dear father Antílochos shouted:
"You two as well get moving, as fast as you can stretch forward—
nevertheless, I do not charge you to contend with the steeds of
405   Tydeus' war-skilled scion, for it is on them that Athena
now has bestowed great speed, and has granted to him to win glory;
overtake swiftly the horses of Atreus' son, do not let them
leave you behind, lest Aithè, a female, shower you both with
mocking opprobrium—why are you thus outstripped, noble horses?
410   For I say to you plainly, and this will indeed be accomplished:
never will there be fodder for you with the shepherd of people,
Nestor, but he will instead kill you straightway with the sharp bronze,
if for your heedlessness we win an inferior prize now;
rather at once come along and as fast as you can hurry forward;
415   I will contrive these things myself—I will think of the way to
slip past him in the road where it narrows, nor will he escape me."
    So he spoke, and the steeds, terrified of their lord's disapproval,
started to run more strongly for some time; quickly a narrow
place in the hollow track Antílochos steadfast in fight saw—
420   there was a break in the ground where a pent-up wintery stream had
broken the track right through, and then that whole place had eroded;
there Meneláos drove to avoid the wheels clashing together.
But Antílochos turned to the side his single-hoofed horses
out of the track and pursued him, to one side swerving a little.
425   Atreus' scion was frightened and thus to Antílochos shouted,
"Recklessly do you drive, Antílochos! Rein in your horses!
Narrow the track is here—it will soon be wider for passing;
see that you not by hitting my chariot injure us both here."
    So he spoke, but Antílochos drove on even more strongly,
430   urging his steeds with the whip, like a man who seems to hear nothing.

Just so far as the range of a discus swung from the shoulder
which some vigorous youth hurls forth as a trial of manhood,
so far onward they ran; but the horses of Atreus' scion
gave way backward, for he of his own will halted the driving,
435 lest on the track those single-hoofed steeds come crashing together,
thus overturning the well-plaited chariots so that the men were
hurled down into the dust in their eager desire for the triumph.
Scolding Antílochos then spoke forth light-haired Meneláos:
"None among men, Antílochos, is more baneful than you are.
440 Damn you, since we Achaians have falsely considered you thoughtful.
Nevertheless, without taking an oath, this prize you will not win."
      So having said, he called to his horses, and thus he addressed them:
"Never at all hold back, never stop, though grieving in spirit;
surely the feet and the limbs of those horses will sooner than yours grow
445 weary, because they both are bereft of their youthful robustness."
      So he spoke, and the steeds, terrified of their lord's disapproval,
started to run more strongly, and quickly were close to the others.
      In the assembly the Argives were sitting and looking toward those
horses that flew along over the flatland, raising a dust-cloud.
450 First caught sight of the horses Idómeneus, lord of the Cretans—
high in a lookout place and away from the throng he was sitting.
Hearing the man far off who was urging his horses ahead he
knew him, and noticed a horse quite clear to the view in the forefront—
chestnut colored it was in the rest of its coat, but upon its
455 forehead there was a white spot round as the moon at its fullest.
Upright at once he stood and in these words spoke to the Argives:
"Oh dear friends and companions, the Argives' leaders and princes,
am I alone in discerning the steeds, or do you too see them?
Others the horses appear to me now that are there in the forefront;
460 also another the charioteer seems. Doubtless the mares that
up to that point were leading have met some harm on the flatland,
since I saw them in front as around the turn-post they were racing;
now nowhere can I see them, as everywhere on the Trojan
plain my eyes keep glancing about and observing the action.
465 Maybe the reins from the charioteer slipped, so that he could not
hold a course well by the post, and he did not manage to round it;
there I imagine was he thrown out and the chariot shattered,
out of the course the mares swerved, their hearts in the grip of a frenzy.
But you stand up also and see for yourselves, for I am not
470 able for sure to distinguish—to me it appears that he is by

birth an Aitolian man, but among the Argives is a leader,
scion of Tydeus tamer of horses, the strong Diomédes."
　　Shamefully scolded him thus swift Ajax, son of Oïleus:
"Why are you ever, Idómeneus, so loudmouthed? For as yet far
475　off are the high-stepping horses as they speed over the great plain.
Neither among the Argives are you so much younger than others,
nor in the least do your eyes look out of your head the most keenly;
yet are you always loudmouthed in speaking, but never at all should
you be loudmouthed, since here others are better than you are.
480　They are the same mares now in front as before were the leaders,
those of Eumélos, and holding the reins inside he is driving."
　　Wrathful at him spoke giving an answer the lord of the Cretans:
"Ajax, best at rebuking, if dull of perception—in all things
else you are worst of the Argives, because your mind is unbending;
485　come then, either a cauldron or tripod now let us wager,
let us as umpire choose Agamemnon, scion of Atreus,
telling us which mares lead, so that you may learn it and pay me."
　　He spoke; straightway arose swift Ajax, son of Oïleus,
angrily onto his feet, to return him an answer in harsh words;
490　now still further the conflict between the two men would have gone on,
had not Achilles himself stood up and a word thus spoken:
"Now no longer continue exchanging your answers in harsh words,
evil ones, Ajax and Lord Idómeneus—it is not seemly.
You yourselves would reprove any other who acted in that way.
495　In the assembly instead keep sitting and watching for all those
horses, and they will themselves, in their eager desire for the triumph,
soon come back here, and straightway you, each one, will discover
which of the Argives' horses are following, which are the leaders."
　　So did he say; then Tydeus' son came close to them, driving,
500　constantly down from the shoulder he struck with the whip, and the horses
lifted their feet up high and thus swiftly accomplished the passage.
Always the charioteer was struck by the dust as it sprinkled
over the chariot, all ornamented with gold and with tin, that
speeded behind those swift-hoofed horses, and not very deep were
505　rutted the tracks that the wheels of the chariot left in the fine dust
after it passed, as the two steeds swiftly and eagerly flew on.
In the assembly he stopped, in its midst, and the sweat of the horses
out of the necks and the chests streamed onto the ground in abundance.
Down to the ground from the glittering chariot leapt Diomédes,
510　leaning his whip-rod there on the yoke, nor a moment's delay did

powerful Sthénelos make, but the prize he eagerly seized on;
giving the high-souled comrades the woman to lead and the two-eared
tripod to carry away, from the yoke he loosed the two horses.
    After him drove up his steeds Antílochos, Neleus' scion,
515 having by guile, not at all by speed, outstripped Meneláos;
close to him, nevertheless, Meneláos had brought his swift horses.
Just so far from the chariot-wheel as a horse that is drawing
over the plain his master and strains with the chariot forward,
so on the rims of the wheels do the hindmost hairs of his tail keep
520 touching, for close in back is the chariot running, and not much
space is between as the horse runs onward across the great flatland,
so far now behind faultless Antílochos was Meneláos
left—though as far as a discus-throw he at first was behind, he
rapidly caught up with him, for the excellent power of fair-maned
525 Aithè, the mare Agamemnon had lent him, was ever increasing;
if yet longer the race between those two men had continued,
he would have passed him then, not even have made it a dead heat.
Mérionés, however, Idómeneus' noble attendant,
followed a spear-cast behind the illustrious lord Meneláos,
530 since his horses with beautiful manes were the slowest of all, while
he himself in the race was the weakest at chariot-driving.
Last to come in was the son of Admétos, behind all the others,
dragging his beautiful chariot, driving his horses before him.
There fleet-footed and noble Achilles observed him and pitied,
535 he stood among the Argives, and in these winged words he addressed them:
"Now in the last place drives his single-hoofed horses the best man;
but come, let us award him a prize, as is fitting and proper,
second—the first prize now let the scion of Týdeus bear off."
    So did he say; they all then assented to what he had bidden.
540 He would have given the mare to him now, the Achaians assenting,
had Antílochos, who was the son of the great-souled Nestor,
not stood answering Peleus' scion Achilles, and rightly:
"Truly, Achilles, with you I will be most wrathful if you make
good on this word, since you of my prize are about to deprive me,
545 thinking of this, how injured his chariot was, and the swift-paced
steeds, and himself, though skillful; but he should have prayed to the deathless
gods—thereby he would not have come last of us all in the running.
If for him you feel sorry, and he to your heart is belovèd,
plenty of gold you have in your cabin, and plenty of bronze-work,
550 plenty of sheep and of handmaids and plenty of single-hoofed horses;

choosing from these, you later can give him a prize even better—
even indeed right now, to incite the Achaians to praise you.
This mare I will not give him; about her let any man make
trial, whoever may wish with his hands to do battle against me."

555   So did he say; swift-footed and noble Achilles, rejoicing,
smiled at Antílochos, seeing that he was his much-loved comrade;
answering him he spoke, and in these winged words he addressed him:
"Truly, Antílochos, if you demand that I give to Eumélos
something else from my stores as a prize, I surely will do it.

560   I will give him the cuirass that I stripped from Ásteropaíos,
brazen and plated about with a bright tin ornamentation,
set in circles upon it; a thing of great worth he will find it."

Thus, and his dear comrade Autómedon he at once bade to
carry it out of the cabin; and he went inside and brought it,

565   putting it into the hands of Eumélos, who gladly received it.

Then among them with grief in his heart stood up Meneláos,
quenchless anger he felt at Antílochos; straightway the herald,
placing the staff in his hands, bade all of the Argives to keep their
silence; and then did the godlike man start speaking among them:

570   "Well, Antílochos, thoughtful before this, what have you now done!
You have disgraced my prowess and skill, my steeds you have thwarted,
thrusting your own to the front in the way, though they were far slower.
But come now, you who are the Argives' leaders and princes,
make an impartial judgment between us, favoring neither,

575   lest in the future will say someone of the bronze-clad Achaians:
'Over Antílochos having prevailed by his lies, Meneláos
went off leading the mare, since, though far slower his horses
proved to be, he was himself far greater in rank and in power.'
Come then, I will myself give judgement, nor will another

580   man of the Dánaäns chide me, I think—it will be straightforward.
Come here now, Zeus-loved Antílochos, duly and fitly
standing before your horses and chariot, grasping the pliant
whip-rod firmly in hand with which you were earlier driving,
touch your horses and swear by the holder and shaker of earth that

585   you did not purposely hinder my chariot, using deception."

Thoughtful Antílochos then spoke out to him, giving an answer:
"Bear with me now, since I am in fact far younger than you are,
Lord Meneláos, and you are the elder in years and the better.
You are aware what sorts of offenses arise in a young man,

590   since too hasty to act is his mind, too slight is his judgment.

Therefore now let your heart endure it, and I of myself will
give you the mare that I won, and if you were to ask for another
thing from my house yet better than this, forthwith I would want to
give it to you, Zeus-loved, much rather than all of my days fall
595   out of your favor and be in the eyes of the gods a transgressor."
       Thus, then leading the mare that scion of great-souled Nestor
gave her into the hands of the lord Meneláos, whose heart grew
warm in the way that the dew on the ears of a ripening crop of
grain grows warm in the sun at the time that the plowlands are bristling;
600   so, Meneláos, did your heart then grow warm in your bosom.
Raising his voice he spoke, and in these winged words he addressed him:
"Now, Antílochos, I of myself give over the wrath I
felt against you, since you were before not flighty of heart nor
foolish of mind—just now did your youth win out over reason.
605   But in the future do not again try outwitting your betters.
Not so soon would another among the Achaians have swayed me,
but as to you, so much have you suffered and much have you labored,
all for my sake, yourself and your excellent father and brother,
so as you make your entreaty will I be swayed, and the mare I
610   give you, though she is mine, so that these men also may know that
mine is a heart that is never excessively proud and unbending."
       Thus, and the mare he gave to Antílochos' comrade Noêmon,
so he could lead it, and then for himself took the shimmering cauldron.
Mérionés took up the two talents of gold for the fourth place,
615   as in the race he had driven, but unclaimed yet was the fifth prize
left, that two-handled urn, and Achilles bestowed it on Nestor;
bearing it through the assembly of Argives, he stood by him, saying:
"There now, this is for you, old sir, let it be a treasure
calling to mind the grave-rites of Patróklos, for never again will
620   he be seen here among the Argives; this prize I bestow on
you just so, since you will not battle in boxing or wrestling,
nor will you enter the javelin contest, nor on your feet will
you be running, for harsh old age now presses upon you."
       So as he spoke, in his hands he placed it; he gladly received it;
625   raising his voice he spoke, and in these winged words he addressed him:
"Certainly all this, son, you speak as is fitting and proper,
since no longer are steady my limbs and feet, friend, and my hands no
longer are nimble, on both sides springing away from the shoulders.
How I wish I were young, and the strength yet steady within me,
630   as at the time the Epeíans were burying strong Amaríngkeus

in Bouprásion—there for the king his sons had set prizes.
Then no man was the equal to me, not among the Epeíans,
nor of the Pylians nor the greathearted Aitolian people.
There in boxing I won over Énops' son Klytomédes,
635   then in wrestling Angkaíos of Pleuron, who stood up to face me;
Íphiklos, good as he was, I then outran in the footrace;
while in the spear-cast I outthrew Polydóros and Phýleus.
Only in chariot-racing the scions of Aktor surpassed me,
driving ahead by numerical force and begrudging me triumph,
640   also because for this contest the best of the prizes remained there.
Those two were in fact twins—one steadily driving the horses,
steadily driving the horses, the other one wielding the whip-rod.
Thus was I once; now it is for men who are younger to face such
labors as these, while I to the prompting of odious old age
645   must give way, who was then outstanding among all the heroes.
But go, honor your comrade too with the funeral contests.
This I gladly receive from your hands, my spirit rejoices,
how as a friend you think of me always and never forget that
honor with which I am fittingly honored among the Achaians.
650   May the gods grant you, as guerdon for these things, plentiful favor."
    So he spoke; through the numerous throng of Achaians the son of
Peleus went, having heard the whole tale of the scion of Neleus.
Next for the painful and dangerous boxing he set out the prizes:
leading a she-mule, sturdy in work, unbroken, of six years—
655   such as is hardest to break—he tethered her in the assembly;
for the defeated contender he set out a two-handled goblet.
There among them he stood, and a word he spoke to the Argives:
"Atreus' sons and you others, the rest of the well-greaved Achaians,
now over these things do we invite two fighters, the best ones,
660   lifting their hands, to contend with their fists; let him whom Apollo
grants the endurance to win, so that all the Achaians perceive it,
lead off the she-mule, sturdy in work, and return to his cabin,
while the defeated contender will bear off the two-handled goblet."
    So he spoke, and at once rose a man stout-bodied and valiant,
665   one most skillful at boxing, Epeíos the son of Panópeus;
holding the she-mule, sturdy in work, he spoke and addressed them:
"Let him approach, whoever will bear off the two-handled goblet;
as for the mule, I say that no other Achaian will take her,
conquering me with his fists, since I claim I am the greatest.
670   Or is it not already enough that in battle I fall short?

Never in all of his acts, it seems, can a man become skillful.
For I say to you plainly, and this thing will be accomplished:
mercilessly his flesh I will tear and his bones I will shatter.
So let those of his kin who care for him stay here together,
675 ready to carry him out, once he at my hands has been vanquished."
        So did he say; then all of the people were hushed in silence.
Only Eurýalos rose to confront him, godlike in manhood—
he was the son of the lordly Mekísteus, Tálaös' scion,
who once journeyed to Thebes for the funeral rites of the fallen
680 Oídipous; there he had vanquished all of the offspring of Kadmos.
Now on this boxer attended the spear-famed scion of Týdeus,
heartening him with his words, as the victory strongly he wished him.
Close to him first he threw down the loincloth, then he provided
him with the thongs well cut from the hide of an ox of the pasture.
685 Girding themselves, those two strode into the midst of the assembly;
straightway lifting their massive hands up against one another
they came crashing together, the huge hands heavily clashing;
dreadfully sounded the gnashing of teeth from the jaws, and the sweat ran
everywhere from their limbs; then noble Epeíos assailed him,
690 striking his cheek as he looked for an opening; not very long he
stood—right there did the glorious limbs give way underneath him.
Just as, under the north wind's ripples, a fish from the water
leaps on a weed-strewn sandbar, and then is concealed in a black wave,
so when struck the man leapt; in his hands greathearted Epeíos
695 grasped him and set him upright, and around him stood his belovèd
comrades, and through the assembly they guided him out, his feet dragging,
spitting out thick blood-clots, with his head off to one side lolling,
dizzy and dazed in his senses, and led him and sat him among them,
then they went to Achilles to fetch him the two-handled goblet.
700   Peleus' son for the third match at once set out other prizes,
letting the Dánaäns see them—the painful and dangerous wrestling:
first for the winner a great tripod to be set over fire whose
value among themselves the Achaians appraised at twelve oxen;
then for the man who would lose he set in the middle a woman
705 skillful in much handwork, whose worth they appraised at four oxen.
There among them he stood, and a word he spoke to the Argives:
"Rise now, two among you who would prove yourselves in this contest."
So did he say; then arose great Ajax, Télamon's scion;
up stood Odysseus of many devices, astute in contrivance;
710 girding themselves, those two strode into the midst of the assembly,

then with their massive hands each grappled the arms of the other
like great rafters a glorious craftsman has fitted together
up in a high-roofed dwelling, resisting the might of the stormwinds.
Both of their backs creaked harshly beneath the inflexible wrenching
715   tugs of the violent hands, and in streams sweat ran from their bodies,
numerous too were the welts that along their ribs and their shoulders
sprang up, swollen and ruddy with blood, as incessantly, always,
those two struggled for triumph, for winning the well-made tripod;
neither Odysseus was able to trip Ajax or to throw him,
720   nor could Ajax achieve it—Odysseus' immense might held firm.
Finally, when they were starting to weary the well-greaved Achaians,
then to Odysseus spoke great Ajax, Télamon's scion:
"Zeus-sprung son of Laërtes, Odysseus of many devices,
lift me, or I will lift you—the whole outcome Zeus will determine."
725   So he said, lifting, but not of his guile was Odysseus forgetful;
aiming a blow at his knee from behind, his limbs he unloosened
so that he fell down backward; upon his breast did Odysseus
fall to the ground, and the people were marveling, gazing upon it.
Trying to lift him then, much-suffering noble Odysseus
730   moved him a little away from the ground yet still did not lift him;
rather inside of his knee he hooked his own leg, so that both men
fell to the ground right next to each other—with dust they were dirtied.
Then for the third time they once more would have leapt up and wrestled,
had not Achilles himself stood up and held back the two fighters:
735   "Strain no longer to fight, nor exhaust yourselves with afflictions;
victory both of you win; so taking equivalent prizes,
go on your way, so that other Achaians may join in the contests."
So did he say; they carefully listened to him and obeyed him,
then they wiped off the dust from their bodies and put on their tunics.
740   Peleus' son for the footrace at once set out other prizes:
first was a wine bowl skillfully fashioned of silver for holding
six full measures of wine, in beauty outstanding above all
others on earth, since clever Sidonian craftsman had made it;
over the seaway, misty and murky, Phoenicians had brought it;
745   coming to land in the harbor, to Thoas they gave it as present;
then to the hero Patróklos Eunéos the scion of Jason
gave it to ransom Lykáon the own dear offspring of Priam.
This as a prize did Achilles to honor his comrade set out
now for the runner who proved on his swift feet lightest and nimblest.
750   Then a huge ox, thick-laden with fat, he set for the second;

gold, a half-talent in weight, he set out there for the last prize.
There among them he stood, and a word he spoke to the Argives:
"Rise now, you who would also prove yourselves in this contest."
    So he said; quickly arose swift Ajax, son of Oïleus,
755 also Odysseus of many devices, and after him Nestor's
son Antílochos, since on his feet he was best of the young men.
They stood there in a row, and Achilles showed them the turn-post.
Stretching away from a line was the course they ran, and Oïleus'
son raced swiftly ahead; close after him noble Odysseus
760 speeded; as near as a shed-rod is to a fair-girdled woman's
bosom, the rod which she with her hands draws back, separating
warp-threads, and then through them pulls the weft-spool—close to her breast she
holds it—as closely behind him Odysseus was running; his feet trod
right in the footsteps of Ajax before dust settled upon them;
765 down on his head was blowing the breath of the noble Odysseus
who kept rapidly running; and all the Achaians were shouting
as for the win he struggled, and urging him on as he speeded.
Finally, when the last leg of the race they were running, Odysseus
quickly addressed this prayer in his spirit to bright-eyed Athena:
770 "Hear me, goddess, and come to me now, for my feet a strong helper."
So he spoke as he prayed; he was heard by Pallas Athena,
who made nimble his limbs, his feet and his hands up above them.
Finally, just as the two were beginning the rush for the first prize,
Ajax slipped as he ran—for Athena disabled him badly—
775 right where the dung was strewn from the killing of bellowing oxen
which swift-footed Achilles had slaughtered to honor Patróklos;
then with the dung of the oxen were filled his mouth and his nostrils.
So much-suffering noble Odysseus took up the wine bowl,
since he had come in first; and the ox then glorious Ajax
780 took and stood holding his hand on the horn of the ox of the pasture,
spitting the dung from his mouth, and he spoke these words to the Argives:
"Well then, now has the goddess disabled my feet—she has always
stood at Odysseus' side like a mother and offered him succor."
    So he spoke, and at him they all began merrily laughing.
785 Taking the gold, Antílochos carried the last of the prizes
off as he smiled; this then is the word he spoke to the Argives:
"Now to you all who know it, friends, I will say that to this day
do the immortals indeed show honor to men who are older,
seeing that Ajax was in his birth but a little before me,
790 while this man was of earlier birth and of earlier people—

his is a green old age, they say—and a difficult man for
any Achaians to match in running, except for Achilles."
        So he spoke and exalted the swift-footed scion of Peleus.
        Speaking in these words answered Achilles, and thus he addressed him:
795   "Not in vain will this praise, Antílochos, prove to be spoken,
but to your prize a half-talent of gold I will add as a present."
        So as he spoke, in his hands he placed it; he gladly received it.
Straightway Peleus' son brought out a long-shadowing spear-shaft;
in the assembly he set it, as well as a shield and a helmet.
800   They were Sarpédon's arms; from his body Patróklos had stripped them.
There among them he stood, and a word he spoke to the Argives:
"Now over these things do we invite two fighters, the best ones,
dressing themselves in armor and grasping the bronze that cuts bodies,
here in front of the host to make proof each one of the other.
805   Who of the two first reaches the beautiful flesh of the other,
touching the inside parts through the armor, as well as the black blood,
he is the one I will give this sword all studded with silver,
beautiful, Thracian in make, that I stripped from Ásteropaíos;
let the two men carry off these arms as a common possession;
810   then I will set out before them an excellent meal in the cabins."
        So he spoke, and then rose great Ajax, Télamon's scion;
after him rose up Tydeus' scion, the strong Diomédes.
Soon as the two, either side of the throng, were armed and accoutered,
both of the men strode into the midspace, avid for battle,
815   glaring their terrible stares, and astonishment seized the Achaians.
When in coming together the men were close to each other,
thrice at each other they leapt, thrice charged in hand-to-hand combat.
Ajax thrust straight down through the circular shield of his foe and
struck but did not reach flesh, for the corselet guarded it inside;
820   Tydeus' son meanwhile kept trying to strike at his neck just
over his great broad shield with the point of his glistening spear-blade.
Then indeed the Achaians, exceedingly fearful for Ajax,
bade them to leave off fighting and take up equivalent prizes.
But to the scion of Tydeus the hero presented the great sword,
825   bringing it over to him with its scabbard and well-cut baldric.
        Peleus' son as a prize then set out a lump of pig iron,
which had aforetime often been hurled by Eêtion's huge strength;
but then, when swift-footed and noble Achilles had killed him,
this he had carried away in his ships with the rest of his plunder.
830   There among them he stood, and a word he spoke to the Argives:

"Rise now, you who would also prove yourselves in this contest.
Even although his fertile plowlands are far at a distance,
five full years of the seasons' revolving the winner will have this,
serving his needs, since never his shepherd or plowman in want of
835 iron will have to go into the city, but this will supply them."
      So as he spoke rose up Polypoítes, steadfast in battle,
also rose up the powerful strength of the godlike Leónteus,
then rose Ajax Télamon's son and the noble Epeíos.
They stood there in a line, and the lump did the noble Epeíos
840 seize, then whirled it and hurled it, and all the Achaians were laughing.
Second at throwing the lump was Leónteus, offshoot of Ares,
then as the third great Ajax the scion of Télamon hurled it
forth from his stout hand—over the marks of them all did he throw it.
But then, seizing the lump, Polypoítes, steadfast in battle,
845 just so far as a staff gets flung on its cord by a cowherd
so that it flies forth whirling and over the herds of his cattle,
so far beyond the whole contest he hurled it, and loudly they shouted.
Rising at once to their feet, the companions of strong Polypoítes
carried the prize of their ruler away to his hollow galleys.
850   Next for the archery contest the dark-blue iron he set out—
ten double-axes and ten single-axes he set as the prizes.
Then faraway on the sands he set up the mast of a dark-prowed
galley, to which he fastened a fluttering dove with a slender
string bound onto its foot—this then he ordered that they should
855 shoot at: "Whoever should strike that fluttering dove with his arrow,
let him receive all these double-axes and carry them homeward.
Then whoever should hit on the string, though the bird he misses,
since his shot is the worse, he will take away these single-axes."
      When these words he had said, then rose up the might of Lord Teukros;
860 Mérionés rose also, Idómeneus' noble attendant.
Taking the two lots up, in a helmet of bronze they shook them.
Teukros it was who drew the first place, and an arrow at once he
let fly mightily forth, but he did not vow to the lord that
firstborn lambs he would offer, a glorious hecatomb, later.
865 Therefore he missed that bird, for Apollo begrudged him the triumph;
rather he struck by the foot on the string which fastened the bird there;
utterly then was the string cut through by the sharp bitter arrow;
up and away to the sky went darting the dove, and the string fell
dangling below toward earth; the Achaians were loudly applauding.
870 Acting in haste then Mérionés snatched out of his hand that

bow, for an arrow before he had held, while Teukros was shooting;
straightway then to the lord far-shooting Apollo he vowed that
firstborn lambs he would offer, a glorious hecatomb, later.
High up under the clouds was the fluttering dove, and he saw her;
875   there as she circled around, square under the wing did he strike her;
straight through went the sharp missile and fell back down and in front of
Mérionés' feet planted itself in the ground, and the bird then
dropped and alighted upon the tall mast of the dark-prowed galley,
letting her neck hang down, and her fine thick feathers were drooping;
880   swiftly the life flew out of her limbs; faraway from the mast she
fell to the ground, and the people were marveling, gazing upon it.
Mérionés took up for himself all ten double-axes;
Teukros carried the singles away to the hollow galleys.

    Straightway Peleus' son brought out a long-shadowing spear-shaft,
885   also an unsmirched cauldron with flower-embossing, an ox-worth;
in the assembly he set them, and then up stood the spear-throwers;
up rose Atreus' son, wide-governing Lord Agamemnon;
Mérionés rose also, Idómeneus' noble attendant.
Then among them spoke thus swift-footed and noble Achilles:
890   "Atreus' son, since we are aware how far you surpass all,
how much you are the best in strength and in throwing a spear-shaft,
now then, take this prize and go back to the hollow galleys,
while to the hero Mérionés this spear let us proffer,
if in your heart you desire it, for so I certainly urge it."
895   He spoke, nor disobeyed him the leader of men Agamemnon;
Mérionés he gave the bronze spear; thereafter the hero
handed his beautiful prize to Talthýbios, who was his herald.

BOOK 24

Then the assembly dissolved, and the people dispersed to the swift ships—
each man went to his own—where most took thought of their dinner
and of their slumber, to take their pleasure; but meanwhile Achilles
wept as he thought of his much-loved comrade, nor was he seized by
5   Sleep, that queller of all, but he turned from one side to the other,
so did he long for Patróklos, his valorous might and his manhood,
thinking of all he had labored with him, what pains he had suffered
cleaving a way through battles of men and the troublesome billows;
mindful of all these things, he shed great tears in abundance;
10 some of the time he would lie on his side, and again at another
time on his back, and again face downward, and then he would rise up
onto his feet, go roaming along the seashore distraught, and the Dawn would
never escape him as she shone bright on the sea and the beaches.
But then, when to the chariot-pole he would yoke the swift horses
15 and to the chariot he would bind Hektor to drag him behind it,
thrice he would drag him around the grave-mound of Menoítios' dead son;
then in his cabin again he would rest, but the corpse he would leave right
there stretched out in the dust face down. From the body Apollo
kept off every shameful defilement—he pitied the fighter
20 even in death, and he covered him wholly about with the golden
aegis so that Achilles would not tear him as he dragged him.
So he sought to defile noble Hektor, savagely raging;
looking upon him the fortunate gods felt pity for Hektor—
they kept urging the keen-eyed slayer of Argos to steal him.
25 This, though pleasing to all of the other gods, never did Hera
nor did Poseidon accept, nor at all did the bright-eyed maiden;
but they held as before holy Ilion hateful to them, and
Priam as well, and his people, for Alexander's delusion—
he had insulted the goddesses when they came to his farmstead,
30 favoring her who imbued him with ruinous sexual craving.

Finally, soon as appeared thereafter the twelfth of the mornings,
standing among the immortals addressed them Phoibos Apollo:
"Gods, you workers of bane, you are merciless! Never did Hektor
burn thigh-pieces of oxen and goats unblemished to please you?

35 Now no heart do you have to preserve him, though a dead body,
so that his bedmate looks upon him, and his child and his mother,
Priam his father as well, and his people, who quickly would burn his
corpse in the blaze of a pyre and provide him funeral honors.
Baneful Achilles instead, you gods, you are eager to succor,

40 him in whom is no mind that is righteous, nor can the purpose
ever be bent in his breast, but he thinks fierce thoughts like a lion
who, any time that he yields to his own great might and his valiant
heart, goes after the sheep flocks of mortals to get him a banquet;
so has Achilles destroyed compassion, and shame and respect no

45 longer he has, which harm men greatly but profit them also.
There is no doubt that a man may have lost someone even dearer,
either a brother by one same mother or even his own son,
yet once he has lamented and wept, he ceases to mourn him,
since mankind is endowed by the Fates with a heart of endurance.

50 Yet he, having bereft of his life noble Hektor, behind his
chariot ties him and drags him around the grave-mound of his much-loved
comrade—nothing at all this gets him of honor or profit.
Let him beware, though valiant he is, lest we become angry,
since in his furious raging the mute earth he is defiling."

55   Wrathfully then in reply thus spoke to him white-armed Hera:
"God of the silvery bow, your word might well be a true one,
should you gods on Achilles and Hektor bestow the same honor.
Hektor is mortal, however, and sucked at the breast of a woman,
while of a goddess Achilles is offspring—I was myself her

60 nurse, and I brought her up, then gave her as bride to her husband,
Peleus, who is exceedingly dear to the hearts of the immortals.
Gods, in the wedding you all took part; you too with your lyre were
feasting among them, friend of iniquities, treacherous always."
    Answering her in return spoke forth the cloud-gathering god Zeus:

65 "Hera, do not with the gods be utterly, bitterly wrathful;
not the same honor will these two have, yet Hektor as well was
dearest of all to the gods, among mortals in Ilion living—
so to myself, for he did not fail to make gifts that were pleasing,
no, since never my altar was lacking a well-shared banquet,

70 savory smoke and libations, for these we get as our prizes.

But now let us give up any theft of the valorous Hektor,
since no way may it happen unknown to Achilles; his mother
always goes to his side in the night and as well in the daytime.
Would that a god might go call Thetis to come to me hither,
75   so that a wise word I may address her, and then that Achilles
may accept presents from Priam and give back Hektor to take home."

He spoke; storm-footed Iris arose to go carry the message;
then midway between Samos and Imbros rugged and rocky,
in the black sea she leapt, and the water resounded above her.
80   Clear down into the depths she plummeted, much as a leaden
weight set onto the shield of a fish-line, the horn of a field ox,
goes down taking their destined death to the ravenous fishes.
Thetis she came upon there in her hollow cave, and the other
sea-goddesses sat gathered around her; she in their midst was
85   making lament for the death of her faultless son, who would soon be
dying in deep-soiled Troy, faraway from the land of his fathers.
Standing beside her there, thus spoke to her swift-footed Iris:
"Rise up, Thetis, for Zeus of infallible purposes calls you."

Thetis the goddess of silvery feet then gave her an answer:
90   "Why does that great god call me? To mingle among the immortals
I am ashamed, since measureless grief I have in my spirit.
Yet will I go—not vain will his word be, whatever he utters."

Soon as she said these words, that splendor of goddesses took her
dark head-scarf—no garment exists any blacker than this was—
95   then she set forth to go; before her swift wind-footed Iris
led her the way, and the waves of the deep sea opened around them.
After they went out onto the shore they leapt up to heaven;
there they found the wide-thundering scion of Kronos and, sitting
gathered around, all the rest of the fortunate gods ever-living.
100 There by Zeus the great father she sat, given place by Athena.
Hera put into her hand a fine goblet of gold, and with cordial
words she greeted her; taking a drink then Thetis returned it.
Speaking among them opened the father of gods and of mankind:
"Thetis divine, you have come to Olympos in spite of your sorrow,
105 having at heart unforgettable grief—of myself do I know it.
Nevertheless, I will tell you why I summoned you hither.
Wrangling for nine days now has arisen among the immortals
both over Hektor's corpse and Achilles the sacker of cities;
they keep urging the keen-eyed slayer of Argos to steal it;
110 but to Achilles instead I grant it to be to his glory,

hoping to keep your respect and your friendship ever hereafter.
Go with all speed to the army and tell your son what I charge him:
say that the gods are resentful of him, and among the immortals
I am indeed most wrathful of all, that with furious spirit
115   he keeps Hektor beside the curved galleys and did not return him—
he may perhaps be frightened of me and so give back Hektor.
Meanwhile to great-souled Priam will I send Iris to bid him
ransom his much-loved son, going down to the ships of the Achaians
carrying gifts for Achilles, that they might soften his temper."
120   He spoke: Thetis of silvery feet did not disobey him,
speedily she came down from the summit of lofty Olympos,
then she arrived at the cabin of her dear son, and she found him
there incessantly groaning; around him his much-loved comrades
eagerly busied themselves, engaged in preparing the breakfast.
125   There in the cabin a great woolly ram lay slaughtered as victim.
Close to the side of her son sat down that lady his mother,
gave him a pat with her hand and said these words, calling upon him:
"How much longer, my child, will you keep on weeping and mourning,
eating your heart out—not in the least are you mindful of food nor
130   even of bed, though it would be good with a woman to join in
love, since not very long, I say, will you live, but already
standing beside you is death and your own irresistible doomsday.
But now quickly obey me—from Zeus I bring you a message:
he says the gods are resentful of you, and among the immortals
135   he is indeed the most wrathful of all, that with furious spirit
you keep Hektor beside the curved galleys and did not return him.
But come, give him back now, for the dead man taking a ransom."
        Answering her in return spoke forth swift-footed Achilles:
"So be it; let whoever brings ransom return with the dead man,
140   if wholeheartedly thus the Olympian ruler commands it."
        So in the place where the galleys were gathered the mother and son were
talking together in many a winged word, each to the other.
Meanwhile to sacred Ilion Kronos' son sent forth Iris:
"Go there at once, swift Iris, and leaving the seat of Olympos,
145   take this message to great-souled Priam in Ilion: bid him
ransom his much-loved son, going down to the ships of the Achaians
carrying gifts for Achilles, that they might soften his temper,
only himself—let go with him no other man of the Trojans.
Let some herald attend him, a man who is older, to guide his
150   mules on the way, and the well-wheeled wagon, and also to carry

back to the city the dead man slaughtered by noble Achilles.
Let not death be a care to his spirit, nor let him be fearful,
such is the guide we will give to escort him, the slayer of Argos,
who will conduct him until to Achilles himself he has brought him;
155 once he has taken him into the cabin of noble Achilles,
then will the lord not kill him, but keep off all of the others,
since not mindless he is, not heedless or given to malice;
rather, a supplicant man he will spare in benevolent kindness."
    He spoke; storm-footed Iris arose to go carry the message.
160 Entering Priam's abode, she found lamentation and wailing.
There in the courtyard around their father his children were sitting,
drenching their clothes with the tears they shed; in the middle the old man
sat wrapped closely about in a mantle, and dung in abundance
lay all over the old man's head and his neck and his shoulders—
165 this with his hands while rolling about on the ground he had scraped up.
All through the palace his daughters and daughters-in-law were lamenting,
thinking about those men, those many and valorous fighters,
who lay dead, having lost their lives at the hands of the Argives.
There Zeus' messenger stood beside Priam; addressing him then she
170 spoke in a small soft voice, yet shivering seized on his body:
"Take heart, Priam the scion of Dárdanos, nor at all fear me,
since not threatening evil to you I come to this dwelling,
rather with kindly intention—to you Zeus' messenger I am;
though at a distance from you, he feels much care and compassion.
175 Now the Olympian bids you to ransom the noble lord Hektor,
carrying gifts for Achilles, that they might soften his temper,
only yourself—let go with you no other man of the Trojans.
Let some herald attend you, a man who is older, to guide your
mules on the way, and the well-wheeled wagon, and also to carry
180 back to the city the dead man slaughtered by noble Achilles.
Let not death be a care to your spirit, nor be at all fearful,
such is the guide who will go as your escort, the slayer of Argos,
who will conduct you until to Achilles himself he has brought you;
once he has taken you into the cabin of noble Achilles,
185 then will the lord not kill you, but keep off all of the others,
since not mindless he is, not heedless or given to malice;
rather, a supplicant man he will spare in benevolent kindness."
    So having spoken her message, the swift-footed Iris departed.
Straightway then he commanded his sons to make ready a well-wheeled
190 mule-drawn wagon and fasten upon it a wickerwork basket.

As for himself, he went downstairs to a sweet-smelling chamber,
high-roofed, fashioned of cedar, and much bright treasure containing;
calling his bedmate Hékabè there, these words he addressed her:
"Dear wife, coming from Zeus an Olympian messenger bade me

195 ransom my much-loved son, going down to the ships of the Achaians
carrying gifts for Achilles, that they might soften his temper.
But come now, tell me this—to your mind what seems to be better?
As for myself, my mind and my spirit are dreadfully urging
me to go there to the galleys among the broad host of Achaians."

200   So he spoke, and his wife cried shrilly, returning an answer:
"Ah me, where has departed the wisdom for which you were famous
ever before among strangers as well as the people you govern?
How can you wish to be going alone to the ships of the Achaians,
there to encounter the eyes of the man who slaughtered and stripped our

205 sons so many and noble? The heart in your breast is of iron,
since if he gets you into his hands, with his eyes he beholds you—
faithless the man is, an eater of raw flesh—he will not pity
you nor respect you at all; now sitting apart in our chambers
let us lament over Hektor. For him irresistible Doom spun

210 things this way with her thread at his birth, when I myself bore him—
he was to glut those fleet-footed dogs, faraway from his parents,
under the hands of a violent man, whose liver inside I
wish I could take in my teeth and devour; then deeds of requital
might be done for my son, since he was not killed as a coward,

215 but for the Trojans and deep-bosomed women of Troy he stood there
making defense, not thinking of flight or of running to shelter."
    Speaking to her made answer the old man, godlike Priam:
"Hold me not back—I am minded to go; do not in my own house
serve as a bird of ill omen for me; you will never persuade me,

220 since if another of those who live on the earth had so urged me,
whether of seers divining from victims, or priests of the temples,
we would declare it a falsehood, and certainly we would reject it;
now, as I heard that goddess myself, to her face I beheld her,
there will I go—not vain will her word be. Then if indeed my

225 portion it is by the ships of the bronze-clad Achaians to perish,
so do I wish it—at once let Achilles kill me, when I have
clasped my son in my arms and relieved my desire for lamenting."
    So he spoke, and he opened the beautiful lids of the coffers;
out of them then he took twelve robes exceedingly lovely,

230 twelve wool mantles to be worn single, as many thick blankets,

so too as many white cloaks, and as well the same number of tunics.
Then, having weighed out gold to a ten full talents, he went out,
bearing as well two glistening tripods and four of his cauldrons,
also a beautiful cup that the Thracian men had bestowed on
235 him when he went on a mission, a great gift—not even this was
spared by the old man now in his house, so much in his heart he
wanted to ransom his much-loved son. Then all of the Trojans
he drove out of the porch, and in harsh words spoke to rebuke them:
"Get out, shameful and infamous wretches! And do you not also
240 have in your own homes wailing, that you come here to afflict me?
Do you think slight this pain Zeus scion of Kronos has given,
losing the noblest of sons? Yet you will yourselves realize it,
since most certainly you will be easier for the Achaian
fighters to kill since that man has perished. But as for myself now,
245 may I, before with my eyes I have seen this city all ransacked,
ravaged and leveled to dust, go into the palace of Hades."

     So he spoke and went after the men with a staff; at the old man's
instance they went outside; to his sons he shouted reproaches,
Hélenos thus he rebuked, noble Ágathon also, and Paris,
250 Pammon, Antíphonos, and the great crier of battle Polítes,
then Deíphobos also, Hippóthoös, excellent Dios—
it was to these nine sons that the old man shouted his orders:
"Hurry up, cowardly children, disgraces, I wish that together
you all beside the swift galleys had been killed rather than Hektor.
255 Ah me, to all bane destined, because I fathered the best sons
in broad Troy, and of them not one, I say, is remaining,
no, not godlike Mestor or Troilos the chariot-fighter,
neither is Hektor, who was a god among men, and he did not
seem the offspring of a man, a mere mortal, but rather a god's son.
260 These men Ares has killed, and remaining are all the disgraces,
liars and dancers, the best in the country at beating a dance floor,
plunderers too of the lambs and the kids of the men in your own land.
Now will you not very quickly for me make ready a wagon,
then put these all upon it, that we may accomplish the journey?"
265   So did he say; then trembling before the rebuke of their father,
they brought out of the stable a well-wheeled mule-drawn wagon,
beautiful, newly constructed; upon it a wickerwork basket
they then fixed; from the hook they took down the yoke for the mule-team,
boxwood, knobbed at the front, well fitted with rings for the rein-guides.
270 Then with the yoke they brought out a yoke-rope of nine full cubits;

423

carefully then they fitted the yoke to the well-polished yoke-pole,
onto its front end, throwing the ring on the peg to secure it,
thrice to each side on the knob they fastened the rope, and at last they
bound it around the yoke-pole, then twisted it under the guard-hook.
275 Out of the storage room they carried and heaped on the polished
wagon the measureless ransom to give for the head of great Hektor;
then they yoked up the strong-hoofed mule-team, toiling in harness,
which once Mysians had given to Priam, a glorious present.
Under the yoke they led up for Priam the horses the old man
280 kept for himself, at a well-polished manger providing them nurture.
       So in the high-roofed house were the teams yoked up for the two men,
Priam as well as the herald, who both had minds full of counsel.
Hékabè came up close to them there, much troubled in spirit;
she in her right hand carried to them red wine, honey-hearted,
285 in a gold goblet, that they might make libation at parting;
standing in front of the horses, she spoke a word, calling upon them:
"Here, pour out a libation to Zeus our father, and pray that
you may return back home from the enemy men, for your heart is
urging you now to the ships, though I do not want you to go there.
290 Nevertheless then, pray to the dark-cloud scion of Kronos
sitting on Ida, the god who oversees all of the Troäd;
ask that an omen, a bird, the swift messenger which is the dearest
bird of them all to himself and the one whose might is the strongest,
show on the right, so that you, with your own eyes seeing the omen,
295 trusting in it may go to the swift-horsed Dánaäns' galleys.
Should wide-thundering Zeus not grant you his messenger-omen,
then for my part, indeed, I would never exhort you or bid you
go to the Argives' ships, though you are excessively eager."
       Answering her in return thus spoke to her godlike Priam:
300 "Wife, I will not disobey you about this thing you are urging,
since it is good to lift hands up to Zeus, in the hope he has pity."
       So did the old man speak, and he ordered the housemaid attending
him to pour over his hands pure water; and quickly the housemaid
stood beside him; in her hands she bore a washbasin and pitcher.
305 Washing his hands and receiving the cup from his wife, in the central
courtyard then he prayed as he stood there pouring the wine out;
looking above toward heaven he raised his voice to say these words:
"Father Zeus, ruling from Ida, the lord most honored and mighty,
grant me to come to Achilles as one to befriend and to pity;
310 send me an omen, a bird, the swift messenger which is the dearest

bird of them all to yourself, and the one whose might is the strongest,
here on the right, so that I, with my own eyes seeing the omen,
trusting in it may go to the swift-horsed Dánaäns' galleys."
　　So he spoke as he prayed; Zeus Counselor heard him and heeded;
315　straightway an eagle he sent, among winged birds surest of omens;
it was a dark one, a hunter, the bird men call the black eagle.
Just so wide as the door of the high-roofed treasury room of
some man wealthy in goods, a door fitted with bars to secure it,
so wide then were the wings of the bird, each side; he appeared to
320　them on the right as he sped through the city, and seeing him they were
gladdened—the hearts in the breasts of them all grew lighter and warmer.
　　Quickly and urgently onto his chariot mounted the old man,
out of the courtyard gate and the echoing portico drove it.
Pulling the four-wheeled wagon ahead of the men was the mule-team
325　which wise-minded Idaíos was driving; behind them the horses
went, and the old man, wielding a whip, kept urging them forward,
rapidly crossing the city; his friends all followed behind him,
uttering loud lamentation as if to his death he was going.
Then when they had gone down from the city and come to the flatland,
330　there did the others return toward Ilion, all of his sons and
sons-in-law; wide-thundering Zeus was aware of the two men
when in the plain they appeared; as he saw the old man, he felt pity;
he at once spoke to his dear son Hermes, and thus he addressed him:
"Hermes, because it is pleasing to you above all of the other
335　gods to be friends with a man, and you hear whomever you want to,
go there, and so guide Priam along to the hollow galleys
of the Achaians that none of the rest of the Dánaäns see him
nor recognize him, until he has come to the scion of Peleus."
　　He spoke, nor was ignored by the messenger, slayer of Argos.
340　Straightway under his feet he fastened his beautiful sandals,
golden, undying, divine, which carry him over the water,
over the measureless surface of earth with the breath of the stormwind,
took up the wand he uses for charming the eyes of whatever
man he wishes, and others again he arouses from slumber;
345　this he held in his hand as he flew, the strong slayer of Argos.
Swiftly to Troy he came and the Hellespont; having arrived there,
he set forth on the way in the form of a prince in his youthful
years with his first mustache, of the age most graceful and pleasing.
　　Driving ahead, they passed the enormous grave-mound of Ilos,
350　then they halted the mules and the horses, that there in the river

425

they might drink, since over the earth now darkness had fallen.
Then as the herald was looking he noticed that Hermes had come up
close to them there, and to Priam he spoke these words and addressed him:
"Take thought, Dárdanos' son—here is work for a mind that is thoughtful.

355 I see a man—I suppose he quickly will tear us to pieces.
But come now, let us flee with the horses, or otherwise let us
clasp his knees and beseech him, that he take pity upon us."
    Thus, and the old man's mind was disquieted, dreadfully he was
frightened, and straight upright on his flexible limbs did the hair stand;

360 stupefied he stood there, but the Runner himself came near him;
taking the old man's hand, he spoke to him, asking a question:
"Where now, father, are you thus guiding the mules and the horses
through the ambrosial night, at a time other mortals are sleeping?
Are you not frightened at all of the violence-breathing Achaians,

365 who are to you so hostile, the enemies who are now nearby?
Should one of them see you through the swift black shadows of nighttime
carrying treasures so great, what counsel indeed would you think of?
You are yourself not young, and the one who attends you is old for
keeping away any man when he first starts doing you outrage.

370 I will myself not do any harm to you but will defend you
even against any other; you seem to me like a dear father."
    Speaking to him then answered the old man godlike Priam:
"So without doubt, dear child, these matters are just as you tell me.
Nevertheless, over me some god still stretches his hand out,

375 one who dispatched so fine a wayfarer as you are to meet me—
omen of good—so wondrous in bodily form and appearance,
thoughtful as well in mind; you are sprung from fortunate parents."
    Speaking to him made answer the messenger, slayer of Argos:
"Yes, of all this, old sir, you speak as is fitting and proper.

380 But come now, tell me this and recount it exactly and fully,
whether you seek to convey these treasures so many and noble
quickly to foreigners, so that for you they remain in safety,
whether instead holy Ilion now you all are forsaking,
being afraid, since such is the fighter, the best, who has perished,

385 your own son, who was never deficient in fighting Achaians."
    Speaking to him then answered the old man, godlike Priam:
"Who are you then, most excellent sir, of what parents the offspring?
Such fine things of the doom of my ill-starred son you have spoken."
    Speaking to him made answer the messenger, slayer of Argos:

390 "Thus, old sir, do you test me, in asking about noble Hektor.

426

Him very often, in fact, in the battle that wins a man glory
I with my own eyes saw, and the time when, driving the Argives
into their ships, he killed them, with sharp bronze wreaking destruction;
we kept standing and marveling there, for Achilles would not let
395 us go into the battle, enraged at the scion of Atreus.
     Yes, his attendant am I—the same strong-built galley conveyed us—
one of the Mýrmidons too. My father is noble Polýktor;
he in possessions is wealthy, an elderly man, just as you are;
six are the sons he has, while I myself am the seventh;
400 shaking my lot among theirs, I was chosen to follow along here.
Now have I come to the plain from the galleys, for early at dawn those
bright-eyed Achaians will start up a battle surrounding the city.
They lack patience to sit there idle, nor can the Achaians'
kings keep holding them back, so avid they are for the battle."
405   Speaking to him then answered the old man, godlike Priam:
"Well then, if an attendant of Peleus' scion Achilles
you are indeed, come, tell me the truth and report it all fully,
whether my son is still by the galleys, or whether Achilles,
hewing him limb from limb, to the dogs already has thrown him."
410   Speaking to him made answer the messenger, slayer of Argos:
"Old sir, not yet either the dogs or the birds have devoured him;
rather he still lies just as he was by the ship of Achilles
ever among his cabins, and this is the twelfth of the days that
he has lain there, and his body does not rot, nor are the maggots
415 eating at it which always consume men slaughtered in battle.
True that around the grave-mound of his much-loved comrade, Achilles
ruthlessly drags him, whenever the sacred Dawn is appearing,
yet he never defiles him; and when you arrive you will marvel
how dew-fresh he is lying and washed quite clean of his bloodstains,
420 nor is he anywhere sullied; and all his wounds are now closed up
where he was struck, since many a man drove into him bronze blades.
So to your son do the fortunate gods keep carefully tending,
though he is now but a corpse, since he to their hearts was belovèd."
     So he spoke, and the old man, gladdened, returned him an answer:
425 "Child, it is surely a good thing to give the immortals the gifts most
fitting to them, since never my son—if he ever existed—
there in the palace forgot those gods who inhabit Olympos;
therefore they in the doom of his death hold him in remembrance.
But come now and receive from my hands this beautiful goblet,
430 give me protection in turn, with the gods' aid act as my escort

always until I arrive at the cabin of Peleus' scion."
 Speaking to him made answer the messenger, slayer of Argos:
"Thus, old sir, do you test me, a younger man, nor will persuade me,
bidding me take your present without the consent of Achilles.

435 He is the man I fear and respect too much in my heart that
I should defraud him, lest some evil befall me hereafter.
Yet as a guide I would go with you even to glorious Argos,
kindly attending to you on foot or upon a swift galley,
never would anyone, scorning your guide, do battle against us."

440 So did he say, then onto the horses and chariot leaping,
quickly the messenger took in his hands both reins and the whip-rod;
strongly he breathed might into the horses and into the mule-team.
When they came to the ramparts and trench which guarded the galleys,
there were the watchmen just on the point of preparing the dinner;

445 sleep was poured on them all by the messenger, slayer of Argos;
hastily then he opened the gates by thrusting the bars back;
Priam he brought inside, and the glorious gifts on the wagon.
Finally, when they arrived at the cabin of Peleus' scion,
lofty of roof, that the Mýrmidon men for their lord had erected,

450 hewing the timbers for it out of fir, and the roof overhead they
covered with thatching of long shaggy reeds they cut from the meadows;
then around it for the lord they had made an enormous courtyard,
fenced it with stakes set thickly; the door was secured with a single
fir beam which three Achaians would drive home into the socket;

455 three men also were needed to draw the huge bar of the doors back—
three of the rest; by himself to the socket Achilles could drive it—
there then Hermes the messenger opened the door for the old man,
brought in the glorious gifts for the swift-footed scion of Peleus,
stepped from the chariot onto the ground, and in these words spoke out:

460 "Old sir, I am a god, an immortal, who thus have arrived here,
Hermes, because my father dispatched me to come and escort you.
But now I will depart to go back—not into Achilles'
vision will I go onward—for it would be shameful for any
mortal to welcome and talk face-to-face with a god, an immortal;

465 you, when you go inside, by his knees clasp Peleus' scion,
then by his father and by his mother of beautiful tresses
and by his child implore him, that deep in his heart you may move him."
 After he said these words, toward lofty Olympos departed
Hermes; but out of the chariot onto the ground leapt Priam,

470 there in the courtyard leaving Idaíos, who stayed to await him

holding the horses and mules; the old man went straight to the dwelling
where Zeus-cherished Achilles was sitting, and him he discovered
there with his comrades sitting apart from him; two of them only,
Álkimos scion of Ares and brave Autómedon, stayed there
475 busily waiting on him; he had just now finished his supper,
eating and drinking, and still his table was standing beside him.
Into the cabin unseen of them came great Priam and stood there
close to Achilles and grasped his knees with his hands, and he kissed those
dread man-slaughtering hands that had killed so many of his sons.
480 As at a time a disastrous delusion takes hold of a man who
kills someone in his land, then goes to a country of strangers,
into a rich man's house, and amazement grips the beholders,
so was Achilles amazed at beholding the godlike Priam;
so were the others amazed, and they stared, each one at another.
485 Then imploring him, Priam in these words spoke and addressed him:
"Noble Achilles resembling the gods, take thought of your father,
who is of years like mine, on the baneful threshold of old age.
He also, I suppose, is afflicted by those who around him
dwell, nor is anyone there who could ward off bane and disaster.
490 Nevertheless he, hearing that you are at least yet alive, is
able at heart to rejoice, and he feels hope every day that
he will be seeing his much-loved son come back from the Troäd;
wholly am I ill-fated, because I fathered the best sons
in broad Troy, and of them not one, I say, is remaining.
495 Fifty of them I had when the sons of Achaians arrived here;
nineteen were from the same womb born to me, all of one mother;
women who dwell in the palace were those who bore me the others.
Furious Ares has loosened the knees of too many among them;
as for the one I had who protected the city and people,
500 him you recently slaughtered as he was defending his country,
Hektor, for whose sake now I have come to the ships of the Achaians,
seeking for you to release him and bringing a measureless ransom.
Honor the gods now, Achilles, and show me pity and mercy,
mindful of your own father, though I am far more to be pitied—
505 I have endured what never an earth-dwelling mortal has suffered,
stretching my hand to the mouth of the man who slaughtered my children."
So he spoke and in him roused longing to weep for his father;
taking the old man's hand, he pushed him away from him gently.
So both men were recalling, the one man-slaughtering Hektor,
510 weeping incessantly, crouched in front of the feet of Achilles,

while for his father Achilles was weeping, and also at other
times for Patróklos; the wails of the two rose up in the dwelling.
Then when noble Achilles had taken his pleasure in weeping,
when the desire for lamenting had left his heart and his body,

515 he at once sprang from the chair; by his hand he lifted the old man,
so for the gray head he felt pity, and so for the gray beard;
raising his voice he spoke, and in these winged words he addressed him:
"Ah, poor wretch! In your heart you have borne so many afflictions!
How did you dare thus coming alone to the ships of the Achaians,

520 here to encounter the eyes of the man who slaughtered and stripped your
sons so many and noble? The heart in your breast is of iron.
But come now, sit down on a chair, and for all of our sorrows,
let us allow them to rest in our hearts, although we are grieving,
seeing that nothing of profit arises from chill lamentation.

525 So have the gods spun out as the portion of miserable mortals
life to be led in sorrow, but they are themselves quite carefree,
since there are two large urns which stand on the floor of the god Zeus,
holding the gifts he gives, one of banes and the other of blessings;
he who is given a mixture of these by the thunderbolt-hurler

530 Zeus sometimes meets evils and other times excellent fortunes,
but to one given the baneful alone, Zeus brings degradation;
over the sacred earth he is driven by ravenous hunger;
ever he wanders and gets no honor from gods or from mortals.
So it was with the glorious gifts that the gods gave Peleus

535 right from the day of his birth, for indeed he surpassed all the people
in his possessions and wealth and was over the Mýrmidons ruler,
then although he was mortal, a goddess they gave him as bedmate;
yet even so upon him did a god bring evil, that never
there in his house was engendered an offspring of powerful children;

540 no, he begot one son who would be short-lived, and I do not
tend him as he grows old, since far from the land of my fathers
here in Troy I sit and bring anguish to you and your children.
And of you too, old man, we hear that before you were happy—
all the men seaward that Lesbos, the seat of old Makar, encloses,

545 Phrygia bounds up-country, the limitless Hellespont northward,
you as they say, old sir, in your sons and your riches surpassed them.
Since that time that the heavenly gods brought evil upon you,
always around your city are battles and slaughters of fighters.
Bear up now, and do not in your heart keep endlessly grieving,

550 nothing at all through sorrowing over your son will you profit,

nor will you raise him, but sooner will suffer another affliction."
    Speaking to him then answered the old man godlike Priam:
"Seat me not on a chair, Zeus-nourished, as long as among these
cabins uncared-for Hektor is lying, but quickly release him

555 so that I look upon him with my eyes, and accept the enormous
ransom that we bring you; then may you enjoy it and go back
home to the land of your fathers, because from the first you have spared me,
so that I go on living and looking on Helios' sunlight."
    Looking from lowering brows spoke forth swift-footed Achilles:

560 "No more provoke me now, old man; I am minded myself to
give back Hektor to you, since bringing a message from Zeus my
mother who bore me came, the Old Man of the Sea's dear daughter.
You too, Priam, I know in my heart, and it does not escape me
that by a god you were led to the swift ships of the Achaians,

565 since no mortal would ever endure, not even a strong youth,
coming among this host—he would never escape from the watchmen,
nor would he easily thrust from our doors that bar that secures them.
Therefore now, do not stir my heart yet more to affliction,
lest not even yourself, old man, I spare in my cabin,

570 supplicant though you are, and so violate Zeus's commandment."
    So he spoke, and the old man feared, and obeyed what he told him.
Out of the doors of the house sprang Peleus' son like a lion,
not by himself, for together with him went two of his henchmen,
Álkimos one, and the hero Autómedon—them did Achilles,

575 after the perished Patróklos, esteem above all of his comrades.
Then from under the yokes they loosened the mules and the horses,
also led in the herald who served as the old man's crier,
seating him there on a bench; from the well-wheeled wagon the comrades
took out the measureless ransom it held for the body of Hektor.

580 Two of the robes and a fine-wove tunic they left, so Achilles,
after he wrapped the dead body, could give it to them to take homeward.
Then he called to the handmaids and bade them to wash and anoint it,
taking it some way off, so that Priam would not see his son yet,
lest in the pain of his spirit he might not hold back his anger,

585 seeing his son, and the heart in Achilles as well would be stirred up,
then he would kill the old man, and so violate Zeus's commandment.
After the handmaids washed it and rubbed it with oil of the olive,
they threw garments about it, a beautiful cloak and a tunic,
then by Achilles himself it was lifted and set on a litter;

590 with the companions, he lifted it onto the well-polished wagon.

431

Then he groaned, and he called by name on his much-loved comrade:
"Feel no rancor, Patróklos, against me, should you discover,
even in Hades' abode as you are, that I gave noble Hektor
back to his father, because no worthless ransom he gave me.
595   I will allot you a share of these treasures, as much as is fitting."
      Thus, and the noble Achilles returned then, into the cabin,
on the elaborate chair he sat whence he had arisen,
close to the opposite wall, and a word he spoke to Lord Priam:
"Back to you now, old man, as you asked, has your son been given;
600   out on a litter he lies, and as soon as the light of the Dawn shines,
you will behold him and take him; but now let us think about dinner,
for about eating her food even fair-haired Níobè took thought
though in her halls she had twelve children that came to destruction,
six of them daughters and six of them sons in the vigor of manhood.
605   Then did Apollo with shafts from his silvery bow in his wrath at
Níobè slaughter the sons, and the daughters the shooter of arrows
Artemis killed, since Níobè likened herself to the fair-cheeked
Leto, who brought forth two, she said, while she had born many;
therefore, though they were two, they destroyed all twelve of her children.
610   Nine days there in their blood they were lying, and nobody gave them
burial rites, since Kronos' son made stones out of the people;
but the Olympian gods on the tenth day buried the children;
Níobè thought about food, for of shedding her tears she was wearied.
Now somewhere in the rocks, high up in the desolate peaks on
615   Sípylos, where, men say, are the couches of goddesses, nymphs who
nimbly meander in dances beside Achelóios' waters,
there, though she is a stone, on her god-sent woes she is brooding.
But come, noble old man, let the two of us also be thinking
now about food; then later again you will grieve for your dear son,
620   having to Ilion brought him—with many a tear will you mourn him."
      Thus; to his feet sprang rapid Achilles and slaughtered a white-fleeced
sheep, and his comrades flayed and prepared it well, in good order;
skillfully cutting it up, on stakes they spitted the pieces;
carefully roasting the meat, they drew off all of the morsels.
625   Taking the bread, on the table Autómedon set out the portions
piled in beautiful baskets; the meat was served by Achilles.
They put forth eager hands to partake of the food lying ready.
When they had quite satisfied their appetites, drinking and eating,
then at Achilles did Priam the scion of Dárdanos marvel,
630   so was he handsome and strong, for the gods themselves he resembled;

432

so did Achilles at Priam the scion of Dárdanos marvel,
seeing his august visage and hearing the words he was saying.
When they had taken their pleasure in gazing upon each other,
first then spoke to Achilles the old man godlike Priam:
635 "Give me a bed now quickly, belovèd of Zeus, so that we may
go to our rest, take pleasure at last in the sweetness of slumber,
never at all have my eyes yet been closed under my eyelids
since when under your hands my son was bereft of his life-breath.
Always rather I wail, brood over my numberless sorrows,
640 out in the well-walled court, while rolling about in the ordure.
Now at last I have tasted of food and the glistening wine have
let flow into my gullet; before this, nothing I tasted."

So he spoke, and Achilles, addressing the comrades and handmaids,
bade them to put beds out in the portico, throwing upon them
645 rugs of a beautiful purple, upon those spread out the covers,
then bring mantles of wool to be drawn up over the sleepers.
Out of the hall the maids went, in their hands all carrying torches;
hastily setting the beds for the two, they carefully spread them.
Then in a bantering voice spoke forth swift-footed Achilles:
650 "Dear old man, lie down outside, lest perhaps an Achaian
counselor-lord should arrive at the cabin, for they are accustomed
always to sit beside me and make plans, as is fitting and proper;
should one of them see you through the swift black shadows of nighttime,
straightway then he would tell Agamemnon, shepherd of people,
655 so would arise a delay in the ransoming of the dead body.
But come now, tell me this and recount it exactly and fully—
how many days you want to be burying noble Lord Hektor,
so that I wait myself, and as well I hold back the army."

Speaking to him then answered the old man godlike Priam:
660 "If those rites you are willing that I should accomplish for noble
Hektor, Achilles, in doing these things you would do me a kindness;
you know how we are penned in the city, and far is the journey,
fetching the wood from the mountains; the Trojans are dreadfully frightened.
We will lament and bewail him for nine days there in the palace,
665 then on the tenth we will hold his rites and the people will banquet.
On the eleventh a funeral mound over him we will heap up;
then on the twelfth we will fight once more, if indeed we must do so."

Answering him then spoke swift-footed and noble Achilles:
"These things too will be done, old Priam, the way you have ordered,
670 since our battle will I hold back as much time as you ask for."

433

So having said these things, he clasped the right hand of the old man,
taking it up by the wrist, lest he in his heart should be frightened.
There on the porch of the house did the two men go to their slumber,
Priam as well as the herald, who both had minds full of counsel,
675   while in the depths of the well-built cabin Achilles was sleeping;
close to his side was lying the fair-cheeked daughter of Bríseus.

So were the rest of the gods and the men who were chariot-marshals
sleeping the whole night through and subdued in a soft mild slumber;
yet no slumber at all took hold of the messenger Hermes,
680   while he revolved in his mind on the way he could guide King Priam
out of the ships unseen by the sacred guards of the gateways;
standing above his head, he spoke this word and addressed him:
"Old man, evil is not any trouble to you, from the way you
sleep here still among enemy men, as Achilles has spared you.
685   Now have you ransomed your much-loved son—a great price you have given;
yet for yourself still alive three times that ransom your sons would
give who survive and are left there behind, in case Agamemnon,
Atreus' scion, should know it, or all the Achaians should know it."

So he spoke; the old man was frightened and roused up the herald.
690   Hermes at once yoked up for the men their horses and mule-team;
lightly himself through the army he drove them, and nobody noticed.
But then, when they arrived at the ford of the beautiful-flowing
river, the eddying Xanthos that deathless Zeus had begotten,
straightway Hermes departed to go toward lofty Olympos.

695   Now all over the earth Dawn saffron-appareled was spreading;
into the city they went with moaning and lamentation,
driving the horses, the mule-team bringing the corpse, nor did any
other discover them first, of the men or the fair-girdled women;
rather, Kassandra, in form like Áphrodítè the golden,
700   having to Pérgamos climbed, looked down and observed that her father
stood in his chariot there, and the herald as well, the town crier;
him also she beheld as he lay on the bier in the mule-cart.
Shrilly she started to cry, then shouted to all of the city:
"Trojans and women of Troy, come hither and look upon Hektor,
705   if as he came from the battle alive you were ever rejoicing,
since he was such great joy to the city and all of the people."

She spoke, nor was a man left there inside of the city,
nor was a woman, for over them all unbearable grief came;
close to the gates they met with the king as he brought in the dead man.
710   First of them all did his own dear wife and the lady his mother,

tearing their hair over him, spring onto the well-wheeled wagon,
weeping and touching his head; and the throng stood wailing about them.
Now would the people for that whole day till the hour of the sunset,
shedding their tears in front of the gates, have been mourning for Hektor,
715 had the old man not spoken to them from the chariot, saying:
"Make way now for the mules to pass through; then later will you have
full satisfaction in wailing, when back to the house I have brought him."
  So did he say; they stood to the sides, made way for the wagon.
Soon as they brought him into the glorious palace, they laid him
720 down on a bedstead corded for bedding, and singers beside him,
leaders of dirge, they placed; these started the sorrowful chanting,
singing a dirge over him, and the women as well were lamenting.
There among them white-armed Andrómachè led in the wailing,
while in her arms embracing the head of man-slaughtering Hektor:
725 "Husband, you have been robbed of your life still young and have left me
widowed here in your halls, and the child no more than an infant
whom you and I brought forth, ill-fated ones! Nor do I think he
ever will reach his manhood, for sooner the city will wholly
be ransacked, since you the protector are lost, who were always
730 guarding it, saving the reverend wives and the innocent children.
Soon those wives will be carried away in the hollow galleys;
I will myself be among them, and you, child, either will go with
me to a place in which you will do ignominious labors,
drudging for some implacable master, or else an Achaian,
735 seizing your arm, from the wall will hurl you, a baneful destruction,
wrathful because of his brother, perhaps, whom Hektor had slaughtered,
or of his father, or even his son, since many Achaian
fighters have bitten the limitless earth at the hands of great Hektor,
since your father would never be gentle in dolorous battle;
740 therefore the people are wailing for him all over the city.
You to your parents have brought unspeakable wailing and sorrow,
Hektor; for me above all will be left this dolorous anguish,
since when dying you did not stretch me your hands from the bedstead,
nor did you speak any word of sagacity, one that I might have
745 called to my mind by night and by day while letting the tears fall."
  So she spoke as she mourned, and the women as well were lamenting.
Hékabè next among them then led in the vehement wailing:
"Hektor, dearest by far to my heart among all of my children,
you were indeed most dear to the gods while you were yet living;
750 so now they in the doom of your death take care of your body.

435

Others among my children as slaves swift-footed Achilles
sold, whomever he took, far over the desolate sea-brine,
either to Samos or Imbros or Lemnos shrouded in vapors;
but you, when with the long-edged bronze your life he had taken,
755 often he dragged you around the grave-mound of his comrade Patróklos,
whom you killed, yet not even so did he ever revive him.
Now dew-fresh in my palace as if just recently killed you
lie like one whom Apollo the god of the silvery bow has
killed by visiting him with his mild and benevolent missiles."
760   So she spoke as she mourned and aroused incessant lamenting.
Third in her turn then Helen among them led in the wailing:
"Hektor, dearest by far to my heart among all of my husband's
brothers! Indeed my husband is that godlike Alexander
who once brought me to Troy—how I wish I sooner had perished!
765 Now already upon me the twentieth year has arrived since
when I started from there and departed the land of my fathers;
yet I never from you heard one word harsh or vindictive.
Rather, if somebody else in the halls spoke words of reproval,
one of my husband's brothers or sisters, perhaps, or a brother's
770 fair-robed wife, or my mother-in-law—your father was always
kind as a father could be—yet you by speaking restrained them,
talked them around with gentle demeanor and gentle persuasion.
So I lament both you and my ill-starred self, in heart-anguish,
since in the broad Troäd no longer is anyone else still
775 gentle to me, or a friend, but they all now shudder to see me."
So she spoke as she mourned, and the countless throng was lamenting.
Then did the old man Priam address this word to his people:
"Now, men of Troy, bring wood to the city. Do not in your hearts feel
fear of a close-laid ambush of Argives, since as Achilles
780 sent me away from the dark-hued ships, such orders he gave them,
not to attack us until the twelfth dawn comes—so he assured me."
So he spoke, and the men yoked up to the wagons the mules and
oxen, and quickly were they all gathered in front of the city.
So for a full nine days they were bringing in plentiful timber,
785 but then, when the tenth dawn shone forth to illuminate mortals,
letting the tears flow down, they brought out valorous Hektor,
high on the pyre they placed the dead body and cast fire upon it.
Soon as the Dawn shone forth rose-fingered at earliest daybreak,
there around glorious Hektor's pyre were the people assembled.
790 Then when they had collected and all were gathered together,

first with glistening wine they extinguished the flames of the whole great
pyre, wherever the might of the fire had extended, and straightway
all the white bones of the hero his brothers and comrades collected,
weeping, and over their cheeks flowed down great tears in abundance.

795 Taking the bones up, into a gold-wrought vessel they put them;
this then carefully wrapping in fine soft mantles of purple,
into the hollow grave they at once set it, and above they
covered it over with ponderous stones set closely together;
quickly the mound they heaped, and on all sides stationed the watchmen,

800 fearing the well-greaved Achaians would too soon come to attack them.
After they heaped up the mound, they returned to the city, and then they
cordially gathered together and dined on a glorious dinner
there in the palace of Priam, the ruler belovèd of heaven.

So were they busied with burying Hektor the tamer of horses.

List of
Proper Names
in the *Iliad*

This list gives the first occurrence of each name in the epic; for some characters two lines are cited, one where they are merely named and the other where they have a part in the action. When two or more characters or places have the same name, they are numbered (in parentheses) in the order of their appearance; within entries these numbers indicate the character so numbered in the main entry. Thus Ajax (1) refers to Ajax son of Télamon. The prize-girls of Agamemnon and Achilles have no entries of their own; the names by which they are usually known, *Chryséïs* and *Briséïs*, are patronymics meaning *daughter of Chryses, daughter of Briseus*, like that of Achilles, *Peléïdes, son of Peleus*. These two are the only major figures in Homeric epic to be named exclusively by their patronymics, that is, by reference to their fathers.

Some "significant names" are glossed in quotation marks. Since one aim of this list is to help readers locate places, I have referred to some regions by their later names—e.g., Asia Minor, Greece, Macedonia, Thessaly. Whether a place was a "town" or a "city" is often uncertain; in many cases we do not know where a place was, let alone whether it was a "city" in the ancient or modern sense.

To keep the rhythm clear, I have put acute accents (´) on accented syllables of proper names that might give trouble in pronunciation. The grave accent (`) signifies that a final *è* constitutes a weak syllable, the dieresis (¨) that the second of two contiguous vowels is to be sounded separately. The ending *-eus* is to be pronounced as one syllable—*eu* is a diphthong; *-es* is a separate syllable except in *Thebes; ch* is pronounced as in *school; g* is hard. Most names are transliterated from Greek; a few are so deeply rooted in English usage that I use familiar forms—for example, *Achilles, Ajax, Athens, Crete, Helen.*

439

The indices of proper names in the Loeb Classical Library edition, translated by A. T. Murray, revised by William F. Wyatt, and in Richmond Lattimore's translation have been of great help in compiling this list. Exhaustive references in Greek may be found in the Oxford Classical Texts edition of the *Iliad*, edited by D. B. Monro and T. W. Allen; the Loeb edition contains references fuller than I can give here, though with little annotation, under the Latinized English form of each name. I am also indebted to the Cambridge commentaries on the *Iliad*, general editor G. S. Kirk, for help with the annotations.

Abántes: people of Euboía; 2.536.

Abarbárea: nymph, consort of Boukólion, mother of the Trojans Aisépos and Pédasos; 6.22.

Abas: Trojan, son of Eurýdamas, killed by Diomédes; 5.148.

Ábioi: people dwelling north of Thrace; 13.6.

Abléros: Trojan killed by Antílochos; 6.32

Abýdos: city on the south shore of the Hellespont, across from Sestos; 2.836.

Achaia, Achaians: Greece and the Greek army; 1.254, 1.2.

Achelóïos: (1) strong river of northwest Greece, 21.194; (2) river in Lydia; 24.616.

Achilles: Achaian hero, lord of the Mýrmidons, son of Peleus and Thetis; 1.1.

Ádamas: Trojan, son of Ásios, killed by Mérionés; 12.140, 13.561.

Admétos: father of Eumélos, husband of Alkéstis; 2.713.

Ádresteía: city of the Troäd; 2.828.

Adréstos: (1) Achaian, king of Síkyon; 2.572; (2) leader of the Ádresteíans; 2.830; (3) Trojan captured by Meneláos, killed by Agamemnon; 6.37; (4) Trojan killed by Patróklos; 16.694.

Ágakles: father of Epeígeus; 16.571.

Agamédè: wife of Moúlios, daughter of Augeías; 11.740.

Agamemnon: chief leader of the Achaians, son of Atreus, brother of Meneláos, husband of Klýtaimnéstra; 1.24.

Agapénor: leader of the Arkádians; 2.609.

Agásthenes: father of Polýxeinos; 2.624.

Agástrophos: Trojan killed by Diomédes; 2.338.

Ágathon: son of Priam; 24.249.

Agaúë: sea-nymph; "luminary"; 18.42.

Ageláos: (1) Trojan killed by Diomédes; 5.257; (2) Achaian killed by Hektor; 11.302.

Agénor: Trojan, son of Anténor, fights Achilles; 4.467, 21.545.

Aglaía: mother of Níreus, 2.672.

Ágrios: son of Portheus, brother of Oíneus; 14.117.

Aíakos: son of Zeus, father of Peleus, grandfather of Achilles; 2.860, 21.189.

Aïdóneus: Hades, god of the underworld; 5.190.

Aigai: city in the region of Achaia where Poseidon is worshipped; 8.203.

Aígaion: the human name of the hundred-handed Briáreus; 1.404.

Aigeus: father of Theseus; 1.265.

Aígialeía: wife of Diomédes, daughter of Adréstos (1); 5.412.

Aigialós: town in Páphlagónia; 2.855.

Aigílips: place in Ithaka; 2.633.

Aigína: island in the Aegean Sea; 2.562.

Aígion: town in the Peloponnese ruled by Agamemnon, 2.574.

Aineías: leader of the Dardánians, son of Aphrodítè and Anchíses (1); 2.819.

Aínios: Paiónian killed by Achilles; 21.210.

Ainos: city in Thrace; 4.520.

Aíolos: father of Sísyphos, great-grandfather of Bellérophon; 6.154.

Aipeía: town in the region of Pylos; 9.152.

Aipy: town near Pylos, 2.592.

Aipýtos: Arkádian hero; 2.604.

Aisépos: (1) river in the Troäd; 2.825; (2) Trojan killed by Eurýalos; 6.21.

Aisyétes: (1) Trojan hero; 2.793; (2) father of Alkáthoös; 13.427.

Aisýmè: city in Thrace; 8.304.

Aísymnos: Achaian killed by Hektor; 11.303.

Aithè: mare lent by Agamemnon to Meneláos, "fiery"; 23.295.

Aithíkes: people of Thessaly; 2.744.

Aithon: one of Hektor's horses, "fiery"; 8.185.

Aithrè: handmaid of Helen, daughter of Píttheus; 3.144.

Aitolians: people of Aitolia, in western Greece; 2.638.

Ajax: (1) Salaminian leader, son of Télamon; 1.138; (2) Lokrian leader, son of Oïleus; 2.527.

Ákamas: (1) Dardánian leader, son of Anténor; 2.823; (2) Thracian leader, son of Eusóros, killed by Ajax; 6.8.

Akessámenos: father of Periboía; 21.142.

Akrísios: father of Dánaë; 14.319.

Aktaíë: sea-nymph, "maid of the seashore"; 18.41.

Aktor: (1) father of Astýochè; 2.513; (2) father of Ktéatos and Eúrytos, the Moliónes; 2.621, 11.750; (3) father of Menoítios, grandfather of Patróklos; 11.785; (4) father of Echékles; 16.189.

Alástor: (1) Pylian leader; 4.295; (2) Lykian killed by Odysseus; 5.677; (3) Salaminian comrade of Ajax (1); 8.333; (4) father of Tros; 20.463.

Alegénor: father of Prómachos; 14.503.

Aleíos: plain in Asia Minor; 6.201.

Aléktryon: father of Léïtos; 17.602.

Alésion: hill on the border of Elis; 2.617.

Alexander: =Paris, son of Priam, consort of Helen, brother of Hektor; 3.16.

Alkándros: Lykian killed by Odysseus; 5.678.

Alkáthoös: Trojan, son of Aisyétes, killed by Idómeneus; 12.93, 13.428.

Alkéstis: daughter of Pélias, wife of Admétos, mother of Eumélos; 2.715.

Alkímedon, Álkimos: Mýrmidon leader, Achilles' comrade, son of Laërkes; 16.197, 19.392.

Alkmáon: Achaian, son of Thestor, killed by Sarpédon; 12.394.

Alkménè: wife of Amphítryon, consort of Zeus, mother of Herakles; 14.323.

Alkýonè: nickname of Kleopatra; 9.562.

Alóeus: father of Ephiáltes and Otos; 5.386.

Álopè: town in Thessaly; 2.682.

Alos: town in Thessaly; 2.682.

Álpheios: river in the western Peloponnese; 2.592.

Altes: father of Laôthoë, grandfather of Lykáon; 21.85.

Althaía: mother of Meleágros; 9.555.

Álybè: city on the Black Sea; 2.857.

Amarýngkeus: earlier king of the Epeíans, father of Dióres; 2.622.

Amatheía: sea-nymph, "sand-maid"; 18.48.

Amazons: warrior women; 3.189.

Ámisodaúros: Lykian, father of Atýmnios and Maris; 16.328.

Amopáon: Trojan, son of Polyaímon, killed by Teukros; 8.276.

Amphídamas: (1) Kytheréan hero; 10.268; (2) man of Opóeis whose son Phoinix killed; 23.87.

Ámphigeneía: town near Pylos; 2.593.

Amphíklos: Trojan, killed by Meges; 16.313.

Amphímachos: (1) Epeían leader, son of Ktéatos; 2.620; (2) Karian leader, son of Nómion; 2.870.

Amphínomè: sea-nymph, "rich in pastures"; 18.44.

Ámphion: Epeían leader; 13.692.

Ámphios: (1) Ádresteían leader, son of Mérops; killed by Diomédes, 2.830; (2) Trojan ally, son of Sélagos, killed by Ajax (1); 5.612.

Amphíthoë: sea-nymph, "swift-whirling"; 18.42.

Amphítryon: husband of Alkmḗnè, putative father of Herakles; 5.392.

Amphóteros: Trojan killed by Patróklos; 16.415.

Ámydon: city of the Paiónians in northern Greece; 2.849.

Amýklai: city near Sparta in Lakedaímon, 2.584.

Amýntor: son of Órmenos, father of Phoinix; 9.448.

Anchíalos: Achaian killed by Hektor; 5.609.

Anchíses: (1) father of Aineías by Aphrodítè; 2.819; (2) father of Echepólos; 23.296.

Andraímon: father of Thoas; 2.638.

Andrómachè: daughter of Eêtion, wife of Hektor; 6.371.

Ánemoreía: town in Phokis; 2.521.

Angkaíos: (1) father of Agapénor; 2.609; (2) wrestler beaten by Nestor; 23.635.

Anteía: wife of Proítos; 6.160.

Anténor: Trojan elder, father of Agénor and many other sons; 2.822.

Anthédon: harbor town in Boiótia; 2.508.

Antheía: town in the region of Pylos; 9.151.

Anthémion: father of Simoeísios; 4.473.

Antílochos: Achaian, comrade of Achilles, son of Nestor; 4.457.

Antímachos: father of Peisándros, Hippólochos, and Hippómachos; 11.123.

Antíphates: Trojan killed by Leónteus; 12.191.

Antíphonos: son of Priam; 24.250.

Ántiphos: (1) leader of the men from Kos, son of Théssalos, grandson of Herakles;

2.678; (2) Maiónian leader, son of Talaímenes; 2.864; (3) son of Priam killed by Agamemnon; 4.489, 11.101.

Antron: town in Thessaly; 2.697.

Apaísos: =Paisos (?) town in the Troäd; 2.828.

Apháreus: Achaian, son of Kalétor, killed by Aineías; 9.83, 13.541.

Aphrodítè: =Cypris, daughter of Zeus and Diónè, mother of Aineías; 2.820.

Apisáon: (1) Trojan killed by Eurýpylos; 11.578; (2) Trojan killed by Lykomédes; 17.348.

Apollo: son of Zeus and Leto, brother of Artemis, cognomen Phoibos; 1.14.

Apseúdes: sea-nymph, "truthful"; 18.46.

Áraithýrea: town in the northern Pelopponese, near Korinth; 2.571.

Archélochos: Dardánian leader, son of Anténor; 2.823.

Árcheptólemos: charioteer of Hektor, Íphitos' son, killed by Teukros; 8.128, 312.

Areïlochos: (1) father of Prothoénor; 14.450; (2) Trojan killed by Patróklos; 16.308.

Áreïthöös: (1) father of Menésthios; 7.8; (2) Trojan killed by Achilles; 20.487.

Arénè: town in the western Pelopponese; 2.591.

Ares: son of Zeus and Hera, cognomen Enyálios; 2.110.

Aretáon: Trojan killed by Teukros; 6.31.

Arétos: Trojan killed by Autómedon; 17.494.

Árgeas: father of Polymélos; 16.417.

Argíssa: town in Thessaly; 2.738.

Argos, Argives: (1) region in northeast Pelopponese; 1.30; (2) city in that region, ruled by Diomédes; 2.558; (3) all of what we call Greece; 2.287; its people=Achaians, Dánaäns; 1.79; (4) region in Thessaly; 2.681.

Ariádnè: daughter of Minos, taken away by Theseus; 18.592.

Árimoi: people of Kilíkia; 2.783.

Aríon: famous race-horse; 23.346.

Arísbas: father of Leiókritos; 17.344.

Arísbè: town on the Hellespont; 2.836.

Arkádia: region in the central Pelopponese; 2.603.

Árkesiláos: Boiótian leader; 2.495.

Arnè: town in Boiótia; 2.507.

Arsínoös: father of Hekamédè; 11.626.

Artemis: daughter of Zeus and Leto, sister of Apollo; 5.51.

Asaíos: Achaian killed by Hektor; 11.301.

Asínè: town in the region of Argos; 2.560.

Ásios: (1) son of Hýrtakos, father of Ádamas and Phainops; killed by Idómeneus; 2.837, 13.384; (2) Trojan, son of Dymas, brother of Hékabè; 16.717.

Askálaphos: Minyan leader, son of Ares by Astýochè, brother of Iálmenos, killed by Deïphobos; 2.512, 13.518.

Askánia: region of Phrygia; 2.863.

Askánios: Phrygian leader; 2.862.

Asklépios: famous healer, father of Podaleírios and Macháon; 2.731.

Asópos: river in Boiótia; 4.383.

Asplédon: town of the Minyans near Orchómenos; 2.511.

Assárakos: son of Tros, grandfather of Anchíses; 20.232.

Astérion: town in Thessaly; 2.735.

Ásteropaíos: Paiónian leader, son of Pélegon, killed by Achilles; 12.102, 21.140.

Astýalos: Trojan killed by Polypoítes, 6.29.

Ástyanáx: infant son of Hektor, "lord of the city"; 6.403.

Astýnoös: (1) Trojan killed by Diomédes; 5.144; (2) Trojan, son of Protiáön; 15.455.

Astýochè: wife of Ázeus, mother of Askálaphos and Iálmenos by Ares; 2.513.

Ástyocheía: mother of Tlepólemos by Herakles; 2.658.

Astýpylos: Paiónian killed by Achilles; 21.209.

Athena: daughter of Zeus; 1.194.

Athens, Athenians: city in Greece and its inhabitants; 2.546, 550.

Athos: promontory-mountain in the northern Aegean Sea; 14.229.

Atreus: father of Agamemnon and Meneláos; 1.7.

Atýmnios: Trojan, father of Mydon, killed by Antílochos; 5.581, 16.318.

Augeíai: (1) town in Lokris; 2.532; (2) town in Lakedaímon; 2.583.

Augeías: lord of Elis, father of Agasthénes, grandfather of Polýxeinos; 2.624.

Aulis: city in Boiótia where the Achaian fleet assembled; 2.303.

Autólykos: maternal grandfather of Odysseus; 10.266.

Autómedon: Achaian, henchman of Achilles; 9.209.

Autónoös: (1) Achaian killed by Hektor; 11.301; (2) Trojan killed by Patróklos; 16.694.

Autóphonos: father of Polyphóntes; 4.395.

Áxios: river in Paiónia; 2.849.

Áxylos: Trojan ally, son of Teuthras, killed by Diomédes; 6.12.

Ázeus: father of Aktor (1), grandfather of Astýochè; 2.513.

Balios: one of Achilles' horses, "dapple"; 16.149.

Báthycles: Mýrmidon killed by Glaukos; 16.594.

Batieía: "hill of the briar" in the Troäd, to the gods "the grave of Myrínè"; 2.813.

Bellérophon: hero from Ephýra=Korinth, son of Glaukos, grandfather of Sarpédon and Glaukos; 6.155.

Bessa: town in Lokris; 2.532.

Bias: (1) Pylian leader; 4.296; (2) Athenian leader; 13.691; (3) father of Dárdanos (2) and Laógonos; 20.460.

Biénor: Trojan killed by Agamemnon; 11.92.

Boágrios: river in Lokris; 2.533.

Boibè, Lake Boibéïs: town and lake in Thessaly; 2.712, 2.711.

Boiótians: people of Boiótia, a region north of the Gulf of Korinth; 2.494.

Boreas: the north wind; 9.5.

Boros: (1) father of Phaistos; 5.43; (2) son of Periéres, husband of Polydóra, putative father of Menésthios; 16.177.

Boudeíon: town in Phthia; 16.572.

Boukólion: consort of Abarbárea, son of Laómedon, father of Aisépos (2) and Pédasos (1); 6.22.

Boúkolos: father of Sphélos; 15.338.

Bouprásion: region or town in the western Pelopponese, near Elis; 2.615.

Briáreos: the gods' name for the hundred-handed giant men call Aigaíon; 1.403.

Bríseus: father of Achilles' prize-girl—see headnote; 1.184.

Bryseíai: town in Lakedaímon; 2.583.

Centaurs: people of Thessaly, half-human, half-horse; 1.268.

Chalkis: (1) city in Euboía; 2.537; (2) town in Aitolia; 2.640; (3) name of a bird, the *kymindis;* 14.291.

Chálkodon: father of Elephénor; 2.541.

Chalkon: father of Báthykles; 16.595.

Charis: wife of Hephaistos; 18.382.

Charópos: father of Níreus; 2.672.

Charops: Trojan, son of Híppasos, killed by Odysseus; 11.427.

Cheiron: Centaur, teacher of Asklépios, Peleus, and Achilles; 4.219.

Chersídamas: Trojan killed by Odysseus; 11.423.

Chimaíra: monster—lion, she-goat, serpent—killed by Bellérophon; 6.179.

Chrómios: (1) Pylian; 4.295; (2) son of Priam killed by Diomédes; 5.160; (3) Lykian killed by Odysseus; 5.677; (4) Trojan killed by Teukros; 8.275; (5) Trojan leader; 17.218.

Chromis: Mysian leader; 2.858.

Chrysè: town in the Troäd; 1.37.

Chryses: priest of Apollo at Chrysè, father of Agamemnon's prize-girl—see headnote; 1.12, 1.111.

Chrysóthemis: daughter of Agamemnon; 9.145.

Crete, Cretans: island in the Mediterranean Sea and its people; 2.645, 2.649.

Cypris: cognomen of Aphrodítè, from the island; 5.330.

Cyprus: island in the eastern Mediterranean Sea; 11.21.

Daídalos: builder of a dance-floor in Crete; 18.592.

Daitor: Trojan killed by Teukros; 8.275.

Dámasos: Trojan killed by Polypoítes; 12.183.

Damástor: father of Tlépolemos (2); 16.416.

Dánaäns: =Achaians, Argives—the Greek army at Troy; 1.42.

Dánaë: daughter of Akrísios, consort of Zeus, mother of Perseus; 14.319.

Dardánia, Dardánians: region of the Troäd; its people, or the descendants of Dárdanos; 20.216, 2.819.

Dárdanos: (1) son of Zeus, ancestor of the Trojan rulers; 11.166; (2) Trojan, son of Bias, killed by Achilles; 20.460.

Dares: Trojan, priest of Hephaistos, father of Phégeus and Idaíos (2); 5.9.

Daulis: town in Phokis; 2.520.

Deïkoön: Dardánian, son of Pérgasos, killed by Agamemnon; 5.534.

Deïochos: Achaian killed by Paris, 15.341.

Déïopítes: Trojan killed by Odysseus, 11.420.

Deïphobos: Trojan leader, son of Priam; 12.94.

Deípylos: Achaian, comrade of Sthénelos; 5.325.

Deípyros: Achaian killed by Hélenos; 9.83, 13.578.

Deisénor: Trojan leader; 17.217.

Deméter: daughter of Kronos and Rheia, sister of Zeus; 2.696.

Demókoön: bastard son of Priam killed by Odysseus; 4.499.

Demóleon: Trojan, son of Anténor, killed by Achilles; 20.396.

Demoúchos: Trojan, son of Philétor, killed by Achilles; 20.457.

Deukálion: (1) son of Minos, father of Idómeneus; 12.177; (2) Trojan killed by Achilles; 20.478.

Déxamené: sea-nymph, "receiver [of prayer and sacrifice?]"; 18.44.

Dexios: father of Iphínoös; 7.14.

Díokles: father of Orsílochos (1) and Krethon, son of Ortílochos; 5.542.

Diomédè: daughter of Phorbas, consort of Achilles from Lesbos; 9.665.

Diomédes: lord of Argos, son of Tydeus, grandson of Oíneus; 2.563.

Dion: town in Euboía; 2.538.

Diónè: consort of Zeus, mother of Aprodítè; 5.370.

Dionýsos: son of Zeus and Sémelè; 6.132.

Dióres: (1) Epeían leader, son of Amaryngkeus, killed by Peíroös; 2.622, 4.517; (2) father of Autómedon; 17.429.

Dios: son of Priam; 24.251.

Dodóna: Thesprotian site of an oracle of Zeus; 2.750.

Dolon: son of Eumédes, Trojan spy killed by Diomédes and Odysseus; 10.314.

Dolopians: people of Phthia ruled by Phoinix; 9.484.

Dolopion: Trojan priest, father of Hypsénor; 5.77.

Dolops: (1) Achaian, son of Klytios, killed by Hektor; 11.302; (2) Trojan, son of Lampos, killed by Meneláos; 15.525.

Dorion: town in Messenia, southwestern Peloponnese; 2.594.

Doris: sea-nymph, "gift"; 18.45.

Dóryklos: bastard son of Priam killed by Ajax; 11.489.

Doto: sea-nymph, "giver"; 18.43.

Doulíchion: island near the west coast of Greece; 2.625.

Drákios: leader of the Epeíans; 13.692.

Dresos: Trojan killed by Euryalos; 6.20.

Dryas: (1) Lapith, hero of earlier times; 1.263; (2) father of Lykoúrgos; 6.130.

Dryops: Trojan killed by Achilles; 20.455.

Dymas: father of Hékabè and Ásios (2); 16.718.

Dynámenè: sea-nymph, "powerful"; 18.43.

Echékles: Mýrmidon, son of Aktor (4), husband of Polymélè; 16.189.

Echéklos: (1) Trojan killed by Patróklos; 16.694; (2) Trojan, son of Agénor, killed by Achilles; 20.474.

Echémmon: Trojan, son of Priam, killed by Diomédes; 5.160.

Echepólos: (1) Trojan, son of Thalýsias, killed by Antílochos; 4.458; (2) Achaian, son of Anchíses (2); 23.296.

Echínai: islands near the west coast of Greece, 2.625.

Échios: (1) father of Mekísteus; 8.333; (2) Achaian killed by Polítes; 15.339; (3) Lykian killed by Patróklos; 16.416.

Éëriboía: stepmother of Ephiáltes and Otos; 5.390.

Eëtion: (1) king of Thébè, father of Andrómachè, killed by Achilles; 1.366; (2) father of Podes; 17.575; (3) lord of Imbros; 21.43.

Eíleithúia: goddess of childbirth; 16.187.

Eilésion: town in Boiótia; 2.499.

Eïónai: town in the region of Argos; 2.561.

Eïóneus: (1) Achaian killed by Hektor; 7.11; (2) father of Rhesos; 10.435.

Élasos: Trojan killed by Patróklos; 16.696.

Élatos: Trojan killed by Agamemnon; 6.33.

Éleon: city in Boiótia; 2.500.

Elephénor: leader of the Euboíans; 2.540.

Elis, Eleíans: region in the western Pelopponese, its inhabitants; 2.615, 11.671.

Elónè: town in Thessaly; 2.739.

Emáthia: place in Macedonia; 14.226.

Énetoi: people of Asia Minor, a tribe of the Páphlagónians; 2.852.

Eniénes: people of western Thessaly; 2.749.

Éniopeús: charioteer of Hektor, son of Thebaíos, killed by Diomédes; 8.120.

Eníspè: town in Arkádia; 2.606.

Énnomos: (1) Mysian leader and soothsayer killed by Achilles; 2.858; (2) Trojan killed by Odysseus; 11.422.

Énopè: town in the region of Pylos; 9.150.

Énops: (1) father of Sátnios and Thestor; 14.443; (2) father of Klytomédes; 23.634.

Enyálios: title of Ares; 2.651.

Enýeus: lord of Skyros; 9.668.

Enýö: war-goddess; 5.333.

Epáltes: Lykian killed by Patróklos; 16.415.

Epeíans: people of Elis; 2.619.

Epeígeus: Mýrmidon, son of Ágakles, killed by Hektor; 16.571.

Epeíos: Achaian boxer, son of Panópeus; 23.665.

Ephiáltes: giant, son of Alóeos, brother of Otos; 5.385.

Ephýra: (1) city in Thesprotia, on the river Selléëis; 2.659; (2) =Korinth, in the region of Argos; 6.152.

Ephýroi: people of the north, probably Thessaly, aided by Ares and Panic; 13.301.

Epidaúros: city in the region of Argos; 2.561.

Epíkles: Lykian, comrade of Sarpédon, killed by Ajax (1); 12.379.

Epístor: Trojan killed by Patróklos; 16.695.

Epístrophos: (1) Phokian leader, son of Íphitos; 2.517; (2) prince of Lyréssos, son of Euénos, killed by Achilles; 2.692; (3) Halizónian leader; 2.856.

Épytos: father of Périphas; 17.324.

Érebos: the underworld; 8.368.

Eréchtheus: ancestral hero of Athens; 2.547.

Erétria: city in Euboía; 2.537.

Ereuthálion: Arkádian killed by Nestor; 4.319.

Erichthónios: son of Dárdanos, ancestor of the Trojan kings; 20.219.

Erínys, Erínyës: avenging goddess(es); 9.454, 571.

Eriópis: wife of Oïleus, stepmother of Médon; 13.697.

Eryláos: Lykian killed by Patróklos; 16.411.

Érymas: (1) Trojan killed by Idómeneus; 16.345; (2) Lykian killed by Patróklos; 16.415.

Erythínoi: town in Asia Minor on the Black Sea where Páphlagónians live; 2.855.

Erýthrai: town in Boiótia; 2.499.

Eteókles: son of Oídipous, brother of Polyneíkes, ruler of Thebes; 4.386.

Eteónos: town in Boiótia; 2.497.

Ethiopians: people near the Ocean with whom the gods banquet; 1.423.

Euaímon: father of Eurýpylos (2); 2.736.

Euboía: island close to the east coast of Greece; 2.535.

Euchénor: Korinthian, son of Polyïdos, killed by Paris; 13.663.

Eudóros: Mýrmidon leader, son of Hermes and Polymélè; 16.179.

Euénos: (1) father of Mynes and Epístrophos (2); 2.693; (2) father of Marpéssa; 9.557.

Euíppos: Lykian killed by Patróklos; 16.417.

Eumédes: father of Dolon; 10.314.

Eumélos: Thessalian leader from Phérai; 2.714.

Eunéos: lord of Lemnos, son of Jason and Hypsípylè; 7.468.

Euphémos: Kikonian leader; 2.846.

Euphétes: lord of Ephýra (1); 15.532.

Euphórbos: Dardánian, son of Pánthoös, strikes Patróklos, killed by Meneláos; 16.808, 17.59.

Eurýalos: Argive leader, son of Mekísteus, comrade of Diomédes; 2.565.

Eurybátes: (1) herald of Agamemnon; 1.320; (2) herald of Odysseus; 2.184.

Eurýdamas: Trojan soothsayer, father of Abas and Polyïdos (1); 5.149.

Eurýmedon: (1) retainer of Agamemnon, son of Ptolemaíos; 4.228; (2) retainer of Nestor; 8.114.

Eurýpylos: (1) ancient hero of Kos; 2.677; (2) Thessalian, son of Euaímon; 2.736.

Eurýstheus: son of Sthénelos, grandson of Perseus, lord of the Argives, taskmaster of Herakles; 8.363, 19.123.

Eúrytos: (1) lord of Oichália; 2.596; (2) son of Aktor (2), father of Thálpios, brother of Ktéatos; 2.621.

Eussóros: father of Ákamas; 6.8.

Eutrésis: town in Boiótia; 2.502.

Exádios: Lapith hero of earlier times; 1.264.

Galateía: sea-nymph, "milky" (as in white sea-foam); 18.45.

Ganymédes: son of Tros, taken by the gods for his beauty; 5.266.

Gárgaros: Zeus' seat on the peak of Mount Ida; 8.48.

Gerenian: common epithet of Nestor, meaning unknown; 2.336.

Gláphyrai: town near Phérai in Thessaly; 2.712.

Glaukè: sea-nymph, "glittering"; 18.39.

Glaukos: (1) Lykian leader, son of Hippólochos, comrade of Sarpédon; 2.876; (2) son of Sísyphos, father of Bellérophon; 6.154.

Glísas: town in Boiótia; 2.504.

Gonoéssa: town in the northern Pelopponese; 2.573.

Gorgon: monster whose stare petrified the onlooker; 5.741.

Gorgýthion: son of Priam and Kástianeíra, killed by Teukros; 8.302.

Gortys: city in Crete; 2.646.

Gouneus: leader of the Eniénes and Peraíboi; 2.748.

Graces: goddesses of indefinite number, embodiments of beauty; 5.338.

Graia: town in Boiótia; 2.498.

Grénikos: river in the Troäd; 12.21.

Gygaía: lake in Maiónia; 2.865.

Gyrtios: father of Hyrtios; 14.511.

Gyrtónè: town in Thessaly; 2.738.

Hades: son of Kronos and Rheia, brother of Zeus, Hera, Poseidon, and Deméter; 1.3.

Haimon: (1) comrade of Nestor; 4.296; (2) father of Maion; 4.394; (3) father of Laérkes; 17.467.

Haliártos: town in Boiótia; 2.503.

Hálië: sea-nymph; "seabrine"; 18.40.

Hálios: Lykian killed by Odysseus; 5.678.

Halizónians: people of eastern Asia Minor; 2.856.

Harma: town in Boiótia; 2.499.

Harmon: father of Tekton, 5.60.

Harpálion: Páphlagónian killed by Mériones; 13.643.

Hebè: daughter of Zeus and Hera, servant of the gods; 4.2.

Hékabè: wife of Priam, daughter of Dymas, mother of Hektor and others; 6.293.

Hekamédè: prize-woman of Nestor from Ténedos, daughter of Arsínoös; 11.624.

Hektor: Trojan hero, son of Priam and Hékabè, husband of Andrómachè, father of Ástyanáx; 1.242.

Helen: daughter of Zeus and Leda, wife of Meneláos, consort of Paris; 2.161.

Hélenos: (1) Achaian killed by Hektor; 5.707; (2) soothsayer, son of Priam; 6.75.

Helikáön: Trojan, son of Anténor, husband of Laódikè; 3.123.

Hélikè: city in Achaia; 2.575.

Helios: sun-god; 3.277.

Hellas, Héllenes: region in Thessaly, its people, ruled by Peleus; 2.683, 684.

Hellespont: the modern Dardanelles, strait between Thrace and the Troäd; 2.845.

Helos: (1) city in Lakedaímon; 2.584; (2) town in the region of Pylos; 2.594.

Hephaistos: god of fire, artificer, son of Hera; 1.571.

Heptáporos: river of the Troäd; 12.20.

Hera: daughter of Kronos and Rhea, sister of Zeus, Poseidon, Hades, and Deméter, wife of Zeus; 1.55.

Herakles: hero, son of Zeus and Alkménè, father of Tlepólemos (1) and Théssalos; 2.653, 14.324.

Hermes: son of Zeus and Maia, messenger and guide, killer of Argos; 2.104.

Hermíonè: town on the south shore of the region of Argos; 2.560.

Hermos: river in Maiónia; 20.392.

Hiketáon: Trojan elder, son of Laómedon, father of Melaníppos (2); 3.147.

Híppasos: (1) father of Chárops and Sokos; 11.426; (2) father of Hypsénor; 13.411.

Hippemólgoi: people dwelling north of Thrace, "horse-milkers"; 13.5.

Hippódamas: Trojan killed by Achilles; 20.401.

Híppodameía: (1) wife of Peiríthoös, mother of Polypoítes; 2.742; (2) daughter of Anchíses (1), wife of Alkáthoös; 13.429.

Hippódamos: Trojan killed by Odysseus; 11.335.

Hippókoön: Thracian, cousin of Rhesos; 10.518.

Hippólochos: (1) son of Bellérophon, father of Glaukos (1); 6.119; (2) Trojan, son of Antímachos, killed by Agamemnon; 11.122.

Hippómachos: Trojan, son of Antímachos, killed by Leónteus; 12.189.

Hippónoös: Achaian killed by Hektor; 11.303.

Hippóthoös: (1) Pelásgian leader, son of Lethos, killed by Ajax (1); 2.840, 17.288; (2) son of Priam; 24.251.

Hippótion: Askánian lord, father of Askánios, Palmys, and Morys; killed by Mérionés; 13.792, 14.514.

Hirè: town in the region of Pylos; 9.150.

Histiaía: city in Euboía; 2.537.

Hýades: group of stars in the constellation Taurus, "rain-bringers"; 18.486.

Hyámpolis: city in Phokis; 2.521.

Hydè: region around Mount Tmolos in Maiónia; 20.385.

Hylè: town in Boiótia; 2.500.

Hyllos: river in Maiónia; 20.392.

Hypeírochos: (1) Trojan killed by Odysseus; 11.335; (2) father of Itómeneus; 11.672.

Hypeíron: Trojan killed by Diomédes; 5.144.

Hypereía: spring in Thessaly, in Eurýpylos' domain, 2.734.

Hyperénor: Dardánian, son of Pánthoös, killed by Meneláos; 14.516.

Hyperésia: city on the Gulf of Korinth, 2.573.

Hypsénor: (1) Trojan, son of Dolópion, killed by Eurýpylos; 5.76; (2) Achaian, son of Híppasos, killed by Deíphobos; 13.411.

Hypsípylè: wife of Jáson, mother of Eunéos; 7.469.

Hyria: town in Boiótia, near Aulis; 2.496.

Hýrminè: town of the Epeíans, in the western Pelopponese; 2.616.

Hýrtakos: father of Ásios (1); 2.837.

Hyrtios: Mysian leader, son of Gyrtios, killed by Mérionés; 14.512.

Iaíra: sea-nymph, "swift maid"; 18.42.

Iálmenos: Minyan leader, son of Ares by Astýochè, brother of Askálaphos; 2.512.

Iálysos: city in Rhodos; 2.656.

Iámenos: Trojan killed by Leónteus; 12.139, 193.

Ianássa: sea-nymph, "powerful protectress"; 18.47.

Ianeíra: sea-nymph, "powerful lady"; 18.47.

Iápetos: Titan in the underworld; 8.479.

Iardános: river in Arkádia or Pylos, by which Pheia is located; 7.135.

Iásos: Achaian killed by Aineías; 15.332.

Ida, Idaían: mountain in the Troäd, epithet of Zeus derived from it; 2.821, 16.604.

Idaíos: (1) herald of Priam; 3.248, 24.325; (2) Trojan, son of Dares, brother of Phégeus, killed by Diomédes; 5.11.

Idómeneus: lord of the Cretans, son of Deukálion; 1.145.

Ikárian seaway: sea south of the island of Ikária and north of Samos; 2.145.

Ilion: =Troy; 1.71.

Ilióneus: Trojan, son of Phorbas, killed by Penéleos; 14.489.

Ilos: hero of Ilion, son of Tros, father of Laómedon, grandfather of Priam; 10.415.

Ímbrasos: father of Peíroös; 4.520.

Ímbrios: Trojan, son of Mentor, killed by Teukros; 13.171.

Imbros: island in the Aegean Sea near Troy; 13.33.

Iólkos: city in Thessaly; 2.712.

Iónians: people associated with, or the same as, the Athenians; 13.685.

Ípheus: Lykian killed by Patróklos; 16.417.

Íphianássa: daughter of Agamemnon; 9.145.

Iphídamas: Trojan, son of Anténor, wounds Agamemnon, who kills him; 11.221.

Íphiklos: father of Podárkes, defeated by Nestor; 2.705, 23.636.

Iphínoös: Achaian, son of Dexios, killed by Glaukos (1); 7.14.

Iphis: prize-girl of Patróklos; 9.667.

Iphítion: Trojan killed by Achilles; 20.382.

Íphitos: (1) father of Schédios (1) and Epístrophos (1), 2.518; (2) father of Árcheptólemos; 8.128.

Iris: messenger of the gods; 2.786.

Isándros: son of Bellérophon; 6.197.

Isos: bastard son of Priam, killed by Agamemnon; 11.101.

Ithaímenes: father of Stheneláos; 16.586.

Ithaka, Ithakan: island west of Greece, home of Odysseus; 2.184, 632.

Ithómè: town in western Thessaly; 2.729.

Iton: town in eastern Thessaly, south of Phérai; 2.696.

Itýmoneus: Eleíans killed by Nestor; 11.673.

Ixion: putative father of Peiríthoös, husband of Dia; 14.317.

Jason: Argonaut, father of Eunéos by Hypsípylè; 7.468.

Kabésos: city allied with Troy, location unknown; 13.363.

Kadmeíans: inhabitants of Thebes, named for Kadmos, the founder; 4.385.

Kaineus: Lapith, hero of Nestor's earlier years, father of Korónos; 1.264.

Kalchas: soothsayer for the Achaians; 1.69.

Kalésios: charioteer of Áxylos; 6.18.

Kalétor: (1) father of Apháreus; 13.541; (2) Trojan, son of Klýtios, killed by Ajax; 15.419.

Kállianássa: sea-nymph, "lovely protectress"; 18.46.

Kállianeíra: sea-nymph, "lovely lady"; 18.44.

Kálliarós: town in Lokris; 2.531.

Kállikolónè: hill in the Troäd, "pleasant hill"; 20.53.

Kalýdnai: islands in the southeast Aegean Sea; 2.677.

Kálydon: city in Aitolia; 2.640.

Kameíros: city in Rhodes; 2.656.

Kápaneus: father of Sthénelos (1); 2.564.

Kapys: son of Assárakos, father of Priam, grandfather of Aineías; 20.239.

Kárdamylè: town in the region of Pylos; 9.150.

Karésos: river in the Troäd; 12.20.

Karians: people of western Asia Minor, in and around Milétos; 2.867.

Karýstos: city in Euboía; 2.539.

Kasos: island in the southeast Aegean Sea; 2.676.

Kassandra: daughter of Priam and Hékabè; 13.366.

Kástianeíra: consort of Priam, mother of Gorgýthion; 8.305.

Kastor: son of Leda and Tyndáreos, brother of Helen and Polydeúkes; 3.237.

Kaukónians: people of Asia Minor; 10.429.

Kaÿstrios: river of Asia Minor that flows into the sea at Ephesos; 2.461.

Kéas: father of Troizénos; 2.847.

Kebríones: bastard son of Priam, killed by Patróklos; 8.318, 16.727.

Kéladon: river in Pylos or Arkadia; 7.133.

Kephallénians: people ruled by Odysseus, in Samos (later Kephallénia) and the islands around it; 2.631.

Kephisian lake: lake in Boiótia, often called Lake Kopáïs; 5.709.

Képhisos: river in Phokis and Boiótia; 2.522.

Kerínthos: town in Boiótia; 2.538.

Kikonians: people of Thrace; 2.846.

Kilíkians: people of Thébè in the Troäd; 6.397.

Killa: town in the Troäd; 1.38.

Kinýras: lord of Cyprus; 11.20.

Kisses: father of Theáno, grandfather of Iphídamas; 6.299, 11.223.

Kleitos: Trojan, Polýdamas' retainer, son of Peisénor, killed by Teukros; 15.445.

Kleóboulos: Trojan killed by Ajax (2); 16.330.

Kleónai: city in the northern Peloponnese; 2.570.

Kleopatra: daughter of Idas and Marpéssa, wife of Meleágros; 9.556.

Klónios: leader of the Boiótians, killed by Agénor; 2.495, 15.340.

Klýmenè: (1) handmaid of Helen; 3.144; (2) sea-nymph, "renowned"; 18.47.

Klýtaimnéstra: wife of Agamemnon; 1.113.

Klýtios: (1) Trojan elder, son of Laómedon; 3.147; (2) father of Dolops; 11.302.

Klytomédes: boxer defeated by Nestor; 23.634.

Knosos: city in Crete; 2.646.

Koíranos: (1) Lykian killed by Odysseus; 5.677; (2) charioteer of Mérionés killed by Hektor; 17.611.

Koön: son of Anténor, killed by Agamemnon after wounding him; 11.248.

Kopai: town in Boiótia; 2.502.

Kópreus: messenger of Eurýstheus, father of Periphétes; 15.639.

Korinth: =Ephýra (2), city in the northern Peloponnese; 2.570.

Koroneía: city in Boiótia; 2.503.

Korónos: father of Leónteus; 2.746.

Kos: island in the southeast Aegean Sea; 2.677.

Kourétes: people of western Greece; 9.529.

Kránaë Island: an island near Lakedaímon; 3.445.

Krápathos: island in the southeast Aegean Sea; 2.676.

Kreion: Father of Lykomédes; 9.84.

Krethon: Achaian, son of Díokles, brother of Orsílochos, killed by Aineías; 5.542.

Krisa: city in Phokis, near Delphi; 2.520.

Kroismos: Trojan killed by Meges; 15.523.

Krokyleía: place in Ithaka; 2.633.

Kromna: town in Páphlagónia; 2.855.

Kronos: Titan, consort of Rheia, father of Zeus, Hades, Poseidon, Hera, and Demeter; 1.398.

Ktéatos: son of Aktor (2), brother of Eúrytos (2), father of Amphímachos (1); 2.621.

Kyllénè: mountain in Arkádia; 2.603.

Kyllénian: from Kyllénè, the port of Elis; 15.518.

Kymíndis: human name for the bird called "chalkis" by the gods; 14.291.

Kýmodoké: sea-nymph, "wave-calming"; 18.39.

Kýmothoë: sea-nymph, "wave-racing"; 18.41.

Kynos: port town in Lokris; 2.531.

Kýparisséëis: town near Pylos; 2.593.

Kyparíssos: town in Phokis; 2.519.

Kyphos: city of Gouneus, in Thessaly; 2.748.

Kýthera: island off Cape Máleia, southern Lakedaímon; 15.432.

Kytóros: town in Páphlagónia; 2.853.

Laäs: city in Lakedaímon; 2.585.

Laȇrkes: father of Alkímedon; 16.197.

Laȇrtes: father of Odysseus; 2.173.

Lakedaímon: region in the southern Pelopponese; 2.581.

Lampos: (1) Trojan elder, son of Laómedon, father of Dolops; 3.147; (2) one of Hektor's horses; 8.185.

Laódamas: Trojan, son of Anténor, killed by Ajax (1); 15.516.

Láodameía: daughter of Bellérophon, consort of Zeus, mother of Sarpédon; 6.197.

Laódikè: (1) daughter of Priam, wife of Helikáön; 3.124; (2) daughter of Agamemnon; 9.145.

Laódokos: (1) Trojan, son of Anténor; 4.87; (2) Achaian, charioteer of Antílochos; 17.699.

Laógonos: (1) Trojan, son of Onétor, killed by Mérionés; 16.604; (2) Trojan, son of Bias, killed by Achilles; 20.460.

Laómedon: King of Troy, father of Priam, Lampos (1), Tithónos, Hiketáon, and Klytios (1); 3.250, 20.236.

Laothoë: daughter of Altes, wife of Priam, mother of Lykáon (2) and Polydóros; 21.85.

Lapiths: people of Thessaly; 12.128.

Laríssa: city of Pelásgians, probably located in the Troäd; 2.841.

Leiókritos: Achaian, son of Arísbas, killed by Aineías; 17.344.

Léïtos: Boiótian leader, son of Aléktryon, wounded by Hektor; 2.494, 17.601.

Lekton: promontory of the Troäd; 14.284.

Léleges: people of Pédasos in the Troäd; 10.429, 21.86.

Lemnos: island in the northern Aegean Sea; 1.593.

Leónteus: leader of the Lapiths, son of Korónos; 2.745.

Lesbos: island and city in the Aegean Sea near Asia Minor; 9.128.

Lethos: lord of Laríssa, father of Hippóthoös (1) and Pylaíos; 2.843.

Leto: consort of Zeus, mother of Apollo and Artemis; 1.9.

Leukos: comrade of Odysseus killed by Ántiphos; 4.491.

Likýmnios: Herakles' uncle killed by Tlepólemos (1), his great-nephew; 2.663.

Lilaía: town in Phokis; 2.523.

Límnoreía: sea-nymph, "harbor-maid"; 18.41.

Lindos: city in Rhodos; 2.656.

Lokrians: people of Lokris, in eastern Greece; 2.527.

Lykáon: (1) father of Pándaros; 2.826; (2) son of Priam and Laóthoè, killed by Achilles; 3.333, 21.35.

Lykástos: city in Crete; 2.647.

Lykia, Lykians: (1) region and people in southwest Asia Minor; 2.876, 5.479; (2) region near Troy; 5.105.

Lykomédes: Achaian, son of Kreion; 9.84.

Lykon: Trojan killed by Penéleos; 16.335.

Lykophóntes: Trojan killed by Teukros; 8.275.

Lýkophron: son of Mastor, Kytheréan comrade of Ajax, killed by Hektor; 15.430.

Lykoúrgos: (1) son of Dryas (2); he attacked the nurses of Dionýsos; 6.130; (2) hero who killed Areíthoös; 7.142.

Lyktos: city in Crete; 2.647.

Lyrnéssos: town in the Troäd, beneath Mount Ida; 2.690.

Lysánder: Trojan killed by Ajax (1); 11.491.

Macháon: Oichálian healer, son of Asklépios, wounded by Paris; 2.732, 11.506.

Magnétes: people of eastern Thessaly; 2.756.

Maiándros: river of western Asia Minor; 2.869.

Maímalos: father of Peisándros (3); 16.194.

Maion: leader of the Kadmeíans, son of Haimon; 4.394.

Maiónia, Maiónians: region and people in western Asia Minor; 3.401, 2.864.

Maíra: sea-nymph, "sparkling"; 18.48.

Makar: lord of Lesbos; 24.544.

Mantineía: city in Arkádia; 2.607.

Maris: Lykian, son of Ámisodáros, killed by Thrasymédes; 16.319.

Marpéssa: daughter of Eúenos, wife of Idas, mother of Kleopatra; 9.557.

Mases: port town in the region of Argos; 2.562.

Mastor: father of Lýkophron; 15.430.

Médeon: town in Boiótia; 2.501.

Médesikástè: bastard daughter of Priam, wife of Ímbrios; 13.173.

Medon: (1) Thessalian leader in Philoktétes' absence, bastard son of Oïleus (1), killed by Aineías; 2.727, 15.332; (2) Trojan ally; 17.216.

Megas: father of Périmos; 16.695.

Meges: Doulíchian leader of the Epeíans, son of Phýleus; 2.627, 13.692.

Mekísteus: (1) one of the Seven against Thebes, son of Tálaös, father of Eurýalos; 2.566; (2) Achaian, son of Échios, killed by Polýdamas; 8.333, 15.339.

Melaníppos: (1) Trojan killed by Teukros; 8.276; (2) Trojan, son of Hiketáon, killed by Antílochos; 15.547; (3) Trojan killed by Patróklos; 16.695; (4) Achaian leader; 19.240.

Melánthios: Trojan killed by Eurýpylos; 6.36.

Melas: son of Portheus, brother of Oíneus, great-uncle of Diomédes; 14.117.

Meleágros: former prince of Kálydon, son of Oíneus; 2.642, 9.543.

Meliboía: town in Thessaly; 2.717.

Mélitè: sea-nymph, "honey-sweet"; 18.42.

Meneláos: Achaian leader, son of Atreus, brother of Agamemnon, husband of Helen, lord of Lakedaímon; 1.159.

Menésthes: Achaian killed by Hektor; 5.609.

Menéstheus: Athenian leader, son of Péteos; 2.552.

Menésthios: (1) Achaian, son of Áreïthóös, killed by Paris; 7.9; (2) Mýrmidon leader, son of Spercheios; 16.173.

Menoítios: son of Aktor (3), father of Patróklos; 1.307.

Menon: Trojan killed by Leónteus; 12.193.

Mentes: leader of the Kikonians; 17.73.

Mentor: father of Ímbrios; 13.171.

Mérionés: Cretan leader, comrade of Idómeneus; 2.651.

Mérmeros: Trojan killed by Antílochos; 14.513.

Merops: father of Adréstos and Ámphios; 2.831.

Messa: town in Lakedaímon; 2.582.

Messëís: spring somewhere in Greece; 6.457.

Mesthles: Maiónian leader, son of Talaímenes; 2.864.

Mestor: son of Priam; 24.257.

Methóna: town in Thessaly; 2.716.

Midéia: town in Boiótia; 2.507.

Milétos: (1) city in Crete; 2.647; (2) city of the Karians in Asia Minor; 2.868.

Minos: king of Crete, son of Zeus and Europa, father of Deukálion, grandfather of Idómeneus; 13.450.

Minyan: pertaining to the Minyans, who live in and around Orchómenos; 2.511.

Minyéïos: river in the western Pelopponese; 11.722.

Mnesos: Paiónian killed by Achilles; 21.210.

Mólion: Trojan comrade of Thymbraíos killed by Odysseus; 11.322.

Moliónes: (presumably a metronymic) Eúrytos (2) and Ktéatos; 11.709.

Molos: father of Mérionés; 10.269.

Morys: Askanian leader, son of Hippótion, killed by Mérionés; 13.792, 14.514.

Moúlios: (1) Epeían killed by Nestor; 11.739; (2) Trojan killed by Patróklos; 16.696; (3) Trojan killed by Achilles; 20.472.

Muse, Muses: goddesses of artistic creation, inspiring the singer of tales; 1.604.

Mydon: (1) Páphlagónian, charioteer of Pylaímenes, son of Atýmnios, killed by Antílochos; 5.581; (2) Paiónian killed by Achilles; 21.209.

Mygdon: Phrygian leader; 3.186.

Mýkalè: promontory near Milétos (2); 2.869.

Mykaléssos: city in Boiótia; 2.498.

Mykénè: city of Agamemnon, north of Argos in the eastern Pelopponese; 2.569.

Mynes: Prince of Lyrnéssos, son of Euénos, former husband of Bríseus' daughter, killed by Achilles; 2.692.

Myrínè: dancer, possibly an Amazon princess, entombed near Troy; 2.814.

Mýrmidons: people of Phthia, ruled by Peleus, led by Achilles; 1.180.

Mýrsinos: city in Elis; 2.616.

Mysians: people of Mysia, just east of the Troäd, or dwelling in Thrace; 2.858, 13.5.

Nastes: Karian leader killed by Achilles; 2.867.

Neleus: king of Pylos, father of Nestor; 2.20.

Némertés: sea-nymph, "infallible"; 18.46.

Neoptólemos: son of Achilles; 19.327.

Néreus: the old man of the sea, father of Thetis and the other sea-nymphs; 18.38.

Nériton: mountain on Ithaka; 2.632.

Nesaía: sea-nymph, "island-maid"; 18.40.

Nestor: Achaian elder from Pylos, father of Antílochos and Thrasymédes; 1.248.

Níobè: mother of twelve children killed by Apollo and Artemis; 24.602.

Níreus: leader from Sýmè famed for beauty, son of Charópos and Aglaía; 2.671.

Nisa: town in Boiótia; 2.508.

Nisýros: island in the southeastern Aegean Sea; 2.676.

Noêmon: (1) Lykian killed by Odysseus; 5.678; (2) comrade of Antílochos; 23.612.

Nómion: father of Nastes and Amphímachos (2); 2.871.

Nysa: mountain of uncertain location, sacred to Dionýsos; 6.133.

Ocean: great river surrounding the world, its god, husband of Tethys, ancestor of the gods; 1.423, 14.201.

Ochésios: father of Périphas; 5.843.

Odios: (1) Halizónian leader; 2.856; (2) Achaian herald; 9.170.

Odysseus: Ithakan leader of the Kephallénians, son of Laërtes, 1.138.

Oichália: city in Thessaly; 2.595.

Oidipous: Hero of Thebes (1); 23.680.

Oïleus: (1) father of Ajax (2) and Médon (1); 2.527; (2) Trojan killed by Agamemnon; 11.93.

Oíneus: Aitolian hero, son of Portheus, father of Tydeus and Meleágros, grandfather of Diomédes; 2.641, 14.117.

Oinómaös: (1) Achaian killed by Hektor; 5.706; (2) Trojan killed by Idómeneus; 12.140, 13.506.

Oinops: father of Hélenos (1); 5.707.

Oítylos: town in Lakedaímon; 2.585.

Okálea: city in Boiótia; 2.501.

Olénian rock: landmark on the border of Elis; 2.617.

Ólenos: town in Aitolia; 2.639.

Olízon: town in Thessaly; 2.717.

Oloösson: city in Thessaly; 2.739.

Olympos, Olympian: mountain in northern Thessaly, abode of the gods; pertaining to it, title of Zeus; 1.18, 44, 353.

Onchéstos: town and sanctuary of Poseidon in Boiótia; 2.506.

Onétor: father of Laógonos (1), priest of Idaían Zeus; 16.604.

Opheléstes: (1) Trojan killed by Teukros; 8.274; (2) Paiónian killed by Achilles; 21.210.

Ophéltios: (1) Trojan killed by Eurýalos; 6.20; (2) Achaian killed by Hektor; 11.302.

Opítes: Achaian killed by Hektor; 11.301.

Opóeis: city in Lokris; 2.531.

Orchómenos: (1) Boiótian city of the Minyans; 2.511; (2) city in Arkádia; 2.605.

Óreithuía: sea-nymph, "mountain-rushing [wind?]"; 18.48.

Orésbios: Boiótian killed by Hektor; 5.707.

Orestes: (1) Achaian killed by Hektor; 5.705; (2) son of Agamemnon; 9.142; (3) Trojan killed by Leónteus; 12.139, 193.

Oríon: constellation; 18.486.

Orménios: town in Thessaly; 2.734.

Órmenos: (1) Trojan killed by Teukros; 8.274; (2) father of Amýntor, grandfather of Phoinix; 9.448; (3) Trojan killed by Polypoítes; 12.187.

Orneíai: town in the northern Peloponese; 2.571.

Oros: Achaian killed by Hektor; 11.303.

Orsílochos: (1) Achaian, son of Díokles, killed by Aineías; 5.542; (2) Trojan killed by Teukros; 8.274.

Ortílochos: son of Álpheios, father of Díokles; 5.546.

Orthaíos: Trojan leader; 13.791.

Orthè: town in Thessaly; 2.739.

Óthryoneús: suitor of Kassandra, from Kabésos, killed by Idómeneus; 13.363.

Otos: (1) giant, son of Alóeos, brother of Ephiáltes; 5.385; (2) Kellénian lord of the Epeíans, killed by Polýdamas; 15.518.

Ótreus: lord of Phrygia; 3.186.

Otrýnteus: father of Iphítion, lord of Hydè; 20.383.

Oukálegon: Trojan elder; 3.148.

Oúranos: ancestor of the gods, "heaven," by his union with Gaia, "Earth"; 5.373.

Paiêon: healing god; 5.401.

Paion: father of Agástrophos; 11.339.

Paiónia, Paiónians: region in Macedonia and its inhabitants; 17.350, 2.848.

Paisos: =Apaísos (?) town in the Troäd; 5.612.

Pallas: title of Athena; 1.200.

Palmys: Askánian leader, son of Hippótion; 13.792.

Pammon: son of Priam; 24.250.

Pándaros: Trojan leader, son of Lykáon (1), shoots Meneláos, killed by Diomédes; 2.827, 4.88, 5.168.

Pándion: retainer of Teukros; 12.372.

Pándokos: Trojan killed by Ajax; 11.490.

Pánopè: sea-nymph, "all-seeing"; 18.45.

Panópeus: (1) city in Phokis; 2.520; (2) father of Epeíos; 23.665.

Pánthoös: Dardánian elder, father of Euphórbos, Polýdamas, and Hyperénor; 3.146.

Páphlagónians: people of Páphlagónia, in northeastern Asia Minor; 2.851.

Paris: =Alexander, son of Priam, consort of Helen, brother of Hektor; 3.39.

Parrhásia: district of western Arkádia; 2.608.

Parthénios: river in Páphlagónia; 2.854.

Pasíthea: one of the Graces; 14.269.

Patróklos: comrade of Achilles, son of Menoítios, killed by Hektor; 1.307.

Pedaíos: (1) Trojan, bastard son of Anténor, killed by Meges; 5.69; (2) town, probably in the Troäd; 13.172.

Pédasos: (1) Trojan, son of Boukólion and Abarbárea, killed by Eurýalos; 6.21; (2) city in the Troäd; 6.35; (3) town in the region of Pylos; 9.152; (4) one of Achilles' horses; 16.152.

Peires: father of Rhigmos; 20.484.

Peiraíos: father of Ptolemaíos, grandfather of Eurýmedon; 4.228.

Peiríthoös: Lapith hero, son of Zeus, father of Polypoítes; 1.263.

Peíroös: Thracian, son of Ímbrasos, kills Dióres, killed by Thoas; 2.844, 4.520.

Peisándros: (1) Trojan, son of Antímachos, killed by Agamemnon; 11.122; (2) Trojan killed by Meneláos; 13.601; (3) Mýrmidon leader, son of Maímalos; 16.193.

Peisénor: father of Kleitos; 15.445.

Pélagon: (1) comrade of Nestor; 4.295; (2) comrade of Sarpédon; 5.694.

Pelásgian, Pelásgians: (1) pertaining to Thessalian Argos, ruled by Peleus; 2.681; (2) people of Asia Minor, in or near the Troäd; 2.840.

Pélegon: father of Ásteropaíos, son of the Áxios River by Periboía; 21.141.

Peleus: son of Aíakos, husband of Thetis, father of Achilles; 1.1.

Pélias: king of Iólkos, father of Alkéstis; 2.715.

Pélion, Pélian: mountain in Thessaly; coming from it; 2.757, 16.143.

Pellénè: town in the northeast Pelopponese; 2.574.

Pelops: lord of the region of Argos (1), father of Atreus, grandfather of Agamemnon and Meneláos; 2.104.

Peneíos: main river of Thessaly; 2.752.

Penéleos: Boiótian leader; 2.494.

Peraíboi: people of Thessaly; 2.749.

Pereía: place where Apollo raised the mares of Pheres; may =Phérai (1); 2.766.

Pérgamos: citadel of Troy; 4.508.

Pérgasos: father of Deïkoön; 5.535.

Periboía: mother of Pélegon by the Áxios River; 21.142.

Periéres: father of Boros; 16.177.

Perimédes: father of Schédios (2); 15.515.

Périmos: Trojan, son of Megas, killed by Patróklos; 16.695.

Périphas: (1) Aitolian, son of Ochésios, killed by Ares; 5.842; (2) son of Épitos, herald of Anchíses (1); 17.323.

Periphétes: (1) Trojan killed by Teukros; 14.515; (2) Achaian, son of Kópreus, killed by Hektor; 15.638.

Perkótè, Perkósian: city on the Hellespont; pertaining to it; 2.831, 835.

Perséphonè: consort of Hades, queen of the underworld; 9.457.

Perseus: hero, son of Zeus and Dánaë, father of Sthénelos, grandfather of Eurýstheus; 14.320, 19.116.

Péteon: town in Boiótia; 2.500.

Péteos: father of Menéstheus; 2.552.

Phainops: (1) father of Xanthos (1) and Thoön (1); 5.152; (2) father of Phorkys; 17.312; (3) guest-friend of Hektor from Abýdos, son of Ásios; 17.583.

Phaistos: (1) city in Crete; 2.648; (2) Maiónian, son of Boros, killed by Idómeneus; 5.43.

Phalkes: Trojan killed by Antílochos; 13.791, 14.513.

Pharis: town in Lakedaímon; 2.582.

Phaúsias: father of Apisáon; 11.578.

Phégeus: Trojan, son of Dares, brother of Idaíos, killed by Diomédes; 5.11.

Pheia: city on the river Iardános; 7.135.

Pheidas: Athenian leader; 13.691.

Pheidíppos: leader from Kos, son of Théssalos, grandson of Herakles; 2.678.

Phéneos: city in Arkádia, under Mount Kyllénè; 2.605.

Phérai: (1) city in Thessaly; 2.711; (2) city in the region of Pylos; 5.543, 9.151.

Phéreklos: Trojan shipwright, son of Tekton, killed by Mériones; 5.59.

Pheres: father of Admétos, grandfather of Eumélos; 2.763.

Pheroúsa: sea-nymph, "carrier [of ships?];" 18.43.

Philétor: father of Demoúchos; 20.457.

Philoktétes: Thessalian leader, archer, bitten by a snake, left on Lemnos; 2.718.

Phlegyan: referring to Lapiths, people of Thessaly; 13.302.

Phoibos: cognomen of Apollo; 1.43.

Phoinix: (1) Achaian elder, comrade and tutor of Achilles, son of Amýntor; 9.168; (2) father of Europa; 14.321.

Phokis, Phokians: region west of Boiótia; its people; 2.517, 525.

Phorbas: (1) father of Diomédè; 9.665; (2) father of Ilióneus; 14.490.

Phorkys: Phrygian leader from Askánia, son of Phainops, killed by Ajax (1); 2.862, 17.312.

Phradmon: father of Ageláos: 8.257.

Phrontis: wife of Pánthoös, mother of Euphórbos, Polýdamas, Hyperénor; 17.40.

Phrygia, Phrygians: region east of Troy; its people; 2.862, 3.184.

Phthia: region in southern Thessaly, Achilles' homeland; 1.155.

Phthires: mountain in western Asia Minor, near Milétos (2); 2.868.

Phýlakè: city of Prótesiláos in Thessaly; 2.695.

Phýlakos: (1) father of Íphiklos, grandfather of Prótesiláos and Podárkes; 2.705; (2) Trojan killed by Leïtos; 6.35.

Phylas: father of Polymélè, grandfather of Eudóros; 16.181.

Phýleus: father of Meges, defeated by Nestor in the spear-throw; 2.628, 23.637.

Phýlomedoúsa: wife of Áreïthóös (1), mother of Menésthios; 7.10.

Pidýtes: Perkósian killed by Odysseus; 6.30.

Piéria: region near Mount Olympos; 14.226.

Píttheus: father of Aithrè; 3.144.

Pityeía: town in the Troäd, on the Hellespont; 2.829.

Plakos: mountain in the Troäd, above Thébè; 6.396.

Plataía: city in Boiótia; 2.504.

Pleíades: group of stars in the constellation Taurus, marking the time for harvest and plowing; 18.486.

Pleuron: town in Aitolia; 2.639.

Podaleírios: healer, Oichálian leader, son of Asklépios; 2.732.

Podárgè: mother by Zephyr of Xanthos (5) and Balios, "fleet-foot"; 16.150.

Podárgos: (1) one of Hektor's horses, "fleet-foot"; 8.185; (2) one of Meneláos' horses; 23.295.

Podárkes: Thessalian leader from Phýlakè, son of Íphiklos, younger brother of Prótesiláos; 2.704.

Podes: son of Eëtion (2), friend of Hektor, killed by Meneláos; 17.575.

Polítes: son of Priam; 2.791.

Polyaímon: father of Amopáon; 8.276.

Pólybos: Trojan leader, son of Anténor; 11.59.

Polýdamas: Trojan leader, Hektor's frequent adviser, son of Pánthoös; 11.57.

Polydeúkes: son of Leda and Tyndáreos, brother of Helen and Kastor; 3.237.

Polydóra: Peleus' daughter, wife of Boros, consort of Spercheios and by him mother of Menésthios; 16.175.

Polydóros: (1) son of Priam killed by Achilles; 20.407; (2) spear-thrower defeated by Nestor; 23.637.

Polyïdos: (1) Trojan, son of Eurýdamas, killed by Diomédes; 5.148; (2) soothsayer, father of Euchénor; 13.663.

Polýktor: father of the Mýrmidon that Hermes pretends to be; 24.397.

Polymélè: daughter of Phylas, mother, by Hermes, of Eudóros; 16.180.

Polymélos: Lykian, son of Árgeas, killed by Patróklos; 16.417.

Polyneíkes: son of Oídipous, brother of Etéokles, leader of the Seven against Thebes; 4.377.

Polyphémos: Lapith, hero of Nestor's earlier years; 1.264.

Polyphétes: Trojan leader; 13.791.

Polyphóntes: leader of the Kadmeíans, son of Autóphonos; 4.395.

Polypoítes: Lapith leader, son of Peiríthoös and Hippodameía; 2.740.

Polýxeinos: Epeían leader, son of Agásthenes; 2.623.

Portheus: father of Ágrios, Melos, and Oíneus, ancestor of Diomédes; 14.115.

Poseidon: god of the sea, son of Kronos and Rheia, brother of Zeus, Deméter, Hera, and Hades; 1.400.

Praktios: river in the Troäd, flowing into the Hellespont; 2.835.

Prámneian wine: used medicinally in a potion, place of origin unknown; 11.639.

Priam: King of Troy, son of Laómedon, husband of Hékabè, father of Hektor and many other children; 1.19.

Proítos: King of Ephýra (2), husband of Anteía; 6.157.

Prómachos: Boiótian killed by Ákamas (1); 14.477.

Pronóös: Trojan killed by Patróklos; 16.399.

Prótesiláos: leader of the Thessalians from Phýlake, first Achaian killed at Troy, son of Phýlakos; 2.698.

Prothoênor: Boiótian, son of Areïlochos, killed by Polýdamas; 2.495, 14.450.

Próthoön: Trojan killed by Teukros; 14.515.

Próthoös: leader of the Magnétes, son of Tenthrédon; 2.756.

Protiãon: father of Astýnoös; 15.455.

Proto: sea-nymph, "foremost"; 18.43.

Prýtanis: Lykian killed by Odysseus; 5.678.

Ptéleon: (1) town in the region of Pylos; 2.594; (2) town in Thessaly, near Phýlakè; 2.697.

Ptolemaíos: son of Peiraíos, father of Eurýmedon; 4.228.

Pygmies: small people attacked by cranes, "fist-like"; 3.6.

Pylaímenes: Páphlagónian leader killed by Meneláos; 2.851, 5.576.

Pylaíos: Pelásgian leader from Laríssa; 2.842.

Pylártes: (1) Trojan killed by Ajax (1); 11.491; (2) Trojan killed by Patróklos; 16.696.

Pylénè: town in Aitólia; 2.639.

Pylon: Trojan killed by Polypoítes; 12.187.

Pylos: city and region in the western Peloponnese, ruled by Nestor; 1.252.

Pyraíchmes: leader of the Paiónians, killed by Patróklos; 2.848, 16.287.

Pýrasos: town in Thessaly, near Phýlakè; 2.695.

Pyris: Trojan killed by Patróklos; 16.416.

Pytho: place in Phokis with a shrine of Apollo, later called Delphoi; 2.519.

Rhadamánthys: Son of Zeus and Europa, brother of Minos; 14.322.

Rheia: Titan, wife of Kronos, mother of Zeus, Poseidon, Hera, Hades, and Demeter; 14.203.

Rhenè: consort of Oïleus (1), mother of Medon (1); 2.728.

Rhesos: (1) king of the Thracians, son of Eióneus, killed by Diomédes; 10.435; (2) river in the Troäd; 12.20.

Rhigmos: Thracian, son of Peires, killed by Achilles; 20.485.

Rhipè: town in Arkádia; 2.606.

Rhodos, Rhodians: island south of Asia Minor and its inhabitants; 2.654.

Rhodios: river in the Troäd; 12.20.

Rhýtion: city in Crete; 2.648.

Sálamis: island near Athens; 2.557.

Samos: (1) island near Ithaka, later called Kephallenia; 2.634; (2) island near Thrace=Samothrace; 13.12.

Sangários: river in Phrygia; 3.187.

Sarpédon: Lord of Lykia, son of Zeus, killed by Patróklos; 2.876, 16.418–505.

Satníoeis: river in the Troäd; 6.34.

Sátnios: Trojan, son of Énops by a Naiad, killed by Ajax (2); 14.444.

Schédios: (1) Phokian leader, son of Íphitos (1), killed by Hektor; 2.517, 17.306; (2) Phokian leader, son of Perimédes, killed by Hektor; 15.515. (This near-duplication may be an error.)

Schoinos: city in Boiótia; 2.497.

Sélagos: father of Ámphios; 5.612.

Selépios: father of Euénos (1), grandfather of Epístrophos (2) and Mynes; 2.693.

Sellëëis: (1) river in Thesprotia; 2.659; (2) river in the Troäd; 2.839.

Selloi: prophets of Zeus living at Dodóna; 16.234.

Sémelè: consort of Zeus, mother of Dionýsos; 14.323.

Sésamos: town in Páphlagónia; 2.853.

Sestos: city on the northern shore of the Hellespont, across from Abýdos; 2.836.

Sidon, Sidonians: city of Phoenicia and its inhabitants; 6.290, 291.

Síkyon: city in the northeast Peloponnese; 2.572.

Símoeis: river in the Troäd; 4.475.

Simoeísios: Trojan, son of Anthémion, killed by Ajax (1); 4.474.

Sintian: of the people of Lemnos; 1.594.

Sípylos: river in Lydia; 24.615.

Sísyphos: hero of Ephýra (2), son of Aíolos, father of Glaukos (2), grandfather of Bellérophon; 6.153.

Skaian Gates: main gate of Troy in the direction of the battlefield; 3.145.

Skamánder: human name for the Xanthos, river of the Troäd, fights Achilles; 2.465, 20.74.

Skamándrios: (1) Trojan, son of Stróphios, killed by Meneláos; 5.49; (2) Hektor's name for his son Ástyanáx; 6.402.

Skandeía: city in Kýthera; 10.268.

Skarphè: town in Lokris; 2.532.

Skolos: town in Boiótia; 2.497.

Skyros: island and city in the Aegean, where Neoptólemos lives; 9.668, 19.326.

Smíntheus: title of Apollo; 1.39.

Sokos: Trojan, son of Híppasos, wounds Odysseus and is killed by him; 11.427.

Sólymoi: people of Asia Minor against whom Bellérophon fought; 6.184.

Sparta: city in Lakedaímon, by which name it is sometimes called; 2.582.

Speio: sea-nymph, "grotto"; 18.40.

Spercheios: river in Phthia, father of Menésthios by Polydóra; 16.174.

Sphelos: son of Boúkolos, father of Íasos; 15.338.

Stentor: loud-voiced Achaian lord impersonated by Hera; 5.785.

Stheneláos: Trojan, son of Ithaímenes, killed by Patróklos; 16.586.

Sthénelos: (1) Argive leader, son of Kápaneus, comrade of Diomédes; 2.564; (2) son of Perseus, father of Eurýstheus; 19.116.

Stíchios: Athenian leader killed by Hektor; 13.195, 15.329.

Strátia: town in Arkádia; 2.606.

Stróphios: father of Skamándrios (1); 5.49.

Stýmphalos: town in Arkádia; 2.608.

Styra: city in Euboía; 2.539.

Styx, Stygian: river in Thesprotia by which gods swear; its waters; 2.755, 8.369.

Symè: island near southeast Asia Minor, north of Rhodos; 2.671.

Talaímenes: father of Mesthles and Ántiphos; 2.865.

Tálaös: father of Mekísteus (1); 2.566.

Talthýbios: herald of Agamemnon; 1.320.

Tarnè: city in Maiónia; 5.44.

Tarphè: town in Lokris; 2.533.

Tártaros: realm beneath Hades' domain, where Iápetos and Kronos reside; 8.13.

Tegéa: city in Arkádia; 2.607.

Tekton: son of Harmon, father of Phéreklos, "joiner, shipwright"; 5.59.

Télamon: father of Ajax (1) and Teukros; 2.528.

Telémachos: son of Odysseus; 2.260.

Ténedos: island near the Troäd; 1.38.

Tenthrédon: father of Próthoös; 2.756.

Tereía: mountain in the Troäd, near the Hellespont; 2.829.

Tethys: wife of Ocean, ancestress of the gods; 14.201.

Teukros: Achaian archer, son of Télamon, brother of Ajax (1); 6.31.

Teútamos: father of Lethos, grandfather of Hippóthoös (1) and Pylaíos; 2.843.

Teuthras: (1) Achaian killed by Hektor; 5.705; (2) father of Áxylos; 6.13.

Thaleía: sea-nymph, "blooming"; 18.39.

Thalpios: Epeían leader, son of Eúrytos (2); 2.620.

Thalýsias: father of Echepólos (1); 4.458.

Thamýris: Thracian singer disabled by the Muses for his boasting; 2.595.

Thaumákia: town in Thessaly; 2.716.

Theáno: daughter of Kisses, wife of Anténor, foster mother of Pedaíos, priestess of Athena; 5.70, 6.299.

Thébè: city of the Troäd; 1.366.

Thebes: (1) city in Boiótia; lower, 2.505; citadel (destroyed at the time of the story), 4.378; (2) city in Egypt; 9.382.

Themis: Titan, goddess of custom and justice; 15.88.

Thersílochos: Paiónian killed by Achilles; 17.216, 21.209.

Thersítes: Achaian of questionable status, disorderly but loquacious; 2.212.

Theseus: Athenian hero of former times, son of Aigeus; 1.265.

Thespeía: city in Boiótia; 2.498.

Théssalos: son of Herakles, father of Pheidíppos and Ántiphos (1); 2.679.

Thestor: (1) father of Kalchas; 1.69; (2) father of Alkmáon; 12.394; (3) Trojan, son of Énops, killed by Patróklos; 16.401.

Thetis: sea-nymph, daughter of Nereus, wife of Peleus, mother of Achilles; 1.413.

Thisbè: town in Boiótia; 2.502.

Thoas: (1) Aitolian leader, son of Andraímon; 2.638; (2) king of Lemnos; 14.230; (3) Trojan killed by Meneláos; 16.311.

Thoë: sea-nymph, "nimble, swift"; 18.40.

Thoön: (1) Trojan, son of Phainops, killed by Diomédes; 5.152; (2) Trojan killed by Odysseus; 11.422; (3) Trojan killed by Antílochos; 12.140, 13.545.

Thŏótes: herald of Menéstheus; 12.342.

Thrace, Thracians: region north of the Aegean Sea; its people; 2.595, 844, 9.5.

Thrásios: Paiónian killed by Achilles; 21.210.

Thrasymédes: son of Nestor; 9.81.

Thrasymélos: retainer of Sarpédon killed by Patróklos; 16.463.

Thrónion: town in Lokris; 2.533.

Thryon, Thryoëssa: town in the region of Pylos, on the Álpheios; 2.592, 11.711.

Thyéstes: son of Pelops, brother of Atreus; 2.106.

Thymbraíos: Trojan killed by Diomédes; 11.320.

Thymbrè: town near Troy; 10.430.

Thymoítes: Trojan elder; 3.146.

Tiryns: city in the region of Argos; 2.559.

Titános: town in Thessaly; 2.735.

Titans: older gods displaced by the Olympian gods, banished to Tártaros; 14.279.

Titaréssos: river in Thessaly; 2.751.

Tithónos: son of Laómedon, brother of Priam, husband of Dawn; 11.1, 20.237.

Tlepólemos: (1) Rhodian, son of Herakles, wounds Sarpédon, is killed by him; 2.653, 5.628; (2) Lykian, son of Damástor, killed by Patróklos; 16.416.

Tmolos: mountain in Maiónia; 2.866.

Trachis: city in Pelásgian Argos; 2.682.

Trechos: Aitolian killed by Hektor; 5.706.

Trikkè: city in Thessaly; 2.729.

Trítogeneía: cognomen of Athena; 4.515.

Troizen: city on the east coast of the region of Argos; 2.561.

Troizénos: son of Kéas, father of Euphémos; 2.847.

Troilos: son of Priam, killed earlier in the war; 24.257.

Tros: (1) Eponymous hero of Troy, son of Érichthónios, father of Ilos, Assárakos, and Ganymédes, ancestor of the lords of Troy; 5.265, 20.230; (2) Trojan, son of Alástor, killed by Achilles; 20.463.

Troy, Trojans: =Ilion, the city and its inhabitants; 1.129, 1.152.

Týchios: Achaian leather-worker, maker of the shield of Ajax (1); 7.220.

Tydeus: son of Oíneus, father of Diomédes; 2.406, 14.114.

Typhóeus: monster created by Gaia, blasted and buried by Zeus; 2.782.

Xanthos: (1) river in Lykia; 2.877; (2) Trojan, son of Phainops, killed by Diomédes; 5.152; (3) the gods' name for the Skamánder, river in the Troäd; 6.4; (4) one of Hektor's horses, "bay"; 8.185; (5) one of Achilles' horses; 16.149.

Zakýnthos: island south of Ithaka, west of Elis; 2.634.

Zeleía: city north of Mount Ida, on the River Aisépos near the Propontis; 2.824.

Zephyr: the west wind; 9.5.

Zeus: Supreme god, son of Kronos and Rheia, brother of Demeter, Hades, Hera, and Poseidon, husband of Hera, father of Apollo, Artemis, Athena, Herakles, Sarpédon, and others, divine and mortal; 1.5.